The Billboard Book of
TOP 40 ALBUMS

REVISED & ENLARGED 3RD EDITION

JOEL WHITBURN

BILLBOARD BOOKS
An imprint of Watson-Guptill Publications/New York

Album covers selected from Joel Whitburn's personal collection
Photography by Malcolm Hjerstedt of Munroe Studios, Inc.
Photograph captions by Dave DiMartino
Chart typesetting by Quantum Imaging, Inc.
Cover design: Bob Fillie, Graphiti Graphics
Graphic production: Hector Campbell
Senior Editor: Paul Lukas
Editor: Liz Harvey

The author wishes to give thanks to his
dedicated Record Research staff:

Bill Hathaway	Troy Kluess
Kim Bloxdorf	Jeanne Olynick
Fran Whitburn	Paul Haney
Brent Olynick	Bobby Desai
Kim Kellen	Oscar Vidotto
Joanne Wagner	

"Dedicated To The One I Love"…
For my wife, Fran
When we met 34 years ago, this was our song.
As newlyweds three years later, our song was "Chapel of Love."
Now, for 31 years of standing by me, I thank you "On Bended Knee."

Revised and enlarged third edition first published 1995 by Billboard
Books, an imprint of Watson-Guptill Publications, a division of BPI
Communications, Inc., 1515 Broadway, New York, NY 10036.

Library of Congress Cataloging in Publication Data
Whitburn, Joel.
    The Billboard Book of top 40 albums / by Joel Whitburn.
    — Rev. & enl. 3rd ed.
        p.   cm.
    Includes index.
    ISBN 0-8230-7631-8
    1. Popular music—Discography.   I. Title.
ML 156.4.P6W43   1995   95-11881
016.78164—dc20   CIP
                                                                MN

Manufactured in the United States of America
First Printing, 1995
1 2 3 4 5 6 7 8 9/02 01 00 99 98 97 96 95

CONTENTS

AUTHOR'S NOTE

If you want to get a good overview of the hottest sounds in America, take a look at a current pop albums chart in *Billboard* magazine, "The Billboard 200." There you will find a broad definition of what makes up today's popular music. This chart is home to a wide variety of musical genres — from Country to Urban to Alternative Rock to Opera and more.

"The Billboard 200" reports which recent albums, whether they are on CD, cassette or vinyl, had the highest sales of the week. Not limited to a particular type of music, the constitution of this chart is decided by the many consumers who, on the average, spend most of their music budget on albums. Therefore, "The Billboard 200" is entirely based on the public's album-buying habits, not the radio-station program directors' playlists.

I know of no commercial radio station of the 1990s with a playlist that could accommodate the wide spectrum of music represented on "The Billboard 200." Ironically, the multi-genre facet of today's pop albums chart was also true with pop radio and the pop singles charts of the 1960's. Back then, the playlists of pop radio stations integrated many types of music, and singles dominated albums in sales.

Today with pop radio segregated into several pop formats (Adult, Urban, etc.) and the higher price and limited release of singles, the pop albums chart has become what the pop singles chart once was: an across-the-board representation of popular music. "The Billboard 200" documents the mega-success of artists who have released no cassette singles, like Garth Brooks and Pearl Jam. It is in this chart's fascinating mix of artists that you can witness the high-stakes race between Snoop Doggy Dogg and Mariah Carey, or Pink Floyd and Tim McGraw, or *Forrest Gump* trying to get an edge on *The Lion King*. With this much variety, "The Billboard 200" is indeed the spiciest of the *Billboard* charts.

JOEL WHITBURN

ABOUT THE AUTHOR
Joel Whitburn

From pastime to passion to profitable enterprise, the growth of Record Research has been the outgrowth of Joel Whitburn's hobby. Whitburn began collecting records as a teenager in the 1950s. As his collection grew, he began to sort, categorize and file each record according to the highest position it reached on Billboard's charts. He went on to publish this information — first on individual artists' cards, then in book form — and a business was born.

Today, Whitburn leads a team of researchers who delve into all of *Billboard*'s music and video charts to an unmatched degree of depth and detail. Widely recognized as the most authoritative historian on charted music, Whitburn has also collaborated with Rhino Records on a series of over 100 cassette and CD albums of America's top charted hits. Whitburn's own record collection remains unrivaled the world over and includes every charted *Hot 100* and pop single (back to 1936), every charted pop album (back to 1945), collections of every charted *Country, R&B, Bubbling Under The Hot 100* and *Adult Contemporary* records, and every video to chart since *Billboard* began its video charts in 1979. Ever the consummate collector, Whitburn also owns one of the world's largest picture-sleeve collections, many of which he displays in the series of books he writes for *Billboard*'s book division.

An avid sports fan, the 6'6" Whitburn played high school, college and semi-pro basketball, and enjoys browsing through his sizable collection of early Topps and Bowman baseball cards. Also among Whitburn's favorite pursuits are motorcycling, snowmobiling, jet skiing, four-wheeling and boating.

SYNOPSIS OF THE *BILLBOARD* POP ALBUM CHARTS 1955-1994

DATE	POSITIONS	CHART TITLE
1/8/55	15	**BEST SELLING POPULAR ALBUMS** (a biweekly chart with the exception of a seven-week gap and several three-week gaps)
3/24/56	10-15-20-30	**BEST SELLING POPULAR ALBUMS** (published weekly with size varying from a top 10 to a top 30)
6/2/56	15	**BEST SELLING POP ALBUMS**
9/2/57	25	**BEST SELLING POP LPs**
5/25/59	50	**BEST SELLING MONOPHONIC LPs**
5/25/59	30	**BEST SELLING STEREOPHONIC LPs** (separate Stereo and Mono charts published through 8/10/63)
1/4/60	40	**MONO ACTION CHARTS** (mono albums charted 39 weeks or less)
1/4/60	30	**STEREO ACTION CHARTS** (stereo albums charted 19 weeks or less; changed to 29 weeks or less on 5/30/60)
1/4/60	25	**ESSENTIAL INVENTORY — MONO** (mono albums charted 40 weeks or more)
1/4/60	20	**ESSENTIAL INVENTORY — STEREO** (stereo albums charted 20 weeks or more; changed to 30 weeks or more on 5/30/60)
1/9/61	25	**ACTION ALBUMS — MONOPHONIC** (mono albums charted nine weeks or less)
1/9/61	15	**ACTION ALBUMS — STEREOPHONIC** (stereo albums charted nine weeks or less)
1/9/61	—	Approximately 200 albums listed by category (no positions) and shown as essential inventory
4/3/61	150	**TOP LPs — MONAURAL**
4/3/61	50	**TOP LPs — STEREO**
8/17/63	150	**TOP LPs** (one chart)
4/1/67	175	**TOP LPs**
5/13/67	200	**TOP LPs**
11/25/67	200	**TOP LPs** (three pages)
2/15/69	200	**TOP LPs** (two pages with A-Z artist listing)
2/19/72	200	**TOP LPs & TAPES**
10/20/84	200	**TOP 200 ALBUMS**
1/5/85	200	**TOP POP ALBUMS**
9/7/91	200	**THE BILLBOARD 200 TOP ALBUMS**
3/14/92	200	**THE BILLBOARD 200**

An album appearing on both the Mono and Stereo charts in the same week is tabulated as one weekly appearance. The album's highest position is determined by the chart (Mono or Stereo) on which the album reached its highest position.

The Essential Inventory charts list albums that have already been charted for months on the Mono and Stereo charts, and, therefore, were not researched for this book.

THE
TOP 40
ALBUMS

HOW TO USE THIS SECTION

This section lists, alphabetically by artist name, every album that hit the Top 40 on *Billboard*'s pop album charts from January 8, 1955, through December 31, 1994 (see chart synopsis on page 6). Each group or artist's charted albums are listed in chronological order. A sequential number is shown in front of each album title to indicate the number of charted albums. If an album contains any singles that appeared in the Top 10 of *Billboard*'s Hot 100 chart, each of those Top 10 singles is listed in italics below the album title. The highest position each single reached is indicated in parenthesis after the title.

EXPLANATION OF HEADINGS & SYMBOLS

DATE: Date album debuted in the Top 40

POS: Album's highest charted position (highlighted in bold type). The number in parentheses after #1 and #2 albums indicates total weeks album held that position.

WKS: Total weeks charted in the Top 40

LABEL & NO.: Original album label and number. Numeral in brackets following the label number indicates the number of records/CD's in the album.

+: Indicates the peak position and/or weeks charted data is subject to change since the album was still accumulating weeks in the Top 40 as of the February 25, 1995 cutoff date.

●   RIAA certified gold album (500,000 units sold)

▲   RIAA certified platinum album (1,000,000 units sold). A superscript number to the right of the platinum triangle indicates the album was awarded multi-platinum status (ex.: $▲^3$ indicates an album was certified triple platinum).

The Record Industry Association of America (RIAA) began certifying gold albums in 1958, platinum albums in 1976 and multi-platinum albums in 1984. Before these dates, there are most certainly some albums that would have qualified for these certifications. Also, some record labels have never requested RIAA certification for albums that would have qualified for these awards.

Letters in brackets after album titles indicate the following types of albums:

C	-	Comedy	E	-	Early Recordings
EP	-	7" Extended Play	F	-	Foreign Language
G	-	Greatest Hits	I	-	Instrumental
K	-	Compilation	L	-	Live
N	-	Novelty	OC	-	Original Cast
S	-	Film Soundtrack	T	-	Talk/Spoken Word
TV	-	Television Show Soundtrack			
M	-	Mini (10" or 12" EP, or lower-priced CD)			
R	-	Reissue or re-release of a previously charted or previously recorded			
X	-	Christmas (If an album also charted on *Billboard*'s special Christmas album charts, a note below the album title indicates the highest position reached and year it made the special Christmas albums chart.) For example, the note *Christmas charts: 5/'67, 10/'68* would indicate that the album hit position 5 on the special Christmas albums chart in 1967 and position 10 on that chart in 1968.			

NEW COMPILATION METHOD

Billboard's compilation of the pop album chart has always been based on album sales. For more than 30 years, *Billboard* tallied the pop album charts from rankings of best-selling albums as reported by a representative sampling of stores nationwide. On May 25, 1991, *Billboard* ushered in a new era in sales-charts compilation. *Billboard* now bases the pop album chart on actual units sold data as collected by point-of-sale scanning machines that read the album's UPC bar code. SoundScan Inc., a music research firm, provides *Billboard* with the actual sales of all albums from a continually revised, representative sampling of stores. It is likely that the pop album chart of the last few years, *The Billboard 200*, is the most accurate ever.

LABEL ABBREVIATIONS

ABC-Para	ABC-Paramount	Morgan Cr.	Morgan Creek
American G.	American Grammaphone	Music Fac.	Music Factory
Ariola Am.	Ariola America	Neighbor.	Neighborhood
Atl. Art.	Atlanta Artists	Next Plat.	Next Plateau
Atlantic/Int.	Atlantic/Interscope	Original Snd.	Original Sound
Audio Fidel.	Audio Fidelity	Paisley P.	Paisley Park
Barking P.	Barking Pumpkin	Phil. Int.	Philadelphia International
Begr. B.	Beggar's Banquet	Private M.	Private Music
Beverly G.	Beverly Glen	Private St.	Private Stock
Canadian-Am.	Canadian-American	Rhyme Synd.	Rhyme Syndicate
Capitol Int.	Capitol International	Rock 'n' R.	Rock 'n' Roll
CBS As. or CBS Assoc.	CBS Associated	Rolling S.	Rolling Stones
Choc. City	Chocolate City	Scotti Br.	Scotti Brothers
Cleve. I.	Cleveland International	Stereo-Fid.	Stereo-Fidelity
Cold Chill.	Cold Chillin'	Stormy F.	Stormy Forest
Death Row/Int.	Death Row/Interscope	Street Know.	Street Knowledge
Def Amer.	Def American	Tetragramm.	Tetragrammaton
Delicious V.	Delicious Vinyl	Tin Pan A.	Tin Pan Apple
EMI-Man.	EMI-Manhattan	Total Exp.	Total Experience
Epic/Assc.	Epic/Associated	United Art.	United Artists
Epic/Chip.	Epic/Chipmunk	Varese S.	Varese Sarabande
Epic Sound.	Epic Soundtrax	Verve F.	Verve Forecast
London P. 4	London Phase 4	Vintertn.	Vintertainment
Luke Sky.	Luke Skyywalker	Wooden N.	Wooden Nickel
Midland Int.	Midland International	World Art.	World Artists

DATE	POS	WKS	ARTIST—RECORD TITLE	LABEL & NO.

A

AALIYAH

Aaliyah (pronounced ah-lee-yah) Haughton. Female singer from Detroit. Fifteen years old in 1994. Married singer/producer R. Kelly on 8/31/94.

DATE	POS	WKS	ARTIST—RECORD TITLE	LABEL & NO.
6/11/94	18	19	▲ Age Ain't Nothing But A Number produced by R. Kelly *Back & Forth (5)/At Your Best (You Are Love) (6)*	Blackground 41533

ABBA

Pop quartet formed in Stockholm, Sweden, in 1970, using their first initials as an acronym. Consisted of Anni-Frid "Frida" Lyngstad and Agnetha Faltskog (vocals), Bjorn Ulvaeus (guitar) and Benny Andersson (keyboards). Andersson and Ulvaeus recorded together in 1966. Ulvaeus and Faltskog married in 1971; divorced in 1979. Andersson and Lyngstad married in 1978; divorced in 1981. Disbanded in the early '80s. Ulvaeus and Andersson co-wrote the *Chess* musical with Tim Rice.

DATE	POS	WKS	ARTIST—RECORD TITLE	LABEL & NO.
2/26/77	20	9	● 1. Arrival *Dancing Queen (1)*	Atlantic 18207
3/25/78	14	17	▲ 2. The Album *Take A Chance On Me (3)*	Atlantic 19164
7/28/79	19	12	● 3. Voulez-Vous *title is French for will you*	Atlantic 16000
12/27/80	17	16	● 4. Super Trouper *The Winner Takes It All (8)*	Atlantic 16023
1/23/82	29	6	5. The Visitors	Atlantic 19332

ABBOTT, Gregory

Soul singer/songwriter from New York. At age eight, member of St. Patrick's Cathedral Choir. Psychology major at Boston University and Stanford; taught English at Berkeley.

DATE	POS	WKS	ARTIST—RECORD TITLE	LABEL & NO.
12/27/86	22	16	● Shake You Down *Shake You Down (1)*	Columbia 40437

ABC

Electro-pop group from Sheffield, England. Formed as Vice Versa with Stephen Singleton and Mark White. Lead singer Martin Fry joined in 1980; group renamed ABC. Singleton left group in 1985.

DATE	POS	WKS	ARTIST—RECORD TITLE	LABEL & NO.
11/20/82	24	20	● 1. the Lexicon of Love	Mercury 4059
10/26/85	30	15	2. how to be a ... Zillionaire! *Be Near Me (9)*	Mercury 824904

ABDUL, Paula

Born on 6/19/62 of Brazilian and French Canadian parentage. Los Angeles singer/choreographer. While still a teen, was choreographer and member of the Los Angeles Lakers cheerleaders. Choreographed Janet Jackson's *Control* videos and TV's "The Tracey Ullman Show." Married actor Emilio Estevez on 4/29/92; split on 5/10/94.

DATE	POS	WKS	ARTIST—RECORD TITLE	LABEL & NO.
1/28/89	1(10)	78	▲7 **1. Forever Your Girl** *Straight Up (1)/Forever Your Girl (1)/Cold Hearted (1)/ (It's Just) The Way That You Love Me (3)/Opposites Attract (1)*	Virgin 90943
6/2/90	7	16	▲ **2. Shut Up And Dance (The Dance Mixes)** **[K]** remixes of Abdul's hits	Virgin 91362

DATE	POS	WKS	ARTIST—RECORD TITLE	LABEL & NO.
6/1/91	**1**(2)	41	▲³ **3. Spellbound** *Rush, Rush* (1)/*The Promise Of A New Day* (1)/ *Blowing Kisses In The Wind* (6)	Virgin 91611
			ABOVE THE LAW	
			Rap outfit led by Don "Cold 187um" Hutchison.	
2/20/93	**37**	1	Black Mafia Life	Ruthless 24477
			AC/DC	
			Hard-rock band formed in Sydney, Australia, in 1974. Consisted of brothers Angus and Malcolm Young (guitars), Ron Belford "Bon" Scott (lead singer), Phil Rudd (drums) and Mark Evans (bass). Cliff Williams replaced Evans in 1977. Bon Scott died on 2/19/80 (age 33) from alcohol abuse; replaced by Brian Johnson. Simon Wright replaced Rudd in 1985. Wright joined Dio in 1989; replaced by Chris Slade of The Firm. Angus and Malcolm are the younger brothers of George Young of The Easybeats.	
9/15/79	**17**	11	▲⁴ **1. Highway To Hell**	Atlantic 19244
8/23/80	**4**	45	▲¹⁰ **2. Back In Black** Brian Johnson replaces Bon Scott as lead singer	Atlantic 16018
4/18/81	**3**	19	▲³ **3. Dirty Deeds Done Dirt Cheap** [E-R] recorded in 1976	Atlantic 16033
12/12/81	**1**(3)	16	▲² **4. For Those About To Rock We Salute You**	Atlantic 11111
9/10/83	**15**	11	● 5. Flick Of The Switch	Atlantic 80100
8/17/85	**32**	5	● 6. Fly On The Wall	Atlantic 81263
8/9/86	**33**	6	▲³ 7. Who Made Who [S-K] soundtrack from the movie *Maximum Overdrive*	Atlantic 81650
3/5/88	**12**	12	▲ 8. Blow Up Your Video	Atlantic 81828
10/13/90	**2**(1)	38	▲³ **9. The Razors Edge**	Atco 91413
11/14/92	**15**	7	▲² 10. Live [L] 14 tracks from album below	Atco 92215
11/14/92	**34**	1	11. Live (Special Collector's Edition) [L] recorded during their 1990-91 world tour	Atco 92212 [2]
			ACE	
			Pub-rock quintet from Sheffield, England, led by vocalist Paul Carrack. Disbanded in 1977. Carrack joined Squeeze in 1981, then Mike + The Mechanics in 1985.	
4/5/75	**11**	11	Five-A-Side (an Ace album) *How Long* (3)	Anchor 2001
			ACE OF BASE	
			Pop quartet from Gothenburg, Sweden: vocalists/sisters Jenny and Linn Berggren with keyboardists Jonas "Joker" Berggren (their brother) and Ulf "Buddha" Ekberg.	
12/18/93	**1**(2)	63+	▲⁷ **The Sign** *All That She Wants* (2)/*The Sign* (1)/*Don't Turn Around* (4)	Arista 18740
			ADAMS, Bryan	
			Born on 11/5/59 in Kingston, Ontario, Canada. Rock singer/songwriter/guitarist based in Vancouver. Lead singer of Sweeney Todd in 1976. Teamed with Jim Vallance in 1977 in songwriting partnership. Cameo appearance in the movie *Pink Cadillac*.	
4/2/83	**8**	24	▲ **1. Cuts Like A Knife** *Straight From The Heart* (10)	A&M 4919
12/1/84	**1**(2)	66	▲⁵ **2. Reckless** *Run To You* (6)/*Heaven* (1)/*Summer Of '69* (5)	A&M 5013

DATE	POS	WKS	ARTIST—RECORD TITLE	LABEL & NO.
4/18/87	7	22	▲ **3. Into The Fire** *Heat Of The Night* (6)	A&M 3907
10/12/91	6	37	▲³ **4. Waking Up The Neighbours** *(Everything I Do) I Do It For You* (1)/ *Can't Stop This Thing We Started* (2)	A&M 5367
11/27/93	6	23	▲³ **5. So Far So Good** [G] *Please Forgive Me* (7)	A&M 0157
			ADAMS, Oleta Native of Yakima, Washington. Discovered by Tears For Fears in Kansas City; backing singer on their *Seeds Of Love* album and tour.	
3/16/91	20	9	● Circle Of One *Get Here* (5)	Fontana 846346
			ADDERLEY, "Cannonball" Born Julian Edwin Adderley on 9/15/28 in Tampa. Died of a stroke on 8/8/75 in Gary, Indiana. Nickname derived from "cannibal" — in tribute to his love of eating. Alto saxophonist/leader of jazz combo featuring brother Nat Adderley (cornet) and Joe Zawinul (piano; left in 1971 to form Weather Report; replaced by George Duke).	
7/7/62	30	5	**1. Nancy Wilson/Cannonball Adderley** **NANCY WILSON/CANNONBALL ADDERLEY**	Capitol 1657
4/13/63	11	11	**2. Jazz Workshop Revisited** [I-L] **CANNONBALL ADDERLEY Sextet**	Riverside 444
3/25/67	13	9	**3. Mercy, Mercy, Mercy!** [I-L] **THE CANNONBALL ADDERLEY Quintet**	Capitol 2663
			AEROSMITH Hard-rock band formed in Sunapee, New Hampshire, in 1970. Consisted of Steven Tyler (born Steven Tallarico; lead singer), Joe Perry and Brad Whitford (guitars), Tom Hamilton (bass) and Joey Kramer (drums). Perry left for own Joe Perry Project in 1979; replaced by Jimmy Crespo. Whitford left in 1981; replaced by Rick Dufay. Original band reunited in April 1984. Tyler's daughter model/actress Liv acted in the movie *Silent Fall*.	
5/31/75	11	30	▲⁶ **1. Toys In The Attic** *Walk This Way* (10)	Columbia 33479
3/20/76	21	8	▲² **2. Aerosmith** *Dream On* (6)	Columbia 32005
5/29/76	3	21	▲³ **3. Rocks**	Columbia 34165
1/7/78	11	8	▲ **4. Draw The Line**	Columbia 34856
11/18/78	13	13	▲ **5. Live! Bootleg** [L]	Columbia 35564 [2]
12/15/79	14	12	▲ **6. Night In The Ruts**	Columbia 36050
10/2/82	32	6	● **7. Rock In A Hard Place**	Columbia 38061
12/14/85	36	5	● **8. Done With Mirrors**	Geffen 24091
10/3/87	11	52	▲⁵ **9. Permanent Vacation** *Angel* (3)	Geffen 24162
9/30/89	5	53	▲⁷ **10. Pump** *Love In An Elevator* (5)/*Janie's Got A Gun* (4)/ *What It Takes* (9)	Geffen 24254
5/8/93	1(1)	69	▲⁶ **11. Get A Grip**	Geffen 24455
11/19/94	6	15+	▲² **12. Big Ones** [G]	Geffen 24716

DATE	POS	WKS	ARTIST—RECORD TITLE	LABEL & NO.
			AFTER 7	
			Indianapolis R&B vocal trio: Keith Mitchell with brothers Kevon and Melvin Edmonds. Keith is cousin of L.A. Reid. Kevon and Melvin are brothers of Babyface.	
7/14/90	**35**	4	▲ After 7	Virgin 91061
			Ready Or Not (7)/*Can't Stop* (6)	
			AFTER THE FIRE	
			English rock band: Andy Piercy, Peter Banks (ex-Yes, ex-Flash), Tim Haywell and Nick Battle.	
4/16/83	**25**	8	ATF	Epic 38282
			Der Kommissar (5)	
			a-ha	
			Pop trio formed in Oslo, Norway: Morten Harket (vocals), Pal Waaktaar (guitar) and Magne "Mags" Furuholmen (keyboards).	
9/7/85	**15**	26	▲ Hunting High And Low	Warner 25300
			Take On Me (1)	
			AIR FORCE — see BAKER, Ginger	
			AIR SUPPLY	
			Melbourne, Australia vocal group featuring Russell Hitchcock (born 6/15/49 in Melbourne) and Graham Russell (born 6/1/50 in Nottingham, England). Disbanded in 1988. Hitchcock and Russell reunited in 1991.	
9/6/80	**22**	19	▲^{2} 1. Lost In Love	Arista 4268
			Lost In Love (3)/*All Out Of Love* (2)/ *Every Woman In The World* (5)	
6/27/81	**10**	25	▲ **2. The One That You Love**	Arista 9551
			The One That You Love (1)/*Here I Am* (5)/*Sweet Dreams* (5)	
7/17/82	**25**	8	▲ 3. Now And Forever	Arista 9587
			Even The Nights Are Better (5)	
9/3/83	**7**	26	▲^{5} **4. Greatest Hits** **[G]**	Arista 8024
			Making Love Out Of Nothing At All (2)	
7/6/85	**26**	8	● 5. Air Supply	Arista 8283
			ALABAMA	
			Country quartet from Fort Payne, Alabama: Randy Owen (vocals, guitar), Jeff Cook (keyboards, fiddle), Teddy Gentry (bass, vocals) and Mark Herndon (drums, vocals). Owen, Cook and Gentry are cousins.	
5/2/81	**16**	42	▲^{4} 1. Feels So Right	RCA 3930
3/20/82	**14**	20	▲^{4} 2. Mountain Music	RCA 4229
3/26/83	**10**	15	▲^{3} **3. The Closer You Get ...**	RCA 4663
2/18/84	**21**	17	▲^{3} 4. Roll On	RCA 4939
3/16/85	**28**	5	▲^{2} 5. 40 Hour Week	RCA 5339
3/8/86	**24**	15	▲^{3} 6. Greatest Hits **[G]**	RCA 7170
			ALARM, The	
			Welsh rock quartet: Mike Peters (lead singer), Dave Sharp, Eddie MacDonald and Nigel Twist. Formed in 1977 by Peters and Twist as The Toilets. MacDonald and Sharp joined in 1978; group renamed Seventeen (after a Sex Pistols song). Renamed The Alarm in 1982.	
2/15/86	**39**	3	Strength	I.R.S. 5666

DATE	POS	WKS	ARTIST—RECORD TITLE	LABEL & NO.
			ALBERT, Morris	
			Born Morris Albert Kaisermann. Brazilian singer/songwriter.	
11/29/75	37	2	Feelings	RCA 1018
			Feelings (6)	
			AL B. SURE!	
			Born Al Brown in Boston and raised in Mount Vernon, New York. R&B singer. Turned down football scholarship to the University of Iowa in order to pursue music career.	
6/11/88	20	25	▲ 1. In Effect Mode	Warner 25662
			Nite And Day (7)	
11/10/90	20	5	● 2. Private Times ... And The Whole 9!	Warner 26005
			ALDRICH, Ronnie, And His Two Pianos	
			British pianist/arranger. In the 1940s, formed The Famous Squadronaires, a popular big band in England. Musical director of the "Benny Hill" TV variety series. Died of prostate cancer on 9/30/93 (age 77).	
11/6/61	20	13	1. Melody And Percussion For Two Pianos [I]	London P. 4 44007
10/20/62	36	2	2. Ronnie Aldrich and his Two Pianos [I]	London P. 4 44018
			ALICE IN CHAINS	
			Male hard-rock band from Seattle: Layne Staley (vocals), Jerry Cantrell, Michael Starr and Sean Kinney. Starr replaced by Mike Inez (former bassist for Ozzy Osbourne) by 1994.	
10/17/92	6	19	▲³ **1. Dirt**	Columbia 52475
2/12/94	1(1)	17	▲¹ **2. Jar Of Flies** [M]	Columbia 57628
			ALLAN, Davie, And The Arrows	
			Born in Los Angeles. Began as a session guitarist for Mike Curb. Formed The Arrows while in high school in Van Nuys, California. Consisted of Allan (Fender lead guitar), Drew Bennett (bass), Jared Hendler (keyboards) and Larry Brown (drums).	
12/3/66	17	13	The Wild Angels [S]	Tower 5043
			ALLEN, Dayton	
			Born on 9/24/19 in New York City. Comedian on TV's "The Steve Allen Show." Voice of "Deputy Dawg" TV cartoon and Phineas T. Bluster of TV's "Howdy Doody."	
12/19/60	35	1	Why Not! [C]	Grand Award 424
			ALLEN, Steve	
			Born on 12/26/21 in New York City. Comedian/actor/songwriter/author. In 1954, became first host of TV's "The Tonight Show." Played title role in 1956 movie *The Benny Goodman Story*. Hosted own variety and talk shows, 1956-80. Married to actress Jayne Meadows.	
5/14/55	7	10	**Music For Tonight** [I]	Coral 57004
			ALL-4-ONE	
			Male vocal quartet based in Southern California: Jamie Jones, Delious Kennedy, Alfred Nevarez and Tony Borowiak.	
5/7/94	7	25	▲² **All-4-One**	Blitzz 82588
			So Much In Love (5)/*I Swear* (1)	
			ALLMAN, Duane	
			Born Howard Duane Allman on 11/20/46. The Allman Brothers Band guitarist. Died on 10/29/71 in a motorcycle mishap near his hometown of Macon, Georgia.	
1/20/73	28	6	● An Anthology [K]	Capricorn 0108 [2]
			features Duane's session work	

DATE	POS	WKS	ARTIST—RECORD TITLE		LABEL & NO.
			ALLMAN, Gregg		
			Born on 12/8/47 in Nashville and raised in Daytona Beach, Florida. Keyboardist/vocalist. In 1965, Greg and brother Duane formed The Allman Joys, which evolved into The Allman Brothers Band by 1969. Married to Cher from 1975-77. Acted in the movie *Rush*.		
12/8/73	**13**	17	● 1. Laid Back		Capricorn 0116
5/2/87	**30**	6	● 2. I'm No Angel		Epic 40531
			THE GREGG ALLMAN BAND		
			ALLMAN BROTHERS BAND, The		
			Southern rock band formed in Macon, Georgia, in 1969. Consisted of brothers Duane (lead guitar) and Gregg Allman (keyboards), Dickey Betts (guitar), Berry Oakley (bass), and the drum duo of Butch Trucks and Jai Johnny Johanson (pronounced Jay Johnny Johnson). Duane and Gregg known earlier as the Allman Joys and Hour Glass. Duane was the top session guitarist at Muscle Shoals studio; he was killed in a motorcycle crash on 10/29/71 (age 24). Oakley died in another cycle accident on 11/11/72 (age 24); replaced by Lamar Williams. Chuck Leavell (keyboards) added in 1972. Group split up in 1976. Gregg formed The Gregg Allman Band. Betts formed Great Southern. Leavell, Williams and Johanson formed fusion-rock band Sea Level. Allman and Betts reunited with new Allman Brothers lineup in 1978. Disbanded in 1981. Allman, Betts, Trucks and Johanson re-grouped with Warren Haynes (guitar), Allen Woody (bass) and Johnny Neel (keyboards) in 1989. Neel left in 1990; replaced by Mark Quinones. Group inducted into the Rock and Roll Hall of Fame in 1995.		
12/5/70	**38**	2	1. Idlewild South		Atco 342
			album named after band's farmhouse in Macon		
7/31/71	**13**	11	▲ 2. At Fillmore East	[L]	Capricorn 802 [2]
3/18/72	**4**	29	● **3. Eat A Peach**	[L]	Capricorn 0102 [2]
			includes Duane's last three studio recordings		
4/7/73	**25**	6	● 4. Beginnings	[R]	Atco 805 [2]
			reissue of album #1 above and LP *The Allman Brothers Band* (1970)		
8/25/73	**1**(5)	24	● **5. Brothers And Sisters**		Capricorn 0111
			Ramblin Man (2)		
9/27/75	**5**	8	● **6. Win, Lose Or Draw**		Capricorn 0156
3/24/79	**9**	13	● **7. Enlightened Rouges**		Capricorn 0218
9/6/80	**27**	6	8. Reach For The Sky		Arista 9535
			ALMEIDA, Laurindo, and The Bossa Nova All Stars		
			Born on 9/2/17 in Sao Paulo, Brazil. Guitarist/bandleader. To U.S. in 1947. Member of Stan Kenton's orchestra until 1950.		
12/8/62	**9**	22	**Viva Bossa Nova!**	[I]	Capitol 1759
			ALPERT, Herb, & The Tijuana Brass		
			Alpert was born on 3/31/35 in Los Angeles. Producer/composer/trumpeter/ bandleader. Played trumpet since age eight. A&R for Keen Records. Produced first Jan & Dean session. Wrote "Wonderful World" hit for Sam Cooke. Recorded as Dore Alpert in 1962. Formed A&M Records with Jerry Moss in 1962. Used studio musicians until early 1965, then formed own band. Alpert and Moss formed the Almo Sounds label in 1994.		
			HERB ALPERT & THE TIJUANA BRASS:		
1/26/63	**10**	51	● **1. The Lonely Bull**	[I]	A&M 101
			The Lonely Bull (6)		
6/12/65	**1**(8)	141	● **2. Whipped Cream & Other Delights** *	[I]	A&M 110
			Taste Of Honey (7)		
11/6/65	**1**(6)	107	● **3. Going Places**	[I]	A&M 112

DATE	POS	WKS	ARTIST—RECORD TITLE		LABEL & NO.
12/18/65	6	52	● 4. South Of The Border *	[I]	A&M 108
3/5/66	17	13	● 5. Herb Alpert's Tijuana Brass, Volume 2 *	[I]	A&M 103
			Alpert's second album, recorded in 1963		
			*HERB ALPERT'S TIJUANA BRASS		
5/21/66	1(9)	59	● 6. What Now My Love	[I]	A&M 4114
12/17/66	2(6)	38	● 7. S.R.O.	[I]	A&M 4119
6/10/67	1(1)	36	● 8. Sounds Like	[I]	A&M 4124
12/30/67	4	18	● 9. Herb Alpert's Ninth	[I]	A&M 4134
5/18/68	1(2)	28	● 10. The Beat Of The Brass	[I]	A&M 4146
			This Guy's In Love With You (1)		
7/19/69	28	7	● 11. Warm	[I]	A&M 4190
12/6/69	30	5	12. The Brass Are Comin'	[I]	A&M 4228
			HERB ALPERT:		
10/20/79	6	19	▲ 13. Rise	[I]	A&M 4790
			Rise (1)		
8/9/80	28	4	14. Beyond	[I]	A&M 3717
4/25/87	18	17	● 15. Keep Your Eye On Me		A&M 5125
			Diamonds (5-featuring Janet Jackson)		
			AMBROSIA		
			Los Angeles-based pop group. Lead singers David Pack and Joe Puerta with Burleigh Drummond and Christopher North (left in 1977).		
7/26/75	22	8	1. Ambrosia		20th Century 434
11/4/78	19	9	2. Life Beyond L.A.		Warner 3135
			How Much I Feel (3)		
5/31/80	25	7	3. One Eighty		Warner 3368
			Biggest Part Of Me (3)		
			AMERICA		
			Trio formed in London in 1969. Consisted of Americans Dan Peek and Gerry Beckley, with Englishman Dewey Bunnell. All played guitars. Met at U.S. Air Force base. Members of Daze in 1970. Moved to U.S. in February 1972. Won 1972 Best New Artist Grammy Award. Peek left in 1976; became popular contemporary Christian artist.		
3/4/72	1(5)	22	▲ 1. America		Warner 2576
			A Horse With No Name (1)/*I Need You* (9)		
12/16/72	9	16	● 2. Homecoming		Warner 2655
			Ventura Highway (8)		
12/1/73	28	5	3. Hat Trick		Warner 2728
8/24/74	3	17	● 4. Holiday		Warner 2808
			Tin Man (4)/*Lonely People* (5)		
4/19/75	4	17	● 5. Hearts		Warner 2852
			Sister Golden Hair (1)		
11/29/75	3	22	▲⁴ 6. History/America's Greatest Hits	[G]	Warner 2894
5/8/76	11	8	● 7. Hideaway		Warner 2932
3/26/77	21	4	8. Harbor		Warner 3017
			AMES, Ed		
			Born Ed Urick on 7/9/27 in Malden, Massachusetts. One of The Ames Brothers. Played Mingo on the "Daniel Boone" TV series.		
3/18/67	4	19	● 1. My Cup Runneth Over		RCA 3774
			My Cup Runneth Over (8)		
1/20/68	24	8	2. When The Snow Is On The Roses		RCA 3913

DATE	POS	WKS	ARTIST—RECORD TITLE	LABEL & NO.
3/23/68	**13**	18	● 3. Who Will Answer? And Other Songs Of Our Time	RCA 3961
			AMES BROTHERS, The	
			Pop vocal group from Malden, Massachusetts, formed in 1947. Family name Urick. Consisted of lead singer Ed Ames (born 7/9/27) and his brothers Gene (born 2/13/25), Joe (born 5/3/24) and Vic (born 5/20/26; died 1/23/78). Own TV series in 1955. Ed recorded solo and acted on Broadway and TV.	
12/2/57	**16**	4	There'll Always Be A Christmas [X]	RCA 1541
			AMOS, Tori	
			Born Myra Ellen Amos on 8/22/63 in North Carolina; raised in Maryland. At age five, she won a piano scholarship to Baltimore's Peabody Conservatory.	
2/19/94	**12**	10	▲ Under The Pink	Atlantic 82567
			ANDERSON, Bill	
			Born James William Anderson III on 11/1/37 in Columbia, South Carolina. Country singer/songwriter/actor. Hosted Nashville Network's TV game show "Fandango." Member of the *Grand Ole Opry* since 1961. Known as "Whispering Bill."	
7/27/63	**36**	5	Still *Still* (8)	Decca 74427
			ANDERSON, Ernestine	
			Born on 11/11/28 in Houston. Jazz singer based in Seattle. Formerly with Eddie Heywood and Lionel Hampton.	
10/20/58	**15**	6	Hot Cargo!	Mercury 20354
			ANDERSON, John	
			Born on 12/13/54 in Apopka, Florida. Honky-tonk country singer.	
10/24/92	**35**	5	▲ Seminole Wind	BNA 61029
			ANDERSON, Lynn	
			Born on 9/26/47 in Grand Forks, North Dakota; raised in Sacramento. Country singer; daughter of country singer Liz Anderson. An accomplished equestrienne, she was the California Horse Show Queen in 1966.	
2/13/71	**19**	12	▲ Rose Garden *Rose Garden* (3)	Columbia 30411
			ANDERSON, BRUFORD, WAKEMAN, HOWE — see YES	
			ANGELS, The	
			Female pop trio from Orange, New Jersey. Formed as The Starlets with sisters Phyllis "Jiggs" & Barbara Allbut, and Linda Jansen (lead singer). Jansen was replaced by Peggy Santiglia in 1962. Studio backing vocalists for Lou Christie and others in the mid-1960s. Disbanded in 1967.	
11/16/63	**33**	3	My Boyfriend's Back *My Boyfriend's Back* (1)	Smash 67039
			ANIMALS, The	
			Rock group formed in Newcastle, England, in 1958 as The Alan Price Combo. Consisted of Eric Burdon (vocals), Alan Price (keyboards), Bryan "Chas" Chandler (bass), Hilton Valentine (guitar) and John Steel (drums). Price left in May 1965; replaced by Dave Rowberry. Chandler pursued a management career and discovered Jimi Hendrix in 1966. Steel left in 1966; replaced by Barry Jenkins. Group disbanded in July 1968. After a period with War, Burdon and the other originals reunited in 1976 and again in 1983. Inducted into the Rock and Roll Hall of Fame in 1994.	
10/3/64	**7**	15	**1. The Animals** *The House Of The Rising Sun* (1)	MGM 4264

DATE	POS	WKS	ARTIST—RECORD TITLE	LABEL & NO.
3/12/66	6	51	● **2. The Best Of The Animals** [G]	MGM 4324
9/24/66	20	12	3. Animalization	MGM 4384
			See See Rider (10)	
1/14/67	33	3	4. Animalism	MGM 4414

ANIMOTION

Techno-pop quintet led by Astrid Plane and Bill Wadhams. Four of five members replaced in 1988, including Plane and Wadhams. New vocalists include Paul Engemann (formerly of Device) and actress/ dancer Cynthia Rhodes (appeared in the movies *Staying Alive* and *Dirty Dancing*; married Richard Marx on 1/8/89). Plane married group's founding bassist, Charles Ottavio, on 10/13/90.

DATE	POS	WKS	ARTIST—RECORD TITLE	LABEL & NO.
4/20/85	28	7	Animotion	Mercury 822580
			Obsession (6)	

ANKA, Paul

Born on 7/30/41 in Ottawa, Canada. Performer since age 12. Father financed first recording, "I Confess," on RPM 472 in 1956. Wrote "She's A Lady" for Tom Jones and the English lyrics to "My Way" for Frank Sinatra. Also wrote theme for TV's "The Tonight Show." Own variety show in 1973. Cameo appearances in the 1962 movie *The Longest Day* and the 1992 movie *Captain Ron*. Longtime popular entertainer in Las Vegas.

DATE	POS	WKS	ARTIST—RECORD TITLE	LABEL & NO.
7/4/60	4	54	**1. Paul Anka Sings His Big 15** [G]	ABC-Para. 323
			Diana (1)/*You Are My Destiny* (7)/*Lonely Boy* (1)/*Put Your Head On My Shoulder* (2)/*It's Time To Cry* (4)/*Puppy Love* (2)	
12/5/60	23	3	2. Anka At The Copa [L]	ABC-Para. 353
9/28/74	9	16	● **3. Anka**	United Art. 314
			(You're) Having My Baby (1)/*One Man Woman/One Woman Man* (7)	
5/24/75	36	3	4. Feelings	United Art. 367
			I Don't Like To Sleep Alone (8)	
1/17/76	22	9	● 5. Times Of Your Life [K]	United Art. 569
			9 of 10 cuts from previous 2 United Artists albums *Times Of Your Life* (7)	

ANNETTE

Born Annette Funicello on 10/22/42 in Utica, New York. Became Mouseketeer in 1955. Acted in several teen movies in the early '60s. Co-starred with Frankie Avalon in the 1987 movie *Back to the Beach*. Diagnosed with multiple sclerosis in 1987.

DATE	POS	WKS	ARTIST—RECORD TITLE	LABEL & NO.
3/21/60	21	9	1. Annette Sings Anka	Buena Vista 3302
9/26/60	38	3	2. Hawaiiannette	Buena Vista 3303
12/14/63	39	1	3. Annette's Beach Party [S]	Buena Vista 3316
			half of the songs are from the movie *Beach Party* starring Annette and Frankie Avalon	

ANOTHER BAD CREATION

Pre-teen R&B/rap vocal quintet managed and produced by Michael Bivins of Bell Biv DeVoe. Made up of Atlanta natives: Chris Sellers, Dave Shelton, Romell Chapman, with brothers Marliss and Demetrius Pugh. Appeared in the movie *The Meteor Man*.

DATE	POS	WKS	ARTIST—RECORD TITLE	LABEL & NO.
3/23/91	7	26	▲ **coolin' at the PLAYGROUND ya' know!**	Motown 6318
			Iesha (9)/*Playground* (10)	

DATE	POS	WKS	ARTIST—RECORD TITLE	LABEL & NO.
			ANT, Adam	
			Born Stuart Goddard on 11/3/54 in London. Formed romantic-punk group Adam & The Ants in 1976. Ant headed new lineup in 1980. Original members Matthew Ashman and Dave Barbarossa founded Bow Wow Wow. Ant went solo in 1982. Appeared in the movies *World Gone Wild* and *Slam Dance* and the TV show "The Equalizer."	
12/11/82	16	16	● Friend Or Foe	Epic 38370
			ANTHONY, Ray	
			Born Raymond Antonini on 1/20/22 in Bentleyville, Pennsylvania, and raised in Cleveland. Big band leader/trumpeter. Joined Al Donahue in 1939, then with Glenn Miller and Jimmy Dorsey from 1940-42. Led U.S. Army band. Own band in 1946. Own TV series in the '50s. Appeared in the movie *Daddy Long Legs* with Fred Astaire in 1955. Wrote "Bunny Hop." Married for a time to actress Mamie Van Doren.	
3/19/55	10	6	**1. Golden Horn** [I]	Capitol 563
6/23/56	15	1	2. Dream Dancing [I]	Capitol 723
10/28/57	11	21	3. Young Ideas [I]	Capitol 866
5/19/58	12	10	4. The Dream Girl [I]	Capitol 969
8/11/62	14	13	5. Worried Mind [I]	Capitol 1752
			ANTHRAX	
			New York hard-rock quintet: Joey Belladonna (vocals), Dan Spitz (guitar), Scott Ian (guitar), Frank Bello (bass) and Charlie Benante (drums). Greg D'Angelo of White Lion was an early member. Band appeared on TV's "Married ... With Children" in 1992. Belladonna left in early 1992.	
10/15/88	30	5	● 1. State Of Euphoria	Island 91004
9/15/90	24	6	● 2. Persistence Of Time	Island 846480
7/13/91	27	7	● 3. Attack Of The Killer B's [K]	Megaforce 848804
			unreleased material and B-sides recorded from 1988-91	
6/12/93	7	4	● **4. Sound Of White Noise**	Elektra 61430
			APPICE, Carmine — see BECK, Jeff	
			APRIL WINE	
			Rock quintet from Montreal: Myles Goodwyn (lead singer, guitar), Brian Greenway (guitar), Steve Lang (bass), Gary Moffet (guitar) and Jerry Mercer (drums). Lang, Moffet and Mercer replaced by Daniel Barbe (keyboards), Jean Pellerin (bass) and Marty Simon (drums) in 1985.	
2/28/81	26	12	▲ 1. The Nature Of The Beast	Capitol 12125
8/7/82	37	3	2. Power Play	Capitol 12218
			ARCADIA	
			English group featuring Duran Duran's Simon LeBon, Nick Rhodes and Roger Taylor.	
12/21/85	23	9	▲ So Red The Rose *Election Day* (6)	Capitol 12428
			ARGENT	
			British rock quartet. Consisted of ex-Zombies member Rod Argent (vocals, keyboards), Jim Rodford (bass; Argent's cousin), Robert Henrit (drums) and Russ Ballard (guitar; later successful songwriter/ producer). Rodford and Henrit were later members of The Kinks.	
9/2/72	23	7	All Together Now *Hold Your Head Up* (5)	Epic 31556

DATE	POS	WKS	ARTIST—RECORD TITLE	LABEL & NO.
			ARMATRADING, Joan	
			Born on 12/9/50 in St. Kitts, West Indies. Vocalist/pianist/guitarist/composer. To Birmingham, England, in 1958. First recorded for Cube in 1971.	
7/26/80	28	5	1. Me Myself I	A&M 4809
5/28/83	32	3	2. The Key	A&M 4912
			ARMSTRONG, Louis	
			Born Daniel Louis Armstrong in New Orleans on 8/4/01 (not 7/4/1900, as Armstrong claimed). Died on 7/6/71 in New York. Nickname: "Satchmo." Joined legendary band of Joe "King" Oliver in Chicago in 1922. By 1929, had become the most widely known black musician in the world. Influenced dozens of singers and trumpet players, both black and white. Numerous appearances on radio and TV and in movies. Won 1972 Lifetime Achievement Grammy Award. Inducted into the Rock and Roll Hall of Fame in 1990 as a forefather of rock music.	
10/1/55	10	2	**1. Satch Plays Fats**	Columbia 708
			LOUIS ARMSTRONG and his All-Stars a tribute to Fats Waller	
12/15/56	12	2	2. Ella And Louis	Verve 4003
			ELLA FITZGERALD and LOUIS ARMSTRONG backing by the Oscar Peterson Trio, plus Buddy Rich	
5/23/64	1 (6)	48	● **3. Hello, Dolly!**	Kapp 3364
			Hello, Dolly! (1)	
			ARNOLD, Eddy	
			Born Richard Edward Arnold on 5/15/18 near Henderson, Tennessee. Ranked as the #1 artist in *Joel Whitburn's Top Country Singles 1944-1993* book. Became popular on Nashville's *Grand Ole Opry* as a singer with Pee Wee King (1940-43). Nicknamed "The Tennessee Plowboy" on all RCA recordings through 1954. Elected to the Country Music Hall of Fame in 1966. Won 1967 Country Music Association Entertainer of the Year Award.	
11/27/65	7	28	● **1. My World**	RCA 3466
			Make The World Go Away (6)	
5/21/66	26	5	2. I Want To Go With You	RCA 3507
3/11/67	36	2	3. Somebody Like Me	RCA 3715
6/24/67	34	2	● 4. The Best Of Eddy Arnold [G]	RCA 3565
11/25/67	34	5	5. Turn The World Around	RCA 3869
			ARRESTED DEVELOPMENT	
			Coed rap outfit from Georgia led by Milwaukee-born, Tennessee-raised Todd "Speech" Thomas. Includes his cousin Aerlee Taree (pronounced early ta-ree), Tim "Headliner" Barnwell, Montsho Eshe, Rasa Don and Baba Oje. Won 1992 Best New Artist Grammy Award. Thomas's parents publish *The Milwaukee Community Journal*.	
7/25/92	7	44	▲ **3 Years, 5 Months & 2 Days In The Life Of ...**	Chrysalis 21929
			title refers to length of time between group's formation and the signing of its recording contract *Tennessee* (6)/*People Everyday* (8)/*Mr. Wendal* (6)	
			ARROWS, The — see ALLAN, Davie	
			ARTISTS UNITED AGAINST APARTHEID	
			Benefit group of 49 superstar artists formed to protest the South African apartheid government; proceeds went to political prisoners in South Africa. Organized by Little Steven and Arthur Baker. Featuring Pat Benatar, Bono (U2), Jackson Browne, Jimmy Cliff, Bob Dylan, Peter Gabriel, Bonnie Raitt, Lou Reed, Bruce Springsteen and many others.	
12/7/85	31	4	Sun City	Manhattan 53019

DATE	POS	WKS	ARTIST—RECORD TITLE	LABEL & NO.
			ASHFORD & SIMPSON	
			Husband-and-wife R&B vocal/songwriting duo: Nickolas Ashford (born 5/4/42, Fairfield, South Carolina) and Valerie Simpson (born 8/26/46, New York City). Recorded as Valerie & Nick in 1964 ("Bubbled Under"). Team wrote for Chuck Jackson and Maxine Brown. Joined staff at Motown and wrote and produced for many of the label's top stars. Simpson recorded solo in 1972. They married in 1974. Simpson's brother, Ray, was the lead singer of Village People.	
9/23/78	20	12	● 1. Is It Still Good To Ya	Warner 3219
9/8/79	23	9	● 2. Stay Free	Warner 3357
9/13/80	38	2	3. A Musical Affair	Warner 3458
2/9/85	29	10	4. Solid	Capitol 12366
			ASIA	
			British rock supergroup: guitarist Steve Howe (Yes), drummer Carl Palmer (Emerson, Lake & Palmer; Atomic Rooster), keyboardist Geoff Downes (Buggles; Yes) and vocalist/bassist John Wetton (King Crimson; Uriah Heep; U.K.). Howe replaced by Mandy Meyer (Krokus) in 1985. Meyer replaced in 1990 by Oakland, California native Pat Thrall (Automatic Man; Pat Travers Band; Hughes/Thrall).	
4/3/82	1 (9)	35	▲⁴ 1. Asia	Geffen 2008
			Heat Of The Moment (4)	
8/27/83	6	11	▲ 2. Alpha	Geffen 4008
			Don't Cry (10)	
			ASSOCIATION, The	
			Group formed in Los Angeles in 1965. Consisted of Terry Kirkman (plays 23 wind, reed and percussion instruments), Gary "Jules" Alexander (guitar), Brian Cole (bass), Jim Yester (guitar), Ted Bluechel, Jr. (drums) and Russ Giguere (percussion). Larry Ramos, Jr., joined in early 1968. Cole died on 8/2/72 of a heroin overdose.	
10/1/66	5	15	● **1. And Then ... Along Comes The Association**	Valiant 5002
			Along Comes Mary (7)/*Cherish* (1)	
3/4/67	34	3	2. Renaissance	Valiant 5004
8/5/67	8	25	● **3. Insight Out**	Warner 1696
			Windy (1)/*Never My Love* (2)	
5/25/68	23	6	4. Birthday	Warner 1733
			Everything That Touches You (10)	
1/25/69	4	23	▲² **5. Greatest Hits** [G]	Warner 1767
10/18/69	32	4	6. The Association	Warner 1800
			ASTLEY, Rick	
			Born on 2/6/66 in Warrington; raised in Manchester, England. Pop singer/guitarist.	
2/13/88	10	39	▲² **1. Whenever You Need Somebody**	RCA 6822
			Never Gonna Give You Up (1)/*Together Forever* (1)/ *It Would Take A Strong Strong Man* (10)	
2/4/89	19	10	● 2. Hold Me In Your Arms	RCA 8589
			She Wants To Dance With Me (6)	
4/27/91	31	4	3. Free	RCA 3004
			Cry For Help (7)	

DATE	POS	WKS	ARTIST—RECORD TITLE	LABEL & NO.
			ATKINS, Chet	
			Born on 6/20/24 in Luttrell, Tennessee. Revered guitarist; began recording for RCA in 1947. Moved to Nashville in 1950 and became prolific studio musician/producer. RCA's A&R manager in Nashville from 1960-68; RCA Vice President from 1968-82. Entered the Country Music Hall of Fame in 1973 as youngest inductee (age 49). Won 1993 Lifetime Achievement Grammy Award.	
6/16/58	21	4	1. Chet Atkins At Home [I]	RCA 1544
2/22/60	16	12	2. Teensville [I]	RCA 2161
2/13/61	7	9	**3. Chet Atkins' Workshop** **[I]**	RCA 2232
4/28/62	31	4	4. Down Home [I]	RCA 2450
10/13/62	33	6	5. Caribbean Guitar [I]	RCA 2549
			ATLANTA RHYTHM SECTION	
			Group formed of musicians from Studio One, Doraville, Georgia, in 1971. Consisted of Rodney Justo (vocals), Barry Bailey and J.R. Cobb (guitars), Paul Goddard (bass), Dean Daughtry (keyboards) and Robert Nix (drums). Justo, Daughtry and Nix were with Roy Orbison's band, The Candymen. Cobb, Daughtry and band manager/producer Buddy Buie were with The Classics IV. Justo left after first album; replaced by Ronnie Hammond.	
3/12/77	11	14	● 1. A Rock And Roll Alternative *So In To You* (7)	Polydor 6080
4/8/78	7	15	▲ **2. Champagne Jam** *Imaginary Lover* (7)	Polydor 6134
7/7/79	26	7	● 3. Underdog	Polydor 6200
			ATLANTIC STARR	
			Soul band formed in 1976 in White Plains, New York, by brothers Wayne, David and Jonathan Lewis. Wayne and David on vocals with Sharon Bryant. In 1984, reduced to a quintet; Barbara Weathers replaced Bryant. Porscha Martin replaced Weathers in 1989. Rachel Oliver replaced Martin in 1991. By 1994, Aisha Tanner replaced Oliver.	
4/17/82	18	7	1. Brilliance	A&M 4883
2/22/86	17	14	● 2. As The Band Turns *Secret Lovers* (3)	A&M 5019
5/16/87	18	15	● 3. All In The Name Of Love *Always* (1)	Warner 25560
			AURRA	
			Ohio soul band: ex-Slave members Steve Washington and Tom Lockett, Jr. (saxophones), with Philip Fields (keyboards) and Starleana Young and Curt Jones (vocalists). Young and Jones later formed the duo Deja.	
4/17/82	38	3	A Little Love	Salsoul 8551
			AUSTIN, Patti	
			Born on 8/10/48 in New York City. R&B backing vocalist in New York. Goddaughter of Quincy Jones. Made Harlem's Apollo Theater debut at age four. In the 1988 movie *Tucker*.	
1/29/83	36	11	Every Home Should Have One *Baby, Come To Me* (1-with James Ingram)	Qwest 3591
			AUTOGRAPH	
			Los Angeles-based rock quintet led by vocalist Steve Plunkett.	
2/23/85	29	12	● Sign in Please	RCA 8040

DATE	POS	WKS	ARTIST—RECORD TITLE	LABEL & NO.
			AVALON, Frankie	
			Born Francis Avallone on 9/18/39 in Philadelphia. Teen idol managed by Bob Marcucci. Worked in bands in Atlantic City, New Jersey, in 1953. Radio and TV with Paul Whiteman, mid-1950s. Singer/trumpet player with Rocco & His Saints in 1957, which included Bobby Rydell. Co-starred in many movies with Annette. Appeared in the movies *Jamboree!* (1957), *Guns of the Timberland* (1960), *The Alamo* (1960) and *Back to the Beach* (1987).	
1/4/60	9	13	**Swingin' On A Rainbow**	Chancellor 5004
			AVERAGE WHITE BAND	
			Vocal/instrumental group formed in Scotland in 1972. Consisted of Alan Gorrie (of Forever More; vocals, bass), Hamish Stuart (vocals, guitar), Onnie McIntyre (vocal, guitar), Malcolm Duncan (saxophone), Roger Ball (keyboards, saxophone) and Robbie McIntosh (drums). McIntosh died of drug poisoning on 9/23/74; replaced by Steve Ferrone. McIntosh and Ferrone were members of Brian Auger's Oblivion Express.	
12/21/74	**1**(1)	17	● **1. AWB**	Atlantic 7308
			Pick Up The Pieces (1)	
5/17/75	39	2	2. Put It Where You Want It [E-R]	MCA 475
			reissue of 1973 album *Show Your Hand*	
7/5/75	4	11	● **3. Cut The Cake**	Atlantic 18140
			Cut The Cake (10)	
7/31/76	9	10	▲ **4. Soul Searching**	Atlantic 18179
2/5/77	28	5	● 5. Person To Person [L]	Atlantic 1002 [2]
8/20/77	33	5	6. Benny And Us	Atlantic 19105
			AVERAGE WHITE BAND & BEN E. KING	
4/22/78	28	5	● 7. Warmer Communications	Atlantic 19162
5/5/79	32	3	8. Feel No Fret	Atlantic 19207
			AYERS, Roy	
			Born on 9/10/40 in Los Angeles. R&B-jazz vibraphone player/keyboardist/ vocalist. At age five, was given pair of mallets by famed vibraphonist Lionel Hampton. With Herbie Mann from 1966-70. In 1970, formed Ubiquity, whose guest players included drummer Billy Cobham, flutist Herbert Laws, guitarist George Benson, trombonist Wayne Henderson (The Crusaders) and vocalist Dee Dee Bridgewater.	
4/15/78	33	3	Let's Do It	Polydor 6126
			# B	
			BABYFACE	
			Vocalist/instrumentalist Kenneth Edmonds, formerly with Manchild and The Deele. Brother of Kevon and Melvin Edmonds of After 7. Prolific writing/ production duo with L.A. Reid.	
9/23/89	14	41	▲² 1. Tender Lover	Solar 45288
			It's No Crime (7)/*Whip Appeal* (6)	
9/4/93	16	14	▲² 2. For The Cool In You	Epic 53558
			When Can I See You (4)	

DATE	POS	WKS	ARTIST—RECORD TITLE	LABEL & NO.
			BABYS, The	
			British rock group: John Waite (vocals), Walt Stocker, Mike Corby and Tony Brock. By 1980, keyboardist Jonathan Cain (later of Journey) replaced Corby, and bassist Ricky Phillips joined group. In 1989, Waite formed Bad English with Phillips and Cain.	
12/17/77	**34**	3	1. Broken Heart	Chrysalis 1150
3/10/79	**22**	10	2. Head First	Chrysalis 1195
			BACHARACH, Burt	
			Born on 5/12/28 in Kansas City. Conductor/arranger/composer. With lyricist Hal David wrote "Close To My," "Raindrops Keep Falling On My Head," "This Guy's In Love With You," "What's New Pussycat" and most of Dionne Warwick's hits. Formerly married to actress Angie Dickinson. Married to songwriter Carole Bayer Sager, 1982-91.	
6/26/71	**18**	12	● Burt Bacharach	A&M 3501
			BACHMAN-TURNER OVERDRIVE	
			Hard-rock group formed in Vancouver, Canada, in 1972. Brothers Randy (vocals, guitar), Tim (guitar) and Robbie Bachman (drums), with C. Fred Turner (vocals, bass). Originally known as Brave Belt. Randy had been in The Guess Who and recorded solo. Tim left in 1973; replaced by Blair Thornton. Randy left in 1977 to form Ironhorse. Randy and Tim re-grouped with Turner in 1984.	
3/9/74	**4**	35	● **1. Bachman-Turner Overdrive II**	Mercury 696
9/14/74	**1**(1)	25	● **2. Not Fragile**	Mercury 1004
			You Ain't Seen Nothing Yet (1)	
6/7/75	**5**	9	● **3. Four Wheel Drive**	Mercury 1027
1/31/76	**23**	7	● 4. Head On	Mercury 1067
9/11/76	**19**	6	▲ 5. Best Of B.T.O. (So Far) [G]	Mercury 1101
			BAD COMPANY	
			British rock band: Paul Rodgers (vocals), Mick Ralphs (guitar), Simon Kirke (drums) and Boz Burrell (bass). Rodgers and Kirke from Free; Ralphs from Mott The Hoople; and Burrell from King Crimson. Rodgers, who left group in late 1982, was member of supergroup The Firm (1984-86) and The Law (since 1991). In 1986, vocalist Brian Howe joined Kirke and Ralphs in group. Bassist Paul Cullen and guitarist Geoffrey Whitehorn joined in 1990. Rick Wills (of Foreigner; bass) joined in late 1992. Lineup in 1993: Ralphs, Kirke, Howe, Wills and Dave Colwell (rhythm guitar). Band named after a 1972 Jeff Bridges movie.	
8/3/74	**1**(1)	15	▲⁵ **1. Bad Company**	Swan Song 8410
			Can't Get Enough (5)	
4/26/75	**3**	11	▲³ **2. Straight Shooter**	Swan Song 8413
			Feel Like Makin' Love (10)	
2/21/76	**5**	15	▲ **3. Run With The Pack**	Swan Song 8415
4/2/77	**15**	8	● 4. Burnin' Sky	Swan Song 8500
3/31/79	**3**	24	▲² **5. Desolation Angels**	Swan Song 8506
9/18/82	**26**	6	6. Rough Diamonds	Swan Song 90001
7/28/90	**35**	4	▲ 7. Holy Water	Atco 91371
10/10/92	**40**	1	● 8. Here Comes Trouble	Atco 91759
			BAD ENGLISH	
			Rock supergroup: John Waite (vocals), Ricky Phillips (bass), Jonathan Cain (keyboards), Neal Schon (guitar) and Deen Castronovo (drums). Waite, Phillips and Cain were members of The Babys. Cain and Schon (ex-Santana) were members of Journey. Schon and Castronovo with Hardline in 1992.	
10/21/89	**21**	22	▲ Bad English	Epic 45083
			When I See You Smile (1)/*Price Of Love* (5)	

Paula Abdul's 1988 smash debut album, *Forever Your Girl*, spent 10 weeks at No. 1 and was, significantly, the first domestically signed success for Virgin Records' American-label operation. *Shut Up And Dance (The Dance Mixes)*, Abdul's 1990 follow-up, was one of pop's very first all-remix collections.

Herb Alpert's Tijuana Brass scored its first No. 1 album with 1965's *Whipped Cream & Other Delights*. Its cover, one of the most memorable of the '60s, was later parodied by hitmakers Soul Asylum on 1988's *Clam Dip & Other Delights*.

Another Bad Creation's 1991 Motown debut, *Coolin' At The Playground Ya' Know*, announced the arrival of a captivating young R&B group in the tradition of Motown's historic Jackson 5. The quintet's initials and the Jacksons' 1970 hit "ABC" bore intriguing similarities.

Asia's eponymous debut marked the career high point of one of the most successful supergroups in pop history. For nine weeks, the 1982 album held the No. 1 slot, a position the group's forebears, Yes, King Crimson and Emerson, Lake & Palmer, never attained.

Joan Baez's 1965 set, *Farewell, Angelina*, was the third (and, so far, last) Top 10 album of her distinguished career. Six years later, the prolific singer had her first Top 5 hit with a cover of The Band's "The Night They Drove Old Dixie Down."

The Beach Boys' extraordinary career has so far resulted in only two No. 1 albums: 1974's oldies collection, *Endless Summer*, and the 1964 live set, *Beach Boys Concert*. The latter was notable for its inclusion of group leader Brian Wilson, who stopped touring with the band only a month after the album's release.

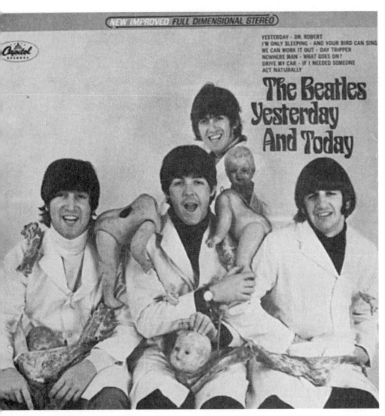

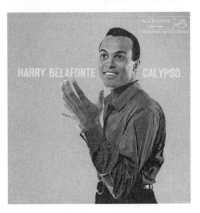

The Beatles' 1966 album, *Yesterday And Today*, bore this eminently collectible cover on a limited number of its first pressings. Now worth many thousands of dollars, the so-called "butcher cover" may be the best-known rarity in all of rock and roll.

The Bee Gees' phenomenal success with the *Saturday Night Fever* soundtrack, which stayed perched at No. 1 for 24 weeks in 1977–78, was a career high from which the much-respected Gibb Brothers have never fully recovered. The trio's white suits, as well as John Travolta's memorable pose, have come to visually represent both an entire decade and the era of disco.

Harry Belafonte's enormous success with 1956's *Calypso*, a No. 1 album for 31 weeks, came nearly 30 years before his high-visibility slot as the spokesperson for USA for Africa's superstar single, "We Are The World."

Tony Bennett's presence on the charts was a given throughout the '60s via such song collections as 1963's *This Is All I Ask*, his fifth charting album. Thirty years later, incredibly enough, he became an MTV sensation.

DATE	POS	WKS	ARTIST—RECORD TITLE	LABEL & NO.
			BADFINGER	
			Welsh rock quartet originally known as The Iveys. Consisted of Pete Ham (guitar), Tom Evans (bass), Joey Molland (guitar; joined in late 1968, after band's first hit single "Maybe Tomorrow") and Mike Gibbins (drums). All but Gibbins share vocals. Ham (born 4/27/47) committed suicide on 4/23/75. Group disbanded from 1976-78. Molland and Evans re-grouped in 1979. Evans committed suicide on 11/23/83 (age 36).	
12/5/70	28	5	1. No Dice	Apple 3367
			No Matter What (8)	
2/19/72	31	3	2. Straight Up	Apple 3387
			produced by Todd Rundgren and George Harrison	
			Day After Day (4)	
			BAEZ, Joan	
			Born Joan Chandos Baez in Staten Island, New York, on 1/9/41 to a Mexican father and British mother. Preeminent folk-song stylist. Became political activist while attending Boston University in late '50s. Made her professional debut in July 1959 at the first Newport Folk Festival. Orientation changed from traditional to popular folk songs in the early '60s. Influential in fostering career of Bob Dylan. Founded the Institute for the Study of Nonviolence in Carmel Valley, California, in 1965. Married to Stanford University student leader David Harris from 1968-71. Appeared in Bob Dylan's Rolling Thunder Revue in 1975 and his 1978 movie *Renaldo and Clara*. Baez's sister Mimi Farina was in a folk-song- writing/singing duo with her husband, the late Richard Farina.	
12/18/61	13	70	● 1. Joan Baez, Vol. 2	Vanguard 2097
4/14/62	15	45	● 2. Joan Baez	Vanguard 2077
			Baez's first album, recorded in 1960	
11/3/62	10	70	● **3. Joan Baez In Concert** [L]	Vanguard 2122
12/14/63	7	23	**4. Joan Baez In Concert, Part 2** [L]	Vanguard 2123
12/5/64	12	28	5. Joan Baez/5	Vanguard 79160
11/13/65	10	9	**6. Farewell, Angelina**	Vanguard 79200
10/14/67	38	2	7. Joan	Vanguard 79240
2/15/69	30	5	● 8. Any Day Now	Vanguard 79306 [2]
			songs of Bob Dylan	
7/26/69	36	2	9. David's Album	Vanguard 79308
			dedicated to her husband, David Harris, imprisoned for draft resistance	
10/2/71	11	10	● 10. Blessed Are	Vanguard 6570 [2]
			The Night They Drove Old Dixie Down (3)	
6/14/75	11	17	● 11. Diamonds & Rust	A&M 4527
3/6/76	34	3	12. From Every Stage [L]	A&M 3704 [2]
			BAILEY, Philip	
			Born on 5/8/51 in Denver. R&B percussionist/co-lead vocalist with Earth, Wind & Fire since 1971.	
1/19/85	22	11	Chinese Wall	Columbia 39542
			Easy Lover (2-with Phil Collins)	
			BAKER, Anita	
			Born on 1/26/58 in Toledo, Ohio; raised in Detroit. Soul singer. Female lead singer of Chapter 8 from 1976-84.	
9/13/86	11	72	▲⁵ 1. Rapture	Elektra 60444
			Sweet Love (8)	
11/5/88	1(4)	28	▲³ **2. Giving You The Best That I Got**	Elektra 60827
			Giving You The Best That I Got (3)	
7/21/90	5	18	▲ **3. Compositions**	Elektra 60922

DATE	POS	WKS	ARTIST—RECORD TITLE	LABEL & NO.
10/1/94	3	16	▲² **4. Rhythm Of Love**	Elektra 61555
			### BAKER('S), Ginger, Air Force	
			Born Peter Baker on 8/19/39 in Lewisham, England. Drummer for Cream and Blind Faith. Got start as replacement for Charlie Watts (who left to join The Rolling Stones) in Alexis Korner's Blues Incorporated in 1962. Then with The Graham Bond Organization. Air Force featured Steve Winwood, Denny Laine (Moody Blues; Wings) and Rick Grech (Family; Traffic; Blind Faith). Joined Masters of Reality in 1992.	
6/6/70	33	3	Ginger Baker's Air Force [L] recorded live at London's Royal Albert Hall	Atco 703 [2]
			### BALIN, Marty	
			Born on 1/30/43 in Cincinnati. Co-founder of Jefferson Airplane/Jefferson Starship/KBC.	
8/15/81	35	3	Balin *Hearts* (8)	EMI America 17054
			### BALL, Kenny, and his Jazzmen	
			Born on 5/22/30 in Ilford, England. Leader of English Dixieland jazz band formed in 1958.	
4/14/62	13	15	Midnight In Moscow [I] *Midnight In Moscow* (2)	Kapp 1276
			### BANANARAMA	
			Female pop-rock trio from London: Sarah Dallin, Keren Woodward and Siobhan Fahey. Group name is combination of the children's TV show "The Banana Splits" and the Roxy Music song "Pyjamarama." Fahey married Dave Stewart (Eurythmics) on 8/1/87; left group in early 1988; replaced by Jacqui O'Sullivan (who left in mid-1991). Fahey later formed duo Shakespear's Sister.	

9/15/84	30	7	1. Bananarama
			    reissued (#820165) October 1984 with new song "Wild Life"
			    Cruel Summer (9)
				London 820036

8/23/86	15	11	● 2. True Confessions *Venus* (1)	London 828013
			### BAND, The	
			Rock group formed in Woodstock, New York, in 1967: Robbie Robertson (guitar), Levon Helm (drums), Rick Danko (bass), Richard Manuel and Garth Hudson (keyboards). All from Canada (except Helm from Arkansas) and all were with Ronnie Hawkins's Hawks. Group's "farewell concert" on Thanksgiving Day in 1976 was documented in the Martin Scorcese movie *The Last Waltz*. Manuel committed suicide on 3/4/86 (age 42). Helm, Danko and Hudson reunited in 1993 with Jim Weider (guitar), Richard Bell (piano) and Randy Ciarlante (drums). Inducted into the Rock and Roll Hall of Fame in 1994.	
10/19/68	30	7	1. Music From Big Pink Big Pink: The Band's communal home in West Saugerties, New York	Capitol 2955
10/18/69	9	24	▲ **2. The Band**	Capitol 132
9/5/70	5	14	● **3. Stage Fright**	Capitol 425
10/16/71	21	5	4. Cahoots	Capitol 651
9/23/72	6	14	● **5. Rock Of Ages** [L]	Capitol 11045 [2]
12/15/73	28	6	6. Moondog Matinee title is the name of Alan Freed's Cleveland radio show, late '50s	Capitol 11214
2/9/74	1(4)	12	**7. Planet Waves** **BOB DYLAN With The Band**	Asylum 1003

DATE	POS	WKS	ARTIST—RECORD TITLE	LABEL & NO.
7/20/74	**3**	10	**8. Before The Flood** [L] **BOB DYLAN/THE BAND**	Asylum 201 [2]
8/2/75	**7**	9	**9. The Basement Tapes** [E] **BOB DYLAN AND THE BAND** recorded in 1967 at the Big Pink, a house rented by The Band in West Saugerties, New York	Columbia 33682 [2]
1/3/76	**26**	5	10. Northern Lights-Southern Cross	Capitol 11440
5/20/78	**16**	8	11. The Last Waltz [S-L] farewell concert at the San Francisco Winterland with guests Bob Dylan, Eric Clapton, Neil Diamond, Ringo Starr and others	Warner 3146 [3]

BANGLES

Female pop-rock quartet formed in Los Angeles in January 1981. Consisted of sisters Vicki (lead guitar) and Debbi Peterson (drums), Michael Steele (bass) and Susanna Hoffs (guitar). Originally named The Bangs. Steele was previously in The Runaways. Disbanded in October 1989.

DATE	POS	WKS	ARTIST—RECORD TITLE	LABEL & NO.
3/8/86	**2**(2)	46	▲³ **1. Different Light** *Manic Monday* (2)/*Walk Like An Egyptian* (1)	Columbia 40039
12/24/88	**15**	24	▲ 2. Everything *In Your Room* (5)/*Eternal Flame* (1)	Columbia 44056

BAR-KAYS

R&B vocal/instrumental combo: Jimmy King (guitar), Ronnie Caldwell (organ), James Alexander (bass), Carl Cunningham (drums), Phalon Jones (saxophone) and Ben Cauley (trumpet). Formed by Al Jackson, drummer with Booker T & The MG's. The plane crash that killed Otis Redding (12/10/67) also claimed the lives of all the Bar-Kays except Alexander (not on plane) and Cauley (survived crash). Alexander re-formed the band. Appeared in the movie *Wattstax*; much session work at Stax. Alexander's son Phalon began solo career in 1990.

DATE	POS	WKS	ARTIST—RECORD TITLE	LABEL & NO.
12/15/79	**35**	4	● Injoy	Mercury 3781

BASIA

Born on 9/30/59; raised in Jaworzno, Poland. Britain-based, female pop-jazz singer/composer Basia Trzetrzelewska (pronounced basha tshet-shel-ev-ska). Former vocalist of the group Matt Bianco.

DATE	POS	WKS	ARTIST—RECORD TITLE	LABEL & NO.
11/12/88	**36**	3	▲ 1. Time And Tide	Epic 40767
3/10/90	**20**	15	▲ 2. London Warsaw New York	Epic 45472
5/21/94	**27**	2	● 3. The Sweetest Illusion	Epic 64255

BASIE, Count

Born William Basie on 8/21/04 in Red Bank, New Jersey. Died on 4/26/84 of pancreatic cancer. World- renowned jazz, big band leader/pianist/organist. Learned music and piano from mother, organ from Fats Waller. First recorded with own band in 1937 for Decca. Appeared in many movies and toured into the '70s. His best-known recording, "One O'Clock Jump" (1937), is in the Grammy Hall of Fame. Won 1981 Trustees Grammy Award.

DATE	POS	WKS	ARTIST—RECORD TITLE	LABEL & NO.
2/9/63	**5**	22	**1. Sinatra-Basie** **FRANK SINATRA/COUNT BASIE**	Reprise 1008
7/20/63	**19**	4	2. This Time By Basie! Hits of the 50's And 60's [I]	Reprise 6070
9/12/64	**13**	15	3. It Might As Well Be Swing **FRANK SINATRA/COUNT BASIE**	Reprise 1012

BASIL, Toni

Born in 1950. Los Angeles-based choreographer/actress/video director. Worked on TV shows "Shindig" and "Hullaballoo." Choreographed the movie *American Graffiti*. Appeared in the movie *Easy Rider* and others.

DATE	POS	WKS	ARTIST—RECORD TITLE	LABEL & NO.
11/27/82	**22**	9	● Word Of Mouth *Mickey* (1)	Chrysalis 1410

DATE	POS	WKS	ARTIST—RECORD TITLE	LABEL & NO.
			BAXTER, Les	
			Born on 3/14/22 in Mexia, Texas. Orchestra leader/arranger. Began as a conductor on radio shows in the '30s. Member of Mel Torme's vocal group, The Mel-Tones. Musical arranger for Capitol Records (Nat King Cole, Margaret Whiting and others) in the '50s. Composed over 100 movie scores.	
1/28/56	6	2	**1. Tamboo!** [I]	Capitol 655
			LES BAXTER/His Chorus and Orchestra	
3/16/57	21	2	2. Skins! [I]	Capitol 774
			BAY CITY ROLLERS	
			Rock group formed in 1967 in Edinburgh, Scotland, as The Saxons. Original members: brothers Alan and Derek Longmuir, Les McKeoun (lead singer), Eric Faulkner and Stuart "Woody" Wood.	
12/13/75	20	9	● 1. Bay City Rollers	Arista 4049
			Saturday Night (1)	
7/24/76	31	4	● 2. Rock N' Roll Love Letter	Arista 4071
			Money Honey (9)	
10/9/76	26	7	● 3. Dedication	Arista 4093
7/30/77	23	7	● 4. It's A Game	Arista 7004
			You Made Me Believe In Magic (10)	
			BEACH BOYS, The	
			Group formed in Hawthorne, California, in 1961. Consisted of brothers Brian (keyboards, bass), Carl (guitar), and Dennis Wilson (drums); their cousin Mike Love (lead vocals, saxophone; formed the group Celebration in 1978), and Al Jardine (guitar). Known in high school as Kenny & The Cadets, Carl & The Passions, then The Pendletones. First recorded for X/Candix in 1961. Jardine replaced by David Marks from March 1962 to March 1963. Brian quit touring with group in December 1964; replaced briefly by Glen Campbell until Bruce Johnston (of Bruce & Terry) joined permanently in April 1965. Johnston and Campbell also recorded in the studio band Sagittarius in 1967. Brian continued to write for and produce group; returned to stage in 1983. Daryl Dragon (of Captain & Tennille) was a keyboardist in the stage band. Dennis Wilson drowned on 12/28/83 (age 39). Lineup of Carl, Brian, Mike, Alan and Bruce continues to perform today. Carnie and Wendy Wilson, daughters of Brian Wilson, are members of Wilson Phillips. Group was inducted into the Rock and Roll Hall of Fame in 1988.	
12/8/62	32	7	1. Surfin' Safari	Capitol 1808
5/18/63	2 (2)	30	● 2. Surfin' U.S.A.	Capitol 1890
			Surfin' U.S.A. (3)	
10/26/63	7	18	● 3. Surfer Girl	Capitol 1981
			Surfer Girl (7)	
12/7/63	4	20	▲ 4. Little Deuce Coupe	Capitol 1998
			Be True To Your School (6)	
5/2/64	13	22	● 5. Shut Down, Volume 2	Capitol 2027
			Fun, Fun, Fun (5)	
			Volume 1 listed in Miscellaneous section: Cars	
8/8/64	4	38	● 6. All Summer Long	Capitol 2110
			I Get Around (1)	
11/21/64	1 (4)	40	● 7. Beach Boys Concert [L]	Capitol 2198
4/17/65	4	29	● 8. The Beach Boys Today!	Capitol 2269
			When I Grow Up (9)/*Dance, Dance, Dance* (8)	
8/7/65	2 (1)	17	● 9. Summer Days (And Summer Nights!!)	Capitol 2354
			Help Me Rhonda (1)/*California Girls* (3)	
12/4/65	6	14	10. Beach Boys' Party!	Capitol 2398
			Barbara Ann (2)	

DATE	POS	WKS	ARTIST—RECORD TITLE	LABEL & NO.
6/11/66	**10**	21	**11. Pet Sounds**	Capitol 2458
			Sloop John B (3)/*Wouldn't It Be Nice* (8)	
8/13/66	**8**	18	▲² **12. Best Of The Beach Boys** [G]	Capitol 2545
1/27/68	**24**	9	13. Wild Honey	Capitol 2859
10/2/71	**29**	7	14. Surf's Up	Brother 6453
3/10/73	**36**	3	15. Holland	Brother 2118
1/5/74	**25**	5	● 16. The Beach Boys In Concert [L]	Brother 6484 [2]
8/3/74	**1**(1)	19	● **17. Endless Summer** [K]	Capitol 11307 [2]
5/17/75	**8**	13	● **18. Spirit Of America** [K]	Capitol 11384 [2]
8/9/75	**25**	5	19. Good Vibrations-Best Of The Beach Boys [G]	Brother 2223
7/24/76	**8**	12	● **20. 15 Big Ones**	Brother 2251
			15: age of band and number of tracks	
			Rock And Roll Music (5)	

BEASTIE BOYS

New York white rap trio formed in 1981, consisting of King Ad-Rock (Adam Horovitz, son of playwright Israel Horovitz), MCA (Adam Yauch) and Mike D (Michael Diamond). Horovitz starred in the movie *Lost Angels* and married actress Ione Skye (daughter of *Donovan*). Their DJ, Doctor Dre, became co-host of *Yo! MTV Raps*. Beastie stands for Boys Entering Anarchistic States Towards Internal Excellence.

DATE	POS	WKS	ARTIST—RECORD TITLE	LABEL & NO.
12/20/86	**1**(7)	37	▲⁵ **1. Licensed To Ill**	Def Jam 40238
			(You Gotta) Fight For Your Right (To Party!) (7)	
8/19/89	**14**	8	● 2. Paul's Boutique	Capitol 91743
			album named after a store in Brooklyn	
5/9/92	**10**	12	▲ **3. Check Your Head**	Capitol 98938
6/18/94	**1**(1)	15	▲ **4. Ill Communication**	Capitol 28599

BEATLES, The

The world's #1 rock group was formed in Liverpool, England, in the late '50s. Known in early forms as The Quarrymen, Johnny & the Moondogs, The Rainbows, and the Silver Beatles. Named The Beatles in 1960. Originally consisted of John Lennon, Paul McCartney, George Harrison (guitars), Stu Sutcliffe (bass) and Pete Best (drums). Sutcliffe left in April 1961 (died 4/10/62 of a brain hemorrhage); McCartney moved to bass. Best replaced by Ringo Starr in August 1962. Group managed by Brian Epstein (died 8/27/67 of sleeping-pill overdose); produced by George Martin. First U.S. tour in February 1964. Won 1964 Best New Artist Grammy Award. Group starred in the movies *A Hard Day's Night* (1964), *Help* (1965), *Magical Mystery Tour* (1967) and *Let It Be* (1970); contributed soundtrack to the animated movie *Yellow Submarine* (1968). Own Apple label in 1968. McCartney publicly announced group's dis- solution on 4/10/70. Won 1972 Trustees Grammy Award. Lennon was shot to death on 12/8/80. Inducted into the Rock and Roll Hall of Fame in 1988.

DATE	POS	WKS	ARTIST—RECORD TITLE	LABEL & NO.
2/8/64	**1**(11)	27	▲⁵ **1. Meet The Beatles!**	Capitol 2047
			I Want To Hold Your Hand (1)	
2/15/64	**2**(9)	26	**2. Introducing ... The Beatles**	Vee-Jay 1062
			1st U.S. album; released July 1963	
			Please Please Me (3)/*Twist And Shout* (2)/	
			Do You Want To Know A Secret (2)/*Love Me Do** (1)/	
			*P.S. I Love You** (10) *only on first pressing	
4/25/64	**1**(5)	26	● **3. The Beatles' Second Album**	Capitol 2080
			She Loves You (1)	
6/20/64	**20**	9	4. The American Tour With Ed Rudy [T]	RadioPulsebeat 2
			interviews with The Beatles	
7/18/64	**1**(14)	40	**5. A Hard Day's Night** [S]	United Art. 6366
			features 8 vocals and 4 instrumentals	
			Can't Buy Me Love (1)/*A Hard Day's Night* (1)	

DATE	POS	WKS	ARTIST—RECORD TITLE	LABEL & NO.
8/15/64	**2**(9)	28	▲ **6. Something New** includes 5 tunes from *A Hard Day's Night* album	Capitol 2108
12/19/64	**7**	9	● **7. The Beatles' Story** [T] narrative featuring bits of their hits	Capitol 2222 [2]
1/9/65	**1**(9)	38	▲² **8. Beatles '65** *I Feel Fine* (1)/*She's A Woman* (4)	Capitol 2228
7/10/65	**1**(6)	21	● **9. Beatles VI** *Eight Days A Week* (1)	Capitol 2358
9/11/65	**1**(9)	33	● **10. Help!** [S] features 7 vocals and 5 instrumentals *Ticket To Ride* (1)/*Help!* (1)	Capitol 2386
1/8/66	**1**(6)	39	▲⁴ **11. Rubber Soul**	Capitol 2442
7/16/66	**1**(5)	15	● **12. "Yesterday" ... And Today** [G] originally featured the "butcher cover" (proper name of photo on cover is "Somnambulant Adventure"), which is valued at $2000-$5000 for a mono copy and $5000-$10,000 for a stereo copy; album quickly withdrawn after its release and a new photo was pasted over the controversial original cover *Yesterday* (1)/*We Can Work It Out* (1)/*Day Tripper* (5)/ *Nowhere Man* (3)	Capitol 2553
9/10/66	**1**(6)	24	▲³ **13. Revolver** *Yellow Submarine* (2)	Capitol 2576
6/24/67	**1**(15)	63	▲⁸ **14. Sgt. Pepper's Lonely Hearts Club Band** 1967 Album of the Year Grammy Award; also see soundtrack of the same name	Capitol 2653
12/30/67	**1**(8)	30	▲⁵ **15. Magical Mystery Tour** [S-G] 6 tunes from the movie and 5 singles hits *Penny Lane* (1)/*Strawberry Fields Forever* (8)/ *All You Need Is Love* (1)/*Hello Goodbye* (1)	Capitol 2835
12/14/68	**1**(9)	25	▲⁷ **16. The Beatles [White Album]** simply titled *The Beatles*; however, because of stark cover, commonly referred to as *The White Album*	Apple 101 [2]
2/15/69	**2**(2)	12	▲ **17. Yellow Submarine** [S] side 1: The Beatles; side 2: instrumentals by George Martin	Apple 153
10/25/69	**1**(11)	32	▲⁹ **18. Abbey Road** Abbey Road is the London studio where group recorded 191 songs *Come Together* (1)/*Something* (3)	Apple 383
3/21/70	**2**(4)	17	▲³ **19. Hey Jude** [G] *Paperback Writer* (1)/*Lady Madonna* (4)/*Hey Jude* (1)/ *The Ballad Of John And Yoko* (8)	Apple 385
6/6/70	**1**(4)	20	● **20. Let It Be** [S] movie features The Beatles during recording sessions *Get Back* (1)/*Let It Be* (1)/*The Long And Winding Road* (1)	Apple 34001
4/21/73	**3**	18	▲⁵ **21. The Beatles/1962-1966** [G]	Apple 3403 [2]
4/21/73	**1**(1)	21	▲⁵ **22. The Beatles/1967-1970** [G]	Apple 3404 [2]
6/26/76	**2**(2)	13	▲ **23. Rock 'N' Roll Music** [K] *Got To Get You Into My Life* (7)	Capitol 11537 [2]
5/21/77	**2**(2)	8	▲ **24. The Beatles At The Hollywood Bowl** [E-L] concert recordings of 8/23/64 and 8/30/65	Capitol 11638
11/19/77	**24**	6	● **25. Love Songs** [K]	Capitol 11711 [2]
4/19/80	**21**	9	**26. Rarities** [K]	Capitol 12060
4/10/82	**19**	8	● **27. Reel Music** [K] tunes from The Beatles' 5 movies	Capitol 12199

DATE	POS	WKS	ARTIST—RECORD TITLE	LABEL & NO.
12/24/94	3	7	▲⁴ **28. Live At The BBC** [E-L] band's recordings and dialog as featured performers on 52 of London's BBC radio programs	Apple 31796 [2]
			BEAU BRUMMELS, The Rock group formed in 1964 in San Francisco. Led by Sal Valentino (born Sal Spaminato on 9/8/42, San Francisco; vocals) and Ron Elliott (born 10/21/43, Haddsburg, California; guitar).	
6/26/65	24	7	Introducing The Beau Brummels produced by Sly Stone *Just A Little* (8)	Autumn 103
			BECK Born Beck Hansen on 7/8/70 near Kansas City. Raised in Los Angeles. Male singer/songwriter/guitarist.	
3/19/94	13	9	● Mellow Gold *Loser* (10)	DGC 24634
			BECK, Jeff Born on 6/24/44 in Surrey, England. Veteran guitarist. With The Yardbirds from 1964-66. Rod Stewart and Ron Wood were members of The Jeff Beck Group from 1967-69. Member of supergroup The Honeydrippers.	
9/14/68	15	14	1. Truth	Epic 26413
8/2/69	15	8	2. Beck-Ola * above 2 with Rod Stewart (vocals)	Epic 26478
6/3/72	19	9	● 3. Jeff Beck Group * ***JEFF BECK GROUP**	Epic 31331
4/28/73	12	11	● 4. Jeff Beck, Tim Bogert, Carmine Appice **BECK, BOGERT, APPICE** Bogert (bass) and Appice (drums) were both formerly with Cactus and Vanilla Fudge; Appice was later with Blue Murder and KGB	Epic 32140
4/26/75	4	11	▲ **5. Blow By Blow** [I]	Epic 33409
7/17/76	16	9	▲ 6. Wired [I]	Epic 33849
4/9/77	23	6	7. Jeff Beck with The Jan Hammer Group Live [I-L]	Epic 34433
7/19/80	21	8	8. There And Back [I]	Epic 35684
8/17/85	39	2	9. Flash *People Get Ready* sung by Rod Stewart	Epic 39483
			BEE GEES Trio of brothers from Manchester, England: Barry Gibb (born 9/1/47) and twins Maurice and Robin Gibb (born 12/22/49). First performed December 1955. To Australia in 1958; performed as The Gibbs, later as BG's, finally the Bee Gees. First recorded for Leedon/Festival in 1963. Returned to England in February 1967, with guitarist Vince Melouney and drummer Colin Peterson. Toured Europe and the U.S. in 1968. Melouney left in December 1968; Robin left for solo career in 1969. When Peterson left in August 1969, Barry and Maurice went solo. After eight months, the brothers reunited. Composed soundtracks for *Saturday Night Fever* and *Staying Alive*. Acted in the movie *Sgt. Pepper's Lonely Hearts Club Band*. Youngest brother Andy Gibb was a successful solo singer (died 3/10/88).	
9/16/67	7	18	**1. Bee Gees' 1st**	Atco 223
2/24/68	12	7	2. Horizontal	Atco 233
9/28/68	17	7	3. Idea *I've Gotta Get A Message To You* (8)/*I Started A Joke* (6)	Atco 253
3/8/69	20	10	4. Odessa	Atco 702 [2]
8/2/69	9	16	● **5. Best Of Bee Gees** [G]	Atco 292

DATE	POS	WKS	ARTIST—RECORD TITLE	LABEL & NO.
2/6/71	**32**	5	6. 2 Years On *Lonely Days* (3)	Atco 353
10/2/71	**34**	6	7. Trafalgar *How Can You Mend A Broken Heart* (1)	Atco 7003
12/16/72	**35**	3	8. To Whom It May Concern	Atco 7012
8/16/75	**14**	22	● 9. Main Course *Jive Talkin'* (1)/*Nights On Broadway* (7)	RSO 4807
10/2/76	**8**	27	▲ **10. Children Of The World** *You Should Be Dancing* (1)/*Love So Right* (3)	RSO 3003
6/4/77	**8**	31	▲ **11. Here At Last ... Bee Gees ... Live** [L]	RSO 3901 [2]
12/10/77	**1**(24)	54	▲[11] **12. Saturday Night Fever** [S] 6 cuts by the Bee Gees/others by various artists; 1978 Album of the Year Grammy Award; the #1-selling soundtrack album of all time (25 million) *How Deep Is Your Love* (1)/*Stayin' Alive* (1)/*Night Fever* (1)/*If I Can't Have You* (1-Yvonne Elliman)	RSO 4001 [2]
2/17/79	**1**(6)	26	▲ **13. Spirits Having Flown** *Too Much Heaven* (1)/*Tragedy* (1)/*Love You Inside Out* (1)	RSO 3041
11/17/79	**1**(1)	17	▲ **14. Bee Gees Greatest** [G] RSO hits only	RSO 4200 [2]
7/30/83	**6**	14	▲ **15. Staying Alive** [S] side 1: Bee Gees; side 2: various artists *Far From Over* (10-Frank Stallone)	RSO 813269

BELAFONTE, Harry

Born Harold George Belafonte, Jr., on 3/1/27 in Harlem to a Jamaican mother and a West Indian father. Actor in American Negro Theater, Drama Workshop, mid-1940s. Started career as a "straight pop" singer. Recorded for Jubilee Records in 1949; shortly afterward began specializing in folk music. Rode the crest of the calypso craze to worldwide stardom. Starred in eight movies from 1953-74. Replaced Danny Kaye in 1987 as UNICEF goodwill ambassador. Father of actress Shari Belafonte.

DATE	POS	WKS	ARTIST—RECORD TITLE	LABEL & NO.
1/28/56	**3**	6	1. **"Mark Twain" And Other Folk Favorites**	RCA 1022
2/25/56	**1**(6)	62	● 2. **Belafonte**	RCA 1150
6/16/56	**1**(31)	72	● 3. **Calypso** *Banana Boat (Day-O)* (5)	RCA 1248
3/30/57	**2**(2)	20	● 4. **An Evening With Belafonte**	RCA 1402
9/16/57	**3**	16	5. **Belafonte Sings Of The Caribbean**	RCA 1505
10/20/58	**16**	12	6. Belafonte Sings The Blues	RCA 1006
5/25/59	**18**	10	7. Love Is A Gentle Thing	RCA 1927
6/22/59	**13**	19	8. Porgy & Bess **LENA HORNE/HARRY BELAFONTE**	RCA 1507
11/16/59	**3**	86	● 9. **Belafonte At Carnegie Hall** [L]	RCA 6006 [2]
3/21/60	**34**	1	10. My Lord What A Mornin' spirituals	RCA 2022
12/26/60	**3**	10	● 11. **Belafonte Returns To Carnegie Hall** [L] with Odetta-Miriam Makeba-Chad Mitchell Trio	RCA 6007 [2]
9/11/61	**3**	40	● 12. **Jump Up Calypso**	RCA 2388
6/2/62	**8**	18	13. **The Midnight Special**	RCA 2449
10/27/62	**25**	13	14. The Many Moods Of Belafonte	RCA 2574
7/13/63	**30**	5	15. Streets I Have Walked	RCA 2695
4/25/64	**17**	10	16. Belafonte At The Greek Theatre [L]	RCA 6009 [2]

DATE	POS	WKS	ARTIST—RECORD TITLE	LABEL & NO.
			BELL & JAMES	
			R&B duo of Leroy Bell and Casey James. Began as songwriting team for Bell's uncle, producer Thom Bell.	
4/7/79	**31**	4	Bell & James	A&M 4728
			BELL BIV DeVOE	
			Trio of New Edition members: Ricky Bell, Michael Bivins and Ronnie DeVoe. Bivins produced Another Bad Creation, Boyz II Men and M.C. Brains; formed own record label, Biv 10, and assembled East Coast Family.	
4/14/90	**5**	54	▲³ **1. Poison**	MCA 6387
			Poison (3)/*Do Me!* (3)	
9/14/91	**18**	9	● 2. WBBD — Bootcity! The Remix Album [K]	MCA 10345
7/10/93	**19**	2	● 3. Hootie Mack	MCA 10682
			CD includes bonus track	
			BENATAR, Pat	
			Born Patricia Andrzejewski in Lindenhurst, Long Island, New York, in 1952. Rock singer. Married her producer/guitarist Neil Giraldo on 2/20/82. Acted in the movie *Union City* and the 1989 ABC Afterschool TV Special "Torn Between Two Fathers."	
1/26/80	**12**	15	▲ 1. In The Heat Of The Night	Chrysalis 1236
8/30/80	**2**(5)	38	▲⁴ **2. Crimes Of Passion**	Chrysalis 1275
			Hit Me With Your Best Shot (9)	
7/25/81	**1**(1)	30	▲² **3. Precious Time**	Chrysalis 1346
11/27/82	**4**	27	▲ **4. Get Nervous**	Chrysalis 1396
10/22/83	**13**	16	▲ 5. Live From Earth [L]	Chrysalis 41444
			2 of the 10 songs are new studio tracks	
			Love Is A Battlefield (5)	
12/1/84	**14**	15	▲ 6. Tropico	Chrysalis 41471
			We Belong (5)	
12/21/85	**26**	9	7. Seven The Hard Way	Chrysalis 41507
			Invincible (10)	
8/6/88	**28**	10	● 8. Wide Awake In Dreamland	Chrysalis 41628
5/4/91	**37**	3	9. True Love	Chrysalis 21805
			CD includes bonus track	
			BENEDICTINE MONKS OF SANTO DOMINGO DE SILOS, The	
			36 monks who live in an 8th-century monastery in north-central Spain. They sing 1,000-year-old Gregorian chants in Latin.	
4/9/94	**3**	24	▲² Chant [F]	Angel 55138
			BENNETT, Tony	
			Born Anthony Dominick Benedetto on 8/13/26 in Queens, New York. One of the top jazz vocalists of the past 40 years. Worked local clubs while in high school; sang in U.S. Army bands. Breakthrough in 1949 with Bob Hope, who suggested that he change his then-stage name, Joe Bari, to Tony Bennett. Audition record of "Boulevard of Broken Dreams" earned a Columbia contract in 1950. Appeared in the movie *The Oscar*.	
2/23/57	**14**	9	1. Tony	Columbia 938
8/25/62	**5**	83	● **2. I Left My Heart In San Francisco**	Columbia 8669
12/8/62	**37**	2	3. Tony Bennett At Carnegie Hall [L]	Columbia 23 [2]
4/6/63	**5**	23	**4. I Wanna Be Around**	Columbia 8800
9/21/63	**24**	8	5. This Is All I Ask	Columbia 8856
3/21/64	**20**	8	6. The Many Moods Of Tony	Columbia 8941

DATE	POS	WKS	ARTIST—RECORD TITLE	LABEL & NO.
10/2/65	**20**	18	● 7. Tony's Greatest Hits, Volume III [G]	Columbia 9173
5/14/66	**18**	12	8. The Movie Song Album	Columbia 9272
			BENSON, George	
			Born on 3/22/43 in Pittsburgh. R&B-jazz guitarist. Played guitar from age eight. Played in Brother Jack McDuff's trio in 1963. House musician at CTI Records to early '70s. Influenced by Wes Montgomery. Member of Fuse One.	
5/22/76	**1**(2)	22	▲³ **1. Breezin'**	Warner 2919
			This Masquerade (10)	
2/19/77	**9**	17	▲ **2. In Flight**	Warner 2983
2/18/78	**5**	19	▲ **3. Weekend In L.A.** [L]	Warner 3139 [2]
			On Broadway (7)	
3/24/79	**7**	13	● **4. Livin' Inside Your Love**	Warner 3277 [2]
8/9/80	**3**	20	▲ **5. Give Me The Night**	Warner 3453
			Give Me The Night (4)	
12/12/81	**14**	14	● 6. The George Benson Collection [G]	Warner 3577 [2]
			Turn Your Love Around (5)	
7/2/83	**27**	11	● 7. In Your Eyes	Warner 23744
			BENTON, Brook	
			Born Benjamin Franklin Peay on 9/19/31 in Camden, South Carolina; died on 4/9/88 of complications from spinal meningitis. R&B singer/songwriter. In The Camden Jubilee Singers. To New York in 1948; joined Bill Langford's Langfordaires. With Jerusalem Stars in 1951. First recorded under own name for Okeh in 1953. Wrote "Looking Back," "A Lover's Question," "The Stroll," "It's Just A Matter Of Time" and "Endlessly."	
12/29/62	**40**	1	1. Singing The Blues — Lie To Me	Mercury 60740
3/28/70	**27**	4	2. Brook Benton Today	Cotillion 9018
			Rainy Night In Georgia (4)	
			BERGEN, Polly	
			Born on 7/4/30 in Knoxville, Tennessee. Real name: Nellie Burgin. Singer/actress in movies and on TV.	
6/10/57	**10**	5	**1. Bergen Sings Morgan**	Columbia 994
			Bergen portrayed '20s "torch singer" Helen Morgan in a TV movie	
11/4/57	**20**	1	2. The Party's Over	Columbia 1031
			BERLIN	
			Los Angeles electro-pop group. Went from a sextet to a trio in 1985 featuring Terri Nunn (vocals), John Crawford (bass) and Rob Brill (drums). Nunn, who as a teen acted on "Lou Grant" and several other TV shows, left band in 1987 and had an Adult Contemporary hit with Paul Carrack in 1989, "Romance."	
3/19/83	**30**	11	▲ 1. Pleasure Victim	Geffen 2036
5/26/84	**28**	4	● 2. Love Life	Geffen 4025
			BERMAN, Shelley	
			Born on 2/3/26 in Chicago. Popular nightclub comedian/actor. Made TV debut on "The Jack Paar Show." In movies The Best Man, The Wheeler Dealer and Divorce American Style.	
4/27/59	**2**(5)	46	**1. Inside Shelley Berman** [C]	Verve 15003
11/30/59	**6**	39	**2. Outside Shelley Berman** [C]	Verve 15007
7/25/60	**4**	24	**3. The Edge Of Shelley Berman** [C]	Verve 15013
12/25/61	**25**	3	4. A Personal Appearance [C]	Verve 15027

DATE	POS	WKS	ARTIST—RECORD TITLE	LABEL & NO.
			BERNSTEIN, Leonard	
			Born on 8/25/18 in Lawrence, Massachusetts. Died on 10/14/90 of emphysema-related heart attack. Conductor/pianist/composer. First classical international superstar from U.S. Conductor of numerous major orchestras worldwide, including the New York Philharmonic (1958-69) and the Vienna Philharmonic. Composed music for *West Side Story*, the movie *On the Waterfront* and others. Won 1985 Lifetime Achievement Grammy Award. Married Chilean actress Felicia Montealegre Cohn in 1951. Retired only five days before his death.	
12/12/60	**13**	7	1. Bernstein Plays Brubeck Plays Bernstein [I]	Columbia 8257
			side 1: New York Philharmonic with the Dave Brubeck Quartet conducted by Leonard Bernstein; side 2: Dave Brubeck Quartet	
			BERRY, Chuck	
			Born Charles Edward Anderson Berry on 10/18/26 in San Jose, California. Grew up in St. Louis. Muddy Waters introduced Berry to Leonard Chess (Chess Records) in Chicago. First recording, "Maybellene," was an instant success. Appeared in the movie *Rock, Rock, Rock* in 1956, and several others. Won 1984 Lifetime Achievement Grammy Award. Inducted into the Rock and Roll Hall of Fame in 1986. Movie documentary/concert tribute to Berry, *Hail! Hail! Rock 'n' Roll*, released in 1987. Acclaimed as one of rock and roll's most influential artists.	
10/5/63	**29**	2	1. Chuck Berry On Stage [L]	Chess 1480
			live audience dubbed in	
8/22/64	**34**	3	2. Chuck Berry's Greatest Hits [G]	Chess 1485
			Maybellene (5)/School Day (3)/Rock & Roll Music (8)/ Sweet Little Sixteen (2)/Johnny B. Goode (8)	
8/5/72	**8**	20	● **3. The London Chuck Berry Sessions** [L]	Chess 60020
			side 1: studio; side 2: live *My Ding-A-Ling* (1)	
			BETTS, Dickey	
			Born on 12/12/43 near Sarasota, Florida. Lead guitarist of The Allman Brothers Band. Wrote "Ramblin' Man" and "Jessica." In the late '70s, formed Great Southern.	
9/28/74	**19**	7	1. Highway Call **RICHARD BETTS** side 1: vocals; side 2: instrumentals	Capricorn 0123
5/21/77	**31**	2	2. Dickey Betts & Great Southern **DICKEY BETTS & GREAT SOUTHERN**	Arista 4123
			B-52'S, The	
			Formed in 1977 in Athens, Georgia, as a new-wave dance band: Cindy Wilson (guitar, vocals) and her brother Ricky Wilson (died of AIDS on 10/12/85; guitar), Kate Pierson (organ, vocals), Fred Schneider (keyboards, vocals) and Keith Strickland (drums; moved to guitar after Ricky's death). Cindy left in 1991; replaced on tour by Julee Cruise. Appeared as The B.C. 52's in the movie *The Flintstones*. B-52 is slang for the bouffant hairstyle worn by Kate and Cindy.	
9/27/80	**18**	9	● 1. Wild Planet	Warner 3471
3/6/82	**35**	4	2. Mesopotamia [M]	Warner 3641
6/4/83	**29**	6	● 3. Whammy!	Warner 23819
9/9/89	**4**	41	▲² **4. Cosmic Thing**	Reprise 25854
			Love Shack (3)/*Roam* (3)	
7/11/92	**16**	4	● 5. Good Stuff	Reprise 26943

DATE	POS	WKS	ARTIST—RECORD TITLE	LABEL & NO.
			BIG BROTHER AND THE HOLDING COMPANY	
			Rock group formed in San Francisco in 1965. Janis Joplin joined as lead singer in 1966. Other members: Peter Albin (bass), James Gurley (guitar), Sam Andrew (guitar) and David Getz (drums). Sensation at the Monterey Pop Festival in 1967. Disbanded in 1972.	
9/14/68	1(8)	29	● **Cheap Thrills**	Columbia 9700
			BIG COUNTRY	
			Rock quartet formed in Dunfermline, Scotland: Stuart Adamson (vocals, guitar), Bruce Watson (guitar), Tony Butler (bass) and Mark Brzezicki (drums).	
10/8/83	18	18	● The Crossing	Mercury 812870
			BIG HEAD TODD AND THE MONSTERS	
			Colorado-based rock trio: Todd Park Mohr (guitar, keyboards), Rob Squires (bass) and Brian Nevin (drums). All share vocals.	
10/15/94	30	1	Strategem	Giant 24580
			BIG MIKE	
			Male rapper from Houston. Member of The Geto Boys.	
7/30/94	40	1	● Somethin' Serious	Rap-A-Lot 53907
			BILK, Mr. Acker	
			Born Bernard Stanley Bilk on 1/28/29 in Somerset, England. Clarinetist/composer.	
5/19/62	3	24	● **Stranger On The Shore** [I]	Atco 129
			Stranger On The Shore (1)	
			BISHOP, Elvin	
			Born on 10/21/42 in Tulsa, Oklahoma. Lead guitarist with The Paul Butterfield Blues Band (1965-68).	
4/24/76	18	8	1. Struttin' My Stuff	Capricorn 0165
			Fooled Around And Fell In Love (3)	
10/8/77	38	2	2. Live! Raisin' Hell [L]	Capricorn 0185 [2]
			BISHOP, Stephen	
			Born on 11/14/51 in San Diego. Pop-rock singer/songwriter. Wrote movie theme for *The China Syndrome*. Cameo role as the "Charming Guy With Guitar" in *National Lampoon's Animal House*.	
10/8/77	34	3	1. Careless	ABC 954
			On And On	
11/4/78	35	4	● 2. Bish	ABC 1082
			BLACK('S), Bill, Combo	
			Bill was born on 9/17/26 in Memphis; died of a brain tumor on 10/21/65. Bass guitarist. Session work in Memphis; backed Elvis Presley (with Scotty Moore, guitar; D.J. Fontana, drums) on most of his early records. Formed own band in 1959. Labeled as "The Untouchable Sound."	
11/14/60	23	6	1. Solid And Raunchy [I]	Hi 12003
3/17/62	35	3	2. Let's Twist Her [I]	Hi 12006
			BLACK, Clint	
			Born on 2/4/62 in Long Branch, New Jersey; raised in Houston. Country singer. Former construction worker. Married actress Lisa Hartman (TV's "Knot's Landing," "Tabitha") on 10/20/91.	
5/19/90	31	8	▲³ 1. Killin' Time	RCA 9668
12/1/90	18	17	▲² 2. Put Yourself In My Shoes	RCA 2372
8/1/92	8	8	▲ **3. The Hard Way**	RCA 66003

DATE	POS	WKS	ARTIST—RECORD TITLE	LABEL & NO.
7/31/93	14	9	▲ 4. No Time To Kill	RCA 66239
10/29/94	37	1	● 5. One Emotion	RCA 66419

BLACK, Stanley, and his Orchestra

Born on 6/14/13 in London. Pianist/arranger/composer. Conducted BBC Dance Orchestra for nine years, beginning in 1944. Wrote many movie scores.

DATE	POS	WKS	ARTIST—RECORD TITLE	LABEL & NO.
3/10/62	30	2	1. Exotic Percussion [I]	London P. 4 44004
10/6/62	33	2	2. Spain [I]	London P. 4 44016

BLACKBYRDS, The

Soul group founded in 1973 by Donald Byrd (born 12/9/32, Detroit) while teaching jazz at Howard University in Washington, D.C.

DATE	POS	WKS	ARTIST—RECORD TITLE	LABEL & NO.
3/8/75	30	7	1. Flying Start	Fantasy 9472
			Walking In Rhythm (6)	
4/3/76	16	9	● 2. City Life	Fantasy 9490
1/29/77	34	4	● 3. Unfinished Business	Fantasy 9518

BLACK CROWES, The

Hard-rock quintet from Atlanta. Led by brothers Chris (vocals) and Rich (guitar) Robinson. Includes Jeff Cease, Steve Gorman and Johnny Colt. Cease left in late 1991; replaced by Marc Ford (ex-Burning Tree).

DATE	POS	WKS	ARTIST—RECORD TITLE	LABEL & NO.
11/10/90	4	49	▲⁴ **1. Shake Your Money Maker**	Def Amer. 24278
			album title is an Elmore James blues song	
5/30/92	1(1)	19	▲ **2. The Southern Harmony And Musical Companion**	Def Amer. 26916
			title derived from a famous book of hymns	
11/19/94	11	2	● 3. Amorica.	American 43000
			also released with less controversial cover on American 43001	

BLACKMORE, Ritchie — see RAINBOW

BLACK SABBATH

Heavy-metal group formed as blues band Earth in Birmingham, England, in 1968. Changed name to Black Sabbath in late 1969. Original lineup included: Ozzy Osbourne (vocals), Tony Iommi (guitar), William Ward (drums) and Terry "Geezer" Butler (bass). Osbourne formed The Blizzard of Ozz in 1979; replaced by Ronnie James Dio (Rainbow). Ward left for a year in 1981; replaced by Vinnie Appice. Ian Gillan (Deep Purple) replaced Dio in 1983. Fluctuating lineup since 1986. Iommi was the only original member in lineups that included vocalists Glenn Hughes (1986; ex-Deep Purple) and Tony Martin (since 1987); bassists Dave Spitz (1986-87), Bob Daisley (1987), Laurence Cottle (1989) and Neil Murray (since 1990); drummers Eric Singer (1986-87), Bev Bevan (1987; The Move; ELO) and Cozy Powell (since 1989; ELP), and keyboardist Geoff Nicholls (1983-89). Singer later joined Kiss. In 1991, reunion of Iommi, Butler, Appice and Dio.

DATE	POS	WKS	ARTIST—RECORD TITLE	LABEL & NO.
11/28/70	23	10	▲ 1. Black Sabbath	Warner 1871
2/20/71	12	34	▲⁴ 2. Paranoid	Warner 1887
9/11/71	8	17	▲ 3. **Master Of Reality**	Warner 2562
11/4/72	13	13	▲ 4. Black Sabbath, Vol. 4	Warner 2602
2/9/74	11	11	▲ 5. Sabbath Bloody Sabbath	Warner 2695
9/13/75	28	4	6. Sabotage	Warner 2822
6/21/80	28	9	▲ 7. Heaven And Hell	Warner 3372
12/5/81	29	8	● 8. Mob Rules	Warner 3605
2/19/83	37	4	9. Live Evil [L]	Warner 23742 [2]
11/5/83	39	2	10. Born Again	Warner 23978

DATE	POS	WKS	ARTIST—RECORD TITLE	LABEL & NO.
			BLACK SHEEP	
			Bronx rap duo of Andre "Dres" Titus and William "Mista Lawnge" (pronounced long) McLean.	
4/4/92	30	6	● A Wolf In Sheep's Clothing	Mercury 848368
			CD includes 2 bonus tracks	
			BLAND, Bobby	
			Born Robert Calvin Bland on 1/27/30 in Rosemark, Tennessee. Nicknamed "Blue." Sang in gospel group The Miniatures in Memphis, late '40s. Member of the Beale Streeters which included Johnny Ace, B.B. King, Rosco Gordon, Earl Forest and Willie Nix in 1949. Driver and valet for B.B. King; appeared in the Johnny Ace Revue, early '50s. First recorded in 1952 for the Modern label.	
8/3/63	11	7	Call On Me/That's The Way Love Is	Duke 77
			BLASTERS, The	
			Los Angeles rockabilly group led by brothers Phil (lead singer, guitar) and Dave (lead guitar) Alvin. Dave was also a member of The Knitters.	
5/1/82	36	4	The Blasters	Slash 3680
			BLIGE, Mary J.	
			Born in Atlanta; raised in Yonkers, New York. Twenty-one years old in 1992. R&B singer.	
8/22/92	6	34	▲² 1. What's The 411?	MCA 10681
			Real Love (7)	
12/17/94	7	11+	▲ 2. My Life	Uptown 11156
			BLIND FAITH	
			Short-lived British rock supergroup: Eric Clapton (The Yardbirds; John Mayall's Bluesbreakers; Cream), Steve Winwood (Spencer Davis Group; Traffic; Ginger Baker's Air Force), Ginger Baker (Cream; Air Force) and Rick Grech (Family; Traffic; Air Force). Formed and disbanded in 1969.	
8/23/69	1 (2)	20	▲ Blind Faith	Atco 304
			BLIND MELON	
			Los Angeles-based band: Shannon Hoon (vocals), Roger Stevens, Christopher Thorn, Brad Smith and Glen Graham. Stevens, Smith and Graham are from West Point, Mississippi.	
8/14/93	3	26	▲² Blind Melon	Capitol 96585
			album jacket features a childhood photo of Glen Graham's sister Georgia dressed in a bee costume; Heather DeLoach appeared as "The Bee Girl" in the group's music videos	
			BLONDIE	
			New York City techno-pop sextet formed in 1975. Consisted of Debbie Harry (lead singer), Chris Stein, Frank Infante, Jimmy Destri, Gary Valentine and Clem Burke. Harry had been in the folk-rock group Wind in the Willows. She did solo work from 1980; appeared in several movies. Group disbanded in 1983.	
3/17/79	6	16	▲ 1. Parallel Lines	Chrysalis 1192
			Heart Of Glass (1)	
10/27/79	17	19	▲ 2. Eat To The Beat	Chrysalis 1225
12/13/80	7	23	▲ 3. Autoamerican	Chrysalis 1290
			The Tide Is High (1)/*Rapture* (1)	
11/21/81	30	11	● 4. The Best Of Blondie [G]	Chrysalis 1337
			Call Me (1)	
6/26/82	33	4	5. The Hunter	Chrysalis 1384

DATE	POS	WKS	ARTIST—RECORD TITLE	LABEL & NO.
			BLOODROCK	
			Rock group from Fort Worth, Texas. Jim Rutledge (lead vocals) headed own production company in the '70s; produced Meri Wilson's top 20 pop single "Telephone Man."	
1/23/71	**21**	8	● 1. Bloodrock 2	Capitol 491
4/17/71	**27**	8	2. Bloodrock 3	Capitol 765
			BLOODSTONE	
			Soul group from Kansas City, Missouri. Formed in 1962 as The Sinceres. Consisted of Charles McCormick, Willis Draffen, Charles Love, Henry Williams and Roger Durham (died 1973 [age 27]).	
6/30/73	**30**	7	Natural High *Natural High* (10)	London 620
			BLOOD, SWEAT & TEARS	
			Pop-jazz group formed by Al Kooper (Royal Teens, Blues Project) in 1968. Nucleus consisted of Kooper (keyboards), Steve Katz (guitar; Blues Project), Bobby Colomby (drums) and Jim Fielder (bass). Kooper replaced by lead singer David Clayton-Thomas in 1969. Clayton-Thomas replaced by Jerry Fisher in 1972. Katz left in 1973. Clayton-Thomas rejoined in 1974. Colomby later worked as television music reporter and executive with Epic, Capitol, EMI and CBS.	
2/1/69	**1**(7)	66	▲³ **1. Blood, Sweat & Tears** 1969 Album of the Year Grammy Award *You've Made Me So Very Happy* (2)/*Spinning Wheel* (2)/ *And When I Die* (2)	Columbia 9720
7/18/70	**1**(2)	19	● **2. Blood, Sweat & Tears 3**	Columbia 30090
7/17/71	**10**	11	● **3. B, S & T; 4**	Columbia 30590
3/25/72	**19**	6	▲ 4. Blood, Sweat & Tears Greatest Hits [G]	Columbia 31170
11/25/72	**32**	7	5. New Blood	Columbia 31780
			BLOOMFIELD, Mike	
			Born on 7/28/44 in Chicago; died on 2/15/81 of a drug overdose. Blues guitarist. With The Paul Butterfield Blues Band and Electric Flag. Later joined KGB.	
10/5/68	**12**	10	● 1. Super Session **MIKE BLOOMFIELD/AL KOOPER/STEVE STILLS**	Columbia 9701
2/15/69	**18**	10	2. The Live Adventures Of Mike Bloomfield And Al Kooper [L] **MIKE BLOOMFIELD & AL KOOPER**	Columbia 6 [2]
			BLOW MONKEYS, The	
			British quartet led by Dr. Robert (Robert Howard). Includes: Mick Anker, Neville Henry and Tony Kiley.	
7/19/86	**35**	5	Animal Magic	RCA 8065
			BLUE CHEER	
			San Francisco hard-rock group: Dickie Peterson (vocals, bass), Leigh Stephens (guitar) and Paul Whaley (drums).	
3/30/68	**11**	11	Vincebus Eruptum	Philips 264

DATE	POS	WKS	ARTIST—RECORD TITLE	LABEL & NO.
			BLUE OYSTER CULT	
			Hard-rock quintet formed in Long Island, New York, in 1970: Donald "Buck Dharma" Roeser (guitar), Eric Bloom (vocal), Allen Lanier (keyboards), and brothers Joe (bass) and Albert Bouchard (drums). Earlier incarnations of band known as Soft White Underbelly, then The Stalk Forrest Group. Drummers Rick Downey and Jimmy Wilcox replaced Albert Bouchard from 1982 until his return to group in 1988. Tommy Zvoncheck filled in for Allen Lanier for a year in 1986. All original members back together since 1988. Bloom is a cousin of New York's shock-radio DJ Howard Stern.	
4/5/75	22	4	● 1. On Your Feet Or On Your Knees [L]	Columbia 33371 [2]
9/25/76	29	9	▲ 2. Agents Of Fortune	Columbia 34164
8/16/80	34	3	3. Cultosaurus Erectus	Columbia 36550
8/1/81	24	11	● 4. Fire Of Unknown Origin	Columbia 37389
6/12/82	29	5	5. Extraterrestrial Live [L]	Columbia 37946 [2]
			BLUES BROTHERS	
			Joliet "Jake" (John Belushi; born 1/24/49, Wheaton, Illinois; died 3/5/82) and Elwood Blues (Dan Aykroyd; born 7/1/52, Ottawa, Ontario); originally created for TV's "Saturday Night Live."	
1/6/79	**1**(1)	16	▲² **1. Briefcase Full Of Blues** [L]	Atlantic 19217
7/5/80	**13**	12	● 2. The Blues Brothers [S]	Atlantic 16017
			with Aretha Franklin, James Brown and Ray Charles	
			BLUES MAGOOS	
			Bronx, New York, psychedelic-rock quintet led by singer/guitarist Peppy Castro (real name: Emil Thielhelm). Originally known as The Bloos Magoos. Castro later became lead singer of Balance.	
2/18/67	**21**	5	Psychedelic Lollipop	Mercury 61096
			(We Ain't Got) Nothin' Yet (5)	
			BODY COUNT	
			Speed-metal band formed by rapper Ice-T (vocals) and Ernie-C (guitar), with D-Roc (guitar), Mooseman (bass) and Beatmaster V (drums). All are alumni of Crenshaw High School in South Central Los Angeles.	
4/18/92	**26**	4	● Body Count	Sire 26878
			national controversy over album due to lyrics of the track "Cop Killer" — releases of album from August on replaced "Cop Killer" with "Freedom Of Speech"	
			BOFILL, Angela	
			Born in West Bronx, New York, in 1954 to a French-Cuban father and Puerto Rican mother. Studied voice at Hartford Conservatory and at Manhattan School of Music. Performed with Dizzy Gillespie and Cannonball Adderley. Featured vocalist for the Dance Theater of Harlem at age 22.	
12/22/79	**34**	8	1. Angel of the Night	GRP 5501
4/2/83	**40**	3	2. Too Tough	Arista 9616
			BOGERT, Tim — see BECK, Jeff	
			BOHN, Rudi, and his Band	
			German conductor of polkas.	
10/16/61	**38**	2	Percussive Oompah [I]	London P. 4 44009

DATE	POS	WKS	ARTIST—RECORD TITLE	LABEL & NO.
			BOLTON, Michael	
			Born Michael Bolotin on 2/26/54 in New Haven, Connecticut. First recorded for Epic in 1969. Lead singer of Blackjack in the late '70s. Big break came when Laura Branigan recorded "How Am I Supposed To Live Without You." Began recording as Michael Bolton in 1983.	
12/23/89	3	50	▲6 1. Soul Provider	Columbia 45012
			How Am I Supposed To Live Without You (1)/ *How Can We Be Lovers* (3)/*When I'm Back On My Feet Again* (7)	
5/11/91	1(1)	77	▲8 2. Time, Love & Tenderness	Columbia 46771
			Love Is A Wonderful Thing (4)/*Time, Love And Tenderness* (7)/ *When A Man Loves A Woman* (1)	
10/17/92	1(1)	25	▲4 3. Timeless (The Classics)	Columbia 52783
12/4/93	3	24	▲3 4. The One Thing	Columbia 53567
			Said I Loved You ... But I Lied (6)	
			BONDS, Gary (U.S.)	
			Born Gary Anderson on 6/6/39 in Jacksonville, Florida. To Norfolk, Virginia, in the mid-1950s. Signed to Legrand by Frank Guida. Wrote "She's All I Got" hit for Johnny Paycheck in 1971.	
8/21/61	6	11	1. Dance 'til Quarter To Three	Legrand 3001
			U.S. BONDS	
			New Orleans (6)/*Quarter To Three* (1)/*School Is Out* (5)	
5/16/81	27	7	2. Dedication	EMI America 17051
			produced by Bruce Springsteen and Steve Van Zant	
			BONE THUGS-N-HARMONY	
			Male rap quintet from Cleveland: Krayzie Bone, Layzie Bone, Bizzy Bone, Wish Bone and Flesh-N-Bone. Discovered by Eazy-E.	
9/10/94	12	18+	▲1 Creepin On Ah Come Up [M]	Ruthless 5526
			BONHAM	
			British hard-rock quartet led by drummer Jason Bonham, the son of Led Zeppelin's drummer, the late John Bonham. Includes Daniel MacMaster (vocals), Ian Hatton (guitar) and John Smithson (keyboards, bass).	
12/16/89	38	6	● The Disregard Of Timekeeping	WTG 45009
			BON JOVI	
			Hard-rock quintet formed in Sayreville, New Jersey: Jon Bon Jovi (born 3/2/62; actual spelling: Bongiovi; lead vocals), Richie Sambora (born 7/11/59; guitar), Dave Bryan (born 2/7/62; keyboards), Alec John Such (born 11/14/56; bass) and Tico Torres (born 10/7/53; drums). Such left in November 1994.	
6/8/85	37	5	▲ 1. 7800 Fahrenheit	Mercury 824509
			title refers to the temperature of an exploding volcano	
9/20/86	1(8)	60	▲11 2. Slippery When Wet	Mercury 830264
			You Give Love A Bad Name (1)/*Livin' On A Prayer* (1)/ *Wanted Dead Or Alive* (7)	
10/8/88	1(4)	52	▲6 3. New Jersey	Mercury 836345
			Bad Medicine (1)/*Born To Be My Baby* (3)/ *I'll Be There For You* (1)/*Lay Your Hands On Me* (7)/ *Living In Sin* (9)	
8/25/90	3	22	▲2 4. Blaze Of Glory/Young Guns II [S]	Mercury 846473
			JON BON JOVI	
			songs from and songs inspired by the movie *Young Guns II* starring Emilio Estevez and Kiefer Sutherland	
			Blaze Of Glory (1)	
11/21/92	5	20	▲2 5. Keep The Faith	Jambco 514045
			Bed Of Roses (10)	

DATE	POS	WKS	ARTIST—RECORD TITLE	LABEL & NO.
11/5/94	8	17+	▲² **6. Cross Road** [G] *Always* (4)	Mercury 526013
			BONOFF, Karla	
			Born on 12/27/51 in Los Angeles. Pop singer/songwriter/pianist.	
10/13/79	31	8	Restless Nights	Columbia 35799
			BOOGIE DOWN PRODUCTIONS	
			Brooklyn-based rap outfit led by Blastmaster KRS One (Kris Parker). Co-founder/DJ Scott "La Rock" Sterling fatally shot on 8/25/87 (age 24) in a scuffle in the Bronx. Rapper Derrick "D-Nice" Jones later recorded solo. Parker is brother-in-law of female rapper Harmony.	
8/5/89	36	4	● 1. Ghetto Music: The Blueprint Of Hip Hop	Jive 1187
9/1/90	32	3	● 2. Edutainment CD includes 3 bonus tracks	Jive 1358
			BOOKER T. & THE MG'S	
			Band formed by sessionmen from Stax Records, Memphis, in 1962. Consisted of Booker T. Jones (born 11/12/44, Memphis), keyboards; Steve Cropper (born 10/21/42, Ozark Mountains, Missouri), guitar; Donald "Duck" Dunn (born 11/24/41, Memphis), bass; and Al Jackson, Jr. (born 11/27/34, Memphis; murdered on 10/1/75), drums. MG stands for Memphis Group. Group disbanded in 1971; reorganized for short time in 1973. Jones produced Willie Nelson's *Stardust* album. Cropper and Dunn joined the Blues Brothers.	
1/12/63	33	2	1. Green Onions [I] *Green Onions* (3)	Stax 701
9/16/67	35	4	2. Hip Hug-Her [I]	Stax 717
			BOONE, Debby	
			Born on 9/22/56 in Hackensack, New Jersey. Third daughter of Shirley and Pat Boone and granddaughter of Red Foley. Worked with The Boone Family from 1969; sang with sisters in the Boones' gospel quartet. Went solo in 1977. Winner of three Grammys, including 1977 Best New Artist Award. Popular contemporary Christian artist. Married Gabriel Ferrer, the son of Rosemary Clooney and Jose Ferrer, in 1982.	
11/12/77	6	10	▲ **You Light Up My Life** *You Light Up My Life* (1)	Warner 3118
			BOONE, Pat	
			Born Charles Eugene Boone on 6/1/34 in Jacksonville, Florida. To Tennessee in 1936. Direct descendant of Daniel Boone. Married country singer Red Foley's daughter, Shirley, on 11/7/53. Won on "Ted Mack's Amateur Hour" and "Arthur Godfrey's Talent Scouts" in 1954. First recorded for Republic Records in 1954. Graduated from New York's Columbia University in 1958. Hosted own TV show, "The Pat Boone-Chevy Showroom," 1957-60. Appeared in 15 movies. Toured with wife and daughters Cherry, Linda, Laura and Debby Boone in the mid-1960s. Recording artist Nick Todd is his younger brother. Pat's trademark: white buck shoes.	
10/27/56	14	4	1. Howdy!	Dot 3030
6/24/57	13	7	2. A Closer Walk with Thee [EP] 7" EP (four sacred songs)	Dot 1056
7/8/57	19	3	3. "Pat"	Dot 3050
9/2/57	5	5	**4. Four By Pat** [EP] 7" EP (four songs)	Dot 1057
10/7/57	20	2	5. Pat Boone Pat's first album *Ain't That A Shame* (1)/*At My Front Door* (7)/*I'll Be Home* (4)	Dot 3012

DATE	POS	WKS	ARTIST—RECORD TITLE	LABEL & NO.
10/21/57	3	36	● 6. Pat's Great Hits [G] *I Almost Lost My Mind* (1)/*Friendly Persuasion* (5)/ *Don't Forbid Me* (1)/*Why Baby Why* (5)/ *Love Letters In The Sand* (1)/*Remember You're Mine* (6)/ *Chains Of Love* (10)	Dot 3071
12/23/57	12	13	7. April Love [S] *April Love* (1)	Dot 9000
12/23/57	21	4	8. Hymns We Love	Dot 3068
7/28/58	2 (1)	32	**9. Star Dust**	Dot 3118
11/24/58	13	2	10. Yes Indeed!	Dot 3121
7/20/59	17	9	11. Tenderly	Dot 3180
5/23/60	26	3	12. Moonglow	Dot 3270
8/7/61	29	6	13. Moody River *Moody River* (1)	Dot 3384
1/13/62	39	1	14. White Christmas [X]	Dot 3222
			BOOTSY'S RUBBER BAND	
			Bootsy is William Collins, born on 10/26/51 in Cincinnati. Member of James Brown's JB's from 1969-71. Bassist of Funkadelic/Parliament in 1972. Featured guitarist with Deee-Lite.	
3/5/77	16	12	● 1. Ahh ... The Name Is Bootsy, Baby!	Warner 2972
3/11/78	16	10	● 2. Bootsy? Player Of The Year	Warner 3093
			BOSS	
			Female rap duo based in Los Angeles. Lichelle "Boss" Laws and Irene "Dee" Moore met at Detroit's Oakland University.	
6/12/93	22	3	Born Gangstaz	DJ West 52903
			BOSTON	
			Rock group from Boston, spearheaded by Tom Scholz (guitars, keyboards) and Brad Delp (lead vocals). Originally a quintet, group also included Barry Goudreau (guitar), Fran Sheehan (bass) and Sib Hashian (drums). Goudreau formed Orion The Hunter. After a long absence from the charts, Boston returned in 1986 as a duo: Scholz and Delp. Delp and Goudreau spearheaded RTZ in 1991.	
10/16/76	3	49	▲¹⁵ **1. Boston** *More Than A Feeling* (5)	Epic 34188
9/2/78	1 (2)	13	▲⁶ **2. Don't Look Back** *Don't Look Back* (4)	Epic 35050
10/18/86	1 (4)	29	▲⁴ **3. Third Stage** *Amanda* (1)/*We're Ready* (9)	MCA 6188
6/25/94	7	5	▲ **4. Walk On**	MCA 10973
			BOSTON POPS ORCHESTRA	
			Conductor Arthur Fiedler was born in Boston on 12/17/1894; died on 7/10/79. Fiedler joined the Boston Pops Orchestra around 1915 as viola player. Began his long reign as conductor in 1930, where he remained until his death. John Williams succeeded Fiedler as conductor in 1980. **BOSTON POPS/ARTHUR FIEDLER:**	
2/2/59	9	16	**1. Offenbach: Gaite Parisienne; Khachaturian:** **Gayne Ballet Suite** [I]	RCA 2267
9/15/62	29	4	2. Pops Roundup [I]	RCA 2595
3/23/63	36	2	3. Our Man In Boston [I]	RCA 2599
4/13/63	5	18	**4. "Jalousie" And Other Favorites In The Latin** **Flavor** [I]	RCA 2661
6/22/63	29	7	5. Star Dust [I]	RCA 2670

DATE	POS	WKS	ARTIST—RECORD TITLE	LABEL & NO.
11/7/64	**18**	12	6. "Pops" Goes The Trumpet [I] **AL HIRT/BOSTON POPS/ARTHUR FIEDLER**	RCA 2729
5/18/63	**17**	7	**BOSTON SYMPHONY Orchestra** Ravel: Bolero/Pavan For A Dead Princess/ La Valse [I] Charles Munch, conductor	RCA 2664
			BOWIE, David Born David Robert Jones on 1/8/47 in London. First recorded as David Jones & The King Bees, Lower Third, and Manish Boys in 1963. Brought highly theatrical values to rock through work with Lindsay Kemp Mime Troupe. Periods of reclusiveness heightened his appeal. Movies *The Man Who Fell to Earth* (1976), *Labyrinth*, *Absolute Beginners* (1986) and others. In Broadway play *The Elephant Man* (1980). Married to Angie Barnet, the subject of The Rolling Stones' song "Angie," from 1970-80. Formed the group Tin Machine in 1988. Married Somalian actress/supermodel Iman on 4/24/92.	
3/3/73	**16**	10	1. Space Oddity [E-R] first released on Mercury 61246 in 1968	RCA 4813
5/26/73	**17**	8	● 2. Aladdin Sane	RCA 4852
11/24/73	**23**	9	3. Bowie Pin Ups Bowie's versions of his favorite pop hits from '64-'67; supermodel Twiggy appears on the cover	RCA 0291
6/22/74	**5**	10	● **4. Diamond Dogs** original cover, which is worth $2000+, features Bowie as a dog with his genitals visible — controversial and quickly withdrawn	RCA 0576
11/9/74	**8**	8	● **5. David Live** [L] recorded at the Tower Theatre, Philadelphia	RCA 0771 [2]
3/29/75	**9**	17	● **6. Young Americans** *Fame* (1)	RCA 0998
2/14/76	**3**	13	● **7. Station To Station** *Golden Years* (10)	RCA 1327
6/26/76	**10**	8	▲ **8. Changesonebowie** [G]	RCA 1732
2/5/77	**11**	7	9. Low	RCA 2030
11/26/77	**35**	3	10. "Heroes"	RCA 2522
6/23/79	**20**	8	11. Lodger	RCA 3254
10/18/80	**12**	12	12. Scary Monsters	RCA 3647
5/7/83	**4**	35	▲ **13. Let's Dance** *Let's Dance* (1)/*China Girl* (10)	EMI America 17093
10/20/84	**11**	11	▲ **14. Tonight** *Blue Jean* (8)	EMI America 17138
5/30/87	**34**	4	● 15. Never Let Me Down features Peter Frampton (lead guitar)	EMI America 17267
5/19/90	**39**	4	▲ 16. Changesbowie [G] Bowie's greatest hits from 1969-90	Rykodisc 20171
4/24/93	**39**	1	17. Black Tie White Noise CD includes 2 bonus tracks	Savage 50212
			BOYS, The Quartet of brothers, ages 9-14 in 1988, from Northridge, California: Khiry (lead), Hakeem, Tajh and Bilal Samad. All are members of performing gymnastic troupes.	
2/4/89	**33**	7	▲ Messages From The Boys	Motown 6260

DATE	POS	WKS	ARTIST—RECORD TITLE	LABEL & NO.
			BOYZ II MEN	
			R&B vocal quartet formed in 1988 at Philadelphia's High School of Creative and Performing Arts: Wanya Morris, Michael McCary, Shawn Stockman and Nathan Morris. Discovered by Michael Bivins (New Edition; Bell Biv DeVoe). Appeared in the 1992 TV mini-series "The Jacksons: An American Dream."	
6/15/91	**3**	70	▲⁵ **1. Cooleyhighharmony**	Motown 6320
			Motownphilly (3)/*It's So Hard To Say Goodbye To Yesterday* (2)	
12/11/93	**19**	5	▲ 2. Christmas Interpretations [X]	Motown 6365
			Christmas charts: 2/'93, 5/'94	
9/17/94	**1**(4)	24+	▲⁷ **3. II**	Motown 0323
			I'll Make Love To You (1)/*On Bended Knee* (1)	
			BRAM TCHAIKOVSKY	
			Rock quartet led by Bram (real name: Peter Bramall; earlier with The Motors). Formed in Lincolnshire, England.	
8/11/79	**36**	4	Strange Man, Changed Man	Polydor 62111
			BRAND NUBIAN	
			Rap outfit from New Rochelle, New York: "Grand Puba" Maxwell, Lord Jamar, and cousins Derek X (aka Sadat X) and DJ Alamo. Grand Puba left with DJ Alamo by 1992. Sincere then joined group.	
2/20/93	**12**	2	In God We Trust	Elektra 61381
			BRANIGAN, Laura	
			Born on 7/3/57 in Brewster, New York. Former backing vocalist with Leonard Cohen. Guest-starred on the TV show "CHiPs" and appeared in the 1984 movie *Mugsy's Girl*.	
11/27/82	**34**	9	● 1. Branigan	Atlantic 19289
			Gloria (2)	
5/14/83	**29**	5	● 2. Branigan 2	Atlantic 80052
			Solitaire (7)	
6/9/84	**23**	19	● 3. Self Control	Atlantic 80147
			Self Control (4)	
			BRASS CONSTRUCTION	
			Nine-man, multi-ethnic disco ensemble. Formed in Brooklyn in 1968 as Dynamic Soul by Guyana-born vocalist Randy Muller. Muller also organized the band Skyy.	
3/20/76	**10**	13	▲ **1. Brass Construction**	United Art. 545
12/4/76	**26**	9	● 2. Brass Construction II	United Art. 677
			BRAXTON, Toni	
			Female singer born in Severn, Maryland. Recorded in 1990 with her younger sisters as The Braxtons. Won 1993 Best New Artist Grammy Award.	
7/31/93	**1**(2)	59	▲⁵ **Toni Braxton**	LaFace 26007
			Another Sad Love Song (7)/*Breathe Again* (3)/ *You Mean The World To Me* (7)	
			BREAD	
			Formed in Los Angeles in 1969. Consisted of leader David Gates (vocals, guitar, keyboards), James Griffin (guitar), Robb Royer (guitar) and Jim Gordon (drums). Originally called Pleasure Faire. Griffin and Royer co-wrote the award-winning hit "For All We Know" with Fred Karlin in 1969. Mike Botts replaced Gordon after first album. Royer replaced by Larry Knechtel (top sessionman; member of Duane Eddy's Rebels) in 1971. Disbanded in 1973; reunited briefly in 1976. All songs written and produced by David Gates.	
8/22/70	**12**	8	● 1. On The Waters	Elektra 74076
			Make It With You (1)	

DATE	POS	WKS	ARTIST—RECORD TITLE	LABEL & NO.
4/10/71	**21**	10	● 2. Manna *If* (4)	Elektra 74086
2/12/72	**3**	20	● **3. Baby I'm-A Want You** *Baby I'm-A Want You* (3)/*Everything I Own* (5)	Elektra 75015
12/2/72	**18**	16	● 4. Guitar Man	Elektra 75047
4/7/73	**2**(1)	23	● **5. The Best Of Bread** [G]	Elektra 75056
7/6/74	**32**	3	● 6. The Best Of Bread, Volume Two [G]	Elektra 1005
2/5/77	**26**	6	● 7. Lost Without Your Love *Lost Without Your Love* (9)	Elektra 1094
			BREATHE Pop group from suburban London: David Glasper (born 1/4/66; vocals), Ian "Spike" Spice, Marcus Lillington and Michael Delahunty (who left in 1988).	
12/3/88	**34**	8	● All That Jazz *Hands To Heaven* (2)/*How Can I Fall?* (3)/*Don't Tell Me Lies* (10)	A&M 5163
			BREEDERS, The Alternative-rock band from Dayton, Ohio: twin sisters/guitarists/vocalists Kim and Kelley Deal, bassist Josephine Wiggs (native of Bedfordshire, England) and drummer Jim MacPherson. Kim was a member of the Pixies. Tanya Donelly (Throwing Muses; Belly) was an early member.	
1/15/94	**33**	6	▲ Last Splash	4 A D 61508
			BREWER & SHIPLEY Folk-rock duo formed in Los Angeles: Mike Brewer (born 1944 in Oklahoma City) and Tom Shipley (born 1942 in Mineral Ridge, Ohio).	
4/24/71	**34**	3	Tarkio *One Toke Over The Line* (10)	Kama Sutra 2024
			BRICK Disco-jazz group formed in Atlanta in 1972. Consisted of Jimmy Brown (vocals), Ray Ransom, Donald Nevins, Reggie Hargis and Eddie Irons. Session work in the early '70s.	
12/25/76	**19**	8	1. Good High *Dazz* (3)	Bang 408
10/8/77	**15**	9	2. Brick	Bang 409
			BRICKELL, Edie, & New Bohemians Vocalist Brickell (pronounced BREE-kell) was born in Oak Cliff, Texas; joined the Dallas-based band in 1985. Varying personnel since then. Brickell's father, Eddie, is a pro bowler. Bohemians' lineup: Brad Houser, Kenny Withrow and John Bush. Joining the band by 1990 were Wes Burt-Martin and Matt Chamberlain. Brickell married Paul Simon on 5/30/92.	
12/3/88	**4**	28	▲ **1. Shooting Rubberbands At The Stars** *What I Am* (7)	Geffen 24192
11/24/90	**32**	3	2. Ghost Of A Dog	Geffen 24304
			BRIDGES, Alicia Born on 7/15/53. Atlanta-based disco singer/songwriter; originally from Lawndale, North Carolina.	
12/16/78	**33**	7	Alicia Bridges *I Love The Nightlife* (5)	Polydor 6158
			BRITNY FOX Philadelphia heavy-metal quartet. "Dizzy" Dean Davidson, vocals.	
10/8/88	**39**	2	● Britny Fox	Columbia 44140

Big Brother And The Holding Company's 1968 album, *Cheap Thrills*, launched the meteoric career of singer Janis Joplin, who left the group and went solo after its climb to No. 1. Two more Big Brother albums followed before Columbia dropped the Joplin-less group.

Blood, Sweat & Tears pioneered the late '60s genre of so-called "jazz-rock," largely through the success of the group's bestselling second album. Bearing no fewer than three No. 2 singles, including "And When I Die," "Spinning Wheel" and "You've Made Me So Very Happy," the album introduced a new singer, Canada's David Clayton-Thomas, to U.S. audiences.

Michael Bolton's late '80s ascension to romantic, soul-crooning superstar, typified by 1991's multi-platinum *Time, Love & Tenderness*, seemed highly unlikely to fans of Blackjack, his earlier hard-rock outfit. Upon his success, earlier material with that band and his previous solo work as Michael Bolotin were swiftly reissued.

Bon Jovi's enormously popular 1986 effort, *Slippery When Wet*, sold more than 9 million copies domestically and established the melodic hard rockers as superstars of the era. Eight years later, the group's greatest-hits set was Poly-Gram Records' biggest seller of the year.

Garth Brooks's phenomenal sales rise in the '90s signaled the prominent return of country music to the pop charts. 1991's *Ropin' The Wind*, his first No. 1 album, didn't sound like the work of a onetime Kiss fan, but his appearance on a later Kiss tribute album proved that it was.

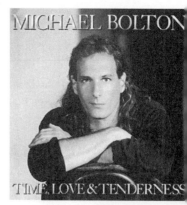

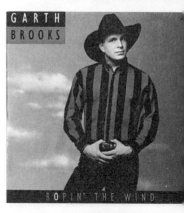

Boyz II Men's 1991 debut, *Cooleyhigh-harmony*, was a sales sensation that showcased vocal harmonies in the tradition of doo-wop and early '60s R&B groups. The Philadelphia-bred quartet broke several significant chart records and easily became Motown's biggest act of the '90s.

Bobby Brown's second solo album, 1988's *Don't Be Cruel*, was a No. 1 hit for six weeks. A former mainstay of the young R&B group New Edition, Brown married superstar Whitney Houston in 1992.

James Brown recorded his vocal hits for the King label in the '60s, but he released a series of instrumental albums, such as 1966's *James Brown Plays New Breed*, for the Smash label during the same period.

Glen Campbell's status as a hitmaking fixture of the '60s took *A New Place In The Sun* to No. 24 in 1968. Of his eight albums to reach the Top 30 during that era, however, it was the only one that failed to attain gold- or platinum-sales status.

Tevin Campbell's solid-gold debut, *T.E.V.I.N.*, signified yet another important discovery for multitalented producer Quincy Jones. The youthful singer, who recorded for Jones's own Qwest label, scored a hit with a remake of the Brothers Johnson's 1977 Top 5 hit, "Strawberry Letter 23."

DATE	POS	WKS	ARTIST—RECORD TITLE	LABEL & NO.
			BRONSKI BEAT	
			British techno-pop trio: Jimmy Somerville (vocals), Steve Bronski and Larry Steinbachek (synthesizers). Somerville formed The Communards in 1986.	
3/2/85	**36**	3	The Age Of Consent	MCA 5538
			BROOKS, Garth	
			Born on 2/7/62 in Luba, Oklahoma; raised in Yukon, Oklahoma. Country singer. Attended Oklahoma State University on a track scholarship (javelin). His mother, Colleen Carroll, signed with Capitol in 1954 and was a regular on Red Foley's "Ozark Jubilee" TV show. Brooks's immense popularity contributed to a resurgence of country music in the '90s.	
9/29/90	**3**	126	▲13 **1. No Fences**	Capitol 93866
5/18/91	**13**	49	▲6 **2. Garth Brooks**	Capitol 90897
9/28/91	**1**(18)	70	▲11 **3. Ropin' The Wind**	Capitol 96330
9/12/92	**2**(1)	20	▲2 **4. Beyond The Season** [X]	Liberty 98742
			Christmas charts: 1/'92, 11/'93, 16/'94	
10/10/92	**1**(7)	35	▲6 **5. The Chase**	Liberty 98743
9/18/93	**1**(5)	25	▲5 **6. In Pieces**	Liberty 80857
12/31/94	**1**(7)	9+	▲5 **7. The Hits** [G]	Liberty 29689
			BROOKS & DUNN	
			Country duo of Kix Brooks (born 5/12/55, Shreveport, Louisiana) and Ronnie Dunn (born 6/1/53, Texas).	
6/27/92	**10**	41	▲4 **1. Brand New Man**	Arista 18658
3/13/93	**9**	18	▲3 **2. Hard Workin' Man**	Arista 18716
10/15/94	**15**	6	▲ 3. Waitin' On Sundown	Arista 18765
			BROTHERS FOUR, The	
			Folk-pop quartet: Dick Foley, Bob Flick, John Paine and Mike Kirkland. Formed while Phi Gamma Delta fraternity brothers at the University of Washington.	
4/18/60	**11**	19	1. The Brothers Four	Columbia 1402
			Greenfields (2)	
2/13/61	**4**	7	**2. B.M.O.C. (Best Music On/Off Campus)**	Columbia 1578
			BROTHERS JOHNSON, The	
			Los Angeles R&B-funk duo of brothers George (born 5/17/53) and Louis Johnson (born 4/13/55). Own band, the Johnson Three + 1, with brother Tommy and cousin Alex Weir. With Billy Preston's band until 1975. Also see Quincy Jones.	
4/17/76	**9**	24	▲ **1. Look Out For #1**	A&M 4567
			I'll Be Good To You (3)	
5/28/77	**13**	26	▲ 2. Right On Time	A&M 4644
			Strawberry Letter 23 (5)	
8/19/78	**7**	10	▲ **3. Blam!!**	A&M 4714
3/15/80	**5**	16	▲ **4. Light Up The Night**	A&M 3716
			Stomp! (7)	
			BROWN, Arthur, The Crazy World Of	
			Born Arthur Wilton on 6/24/44 in Whitby, England. Theatrical rock singer. Band included drummer Carl Palmer, later of Atomic Rooster, Emerson, Lake & Palmer and Asia. Since 1992, has been a partner in Healing Songs Therapy, a music-therapy practice.	
10/12/68	**7**	10	**The Crazy World Of Arthur Brown**	Track 8198
			Fire (2)	

DATE	POS	WKS	ARTIST—RECORD TITLE	LABEL & NO.
			BROWN, Bobby	
			Born on 2/5/69 in Boston. Former member of the teen R&B-pop group New Edition. Had a bit part in the movie *Ghostbusters II*. Established own Bosstown recording studio and label in Atlanta in 1991. Married Whitney Houston on 7/18/92.	
8/13/88	1 (6)	69	▲⁶ 1. Don't Be Cruel	MCA 42185
			Don't Be Cruel (8)/My Prerogative (1)/Roni (3)/ Every Little Step (3)/Rock Wit'cha (7)	
12/16/89	9	17	▲ 2. Dance! ... Ya Know It! [K]	MCA 6342
			previously unreleased, remixed versions of Brown's hits	
9/12/92	2 (1)	29	▲² 3. Bobby	MCA 10417
			Humpin' Around (3)/Good Enough (7)	
			BROWN, Chuck, & The Soul Searchers	
			Washington, D.C.-based, nine-member R&B group.	
3/10/79	31	5	● Bustin' Loose	Source 3076
			BROWN, James	
			Born on 5/3/28 in Macon, Georgia. Raised in Augusta. Formed own vocal group, The Famous Flames. Cut a demo record of own composition "Please Please Please" in November 1955, at radio station WIBB in Macon. Signed to King/Federal Records in January 1956 and re-recorded the song. Cameo appearances in movies *The Blues Brothers* and *Rocky IV*. One of the originators of "soul" music; variously billed on Polydor hits as "Soul I," "The Creator," "The Godfather of Soul," "The Hit Man" and "Minister of New New Super Heavy Funk." His backing group, The JB's, featured various personnel, including Nat Kendrick, Bootsy Collins, Maceo Parker and Fred Wesley. Inducted into the Rock and Roll Hall of Fame in 1986. On 12/15/88, received a six-year prison sentence after leading police on an interstate car chase; released from prison on 2/27/91. Won 1992 Lifetime Achievement Grammy Award. Ranked as the #1 artist in *Joel Whitburn's Top R&B Singles 1942-1988* book.	
7/6/63	2 (2)	33	1. Live At The Apollo [L]	King 826
			recorded at the Apollo Theater, New York City, 10/24/62	
3/28/64	10	13	2. Pure Dynamite! Live At The Royal [L]	King 883
			recorded at the Royal Theater, Baltimore, Maryland	
12/4/65	26	8	3. Papa's Got A Brand New Bag	King 938
			Papa's Got A Brand New Bag (8)	
2/26/66	36	4	4. I Got You (I Feel Good)	King 946
			I Got You (I Feel Good) (3)	
10/28/67	35	2	5. Cold Sweat	King 1020
			Cold Sweat (7)	
4/13/68	17	6	6. I Can't Stand Myself (When You Touch Me)	King 1030
12/14/68	32	7	7. Live At The Apollo, Volume II [L]	King 1022 [2]
9/13/69	26	7	8. It's A Mother	King 1063
9/27/69	40	1	9. James Brown plays & directs The Popcorn [I]	King 1055
10/24/70	29	6	10. Sex Machine [L]	King 1115 [2]
9/18/71	22	7	11. Hot Pants	Polydor 4054
1/29/72	39	2	12. Revolution Of The Mind — Live At The Apollo, Volume III [L]	Polydor 3003 [2]
4/7/73	31	5	13. Black Caesar [S]	Polydor 6014
3/30/74	34	8	● 14. The Payback	Polydor 3007 [2]
9/7/74	35	2	15. Hell	Polydor 9001 [2]

DATE	POS	WKS	ARTIST—RECORD TITLE	LABEL & NO.
			BROWN, Les, and His Band of Renown	
			Born on 3/14/12 in Reinerton, Pennsylvania. Big band leader/clarinetist. Worked as arranger for Jimmy Dorsey, Larry Clinton and others before own band's success. In the '50s, Brown's band was featured on "The Steve Allen Show." Worked on Bob Hope's programs and overseas tours for over two decades.	
2/19/55	15	2	Concert At The Palladium [I-L]	Coral CX-1 [2]
			recorded at the Hollywood Palladium, September 1953	
			BROWN, Peter	
			Born on 7/11/53 in Blue Island, Illinois. R&B vocalist/keyboardist/producer.	
4/1/78	11	19	A Fantasy Love Affair	Drive 104
			Dance With Me (8)	
			BROWNE, Jackson	
			Born on 10/9/48 in Heidelberg, Germany. Rock singer/guitarist/pianist/ composer. To Los Angeles in 1951. With Tim Buckley and Nico in 1967 in New York City. Returned to Los Angeles; concentrated on songwriting. His songs were recorded by Linda Ronstadt, Tom Rush, Joe Cocker, The Byrds, Johnny Rivers, Bonnie Raitt and many others. Worked with The Eagles. Produced Warren Zevon's first album. Wife Phyllis committed suicide on 3/25/76. Activist against nuclear power.	
11/2/74	14	12	▲ 1. Late For The Sky	Asylum 1017
11/27/76	5	18	▲ **2. The Pretender**	Asylum 1079
1/7/78	3	25	▲ **3. Running On Empty**	Asylum 113
7/19/80	1(1)	21	▲ **4. Hold Out**	Asylum 511
8/27/83	8	12	● **5. Lawyers In Love**	Asylum 60268
3/22/86	23	9	● 6. Lives In The Balance	Asylum 60457
11/13/93	40	1	7. I'm Alive	Elektra 61524
			BROWNE, Tom	
			Jazz-funk trumpeter. First played classical music at the High School of Music and Art in New York City. With Weldon Ervine in 1975, Sonny Fortune and Fatback Band in 1976. Member of Fuse One.	
9/20/80	18	9	● 1. Love Approach [I]	GRP 5008
3/21/81	37	2	2. Magic	GRP 5503
			BRUBECK, Dave, Quartet	
			Born David Warren on 12/6/20 in Concord, California. Leader of jazz quartet consisting of Brubeck (piano), Paul Desmond (alto sax), Joe Morello (drums) and Eugene Wright (bass). One of America's all-time most popular jazz groups on college campuses.	
2/5/55	8	6	**1. Dave Brubeck At Storyville: 1954** [I-L]	Columbia 590
3/19/55	5	22	**2. Brubeck Time** [I]	Columbia 622
11/12/55	7	3	**3. Jazz: Red Hot And Cool** [I-L]	Columbia 699
7/8/57	18	1	4. Jazz Impressions of the U.S.A. [I]	Columbia 984
9/30/57	24	1	5. Jazz Goes To Junior College [I-L]	Columbia 1034
11/28/60	2(1)	86	● **6. Time Out Featuring "Take Five"** [I]	Columbia 8192
12/12/60	13	7	7. Bernstein Plays Brubeck Plays Bernstein [I]	Columbia 8257
			side 1: New York Philharmonic with the Dave Brubeck Quartet conducted by Leonard Bernstein; side 2: Dave Brubeck Quartet	
1/27/62	8	31	**8. Time Further Out** [I]	Columbia 8490
7/7/62	24	9	9. Countdown — Time In Outer Space [I]	Columbia 8575
3/23/63	14	10	10. Bossa Nova U.S.A. [I]	Columbia 8798
8/3/63	37	2	11. The Dave Brubeck Quartet At Carnegie Hall [I-L]	Columbia 826 [2]

DATE	POS	WKS	ARTIST—RECORD TITLE	LABEL & NO.
			BRYSON, Peabo	
			Born Robert Peabo Bryson on 4/13/51 in Greenville, South Carolina. R&B singer with Al Freeman & The Upsetters in 1965; with Moses Dillard & The Tex-Town Display from 1968-73. First solo recording for Bang in 1970. Married Juanita Leonard, former wife of boxer Sugar Ray Leonard, in 1992.	
2/10/79	35	4	● 1. Crosswinds	Capitol 11875
2/27/82	40	2	2. I Am Love	Capitol 12179
9/10/83	25	14	● 3. Born To Love	Capitol 12284
			PEABO BRYSON/ROBERTA FLACK	
			B.T. EXPRESS	
			Brooklyn, New York, R&B-disco outfit earlier known as Brooklyn Trucking Express. Keyboardist Michael Jones, who joined group at age 15, later recorded solo as techno-funk musician Kashif.	
12/14/74	5	18	● **1. Do It ('Til You're Satisfied)**	Roadshow 5117
			Do It ('Til You're Satisfied) (2)/*Express* (4)	
8/23/75	19	8	2. Non-Stop	Roadshow 41001
			BUCKINGHAM, Lindsey	
			Born on 10/3/47 in Palo Alto, California. Rock guitarist/vocalist/songwriter. In group Fritz from 1967-71; with Stevie Nicks (Fritz lead singer) formed duo, Buckingham Nicks, in early '70s. Both joined Fleetwood Mac in 1975. Buckingham left Fleetwood Mac in 1987. His grandfather founded Keystone Coffee; his father founded Alta Coffee. Buckingham's brother Gregg won a silver medal in swimming in the 1968 Olympics.	
11/28/81	32	6	Law And Order	Asylum 561
			Trouble (9)	
			BUCKNER & GARCIA	
			Atlanta-based duo: Jerry Buckner and Gary Garcia. Recorded as Willis "The Guard" & Vigorish in 1980.	
5/8/82	24	5	● Pac-Man Fever [N]	Columbia 37941
			album inspired by popular video games	
			Pac-Man Fever (9)	
			BUFFETT, Jimmy	
			Born on 12/25/46 in Mobile, Alabama. Has BS degree in history and journalism from the University of Southern Mississippi. After working in New Orleans, moved to Nashville in 1969. Staff reporter at *Billboard*, 1969-70. Settled in Key West in 1971. Owns a store called Margaritaville and has his own line of tropical clothing.	
3/29/75	25	4	1. A1A	Dunhill 50183
			A1A: beach access road off U.S. 1 in Florida	
3/26/77	12	19	▲ 2. Changes In Latitudes, Changes In Attitudes	ABC 990
			Margaritaville (8)	
4/15/78	10	9	▲ **3. Son Of A Son Of A Sailor**	ABC 1046
9/22/79	14	11	● 4. Volcano	MCA 5102
3/14/81	30	4	5. Coconut Telegraph	MCA 5169
1/30/82	31	6	6. Somewhere Over China	MCA 5285
6/11/94	5	8	▲ **7. Fruitcakes**	Margaritaville 11043
			BULLETBOYS	
			Los Angeles hard-rock quartet: Marq Torien (vocals), Mick Sweda, Lonnie Vencent and Jimmy D'Anda.	
2/4/89	34	5	● BulletBoys	Warner 25782

DATE	POS	WKS	ARTIST—RECORD TITLE	LABEL & NO.
7/11/70	**18**	13	**BURDON, Eric, and War** Burdon was born on 5/11/41 in Newcastle-On-Tyne, England. Lead singer of The Animals. Eric Burdon Declares "War" *Spill The Wine* (3)	MGM 4663
11/9/85 11/20/93	**30** **28**	6 1	**BUSH, Kate** Born on 7/30/58 in Bexley, Kent, England. Discovered by David Gilmour of Pink Floyd. Signed to EMI at age 16. 1. Hounds Of Love 2. The Red Shoes	EMI America 17171 Columbia 53737
5/26/56	**14**	1	**BUSHKIN, Joe** Born on 11/7/16 in New York City. Pianist/composer. Midnight Rhapsody [I]	Capitol 711
10/24/92	**32**	1	**BUSHWICK BILL** Born Richard Stephen Shaw on 12/8/66 in Jamaica. Member of Houston-based rap group The Geto Boys. Lost his right eye in shooting on 5/10/91. Little Big Man	Rap-A-Lot 57189
5/10/69	**29**	6	**BUTLER, Jerry** Born on 12/8/39 in Sunflower, Mississippi. Older brother of soul singer Billy Butler. Sang in the Northern Jubilee Gospel Singers, with Curtis Mayfield. Later with the Quails. In 1957, Butler and Mayfield joined the Roosters with Sam Gooden and brothers Arthur and Richard Brooks. Changed name to The Impressions in 1957. Left for solo career in autumn of 1958. Dubbed "The Ice Man." Also works as the Cook Country Commissioner in Illinois. The Ice Man Cometh *Only The Strong Survive* (4)	Mercury 61198
			BUTTERFIELD, Billy — see CONNIFF, Ray	
10/13/62	**1**(1)	44	**BYRD, Charlie** Born on 9/16/25 in Chuckatuch, Virginia. Jazz and classical-guitar virtuoso. Studied under classical master guitarist Segovia. With Woody Herman in 1959. Own tour of Latin America in 1961. **Jazz Samba** [I] **STAN GETZ/CHARLIE BYRD**	Verve 8432
7/14/73 5/11/74	**36** **33**	2 3	**BYRD, Donald** Born on 12/9/32 in Detroit. R&B-jazz trumpeter/flugelhorn player. With Air Force bands, 1951-53, and George Wallington in 1955. With Art Blakey Jazz Messengers in the mid-1950s. Own bands from the '60s. Founded The Blackbyrds in 1973 while teaching jazz at Howard University in Washington, D.C. 1. Black Byrd 2. Street Lady [I]	Blue Note 047 Blue Note 140

DATE	POS	WKS	ARTIST—RECORD TITLE	LABEL & NO.
			BYRDS, The	
			Folk-rock group formed in Los Angeles in 1964. Consisted of James "Roger" McGuinn, (12-string guitar), David Crosby (guitar), Gene Clark (percussion), Chris Hillman (bass) and Mike Clarke (drums). McGuinn, who changed his name to Roger in 1968, had been with Bobby Darin and The Chad Mitchell Trio. Clark had been with The New Christy Minstrels. All except Clarke had folk-music background. First recorded as The Beefeaters for Elektra in 1964. Also recorded as The Jet Set. Professional debut in March 1965. Clark left after "Eight Miles High." Crosby left in late 1967 to form Crosby, Stills & Nash. Re-formed in 1968 with McGuinn, Hillman, Kevin Kelly (drums) and Gram Parsons (guitar). Hillman and Parsons left that same year to form The Flying Burrito Brothers. McGuinn again re-formed with Clarence White (guitar), John York (bass) and Gene Parsons (drums). Reunions with original members in 1973 and 1979. Gram Parsons died on 9/19/73 (age 26) of a heroin overdose. McGuinn, Clark and Hillman later recorded as a trio. In 1986, Hillman formed popular country group, The Desert Rose Band. McGuinn, Crosby and Hillman reunited on stage on 2/24/90 for a Roy Orbison tribute. Clark died on 5/24/91 (age 46) of natural causes. Clarke, also with The Flying Burrito Brothers and Firefall, died of liver failure on 12/19/93 (age 49). Group inducted into the Rock and Roll Hall of Fame in 1991.	
7/17/65	6	4	**1. Mr. Tambourine Man**	Columbia 9172
			Mr. Tambourine Man (1)	
2/12/66	17	10	2. Turn! Turn! Turn!	Columbia 9254
			Turn! Turn! Turn! (1)	
9/17/66	24	8	3. Fifth Dimension	Columbia 9349
4/22/67	24	5	4. Younger Than Yesterday	Columbia 9442
9/16/67	6	15	▲ **5. The Byrds' Greatest Hits** [G]	Columbia 9516
1/10/70	36	3	6. Ballad Of Easy Rider	Columbia 9942
11/28/70	40	2	7. The Byrds (Untitled) [L]	Columbia 30127 [2]
			record 1: live; record 2: studio	
4/14/73	20	7	8. Byrds	Asylum 5058
			reunion of original 5 Byrds	

C

DATE	POS	WKS	ARTIST—RECORD TITLE	LABEL & NO.
			CAFFERTY, John, and The Beaver Brown Band	
			Rock sextet from Narrangansett, Rhode Island. Band, led by singer/guitarist Cafferty, includes Bob Cotoia, Gary Gramolini, Kenny Jo Silva, Pat Lupo and Michael Antunes.	
8/25/84	9	24	▲² **1. Eddie And The Cruisers** [S]	Scotti Br. 38929
			On The Dark Side (7)	
7/6/85	40	3	2. Tough All Over	Scotti Br. 39405
			CALDWELL, Bobby	
			Born on 8/15/51 in New York City. Raised in Florida. Multi-instrumentalist/songwriter. Percussionist with Johnny Winter, Rick Derringer, Captain Beyond and Armageddon. Wrote tracks for "The New Mickey Mouse Club" TV show, commercials, and Peter Cetera and Amy Grant's "The Next Time I Fall."	
2/17/79	21	10	Bobby Caldwell	Clouds 8804
			What You Won't Do For Love (9)	

DATE	POS	WKS	ARTIST—RECORD TITLE	LABEL & NO.
			CAMEO	
			New York City soul-funk group, formed in 1974 as The New York City Players by Larry "Mr. B" Blackmon (drums) and Gregory "Straps" Johnson (keyboards). Vocals by Wayne Cooper and Tomi "Tee" Jenkins. By 1985, group pared down to trio of Blackmon, Jenkins and Nathan Leftenant.	
7/12/80	25	10	● 1. Cameosis	Choc. City 2011
4/24/82	23	6	● 2. Alligator Woman	Choc. City 2021
4/7/84	27	9	● 3. She's Strange	Atl. Art. 814984
10/11/86	8	31	▲ **4. Word Up!**	Atl. Art. 830265
			Word Up (6)	
			CAMPBELL, Glen	
			Born on 4/22/36 in Billstown, Arkansas. Vocalist/guitarist/composer. With his uncle Dick Bills's band, 1954-58. To Los Angeles; recorded with The Champs in 1960. Became prolific studio musician; with The Hondells in 1964, The Beach Boys in 1965 and Sagittarius in 1967. Own TV show "The Glen Campbell Goodtime Hour," 1968-72. In movies *True Grit*, *Norwood* and *Strange Homecoming*; voice in the animated movie *Rock-A-Doodle*.	
4/27/68	15	35	▲ 1. By The Time I Get To Phoenix	Capitol 2851
			1968 Album of the Year Grammy Award	
6/8/68	26	4	● 2. Hey, Little One	Capitol 2878
8/10/68	5	40	▲ **3. Gentle On My Mind**	Capitol 2809
9/14/68	24	5	4. A New Place In The Sun	Capitol 2907
11/9/68	11	13	● 5. Bobbie Gentry & Glen Campbell	Capitol 2928
			BOBBIE GENTRY & GLEN CAMPBELL	
11/30/68	1(5)	29	▲² **6. Wichita Lineman**	Capitol 103
			Wichita Lineman (3)	
4/12/69	2(1)	18	▲ **7. Galveston**	Capitol 210
			Galveston (4)	
9/27/69	13	14	● 8. Glen Campbell — "Live" [L]	Capitol 268 [2]
2/14/70	12	11	● 9. Try A Little Kindness	Capitol 389
6/20/70	38	3	10. Oh Happy Day	Capitol 443
			inspirational songs	
10/31/70	27	5	11. The Glen Campbell Goodtime Album	Capitol 493
			It's Only Make Believe (10)	
5/29/71	39	1	▲ 12. Glen Campbell's Greatest Hits [G]	Capitol 752
9/6/75	17	13	● 13. Rhinestone Cowboy	Capitol 11430
			Rhinestone Cowboy (1)	
4/16/77	22	7	● 14. Southern Nights	Capitol 11601
			Southern Nights (1)	
			CAMPBELL, Tevin	
			Born on 11/12/78 in Waxahachie, Texas. Won role in 1988 for the TV show "Wally & The Valentines." Discovered by Quincy Jones. Appeared in the movie *Graffiti Bridge*.	
2/22/92	38	3	▲ 1. T.E.V.I.N.	Qwest 26291
			Tell Me What You Want Me To Do (6)	
11/13/93	18	27	▲² 2. I'm Ready	Qwest 45388
			Can We Talk (9)/*I'm Ready* (9)	

DATE	POS	WKS	ARTIST—RECORD TITLE	LABEL & NO.
			C & C MUSIC FACTORY	
			Dance outfit led by producers/songwriters Robert Clivilles (percussion, New York native) and David Cole (keyboards, Tennessee native). Featured vocalists include Freedom Williams and Deborah Cooper (Fatback; Change). Martha Wash (Two Tons O' Fun; The Weather Girls) is the actual vocalist of "Gonna Make You Sweat," lip-synched in video by Liberian-born Zelma Davis. Cole died of spinal meningitis on 1/25/95 (age 32).	
1/26/91	**2**(7)	60	▲⁵ **Gonna Make You Sweat**	Columbia 47093
			Gonna Make You Sweat (1)/*Here We Go* (3)/ *Things That Make You Go Hmmmm ...* (4)	
			CANDLEBOX	
			Seattle-based hard-rock band: Kevin Martin (vocals), Peter Klett, Bardi Martin and Scott Mercado.	
5/7/94	**7**	41	▲³ **Candlebox**	Maverick 45313
			CANDYMAN	
			Rapper from Los Angeles born on 6/25/68. Backing rapper/dancer with Tone Loc.	
2/16/91	**40**	1	● Ain't No Shame In My Game	Epic 46947
			Knockin' Boots (9)	
			CANNED HEAT	
			Blues-rock band formed in Los Angeles in 1966. Consisted of Bob "The Bear" Hite (vocals, harmonica), Alan "Blind Owl" Wilson (guitar, harmonica, vocals), Henry Vestine (guitar), Larry Taylor (bass) and Frank Cook (drums). Cook replaced by Fito de la Parra in 1968. Vestine replaced by Harvey Mandel in 1969. Wilson died of a drug overdose on 9/3/70 (age 27). Hite died of a drug-related heart attack on 4/6/81 (age 36).	
9/7/68	**16**	14	1. Boogie With Canned Heat	Liberty 7541
12/28/68	**18**	9	2. Living The Blues [L]	Liberty 27200 [2]
			the second LP is live	
8/30/69	**37**	2	3. Hallelujah	Liberty 7618
			CANO, Eddie	
			Born on 6/6/27 in Los Angeles; died on 1/30/88. Latin-jazz pianist/ bandleader. Played with Latin bandleader Miguilito Valdez in the late '40s.	
9/1/62	**31**	3	Eddie Cano At P.J.'s [I]	Reprise 6030
			CAPTAIN & TENNILLE	
			Daryl "The Captain" Dragon (born 8/27/42, Los Angeles) and his wife, Toni Tennille (born 5/8/43, Montgomery, Alabama). Dragon is the son of noted conductor Carmen Dragon; nicknamed "The Captain" by Mike Love. Duo had own TV show on ABC from 1976-77.	
6/21/75	**2**(1)	14	● **1. Love Will Keep Us Together**	A&M 3405
			Love Will Keep Us Together (1)/*The Way I Want To Touch You* (4)	
3/27/76	**9**	16	▲ **2. Song Of Joy**	A&M 4570
			Lonely Night (3)/*Shop Around* (4)/*Muskrat Love* (4)	
4/23/77	**18**	7	● 3. Come In From The Rain	A&M 4700
1/5/80	**23**	9	● 4. Make Your Move	Casablanca 7188
			Do That To Me One More Time (1)	

DATE	POS	WKS	ARTIST—RECORD TITLE	LABEL & NO.
			CAREY, Mariah	
			Born on 3/27/70 of Irish American and Black Venezuelan parentage. Native of Long Island, New York. Her mother is Patricia Carey, former singer with the New York City Opera. Carey sang backup for Brenda K. Starr. Won 1990 Best New Artist Grammy Award. Married Tommy Mottola, president of Sony Music Entertainment, on 6/5/93.	
7/14/90	**1**(11)	66	▲⁸ **1. Mariah Carey**	Columbia 45202
			Vision Of Love (1)/*Love Takes Time* (1)/*Someday* (1)/ *I Don't Wanna Cry* (1)	
10/5/91	**4**	34	▲⁴ **2. Emotions**	Columbia 47980
			Emotions (1)/*Can't Let Go* (2)/*Make It Happen* (5)	
6/20/92	**3**	17	▲³ **3. MTV Unplugged EP** [L-M]	Columbia 52758
			recorded on 3/16/92 for the MTV program "Unplugged" *I'll Be There* (1)	
9/18/93	**1**(8)	50	▲⁸ **4. Music Box**	Columbia 53205
			Dreamlover (1)/*Hero* (1)/*Without You* (3)	
11/19/94	**3**	9	▲³ **5. Merry Christmas** [X]	Columbia 64222
			Christmas charts: 1/'94	
			CARLIN, George	
			Born on 5/12/37 in New York City. Comedian/actor. In movies *Bill & Ted's Excellent Adventure*, *Outrageous Fortune*, *Car Wash* and *Americathon*. Replaced Ringo Starr as Mr. Conductor on PBS-TV's "Shining Time Station" in 1991. Current star of own Fox-TV series.	
3/18/72	**13**	16	● 1. FM & AM [C]	Little David 7214
10/28/72	**22**	10	● 2. Class Clown [C]	Little David 1004
12/1/73	**35**	5	● 3. Occupation: Foole [C]	Little David 1005
1/4/75	**19**	7	● 4. Toledo Window Box [C]	Little David 3003
12/27/75	**34**	3	5. An Evening With Wally Londo Featuring Bill Slaszo [C]	Little David 1008
			CARLISLE, Belinda	
			Born on 8/17/58 in Hollywood. Lead singer of The Go-Go's, 1978-84. Married to Morgan Mason, son of late actor James Mason.	
7/5/86	**13**	16	● 1. Belinda	I.R.S. 5741
			Mad About You (3)	
11/7/87	**13**	35	▲ 2. Heaven On Earth	MCA 42080
			Heaven Is A Place On Earth (1)/*I Get Weak* (2)/ *Circle In The Sand* (7)	
12/9/89	**37**	2	● 3. Runaway Horses	MCA 6339
			CARLOS, Walter	
			Born in 1939 in Pawtucket, Rhode Island. Classical musician who performs on the Moog synthesizer. Had a sex change; known as Wendy Carlos by 1992.	
3/1/69	**10**	17	● Switched-On Bach [I]	Columbia 7194
			CARLTON, Carl	
			Born in 1952 in Detroit. Soul singer. First recorded for Lando Records in 1964.	
10/3/81	**34**	3	Carl Carlton	20th Century 628
			CARMEN, Eric	
			Born on 8/11/49 in Cleveland. Classical training at the Cleveland Institute of Music from early years to mid-teens. Lead singer of The Raspberries from 1970-74.	
2/21/76	**21**	8	● Eric Carmen	Arista 4057
			All By Myself (2)	

DATE	POS	WKS	ARTIST—RECORD TITLE	LABEL & NO.
			CARNES, Kim	
			Born on 7/20/45 in Los Angeles. Vocalist/pianist/composer. Member of The New Christy Minstrels with husband/co-writer Dave Ellingson and Kenny Rogers, late '60s. Wrote for and performed in commercials. Co-wrote "Love Comes From Unexpected Places," which won the 1977 American Song Festival and was later recorded by Barbra Streisand.	
5/9/81	**1**(4)	23	▲ **Mistaken Identity**	EMI America 17052
			Bette Davis Eyes (1)	
			CARPENTER, Mary-Chapin	
			Born on 2/21/58 in Princeton, New Jersey. Moved to Washington, D.C., in 1974. Graduated from Brown University with an American Civilization degree. Pursued folk music before she became a top country vocalist.	
8/1/92	**31**	7	▲³ 1. **Come On Come On**	Columbia 48881
10/22/94	**10**	9	▲ 2. **Stones In The Road**	Columbia 64327
			MARY CHAPIN CARPENTER	
			CARPENTERS	
			Richard Carpenter (born 10/15/46) and sister Karen (born 3/2/50; died 2/4/83 of heart failure due to anorexia nervosa). From New Haven, Connecticut. Richard played piano from age nine. To Downey, California in 1963. Karen played drums in group with Richard and bass player Wes Jacobs in 1965. Trio recorded for RCA in 1966. After a period with the band Spectrum, the Carpenters recorded as a duo for A&M in 1969. Won 1970 Best New Artist Grammy Award. Hosts of the TV variety show "Make Your Own Kind of Music" in 1971. 1988 TV movie "The Karen Carpenter Story" was based on Karen's life.	
9/26/70	**2**(1)	53	● 1. **Close To You**	A&M 4271
			Close To You (1)/*We've Only Just Begun* (2)	
6/5/71	**2**(2)	39	● 2. **Carpenters**	A&M 3502
			For All We Know (3)/*Rainy Days And Mondays* (2)/*Superstar* (2)	
7/8/72	**4**	19	● 3. **A Song For You**	A&M 3511
			Hurting Each Other (2)/*Goodbye To Love* (7)	
6/9/73	**2**(1)	19	● 4. **Now & Then**	A&M 3519
			side 2: medley of '60s hits with D.J. Tony Peluso	
			Sing (3)/*Yesterday Once More* (2)	
12/8/73	**1**(1)	17	▲⁴ 5. **The Singles 1969-1973** [G]	A&M 3601
			Top Of The World (1)	
6/28/75	**13**	11	● 6. Horizon	A&M 4530
			Please Mr. Postman (1)/*Only Yesterday* (4)	
7/31/76	**33**	5	● 7. A Kind Of Hush	A&M 4581
			CARR, Vikki	
			Born Florencia Martinez Cardona on 7/19/41 in El Paso, Texas. Regular on TV's "The Ray Anthony Show," 1962.	
12/2/67	**12**	16	1. It Must Be Him	Liberty 7533
			It Must Be Him (3)	
6/7/69	**29**	7	2. For Once In My Life [L]	Liberty 7604
			CARRERAS, Jose	
			Born in 1946 in Barcelona, Spain. Operatic tenor. Began performing opera as a child. Battled leukemia in 1991.	
3/2/91	**35**	6	▲ 1. CARRERAS DOMINGO PAVAROTTI in concert [L]	London 430433
			CARRERAS DOMINGO PAVAROTTI	
			concert on 7/7/90 of opera tenors: Jose Carreras, Placido Domingo and Luciano Pavarotti with orchestra conducted by Zubin Mehta at the Baths of Caracalla in Rome	

DATE	POS	WKS	ARTIST—RECORD TITLE	LABEL & NO.
9/17/94	4	13	▲ **2. The 3 Tenors In Concert 1994** **[L]** **CARRERAS, DOMINGO, PAVAROTTI with MEHTA** concert on 7/16/94 of opera tenors Jose Carreras, Placido Domingo and Luciano Pavarotti with orchestra conducted by Zubin Mehta at Dodger Stadium in Los Angeles	Atlantic 82614
			### CARROLL, David, and His Orchestra	
			Born Nook Schrier on 10/15/13 in Chicago. Arranger/conductor since 1951 for many top Mercury artists.	
6/1/59	21	6	1. Let's Dance	Mercury 60001
1/11/60	6	30	**2. Let's Dance Again**	Mercury 60152
			### CARS, The	
			Rock group formed in Boston in 1976. Consisted of Ric Ocasek (lead vocals, guitar), Benjamin Orr (bass, vocals), Elliot Easton (guitar), Greg Hawkes (keyboards) and David Robinson (drums; formerly with The Modern Lovers). Ocasek, Orr and Hawkes had been in trio in the early '70s. Group named by Robinson; got start at the Rat Club in Boston. Disbanded in 1988.	
9/23/78	18	37	▲ 1. The Cars	Elektra 135
7/7/79	3	21	▲ **2. Candy-O**	Elektra 507
9/6/80	5	11	▲ **3. Panorama**	Elektra 514
11/28/81	9	24	▲ **4. Shake It Up** *Shake It Up* (4)	Elektra 567
4/7/84	3	48	▲³ **5. Heartbeat City** *You Might Think* (7)/*Drive* (3)	Elektra 60296
11/23/85	12	16	▲ 6. The Cars Greatest Hits **[G]** *Tonight She Comes* (7)	Elektra 60464
9/26/87	26	8	● 7. Door To Door	Elektra 60747
			### CASH, Johnny	
			Born on 2/26/32 in Kingsland, Arkansas. To Dyess, Arkansas, at age three. Brother Roy led The Dixie Rhythm Ramblers band in late '40s. In U.S. Air Force, 1950-54. Formed trio with Luther Perkins (guitar) and Marshall Grant (bass) in 1955. First recorded for Sun in 1955. On *Louisiana Hayride* and *Grand Ole Opry* in 1957. Own TV show for ABC from 1969-71. Worked with June Carter from 1961; married her in March 1968. Elected to the Country Music Hall of Fame in 1980. Won 1990 Living Legends Grammy Award. Daughter Rosanne Cash and stepdaughter Carlene Carter currently enjoying successful singing careers. According to *Joel Whitburn's Top Country Singles*, Johnny ranks within the top three artists of the country charts. Acted in the TV series "Dr. Quinn, Medicine Woman" in 1993 and TV movies. Also see *Highwayman* in Concept Albums.	
12/8/58	19	9	1. The Fabulous Johnny Cash	Columbia 1253
9/14/63	26	9	● 2. Ring Of Fire (The Best Of Johnny Cash) **[K]**	Columbia 8853
7/20/68	13	39	▲² 3. Johnny Cash At Folsom Prison **[L]**	Columbia 9639
7/12/69	1(4)	35	▲² **4. Johnny Cash At San Quentin** **[L]** *A Boy Named Sue* (2)	Columbia 9827
2/21/70	6	17	● **5. Hello, I'm Johnny Cash**	Columbia 9943
			### CASH, Rosanne	
			Born on 5/24/55 in Memphis. Daughter of Johnny Cash and Vivian Liberto. Raised by her mother in California; then moved to Nashville after high- school graduation. Worked in the Johnny Cash Road Show. Married to Rodney Crowell from 1979-92.	
6/6/81	26	9	● Seven Year Ache	Columbia 36965

DATE	POS	WKS	ARTIST—RECORD TITLE	LABEL & NO.
			CASSIDY, David	
			Born on 4/12/50 in New York City. Son of actor Jack Cassidy and actress Evelyn Ward. Played Keith Partridge, the lead singer of TV's "The Partridge Family." Married to actress Kay Lenz from 1977-81. Co-starred with his half-brother Shaun Cassidy on Broadway's *Blood Brothers* in 1993.	
2/19/72	**15**	8	● Cherish	Bell 6070
			Cherish (9)	
			CASSIDY, Shaun	
			Born on 9/27/59 in Los Angeles. Son of actor Jack Cassidy and actress Shirley Jones of TV's "The Partridge Family." Played Joe Hardy on TV's "The Hardy Boys." Shaun and David Cassidy are half-brothers. Cast member of the TV soap "General Hospital" in 1987. Married to model Ann Pennington, 1979-91.	
7/9/77	**3**	26	▲ **1. Shaun Cassidy**	Warner 3067
			Da Doo Ron Ron (1)/*That's Rock 'N' Roll* (3)	
12/3/77	**6**	11	▲ **2. Born Late**	Warner 3126
			Hey Deanie (7)	
9/2/78	**33**	4	▲ 3. Under Wraps	Warner 3222
			CASTOR, Jimmy, Bunch	
			Born on 6/2/43 in New York City. R&B singer/saxophonist/composer/arranger. Formed The Jimmy Castor Bunch in 1972, with Gerry Thomas (keyboards), Doug Gibson (bass), Harry Jensen (guitar), Lenny Fridie, Jr. (congas) and Bobby Manigault (drums).	
6/24/72	**27**	6	It's Just Begun	RCA 4640
			Troglodyte (6)	
			CETERA, Peter	
			Born on 9/13/44 in Chicago. Lead singer/bass guitarist of Chicago from 1967-85.	
7/26/86	**23**	25	● Solitude/Solitaire	Warner 25474
			Glory Of Love (1)/*The Next Time I Fall* (1-with Amy Grant)	
			CHACKSFIELD, Frank, And His Orchestra	
			Born on 5/9/14 in Sussex, England.	
1/9/61	**36**	1	Ebb Tide	Richmond 30078
			CHAD & JEREMY	
			Folk-rock duo formed in the early '60s: Chad Stuart (born 12/10/43, England) and Jeremy Clyde (born 3/22/44, England). Broke up in 1967. Re-formed briefly in 1982.	
1/23/65	**22**	11	1. Yesterday's Gone	World Art. 2002
			A Summer Song (7)	
8/21/65	**37**	3	2. Before And After	Columbia 9174
			CHAKIRIS, George	
			Born on 9/16/34 in Norwood, Ohio. Portrayed Bernardo, leader of the Sharks gang, in the movie *West Side Story*.	
9/15/62	**28**	4	George Chakiris	Capitol 1750
			CHAMBERLAIN, Richard	
			Born on 3/31/35 in Los Angeles. Leading movie, theater and TV actor. Played lead role in TV's "Dr. Kildare," 1961-66.	
2/16/63	**5**	24	**Richard Chamberlain Sings**	MGM 4088
			Theme From Dr. Kildare (10)	

DATE	POS	WKS	ARTIST—RECORD TITLE	LABEL & NO.
			CHAMBERS BROTHERS, The	
			Four Mississippi-born brothers: George (bass), Willie (guitar), Lester (harmonica) and Joe Chambers (guitar). Formed as a gospel group in Los Angeles in 1954. Drummer Brian Keenan added in 1965.	
9/14/68	4	17	● **1. The Time Has Come**	Columbia 9522
11/23/68	16	6	2. A New Time-A New Day	Columbia 9671
			CHANGE	
			European American studio group formed by Italian producer Jacques Fred Petrus. Led by Paolo Granolio (guitar) and David Romani (bass). Luther Vandross sang on several songs for group's first two albums. Later group, based in New York, included lead vocals by James Robinson and Deborah "Crab" Cooper (later with C & C Music Factory). One-time band member Rick Gallwey married Sharon Bryant, former lead singer of Atlantic Starr.	
6/21/80	29	7	● The Glow Of Love	RFC 3438
			CHANGING FACES	
			Female vocal duo: Bronx-born Charisse Rose and Manhattan-born Cassandra Lucas.	
9/10/94	25	5	● Changing Faces *Stroke You Up* (3)	Big Beat 92369
			CHANTAY'S	
			Teenage surf-rock quintet from Santa Ana, California: Bob Spickard (lead guitar), Brian Carman (rhythm guitar), Rob Marshall (piano), Warren Waters (bass) and Bob Welsh (drums).	
6/22/63	26	4	Pipeline [I] *Pipeline* (4)	Dot 25516
			CHAPIN, Harry	
			Born on 12/7/42 in New York City. Died in an auto accident on 7/16/81. Folk-rock balladeer. As a child, was a member of the Brooklyn Heights Boys Choir. Documentary moviemaker in the '60s. Signed to Elektra in 1971.	
10/26/74	4	17	● **Verities & Balderdash** *Cat's In The Cradle* (1)	Elektra 1012
			CHAPMAN, Tracy	
			Born in Cleveland. Boston-based singer/songwriter. Graduated from Tufts University in 1986 with an anthropology degree. Won 1988 Best New Artist Grammy Award.	
6/4/88	1(1)	46	▲³ **1. Tracy Chapman** *Fast Car* (6)	Elektra 60774
10/28/89	9	14	▲ **2. Crossroads**	Elektra 60888
			CHARLENE	
			Pop singer Charlene Duncan (nee: D'Angelo). Born on 6/1/50 in Hollywood.	
6/5/82	36	3	I've Never Been To Me *I've Never Been To Me* (3)	Motown 6009

DATE	POS	WKS	ARTIST—RECORD TITLE	LABEL & NO.
			CHARLES, Ray	
			Born Ray Charles Robinson on 9/23/30 in Albany, Georgia. To Greenville, Florida, while still an infant. Partially blind at age five; completely blind at seven (glaucoma). Studied classical piano and clarinet at State School for Deaf and Blind Children, St. Augustine, Florida, 1937-45. With local Florida bands; moved to Seattle in 1948. Formed The McSon Trio (also known as The Maxim Trio and The Maxine Trio) with Gossady McGhee (guitar) and Milton Garred (bass). First recordings were very much in the King Cole Trio style. Formed own band in 1954. The '50s female vocal group, The Cookies, became his backing group, The Raeletts. Inducted into the Rock and Roll Hall of Fame in 1986. Won 1987 Lifetime Achievement Grammy Award. Popular performer with many TV and movie appearances.	
2/15/60	**17**	37	1. The Genius Of Ray Charles	Atlantic 1312
7/18/60	**13**	18	2. Ray Charles In Person [L]	Atlantic 8039
			recorded on 5/28/59 at Herndon Stadium, Atlanta	
10/10/60	**9**	13	**3. The Genius Hits The Road**	ABC-Para. 335
			Georgia On My Mind (1)	
3/6/61	**11**	16	4. Dedicated To You	ABC-Para. 355
3/27/61	**4**	29	**5. Genius + Soul = Jazz**	Impulse! 2
			featuring top jazz artists, including Count Basie's band *One Mint Julep* (8)	
1/20/62	**11**	24	6. Do The Twist! [K]	Atlantic 8054
5/12/62	**1(14)**	59	● **7. Modern Sounds In Country And Western Music**	ABC-Para. 410
			I Can Stop Loving You (1)/*You Don't Know Me* (2)	
6/23/62	**20**	4	8. What'd I Say [K]	Atlantic 8029
			What'd I Say (6)	
9/1/62	**5**	23	● **9. Ray Charles' Greatest Hits** [G]	ABC-Para. 415
			Hit The Road Jack (1)/*Unchain My Heart* (9)	
9/1/62	**14**	9	10. The Ray Charles Story [K]	Atlantic 900 [2]
			all of above Atlantic albums recorded 1952-59	
11/10/62	**2(2)**	38	● **11. Modern Sounds In Country And Western Music (Volume Two)**	ABC-Para. 435
			You Are My Sunshine (7)/*Take These Chains From My Heart* (8)	
9/14/63	**2(2)**	21	**12. Ingredients In A Recipe For Soul**	ABC-Para. 465
			Busted (4)	
4/4/64	**9**	11	**13. Sweet & Sour Tears**	ABC-Para. 480
9/26/64	**36**	5	14. Have A Smile With Me	ABC-Para. 495
4/30/66	**15**	20	15. Crying Time	ABC-Para. 544
			Crying Time (6)	
			CHARLES, Ray, Singers	
			Born Charles Raymond Offenberg on 9/13/18 in Chicago. Arranger/conductor for many TV shows, including "The Perry Como Show," "The Glen Campbell Goodtime Hour" and "Sha-Na-Na." Winner of two Emmy Awards.	
5/30/64	**11**	15	Something Special For Young Lovers	Command 866
			Love Me With All Your Heart (3)	
			CHARLESTON CITY ALL-STARS	
			Conducted by Enoch Light.	
9/2/57	**16**	14	1. The Roaring 20's, Volume 2 [I]	Grand Award 340
9/2/57	**17**	2	2. The Roaring 20's, Volume 3 [I]	Grand Award 353

DATE	POS	WKS	ARTIST—RECORD TITLE		LABEL & NO.
			CHASE		
			Jazz-rock band organized by trumpeter Bill Chase (formerly with Woody Herman and Stan Kenton). Chase and three other members were killed in a plane crash on 8/9/74.		
7/3/71	**22**	10	Chase		Epic 30472
			CHEAP TRICK		
			Rock quartet from Rockford, Illinois, founded by Rick Nielsen (guitar) and Tom Petersson (bass), with Bun E. Carlos (real name: Brad Carlson; drums) and Robin Zander (vocals). Discovered by Aerosmith's producer Jack Douglas. Petersson replaced by Jon Brant in 1980; returned in 1988, replacing Brant.		
3/3/79	**4**	30	▲³ **1. Cheap Trick At Budokan** [L]		Epic 35795
			I Want You To Want Me (7)		
10/6/79	**6**	10	▲ **2. Dream Police**		Epic 35773
7/19/80	**39**	2	3. Found All The Parts [M]		Epic 36453
			10" mini LP; recorded 1976-79		
11/22/80	**24**	7	● 4. All Shook Up		Epic 36498
6/19/82	**39**	10	● 5. One On One		Epic 38021
10/5/85	**35**	4	6. Standing On The Edge		Epic 39592
5/21/88	**16**	28	▲ 7. Lap Of Luxury		Epic 40922
			The Flame (1)/*Don't Be Cruel* (4)		
			CHECKER, Chubby		
			Born Ernest Evans on 10/3/41 in Philadelphia. Did impersonations of famous singers. First recorded for Parkway in 1959. Dick Clark's then-wife Bobbie suggested that Evans change his name to Chubby Checker because he resembled a teenage Fats Domino. Cover version of Hank Ballard's "The Twist" started worldwide dance craze. On 4/12/64, married Miss World 1962, Dutch-born Catharina Lodders ("Loddy Lo" written for her). In the movies *Don't Knock the Twist* and *Twist Around the Clock*.		
10/31/60	**3**	42	**1. Twist With Chubby Checker**		Parkway 7001
			The Twist (1)		
12/4/61	**11**	16	2. Let's Twist Again		Parkway 7004
			Let's Twist Again (8)		
12/18/61	**2**(6)	36	**3. Your Twist Party** [K]		Parkway 7007
			features songs from above 2 albums		
12/25/61	**7**	11	**4. Bobby Rydell/Chubby Checker**		Cameo 1013
			BOBBY RYDELL/CHUBBY CHECKER		
1/20/62	**8**	22	**5. For Twisters Only**		Parkway 7002
4/14/62	**17**	17	6. For Teen Twisters Only		Parkway 7009
			The Fly (7)/*Slow Twistin'* (3)		
7/21/62	**29**	3	7. Don't Knock The Twist [S]		Parkway 7011
			6 cuts by Checker, who also stars in the movie		
11/10/62	**23**	8	8. All The Hits (For Your Dancin' Party)		Parkway 7014
			Limbo Rock (2)		
12/29/62	**11**	19	9. Limbo Party		Parkway 7020
2/9/63	**27**	8	10. Chubby Checker's Biggest Hits [G]		Parkway 7022
			Popeye The Hitchhiker (10)		

DATE	POS	WKS	ARTIST—RECORD TITLE	LABEL & NO.
			CHEECH & CHONG	
			Comedians Richard "Cheech" Marin (born 7/13/46, Watts, California) and Thomas Chong (born 5/24/38, Edmonton, Alberta, Canada). Starred in movies since 1978. Chong, the father of actress Rae Dawn Chong, was guitarist of Bobby Taylor & The Vancouvers. Cheech was a cast member of TV's "Golden Palace."	
1/29/72	28	10	● 1. Cheech And Chong [C]	Ode 77010
7/15/72	2(1)	20	● **2. Big Bambu** [C]	Ode 77014
9/8/73	2(1)	29	● **3. Los Cochinos** [C]	Ode 77019
			title is Spanish for the pigs	
10/26/74	5	9	● **4. Cheech & Chong's Wedding Album** [C]	Ode 77025
			Earache My Eye (Featuring Alice Bowie) (9)	
7/10/76	25	6	5. Sleeping Beauty [C]	Ode 77040
			CHER	
			Born Cherilyn LaPierre on 5/20/46 in El Centro, California. Worked as backup singer for Phil Spector. Recorded as "Bonnie Jo Mason" and "Cherilyn" in 1964. Recorded with Sonny Bono as "Caesar & Cleo" in 1963, then as Sonny & Cher from 1965-73. Married to Bono from 1963-74. Married to Gregg Allman from 1975-77. Own TV series with Bono from 1971-77. Member of the group Black Rose in 1980. Acclaimed movie actress (won 1987 Best Actress Oscar for *Moonstruck*).	
10/16/65	16	10	1. All I Really Want To Do	Imperial 12292
6/18/66	26	7	2. The Sonny Side Of Cher	Imperial 12301
			Bang Bang (9)	
10/30/71	16	11	● 3. Gypsys, Tramps & Thieves	Kapp 3649
			Gypsys, Tramps & Thieves (1)/*The Way Of Love* (7)	
			original pressing simply titled *Cher*	
10/27/73	28	4	● 4. Half-Breed	MCA 2104
			Half-Breed (1)	
4/14/79	25	6	● 5. Take Me Home	Casablanca 7133
			Take Me Home (8)	
3/19/88	32	12	▲ 6. Cher	Geffen 24164
			I Found Someone (10)	
8/26/89	10	31	▲² **7. Heart Of Stone**	Geffen 24239
			After All (6-with Peter Cetera)/*If I Could Turn Back Time* (3)/ *Just Like Jesse James* (8)	
			CHERRELLE	
			Born Cheryl Norton in Los Angeles. Soul vocalist/drummer. Cousin of vocalist Pebbles. Moved to Detroit in 1979. Discovered by Michael Henderson.	
4/12/86	36	1	High Priority	Tabu 40094
			accompanied by The Secrets: Jimmy *Jam* Harris, Terry Lewis and Monte Moir (all ex-members of Time)	
			CHERRY, Don	
			Born on 1/11/24 in Wichita Falls, Texas. Studied voice after the service in mid-1940s. Vocalist with Jan Garber band in the late '40s. Accomplished professional golfer.	
9/22/56	15	7	Swingin' For Two	Columbia 893
			with Ray Conniff & His Orchestra	

DATE	POS	WKS	ARTIST—RECORD TITLE		LABEL & NO.
			CHERRY, Neneh		
			Born on 8/10/64 in Stockholm, of Swedish and West African parentage and raised in New York City. London-based R&B singer. Stepdaughter of jazz trumpeter Don Cherry.		
9/16/89	**40**	1	Raw Like Sushi		Virgin 91252
			Buffalo Stance (3)/Kisses On The Wind (8)		
			CHIC		
			R&B-disco group formed in New York City by prolific producers Bernard Edwards (bass) and Nile Rodgers (guitar). Vocalists: Norma Jean Wright (replaced by Alfa Anderson) and Luci Martin; drums: Tony Thompson. Wright began solo career in 1978 as Norma Jean. Edwards recorded with the studio group Roundtree in 1978. Rodgers joined The Honeydrippers in 1984. Thompson joined The Power Station in 1985, and Edwards became their producer. Wright along with supporting Chic member Raymond Jones formed State Of Art in 1991. Rodgers and Edwards re-grouped as Chic in 1992 with female lead vocalists/South Carolina natives Sylvester Logan Sharp and Jenn Thomas.		
2/4/78	**27**	9	● 1. Chic		Atlantic 19153
			Dance, Dance, Dance (6)		
12/9/78	**4**	22	▲ 2. C'est Chic		Atlantic 19209
			Le Freak (1)/I Want Your Love (7)		
8/25/79	**5**	11	▲ 3. Risqué		Atlantic 16003
			Good Times (1)		
8/23/80	**30**	3	4. Real People		Atlantic 16016
			CHICAGO		
			Jazz-oriented rock group formed in Chicago in 1967. Consisted of Peter Cetera (lead singer, bass guitar), Robert Lamm (keyboards), James Pankow (trombone), Lee Loughnane (trumpet), Terry Kath (died 1/23/78 [age 31] of accidental self-inflicted gunshot; guitar), Walt Parazaider (reeds) and Danny Seraphine (drums). Originally called The Big Thing; later Chicago Transit Authority. To Los Angeles in the late '60s. Kath replaced by Donnie Dacus (left in 1979). Bill Champlin (keyboards) joined in 1982. Cetera left in 1985; replaced by Jason Scheff. Seraphine left in 1989; guitarist DaWayne Bailey added.		
5/31/69	**17**	42	▲² 1. Chicago Transit Authority		Columbia 8 [2]
			Does Anybody Really Know What Time It Is? (7)/Beginnings (7)		
2/21/70	**4**	53	● 2. Chicago II		Columbia 24 [2]
			Make Me Smile (9)/25 Or 6 To 4 (4)		
1/30/71	**2**(2)	22	▲ 3. Chicago III		Columbia 30110 [2]
11/20/71	**3**	19	▲ 4. Chicago At Carnegie Hall	[L]	Columbia 30865 [4]
7/29/72	**1**(9)	20	▲² 5. Chicago V		Columbia 31102
			Saturday In The Park (3)		
7/21/73	**1**(5)	27	▲² 6. Chicago VI		Columbia 32400
			Feelin' Stronger Every Day (10)/Just You 'N' Me (4)		
4/6/74	**1**(1)	35	▲ 7. Chicago VII		Columbia 32810 [2]
			(I've Been) Searchin' So Long (9)/Call On Me (6)		
4/12/75	**1**(2)	15	▲ 8. Chicago VIII		Columbia 33100
			Old Days (5)		
11/29/75	**1**(5)	22	▲⁵ 9. Chicago IX — Chicago's Greatest Hits	[G]	Columbia 33900
7/4/76	**3**	30	▲² 10. Chicago X		Columbia 34200
			If You Leave Me Now (1)		
10/1/77	**6**	10	▲ 11. Chicago XI		Columbia 34860
			Baby, What A Big Surprise (4)		
10/21/78	**12**	11	▲ 12. Hot Streets		Columbia 35512

DATE	POS	WKS	ARTIST—RECORD TITLE	LABEL & NO.
9/8/79	21	5	● 13. Chicago 13	Columbia 36105
7/17/82	9	18	▲ **14. Chicago 16**	Full Moon 23689
			Hard To Say I'm Sorry (1)	
6/16/84	4	44	▲⁵ **15. Chicago 17**	Full Moon 25060
			Hard Habit To Break (3)/*You're The Inspiration* (3)	
2/21/87	35	4	● 16. Chicago 18	Warner 25509
			Will You Still Love Me? (3)	
1/7/89	37	4	▲ 17. 19	Reprise 25714
			I Don't Wanna Live Without Your Love (3)/*Look Away* (1)/	
			You're Not Alone (10)	
1/20/90	37	5	▲² 18. Greatest Hits 1982-1989 [G]	Reprise 26080
			What Kind Of Man Would I Be? (5)	
			CHI-LITES, The	
			R&B vocal group from Chicago. Consisted of Eugene Record (lead vocals), Robert "Squirrel" Lester (tenor), Marshall Thompson (baritone) and Creadel "Red" Jones (bass). First recorded as The Hi-Lites on Daran in 1963. Eugene Record (husband of Barbara Acklin) went solo in 1976.	
9/25/71	12	14	1. (For God's Sake) Give More Power To The People	Brunswick 754170
			Have You Seen Her (3)	
5/13/72	5	16	**2. A Lonely Man**	Brunswick 754179
			Oh Girl (1)	
			CHIPMUNKS, The	
			Characters created by Ross Bagdasarian ("David Seville") who named Alvin, Simon and Theodore after Liberty executives Alvin Bennett, Simon Waronker and Theodore Keep. The Chipmunks starred in own prime-time, animated TV show in the early '60s and a Saturday-morning cartoon series in the mid-1980s. Bagdasarian died on 1/16/72 (age 52). His son, Ross, Jr., resurrected the act in 1980.	
			DAVID SEVILLE AND THE CHIPMUNKS:	
12/7/59	4	28	**1. Let's All Sing With The Chipmunks** [N]	Liberty 3132
			The Chipmunk Song (1)/*Alvin's Harmonica* (3)	
6/20/60	31	5	2. Sing Again With The Chipmunks [N]	Liberty 3159
			THE CHIPMUNKS With DAVID SEVILLE:	
9/19/64	14	11	3. The Chipmunks Sing The Beatles Hits [N]	Liberty 7388
			THE CHIPMUNKS:	
8/23/80	34	6	● 4. Chipmunk Punk [N]	Excelsior 6008
			ALVIN & THE CHIPMUNKS:	
12/19/92	21	4	● 5. Chipmunks In Low Places [N]	Epic/Chip. 53006
			with special guests Billy Ray Cyrus, Aaron Tippin, Tammy Wynette, Charlie Daniels, Alan Jackson and Waylon Jennings	
			CHRISTY, June	
			Born Shirley Luster on 11/20/25 in Springfield, Illinois. Died on 6/21/90 of kidney failure. Jazz singer. Achieved national fame with The Stan Kenton Band. Orchestra conducted by Pete Rugolo.	
9/29/56	14	4	1. The Misty Miss Christy	Capitol 725
7/22/57	16	4	2. June — Fair and Warmer!	Capitol 833
			CINDERELLA	
			Pennsylvania-based, heavy-metal band consisting of Tom Keifer (vocals, guitar), Jeff LaBar (guitar), Eric Brittingham (bass) and Fred Coury (drums; left in 1992 and formed Arcade).	
8/23/86	3	49	▲³ **1. Night Songs**	Mercury 830076

DATE	POS	WKS	ARTIST—RECORD TITLE	LABEL & NO.
7/30/88	**10**	32	▲² **2. Long Cold Winter**	Mercury 834612
12/15/90	**19**	12	▲ 3. Heartbreak Station	Mercury 848018

CLAPTON, Eric

Born Eric Patrick Clapp on 3/30/45 in Ripley, England. Prolific rock-blues guitarist/vocalist. With The Roosters in 1963; The Yardbirds, 1963-65; and John Mayall's Bluesbreakers, 1965-66. Formed Cream with Jack Bruce and Ginger Baker in 1966. Formed Blind Faith in 1968; worked with John Lennon's Plastic Ono Band, and Delaney & Bonnie. Formed Derek and The Dominos in 1970. After two years of reclusion (1971-72), Clapton performed his comeback concert at London's Rainbow Theatre in January 1973. Began actively recording and touring again in 1974. Clapton's four-year-old son, Conor, died on 3/20/91 in a 53-floor fall in New York City. Nicknamed "Slowhand" in 1964 while with The Yardbirds.

DATE	POS	WKS	ARTIST—RECORD TITLE	LABEL & NO.
8/8/70	13	10	1. Eric Clapton	Atco 329
11/28/70	16	19	● 2. Layla **DEREK AND THE DOMINOS** *Layla* (10)	Atco 704 [2]
4/22/72	**6**	22	● **3. History Of Eric Clapton** [K] recordings with groups listed in above artist notes	Atco 803 [2]
2/17/73	20	9	● 4. Derek & The Dominos In Concert [L] **DEREK AND THE DOMINOS**	RSO 8800 [2]
10/6/73	18	6	5. Eric Clapton's Rainbow Concert [L] Clapton's comeback concert at London's Rainbow Theatre with Pete Townshend, Steve Winwood, Ron Wood, Jim Capaldi and Rick Grech	RSO 877
7/27/74	**1**(4)	14	● **6. 461 Ocean Boulevard** address where recorded in Miami, Florida *I Shot The Sheriff* (1)	RSO 4801
4/26/75	21	5	7. There's One In Every Crowd	RSO 4806
9/13/75	20	7	8. E.C. Was Here [L]	RSO 4809
10/16/76	15	12	9. No Reason To Cry	RSO 3004
12/24/77	**2**(5)	30	▲³ **10. Slowhand** *Lay Down Sally* (3)	RSO 3030
12/2/78	**8**	17	▲ **11. Backless** *Promises* (9)	RSO 3039
5/10/80	**2**(6)	19	● **12. Just One Night** [L] recorded at the Budokan Theatre, Japan	RSO 4202 [2]
3/21/81	**7**	13	● **13. Another Ticket** *I Can't Stand It* (10)	RSO 3095
2/26/83	16	10	14. Money And Cigarettes	Duck 23773
4/13/85	34	7	● 15. Behind the Sun	Duck 25166
2/21/87	37	5	● 16. August	Duck 25476
5/14/88	34	3	▲² 17. Crossroads [K] contains 73 digitally mastered tracks of Clapton's 25-year career	Polydor 835261 [6]
12/2/89	16	26	▲² 18. Journeyman	Duck 26074
10/26/91	38	1	● 19. 24 Nights [L] recorded over 24 nights at The Royal Albert Hall, London, 1990-91, with a 4-piece band, 9-piece band, band of blues legends and an orchestra; with guests: Phil Collins, Buddy Guy, Jimmie Vaughan, Joey Spampinato (NRBQ), Katie Kissoon, Robert Cray and others	Duck 26420 [2]
2/1/92	**24**	14	● 20. Rush [S+I] *Tears In Heaven* (2)	Reprise 26794

DATE	POS	WKS	ARTIST—RECORD TITLE	LABEL & NO.
9/12/92	1(3)	52	▲⁷ **21. Unplugged** [L] Clapton's 3/12/92 performance on the MTV program "Unplugged"; 1992 Album of the Year Grammy Award	Duck 45024
10/1/94	1(1)	18	▲² **22. From The Cradle** [L] "live" studio session of songs by Willie Dixon, Elmore James, Muddy Waters and other blues greats	Duck 45735
			### CLARK, Dave, Five Clark formed the rock group in Tottenham, England, in 1960. Consisted of Clark (drums), Mike Smith (lead singer, keyboards), Lenny Davidson (guitar), Denny Payton (sax) and Rick Huxley (bass). First recorded for Ember/Pye in 1962. On "The Ed Sullivan Show" in March 1964. In the movie *Having a Wild Weekend* in 1965. Disbanded in 1973. Clark had been a stuntman in movies; formed group to raise money for his soccer team, The Tottenham Hotspurs. Clark wrote the 1986 London stage musical *Time*.	
4/25/64	3	25	● **1. Glad All Over** *Glad All Over* (6)/*Bits And Pieces* (4)	Epic 26093
7/4/64	5	13	**2. The Dave Clark Five Return!** *Can't You See That She's Mine* (4)	Epic 26104
9/5/64	11	9	3. American Tour *Because* (3)	Epic 26117
1/16/65	6	13	**4. Coast To Coast**	Epic 26128
5/15/65	24	6	5. Weekend In London	Epic 26139
9/18/65	15	11	6. Having A Wild Weekend [S] The Dave Clark Five star in the movie *Catch Us If You Can* (4)	Epic 26162
1/22/66	32	6	7. I Like It Like That *I Like It Like That* (7)	Epic 26178
4/2/66	9	20	● **8. The Dave Clark Five's Greatest Hits** [G] *Over And Over* (1)	Epic 26185
			### CLARK, Dick — see COMPILATIONS BY DISC ### JOCKEYS	
			### CLARK, Petula Born on 11/15/32 in Epsom, England. Pop singer/actress. On radio at age nine; own show *Pet's Parlour* at age 11. TV series in England in 1950. First U.S. record release for Coral in 1953. Appeared in over 20 British movies from 1944-57; revived her movie career in the late '60s, starring in *Finian's Rainbow* and *Goodbye Mr. Chips*.	
3/20/65	21	16	1. Downtown *Downtown* (1)	Warner 1590
9/23/67	27	10	2. These Are My Songs *This Is My Song* (3)/*Don't Sleep In The Subway* (5)	Warner 1698
5/24/69	37	3	3. Portrait Of Petula	Warner 1789
			### CLARKE, Stanley Born on 6/30/51 in Philadelphia. R&B-jazz bassist/violinist/cellist. With Chick Corea in Return To Forever in 1973. Much session work; solo debut in 1974. Member of Fuse One in 1982 and Animal Logic in 1989.	
11/29/75	34	3	1. Journey To Love [I]	Nemperor 433
10/23/76	34	4	2. School Days [I]	Nemperor 439
6/6/81	33	8	3. The Clarke/Duke Project **STANLEY CLARKE/GEORGE DUKE**	Epic 36918

DATE	POS	WKS	ARTIST—RECORD TITLE	LABEL & NO.
			CLASH, The	
			Eclectic new-wave rock group formed in London in 1976. Consisted of John "Joe Strummer" Mellor (vocals), Mick Jones (guitar), Paul Simonon (bass) and Nicky "Topper" Headon (drums). Political activists, they wrote songs protesting racism and oppression. Headon left in May 1983; replaced by Peter Howard. Jones (not to be confused with Mick Jones of Foreigner) left band in 1984 to form Big Audio Dynamite. Strummer disbanded The Clash in early 1986; appeared in the 1987 movie *Straight to Hell*.	
3/8/80	27	9	● 1. London Calling	Epic 36328 [2]
2/21/81	24	5	2. Sandinista!	Epic 37037 [3]
6/26/82	7	39	▲ 3. Combat Rock	Epic 37689
			Rock The Casbah (8)	
			CLAY, Andrew Dice	
			Comedian from Brooklyn. Appeared in the movies *Pretty in Pink*, *Casual Sex*, *The Adventures of Ford Fairlane* and TV's "Crime Story."	
6/2/90	39	2	The Day The Laughter Died [C]	Def Amer. 24287 [2]
			recorded at Dangerfield's in New York City on 12/26-27/89	
			CLIBURN, Van	
			Born Harvey Lavan Cliburn, Jr., on 7/12/34 in Shreveport, Louisiana. Classical pianist.	
8/4/58	1(7)	76	▲ 1. Tchaikovsky: Piano Concerto No. 1 [I]	RCA 2252
			Kiril Kondrashin, conductor	
7/13/59	10	37	2. Rachmaninoff: Piano Concerto No. 3 [I-L]	RCA 2355
			Carnegie Hall performance of 5/19/58	
3/24/62	25	7	3. Brahms: Piano Concerto No. 2 [I]	RCA 2581
			Fritz Reiner conducts The Chicago Symphony Orchestra	
			CLIFFORD, Linda	
			Black vocalist from Brooklyn. Former Miss New York State. With Jericho Jazz Singers; own trio in 1967.	
7/1/78	22	5	1. If My Friends Could See Me Now	Curtom 5021
4/21/79	26	8	2. Let Me Be Your Woman	RSO 3902 [2]
			CLIMAX BLUES BAND	
			Blues-rock band formed in Stafford, England. Nucleus consisted of Colin Cooper (sax, vocals), Peter Haycock (guitar, vocals), Derek Holt (bass) and John Cuffley (drums).	
10/5/74	37	2	1. Sense Of Direction	Sire 7501
6/11/77	27	6	2. Gold Plated	Sire 7523
			Couldn't Get It Right (3)	
			CLINE, Patsy	
			Born Virginia Patterson Hensley on 9/8/32 in Winchester, Virginia. Killed in a plane crash with Cowboy Copas and Hawkshaw Hawkins on 3/5/63 near Camden, Tennessee. Elected to the Country Music Hall of Fame in 1973. Jessica Lange played Cline in the 1985 biographical movie *Sweet Dreams*.	
12/7/85	29	5	● Sweet Dreams — The Life And Times Of Patsy Cline [S]	MCA 6149
			featuring Cline's original vocals	

DATE	POS	WKS	ARTIST—RECORD TITLE	LABEL & NO.
			CLINTON, George	
			Born on 7/22/40 in Plainfield, Ohio. Lead singer of The Parliaments. Became leader/producer of Funkadelic and Parliament. Headed "A Parliafunkadelicament Thang," a corporation of nearly 40 musicians that recorded as Parliament and Funkadelic plus various offshoot bands: Bootsy's Rubber Band, The Brides Of Funkenstein, Horny Horns, Parlet and The P. Funk All Stars. Appeared in the movie *House Party*.	
4/30/83	40	1	Computer Games	Capitol 12246
			CLOONEY, Rosemary	
			Born on 5/23/28 in Maysville, Kentucky. One of the most popular singers of the '50s, Clooney and sister Betty sang with The Tony Pastor Band in the late '40s before her solo career was launched. Rosemary was featured in *White Christmas* and several other '50s movies. After a period of personal difficulties, she re-emerged in the late '70s as a successful jazz and ballad singer. Married for a time to actor Jose Ferrer; their son Gabriel married Debby Boone.	
7/22/57	14	7	Ring Around The Rosie **ROSEMARY CLOONEY AND THE HI-LO'S**	Columbia 1006
			CLUB NOUVEAU	
			Sacramento-based, dance-disco group formed and fronted by Jay King (producer/owner of King Jay Records; produced The Timex Social Club).	
2/28/87	6	18	▲ **Life, Love & Pain** *Lean On Me* (1)	Warner 25531
			COBHAM, Billy	
			Born on 5/16/44 in Panama; raised in New York City. Jazz-rock drummer. Formerly with Miles Davis and John McLaughlin.	
1/12/74	26	9	1. Spectrum [I]	Atlantic 7268
5/25/74	23	6	2. Crosswinds [I]	Atlantic 7300
1/25/75	36	1	3. Total Eclipse [I]	Atlantic 18121
			COCKER, Joe	
			Born John Robert Cocker on 5/20/44 in Sheffield, England. Own skiffle band, The Cavaliers, late '50s; later reorganized as Vance Arnold & The Avengers. Assembled The Grease Band in the mid-1960s. Performed at Woodstock in 1969. Successful tour with 43-piece revue, Mad Dogs & Englishmen, in 1970. Notable spastic stage antics were based on Ray Charles's movements at the piano.	
7/19/69	35	3	● 1. With A Little Help From My Friends with Jimmy Page and Stevie Winwood	A&M 4182
11/29/69	11	26	● 2. Joe Cocker! with Leon Russell and The Grease Band	A&M 4224
9/5/70	2(1)	16	● **3. Mad Dogs & Englishmen** [S-L] title refers to Cocker's 1970 concert tour with an entourage of 43 including Leon Russell and Chris Stainton *The Letter* (7)	A&M 6002 [2]
12/30/72	30	7	4. Joe Cocker	A&M 4368
9/21/74	11	10	5. I Can Stand A Little Rain *You Are So Beautiful* (5)	A&M 3633
			COFFEY, Dennis, And The Detroit Guitar Band	
			Detroit native Coffey was a session guitarist for The Temptations, The Jackson 5 and others. Coffey later formed C.J. & Co.	
1/8/72	36	4	Evolution [I] *Scorpio* (6)	Sussex 7004

DATE	POS	WKS	ARTIST—RECORD TITLE	LABEL & NO.
			COHN, Marc	
			Cleveland-born singer/songwriter. Formed a 14-piece band in New York, The Supreme Court, which was discovered by Carly Simon and played at Caroline Kennedy's wedding. Won 1991 Best New Artist Grammy Award.	
3/14/92	**38**	1	● Marc Cohn	Atlantic 82178
			COLD BLOOD	
			Bay-area rock group led by Lydia Pense (vocals). Original members Raul Matute (piano), Rod Ellicott (bass) and Danny Hull (sax) were longtime members of everchanging personnel. Max Haskett (trumpet) and Michael Sasaki (guitar) were also regular members.	
3/7/70	**23**	6	Cold Blood	San Francisco 200
			COLE, Natalie	
			Born on 2/6/50 in Los Angeles. Daughter of Nat "King" Cole. Professional debut at age 11. Married for a time to her producer, Marvin Yancey, Jr. Later married Andre Fischer, former drummer of Rufus and producer for Brenda Russell, Michael Franks and Andre Crouch, until 1992. Won 1975 Best New Artist Grammy Award. Hosted own syndicated variety TV show "Big Break" in 1990.	
11/1/75	**18**	8	● 1. Inseparable	Capitol 11429
			This Will Be (6)	
6/5/76	**13**	11	● 2. Natalie	Capitol 11517
3/12/77	**8**	13	▲ **3. Unpredictable**	Capitol 11600
			I've Got Love On My Mind (5)	
1/28/78	**16**	17	▲ 4. Thankful	Capitol 11708
			Our Love (10)	
8/5/78	**31**	7	● 5. Natalie … Live! [L]	Capitol 11709 [2]
6/29/91	**1**(5)	49	▲⁵ **6. Unforgettable With Love**	Elektra 61049
			sings her father's (Nat "King" Cole) classics from 1944-64	
7/3/93	**26**	5	● 7. Take A Look	Elektra 61496
12/24/94	**36**	1	8. Holly & Ivy [X]	Elektra 61704
			Christmas charts: 6/'94	
			COLE, Nat "King"	
			Born Nathaniel Adams Coles on 3/17/17 in Montgomery, Alabama; raised in Chicago. Died of lung cancer on 2/15/65 in Santa Monica, California. Own band, The Royal Dukes, at age 17. First recorded in 1936 in band led by brother Eddie. Toured with "Shuffle Along" musical revue; lived in Los Angeles. Formed The King Cole Trio in 1939: Nat (piano), Oscar Moore (guitar; later joined brother's group, Johnny Moore's Three Blazers) and Wesley Prince (bass; replaced several years later by Johnny Miller). Long series of top-selling records led to his solo career in 1950. In movies *St. Louis Blues*, *Cat Ballou*, and many others. The first major black performer to star in a network (NBC) TV variety series (1956-57). Stopped performing in 1964 due to ill health. His daughter Natalie Cole is a recording artist. Won 1990 Lifetime Achievement Grammy Award.	
4/28/56	**16**	2	1. Ballads Of The Day	Capitol 680
			Darling Je Vous Aime Beaucoup (7)/*A Blossom Fell* (2)	
3/9/57	**13**	2	2. After Midnight	Capitol 782
			with the King Cole Trio	
4/6/57	**1**(8)	55	▲ **3. Love Is The Thing**	Capitol 824
9/23/57	**18**	3	4. This Is Nat "King" Cole	Capitol 870
12/16/57	**18**	6	5. Just One Of Those Things	Capitol 903
5/5/58	**18**	3	6. St. Louis Blues [S]	Capitol 993
			Cole portrayed W.C. Handy in the movie about Handy's life	
9/22/58	**12**	5	7. Cole Espanol [F]	Capitol 1031

DATE	POS	WKS	ARTIST—RECORD TITLE	LABEL & NO.
12/1/58	17	2	8. The Very Thought Of You	Capitol 1084
4/18/60	33	2	9. Tell Me All About Yourself	Capitol 1331
10/24/60	4	11	**10. Wild Is Love**	Capitol 1392
5/12/62	27	9	11. Nat King Cole sings / George Shearing plays	Capitol 1675
9/29/62	3	53	▲ **12. Ramblin' Rose**	Capitol 1793
			Ramblin' Rose (2)	
1/5/63	24	10	13. Dear Lonely Hearts	Capitol 1838
7/20/63	14	9	14. Those Lazy-Hazy-Crazy Days Of Summer	Capitol 1932
			Those Lazy-Hazy-Crazy Days Of Summer (6)	
8/22/64	18	4	15. I Don't Want To Be Hurt Anymore	Capitol 2118
3/6/65	4	25	**16. L-O-V-E**	Capitol 2195
5/8/65	30	11	▲ 17. Unforgettable [R]	Capitol 357
			reissue of Cole's 1953 10" album	

COLLECTIVE SOUL

Quintet from Stockbridge, Georgia: brothers Ed (vocals) and Dean Roland with Ross Childress, Will Turpin and Shane Evans. Group name taken from a reference in Ayn Rand's novel *The Fountainhead*.

DATE	POS	WKS	ARTIST—RECORD TITLE	LABEL & NO.
5/21/94	15	19	▲ Hints Allegations And Things Left Unsaid	Atlantic 82596

COLLINS, "Bootsy" — see BOOTSY'S RUBBER BAND

COLLINS, Judy

Born on 5/1/39 in Seattle. Contemporary folk singer/songwriter. Began studying classical piano at age five. Moved to Los Angeles, then to Denver at age nine, where her father, Chuck Collins, was a radio personality. Classical debut at 13, playing with The Denver Businessmen's Symphony Orchestra. Discovered folk music at 15. Signed to Elektra in 1961. Her cover versions gave exposure to then-unknown songwriters Leonard Cohen, Joni Mitchell, Randy Newman and Sandy Denny. Stephen Stills wrote "Suite: Judy Blue Eyes" for her. Appeared in the New York Shakespeare Festival's production of *Peer Gynt*. Nominated for a 1974 Academy Award for co-directing *Antonia: A Portrait of the Woman*, a documentary about Collins's former classical mentor and pioneer female orchestra conductor, Dr. Antonia Brico.

DATE	POS	WKS	ARTIST—RECORD TITLE	LABEL & NO.
7/13/68	5	18	● **1. Wildflowers**	Elektra 74012
			Both Sides Now (8)	
2/1/69	29	11	● 2. Who Knows Where The Time Goes	Elektra 74033
10/11/69	29	3	3. Recollections [K]	Elektra 74055
			recordings from 1963-65	
12/12/70	17	16	● 4. Whales & Nightingales	Elektra 75010
7/1/72	37	3	● 5. Colors Of The Day / The Best Of Judy Collins [G]	Elektra 75030
3/24/73	27	4	6. True Stories And Other Dreams	Elektra 75053
5/3/75	17	17	● 7. Judith	Elektra 1032
9/25/76	25	4	8. Bread & Roses	Elektra 1076

COLLINS, Phil

Born on 1/30/51 in London. Pop vocalist/multi-instrumentalist/composer. Stage actor as a young child; played the Artful Dodger in the London production of *Oliver*. With group Flaming Youth in 1969. Joined Genesis as its drummer in 1970; became lead singer in 1975. Also with jazz-rock group Brand X. First solo album in 1981. Starred in the 1988 movie *Buster* and appeared in *Hook* and *Frauds*.

DATE	POS	WKS	ARTIST—RECORD TITLE	LABEL & NO.
4/4/81	7	26	▲⁴ **1. Face Value**	Atlantic 16029
12/4/82	8	21	▲² **2. Hello, I Must Be Going!**	Atlantic 80035
			You Can't Hurry Love (10)	

DATE	POS	WKS	ARTIST—RECORD TITLE		LABEL & NO.
3/9/85	**1**(7)	70	▲[7]	**3. No Jacket Required**	Atlantic 81240
				1985 Album of the Year Grammy Award *One More Night* (1)/*Sussudio* (1)/*Don't Lose My Number* (4)/ *Take Me Home* (7)	
12/9/89	**1**(3)	50	▲[4]	**4. ... But Seriously**	Atlantic 82050
				Another Day In Paradise (1)/*I Wish It Would Rain Down* (3)/ *Do You Remember?* (4)/*Something Happened On The Way To Heaven* (4)	
12/1/90	**11**	19	▲[2]	5. Serious Hits ... Live! [L]	Atlantic 82157
				recorded during his "Serious Tour 1990"; 22-page booklet included	
11/27/93	**13**	8	▲	6. Both Sides	Atlantic 82550

			COLOR ME BADD		
			New York City-based dance vocal quartet: Bryan Abrams, Sam Watters, Mark Calderon and Kevin Thornton. Formed while in high school in Oklahoma City.		Giant 24429
8/10/91	**3**	49	▲[3]	**C.M.B.**	
				I Wanna Sex You Up (2)/*I Adore Mi Amor* (1)/*All 4 Love* (1)	

			COLTER, Jessi — see CONCEPT ALBUMS		

			COMMAND ALL-STARS — see LIGHT, Enoch		

			COMMITMENTS, The — see SOUNDTRACKS **(*The Commitments*)**		

			COMMODORES		
			R&B group formed in Tuskegee, Alabama, in 1970. Consisted of Lionel Richie (vocals, saxophone), William King (trumpet), Thomas McClary (guitar), Milan Williams (keyboards), Ronald LaPread (bass) and Walter "Clyde" Orange (drums). First recorded for Motown in 1972. In the movie *Thank God It's Friday*. Richie began solo work in 1981; left group in 1982.		
7/5/75	**26**	5		1. Caught In The Act	Motown 820
11/29/75	**29**	9		2. Movin' On	Motown 848
				Sweet Love (5)	
8/7/76	**12**	25		3. Hot On The Tracks	Motown 867
				Just To Be Close To You (7)	
4/16/77	**3**	31		**4. Commodores**	Motown 884
				Easy (4)/*Brick House* (5)	
11/12/77	**3**	16		**5. Commodores Live!** [L]	Motown 894 [2]
6/3/78	**3**	23	▲	**6. Natural High**	Motown 902
				Three Times A Lady (1)	
12/23/78	**23**	6		7. Commodores' Greatest Hits [G]	Motown 912
8/18/79	**3**	30		**8. Midnight Magic**	Motown 926
				Sail On (4)/*Still* (1)	
6/28/80	**7**	15	▲	**9. Heroes**	Motown 939
7/11/81	**13**	19	▲	10. In The Pocket	Motown 955
				Lady (You Bring Me Up) (8)/*Oh No* (4)	
1/15/83	**37**	4		11. All The Great Hits [G]	Motown 6028
3/23/85	**12**	15	●	12. Nightshift	Motown 6124
				Nightshift (3)	

DATE	POS	WKS	ARTIST—RECORD TITLE	LABEL & NO.
			COMO, Perry	
			Born Pierino Como on 5/18/12 in Canonsburg, Pennsylvania. Owned barbershop in hometown. With The Freddy Carlone Band in 1933; with Ted Weems, 1936-42. In the movies *Something For the Boys*, *Doll Face*, *If I'm Lucky* and *Words and Music*, 1944-48. Own *Supper Club* radio series to late '40s. Television shows (15 minutes) from 1948-55. Host of hourly TV shows from 1955-63. Winner of five Emmy Awards. One of the most popular singers of the past 50 years.	
10/15/55	7	15	**1. So Smooth**	RCA 1085
9/2/57	8	10	**2. We Get Letters**	RCA 1463
12/16/57	11	9	3. Dream Along With Me	RCA Camden 403
6/23/58	18	2	4. Saturday Night With Mr. C.	RCA 1004
9/1/58	24	2	5. Como's Golden Records [G]	RCA 1007
			Hot Diggity (1)/*Round And Round* (1)/*Catch A Falling Star* (1)/ *Magic Moments* (4)	
1/5/59	16	7	6. When You Come To The End Of The Day	RCA 1885
11/2/59	17	12	7. Como Swings	RCA 2010
12/8/62	32	3	8. By Request	RCA 2567
2/6/71	22	12	9. It's Impossible	RCA 4473
			It's Impossible (10)	
7/7/73	34	4	● 10. And I Love You So	RCA 0100
			CHRISTMAS ALBUMS:	
12/16/57	8	5	● **11. Merry Christmas Music** [X]	RCA 1243
12/15/58	9	4	**12. Merry Christmas Music** [X-R]	RCA 1243
			Christmas charts: 17/'63, 15/'64, 53/'65, 63/'66, 16/'67, 16/'68	
1/4/60	22	1	● 13. Season's Greetings [X]	RCA 2066
12/31/60	27	1	14. Season's Greetings [X-R]	RCA 2066
1/13/62	33	1	15. Season's Greetings [X-R]	RCA 2066
			CON FUNK SHUN	
			Soul band formed as Project Soul in Vallejo, California, in 1968 by high-school classmates Michael Cooper (lead vocals, guitar) and Louis McCall (drums). Moved to Memphis in 1972; changed name to Con Funk Shun. Session work for Stax Records. Included Karl Fuller, Paul Harrell, Felton Pilate II, Danny Thomas, Cedric Martin and Peto Escovedo (son of Azteca's Pete Escovedo and brother of Sheila E).	
8/5/78	32	7	● 1. Loveshine	Mercury 3725
5/10/80	30	5	● 2. Spirit Of Love	Mercury 3806
			CONNICK, Harry, Jr.	
			Born on 9/11/67. Jazz-pop pianist/vocalist from New Orleans. Studied jazz under Ellis Marsalis, the father of Wynton and Branford. Acted in the movies *Memphis Belle* and *Little Man Tate*.	
8/4/90	22	0	▲² 1. We Are In Love	Columbia 46146
10/12/91	17	23	▲² 2. Blue Light, Red Light	Columbia 48685
12/19/92	19	4	▲ 3. 25	Columbia 53172
			classic tunes written by Hoagy Carmichael, Frederick Lowe & Alan Lerner, Johnny Mercer, John Coltrane, Duke Ellington and others; recorded at age 25	
12/11/93	13	5	▲ 4. When My Heart Finds Christmas [X]	Columbia 57550
			Christmas charts: 1/'93, 3/'94	
7/30/94	16	11	▲ 5. She	Columbia 64376

Mariah Carey's meteoric 1990 debut held the No. 1 slot for 11 weeks and stayed on the charts for more than two years. The powerful singer later married Sony Music president Tommy Mottola.

Johnny Cash, the longtime "Man in Black," saw renewed success in, remarkably, his fifth decade of recording, upon signing with producer Rick Rubin's adventurous American label. *American Recordings*, Cash's comeback effort, was nominated for a 1994 Grammy Award.

Ray Charles's sole No. 1 album, 1962's *Modern Sounds In Country And Western Music*, bore the Top 40 hits "I Can't Stop Loving You" and "You Don't Know Me," which reached the No. 1 and No. 2 positions, respectively.

Chicago's 1978 set, *Hot Streets*, was historic for two reasons: it was the first to feature guitarist Donnie Dacus, who left within a year, and perhaps more notably, it was the first album since the group's debut to bear an actual name, rather than number, for its title.

Eric Clapton's post-Cream debut, 1970's *Eric Clapton*, proved the singer/guitarist could function viably as a solo artist. Nonetheless, his next effort, the same year's hugely popular *Layla*, arrived credited to his new band, Derek & the Dominoes.

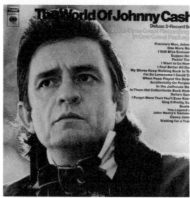

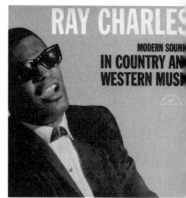

Van Cliburn put Tchaikovsky at the top of the pop charts via his historic 1958 album, *Tchaikovsky: Piano Concerto No. 1*. The platinum disc stayed on the charts for 125 weeks.

Nat "King" Cole's final Top 5 album, 1965's *L-O-V-E*, entered the charts scant weeks before he died of lung cancer. Soon after his death, Capitol Records appropriately reissued his classic 1953 album, *Unforgettable*.

Phil Collins's *No Jacket Required*, which won the 1985 Album of the Year Grammy Award, was the singer's first No. 1 album and remains his all-time bestseller. Ironically, Genesis, his long-time group, has yet to match that chart feat; *Invisible Touch*, its 1986 effort, peaked at No. 3.

Perry Como's *We Get Letters*, released in 1957, was the television and radio star's second Top 10 album. His last appearance on the pop charts came via his cover of Don McLean's "And I Love You So" in 1973.

Bill Cosby's recording career began with a string of comedy albums for Warner Bros., including 1968's *To Russell, My Brother, Whom I Slept With*, which reached No. 7. In 1990, the beloved actor/comedian struck a deal with Verve, resulting in that label's Bill Cosby Jazz Series.

DATE	POS	WKS	ARTIST—RECORD TITLE	LABEL & NO.
			CONNIFF, Ray, And His Orchestra	
			Born on 11/6/16 in Attleboro, Massachusetts. Trombonist/arranger with The Bunny Berigan, Bob Crosby, Harry James, Vaughn Monroe and Artie Shaw Bands. Long string of hit albums beginning in 1957. Conniff's non-instrumental albums feature The Ray Charles Singers.	
3/23/57	11	7	1. 'S Wonderful! [I]	Columbia 925
12/23/57	10	31	● **2. 'S Marvelous** [I]	Columbia 1074
6/23/58	9	43	**3. 'S Awful Nice** [I]	Columbia 1137
9/29/58	9	39	● **4. Concert In Rhythm** [I]	Columbia 1163
7/6/59	29	5	5. Hollywood In Rhythm [I]	Columbia 1310
12/14/59	8	32	**6. Conniff Meets Butterfield** [I]	Columbia 1346
			RAY CONNIFF & BILLY BUTTERFIELD M (jazz trumpeter)	
1/4/60	14	1	● 7. Christmas With Conniff [X]	Columbia 1390
2/15/60	8	32	**8. It's The Talk Of The Town**	Columbia 1334
3/7/60	13	16	9. Concert In Rhythm — Volume II [I]	Columbia 1415
8/15/60	6	13	**10. Young At Heart**	Columbia 1489
10/10/60	4	28	**11. Say It With Music (A Touch Of Latin)** [I]	Columbia 1490
12/31/60	15	1	12. Christmas With Conniff [X-R]	Columbia 1390
2/13/61	4	27	● **13. Memories Are Made Of This** [I]	Columbia 1574
3/27/61	10	3	**14. Broadway In Rhythm** [I]	Columbia 1252
9/18/61	14	21	15. Somebody Loves Me	Columbia 1642
1/6/62	16	3	16. Christmas With Conniff [X-R]	Columbia 1390
			Christmas charts: 39/'65, 35/'67, 11/'68, 7/'69	
2/17/62	5	23	● **17. So Much In Love**	Columbia 1720
5/12/62	6	18	**18. 'S Continental** [I]	Columbia 1776
10/27/62	28	5	19. Rhapsody In Rhythm [I]	Columbia 1878
12/22/62	32	2	▲ 20. We Wish You A Merry Christmas [X]	Columbia 1892
			Christmas charts: 7/'63, 10/'64, 13/'65, 20/'66, 12/'67, 18/'68, 5/'72	
3/9/63	20	8	21. The Happy Beat [I]	Columbia 8749
11/14/64	23	11	22. Invisible Tears	Columbia 9064
7/10/65	34	6	23. Music From Mary Poppins, The Sound Of Music, My Fair Lady, & Other Great Movie Themes	Columbia 9166
7/30/66	3	41	▲ **24. Somewhere My Love**	Columbia 9319
			Somewhere, My Love (9)	
7/8/67	30	6	25. This Is My Song	Columbia 9476
1/6/68	39	2	26. Hawaiian Album	Columbia 9547
3/30/68	25	13	● 27. It Must Be Him	Columbia 9595
7/27/68	22	9	● 28. Honey	Columbia 9661
			CONNORS, Norman	
			Born on 3/1/48 in Philadelphia. Jazz drummer with Archie Shepp, John Coltrane, Pharoah Sanders and others. Own group on Buddah in 1972. Featured vocalists are Michael Henderson, Jean Carn and Phyllis Hyman. Formed disco group Aquarian Dream.	
10/9/76	39	1	● You Are My Starship	Buddah 5655

DATE	POS	WKS	ARTIST—RECORD TITLE	LABEL & NO.
			COOKE, Sam	
			Born on 1/2/31 in Clarksdale, Mississippi; raised in Chicago. Died from a gunshot wound on 12/11/64 in Los Angeles; shot by a female motel manager under mysterious circumstances. Son of a Baptist minister. Sang in choir from age six. Joined gospel group The Highway Q.C.'s. Lead singer of The Soul Stirrers from 1950-56. First recorded secular songs in 1956 as "Dale Cook" on Specialty. String of hits on Keen label led to contract with RCA. Nephew is singer R.B. Greaves. Inducted into the Rock and Roll Hall of Fame in 1986. Revered as the definitive soul singer.	
3/10/58	**16**	2	1. Sam Cooke	Keen 2001
			You Send Me (1)	
11/3/62	**22**	7	2. The Best Of Sam Cooke [G]	RCA 2625
			Chain Gang (2)	
7/4/64	**34**	3	3. Ain't That Good News	RCA 2899
			Another Saturday Night (10)	
2/20/65	**29**	5	4. Sam Cooke At The Copa [L]	RCA 2970
			COOLIDGE, Rita	
			Born on 5/1/44 in Nashville. Had own group, R.C. and The Moonpies, at Florida State University. Moved to Los Angeles in the late '60s. Did backup work for Delaney & Bonnie, Leon Russell, Joe Cocker and Eric Clapton. With Kris Kristofferson from 1971; married to him from 1973-80. Known as "The Delta Lady," for whom Leon Russell wrote song of the same name.	
10/13/73	**26**	6	● 1. Full Moon	A&M 4403
			KRIS KRISTOFFERSON & RITA COOLIDGE	
7/9/77	**6**	21	▲ 2. Anytime ... Anywhere	A&M 4616
			(Your Love Has Lifted Me) Higher And Higher (2)/ *We're All Alone* (7)	
7/15/78	**32**	5	● 3. Love Me Again	A&M 4699
			COOLIO	
			Coolio is Artis Ivey, a rapper from Compton, California. His DJ partner is Bryan "Wino" Dobbs. Coolio is a member of WC and The MAAD Circle.	
8/6/94	**8**	9	▲ **It Takes A Thief**	Tommy Boy 1083
			Fantastic Voyage (3)	
			COOPER, Alice	
			Born Vincent Furnier on 2/4/48 in Detroit. Formed rock group in Phoenix in 1965; in 1966, adopted his stage name from a 16th-century witch. To Los Angeles in 1968, then to Detroit in 1969. Known primarily for his bizarre stage antics. Appeared in the movies *Prince of Darkness* and *Wayne's World*, among others.	
4/3/71	**35**	6	● 1. Love It To Death	Warner 1883
12/18/71	**21**	16	▲ 2. Killer	Warner 2567
7/15/72	**2**(3)	15	▲ **3. School's Out**	Warner 2623
			School's Out (7)	
3/24/73	**1**(1)	23	▲ **4. Billion Dollar Babies**	Warner 2685
12/15/73	**10**	10	● **5. Muscle Of Love**	Warner 2748
9/28/74	**8**	10	▲ **6. Alice Cooper's Greatest Hits** [G]	Warner 2803
3/29/75	**5**	17	▲ **7. Welcome To My Nightmare**	Atlantic 18130
8/21/76	**27**	7	● 8. Alice Cooper Goes To Hell	Warner 2896
9/16/89	**20**	22	▲ 9. Trash	Epic 45137
			Poison (7)	

DATE	POS	WKS	ARTIST—RECORD TITLE	LABEL & NO.
			CORNELIUS BROTHERS & SISTER ROSE	
			Family group from Dania, Florida. Consisted of Edward, Carter and Rose. Billie Jo was added in 1973. All 15 Cornelius children play instruments or sing. Carter died on 11/7/91 (age 43).	
9/30/72	29	6	Cornelius Brothers & Sister Rose *Treat Her Like A Lady* (3)/*Too Late To Turn Back Now* (2)	United Art. 5568
			COSBY, Bill	
			Born on 7/12/38 in Philadelphia. Top comedian who has appeared in nightclubs and movies and on TV. His first seven comedy albums were all million sellers. Played Alexander Scott on TV series "I Spy." Star of highly rated NBC-TV series "The Cosby Show." Winner of five Emmy Awards and nine Grammy Awards.	
2/6/65	32	5	▲ 1. I Started Out As A Child [C]	Warner 1567
10/23/65	19	55	● 2. Why Is There Air? [C]	Warner 1606
6/18/66	7	54	▲ **3. Wonderfulness** **[C]**	Warner 1634
7/9/66	21	34	▲ 4. Bill Cosby Is A Very Funny Fellow, Right! [C]	Warner 1518
5/20/67	2 (1)	28	● **5. Revenge** **[C]**	Warner 1691
9/9/67	18	12	6. Bill Cosby Sings/Silver Throat *Little Ole Man* (4)	Warner 1709
4/13/68	7	23	● **7. To Russell, My Brother, Whom I Slept With** **[C]**	Warner 1734
11/16/68	16	11	● 8. 200 M.P.H. [C]	Warner 1757
3/8/69	37	3	9. It's True! It's True! [C]	Warner 1770
7/5/86	26	4	● 10. Those Of You With Or Without Children, You'll Understand [C]	Geffen 24104
			COSTELLO, Elvis	
			Born Declan McManus in Liverpool, England, on 8/25/54. Changed name to Elvis Costello in 1976; Costello is his mother's maiden name. Formed backing band The Attractions in 1977. Appeared in the 1987 movie *Straight to Hell*. Married Cait O'Riordan, former bassist with The Pogues, on 5/16/86. Leading eclectic rock singer.	
3/4/78	32	5	▲ 1. My Aim Is True	Columbia 35037
5/6/78	30	4	● 2. This Year's Model	Columbia 35331
2/3/79	10	11	● **3. Armed Forces**	Columbia 35709
3/22/80	11	8	4. Get Happy!!	Columbia 36347
10/25/80	28	3	5. Taking Liberties [K] previously released and unreleased tracks	Columbia 36839
2/21/81	28	4	6. Trust	Columbia 37051
8/28/82	30	7	7. Imperial Bedroom	Columbia 38157
8/20/83	24	12	8. Punch The Clock	Columbia 38897
7/21/84	35	3	9. Goodbye Cruel World	Columbia 39429
4/5/86	39	3	10. The Costello Show (Featuring Elvis Costello) — King Of America	Columbia 40173
3/18/89	32	11	● 11. Spike	Warner 25848
3/26/94	34	1	12. Brutal Youth	Warner 45535
			COUGAR, John — see MELLENCAMP	
			COUNTING CROWS	
			San Francisco Bay-area alternative-rock band: Adam Duritz (vocals), Matt Malley, Charlie Gillingham, Steve Bowman and David Bryson.	
1/29/94	4	52	▲⁵ **August and Everything After**	DGC 24528

DATE	POS	WKS	ARTIST—RECORD TITLE	LABEL & NO.
			COUNTRY JOE AND THE FISH	
			Country Joe (Joseph McDonald, born 1/1/42, El Monte, California) and The Fish was San Francisco's leading political rock band of the '60s.	
9/23/67	39	3	1. Electric Music For The Mind And Body	Vanguard 79244
7/27/68	23	7	2. Together	Vanguard 79277
			COVERDALE/PAGE	
			British hard-rock veterans David Coverdale (vocals; Deep Purple; Whitesnake) and Jimmy Page (guitar; Yardbirds; Led Zeppelin; The Firm). Backed by Miami studio musicians Lester Mendez and Jorge Casas, Denny Carmassi (drums; Heart) and Ricky Phillips (bass; Bad English).	
4/3/93	5	9	● **Coverdale/Page**	Geffen 24487
			COWARD, Noel	
			Born on 12/16/1899 in Teddington, England; died on 3/26/73. Enormously popular and enduring actor/playwright/personality in England. Knighted by Queen Elizabeth II in 1970.	
1/28/56	14	2	Noel Coward At Las Vegas [L]	Columbia 5063
			COWBOY JUNKIES	
			Canadian country-punk quartet: vocalist Margo Timmins with brothers Michael and Peter Timmins, and Alan Anton.	
3/11/89	26	9	● The Trinity Session	RCA 8568
			COWSILLS, The	
			Family pop group from Newport, Rhode Island. Consisted of five brothers (Bill, Bob, Paul, Barry and John), with their younger sister (Susan) and mother (Barbara, died 1/31/85 [age 56]). Bob, Paul, John and Susan reunited for touring in 1990. Susan married Peter Holsapple of The dB's on 4/18/93. Group was inspiration for TV's "The Partridge Family."	
12/9/67	31	7	1. The Cowsills *The Rain, The Park & Other Things* (2)	MGM 4498
5/17/69	16	10	2. The Cowsills In Concert [L] *Hair* (2)	MGM 4619
			CRANBERRIES, The	
			Band from Limerick, Ireland: Dolores O'Riordan (vocals), Noel and Mike Hogan, and Fergal Lawler. O'Riordan married Don Burton, assistant tour manager for Duran Duran, on 7/18/94.	
10/16/93	18	22	▲ 1. Everybody Else Is Doing It, So Why Can't We? *Linger* (8)	Island 514156
10/22/94	6	19+	▲² **2. No Need To Argue**	Island 524050
			CRANE, Les	
			Born in 1935 in San Francisco. Hosted TV talk show "ABC's Nightlife" in 1964. Formerly married to actress Tina Louise.	
12/25/71	32	4	Desiderata [T] Crane talks, accompanied by a musical background *Desiderata* (8)	Warner 2570
			CRASH TEST DUMMIES	
			Band from Winnipeg, Canada: lead vocalist Brad Roberts and his younger brother Dan (bass) with Ellen Reid (keyboards) and Benjamin Darvill (harmonica). Drummer Mitch Dorge joined after group's first album.	
3/5/94	9	18	▲ **God Shuffled His Feet** co-produced by Jerry Harrison (Talking Heads) *Mmm Mmm Mmm Mmm* (4)	Arista 16531

DATE	POS	WKS	ARTIST—RECORD TITLE	LABEL & NO.
			CRAWFORD, Johnny	
			Born on 3/26/46 in Los Angeles. One of the original Mouseketeers. Played Chuck Connors' son (Mark McCain) in the TV series "The Rifleman," 1958-63.	
9/22/62	**40**	1	A Young Man's Fancy	Del-Fi 1223
			Cindy's Birthday (8)	
			CRAWFORD, Michael	
			Born Michael Dumble-Smith on 1/19/42 in Salisbury, Wiltshire, England. Theater/movie/TV actor. Tony Award-winning lead in 1987 musical *Phantom of the Opera*.	
10/23/93	**39**	2	● A Touch Of Music In The Night	Atlantic 82531
			CRAY, Robert, Band	
			Born on 8/1/53 in Columbus, Georgia. Blues guitarist/vocalist. Played bass with fictional band, Otis Day & The Knights, in the movie *Animal House*. Band formed in 1974 as backing tour group for Albert Collins. 1988 lineup: Richard Cousins, Peter Boe and David Olson. 1990 lineup: Cousins, Jimmy Pugh, Kevin Hayes and Tim Kaihatsu.	
1/31/87	**13**	26	▲ 1. Strong Persuader	Mercury 830568
9/10/88	**32**	7	● 2. Don't Be Afraid Of The Dark	Mercury 834923
			CRAZY OTTO	
			German honky-tonk pianist Fritz Schulz-Reichel. Born on 7/4/12. Wrote original German version of 1954 hit "The Man With The Banjo."	
4/16/55	**1**(2)	20	**Crazy Otto** **[I]**	Decca 8113
			CREAM	
			British rock supergroup: Eric Clapton (guitar), Ginger Baker (drums) and Jack Bruce (bass). Baker and Bruce had been in Alexis Korner's Blues Inc. and The Graham Bond Organization. Clapton and Bruce were in John Mayall's Bluesbreakers. After Cream disbanded, Clapton and Baker formed Blind Faith. Cream inducted into the Rock and Roll Hall of Fame in 1993.	
12/23/67	**4**	50	▲ **1. Disraeli Gears**	Atco 232
			Sunshine Of Your Love (5)	
7/20/68	**1**(4)	30	● **2. Wheels Of Fire** **[L]**	Atco 700 [2]
			record 1: studio; record 2: Live At The Fillmore	
			White Room (6)	
8/31/68	**39**	1	● 3. Fresh Cream	Atco 206
3/15/69	**2**(2)	20	● 4. Goodbye	Atco 7001
7/26/69	**3**	20	● 5. Best Of Cream **[G]**	Atco 291
5/9/70	**15**	9	6. Live Cream **[L]**	Atco 328
4/15/72	**27**	5	7. Live Cream — Volume II **[L]**	Atco 7005
			CREEDENCE CLEARWATER REVIVAL	
			Rock group formed while members attended high school at El Cerrito, California. Consisted of John Fogerty (vocals, guitar), brother Tom Fogerty (guitar), Stu Cook (keyboards, bass) and Doug Clifford (drums). First recorded as The Blue Velvets for the Orchestra label in 1959. Recorded as The Golliwogs for Fantasy in 1964. Renamed Creedence Clearwater Revival in 1967. Tom left for a solo career in 1971 and group disbanded in October 1972. Tom died on 9/6/90 (age 48) of respiratory failure. Group inducted into the Rock and Roll Hall of Fame in 1993.	
3/1/69	**7**	37	▲² **1. Bayou Country**	Fantasy 8387
			Proud Mary (2)	
9/20/69	**1**(4)	23	▲³ **2. Green River**	Fantasy 8393
			Bad Moon Rising (2)/*Green River* (2)	
12/20/69	**3**	24	▲² **3. Willy and the Poorboys**	Fantasy 8397
			Down On The Corner (3)	

DATE	POS	WKS	ARTIST—RECORD TITLE	LABEL & NO.
7/25/70	1(9)	26	▲⁴ **4. Cosmo's Factory**	Fantasy 8402
			Cosmo is New Orleans record producer Cosmo Matassa	
			Travelin' Band (2)/*Up Around The Bend* (4)/	
			Lookin' Out My Back Door (2)	
12/26/70	5	22	▲ **5. Pendulum**	Fantasy 8410
			Have You Ever Seen The Rain (8)	
5/6/72	12	12	● 6. Mardi Gras	Fantasy 9404
			Sweet Hitch-Hiker (6)	
1/6/73	15	6	▲ 7. Creedence Gold [G]	Fantasy 9418
			### CRICKETS, The — see HOLLY, Buddy	
			### CROCE, Jim	
			Born on 1/10/43 in Philadelphia; killed in a plane crash on 9/20/73 in Natchitoches, Louisiana. Vocalist/guitarist/composer. Recorded with wife, Ingrid, for Capitol in 1968. Lead guitarist on his hits, Maury Muehleisen, was killed in the same crash.	
9/9/72	1(5)	42	● **1. You Don't Mess Around With Jim**	ABC 756
			You Don't Mess Around With Jim (8)/*Time In A Bottle* (1)	
7/21/73	7	26	● **2. Life And Times**	ABC 769
			Bad, Bad Leroy Brown (1)	
12/22/73	2(2)	26	● **3. I Got A Name**	ABC 797
			I Got A Name (10)/*I'll Have To Say I Love You In A Song* (9)	
10/12/74	2(2)	15	▲ **4. Photographs & Memories/His Greatest Hits [G]**	ABC 835
			### CROSBY, Bing	
			Born Harry Lillis Crosby on 5/3/03 in Tacoma, Washington. Died of a heart attack on 10/14/77 on a golf course near Madrid, Spain. One of the most popular entertainers of the 20th century. Crosby and singing partner Al Rinker were hired in 1926 by Paul Whiteman; with Harry Barris they became The Rhythm Boys and gained an increasing following. The trio split from Whiteman in 1930, and Crosby sang briefly with Gus Arnheim's band. His early-1931 smash with Arnheim, "I Surrender, Dear," earned Crosby a CBS radio contract and launched an unsurpassed solo career. Over the next three decades the resonant Crosby baritone and breezy persona sold more than 300 million records and was featured in over 50 movies (won Academy Award for *Going My Way*, 1944). Won 1962 Lifetime Achievement Grammy Award. Ranked as the #1 artist in *Joel Whitburn's Pop Memories 1890-1954* book, Crosby had over 150 hits from 1931-39. Married to actress Dixie Lee from 1930 until her death in 1952; their son, Gary, began recording in 1950. Married to actress Kathryn Grant from 1957 until his death; their daughter, Mary, became an actress. Crosby's youngest brother, Bob Crosby, was popular swing-era bandleader.	
3/31/58	13	2	1. Shillelaghs and Shamrocks	Decca 8207
			CHRISTMAS ALBUMS:	
12/22/56	21	1	2. A Christmas Sing With Bing Around The World [X]	Decca 8419
			from the CBS Radio Program; features various choirs	
12/2/57	1(1)	7	● **3. Merry Christmas** [X-R]	Decca 8128
			first charted in 1945	
12/15/58	2(1)	4	**4. Merry Christmas** [X-R]	Decca 8128
12/28/59	17	2	5. Merry Christmas [X-R]	Decca 8128
12/19/60	9	3	**6. Merry Christmas** [X-R]	Decca 8128
1/6/62	22	3	7. Merry Christmas [X-R]	Decca 8128

DATE	POS	WKS	ARTIST—RECORD TITLE	LABEL & NO.
			CROSBY, David	
			Born David Van Cortland on 8/14/41 in Los Angeles. Vocalist/guitarist with The Byrds from 1964-68 and later Crosby, Stills & Nash. Frequent troubles with the law due to drug charges. Movie cameos in *Backdraft*, *Hook* and *Thunderheart*; appeared on TV's "Roseanne." Underwent a successful liver transplant on 11/19/94.	
3/20/71	**12**	10	● 1. If I Could Only Remember My Name	Atlantic 7203
			with West Coast guests Jerry Garcia, Grace Slick and Joni Mitchell	
			DAVID CROSBY/GRAHAM NASH:	
4/29/72	**4**	14	● 2. Graham Nash/David Crosby	Atlantic 7220
10/25/75	**6**	12	● 3. Wind On The Water	ABC 902
8/21/76	**26**	6	● 4. Whistling Down The Wire	ABC 956
			CROSBY, STILLS & NASH	
			Trio formed in Laurel Canyon, California, in 1968. Consisted of David Crosby (guitar), Stephen Stills (guitar, keyboards, bass) and Graham Nash (guitar). Crosby had been in The Byrds, Stills had been in Buffalo Springfield, and Nash was with The Hollies. Trio won 1969 Best New Artist Grammy Award. Neil Young (guitar), formerly with Buffalo Springfield, joined group in 1969; left in 1974. Reunion in 1988.	
7/5/69	**6**	40	● 1. Crosby, Stills & Nash	Atlantic 8229
4/4/70	**1**(1)	38	▲^{7} 2. Deja Vu *	Atlantic 7200
4/24/71	**1**(1)	26	▲^{4} 3. 4 Way Street * [L]	Atlantic 902 [2]
9/14/74	**1**(1)	12	▲^{6} 4. So Far * [G]	Atlantic 18100
7/16/77	**2**(4)	20	▲^{4} 5. CSN	Atlantic 19104
			Just A Song Before I Go (7)	
7/31/82	**8**	30	▲ 6. Daylight Again	Atlantic 19360
			Wasted On The Way (9)	
12/10/88	**16**	11	▲ 7. American Dream *	Atlantic 81888
			*CROSBY, STILLS, NASH & YOUNG	
			CROSS, Christopher	
			Born Christopher Geppert on 5/3/51 in San Antonio, Texas. Formed own group with Rob Meurer (keyboards), Andy Salmon (bass) and Tommy Taylor (drums) in 1973. Won 1980 Best New Artist Grammy Award.	
3/29/80	**6**	81	▲^{5} 1. Christopher Cross	Warner 3383
			1980 Album of the Year Grammy Award	
			Ride Like The Wind (2)/*Sailing* (1)	
2/26/83	**11**	11	● 2. Another Page	Warner 23757
			Think Of Laura (9)	
			CROW, Sheryl	
			Born on 2/11/63. Native of Kennett, Missouri. After attending the University of Missouri, worked as a grade-school music teacher until moving to Los Angeles in 1986. Worked as backing singer for Michael Jackson, Don Henley, George Harrison and others. Her compositions covered by Eric Clapton and Wynonna Judd.	
9/3/94	**8**	26+	▲^{2} Tuesday Night Music Club	A&M 0126
			album named for the informal weekly jam sessions held at producer Bill Bottrell's L.A. studio with Crow, David & David and others	
			All I Wanna Do (2)	

DATE	POS	WKS	ARTIST—RECORD TITLE	LABEL & NO.
			CROWDED HOUSE	
			New Zealand/Australian trio founded by former Split Enz members Neil Finn (vocals, guitar, piano) and Paul Hester (drums), with Nick Seymour (bass). Neil's brother, Tim Finn (also of Split Enz), joined band in 1991; left in 1993; replaced by Mark Hart. Hester left band in April 1994.	
3/21/87	**12**	24	▲ 1. Crowded House	Capitol 12485
			Don't Dream It's Over (2)/*Something So Strong* (7)	
8/13/88	**40**	2	2. Temple of Low Men	Capitol 48763
			CRUSADERS, The	
			Instrumental jazz-oriented group formed in Houston, as The Swingsters, in the early '50s. To California in the early '60s; name changed to The Jazz Crusaders. Became The Crusaders in 1971. Included Joe Sample (keyboards), Wilton Felder (reeds), Nesbert "Stix" Hooper (drums) and Wayne Henderson (trombone). Henderson left in 1975. Hooper left in 1983. Sample and Felder reunited with new lineup in 1991.	
12/21/74	**31**	3	● 1. Southern Comfort [I]	Blue Thumb 9002 [2]
9/13/75	**26**	5	2. Chain Reaction [I]	Blue Thumb 6022
7/10/76	**38**	3	3. Those Southern Knights [I]	Blue Thumb 6024
8/12/78	**34**	8	● 4. Images [I]	Blue Thumb 6030
6/23/79	**18**	17	● 5. Street Life [I]	MCA 3094
			with guest vocalist Randy Crawford on "Street Life"	
8/2/80	**29**	4	6. Rhapsody And Blues [I]	MCA 5124
			with guest vocalist Bill Withers on "Soul Shadows"	
			CULT, The	
			Nucleus of British rock group: Ian Astbury (vocals), Billy Duffy (guitar) and Jamie Stewart (bass; left in 1989). One-time drummer Matt Sorum joined Guns N' Roses in 1990.	
5/16/87	**38**	4	● 1. Electric	Sire 25555
5/6/89	**10**	20	▲ **2. Sonic Temple**	Sire 25871
10/12/91	**25**	2	3. Ceremony	Sire 26673
			CULTURE CLUB	
			Formed in London in 1981. Consisted of George "Boy George" O'Dowd (born 6/14/61; vocals), Roy Hay (guitar, keyboards), Michael Craig (bass) and Jon Moss (drums). Designer Sue Clowes originated distinctive costuming for the group. Won 1983 Best New Artist Grammy Award. Boy George went solo in 1987.	
2/12/83	**14**	38	▲ 1. Kissing To Be Clever	Epic 38398
			Do You Really Want To Hurt Me (2)/ *Time (Clock Of The Heart)* (2)/*I'll Tumble 4 Ya* (9)	
11/12/83	**2**(6)	38	▲⁴ **2. Colour By Numbers**	Epic 39107
			Church Of The Poison Mind (10)/*Karma Chameleon* (1)/ *Miss Me Blind* (5)	
11/24/84	**26**	9	▲ 3. Waking Up With The House On Fire	Virgin 39881
5/10/86	**32**	6	4. From Luxury To Heartache	Virgin 40345
			CUMMINGS, Burton	
			Born on 12/31/47 in Winnipeg, Canada. Lead singer of The Guess Who.	
12/18/76	**30**	7	Burton Cummings	Portrait 34261
			Stand Tall (10)	

DATE	POS	WKS	ARTIST—RECORD TITLE	LABEL & NO.
			CURE, The	
			British techno-rock group formed in 1977 by Robert Smith (born 4/21/59; vocals, guitar) and Laurence "Lol" Tolhurst (drums). Since 1983, members have included Smith, Tolhurst (until 1990), Porl Thompson, Simon Gallup, Andy Anderson (1984), Boris Williams and Roger O'Donnell (1989). Perry Bamonte joined in 1992. Smith was also touring member of Siouxsie And The Banshees in the early '80s.	
7/4/87	35	8	▲ 1. Kiss Me, Kiss Me, Kiss Me	Elektra 60737 [2]
5/27/89	12	26	▲ 2. Disintegration	Elektra 60855
			Love Song (2)	
11/17/90	14	13	▲ 3. Mixed Up [G]	Elektra 60978
			extended mixes of most of group's hits	
5/9/92	2(1)	14	▲ **4. Wish**	Fiction 61309
			CUTTING CREW	
			British rock group led by singer Nick Van Eede, with Kevin Scott MacMichael (guitar; from Canada), Colin Farley (bass) and Martin Beedle (drums).	
4/18/87	16	10	● Broadcast	Virgin 90573
			(I Just) Died In Your Arms (1)/*I've Been In Love Before* (9)	
			CYPRESS HILL	
			Rap trio based in Los Angeles: Sen "Sen Dog" Reyes (Cuban-born; older brother of Mellow Man Ace), Louis "B-Real" Freeze and Lawrence "Mixmaster Muggs" Muggerud (former member of The 7A3). Band named for Cypress Street in the Southgate section of Los Angeles. Appeared in the movie *The Meteor Man*.	
3/21/92	31	8	▲ 1. Cypress Hill	Ruffhouse 47889
8/7/93	1(2)	18	▲² **2. Black Sunday**	Ruffhouse 53931
			CYRUS, Billy Ray	
			Born on 8/25/61 in Flatwoods, Kentucky. Country singer.	
6/6/92	1(17)	59	▲⁸ **1. Some Gave All**	Mercury 510635
			Achy Breaky Heart (4)	
7/10/93	3	13	▲ **2. It Won't Be The Last**	Mercury 514758

D

DATE	POS	WKS	ARTIST—RECORD TITLE	LABEL & NO.
			DA BRAT	
			Female rapper Shawntae Harris. Began professional career after winning rap contest at a Kris Kross concert in Chicago.	
7/16/94	11	10	▲ Funkdafied	So So Def/Chaos 66164
			Funkdafied (6)	
			DA LENCH MOB	
			Rap trio: Terry "T-Bone" Gray, "J-Dee" DeSean L. Cooper and Shorty. Cooper was jailed in summer of 1993 in connection with fatal shooting. Gray was arrested on 3/10/94 for a 2/18/94 murder. Cooper was replaced in 1994 by Maulkie.	
10/10/92	24	5	● Guerillas In Tha Mist	Street Know. 92206
			produced by Ice Cube	

DATE	POS	WKS	ARTIST—RECORD TITLE	LABEL & NO.
			DALTREY, Roger	
			Born on 3/1/44 in London. Formed band The Detours, which later became The Who. Daltrey was The Who's lead singer and starred in the movies *Tommy*, *Lisztomania*, *The Legacy* and *McVicar*.	
8/30/75	**28**	5	1. Ride A Rock Horse	MCA 2147
8/30/80	**22**	6	2. McVicar [S]	Polydor 6284
			soundtrack features all members of The Who; movie based on the autobiography of British convict John McVicar (Daltry's role)	
			DAMN YANKEES	
			Superstar rock group: Ted Nugent (guitar; Amboy Dukes), Jack Blades (bass, vocals; Night Ranger), Tommy Shaw (guitar, vocals; Styx) and Michael Cartellone (drums).	
5/12/90	**13**	25	▲² 1. Damn Yankees	Warner 26159
			High Enough (3)	
8/29/92	**22**	3	● 2. Don't Tread	Warner 45025
			DAMONE, Vic	
			Born Vito Farinola on 6/12/28 in Brooklyn. Damone is among the most popular of postwar ballad singers. Appeared in the movies *Kismet*, *Meet Me In Las Vegas* and *Hell To Eternity*. Hosted own TV series (1956-57). Married actress Diahann Carroll on 1/3/87.	
10/13/56	**14**	8	That Towering Feeling!	Columbia 900
			DANA, Bill — see JIMENEZ, Jose	
			DANA, Vic	
			Born on 8/26/42 in Buffalo, New York. Moved to California as teen. Adult Contemporary artist.	
5/1/65	**13**	11	Red Roses For A Blue Lady	Dolton 8034
			Red Roses For A Blue Lady (10)	
			DANGERFIELD, Rodney	
			Born Jack Roy on 11/22/21 in Babylon, New York. Comedian and star of the movies *Caddyshack*, *Easy Money*, *Back To School* and others. Owner of Dangerfields, a club in New York City.	
12/24/83	**36**	3	Rappin' Rodney [C]	RCA 4869
			DANIELS, Charlie, Band	
			Daniels (born 10/28/36, Wilmington, North Carolina; vocals, guitar, fiddle) formed band in Nashville in 1971. Included Tom Crain (guitar), Joe "Taz" DiGregorio (keyboards), Charles Hayward (bass) and James W. Marshall (drums). Daniels led The Jaguars from 1958-67. Went solo in 1968; worked as a session musician in Nashville. Played on Bob Dylan's *Nashville Skyline* hit album. In the movie *Urban Cowboy*.	
3/15/75	**38**	2	▲ 1. Fire On The Mountain	Kama Sutra 2603
6/19/76	**35**	3	● 2. Saddle Tramp	Epic 34150
6/30/79	**5**	17	▲² **3. Million Mile Reflections**	Epic 35751
			The Devil Went Down To Georgia (3)	
8/16/80	**11**	9	▲ 4. Full Moon	Epic 36571
4/24/82	**26**	6	● 5. Windows	Epic 37694
			DANZIG	
			Heavy-metal quartet led by singer/songwriter Glenn Danzig (born 6/23/59). Includes John Christ (guitar), Eerie Von (bass) and Chuck Biscuits (drums). Biscuits (formerly with Black Flag; The Circle Jerks) replaced by Joey Castillo in 1994.	
8/1/92	**24**	1	1. Danzig III — How The Gods Kill	Def Amer. 26914
10/22/94	**29**	1	2. Danzig 4	American 45647

DATE	POS	WKS	ARTIST—RECORD TITLE	LABEL & NO.
			D'ARBY, Terence Trent	
			Born on 3/15/62 in New York City. England-based, soul-pop singer. Last name originally spelled Darby. Was member of U.S. Army boxing team.	
3/5/88	4	32	▲ **Introducing The Hardline According To Terence Trent D'Arby** *Wishing Well* (1)/*Sign Your Name* (4)	Columbia 40964
			DARIN, Bobby	
			Born Walden Robert Cassotto on 5/14/36 in the Bronx; died of heart failure on 12/20/73 in Los Angeles. Vocalist/pianist/guitarist/drummer. First recorded in 1956 with The Jaybirds (Decca). First appeared on TV in March 1956 on "The Tommy Dorsey Show." Won 1959 Best New Artist Grammy Award. Married to actress Sandra Dee from 1960-67. Nominated for an Oscar for his performance in the movie *Captain Newman, MD* (1963). Formed own record company, Direction. Inducted into the Rock and Roll Hall of Fame in 1990.	
10/5/59	7	39	**1. That's All** *Mack The Knife* (1)/*Beyond The Sea* (6)	Atco 104
3/7/60	6	38	**2. This Is Darin**	Atco 115
10/17/60	9	12	**3. Darin At The Copa** [L]	Atco 122
6/26/61	18	20	4. The Bobby Darin Story [G] *Splish Splash* (3)/*Queen Of The Hop* (9)/*Dream Lover* (2)	Atco 131
			DAS EFX	
			Rap duo of Andre "Dray" Weston (born 9/9/70) and Willie "Skoob" Hines (born 11/27/70) formed at Virginia State. DAS is an acronym for Dray And Skoob (which is "books" spelled backward).	
5/23/92	16	10	▲ 1. Dead Serious	EastWest 91827
12/4/93	20	1	2. Straight Up Sewaside	EastWest 92265
			DAVID & DAVID	
			Los Angeles duo: David Baerwald and David Ricketts.	
12/6/86	39	2	Boomtown	A&M 5134
			DAVIDSON, John	
			Born on 12/13/41 in Pittsburgh. Singer/actor. Hosted own TV talk show, 1980-82. Co-hosted TV's "That's Incredible" and hosted the new "Hollywood Squares."	
11/19/66	19	10	The Time Of My Life!	Columbia 9380
			DAVIS, Mac	
			Born on 1/21/42 in Lubbock, Texas. Vocalist/guitarist/composer. Worked as a regional rep for Vee-Jay and Liberty Records. Wrote "In the Ghetto" and "Don't Cry Daddy," hits for Elvis Presley. Host of own musical variety TV series from 1974-76. Appearances in several movies, including *North Dallas Forty* in 1979.	
9/30/72	11	13	▲ 1. Baby Don't Get Hooked On Me *Baby Don't Get Hooked On Me* (1)	Columbia 31770
8/10/74	13	15	● 2. Stop And Smell The Roses *Stop And Smell The Roses* (9)	Columbia 32582
3/8/75	21	5	● 3. All The Love In The World	Columbia 32927

DATE	POS	WKS	ARTIST—RECORD TITLE	LABEL & NO.
			DAVIS, Miles	
			Born on 5/26/26 in Alton, Illinois. Died on 9/28/91 of a stroke and pneumonia. Innovative jazz trumpeter who influenced jazz-fusion movement. Began career in 1944 with Billy Eckstine's orchestra. With Six Brown Cats group in 1944. With Charlie Parker and Coleman Hawkins. Recorded with Parker on Parker on Savoy and Dial from 1945-46. Formed own quintet in 1955. Band members included Herbie Hancock and Wayne Shorter. Received 28 Grammy nominations; won 1990 Lifetime Achievement Grammy Award. Married to actress Cicely Tyson from 1981-88.	
6/27/70	35	4	● Bitches Brew [I]	Columbia 26 [2]
			DAVIS, Sammy Jr.	
			Born on 12/8/25 in New York City. Died of throat cancer on 5/16/90. Vocalist/dancer/actor. With father and uncle in dance act, The Will Mastin Trio, from the early '40s. First recorded for Capitol in 1950. Lost his left eye and had his nose smashed in an auto accident near San Bernardino, California, on 11/19/54; returned to performing in January 1955. Frequent appearances on TV and Broadway and in movies. One of the first black entertainers to gain widespread acclaim from white audiences.	
5/14/55	**1**(6)	27	**1. Starring Sammy Davis, Jr.**	Decca 8118
10/15/55	**5**	9	**2. Just For Lovers**	Decca 8170
11/17/62	**14**	9	3. What Kind Of Fool Am I and Other Show-Stoppers	Reprise 6051
5/23/64	**26**	6	4. The Shelter Of Your Arms	Reprise 6114
3/15/69	**24**	8	5. I've Gotta Be Me	Reprise 6324
6/17/72	**11**	8	6. Sammy Davis Jr. Now	MGM 4832
			The Candy Man (1)	
			DAWN	
			Pop vocal trio formed in New York City: Tony Orlando (born 4/3/44, New York City), Telma Hopkins (born 10/28/48, Louisville) and Joyce Vincent (born 12/14/46, Detroit). Orlando had recorded solo from 1961-63; Hopkins and Vincent had been backup singers. Orlando was manager for April-Blackwood Music at the time of trio's first hit. Own TV show from 1974-76. All of its hits produced by Hank Medress (The Tokens) and Dave Appell (The Applejacks). Hopkins appeared on TV's "Bosom Buddies," "Gimme A Break" and "Family Matters."	
1/30/71	**35**	3	1. Candida	Bell 6052
			Candida (3)/*Knock Three Times* (1)	
			DAWN featuring TONY ORLANDO:	
5/26/73	**30**	5	● 2. Tuneweaving	Bell 1112
			Tie A Yellow Ribbon Round The Ole Oak Tree (1)	
			TONY ORLANDO & DAWN:	
1/11/75	**16**	8	3. Prime Time	Bell 1317
5/31/75	**20**	4	4. He Don't Love You (Like I Love You)	Elektra 1034
			He Don't Love You (Like I Love You) (1)	
8/2/75	**16**	6	● 5. Greatest Hits [G]	Arista 4045
			DAY, Doris	
			Born Doris Kappelhoff on 4/3/22 in Cincinnati. Day sang briefly with Bob Crosby in 1940 and shortly thereafter became major star with The Les Brown Band (she had 12 charted hits with Brown). Her great solo recording success was soon transcended by Hollywood as Day became the #1 box-office star of the late '50s and early '60s. Star of own popular TV series from 1968-73. Her son, Terry Melcher, was a member of The Rip Chords and Bruce and Terry, and a prolific producer (The Beach Boys).	
2/5/55	**15**	2	1. Young At Heart [S]	Columbia 6339
			10" album; 6 cuts by Day, 2 by Frank Sinatra: "One For My Baby (And One More For The Road)" and "Someone To Watch Over Me"	

DATE	POS	WKS	ARTIST—RECORD TITLE	LABEL & NO.
6/25/55	1(17)	28	**2. Love Me Or Leave Me** **[S]** *Day portrayed singer Ruth Etting in the movie*	Columbia 710
2/9/57	11	6	3. Day By Day	Columbia 942
5/30/60	26	7	4. Listen To Day	Columbia DD1
			DAY, Morris Born in Springfield, Illinois, and raised in Minneapolis (in local band Grand Central with schoolmate Prince). Leader of Minneapolis funk group The Time (formerly Prince's backing band). Acted in the movies *Purple Rain*, *The Adventures of Ford Fairlane* and *Graffiti Bridge*.	
11/16/85	37	3	Color Of Success	Warner 25320
			DAYNE, Taylor Born Leslie Wonderman on 7/3/62 in Long Island, New York. Female pop singer.	
2/20/88	21	34	▲² 1. Tell It To My Heart *Tell It To My Heart* (7)/*Prove Your Love* (7)/ *I'll Always Love You* (3)/*Don't Rush Me* (2)	Arista 8529
1/6/90	25	36	▲ 2. Can't Fight Fate *With Every Beat Of My Heart* (5)/*Love Will Lead You Back* (1)/ *I'll Be Your Shelter* (4)	Arista 8581
			DAZZ BAND Cleveland ultrafunk band; formerly Kinsman Dazz. "Dazz" means "danceable jazz." Formed by Bobby Harris (vocalist, saxophone) by merging Bell Telefunk and the house band at Cleveland's Kinsman Grill. Included Pierre DeMudd, Sennie "Skip" Martin III, Eric Fearman, Kevin Frederick, Kenny Pettus, Michael Wiley and Isaac Wiley.	
5/29/82	14	11	● Keep It Live *Let It Whip* (5)	Motown 6004
			DEAD OR ALIVE Dance outfit formed in Liverpool, England, by lead singer Pete Burns (born 8/5/59). Wayne Hussey (later a member of Sisters Of Mercy and Mission) was an early member.	
8/17/85	31	6	● Youthquake	Epic 40119
			DEAN, Jimmy Born on 8/10/28 in Plainview, Texas. Country vocalist/pianist/guitarist/composer. With Tennessee Haymakers in Washington, D.C., in 1948. Own Texas Wildcats in 1952. Recorded for Four Star in 1952. Own CBS-TV series, 1957-58; ABC-TV series, 1963-66. Business interests include a restaurant chain and a line of pork sausage. Married country singer Donna Meade on 10/27/91.	
12/11/61	23	11	Big Bad John And Other Fabulous Songs And Tales *Big Bad John* (1)	Columbia 8535
			DEAUVILLE, Ronnie Lead singer with The Ray Anthony Band, 1950-51. Made miraculous recovery from tuberculosis.	
12/9/57	13	2	Smoke Dreams	Era 20002
			DeBARGE Family group from Grand Rapids, Michigan. Consisted of lead vocalist El (keyboards), Mark (trumpet, saxophone), James (keyboards), Randy (bass) and Bunny DeBarge (vocals). Brothers Bobby and Tommy were in Switch. James was briefly married to Janet Jackson in 1984.	
5/28/83	24	7	● 1. All This Love	Gordy 6012
2/4/84	36	5	● 2. In A Special Way	Gordy 6061

DATE	POS	WKS	ARTIST—RECORD TITLE	LABEL & NO.
4/20/85	**19**	24	• 3. Rhythm Of The Night *Rhythm Of The Night* (3)/*Who's Holding Donna Now* (6)	Gordy 6123
6/21/86	**24**	11	### DeBARGE, El Eldra DeBarge (born 6/4/61), lead singer of family group DeBarge. • El DeBarge *Who's Johnny* (3)	Gordy 6181
5/30/87	**25**	8	### DeBURGH, Chris Born Christopher John Davidson on 10/15/48 in Argentina of Irish parentage. British pop-rock singer. • Into The Light *The Lady In Red* (3)	A&M 5121
12/25/61 3/10/62	**2**(6) **18**	36 13	### DEE, Joey, & the Starliters Born Joseph DiNicola on 6/11/40 in Passaic, New Jersey. In September 1960, Joey & The Starlighters became the house band at The Peppermint Lounge, New York City. After 1964, group included three members who later formed The Young Rascals, plus guitarist Jimi Hendrix. In the movies *Hey, Let's Twist* and *Two Tickets to Paris.* 1. Doin' The Twist At The Peppermint Lounge [L] *Peppermint Twist-Part 1* (1)/*Shout* (6) 2. Hey, Let's Twist! [S] with Jo-Ann Campbell, Teddy Randazzo and Kay Armen; filmed at New York's Peppermint Lounge	Roulette 25166 Roulette 25168
12/7/74	**28**	4	### DEE, Kiki, Band Born Pauline Matthews on 3/6/47 in Yorkshire, England. I've Got The Music In Me	Rocket 458
7/9/55	**11**	6	### DEE, Lenny Organist, born in the '20s in Illinois and raised in Florida. Discovered by Red Foley. Dee-lightful! [I]	Decca 8114
11/3/90	**20**	15	### DEEE-LITE New York-based dance trio: Super DJ Dmitry Brill (from Kiev, Soviet Union), Jungle DJ Towa "Towa" Tei (from Tokyo, Japan) and vocalist Lady Miss Kier (Kier Kirby from Youngstown, Ohio). Group's name inspired by the tune "It's De-lovely" from the 1936 Cole Porter musical *Red, Hot & Blue.* Brill and Kier are married. Tei left by 1994; replaced by Ani. • World Clique *Groove Is In The Heart* (4)	Elektra 60957
10/12/68	**24**	10	### DEEP PURPLE British pioneer heavy-metal band: Ritchie Blackmore (guitar), Rod Evans (vocals), Jon Lord (keyboards), Ian Paice (drums) and Nicky Simper (bass). Evans and Simper left in 1969; replaced by Ian Gillan (vocals) and Roger Glover (bass). Evans formed Captain Beyond. Gillan and Glover left in late 1973; replaced by David Coverdale (vocals) and Glenn Hughes (bass). Blackmore left in early 1975 to form Rainbow (which Glover later joined); replaced by American Tommy Bolin (died 12/4/76; ex-James Gang guitarist). Band split in July 1976. Coverdale, Lord and Paice formed Whitesnake. Blackmore, Lord, Paice, Gillan and Glover reunited in 1984. Hughes joined Black Sabbath. Gillan (who joined Black Sabbath for 1983 *Born Again* album) left in 1989 to form Garth Rockett & The Moonshiners. 1990 lineup featured former Rainbow vocalist Joe Lynn Turner, with Blackmore, Lord, Paice and Glover. Gillan replaced Turner by mid-1993. 1. Shades Of Deep Purple *Hush* (4)	Tetragramm. 102

DATE	POS	WKS	ARTIST—RECORD TITLE	LABEL & NO.
9/4/71	32	3	2. Fireball	Warner 2564
5/6/72	7	30	▲² **3. Machine Head**	Warner 2607
			Smoke On The Water (4)	
2/10/73	15	14	● 4. Who Do We Think We Are!	Warner 2678
5/12/73	6	23	▲ **5. Made In Japan** [L]	Warner 2701 [2]
3/23/74	9	12	● **6. Burn**	Warner 2766
12/14/74	20	6	● 7. Stormbringer	Warner 2832
12/8/84	17	18	▲ **8. Perfect Strangers**	Mercury 824003
2/14/87	34	4	9. The House Of Blue Light	Mercury 831318
			DEF LEPPARD	
			Hard-rock quintet formed in Sheffield, England, in 1977: Joe Elliott (lead singer), Pete Willis and Steve Clark (lead guitars), Rick Savage (bass) and Rick Allen (drums; lost his left arm in auto accident on New Year's Eve in 1984). Phil Collen replaced Willis in late 1982. Clark died on 1/8/91 (age 30) of alcohol-related respiratory failure. Guitarist Vivian Campbell (Whitesnake; Dio; Riverdogs; Shadow King) joined in April 1992.	
10/3/81	38	3	▲² 1. High 'n' Dry	Mercury 4021
2/12/83	2(2)	58	▲⁹ **2. Pyromania**	Mercury 810308
8/22/87	1(6)	96	▲¹¹ **3. Hysteria**	Mercury 830675
			Hysteria (10)/*Pour Some Sugar On Me* (2)/*Love Bites* (1)/ *Armageddon It* (3)	
4/18/92	1(5)	31	▲³ **4. Adrenalize**	Mercury 512185
10/23/93	9	6	▲ **5. Retro Active**	Mercury 518305
			DELANEY & BONNIE	
			Delaney Bramlett (born 7/1/39, Pontotoc County, Mississippi) and Bonnie Lynn Bramlett (born 11/8/44, Acton, Illinois). Married in 1967. Friends (backing artists) included, at various times, Leon Russell, Rita Coolidge, Dave Mason, Eric Clapton, Duane Allman (The Allman Brothers Band) and many others. Friends Bobby Whitlock, Carl Radle and Jim Gordon later became Eric Clapton's Dominos. Delaney & Bonnie dissolved their marriage and group in 1972. Their daughter Bekka was lead singer of Mick Fleetwood's Zoo; joined Fleetwood Mac in 1993.	
4/25/70	29	6	Delaney & Bonnie & Friends On Tour with Eric Clapton [L]	Atco 326
			DE LA SOUL	
			Psychedelic-rap trio from Amityville, Long Island, New York: Posdnuos (Kelvin Mercer), Trugoy the Dove (David Jolicoeur) and P.A. Pasemaster Mase (Vincent Mason, Jr.).	
5/20/89	24	10	● 1. 3 Feet High And Rising	Tommy Boy 1019
6/1/91	26	4	● 2. De La Soul Is Dead	Tommy Boy 1029
10/9/93	40	1	3. Buhloone Mindstate	Tommy Boy 1063
			DELLS, The	
			R&B vocal group formed at Thornton Township High School in Harvey, Illinois: Johnny Funches (lead), Marvin Junior (baritone lead), Verne Allison (tenor), Mickey McGill (baritone) and Chuck Barksdale (bass). First recorded as the El-Rays for Chess in 1953. Signed with Vee-Jay in 1955. Group remained intact into the '80s, with the exception of Funches, who was replaced by Johnny Carter (ex-Flamingos) in 1960.	
8/10/68	29	5	There Is	Cadet 804
			Stay In My Corner (10)	

DATE	POS	WKS	ARTIST—RECORD TITLE		LABEL & NO.
			DENNY, Martin		
			Born on 4/10/11 in New York City. Composer/arranger/pianist. Originated "The Exotic Sounds of Martin Denny" in Hawaii, featuring Julius Wechter (Baja Marimba Band) on vibes and marimba.		
5/4/59	**1**(5)	46	**1. Exotica**	[I]	Liberty 7034
			The Exciting Sounds Of MARTIN DENNY *Quiet Village* (4)		
9/14/59	**8**	31	**2. Quiet Village**	[I]	Liberty 7122
			The Exotic Sounds of MARTIN DENNY		
10/6/62	**6**	21	**3. A Taste Of Honey**	[I]	Liberty 7237
			DENVER, John		
			Born John Henry Deutschendorf on 12/31/43 in Roswell, New Mexico. To Los Angeles in 1964. With The Chad Mitchell Trio from 1965-68. Wrote "Leaving On A Jet Plane." Starred in the 1977 movie *Oh, God.* Won 1975 Emmy Award for TV special "An Evening with John Denver."		
6/19/71	**15**	31	● 1. Poems, Prayers & Promises		RCA 4499
			Take Me Home, Country Roads (2)		
11/11/72	**4**	27	● **2. Rocky Mountain High**		RCA 4731
			Rocky Mountain High (9)		
6/30/73	**16**	13	● 3. Farewell Andromeda		RCA 0101
12/22/73	**1**(3)	45	● **4. John Denver's Greatest Hits**	[G]	RCA 0374
			Sunshine On My Shoulders (1)		
7/6/74	**1**(1)	37	● **5. Back Home Again**		RCA 0548
			Annie's Song (1)/*Back Home Again* (5)		
3/8/75	**2**(2)	19	● **6. An Evening With John Denver**	[L]	RCA 0764 [2]
			Thank God I'm A Country Boy (1)		
10/4/75	**1**(2)	22	● **7. Windsong**		RCA 1183
			I'm Sorry (1)/*Calypso* (2)		
12/6/75	**14**	6	● 8. Rocky Mountain Christmas	[X]	RCA 1201
9/4/76	**7**	14	▲ 9. Spirit		RCA 1694
3/5/77	**6**	7	▲ **10. John Denver's Greatest Hits, Volume 2**	[G]	RCA 2195
2/10/79	**25**	6	● 11. John Denver		RCA 3075
12/22/79	**26**	4	▲ 12. A Christmas Together	[X]	RCA 3451
			JOHN DENVER & THE MUPPETS Christmas charts: 10/'83		
4/19/80	**39**	2	13. Autograph		RCA 3449
9/5/81	**32**	4	● 14. Some Days Are Diamonds		RCA 4055
5/22/82	**39**	2	● 15. Seasons Of The Heart		RCA 4256
			DEODATO		
			Born Eumir De Almeida Deodato on 6/21/42 in Rio de Janeiro, Brazil. Keyboardist/composer/producer/ arranger. Kool & The Gang's producer from 1979-82.		
2/24/73	**3**	13	**1. Prelude**	[I]	CTI 6021
			Also Sprach Zarathustra (2001) (2)		
9/8/73	**19**	10	2. Deodato 2	[I]	CTI 6029
			DEPECHE MODE		
			All-synthesized rock band formed in Basildon, England, consisting of David Gahan (vocals), Martin Gore, Vince Clarke and Andy Fletcher. Clarke left in 1982 (formed Yaz, then Erasure); replaced by Alan Wilder. Group name is French for fast fashion.		
11/14/87	**35**	3	▲ 1. Music For The Masses		Sire 25614

DATE	POS	WKS	ARTIST—RECORD TITLE	LABEL & NO.
4/14/90	7	31	▲² **2. Violator**	Sire 26081
			Enjoy The Silence (8)	
4/10/93	**1**(1)	8	▲ **3. Songs Of Faith And Devotion**	Sire 45243
			DEREK AND THE DOMINOS — see CLAPTON, Eric	
			DERRINGER, Rick	
			Born Richard Zehringer on 8/5/47 in Celina, Ohio. Lead singer/guitarist of The McCoys. Performed on and produced sessions for both Edgar and Johnny Winter's bands; also a producer for "Weird Al" Yankovic.	
2/9/74	**25**	8	All American Boy	Blue Sky 32481
			DESMOND, Johnny — see MILLER, Glenn	
			DEVO	
			Robotic rock group formed in Akron, Ohio, consisting of brothers Mark and Bob Mothersbaugh, brothers Jerry and Bob Casale, and Alan Myers. David Kendrick replaced Myers by 1988. Mark and Jerry met while both were art students at Kent State. Devo is short for their theory of "de-evolution" (the regression of mankind).	
10/11/80	**22**	16	▲ 1. Freedom Of Choice	Warner 3435
10/17/81	**23**	6	2. New Traditionalists	Warner 3595
			DEXYS MIDNIGHT RUNNERS	
			Kevin Rowland (born 8/17/53, Wolverhampton, England), leader of eight-piece Birmingham, England, band.	
3/19/83	**14**	12	Too-Rye-Ay	Mercury 4069
			Kevin Rowland & DEXYS MIDNIGHT RUNNERS	
			Come On Eileen (1)	
			DeYOUNG, Dennis	
			Born on 2/18/47 in Chicago. Lead singer/keyboardist of Styx.	
11/10/84	**29**	4	Desert Moon	A&M 5006
			Desert Moon (10)	
			DIAMOND, Neil	
			Born on 1/24/41 in Brooklyn. Vocalist/guitarist/prolific composer. Worked as songplugger/staff writer in New York City; also wrote under pseudonym Mark Lewis. His real name is Neil Diamond; however, he considered changing his name to Noah Kaminsky early in his career. First recorded for Duel in 1961. Wrote for "The Monkees" TV show. Wrote score for the movie *Jonathan Livingston Seagull*. Starred in and composed the music for *The Jazz Singer* in 1980.	
1/17/70	**30**	6	● 1. Touching You Touching Me	Uni 73071
			Holly Holy (6)	
8/29/70	**10**	19	▲² **2. Neil Diamond/Gold** [L]	Uni 73084
			recorded at the Troubadour in Hollywood	
11/21/70	**13**	14	▲ 3. Tap Root Manuscript	Uni 73092
			Cracklin' Rosie (1)	
11/20/71	**11**	13	● 4. Stones	Uni 93106
			I Am ... I Said (4)	
7/22/72	**5**	24	▲ **5. Moods**	Uni 93136
			Song Sung Blue (1)	
12/23/72	**5**	19	▲² **6. Hot August Night** [L]	MCA 8000 [2]
			recorded 8/24/72 at the Greek Theatre, Los Angeles	
3/10/73	**36**	4	7. Double Gold [K]	Bang 227 [2]
9/29/73	**35**	4	● 8. Rainbow [K]	MCA 2103
			reissue of cuts from Uni albums	

DATE	POS	WKS	ARTIST—RECORD TITLE	LABEL & NO.
11/17/73	2 (1)	16	▲² **9. Jonathan Livingston Seagull** [S]	Columbia 32550
6/29/74	29	7	▲⁴ 10. Neil Diamond / His 12 Greatest Hits [G]	MCA 2106
11/9/74	3	19	▲ **11. Serenade**	Columbia 32919
			Longfellow Serenade (5)	
7/4/76	4	16	▲ **12. Beautiful Noise**	Columbia 33965
			produced by Robbie Robertson	
3/5/77	8	9	▲² **13. Love At The Greek** [L]	Columbia 34404 [2]
			recorded August 1976 at the Greek Theatre	
12/10/77	6	14	▲² **14. I'm Glad You're Here With Me Tonight**	Columbia 34990
12/16/78	4	12	▲² **15. You Don't Bring Me Flowers**	Columbia 35625
			You Don't Bring Me Flowers (1-with Barbra Streisand)	
1/19/80	10	10	▲ **16. September Morn**	Columbia 36121
11/29/80	3	32	▲⁵ **17. The Jazz Singer** [S]	Capitol 12120
			movie is remake of Al Jolson's 1927 classic	
			Love On The Rocks (2)/*Hello Again* (6)/*America* (8)	
12/5/81	17	11	▲ **18. On The Way To The Sky**	Columbia 37628
10/23/82	9	19	▲ **19. Heartlight**	Columbia 38359
			Heartlight (5)	
9/1/84	35	5	● 20. Primitive	Columbia 39199
5/31/86	20	11	● 21. Headed For The Future	Columbia 40368
12/12/92	8	5	▲ **22. The Christmas Album** [X]	Columbia 52914
			Christmas charts: 3/'92, 7/'93, 17/'94	
10/16/93	28	1	● 23. Up On The Roof — Songs From The Brill Building	Columbia 57529
			Diamond sings the hits of his contemporaries, the prolific songwriters of the late '50s and early '60s of New York's Tin Pan Alley	

DIGABLE PLANETS

Rap outfit from Washington, D.C.: Ishmael "Butterfly" Butler, Mary Ann "Ladybug" Vierra and Craig "Doodle Bug" Irving.

DATE	POS	WKS	ARTIST—RECORD TITLE	LABEL & NO.
2/27/93	15	10	● 1. Reachin' (A New Refutation Of Time And Space)	Pendulum 61414
11/5/94	32	1	2. Blowout Comb	Pendulum / EMI 30654

DIGITAL UNDERGROUND

Rap-funk crew based in Northern California. Formed by Gregory E. "Shock-G" Jacobs (keyboards, vocals) and Chopmaster J (samples, percussion). Features vocalists Eddie "Humpty-Hump" Humphrey and Ron "Money-B" Brooks. Varying members include Tupac "2 Pac" Shakur, Earl "Schmoovy-Schmoov" Cook, "Clee" Askew, "Saafir" The Saucee Nomad and Michael "Dirty-Red" Boston. Appeared in the movie *Nothing But Trouble*. Chopmaster J later formed Force One Network. Money-B later formed Raw Fusion.

DATE	POS	WKS	ARTIST—RECORD TITLE	LABEL & NO.
4/21/90	24	18	▲ 1. Sex Packets	Tommy Boy 1026
2/16/91	29	8	● 2. This Is An E.P. Release [M]	Tommy Boy 964
			2 of the 6 tracks are from the movie *Nothing But Trouble* starring Dan Aykroyd and Chevy Chase	

DINO

Born Dino Esposito on 7/20/63 in Encino, California; raised in Hawaii and Connecticut. Former DJ/music director at KCEP in Las Vegas.

DATE	POS	WKS	ARTIST—RECORD TITLE	LABEL & NO.
8/26/89	34	6	● 24/7	4th & B'way 4011
			I Like It (7)	

DATE	POS	WKS	ARTIST—RECORD TITLE	LABEL & NO.
			DIO	
			Ronnie James Dio, born Ronald Padavona on 7/10/49 in Portsmouth, New Hampshire; raised in Cortland, New York. Former lead singer of hard-rock groups Black Sabbath and Rainbow.	
7/28/84	23	10	▲ 1. The Last In Line	Warner 25100
9/14/85	29	10	● 2. Sacred Heart	Warner 25292
			DION	
			Born Dion DiMucci on 7/18/39 in the Bronx. Formed Dion & The Timberlanes in 1957, then Dion & The Belmonts in 1958. The Belmonts included: Angelo D'Aleo, Freddie Milano and Carlo Mastrangelo. Group named for Belmont Avenue in the Bronx. Dion went solo in 1960. Brief reunion with The Belmonts in 1967 and 1972; periodically since then. He currently records contemporary Christian songs. Inducted into the Rock and Roll Hall of Fame in 1989.	
12/4/61	11	21	1. Runaround Sue	Laurie 2009
			Runaround Sue (1)/*The Wanderer* (2)	
7/28/62	12	12	2. Lovers Who Wander	Laurie 2012
			Lovers Who Wander (3)/*Little Diane* (8)	
2/23/63	29	3	3. Dion Sings His Greatest Hits [G]	Laurie 2013
			2 cuts by Dion; 10 cuts by Dion & The Belmonts	
			A Teenager In Love (5)/*Where Or When* (3)	
4/6/63	20	6	4. Ruby Baby	Columbia 8810
			Ruby Baby (2)	
			DION, Celine	
			Born on 3/30/68 in Charlemagne, Quebec. Popular singer in France and Canada since her teens. Youngest of 14 children. Married her longtime manager, Rene Angelil, late 1994.	
6/13/92	34	4	▲ 1. Celine Dion	Epic 52473
			Beauty And The Beast (9-with Peabo Bryson)/ *If You Asked Me To* (4)	
1/22/94	4	29	▲³ **2. The Colour Of My Love**	550 Music 57555
			The Power Of Love (1)	
			DIRE STRAITS	
			Rock group formed in London by songwriter/producer Mark Knopfler (lead vocals, lead guitar) and his brother David (guitar), with John Illsley (bass) and Pick Withers (drums). David left in mid-1980; replaced by Hal Lindes (left in 1985). Added keyboardist Alan Clark in 1982. Terry Williams replaced Withers in 1983. Guitarist Guy Fletcher added in 1984. Mark and Fletcher were also members of The Notting Hillbillies in 1990. Dire Straits' 1991 lineup: Knopfler, Illsley, Fletcher and Clark with Chris White (sax), Paul Franklin (pedal steel), Danny Cummings (percussion), Phil Palmer (guitar) and Chris Whitten (drums).	
2/3/79	2 (1)	21	▲² **1. Dire Straits**	Warner 3266
			Sultans Of Swing (4)	
7/7/79	11	9	● 2. Communique	Warner 3330
11/22/80	19	17	● 3. Making Movies	Warner 3480
10/16/82	19	8	● 4. Love Over Gold	Warner 23728
6/15/85	1 (9)	55	▲⁷ **5. Brothers In Arms**	Warner 25264
			Money For Nothing (1)/*Walk Of Life* (7)	
9/28/91	12	8	▲ 6. On Every Street	Warner 26680

DATE	POS	WKS	ARTIST—RECORD TITLE	LABEL & NO.
			DIRKSEN, Senator Everett McKinley	
			Born on 1/4/1896 in Pekin, Illinois; died on 9/7/69. U.S. senator from Illinois, 1950-69.	
1/28/67	**16**	8	Gallant Men [T]	Capitol 2643
			features patriotic stories and recitations to a musical background	
			DISCO-TEX & HIS SEX-O-LETTES	
			Disco studio group assembled by producer Bob Crewe. Featuring lead voice Sir Monti Rock III (real name: Joseph Montanez, Jr.), owner of a chain of hairdressing salons.	
8/23/75	**36**	3	Disco Tex & His Sex-O-Lettes	Chelsea 505
			Get Dancin' (10)	
			DIVINYLS	
			Vocalist Christina Amphlett and guitarist Mark McEntee formed Australian rock group in 1981. Bassist Rick Grossman joined The Hoodoo Gurus in 1989.	
3/30/91	**15**	9	● DiVINYLS	Virgin 91397
			I Touch Myself (4)	
			D.J. JAZZY JEFF & THE FRESH PRINCE	
			Philadelphia rap duo: D.J. Jeff Townes and rapper Will Smith. Smith stars in the hit TV sitcom "Fresh Prince of Bel Aire"; appeared in the movies *Made in America* and *Six Degrees of Separation*.	
6/18/88	**4**	23	▲³ **1. He's The D.J., I'm The Rapper**	Jive 1091 [2]
12/2/89	**39**	7	● 2. And In This Corner ...	Jive 1188
7/27/91	**12**	13	▲ 3. Homebase	Jive 1392
			Summertime (4)	
			DJ QUIK	
			Born in 1971. Rapper from Compton, California.	
5/25/91	**29**	13	● 1. Quik Is The Name	Profile 1402
8/8/92	**10**	5	● **2. Way 2 Fonky**	Profile 1430
			D.O.C., The	
			Pronounced dock. Dallas rapper Tray Curry.	
9/2/89	**20**	10	▲ No One Can Do It Better	Ruthless 91275
			DR. BUZZARD'S ORIGINAL "SAVANNAH" BAND	
			New York City '30s-styled disco group formed by brothers Stony Browder and August Darnell (real name: Thomas August Darnell Browder), with Cory Daye, lead singer. Darnell left in 1980 to form Kid Creole & The Coconuts.	
10/9/76	**22**	18	● 1. Dr. Buzzard's Original Savannah Band	RCA 1504
3/11/78	**36**	3	2. Dr. Buzzard's Original Savannah Band Meets King Penett	RCA 2402
			DR. DRE	
			Real name: Andre Young, co-founder of N.W.A. and World Class Wreckin' Cru. Raised in Compton, California. Produced Eazy-E, The D.O.C. and Michel'le. Founded Death Row Records in 1992. Half-brother of Warren G.	
1/2/93	**3**	44	▲³ **The Chronic**	Death Row 57128
			title is slang for an especially potent strain of marijuana	
			Nuthin' But A "G" Thang (2)/*Dre Day* (8)	

DATE	POS	WKS	ARTIST—RECORD TITLE	LABEL & NO.
			DR. JOHN	
			Born Malcolm "Mac" Rebennack on 11/21/40 in New Orleans. Pioneer "swamp-rock"-styled instrumentalist. With Leonard James & The Nighttrainers and Paul Gayten in 1955. Session work in the mid-1950s. Recorded with Ronnie Baron as "Drits & Dravy." Moved to Los Angeles in the mid-1960s. Character "Dr. John the Night Tripper" is based on act originated by Lawrence "Prince Lala" Nelson.	
6/9/73	24	9	In The Right Place	Atco 7018
			Right Place Wrong Time (9)	
			DOKKEN	
			Los Angeles-based, hard-rock band: Don Dokken (lead vocals), George Lynch (guitar), Jeff Pilson (bass) and Mick Brown (drums). Disbanded in 1988. Dokken assembled new self-named band in 1990 with John Norum (guitar), Billy White (guitar), Peter Baltes (bass) and Mikkey Dee (drums). Lynch and Brown formed Lynch Mob in 1990.	
2/1/86	32	5	▲ 1. Under Lock And Key	Elektra 60458
12/5/87	13	15	▲ 2. Back For The Attack	Elektra 60735
12/17/88	33	4	● 3. Beast From The East [L]	Elektra 60823 [2]
			recorded live in Japan in April 1988	
			DOLBY, Thomas	
			Born Thomas Morgan Dolby Robertson of British parentage on 10/14/58 in Cairo, Egypt. Master of computer-generated rock music and self-directed videos. Keyboardist of Bruce Woolley & The Camera Club, and The Lene Lovich band (1979-80). Movie *Howard the Duck* featured Dolby's music under moniker Dolby's Cube. Married to actress Kathleen Beller (Kirby Colby of TV's "Dynasty").	
3/12/83	20	11	1. Blinded By Science [M]	Harvest 15007
			She Blinded Me With Science (5)	
4/23/83	13	13	2. The Golden Age Of Wireless	Capitol 12271
4/14/84	35	3	3. The Flat Earth	Capitol 12309
			DOMINGO, Placido	
			Born on 1/21/41 in Madrid. One of the world's leading operatic tenors. Emigrated to Mexico in 1950. Debuted at the New York Metropolitan Opera in 1968.	
12/26/81	18	8	▲ 1. Perhaps Love	CBS 37243
			with John Denver on the title cut	
3/2/91	35	6	▲ 2. CARRERAS DOMINGO PAVAROTTI in concert [L]	London 430433
			CARRERAS DOMINGO PAVAROTTI concert on 7/7/90 of opera tenors: Jose Carreras, Placido Domingo and Luciano Pavarotti with orchestra conducted by Zubin Mehta at the Baths of Caracalla in Rome	
9/17/94	4	13	3. The 3 Tenors In Concert 1994 [L]	Atlantic 82614
			CARRERAS, DOMINGO, PAVAROTTI with MEHTA concert on 7/16/94 of opera tenors Jose Carreras, Placido Domingo and Luciano Pavarotti with orchestra conducted by Zubin Mehta at Dodger Stadium in Los Angeles	
			DOMINO	
			St. Louis-born rapper Shawn Ivy. Raised in Long Beach, California.	
2/19/94	39	1	● Domino	Outburst 57701
			Getto Jam (7)	

DATE	POS	WKS	ARTIST—RECORD TITLE	LABEL & NO.
			DOMINO, Fats	
			Born Antoine Domino on 2/26/28 in New Orleans. Classic New Orleans R&B piano-playing vocalist; heavily influenced by Fats Waller and Albert Ammons. Joined The Dave Bartholomew Band in the mid-1940s. Signed to Imperial record label in 1949. His first recording "The Fat Man" reportedly was a million seller. Heard on many sessions cut by other R&B artists, including Lloyd Price and Joe Turner. In the movies *Shake, Rattle and Roll, Jamboree!, The Big Beat* and *The Girl Can't Help It*. Teamed with co-writer Dave Bartholomew on majority of his hits. Lives in New Orleans with wife, Rosemary, and eight children. Frequently appears in Las Vegas. Inducted into the Rock and Roll Hall of Fame in 1986. Winner of 1987 Hall of Fame and 1987 Lifetime Achievement Grammy Awards.	
11/10/56	18	6	1. Fats Domino — Rock And Rollin'	Imperial 9009
			I'm In Love Again (3)	
2/23/57	19	2	2. This Is Fats Domino!	Imperial 9028
			Blueberry Hill (2)/*Blue Monday* (5)	
3/23/57	17	4	3. Rock And Rollin' With Fats Domino	Imperial 9004
			Domino's first album	
			Ain't That A Shame (10)	
			DONOVAN	
			Born Donovan Phillip Leitch on 5/10/46 near Glasgow, Scotland. Singer/songwriter/guitarist. To London at age 10. Worked Newport Folk Festival in 1965. Wrote score for the movie *If It's Tuesday This Must Be Belgium*. In movies *The Pied Piper of Hamlin* (1972) and *Brother Sun, Sister Moon* (1973). Father of actress Ione Skye (*Say Anything*; married Adam Horovitz [Beastie Boys]) & actor Donovan Leitch, Jr.	
10/30/65	30	4	1. Catch The Wind	Hickory 123
10/15/66	11	12	2. Sunshine Superman	Epic 26217
			Sunshine Superman (1)	
3/11/67	14	8	3. Mellow Yellow	Epic 26239
			Mellow Yellow (2)	
1/27/68	19	7	● 4. A Gift From A Flower To A Garden	Epic 171 [2]
			deluxe box set of the albums *Wear Your Love Like Heaven* and *For Little Ones*	
8/10/68	18	14	5. Donovan In Concert [L]	Epic 26386
11/16/68	20	9	6. The Hurdy Gurdy Man	Epic 26420
			Hurdy Gurdy Man (5)	
3/1/69	4	33	▲ **7. Donovan's Greatest Hits** [G]	Epic 26439
10/11/69	23	6	8. Barabajagal	Epic 26481
			with The Jeff Beck Group on 2 cuts	
			Atlantis (7)	
7/25/70	16	6	9. Open Road	Epic 30125
5/5/73	25	8	10. Cosmic Wheels	Epic 32156
			DOOBIE BROTHERS, The	
			Rock/R&B-styled group formed in San Jose, California, in 1970: Patrick Simmons (vocals, guitar), Tom Johnston (lead vocals, guitar, keyboards), John Hartman (percussion) and Dave Shogren (bass). First recorded for Warner in 1971. Shogren replaced by Tiran Porter (bass). Mike Hossack (percussion) added in 1972; later replaced by Keith Knudsen. Jeff "Skunk" Baxter (slide guitar), formerly with Steely Dan, added in 1974. Michael McDonald (lead vocals, keyboards) added in 1975. Johnston left in 1978. Baxter and Hartman replaced by Cornelius Bumpus (keyboards, saxophone), John McFee (guitar) and Chet McCracken (drums) in 1979. Johnston wrote majority of hits from 1972-75; McDonald, from 1976-83. Disbanded in 1983. Re-formed in early 1988 with Johnston, Simmons, Hartman, Porter, Hossack, and Bobby LaKind (died 12/24/92 of cancer; percussion).	
10/28/72	21	9	▲ 1. Toulouse Street	Warner 2634

DATE	POS	WKS	ARTIST—RECORD TITLE	LABEL & NO.
4/28/73	7	33	▲² 2. The Captain And Me *Long Train Runnin'* (8)	Warner 2694
3/23/74	4	30	▲ 3. What Were Once Vices Are Now Habits *Black Water* (1)	Warner 2750
5/24/75	4	13	● 4. Stampede	Warner 2835
4/24/76	8	10	▲ 5. Takin' It To The Streets	Warner 2899
11/27/76	5	14	▲⁷ 6. Best Of The Doobies [G]	Warner 2978
9/24/77	10	8	● 7. Livin' On The Fault Line	Warner 3045
1/6/79	1 (5)	30	▲³ 8. Minute By Minute *What A Fool Believes* (1)	Warner 3193
10/11/80	3	18	▲ 9. One Step Closer *Real Love* (5)	Warner 3452
12/5/81	39	3	● 10. Best Of The Doobies, Volume II [G]	Warner 3612
6/17/89	17	11	● 11. Cycles *The Doctor* (9)	Capitol 90371

DOORS, The

Rock group formed in Los Angeles in 1965. Consisted of Jim Morrison (born 12/8/43, Melbourne, Florida; died 7/3/71, Paris; lead singer), Ray Manzarek (keyboards), Robby Krieger (guitar) and John Densmore (drums). Controversial onstage performances by Morrison caused several arrests and cancellations. Morrison left group on 12/12/70. In the movie *A Feast of Friends*. Group disbanded in 1973. 1991 movie based on group's career, *The Doors*, starred Val Kilmer as Morrison. Group inducted into the Rock and Roll Hall of Fame in 1993.

DATE	POS	WKS	ARTIST—RECORD TITLE	LABEL & NO.
6/24/67	2 (2)	53	▲² 1. The Doors *Light My Fire* (1)	Elektra 74007
11/11/67	3	23	● 2. Strange Days	Elektra 74014
8/17/68	1 (4)	14	▲ 3. Waiting For The Sun *Hello, I Love You* (1)	Elektra 74024
8/9/69	6	2	▲ 4. The Soft Parade *Touch Me* (3)	Elektra 75005
3/14/70	4	12	● 5. Morrison Hotel/Hard Rock Cafe	Elektra 75007
8/15/70	8	12	● 6. Absolutely Live [L]	Elektra 9002 [2]
12/26/70	25	7	▲ 7. 13 [G]	Elektra 74079
5/15/71	9	22	▲² 8. L.A. Woman	Elektra 75011
11/27/71	31	5	9. Other Voices trio of Manzarek, Krieger and Densmore	Elektra 75017
11/15/80	17	17	▲² 10. The Doors Greatest Hits [G]	Elektra 515
11/19/83	23	9	● 11. Alive, She Cried [E-L] recorded 1968-1970	Elektra 60269
3/23/91	8	9	● 12. The Doors [S] 12 tracks performed by The Doors; one track by Velvet Underground & Nico; and an introduction by the Atlanta Symphony Orchestra CD includes bonus track	Elektra 61047
4/13/91	32	4	13. The Best Of The Doors [G] features 18 digitally remastered Doors classics; CD includes bonus track	Elektra 60345 [2]

DATE	POS	WKS	ARTIST—RECORD TITLE	LABEL & NO.
			DORATI, Antal	
			Born on 4/9/06 in Budapest, Hungary. Principal conductor of BBC Symphony from 1962-66 and of Stockholm Philharmonic from 1966-74; music director of Washington National Symphony from 1970-77; principal conductor of Britain's Royal Philharmonic from 1975-78; music director of Detroit Symphony from 1977-81.	
3/16/59	3	46	● 1. **Tchaikovsky: 1812 Festival Overture/Capriccio Italien** [I] with the Minneapolis Symphony Orchestra	Mercury 50054
7/3/61	20	8	2. Beethoven: Wellington's Victory/Leonore Overture No. 3/Prometheus Overture [I] with the London Symphony Orchestra	Mercury 9000
			DORSEY, Jimmy, Orchestra	
			Born on 2/29/04 in Shenandoah, Pennsylvania. Died of cancer on 6/12/57. Esteemed alto sax and clarinet soloist/bandleader. Recorded with his brother Tommy Dorsey in The Dorsey Brothers Orchestra, 1928-35 and 1953-56. Also see Tommy Dorsey.	
10/7/57	19	4	The Fabulous Jimmy Dorsey 8 of 12 cuts were recorded after Jimmy's death *So Rare* (2)	Fraternity 1008
			DORSEY, Tommy, Orchestra	
			Born on 11/19/05 in Mahanoy Plane, Pennsylvania. Choked to death on 11/26/56. Esteemed trombonist/band leader. Tommy and brother Jimmy Dorsey recorded together as The Dorsey Brothers Orchestra from 1928-35 and 1953-56. They hosted musical variety TV show "Stage Show," 1954 and 1955-56. Warren Covington fronted band after Tommy's death.	
5/19/58	15	6	1. The Fabulous Dorseys In Hi-Fi [I] **TOMMY DORSEY and his orchestra featuring JIMMY DORSEY**	Columbia 1190
6/1/59	38	1	2. Tea For Two Cha Chas [I] band led by Warren Covington *Tea For Two Cha Cha* (7)	Decca 8842
			DOUBLE	
			Swiss Pop duo (pronounced doo-BLAY) of Kurt Maloo and Felix Haug. Both were in jazz trio Ping Pong.	
9/13/86	30	6	Blue	A&M 5133
			DOUGLAS, Carl	
			Born in Jamaica, West Indies; raised in California. Studied engineering in the U.S. and in England.	
1/25/75	37	2	Kung Fu Fighting And Other Great Love Songs *Kung Fu Fighting* (1)	20th Century 464
			DOVE, Ronnie	
			Born on 9/7/40 in Herndon, Virginia. Discovered while singing in Baltimore. Nearly all of Dove's hits were produced by Phil Kahl (vice president of Diamond Records); most were arranged by Bill Justis.	
6/4/66	35	6	The Best Of Ronnie Dove [G]	Diamond 5005
			DRAGON, Carmen	
			Born on 7/28/14 in Antioch, California; died on 3/28/84. Dragon conducted the Capitol Symphony Orchestra. Father of Daryl Dragon (of Captain & Tennille). Also see Leonard Pennario.	
4/28/62	36	3	Nightfall [I] classical melodies	Capitol 8575

Creedence Clearwater Revival's second No. 1 album, *Cosmo's Factory*, stayed at the top slot for nine weeks in 1970. When the group was inducted into the Rock and Roll Hall of Fame in 1993, a long-hoped-for reunion of bandleader John Fogerty, Doug Clifford and Stu Cook failed to materialize.

Billy Ray Cyrus started a dance sensation with his country hit, "Achy Breaky Heart," in 1992. The resulting stir propelled *Some Gave All*, his debut album, to No. 1 for 17 weeks.

John Denver's *Rocky Mountain Christmas* entered the pop charts three times: in 1975, reaching No. 14; also in 1975 as part of a special giftpak, reaching No. 138; and in 1976, peaking at No. 115. In 1979, another holiday album paired the popular singer with no less than the Muppets.

Neil Diamond's first greatest-hits collection, released in 1968, has since been followed by at least six other similar compilations. The prolific singer's last appearance in the Top 10 came as recently as 1992 via his popular Christmas album.

Dire Straits' 1985 album, *Brothers In Arms*, the British group's all-time bestseller, held the No. 1 slot for nine weeks. A major reason for its success was the huge hit "Money For Nothing," penned by guitarist Mark Knopfler with The Police's solo-artist-to-be, Sting, who also sang on the MTV-conscious track.

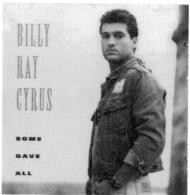

Dr. Dre's 1992 rap classic, *The Chronic*, was a multi-platinum sensation that peaked at No. 3. A critical as well as a commercial hit, the album scored points for introducing the world to Snoop Doggy Dogg, Dre's associate, who wrote and performed the hit "Nuthin' But A 'G' Thang."

Bob Dylan's 1970 disc, *New Morning*, was praised by many critics who regarded it as a return to form after the controversial double set, *Self Portrait*, released only four months earlier. *New Morning* included Dylan's "If Not For You," which was covered by George Harrison and became a Top 25 hit for Olivia Newton-John the next year.

Earth, Wind & Fire's 1974 album *Open Our Eyes* became the group's first platinum effort, helping set the stage for *That's The Way Of The World*, the massive No. 1 follow-up that came out a year later.

Duane Eddy's *Girls! Girls! Girls!*, released on Jamie Records in 1961, was the last album the famed guitar twanger recorded for the small, Philadelphia-based label before moving on to RCA. His greatest tracks were collected on Rhino Records' *Twang Thang: The Duane Eddy Anthology* in 1993.

En Vogue's platinum 1990 debut, *Born To Sing*, laid the groundwork for 1992's *Funky Divas*, the quartet's even more successful follow-up. The group's constant presence on MTV led many to compare its look, style and crossover appeal to those of such Motown greats as The Supremes.

DATE	POS	WKS	ARTIST—RECORD TITLE	LABEL & NO.
			DRAMATICS, The	
			Soul group from Detroit. First recorded for Wingate as The Dynamics, 1966. Members in 1971: Ron Banks (lead singer), William Howard, Larry Demps, Willie Ford and Elbert Wilkins. Howard and Wilkins replaced by L.J. Reynolds and Lenny Mayes in 1973. Reynolds, formerly of Chocolate Syrup, began solo career in 1981. Banks recorded solo in 1983. Drummer Carl Smalls was a member of Undisputed Truth and Sweat Band.	
3/4/72	20	11	1. Whatcha See Is Whatcha Get	Volt 6018
			Whatcha See Is Whatcha Get (9)/*In The Rain* (5)	
5/17/75	31	3	2. The Dramatic Jackpot	ABC 867
			DREAM ACADEMY, The	
			English pop-rock trio: Nick Laird-Clowes (guitar, vocals), Gilbert Gabriel (keyboards) and Kate St. John (vocals).	
2/8/86	20	9	The Dream Academy	Warner 25265
			Life In A Northern Town (7)	
			DREAM THEATER	
			Hard-rock band: James LaBrie (vocals), Kevin Moore, John Myung, John Petrucci and Mike Portnoy. Moore left in September 1994.	
10/22/94	32	1	Awake	EastWest 90126
			DRIFTERS, The	
			R&B vocal group formed in 1953 to showcase lead singer Clyde McPhatter, who went solo in 1955. Various lead singers until 1958, when manager George Treadwell disbanded group, brought in The Five Crowns and renamed them The Drifters. Among many personnel changes, lead singers were Ben E. King (1959-60), Rudy Lewis (1961-63; died 1963) and Johnny Moore (1957, 1964-66). Inducted into the Rock and Roll Hall of Fame in 1988.	
11/7/64	40	2	Under The Boardwalk	Atlantic 8099
			On Broadway (9)/*Under The Boardwalk* (4)	
			D.R.S.	
			Male vocal quintet: Endo, Pic, Jail Bait, Deuce Deuce and Blunt. D.R.S. stands for Dirty Rotten Scoundrels.	
11/20/93	34	1	Gangsta Lean	Capitol 81445
			Gangsta Lean (4)	
			DUCHIN, Eddy — see SOUNDTRACKS (*The Eddy Duchin Story*)	
			DUKE, George	
			Born on 1/12/46 in San Rafael, California. Top jazz-rock keyboardist. Own group in San Francisco during the mid-1950s. With The Don Ellis Big Band and Jean-Luc Ponty. With Frank Zappa's Mothers Of Invention from 1971-75. Also with Cannonball Adderley from 1972-75. Own group from 1977. With Stanley Clarke in The Clarke/Duke Project.	
12/3/77	25	9	● 1. Reach For It	Epic 34883
7/8/78	39	1	2. Don't Let Go	Epic 35366
6/6/81	33	8	3. The Clarke/Duke Project	Epic 36918
			STANLEY CLARKE/GEORGE DUKE	
			DUKES OF DIXIELAND	
			New Orleans dixieland jazz combo led by brothers: Fred (died 4/21/66; trombone) and Frank (died 2/25/74; trumpet) Assunto.	
9/9/57	6	26	1. Marching Along With The Dukes Of Dixieland, Vol. 3 [I]	Audio Fidel. 1851
12/11/61	10	21	2. The Best Of The Dukes Of Dixieland [G-I]	Audio Fidel. 1956

DATE	POS	WKS	ARTIST—RECORD TITLE	LABEL & NO.
			DULFER, Candy	
			Born on 9/19/69 in Amsterdam. Saxophonist.	
8/3/91	22	9	● Saxuality [I] several tracks feature backing vocals and raps	Arista 8674
			DURAN DURAN	
			Synth-pop-dance band formed in Birmingham, England, in 1980. Consisted of Simon LeBon (born 10/27/58; vocals), Andy Taylor (born 2/16/61; guitar), Nick Rhodes (born Nicholas James Bats on 6/8/62; keyboards), John Taylor (born 6/20/60; bass) and Roger Taylor (born 4/26/60; drums). None of the Taylors are related. Group named after a villain in the Jane Fonda movie *Barbarella*. In 1984, Andy and Roger left group. In 1985, Andy and John recorded with supergroup The Power Station; Simon, Nick and Roger recorded as Arcadia. Duran Duran reduced to a trio in 1986 of Simon, Nick and John. Expanded to quintet in 1990 with the addition of Warren Cuccurullo (ex-guitarist of Missing Persons) and Sterling Campbell (left by 1993).	
1/29/83	6	21	▲² **1. Rio** *Hungry Like The Wolf* (3)	Harvest 12211
7/2/83	10	14	▲ **2. Duran Duran** [E-R] group's first album, released in 1981	Capitol 12158
12/10/83	8	41	▲² **3. Seven And The Ragged Tiger** *Union Of The Snake* (3)/*New Moon On Monday* (10)/ *The Reflex* (1)	Capitol 12310
12/8/84	4	15	▲² **4. Arena** [L] *The Wild Boys* (2)	Capitol 12374
12/20/86	12	14	▲ 5. Notorious *Notorious* (2)	Capitol 12540
11/12/88	24	14	● 6. Big Thing **DURANDURAN** *I Don't Want Your Love* (4)	Capitol 90958
3/13/93	7	26	▲ **7. Duran Duran** *Ordinary World* (3)/*Come Undone* (7)	Capitol 98876
			DURANTE, Jimmy	
			Born on 2/10/1893 in New York City. Died on 1/29/80. Much-beloved comedian who started in vaudeville and became star of many Broadway shows and movies as well as his own TV show (1954-56).	
10/26/63	30	4	September Song serious singing by the great comedian	Warner 1506
			DYLAN, Bob	
			Born Robert Allen Zimmerman on 5/24/41 in Duluth, Minnesota. Singer/ songwriter/guitarist/harmonica player. Took stage name from poet Dylan Thomas. To New York City in December 1960. Worked Greenwich Village folk clubs. Signed to Columbia Records in October 1961. Innovator of folk-rock style. Motorcycle crash on 7/29/66 led to short retirement. Movies *Don't Look Back* (1965), *Eat the Document* (1969) and *Pat Garrett and Billy the Kid* (1973). Made movie *Renaldo and Clara* (1978). Newly found Christian faith reflected in his recordings of 1979. Co-starred with Fiona in the 1987 movie *Hearts of Fire*. Member of the supergroup Traveling Wilburys. Inducted into the Rock and Roll Hall of Fame in 1988. Won 1991 Lifetime Achievement Grammy Award. Peter Himmelman married his daughter Maria. Star players who frequently appeared on his albums include Charlie McCoy, Al Kooper, Jim Keltner, Sly Dunbar, Robbie Shakespeare, Mick Taylor, Mark Knopfler and Tom Petty's Heartbreakers. Also see Concerts/Festivals.	
9/28/63	22	14	● 1. The Freewheelin' Bob Dylan	Columbia 8786
3/28/64	20	5	● 2. The Times They Are A-Changin'	Columbia 8905
5/15/65	6	32	● **3. Bringing It All Back Home**	Columbia 9128

DATE	POS	WKS	ARTIST—RECORD TITLE		LABEL & NO.
10/9/65	3	24	●	**4. Highway 61 Revisited** *Like A Rolling Stone* (2)	Columbia 9189
8/6/66	9	15	●	**5. Blonde On Blonde** *Rainy Day Women #12 & 35* (2)	Columbia 841 [2]
5/20/67	10	21	▲²	**6. Bob Dylan's Greatest Hits** [G] *Positively 4th Street* (7)	Columbia 9463
2/10/68	2 (4)	21	●	**7. John Wesley Harding**	Columbia 9604
5/3/69	3	31	▲	**8. Nashville Skyline** guests include Johnny Cash and Charlie Daniels *Lay Lady Lay* (7)	Columbia 9825
7/11/70	4	12	●	**9. Self Portrait**	Columbia 30050 [2]
11/14/70	7	12	●	**10. New Morning**	Columbia 30290
12/11/71	14	17	▲²	**11. Bob Dylan's Greatest Hits, Vol. II** [G]	Columbia 31120 [2]
9/1/73	16	14		12. Pat Garrett & Billy The Kid [S] Dylan appeared as Alias in the movie; 3 vocals by Dylan	Columbia 32460
1/5/74	17	7	●	13. Dylan [K] outtake recordings from 1969-70	Columbia 32747
2/9/74	1 (4)	12	●	**14. Planet Waves** **BOB DYLAN With The Band**	Asylum 1003
7/20/74	3	10	●	**15. Before The Flood** [L] **BOB DYLAN/THE BAND**	Asylum 201 [2]
2/8/75	1 (2)	14	▲²	**16. Blood On The Tracks**	Columbia 33235
8/2/75	7	9		**17. The Basement Tapes** [E] **BOB DYLAN AND THE BAND** recorded in 1967 at the Big Pink, a house rented by The Band in West Saugerties, New York	Columbia 33682 [2]
1/24/76	1 (5)	17	▲	**18. Desire**	Columbia 33893
10/9/76	17	5	●	19. Hard Rain [L] recorded during Dylan's tour, the *Rolling Thunder Revue*	Columbia 34349
7/15/78	11	8	●	20. Street-Legal	Columbia 35453
5/19/79	13	7		21. Bob Dylan At Budokan [L] recorded in Japan on 3/1/78	Columbia 36067 [2]
9/15/79	3	13	▲	**22. Slow Train Coming**	Columbia 36120
7/19/80	24	5		23. Saved	Columbia 36553
9/19/81	33	3		24. Shot Of Love guests include Ringo Starr, Donald "Duck" Dunn and Ron Wood	Columbia 37496
11/26/83	20	10	●	25. Infidels	Columbia 38819
6/29/85	33	6		26. Empire Burlesque	Columbia 40110
1/11/86	33	2	▲	27. Biograph [K] consists of a 53-song collection from 1962-81 (18 songs previously unreleased)	Columbia 38830 [5]
2/25/89	37	3	●	28. Dylan & The Dead [L] **BOB DYLAN & GRATEFUL DEAD** recordings from 6 concert dates in July 1987	Columbia 45056
10/14/89	30	6		29. Oh Mercy	Columbia 45281
10/6/90	38	1		30. Under The Red Sky guests include David Crosby, George Harrison, Bruce Hornsby, Elton John, Slash (Guns N' Roses) and Jimmie and Stevie Ray Vaughan	Columbia 46794

DATE	POS	WKS	ARTIST—RECORD TITLE	LABEL & NO.

E

EAGLES

Rock-country group formed in Los Angeles in 1971. Consisted of Glenn Frey (vocals, guitar), Don Henley (drums), Randy Meisner (bass) and Bernie Leadon (guitar). Meisner founded Poco; Leadon had been in The Flying Burrito Brothers; Frey and Henley were with Linda Ronstadt. Debut album recorded in England in 1972. Don Felder (guitar) added in 1975. Leadon replaced by Joe Walsh in 1975. Meisner replaced by Timothy B. Schmit in 1977. Frey and Henley were only members to play on all recordings. Disbanded in 1982. Henley, Frey, Felder, Walsh and Schmidt reunited for a tour in 1994. Also see Various Artists-Tribute Recordings (*Common Thread*).

DATE	POS	WKS	ARTIST—RECORD TITLE	LABEL & NO.
7/22/72	**22**	7	● 1. Eagles	Asylum 5054
			Witchy Woman (9)	
4/27/74	**17**	24	● 2. On The Border	Asylum 1004
			Best Of My Love (1)	
6/28/75	**1**(5)	43	● **3. One Of These Nights**	Asylum 1039
			One Of These Nights (1)/*Lyin' Eyes* (2)/*Take It To The Limit* (4)	
3/6/76	**1**(5)	57	▲¹² **4. Eagles/Their Greatest Hits 1971-1975**　　[G]	Asylum 1052
12/25/76	**1**(8)	32	▲¹⁰ **5. Hotel California**	Asylum 1084
			New Kid In Town (1)/*Hotel California* (1)	
10/20/79	**1**(9)	36	▲⁴ **6. The Long Run**	Asylum 508
			Heartache Tonight (1)/*The Long Run* (8)/*I Can't Tell You Why* (8)	
11/29/80	**6**	16	▲² **7. Eagles Live**　　[L]	Asylum 705 [2]
11/26/94	**1**(2)	14+	▲⁴ **8. Hell Freezes Over**　　[L]	Geffen 24725
			11 previous "live" hits and 4 new studio songs	

EARTH, WIND & FIRE

Los Angeles-based R&B group formed by Chicago-bred producer/songwriter/vocalist/percussionist/kalimba player Maurice White. In 1969, White, former session drummer for Chess Records and member of The Ramsey Lewis Trio, formed The Salty Peppers; recorded for Capitol. White's brother Verdine White was the group's bassist. Eighteen months later, the brothers hired a new band and recorded as Earth, Wind & Fire—named for the three elements of Maurice's astrological sign. Co-lead singer Philip Bailey joined in 1971. Group generally contained 8 to 10 members, with frequent personnel shuffling. Appeared in the movies *That's the Way of the World* (1975) and *Sgt. Pepper's Lonely Hearts Club Band* (1978). Elaborate stage shows featured an array of magic acts and pyrotechnics. Group members Bailey, Wade Flemons, Ronnie Laws and Maurice White had solo hits.

DATE	POS	WKS	ARTIST—RECORD TITLE	LABEL & NO.
7/14/73	**27**	10	● 1. Head To The Sky	Columbia 32194
4/13/74	**15**	18	▲ 2. Open Our Eyes	Columbia 32712
3/22/75	**1**(3)	29	▲² **3. That's The Way Of The World**　　[S]	Columbia 33280
			group portrayed a rock band in the movie	
			Shining Star (1)	
12/13/75	**1**(3)	21	▲² **4. Gratitude**　　[L]	Columbia 33694 [2]
			contains some studio cuts	
			Sing A Song (5)	
10/16/76	**2**(2)	18	▲² **5. Spirit**	Columbia 34241
12/10/77	**3**	18	▲³ **6. All 'N All**	Columbia 34905
12/2/78	**6**	18	▲ **7. The Best Of Earth, Wind & Fire, Vol. I**　　[G]	ARC 35647
			Got To Get You Into My Life (9)/*September* (8)	
6/23/79	**3**	20	▲² **8. I Am**	ARC 35730
			Boogie Wonderland (6)/*After The Love Has Gone* (2)	

DATE	POS	WKS	ARTIST—RECORD TITLE	LABEL & NO.
11/22/80	**10**	12	● **9. Faces**	ARC 36795 [2]
11/14/81	**5**	18	▲ **10. Raise!**	ARC 37548
			Let's Groove (3)	
3/12/83	**12**	12	● 11. Powerlight	Columbia 38367
1/7/84	**40**	2	12. Electric Universe	Columbia 38980
12/5/87	**33**	6	● 13. Touch The World	Columbia 40596
10/2/93	**39**	1	14. Millennium	Reprise 45274
			### EASTON, Sheena	
			Born on 4/27/59 in Glasgow, Scotland. Real last name is Orr. Vocalist/ actress. Portrayed singer in the 1980 BBC-TV documentary *The Big Time*. Won 1981 Best New Artist Grammy Award. Portrayed Sonny Crockett's wife in five episodes of TV's "Miami Vice."	
5/2/81	**24**	8	● 1. Sheena Easton	EMI America 17049
			Morning Train (Nine To Five) (1)	
10/1/83	**33**	9	2. Best Kept Secret	EMI America 17101
			Telefone (Long Distance Love Affair) (9)	
11/24/84	**15**	22	▲ 3. A Private Heaven	EMI America 17132
			Strut (7)/*Sugar Walls* (9)	
12/14/85	**40**	2	4. Do You	EMI America 17173
			### EAZY-E	
			Born Eric Wright on 9/7/73. Rapper/producer from Compton, California. Formerly with N.W.A.	
11/6/93	**5**	8	▲[1] **It's On (Dr. Dre) 187um Killa** **[M]**	Ruthless 5503
			187 is slang for murder	
			### EDDY, Duane	
			Born on 4/26/38 in Corning, New York. Began playing guitar at age five. At age 13, moved to Tucson, then to Coolidge, Arizona. To Phoenix in 1955; began long association with producer/songwriter Lee Hazlewood. Eddy's backing band, The Rebels, included top sessionmen: Larry Knechtel (piano; later with Bread), saxmen Plas Johnson, Jim Horn and Steve Douglas (died 4/19/93 [age 55] of heart failure), guitarists Al Casey, his wife, Corky Casey, and Donnie Owens, and drummers Jimmy Troxel and Mike Bermani. Billed on most of his records as: "DUANE EDDY His 'Twangy' Guitar and The Rebels." Movies *Because They're Young*, *A Thunder of Drums*, *The Wild Westerners*, *The Savage Seven* and *Kona Coast*. Married to Jessi Colter from 1962-68. Eddy originated the "twangy" guitar sound with his '56 red Gretsch 6120 guitar, and is the all-time #1 rock-and-roll instrumentalist. Inducted into the Rock and Roll Hall of Fame in 1994.	
1/19/59	**5**	42	**1. Have 'Twangy' Guitar-Will Travel** **[I]**	Jamie 3000
			Rebel-'Rouser (6)	
8/17/59	**24**	13	2. Especially For You ... [I]	Jamie 3006
1/25/60	**18**	13	3. The "Twangs" The "Thang" [I]	Jamie 3009
12/26/60	**10**	9	**4. $1,000,000.00 Worth Of Twang** **[G-I]**	Jamie 3014
			Forty Miles Of Bad Road (9)/*Because They're Young* (4)	
			### EDWARDS, Vincent	
			Born Vincento Eduardo Zoine on 7/9/28 in New York City. Stage, movie and TV actor. Best known as star of the TV series "Ben Casey."	
7/21/62	**5**	11	**Vincent Edwards Sings**	Decca 4311
			### ELECTRIC FLAG	
			Chicago rock-blues band formed by Mike Bloomfield and Buddy Miles.	
5/11/68	**31**	5	A Long Time Comin'	Columbia 9597

DATE	POS	WKS	ARTIST—RECORD TITLE	LABEL & NO.
			ELECTRIC LIGHT ORCHESTRA	
			Orchestral rock band formed in Birmingham, England, in 1971, by Roy Wood, Bev Bevan and Jeff Lynne of The Move. Wood left after first album, leaving Lynne as group's leader. Much personnel shuffling from then on. Among various members: Kelly Groucutt (keyboards) and Mike Kaminski (violin). From a group size of eight in 1971, the 1986 ELO consisted of three members: Lynne (vocals, guitar, keyboards), Bevan (drums) and Richard Tandy (keyboards, guitar). Bevan also recorded with Black Sabbath in 1987. Lynne was a member of supergroup The Traveling Wilburys.	
11/9/74	16	17	● 1. Eldorado	United Art. 339
			Can't Get It Out Of My Head (9)	
11/8/75	8	24	● 2. Face The Music	United Art. 546
			Evil Woman (10)	
7/17/76	32	5	● 3. Ole ELO [K]	United Art. 630
11/13/76	5	44	▲ 4. A New World Record	United Art. 679
			Telephone Line (7)	
11/26/77	4	21	▲ 5. Out Of The Blue	Jet 823 [2]
6/23/79	5	17	▲ 6. Discovery	Jet 35769
			Shine A Little Love (8)/*Don't Bring Me Down* (4)	
12/15/79	30	8	▲² 7. ELO's Greatest Hits [G]	Jet 36310
8/9/80	4	15	▲ 8. Xanadu [S]	MCA 6100
			side 1: Olivia Newton-John; side 2: Electric Light Orchestra	
			Xanadu (8-with Olivia Newton-John)	
8/22/81	16	12	● 9. Time	Jet 37371
			Hold On Tight (10)	
8/20/83	36	1	10. Secret Messages	Jet 38490
			ELFMAN, Danny	
			Born on 5/29/53 in Los Angeles. Lead singer of Oingo Boingo.	
9/2/89	30	4	1. Batman Original Motion Picture Score [S-I]	Warner 25977
			Elfman-composed music performed by the Sinfonia of London Orchestra; songs from and songs inspired by the movie *Batman*	
			ELGART, Larry, And His Manhattan Swing Orchestra	
			Elgart was born on 3/20/22 in New London, Connecticut. Alto saxman in own band and in brother Les Elgart's band.	
7/3/82	24	15	▲ Hooked On Swing [I]	RCA 4343
			ELGART, Les, And His Orchestra	
			Elgart was born on 8/3/18 in New Haven, Connecticut. Trumpeter/bandleader since 1945. His 1954 recording (Columbia 40180) of "Bandstand Boogie" was the long-running theme song for Dick Clark's "American Bandstand" TV show.	
11/3/56	13	7	1. The Elgart Touch [I]	Columbia 875
8/19/57	14	7	2. For Dancers Also [I]	Columbia 1008
			ELLIMAN, Yvonne	
			Born on 12/29/51 in Honolulu. Portrayed Mary Magdalene on concept album and in rock opera and movie *Jesus Christ Superstar*. Joined Eric Clapton during his 1974 comeback tour.	
4/29/78	40	2	Night Flight	RSO 3031
			If I Can't Have You (1)	

DATE	POS	WKS	ARTIST—RECORD TITLE	LABEL & NO.
			ELLINGTON, Duke	
			Born Edward Kennedy Ellington on 4/29/1899 in Washington, D.C.; died on 5/24/74. One of jazz music's leading bandleader/composer/arrangers. Won 1966 Lifetime Achievement Grammy Award and 1968 Trustees Grammy Award.	
6/24/57	14	1	Ellington At Newport　　　　　　　　　[I-L]	Columbia 934
			recorded at the Newport Jazz Festival on 7/7/56	
			EMERSON, LAKE & PALMER	
			English classical-oriented rock trio formed in 1969. Consisted of Keith Emerson (keyboards; with The Nice), Greg Lake (vocals, bass, guitars; King Crimson) and Carl Palmer (drums; Atomic Rooster; Crazy World of Arthur Brown). Group split up in 1979, with Palmer joining supergroup Asia. Emerson and Lake re-grouped in 1986 with new drummer Cozy Powell. Palmer returned in 1987, replacing Powell who joined Black Sabbath in 1990.	
2/27/71	18	18	● 1. Emerson, Lake & Palmer	Cotillion 9040
7/10/71	9	11	● 2. Tarkus	Cotillion 9900
1/29/72	10	12	● 3. Pictures At An Exhibition　　　　[L]	Cotillion 66666
			based on Mussorgsky's classical composition	
8/5/72	5	20	● 4. Trilogy	Cotillion 9903
12/29/73	11	16	● 5. Brain Salad Surgery	Manticore 66669
9/14/74	4	11	● 6. Welcome back, my friends, to the show that never ends — Ladies and Gentlemen　[L]	Manticore 200 [3]
4/16/77	12	10	● 7. Works, Volume 1	Atlantic 7000 [2]
1/7/78	37	3	● 8. Works, Volume 2	Atlantic 19147
			above 2 albums feature mostly solo material	
6/28/86	23	12	9. Emerson, Lake & Powell	Polydor 829297
			EMERSON, LAKE & POWELL	
			EMF	
			Techno-funk band from Forest of Dean, England: James Atkin (vocals), Ian Dench, Mark Decloedt, Zac Foley and Derry Brownson. EMF stands for the name of New Order groupies called The Epson Mad Funkers.	
6/1/91	12	19	▲ Schubert Dip	EMI 96238
			Unbelievable (1)	
			EMOTIONS, The	
			Black female trio from Chicago, consisting of sisters Wanda (lead), Sheila and Jeanette Hutchinson. First worked as a child gospel group called The Heavenly Sunbeams. Left gospel; became The Emotions in 1968. Jeanette replaced by cousin Theresa Davis in 1970; later by sister Pamela. Jeanette returned to group in 1978.	
7/2/77	7	21	▲ 1. Rejoice	Columbia 34762
			Best Of My Love (1)	
9/9/78	40	3	● 2. Sunbeam	Columbia 35385
			ENGLAND DAN & JOHN FORD COLEY	
			Pop duo from Austin, Texas: Dan Seals (born 2/8/48) and Coley (born 10/13/48). In the late '60s, both were members of Southwest F.O.B. Seals, currently a top country artist, is brother of Jim Seals of Seals & Crofts and cousin of country singers Johnny Duncan, Troy Seals (Jo Ann & Troy) and Brady Seals (Little Texas).	
9/25/76	17	12	● Nights Are Forever	Big Tree 89517
			I'd Really Love To See You Tonight (2)/ Nights Are Forever Without You (10)	

DATE	POS	WKS	ARTIST—RECORD TITLE	LABEL & NO.
			ENGLISH BEAT	
			English "ska" (reggae/R&B) sextet led by Dave Wakeling and Ranking Roger (Roger Charley). Disbanded in 1983. Wakeling and Roger formed General Public. Cox and Steele formed Fine Young Cannibals.	
4/9/83	39	3	Special Beat Service	I.R.S. 70032
			ENIGMA	
			Enigma is producer Michael Cretu. Born on 5/18/57 in Bucharest, Romania. Moved to Germany in 1975. Worked with Vangelis and The Art Of Noise. Featured vocalist is Cretu's wife, Sandra.	
3/16/91	6	17	▲² 1. MCMXC a.D.	Charisma 91642
			title is the Roman numeral for the year 1990 *Sadeness Part 1* (5)	
2/26/94	9	20	▲ 2. ENIGMA 2 the CROSS of changes	Charisma 39236
			Return To Innocence (4)	
			EN VOGUE	
			Female vocal quartet from the San Francisco Bay area. Formed by production team of Denzil Foster and Thomas McElroy. Consists of Dawn Robinson, Terry Ellis, Cindy Herron and Maxine Jones. Herron married pro baseball player Glenn Braggs in June 1993 and acted in the movie *Juice*.	
5/26/90	21	19	▲ 1. Born To Sing	Atlantic 82084
			Hold On (2)	
4/11/92	8	53	▲³ 2. Funky Divas	EastWest 92121
			My Lovin' (You're Never Gonna Get It) (2)/ *Giving Him Something He Can Feel* (6)/*Free Your Mind* (8)	
			ENYA	
			Born Eithne Ni Bhraonain (Gaelic spelling of Brennan) in Donegal, Ireland. From 1980-82, was member of her siblings' folk-rock group Clannad.	
3/11/89	25	13	▲² 1. Watermark	Geffen 24233
1/11/92	17	27	▲⁴ 2. Shepherd Moons	Reprise 26775
			EPMD	
			Long Island rap duo: Erick Sermon and Parrish Smith. EPMD: Erick and Parrish Making Dollars. Smith was a football tight end at Southern Connecticut State University. By 1994, duo broke up and Smith recorded as PMD.	
2/16/91	36	3	● 1. Business As Usual	Def Jam 47067
8/15/92	14	4	● 2. Business Never Personal	RAL/Def Jam 52848
			EPPS, Preston	
			Bongo player born in 1931 in Oakland. Discovered by Original Sound owner/ Los Angeles DJ, Art Laboe.	
8/15/60	35	1	Bongo Bongo Bongo [I]	Original Snd. 5002
			ERASURE	
			British techno-soul duo of composer/producer/multi-instrumentalist Vince Clarke and lyricist/vocalist Andy Bell. Clarke was a member of Depeche Mode and half of the duo Yaz.	
11/2/91	29	1	1. Chorus	Sire 26668
6/4/94	18	2	2. I Say I Say I Say	Mute/Elektra 61633
			ERIC B. & RAKIM	
			Rap duo: DJ Eric Barrier from Elmhurst, New York, and rapper William Griffin, Jr., from Long Island, New York.	
8/20/88	22	7	● 1. Follow The Leader	Uni 3
7/14/90	32	3	● 2. Let The Rhythm Hit 'Em	MCA 6416

DATE	POS	WKS	ARTIST—RECORD TITLE	LABEL & NO.
7/11/92	**22**	2	3. Don't Sweat The Technique	MCA 10594

ESCAPE CLUB, The

London-based rock quartet formed in 1983: Trevor Steel (vocals), John Holliday (guitar), Johnnie Christo (bass) and Milan Zekavica (drums).

DATE	POS	WKS	ARTIST—RECORD TITLE	LABEL & NO.
10/29/88	**27**	14	● Wild Wild West *Wild, Wild West* (1)	Atlantic 81871

ESSEX, David

Born David Cook on 7/23/47 in London. Portrayed Christ in London production of *Godspell*. Star of British movies since 1970.

DATE	POS	WKS	ARTIST—RECORD TITLE	LABEL & NO.
3/9/74	**32**	3	Rock On *Rock On* (5)	Columbia 32560

ESTEFAN, Gloria/Miami Sound Machine

Latin American-flavored pop band based in Miami, led by singer Gloria Estefan with her husband, percussionist Emilio Estefan, Jr. Band formed in 1975. Gloria (born Gloria Fajardo on 12/1/57) came to Miami in 1960 from Cuba where her father was a bodyguard for President Fulgencio Batista. Emilio emigrated in 1965. On 3/20/90, both were involved in serious crash involving their tour bus, in which Gloria suffered a broken vertebra but fully recovered within a year.

MIAMI SOUND MACHINE:

DATE	POS	WKS	ARTIST—RECORD TITLE	LABEL & NO.
3/1/86	**21**	34	▲² 1. Primitive Love *Conga* (10)/*Bad Boy* (8)/*Words Get In The Way* (5)	Epic 40131

GLORIA ESTEFAN and MIAMI SOUND MACHINE:

DATE	POS	WKS	ARTIST—RECORD TITLE	LABEL & NO.
7/4/87	**6**	48	▲³ 2. Let It Loose *Rhythm Is Gonna Get You* (5)/*Can't Stay Away From You* (6) *Anything For You* (1)/*1-2-3* (3)	Epic 40769

GLORIA ESTEFAN:

DATE	POS	WKS	ARTIST—RECORD TITLE	LABEL & NO.
8/5/89	**8**	41	▲³ 3. Cuts Both Ways cassette and CD versions contain Spanish versions of 2 tracks *Don't Wanna Lose You* (1)/*Here We Are* (6)	Epic 45217
2/23/91	**5**	16	▲² 4. Into The Light *Coming Out Of The Dark* (1)	Epic 46988
11/21/92	**15**	16	▲² 5. Greatest Hits [G]	Epic 53046
7/17/93	**27**	7	▲ 6. Mi Tierra [F] title is Spanish for my country	Epic 53807
11/5/94	**9**	15+	▲ 7. Hold Me, Thrill Me, Kiss Me	Epic 66205

ETHERIDGE, Melissa

Born on 5/29/61 in Leavenworth, Kansas. Singer/guitarist. Studied guitar at Boston's Berklee College of Music. Discovered in Long Beach, California, by Island Records' founder Chris Blackwell.

DATE	POS	WKS	ARTIST—RECORD TITLE	LABEL & NO.
3/25/89	**22**	14	▲ 1. Melissa Etheridge	Island 90875
10/14/89	**22**	10	▲ 2. Brave And Crazy	Island 91285
4/4/92	**21**	4	● 3. Never Enough	Island 512120
10/9/93	**16**	30+	▲³ 4. Yes I Am *I'm The Only One* (8)	Island 848660

EUROPE

Swedish rock quintet: Joey Tempest (vocals), Kee Marcello (guitar), John Leven (bass), Mic Michaeli (keyboards) and Ian Haugland (drums).

DATE	POS	WKS	ARTIST—RECORD TITLE	LABEL & NO.
2/7/87	**8**	42	▲³ 1. The Final Countdown *The Final Countdown* (8)/*Carrie* (3)	Epic 40241
9/3/88	**19**	11	▲ 2. Out Of This World	Epic 44185

DATE	POS	WKS	ARTIST—RECORD TITLE	LABEL & NO.
			EURYTHMICS	
			Synth-pop duo: Annie Lennox (born 12/25/54, Aberdeen, Scotland; vocals, keyboards, flute, composer) and David Stewart (born 9/9/52, England; keyboards, guitar, synthesizer, composer). Both had been in The Tourists from 1977-80. First album recorded in Cologne, Germany, with drummer Clem Burke (formerly of Blondie). Stewart married Siobhan Fahey of Bananarama on 8/1/87. Lennox appeared in TV movie "The Room."	
7/16/83	15	17	● 1. Sweet Dreams (Are Made Of This)	RCA 4681
			Sweet Dreams (Are Made Of This) (1)	
2/11/84	7	23	▲ 2. Touch	RCA 4917
			Here Comes The Rain Again (4)	
6/1/85	9	24	▲ 3. Be Yourself Tonight	RCA 5429
			Would I Lie To You? (5)	
8/16/86	12	15	● 4. Revenge	RCA 5847
11/18/89	34	9	5. We Too Are One	Arista 8606
			EVERLY BROTHERS, The	
			Donald (real name: Isaac Donald) born on 2/1/37 in Brownie, Kentucky; Philip on 1/19/39 in Chicago. Vocal duo/guitarists/songwriters. Parents were folk and country singers. Don (beginning at age eight) and Phil (age six) sang with parents through high school. Invited to Nashville by Chet Atkins and first recorded there for Columbia in 1955. Signed to Archie Bleyer's Cadence Records in 1957. Phil was married for a time to the daughter of Janet Bleyer (Chordettes). Duo split up in July 1973; reunited in September 1983. Inducted into the Rock and Roll Hall of Fame in 1986. Don's daughter Erin was married for short time to Axl Rose of Guns N' Roses in 1990.	
2/10/58	16	3	1. The Everly Brothers	Cadence 3003
			Bye Bye Love (2)/*Wake Up Little Susie* (1)	
5/23/60	9	10	**2. It's Everly Time!**	Warner 1381
			So Sad (To Watch Good Love Go Bad) (7)	
8/22/60	23	8	3. The Fabulous Style Of The Everly Brothers [K]	Cadence 3040
			('Til) I Kissed You (4)/*Let It Be Me* (7)/ *When Will I Be Loved* (8)	
12/5/60	9	9	**4. A Date With The Everly Brothers**	Warner 1395
			Cathy's Clown (1)	
9/15/62	35	3	5. The Golden Hits Of The Everly Brothers [G]	Warner 1471
			Ebony Eyes (8)/*Walk Right Back* (7)/*Crying In The Rain* (6)/ *That's Old Fashioned* (9)	
10/27/84	38	3	6. EB 84	Mercury 822431
			EXILE	
			Band formed in Lexington, Kentucky, in 1963 as The Exiles. J.P. Pennington, lead singer. Toured with Dick Clark in 1965. Changed name to Exile in 1973. Pennington left band in early 1989; replaced by Paul Martin. A top country act since 1983.	
9/23/78	14	8	● Mixed Emotions	Warner 3205
			Kiss You All Over (1)	
			EXPOSE	
			Miami-based, vocal dance trio assembled by producer/songwriter Lewis Martinee. Consists of Miami native Ann Curless, Los Angeles native Jeanette Jurado and Italian-born, New York-raised Gioia Bruno (replaced by Fairbanks, Alaska, native Kelly Moneymaker in 1992).	
3/21/87	16	52	▲² 1. Exposure	Arista 8441
			Come Go With Me (5)/*Point Of No Return* (5)/ *Let Me Be The One* (7)/*Seasons Change* (1)	

DATE	POS	WKS	ARTIST—RECORD TITLE	LABEL & NO.
7/22/89	33	6	● 2. What You Don't Know *What You Don't Know* (8)/*When I Looked At Him* (10)/ *Tell Me Why* (9)	Arista 8532
			EXTREME	
			Boston metal-funk band: Gary Cherone (vocals), Nuno Bettencourt (born in Portugal; guitar), Pat Badger (bass) and Paul Geary (drums).	
5/11/91	10	28	▲² 1. Pornograffitti *More Than Words* (1)/*Hole Hearted* (4)	A&M 5313
10/10/92	10	5	● 2. III Sides To Every Story	A&M 40006

F

			FABIAN	
			Born Fabiano Forte on 2/6/43 in Philadelphia. Discovered at age 14 (because of his good looks and intriguing name) by chance meeting with Bob Marcucci, owner of Chancellor Records. Began acting career in 1959 with the movie *Hound Dog Man*.	
5/18/59	5	18	**1. Hold That Tiger!** *Turn Me Loose* (9)	Chancellor 5003
12/28/59	3	19	**2. Fabulous Fabian**	Chancellor 5005
			FABRIC, Bent, and His Piano	
			Born Bent Fabricius-Bjerre on 12/7/24 in Copenhagen. Head of Metronome Records in Denmark.	
11/24/62	13	22	Alley Cat [I] *Alley Cat* (7)	Atco 148
			FABULOUS THUNDERBIRDS, The	
			Austin, Texas, rock-and-roll group: Kim Wilson (lead singer), Jimmie Vaughan (guitar; older brother of Stevie Ray Vaughan), Preston Hubbard (bass) and Fran Christina (drums). Vaughan appeared in the 1989 movie *Great Balls of Fire* and recorded in The Vaughan Brothers in 1990. Disbanded in June 1990. Reorganized in 1991 with Wilson, Hubbard, Christina and guitarists Duke Robillard and Kid Bangham.	
4/26/86	13	25	▲ Tuff Enuff *Tuff Enuff* (10)	CBS Assoc. 40304
			FACES	
			With the departure of lead singer Steve Marriott who formed Humble Pie, the British rock group Small Faces added, in 1969, former Jeff Beck Group members: Rod Stewart (vocals) and Ron Wood (bass; joined The Rolling Stones in 1976). Other members were Ian McLagen, Kenney Jones (joined The Who in 1978; formed The Law in 1991) and Ronnie Lane (left in 1973; replaced by ex-Free bassist Tetsu Yamauchi). Disbanded in late 1975.	
4/3/71	29	5	1. Long Player	Warner 1892
1/1/72	6	14	● 2. A Nod Is As Good As A Wink ... To A Blind Horse	Warner 2574
5/12/73	21	7	3. Ooh La La	Warner 2665

DATE	POS	WKS	ARTIST—RECORD TITLE	LABEL & NO.
			FAGEN, Donald	
			Born on 1/10/48 in Passaic, New Jersey. Backup keyboardist/vocalist with Jay & The Americans. At New York's Bard College, formed band with Walter Becker and drummer-turned-comic-actor Chevy Chase. Fagen and Becker formed Steely Dan in 1972.	
11/6/82	11	10	● 1. The Nightfly	Warner 23696
			an account of one night at the fictional jazz radio station WJAZ	
6/12/93	10	6	● 2. Kamakiriad	Reprise 45230
			FAITH, Percy	
			Born on 4/7/08 in Toronto. Died of cancer on 2/9/76. Orchestra leader. Moved to the U.S. in 1940. Joined Columbia Records in 1950 as conductor/arranger for company's leading singers (Tony Bennett, Doris Day, Rosemary Clooney, Johnny Mathis and others).	
7/28/56	18	2	1. Passport To Romance [I]	Columbia 880
4/29/57	8	2	**2. My Fair Lady** [I]	Columbia 895
5/25/59	17	14	3. Porgy And Bess [I]	Columbia 8105
1/11/60	7	17	● **4. Bouquet** [I]	Columbia 8124
11/28/60	7	8	**5. Jealousy** [I]	Columbia 8292
1/9/61	6	10	**6. Camelot** [I]	Columbia 8370
11/6/61	38	1	7. Mucho Gusto! More Music Of Mexico [I]	Columbia 8439
4/14/62	26	5	8. Bouquet Of Love [I]	Columbia 8481
6/29/63	12	13	● 9. Themes for Young Lovers [I]	Columbia 8823
			FAITHFULL, Marianne	
			Born on 12/29/46 in Hampstead, London. Discovered by The Rolling Stones' manager, Andrew Loog Oldham. Involved in long, tumultuous relationship with Mick Jagger. Acted in several stage and screen pro-ductions. Married British art-gallery owner John Dunbar, Vibrators bassist Ben Brierly and American playwright Giorgio Dellaterza.	
8/14/65	12	15	Marianne Faithfull	London 423
			FAITH NO MORE	
			San Francisco rock quintet: Michael "Vlad Dracula" Patton (vocals), Jim Martin (guitar), Roddy Bottum (keyboards), Billy Gould (bass) and Mike Bordin (drums). Martin left band in early 1994.	
7/7/90	11	21	▲ 1. The Real Thing	Slash 25878
			Epic (9)	
7/4/92	10	7	● 2. Angel Dust	Slash 26785
			FALCO	
			Falco (Johann Holzel) was born on 2/19/57 in Vienna, Austria.	
3/15/86	3	18	● **Falco 3**	A&M 5105
			Rock Me Amadeus (1)	
			FARRELL, Eileen	
			Born on 2/13/20 in Willimantic, Connecticut. Operatic soprano. Major debut with The San Francisco Opera in 1956. Metropolitan Opera debut in February 1960. ●	
1/9/61	15	7	I've Got A Right To Sing The Blues	Columbia 1465
			FASTWAY	
			British rock group led by Motorhead's Fast Eddie Clarke (guitar) with David King (vocals), Jerry Shirley (drums) and Charlie McCracken (bass; joined in 1984).	
8/13/83	31	6	Fastway	Columbia 38662

DATE	POS	WKS	ARTIST—RECORD TITLE	LABEL & NO.
			FAT BOYS	
			Brooklyn-born rap trio: Mark "Prince Markie Dee" Morales, Darren "The Human Beat Box" Robinson and Damon "Kool Rock-ski" Wimbley. Combined weight of over 750 pounds. Appeared in the 1987 movie *Disorderlies*.	
7/11/87	8	21	▲ 1. Crushin'	Tin Pan A. 831948
7/30/88	33	5	● 2. Coming Back Hard Again	Tin Pan A. 835809
			FELICIANO, Jose	
			Born on 9/8/45 in Puerto Rico; raised in New York City. Blind since birth. Virtuoso acoustic guitarist. Composed score for TV's "Chico and the Man." Won 1968 Best New Artist Grammy Award.	
8/17/68	2 (3)	26	● 1. Feliciano!	RCA 3957
			Light My Fire (3)	
1/11/69	24	4	2. Souled	RCA 4045
8/2/69	16	13	● 3. Feliciano/10 To 23	RCA 4185
			featuring a recording by Feliciano at age 10	
1/3/70	29	4	● 4. Alive Alive-O! [L]	RCA 6021 [2]
			in concert at the London Palladium	
			FENDER, Freddy	
			Born Baldemar Huerta on 6/4/37 in San Benito, Texas. Mexican-American singer/guitarist. First recorded in Spanish under real name for Falcon in 1956. In the movie *The Milagro Beanfield War*. Joined The Texas Tornados in 1990.	
6/7/75	20	11	● Before The Next Teardrop Falls	ABC/Dot 2020
			Before The Next Teardrop Falls (1)/ *Wasted Days And Wasted Nights* (8)	
			FERGUSON, Maynard	
			Born on 5/4/28 in Verdun, Quebec, Canada. Jazz trumpeter. Moved to the U.S. in 1949. Played for Charlie Barnet and then The Stan Kenton Band (1950-56).	
5/21/77	22	7	● Conquistador [I]	Columbia 34457
			FERRANTE & TEICHER	
			Piano duo: Arthur Ferrante (born 9/7/21, New York City) and Louis Teicher (born 8/24/24, Wilkes-Barre, Pennsylvania). Met as children while attending Manhattan's performing-arts academy Juilliard School. First recorded for Columbia in 1953.	
12/11/61	10	27	1. West Side Story & Other Motion Picture & Broadway Hits [I]	United Art. 6166
			Tonight (8)	
12/25/61	23	7	2. Love Themes [I]	United Art. 8514
3/24/62	30	2	3. Golden Piano Hits [I]	United Art. 8505
			Exodus (2)	
3/31/62	11	25	4. Tonight [I]	United Art. 6171
7/13/63	23	8	5. Love Themes From Cleopatra [I]	United Art. 6290
1/2/65	35	6	6. The People's Choice [I]	United Art. 6385
			FIELDS, Richard "Dimples"	
			R&B vocalist. Owner of The Cold Duck Music Lounge in San Francisco.	
8/29/81	33	4	Dimples	Boardwalk 33232

DATE	POS	WKS	ARTIST—RECORD TITLE	LABEL & NO.
			FIELDS, W.C.	
			Born on 2/20/1879 in Philadelphia; died on 12/25/46. Classic comedian of American movies.	
2/8/69	**30**	11	The Original Voice Tracks From His Greatest Movies [C]	Decca 79164
			5TH DIMENSION, The	
			Los Angeles-based R&B vocal group formed in 1966: Marilyn McCoo, Billy Davis, Jr., Florence LaRue, Lamont McLemore and Ron Townson. McLemore and McCoo had been in The Hi-Fi's; Townson and Davis had been with groups in St. Louis. First called The Versatiles. McCoo and Davis married in 1969; recorded as duo since 1976.	
7/8/67	**8**	11	● 1. Up, Up And Away	Soul City 92000
			Up-Up And Away (7)	
9/28/68	**21**	8	2. Stoned Soul Picnic	Soul City 92002
			Stoned Soul Picnic (3)	
5/31/69	**2**(2)	30	● 3. The Age Of Aquarius	Soul City 92005
			Aquarius/Let The Sunshine In (1)/*Wedding Bell Blues* (1)	
5/23/70	**5**	18	● 4. The 5th Dimension/Greatest Hits [G]	Soul City 33900
5/23/70	**20**	16	● 5. Portrait	Bell 6045
			One Less Bell To Answer (2)	
3/27/71	**17**	8	● 6. Love's Lines, Angles And Rhymes	Bell 6060
11/13/71	**32**	4	● 7. The 5th Dimension/Live!! [L]	Bell 9000 [2]
10/14/72	**14**	10	● 8. Greatest Hits On Earth [G]	Bell 1106
			greatest hits from both Soul City and Bell labels	
			50 GUITARS OF TOMMY GARRETT — see GARRETT, Tommy	
			FINE YOUNG CANNIBALS	
			Pop trio from Birmingham, England: Roland Gift (vocals) and English Beat members David Steele (bass) and Andy Cox (guitar). Group appeared in the movie *Tin Men*; Gift was in the movies *Sammy and Rosie Get Laid* and *Scandal*.	
3/18/89	**1**(7)	40	▲² The Raw & The Cooked	I.R.S. 6273
			She Drives Me Crazy (1)/*Good Thing* (1)	
			FIREBALLS, The — see GILMER, Jimmy	
			FIREFALL	
			Mellow rock group formed in Boulder, Colorado. Original lineup: Rick Roberts (lead singer), Larry Burnett (guitar), Jack Bartley (lead guitar), Mark Andes (bass; Spirit; Jo Jo Gunne) and Mike Clarke (drums; ex-Byrds). David Muse (keyboards) joined in 1977. Andes joined Heart in 1980. Roberts and Clarke were members of The Flying Burrito Brothers. Clarke died on 12/19/93 (age 49) of liver failure.	
7/4/76	**28**	14	● 1. Firefall	Atlantic 18174
			You Are The Woman (9)	
9/3/77	**27**	5	● 2. Luna Sea	Atlantic 19101
12/2/78	**27**	7	▲ 3. Elan	Atlantic 19183
			FIREHOUSE	
			Hard-rock quartet from North Carolina: C.J. Snare (vocals), Bill Leverty, Perry Richardson and Michael Foster.	
5/25/91	**21**	25	▲² 1. Firehouse	Epic 46186
			Love Of A Lifetime (5)	
7/4/92	**23**	4	● 2. Hold Your Fire	Epic 48615
			When I Look Into Your Eyes (8)	

DATE	POS	WKS	ARTIST—RECORD TITLE	LABEL & NO.
			FIRM, The	
			British supergroup: Jimmy Page (guitar; Yardbirds; Led Zeppelin; Honeydrippers), Paul Rodgers (vocals; Free; Bad Company), Chris Slade (drums; Manfred Mann) and Tony Franklin (keyboards). Disbanded in 1986. Franklin joined Blue Murder in 1989. Slade joined AC/DC in 1990. Rodgers joined The Law in 1991.	
3/9/85	**17**	16	● 1. The Firm	Atlantic 81239
3/1/86	**22**	7	2. Mean Business	Atlantic 81628
			FIRST EDITION, The — see ROGERS, Kenny	
			FISHER, Eddie	
			Born Edwin Jack Fisher on 8/10/28 in Philadelphia. Performed at Copacabana night club in New York at age 17. With Buddy Morrow and Charlie Ventura in 1946. On Eddie Cantor's radio show in 1949. In the Armed Forces Special Services, 1952-53. Married to Debbie Reynolds from 1955-59. Other marriages to Elizabeth Taylor and Connie Stevens. Daughter with Reynolds is actress Carrie Fisher. Daughter with Stevens is singer Tricia Leigh Fisher. Own "Coke Time" 15-minute TV series, 1953-57. In movies *All About Eve* (1950), *Bundle of Joy* (1956) and *Butterfield 8* (1960). Eddie was the #1 idol of bobby- soxers during the early '50s.	
4/30/55	**8**	10	**I Love You**	RCA 1097
			FITZGERALD, Ella	
			Born on 4/25/18 in Newport News, Virginia. The most-honored jazz singer of all time. Discovered after winning on the *Harlem Amateur Hour* in 1934, she was hired by Chick Webb and in 1938 created popular sensation with "A-Tisket, A-Tasket." Following Webb's death in 1939, Fitzgerald took over the band for three years. Appeared in several movies. Won 1967 Lifetime Achievement Grammy Award. Winner of the *Down Beat* poll as top female vocalist more than 20 times and winner of 12 Grammy Awards, she remains among the undisputed royalty of 20th-century popular music. Because of complications from diabetes, had both legs amputated below the knee in 1993.	
9/17/55	**7**	10	**1. Songs from Pete Kelly's Blues** **PEGGY LEE & ELLA FITZGERALD** songs from the movie in which Fitzgerald and Lee had supporting roles; also see Ray Heindorf and Jack Webb	Decca 8166
7/28/56	**15**	1	2. Ella Fitzgerald sings the Cole Porter Song Book	Verve 4001 [2]
12/15/56	**12**	2	3. Ella And Louis **ELLA FITZGERALD and LOUIS ARMSTRONG** backing by The Oscar Peterson Trio, plus Buddy Rich	Verve 4003
3/16/57	**11**	4	4. Ella Fitzgerald sings the Rodgers and Hart Song Book albums #2 & 4 above arranged and conducted by Buddy Bregman	Verve 4002 [2]
9/12/60	**11**	20	5. Mack The Knife — Ella In Berlin [L] accompanied by The Paul Smith Quartet	Verve 4041
1/6/62	**35**	1	6. Ella In Hollywood [L]	Verve 4052
			FIXX, The	
			London-based, techno-pop group: Cy Curnin (lead singer, piano), Jamie West-Oram (guitars), Rupert Greenall (keyboards), Adam Woods (drums) and Dan K. Brown (bass).	
11/26/83	**8**	28	▲ 1. Reach The Beach *One Thing Leads To Another* (4)	MCA 39001
9/15/84	**19**	10	● 2. Phantoms	MCA 5507
7/5/86	**30**	8	3. Walkabout	MCA 5705

DATE	POS	WKS	ARTIST—RECORD TITLE	LABEL & NO.
			FLACK, Roberta	
			Born on 2/10/39 in Asheville, North Carolina; raised in Arlington, Virginia. Played piano from an early age. Music scholarship to Howard University at age 15; classmate of Donny Hathaway. Worked as high-school music teacher in North Carolina. Discovered by jazz musician Les McCann. Signed to Atlantic in 1969.	
10/17/70	**33**	13	● 1. Chapter Two	Atlantic 1569
12/11/71	**18**	21	● 2. Quiet Fire	Atlantic 1594
3/25/72	**1**(5)	26	● **3. First Take**	Atlantic 8230
			The First Time Ever I Saw Your Face (1)	
5/20/72	**3**	21	● **4. Roberta Flack & Donny Hathaway**	Atlantic 7216
			ROBERTA FLACK & DONNY HATHAWAY	
			Where Is The Love (5)	
9/1/73	**3**	14	● **5. Killing Me Softly**	Atlantic 7271
			Killing Me Softly With His Song (1)	
4/19/75	**24**	5	6. Feel Like Makin' Love	Atlantic 18131
			Feel Like Makin' Love (1)	
2/18/78	**8**	17	● **7. Blue Lights In The Basement**	Atlantic 19149
			The Closer I Get To You (2-with Donny Hathaway)	
4/26/80	**25**	10	● 8. Roberta Flack Featuring Donny Hathaway	Atlantic 16013
			features 2 duets by Roberta and Donny; rest are Roberta solo	
9/10/83	**25**	14	● 9. Born To Love	Capitol 12284
			PEABO BRYSON/ROBERTA FLACK	
			FLASH	
			English rock quartet led by Peter Banks (guitar; Yes) and Colin Carter (vocals).	
8/26/72	**33**	5	Flash	Capitol 11040
			FLEETWOOD MAC	
			Formed as British blues band in 1967 by ex-John Mayall's Bluesbreakers Peter Green (guitar), Mick Fleetwood (drums) and John McVie (bass), along with guitarist Jeremy Spencer. Many lineup changes followed as group headed toward rock superstardom. Green and Spencer left in 1970. Christine McVie (keyboards) joined in August 1970. Bob Welch (guitar) joined in April 1971; stayed through 1974. Group relocated to California in 1974, whereupon Americans Lindsey Buckingham (guitar) and Stevie Nicks (vocals) joined in January 1975. Buckingham left in summer of 1987. Guitarists/vocalists Billy Burnette (son of Dorsey Burnette) and Rick Vito joined in July 1987. Christine McVie and Nicks quit touring with the band at the end of 1990. Vito left in 1991. In early 1993, Nicks and Burnette left. In late 1993, Bekka Bramlett (leader of The Zoo and daughter of Delaney & Bonnie Bramlett) and Dave Mason joined Fleetwood, John and Christine in band.	
11/16/74	**34**	2	1. Heroes Are Hard To Find	Reprise 2196
8/23/75	**1**(1)	68	▲⁵ **2. Fleetwood Mac**	Reprise 2225
			Americans Stevie Nicks and Lindsey Buckingham join group	
2/26/77	**1**(31)	60	▲¹⁷ **3. Rumours**	Warner 3010
			1977 Album of the Year Grammy Award	
			Go Your Own Way (10)/*Dreams* (1)/*Don't Stop* (3)/	
			You Make Loving Fun (9)	
11/3/79	**4**	22	▲² **4. Tusk**	Warner 3350 [2]
			Tusk (8)/*Sara* (7)	
1/10/81	**14**	8	● 5. Fleetwood Mac Live [L]	Warner 3500 [2]
7/24/82	**1**(5)	21	▲² **6. Mirage**	Warner 23607
			Hold Me (4)	
5/9/87	**7**	44	▲² **7. Tango In The Night**	Warner 25471
			Big Love (5)/*Little Lies* (4)	

DATE	POS	WKS	ARTIST—RECORD TITLE	LABEL & NO.
12/24/88	**14**	12	▲³ 8. Greatest Hits [G]	Warner 25801
5/5/90	**18**	9	● 9. Behind The Mask	Warner 26111

FLOATERS, The

Detroit soul group discovered by The Detroit Emeralds: Charles Clarke (lead), Larry Cunningham and brothers Paul and Ralph Mitchell.

DATE	POS	WKS	ARTIST—RECORD TITLE	LABEL & NO.
7/23/77	**10**	13	▲ **Floaters** *Float On* (2)	ABC 1030

FLOCK OF SEAGULLS, A

British new-wave group formed by brothers Mike (vocals) and Ali (keyboards, drums) Score. Quartet until 1988 when three Philadelphia natives joined group.

DATE	POS	WKS	ARTIST—RECORD TITLE	LABEL & NO.
7/3/82	**10**	25	● **1. A Flock Of Seagulls** *I Ran (So Far Away)* (9)	Jive 66000
6/4/83	**16**	11	2. Listen	Jive 8013

FOCUS

Dutch progressive-rock quartet led by guitar virtuoso Jan Akkerman and flutist Thijs van Leer.

DATE	POS	WKS	ARTIST—RECORD TITLE	LABEL & NO.
3/3/73	**8**	21	● **1. Moving Waves** [I] *Hocus Pocus* (9)	Sire 7401
6/9/73	**35**	4	● 2. Focus 3 [I]	Sire 3901 [2]

FOGELBERG, Dan

Born on 8/13/51 in Peoria, Illinois. Vocalist/composer. Worked as folk singer in Los Angeles. With Van Morrison in the early '70s. Session work in Nashville.

DATE	POS	WKS	ARTIST—RECORD TITLE	LABEL & NO.
1/18/75	**17**	11	▲² 1. Souvenirs Joe Walsh, producer and guitarist	Full Moon 33137
10/18/75	**23**	6	▲ 2. Captured Angel	Full Moon 33499
6/18/77	**13**	12	▲² 3. Nether Lands	Full Moon 34185
9/23/78	**8**	13	▲ **4. Twin Sons Of Different Mothers** **DAN FOGELBERG & TIM WEISBERG**	Full Moon 35339
12/15/79	**3**	27	▲ **5. Phoenix** *Longer* (2)	Full Moon 35634
9/19/81	**6**	31	▲ **6. The Innocent Age** *Same Old Lang Syne* (9)/*Hard To Say* (7)/ *Leader Of The Band* (9)	Full Moon 37393 [2]
11/20/82	**15**	12	▲ 7. Dan Fogelberg/Greatest Hits [G]	Full Moon 38308
2/25/84	**15**	10	● 8. Windows and Walls	Full Moon 39004
5/25/85	**30**	5	● 9. High Country Snows	Full Moon 39616

FOGERTY, John

Born on 5/28/45 in Berkeley, California. Lead vocalist of Creedence Clearwater Revival. Multi- instrumentalist. Wrote "Proud Mary," "Have You Ever Seen The Rain," "Bad Moon Rising," "Lookin' Out My Back Door" and many others. Went solo in 1972 and recorded as one-man band, The Blue Ridge Rangers.

DATE	POS	WKS	ARTIST—RECORD TITLE	LABEL & NO.
2/2/85	**1** (1)	28	▲² **1. Centerfield** *The Old Man Down The Road* (10)	Warner 25203
10/18/86	**26**	6	● 2. Eye Of The Zombie	Warner 25449

DATE	POS	WKS	ARTIST—RECORD TITLE	LABEL & NO.
			FOGHAT	
			British rock quartet: Lonesome Dave Peverett (vocals, guitar; formerly with Savoy Brown), Rod Price (guitar), Tony Stevens (bass) and Roger Earl (drums). Settled in New York City in 1975; many bass player changes since. Price replaced by Erik Cartwright in 1981.	
3/16/74	34	3	● 1. Energized	Bearsville 6950
11/30/74	40	2	● 2. Rock And Roll Outlaws	Bearsville 6956
3/6/76	23	7	▲ 3. Fool For The City	Bearsville 6959
12/11/76	36	2	● 4. Night Shift	Bearsville 6962
9/24/77	11	9	▲² 5. Foghat Live [L]	Bearsville 6971
6/10/78	25	7	● 6. Stone Blue	Bearsville 6977
10/20/79	35	3	7. Boogie Motel	Bearsville 6990
			FONDA, Jane — see AEROBICS section	
			FONTAINE, Frank	
			Born on 4/19/20 in Cambridge, Massachusetts; died on 8/4/78. Comedian/singer/actor. Played Crazy Guggenheim on TV's "The Jackie Gleason Show."	
2/23/63	1(5)	28	● **Songs I Sing On The Jackie Gleason Show**	ABC-Para. 442
			FORBERT, Steve	
			Born in 1955 in Meridian, Mississippi. Moved to New York City in 1976.	
2/2/80	20	6	Jackrabbit Slim	Nemperor 36191
			FORD, Lita	
			Born on 9/23/59 in London. Lead guitarist of Los Angeles-based female rock group The Runaways, 1975-79.	
4/23/88	29	23	▲ Lita	RCA 6397
			Close My Eyes Forever (8-with Ozzy Osbourne)	
			FORD, "Tennessee" Ernie	
			Born Ernest Jennings Ford on 2/13/19 in Bristol, Tennessee; died on 10/17/91 of liver disease. Country singer. Revered as America's favorite hymn singer. Began career as DJ. Host of musical variety TV shows 1955-65. Favorite expression: "Bless your little pea-pickin' hearts."	
4/28/56	12	3	1. This Lusty Land!	Capitol 700
1/5/57	2(3)	138	▲ **2. Hymns**	Capitol 756
5/6/57	5	39	● **3. Spirituals**	Capitol 818
6/9/58	5	49	● **4. Nearer The Cross**	Capitol 1005
5/2/60	23	14	5. Sing A Hymn With Me	Capitol 1332
			includes a hymn book	
			CHRISTMAS ALBUM:	
12/22/58	4	3	▲ **6. The Star Carol** [X]	Capitol 1071
12/28/59	7	2	**7. The Star Carol** [X-R]	Capitol 1071
12/31/60	28	1	8. The Star Carol [X-R]	Capitol 1071
			Christmas charts: 15/'64, 25/'65, 56/'66, 41/'67	

DATE	POS	WKS	ARTIST—RECORD TITLE	LABEL & NO.
			FOREIGNER	
			British-American rock group formed in New York City in 1976. Consisted of Mick Jones (guitar; not to be confused with Mick Jones of The Clash and Big Audio Dynamite), Lou Gramm (vocals), Ian McDonald (guitar, keyboards), Ed Gagliardi (bass), Al Greenwood (keyboards) and Dennis Elliott (drums). Gagliardi, Gramm and Greenwood are from New York. Most of material written by Jones (Spooky Tooth) and Gramm. Rick Wills (Roxy Music; Small Faces) replaced Gagliardi in 1979. Greenwood and McDonald (King Crimson) left in 1980. Gramm left in 1991 to form Shadow King; replaced by Johnny Edwards. Gramm returned in mid-1992. Wills left in 1992 to join Bad Company; Elliott left to open woodworking business.	
5/7/77	4	43	▲⁴ **1. Foreigner**	Atlantic 18215
			Feels Like The First Time (4)/*Cold As Ice* (6)	
7/8/78	3	37	▲⁵ **2. Double Vision**	Atlantic 19999
			Hot Blooded (3)/*Double Vision* (2)	
9/29/79	5	22	▲² **3. Head Games**	Atlantic 29999
7/25/81	1(10)	52	▲⁶ **4. 4**	Atlantic 16999
			Urgent (4)/*Waiting For A Girl Like You* (2)	
12/25/82	10	12	▲³ **5. Foreigner Records** [G]	Atlantic 80999
1/5/85	4	24	▲² **6. Agent Provocateur**	Atlantic 81999
			I Want To Know What Love Is (1)	
1/9/88	15	14	▲ 7. Inside Information	Atlantic 81808
			Say You Will (6)/*I Don't Want To Live Without You* (5)	
			FOUNTAIN, Pete	
			Born on 7/3/30 in New Orleans. Top jazz clarinetist. With Al Hirt, 1956-57. Performed on "The Lawrence Welk Show," 1957-59. Own club in New Orleans, The French Quarter Inn.	
2/22/60	8	31	**1. Pete Fountain's New Orleans** [I]	Coral 57282
5/9/60	31	4	2. Pete Fountain Day [I-L]	Coral 57313
8/4/62	30	4	3. Music From Dixie [I]	Coral 57401
			FOUR FRESHMEN, The	
			Jazz-styled vocal and instrumental group formed in 1948 while at Arthur Jordan Conservatory of Music in Indianapolis. Consisted of brothers Ross and Don Barbour (now deceased), their cousin Bob Flanigan and Ken Errair.	
2/25/56	6	33	**1. Four Freshmen and 5 Trombones**	Capitol 683
10/13/56	11	8	2. Freshmen Favorites [G]	Capitol 743
3/2/57	9	7	**3. 4 Freshmen and 5 Trumpets**	Capitol 763
11/18/57	25	1	4. Four Freshmen and Five Saxes	Capitol 844
9/29/58	17	1	5. The Four Freshmen In Person [L]	Capitol 1008
11/3/58	11	6	6. Voices In Love	Capitol 1074
1/11/60	40	1	7. The Four Freshmen and Five Guitars	Capitol 1255
			FOUR LADS, The	
			Toronto vocal quartet: Bernie Toorish, Jimmie Arnold, Frankie Busseri and Connie Codarini. Backed Johnny Ray on his #1 single "Cry."	
10/6/56	14	2	On The Sunny Side	Columbia 912
			4 NON BLONDES	
			San Francisco-based rock band: Linda Perry (vocals), Christa Hillhouse (bass), Dawn Richardson (drums) and Roger Rocha (guitar; replaced Louis Metoyer who played on debut album).	
6/5/93	13	19	▲ Bigger, Better, Faster, More!	Interscope 92112

DATE	POS	WKS	ARTIST—RECORD TITLE	LABEL & NO.
			FOUR PREPS, The	
			Vocal group formed while at Hollywood High School: Bruce Belland, Glen Larson, Ed Cobb and Marvin Ingraham. Belland, who was later in duo with Dave Somerville of The Diamonds, is the father of Tracey and Melissa Belland of Voice of the Beehive. Larson's production company was a creative force behind numerous TV series during the '70s, including "BJ & The Bear," "Battlestar Galactica," "McCloud" and "Quincy."	
9/4/61	8	13	**1. The Four Preps On Campus** [L]	Capitol 1566
5/12/62	40	1	2. Campus Encore [L]	Capitol 1647
			4 SEASONS, The	
			Vocal group formed in Newark, New Jersey. In 1955, lead singer Frankie Valli (Francis Castelluccio) formed The Variatones with brothers Nick and Tommy DeVito, and Hank Majewski. Changed name to The Four Lovers in 1956. Bob Gaudio (of The Royal Teens) joined as keyboardist/songwriter in 1959, replacing Nick DeVito. Nick Massi replaced Majewski, and the 1961 lineup was set: Valli, Gaudio, Massi and Tommy DeVito. Group had been doing session work for their producer Bob Crewe and took their new name from a New Jersey bowling alley, The Four Seasons. In 1965, Nick Massi was replaced by the group's arranger Charlie Calello and then by Joe Long. In 1971, Tommy DeVito retired; Gaudio left (as a performer) the following year. Numerous personnel changes from then on. The songwriting/producing/arranging team of Crewe, Gaudio and Calello helped rank The 4 Seasons as one of the top American groups of the '60s. Inducted into the Rock and Roll Hall of Fame in 1990. Also recorded as The Wonder Who?	
11/3/62	6	20	**1. Sherry & 11 others** *Sherry* (1)/*Big Girls Don't Cry* (1)	Vee-Jay 1053
3/16/63	8	10	**2. Big Girls Don't Cry and Twelve others** *Walk Like A Man* (1)	Vee-Jay 1056
10/5/63	15	11	3. Golden Hits of the 4 Seasons [G]	Vee-Jay 1065
4/4/64	6	10	**4. Dawn (Go Away) and 11 other great songs** *Dawn (Go Away)* (3)	Philips 124
8/15/64	7	13	**5. Rag Doll** *Ronnie* (6)/*Rag Doll* (1)/*Save It For Me* (10)	Philips 146
1/15/66	10	22	● **6. The 4 Seasons' Gold Vault of Hits** [G] *Let's Hang On!* (3)	Philips 196
1/7/67	22	10	● 7. 2nd Vault Of Golden Hits [G] 9 of 12 cuts are Vee-Jay hits *I've Got You Under My Skin* (9)	Philips 221
7/22/67	37	2	8. New Gold Hits *Tell It To The Rain* (10)/*C'mon Marianne* (9)	Philips 243
3/1/69	37	2	● 9. Edizione D'Oro (The 4 Seasons Gold Edition-29 Gold Hits) [G]	Philips 6501 [2]
1/24/76	38	2	10. Who Loves You *Who Loves You* (3)/*December, 1963 (Oh, What A Night)* (1)	Warner 2900
			FOUR TOPS	
			Detroit R&B vocal group formed in 1953 as The Four Aims. Consisted of Levi Stubbs (lead singer), Renaldo "Obie" Benson, Lawrence Payton and Abdul "Duke" Fakir. First recorded for Chess in 1956, then Red Top and Columbia, before signing with Motown in 1963. Group has had no personnel changes since its formation. Stubbs was the voice of Audrey II (the voracious vegetation) in the 1986 movie *Little Shop of Horrors*. Group inducted into the Rock and Roll Hall of Fame in 1990. The Supremes, The Temptations, The Miracles and the Four Tops were the "big 4" of the Motown "group sound."	
1/8/66	20	8	1. Four Tops Second Album *I Can't Help Myself* (1)/*It's The Same Old Song* (5)	Motown 634
10/29/66	32	5	2. 4 Tops On Top	Motown 647

DATE	POS	WKS	ARTIST—RECORD TITLE	LABEL & NO.
1/28/67	**17**	18	3. Four Tops Live! [L]	Motown 654
8/19/67	**11**	14	4. Four Tops Reach Out	Motown 660
			Reach Out I'll Be There (1)/ *Standing In The Shadows Of Love* (6)/*Bernadette* (4)	
10/7/67	**4**	37	**5. The Four Tops Greatest Hits** [G]	Motown 662
6/27/70	**21**	14	6. Still Waters Run Deep	Motown 704
12/30/72	**33**	3	7. Keeper Of The Castle	Dunhill 50129
			Keeper Of The Castle (10)/ *Ain't No Woman (Like The One I've Got)* (4)	
10/31/81	**37**	4	8. Tonight!	Casablanca 7258
			FOX, Samantha	
			British singer born on 4/15/66. Rose to stardom as topless model for the U.K. *Daily Sun* newspaper.	
1/31/87	**24**	11	● 1. Touch Me	Jive 1012
			Touch Me (I Want Your Body) (4)	
2/11/89	**37**	4	● 2. I Wanna Have Some Fun	Jive 1150
			I Wanna Have Some Fun (8)	
			FOXY	
			Miami-based Latino dance band. Four of group's five members came to Florida with the Cuban emigres of 1959. Lead vocalist/guitarist Ish Ledesma later founded and produced Oxo and Company B. Percussionist Richie Puente is son of luminary Latin bandleader Tito Puente.	
8/26/78	**12**	12	1. Get Off	Dash 30005
			Get Off (9)	
4/28/79	**29**	6	2. Hot Numbers	Dash 30010
			FRAMPTON, Peter	
			Born on 4/22/50 in Beckenham, England. Vocalist/guitarist/composer. Joined British band The Herd at age 16, before forming Humble Pie in 1969, which he left in 1971 to form Frampton's Camel. Went solo in 1974. Played Billy Shears in the 1978 movie *Sgt. Pepper's Lonely Hearts Club Band*. Near-fatal car crash on 6/29/78 temporarily sidelined his career.	
5/10/75	**32**	3	● 1. Frampton	A&M 4512
2/14/76	**1**(10)	55	▲⁶ **2. Frampton Comes Alive!** [L]	A&M 3703 [2]
			Show Me The Way (6)/*Do You Feel Like We Do* (10)	
6/25/77	**2**(4)	15	▲ 3. I'm In You	A&M 4704
			I'm In You (2)	
6/30/79	**19**	7	● 4. Where I Should Be	A&M 3710
			FRANCHI, Sergio	
			Italian tenor. Starred in Broadway's *Do I Hear a Waltz?* (1965) and *Nine* (1982). Died of cancer on 5/1/90 (age 57) in Stonington, Connecticut.	
12/8/62	**17**	9	Sergio Franchi	RCA 2640
			FRANCIS, Connie	
			Born Concetta Rosa Maria Franconero on 12/12/38 in Newark, New Jersey. First recorded for MGM in 1955. From 1961-65, appeared in the movies *Where the Boys Are*, *Follow the Boys*, *Looking for Love* and *When the Boys Meet the Girls*. Francis stopped performing after she was raped on 11/8/74. Began comeback with a performance on "Dick Clark's Live Wednesday" TV show in 1978. Pop music's #1 female vocalist from the late '50s to the mid-1960s.	
2/8/60	**4**	48	**1. Italian Favorites** [F]	MGM 3791
			Mama (8)	

DATE	POS	WKS	ARTIST—RECORD TITLE	LABEL & NO.
2/22/60	**17**	25	2. Connie's Greatest Hits [G] *Who's Sorry Now* (4)/*My Happiness* (2)/ *Lipstick On Your Collar* (5)/*Frankie* (9)	MGM 3793
12/12/60	**9**	11	**3. More Italian Favorites** [F]	MGM 3871
9/25/61	**39**	1	4. More Greatest Hits [G] *Among My Souvenirs* (7)/*Everybody's Somebody's Fool* (1)/ *My Heart Has A Mind Of Its Own* (1)/*Many Tears Ago* (7)/ *Where The Boys Are* (4)	MGM 3942
11/6/61	**11**	23	5. Never On Sunday and other title songs from motion pictures	MGM 3965
10/27/62	**22**	2	6. Country Music Connie Style	MGM 4079
			FRANKE & THE KNOCKOUTS Soft-rock quintet led by vocalist Franke Previte of New Brunswick, New Jersey.	
5/23/81	**31**	5	Franke & The Knockouts *Sweetheart* (10)	Millennium 7755
			FRANKIE GOES TO HOLLYWOOD Dance-rock quintet from Liverpool, England. Vocals by William "Holly" Johnson and Paul Rutherford. Group's name inspired by publicity recounting Frank Sinatra's move into the movie industry.	
12/8/84	**33**	14	Welcome To The Pleasuredome *Relax* (10)	Island 90232 [2]
			FRANKLIN, Aretha Born on 3/25/42 in Memphis; raised in Buffalo and Detroit. Daughter of Rev. Cecil L. Franklin, pastor of New Bethel Church in Detroit. Taught to sing gospel at age 9 by Rev. James Cleveland (died 2/9/91, age 59). First recorded for JVB/Battle in 1956. Signed to Columbia Records in 1960 by John Hammond, then dramatic turn in style and success after signing with Atlantic and working with producer Jerry Wexler. Appeared in the 1980 movie *The Blues Brothers*. Winner of 15 Grammy Awards. In 1987, became first woman to be inducted into the Rock and Roll Hall of Fame. Won 1990 Living Legends Grammy Award. The all-time Queen of Soul Music.	
4/29/67	**2**(3)	28	● **1. I Never Loved A Man The Way I Love You** *I Never Loved A Man (The Way I Love You)* (9)/*Respect* (1)	Atlantic 8139
9/2/67	**5**	18	**2. Aretha Arrives** *Baby I Love You* (4)	Atlantic 8150
2/24/68	**2**(2)	33	● **3. Aretha: Lady Soul** *A Natural Woman* (8)/*Chain Of Fools* (2)/ *(Sweet Sweet Baby) Since You've Been Gone* (5)	Atlantic 8176
7/20/68	**3**	20	● **4. Aretha Now** *Think* (7)/*I Say A Little Prayer* (10)	Atlantic 8186
12/7/68	**13**	9	5. Aretha In Paris [L] recorded at the Olympia Theatre in Paris on 5/7/68	Atlantic 8207
2/22/69	**15**	12	6. Aretha Franklin: Soul '69	Atlantic 8212
7/26/69	**18**	11	7. Aretha's Gold [G] *The House That Jack Built* (6)	Atlantic 8227
2/21/70	**17**	13	8. This Girl's In Love With You	Atlantic 8248
9/26/70	**25**	8	9. Spirit In The Dark	Atlantic 8265
6/12/71	**7**	18	● **10. Aretha Live At Fillmore West** [L]	Atlantic 7205
10/9/71	**19**	10	11. Aretha's Greatest Hits [G] *Bridge Over Troubled Water* (6)/*Spanish Harlem* (2)	Atlantic 8295
2/26/72	**11**	17	● **12. Young, Gifted & Black** *Rock Steady* (9)/*Day Dreaming* (5)	Atlantic 7213

DATE	POS	WKS	ARTIST—RECORD TITLE	LABEL & NO.
7/1/72	7	11	▲² **13. Amazing Grace** [L] with James Cleveland & The Southern California Community Choir	Atlantic 906 [2]
8/11/73	30	7	14. Hey Now Hey (The Other Side Of The Sky)	Atlantic 7265
3/30/74	14	11	15. Let Me In Your Life *Until You Come Back To Me (That's What I'm Gonna Do)* (3)	Atlantic 7292
7/4/76	18	11	● 16. Sparkle [S]	Atlantic 18176
9/26/81	36	3	17. Love All The Hurt Away	Arista 9552
9/4/82	23	9	● 18. Jump To It	Arista 9602
8/20/83	36	3	19. Get It Right *above 2 produced by Luther Vandross*	Arista 8019
8/10/85	13	35	▲ 20. Who's Zoomin' Who? *Freeway Of Love* (3)/*Who's Zoomin' Who* (7)	Arista 8286
12/13/86	32	8	● 21. Aretha *I Knew You Were Waiting (For Me)* (1-with George Michael)	Arista 8442
			FREBERG, Stan Born on 8/7/26 in Pasadena, California. Did cartoon voices for major movie studios. Launched highly successful advertising career in the early '60s; winner of 21 Clio Awards (outstanding achievement award of the radio and TV ad industry).	
7/24/61	34	3	Stan Freberg Presents The United States Of America [C] with Jesse White and Paul Frees; musical score by Billy May	Capitol 1573
			FREDDIE AND THE DREAMERS Lead singer Freddie Garrity was born on 11/14/40 in Manchester, England. Formed The Dreamers in 1961 with Derek Quinn (lead guitar), Roy Crewsdon (guitar), Peter Birrell (bass) and Bernie Dwyer (drums).	
5/22/65	19	7	Freddie & The Dreamers	Mercury 61017
			FREE British rock band formed in 1968: Paul Rodgers (vocals), Paul Kossoff (guitar), Simon Kirke (drums) and Andy Fraser (bass). Kossoff and Fraser left in 1972; replaced by Tetsu Yamauchi (bass; later with Faces) and John "Rabbit" Bundrick (keyboards). Kossoff (died 3/19/76 of drug-induced heart failure) formed Back Street Crawler. Rodgers and Kirke formed Bad Company in 1974. Rodgers was lead singer of The Firm (1984-85) and The Law (since 1991).	
9/26/70	17	11	Fire And Water *All Right Now* (4)	A&M 4268
			FREHLEY, Ace Born on 4/27/51 in the Bronx. Lead guitarist of Kiss until 1983. Formed own band, Frehley's Comet.	
11/25/78	26	10	▲ Ace Frehley	Casablanca 7121
			FREY, Glenn Born on 11/6/48 in Detroit. Singer/songwriter/guitarist. Founding member of the Eagles. Appeared in episodes of TV's "Miami Vice" and "Wiseguy"; starred in short-lived CBS series "South of Sunset" in 1993.	
7/24/82	32	11	● 1. No Fun Aloud	Asylum 60129
8/25/84	22	14	● 2. The Allnighter	MCA 5501
10/8/88	36	7	3. Soul Searchin'	MCA 6239

DATE	POS	WKS	ARTIST—RECORD TITLE	LABEL & NO.
			FRIENDS OF DISTINCTION, The	
			Los Angeles-based, soul-MOR group. Original lineup: Floyd Butler, Harry Elston, Jessica Cleaves and Barbara Jean Love. Butler and Elston were in The Hi-Fi's with LaMonte McLemore and Marilyn McCoo (later with The 5th Dimension).	
7/5/69	**35**	3	Grazin'	RCA 4149
			Grazing In The Grass (3)	
			FRIJID PINK	
			Rock group formed in Detroit: Kelly Green (lead singer), Gary Thompson (guitar), Tom Beaudry (bass) and Rich Stevens (drums).	
3/7/70	**11**	12	Frijid Pink	Parrot 71033
			House Of The Rising Sun (7)	
			FRYE, David	
			Comedian/impressionist. Best known for his impression of President Nixon.	
1/10/70	**19**	8	I Am The President [C]	Elektra 75006
			FUNKADELIC	
			Funk aggregation formed in 1968. Consisted of The Parliaments plus a backing band. While recording for Westbound, group also recorded for Invictus as Parliament in 1971. Formed corporation, "A Parliafunka-delicament Thang," through which they recorded under both names. By 1974, leader/producer George Clinton reorganized the Parliament/Funkadelic corporation to include varying membership. Three of the original members of The Parliaments left the corporation in 1977; recorded as Funkadelic for LAX Records in 1981, not in association with Clinton. Also see Parliament.	
10/7/78	**16**	9	▲ 1. One Nation Under A Groove	Warner 3209
10/20/79	**18**	6	● 2. Uncle Jam Wants You	Warner 3371

G

DATE	POS	WKS	ARTIST—RECORD TITLE	LABEL & NO.
			GABRIEL, Peter	
			Born on 2/13/50 in London. Lead singer of Genesis from 1966-75. Scored movies *Birdy* and *The Last Temptation of Christ*. In 1982, financed the World of Music Arts and Dance (WOMAD) festival.	
4/30/77	**38**	2	1. Peter Gabriel	Atco 147
7/5/80	**22**	14	2. Peter Gabriel	Mercury 3848
10/16/82	**28**	12	● 3. Peter Gabriel (Security)	Geffen 2011
6/14/86	**2 (3)**	47	▲⁴ **4. So**	Geffen 24088
			Sledgehammer (1)/*Big Time* (8)	
10/17/92	**2 (1)**	7	▲ **5. Us**	Geffen 24473
10/1/94	**23**	2	6. Secret World Live [L]	Geffen 24722 [2]
			recorded in Modena, Italy, on 11/16-17/93	
			GANG STARR	
			Brooklyn-based rap duo: Christopher "DJ Premier" Martin and Keith "The Guru" Elam.	
3/26/94	**25**	2	Hard To Earn	Chrysalis 28435

Gloria Estefan's steady mid-1980s success with the Miami Sound Machine resulted in Columbia's value-packed *Greatest Hits*, a 14-track compilation featuring the Cuban-born singer's best-known work. Despite a serious tour-bus accident in 1990, the much-loved singer quickly recovered from a back injury to release 1991's *Into The Light*.

The Everly Brothers' historic and influential work was lovingly compiled on Rhino Records' spectacular compilation *Heartaches & Harmonies*, issued in 1994. The 4-CD set featured tracks the pair had recorded for Columbia, Cadence, Warner Brothers, RCA and Mercury.

Percy Faith's smooth orchestral sound, typified by the 1967 album, *Today's Themes For Young Lovers*, was a dominant chart presence for nearly 20 years. Between 1956 and 1972, the Canadian-born bandleader released 30 charting albums for Columbia.

Ferrante & Teicher, a piano duo with considerable MOR appeal, blazed its way through the '60s via 24 charting albums. 1965's *Only The Best* featured instrumental versions of "Chim Chim Cher-ee," "Cast Your Fate To The Wind" and "Fiddler On The Roof," among other favorites.

Fine Young Cannibals' double-platinum 1989 album, *The Raw & The Cooked*, led many to expect big things from the persuasive British trio. Oddly, despite that success, the group never released a follow-up album.

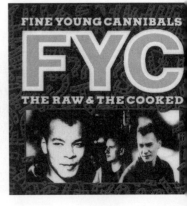

Fleetwood Mac's all-time sales pinnacle, *Rumours*, one of the biggest-selling records in pop history, held the No. 1 slot for an astounding 31 weeks in 1977. It was only the second of the long-lived band's albums to feature Lindsey Buckingham and Stevie Nicks.

The 4 Seasons' high-pitched vocals took America by storm in the early '60s. *Sherry & 11 Others*, which featured two gigantic No. 1 hits: "Sherry" and "Big Girls Don't Cry." The album climbed to No. 6 on the strength of that memorable hit.

The Four Tops, one of Motown's most compelling groups of the '60s, featured the gripping lead vocals of Levi Stubbs. Something of a career diversion, the quartet's 1967 album, *On Broadway*, featured Stubbs singing the likes of "Mame," "The Sound Of Music" and "My Way."

Peter Frampton's phenomenal success with *Frampton Comes Alive* brought him tremendous fame; the album stayed at No. 1 for 10 weeks in 1976. Eventually, however, it became something of a millstone from which his career never recovered. Within 10 years, the guitarist was a member of David Bowie's road band.

Connie Francis's 1961 collection, *More Greatest Hits*, contained that year's Top 5 hit "Where The Boys Are," taken from the film of the same name. The track was the tenth Top 10 single that Francis, an enormously popular singer, had produced in less than three years.

Aretha Franklin's all-time highest-charting album, 1967's *I Never Loved A Man the Way I Love You*, was considerably boosted by the powerhouse presence of her No. 1 smash hit, "Respect." Within four months, Atlantic Records shipped out *Aretha Arrives*, the suitably titled Top 5 follow-up.

DATE	POS	WKS	ARTIST—RECORD TITLE	LABEL & NO.
			GAP BAND, The	
			Soul trio from Tulsa, Oklahoma, consisting of brothers Charles, Ronnie and Robert Wilson. Group named for three streets in Tulsa: Greenwood, Archer and Pine. Cousins of Bootsy Collins. Charles is member of The Eurythmics' backing band.	
2/14/81	**16**	17	▲ 1. The Gap Band III	Mercury 4003
6/26/82	**14**	17	▲ 2. Gap Band IV	Total Exp. 3001
9/24/83	**28**	7	● 3. Gap Band V — Jammin'	Total Exp. 3004
			GARCIA, Jerry	
			Born on 8/1/42 in San Francisco. Founder/lead guitarist of the Grateful Dead. Before forming The Grateful Dead, played banjo in Mother McCree's Uptown Jug Champions. Produced and acted in the movie *Hells Angels Forever*. Ben & Jerry's Cherry Garcia ice cream named after him. Married moviemaker Deborah Koons on 2/14/94.	
2/12/72	**35**	3	Garcia	Warner 2582
			GARDNER, Dave	
			Comedian "Brother Dave" born on 6/11/26 in Jackson, Tennessee. Now deceased.	
6/20/60	**5**	28	**1. Rejoice, Dear Hearts!** [C]	RCA 2083
8/29/60	**5**	19	**2. Kick Thy Own Self** [C]	RCA 2239
9/18/61	**15**	10	3. Ain't That Weird? [C]	RCA 2335
5/18/63	**28**	5	4. It Don't Make No Difference [C]	Capitol 1867
			GARFUNKEL, Art	
			Born on 11/5/41 in Queens, New York. Half of Simon & Garfunkel duo. Appeared in movies *Catch 22*, *Carnal Knowledge* and *Bad Timing*. Has Master's degree in mathematics from Columbia University.	
10/6/73	**5**	13	● 1. Angel Clare	Columbia 31474
			All I Know (9)	
11/1/75	**7**	15	▲ 2. Breakaway	Columbia 33700
			My Little Town (9-Simon & Garfunkel)	
2/11/78	**19**	9	● 3. Watermark	Columbia 34975
			GARLAND, Judy	
			Born Frances Gumm on 6/10/22 in Grand Rapids, Minnesota; died on 1/22/69. Star of MGM movie musicals from 1935-54. Most famous movie role was Dorothy in 1939's *The Wizard of Oz*. Hosted own TV variety series 1963-64. Married to director Vincente Minnelli; their daughter is Liza Minnelli.	
10/29/55	**5**	7	**1. Miss Show Business**	Capitol 676
11/10/56	**17**	5	2. Judy	Capitol 734
6/17/57	**17**	3	3. Alone	Capitol 835
8/7/61	**1**(13)	73	● **4. Judy At Carnegie Hall** [L]	Capitol 1569 [2]
			1961 Album of the Year Grammy Award	
9/8/62	**33**	5	5. The Garland Touch	Capitol 1710
			GARNER, Erroll	
			Born on 6/15/21 in Pittsburgh; died on 1/2/77. Jazz pianist/composer. No formal piano training; could not read music. Composer of "Misty," later a hit for Johnny Mathis and others.	
11/25/57	**16**	2	1. Other Voices [I]	Columbia 1014
3/10/58	**12**	7	2. Concert By The Sea [I-L]	Columbia 883
			recorded in 1956 in Carmel, California	
6/26/61	**35**	2	3. Dreamstreet [I]	ABC-Para. 365

DATE	POS	WKS	ARTIST—RECORD TITLE	LABEL & NO.
			GARRETT, Leif	
			Born on 11/8/61 in Hollywood. Began movie career in 1969. Appeared in all three *Walking Tall* movies, as well as *Macon County Line*, *Bob and Carol and Ted and Alice* and *The Outsiders*.	
2/4/78	**37**	3	● 1. Leif Garrett	Atlantic 19152
1/20/79	**34**	5	● 2. Feel The Need	Scotti Br. 7100
			I Was Made For Dancin' (10)	
			GARRETT, Tommy, 50 Guitars Of	
			Born in 1939 in Dallas. A&R man/producer for Liberty, 1958-66; known as "Snuff" Garrett. 50 Guitars featured guitar solos by Tommy Tedesco.	
1/20/62	**36**	1	50 Guitars Go South Of The Border [I]	Liberty 14005
			GARY, John	
			Born in Watertown, New York, on 11/29/32. Singer on Don McNeill's radio program, *Breakfast Club*.	
11/30/63	**19**	27	1. Catch A Rising Star	RCA 2745
3/7/64	**16**	10	2. Encore	RCA 2804
3/20/65	**17**	8	3. A Little Bit Of Heaven	RCA 2994
8/14/65	**11**	13	4. The Nearness Of You	RCA 3349
12/4/65	**21**	7	5. Your All-Time Favorite Songs	RCA 3411
			GAYE, Marvin	
			Born Marvin Pentz Gay, Jr., on 4/2/39 in Washington, D.C. Fatally shot by his father after a quarrel on 4/1/84 in Los Angeles. Sang in his father's Apostolic church. In vocal groups The Rainbows and The Marquees. Joined Harvey Fuqua in the re-formed Moonglows. To Detroit in 1960. Session work as drummer at Motown; married to Berry Gordy's sister Anna, 1961-75. First recorded under own name for Tamla in 1961. In seclusion for several months following the death of Tammi Terrell, 1970. Problems with drugs and the IRS led to his moving to Europe for three years. Inducted into the Rock and Roll Hall of Fame in 1987.	
6/28/69	**33**	4	1. M.P.G.	Tamla 292
			Too Busy Thinking About My Baby (4)/ *That's The Way Love Is* (7)	
6/26/71	**6**	27	● **2. What's Going On**	Tamla 310
			What's Going On (2)/*Mercy Mercy Me* (4)/ *Inner City Blues* (9)	
1/13/73	**14**	11	3. Trouble Man [S-I]	Tamla 322
			includes 1 vocal by Marvin *Trouble Man* (7)	
9/15/73	**2**(1)	18	**4. Let's Get It On**	Tamla 329
			Let's Get It On (1)	
12/8/73	**26**	5	5. Diana & Marvin	Motown 803
			DIANA ROSS & MARVIN GAYE	
7/27/74	**8**	13	**6. Marvin Gaye Live!** [L]	Tamla 333
4/10/76	**4**	15	**7. I Want You**	Tamla 342
4/16/77	**3**	19	**8. Marvin Gaye Live At The London Palladium** [L]	Tamla 352 [2]
			Got To Give It Up (1)	
1/20/79	**26**	7	9. Here, My Dear	Tamla 364 [2]
2/28/81	**32**	4	10. In Our Lifetime	Tamla 374
11/20/82	**7**	13	▲² **11. Midnight Love**	Columbia 38197
			Sexual Healing (3)	

DATE	POS	WKS	ARTIST—RECORD TITLE	LABEL & NO.
			GAYLE, Crystal	
			Born Brenda Gail Webb on 1/9/51 in Paintsville, Kentucky; raised in Wabash, Indiana. Youngest sister of Loretta Lynn. First country artist to tour China (1979).	
10/22/77	12	10	▲ 1. We Must Believe In Magic	United Art. 771
			Don't It Make My Brown Eyes Blue (2)	
11/24/79	36	4	● 2. Miss The Mississippi	Columbia 36203
			GAYNOR, Gloria	
			Born on 9/7/49 in Newark, New Jersey. Disco singer. With The Soul Satisfiers in 1971.	
2/22/75	25	5	1. Never Can Say Goodbye	MGM 4982
			Never Can Say Goodbye (9)	
2/3/79	4	15	▲ 2. Love Tracks	Polydor 6184
			I Will Survive (1)	
			GEILS, J., Band	
			Formed in Boston in 1967, guitarist Jerome Geils led rock band consisting of Peter "Wolf" Blankfield (vocals), "Magic Dick" Salwitz (harmonica), Seth Justman (keyboards), Danny Klein (bass) and Stephen Jo Bladd (drums). First recorded for Atlantic in 1969. Wolf left for solo career in Fall 1983.	
5/19/73	10	14	● 1. Bloodshot	Atlantic 7260
11/23/74	26	4	2. Nightmares ... and other tales from the vinyl jungle	Atlantic 18107
10/25/75	36	2	3. Hotline	Atlantic 18147
6/26/76	40	1	4. Live — Blow Your Face Out [L]	Atlantic 507 [2]
3/8/80	18	17	● 5. Love Stinks	EMI America 17016
11/21/81	1 (4)	29	▲ 6. Freeze-Frame	EMI America 17062
			Centerfold (1)/*Freeze-Frame* (4)	
12/18/82	23	10	● 7. Showtime! [L]	EMI America 17087
			GENERAL PUBLIC	
			Fronted by former English Beat vocalists Dave Wakeling and Ranking Roger (Roger Charley). Disbanded in March 1987. Roger recorded solo in 1988; Wakeling, in 1991. Roger and Wakeling reunited in 1994.	
1/19/85	26	11	... All The Rage	I.R.S. 70046
			GENESIS	
			Formed as progressive-rock group in England in 1967. Consisted of Peter Gabriel (lead vocals), Anthony Phillips (guitar), Tony Banks (keyboards), Michael Rutherford (guitar, bass) and Chris Stewart (drums; replaced by John Silver in 1968, then John Mayhew in 1969). Phillips and Mayhew left in 1970; replaced by Steve Hackett (guitar) and Phil Collins (drums). Gabriel left in June 1975, with Collins replacing him as new lead singer. Hackett went solo in 1977, leaving group as a trio: Collins, Rutherford and Banks. Added regular members for touring: Americans Chester Thompson (drums), in 1977 and Daryl Stuermer (guitar) in 1978. Collins also recorded in jazz-fusion group Brand X. Rutherford also in own group, Mike + The Mechanics, formed in 1985. Hackett later formed group GTR.	
5/1/76	31	6	● 1. A Trick Of The Tail	Atco 129
2/19/77	26	8	● 2. Wind & Wuthering	Atco 144
4/29/78	14	8	▲ 3. And Then There Were Three ...	Atlantic 19173
			from here on, group consists of Banks, Collins and Rutherford	
5/3/80	11	21	▲ 4. Duke	Atlantic 16014
10/24/81	7	29	▲² 5. Abacab	Atlantic 19313
7/10/82	10	11	● 6. Three Sides Live [L]	Atlantic 2000 [2]
			side 4: studio cuts from 1979-81	

DATE	POS	WKS	ARTIST—RECORD TITLE	LABEL & NO.
11/5/83	**9**	27	▲³ **7. Genesis**	Atlantic 80116
			That's All! (6)	
6/28/86	**3**	61	▲⁵ **8. Invisible Touch**	Atlantic 81641
			Invisible Touch (1)/*Throwing It All Away* (4)/	
			Land Of Confusion (4)/*Tonight, Tonight, Tonight* (3)/	
			In Too Deep (3)	
11/30/91	**4**	45	▲³ **9. We Can't Dance**	Atlantic 82344
			I Can't Dance (7)	
12/19/92	**35**	5	● 10. Live/The Way We Walk — Volume One: The Shorts [L]	Atlantic 82452
2/27/93	**20**	2	11. Live/The Way We Walk — Volume Two: The Longs [L]	Atlantic 82461
			above 2 recorded during the 1992 *We Can't Dance* tour	

GENTRY, Bobbie

Born Roberta Streeter on 7/27/44 in Chickasaw County, Mississippi; raised in Greenwood, Mississippi. Singer/songwriter. Won 1967 Best New Artist Grammy Award. Married singer Jim Stafford on 10/15/78.

DATE	POS	WKS	ARTIST—RECORD TITLE	LABEL & NO.
9/23/67	**1**(2)	18	● **1. Ode To Billie Joe**	Capitol 2830
			Ode To Billie Joe (1)	
11/9/68	**11**	13	● 2. Bobbie Gentry & Glen Campbell	Capitol 2928
			BOBBIE GENTRY & GLEN CAMPBELL	

GEORGIA SATELLITES

Rock quartet formed in Atlanta in 1980, led by dual guitarists/vocalists Dan Baird and Rick Richards, with bassist Rich Price and drummer Mauro Magellan (born Rio de Janeiro). By 1992, Baird left and Richards joined Izzy Stradlin & The Ju Ju Hounds.

DATE	POS	WKS	ARTIST—RECORD TITLE	LABEL & NO.
12/20/86	**5**	20	▲ **Georgia Satellites**	Elektra 60496
			Keep Your Hands To Yourself (2)	

GERARDO

Born Gerardo Mejia III in Guayaquil, Ecuador, on 4/16/65. Rapper/actor. To Glendale, California, at age 12. Raps in Spanglish (half Spanish, half English). Appeared in the movies *Can't Buy Me Love* and *Colors*.

DATE	POS	WKS	ARTIST—RECORD TITLE	LABEL & NO.
5/25/91	**36**	5	● Mo' Ritmo	Interscope 91619
			ritmo is Spanish for rhythm	
			Rico Suave (7)	

GERRY AND THE PACEMAKERS

Pop-rock group formed in Liverpool, England, in 1959: Gerry Marsden (born 9/24/42; vocals, guitar), Leslie Maguire (piano), Les Chadwick (bass) and Freddie Marsden (drums). The Marsden brothers had been in skiffle bands; Gerry had own rock band Mars-Bars. Signed in 1962 by The Beatles' manager Brian Epstein.

DATE	POS	WKS	ARTIST—RECORD TITLE	LABEL & NO.
8/15/64	**29**	5	1. Don't Let The Sun Catch You Crying	Laurie 2024
			Don't Let The Sun Catch You Crying (4)/	
			How Do You Do It? (9)	
4/3/65	**13**	12	2. Ferry Cross The Mersey [S]	United Art. 6387
			9 of 12 songs by Gerry & The Pacemakers (they star in the movie, which was set in Liverpool)	
			Ferry Cross The Mersey (6)	

DATE	POS	WKS	ARTIST—RECORD TITLE	LABEL & NO.
			GETO BOYS, The	
			Houston-based rap outfit: Richard "Bushwick Bill" Shaw, William "Willie Dee" Dennis, Brad "Scarface" Jordan & Collins "DJ Ready Red" Lyaseth (left group in early 1991; replaced by Big Mike). Group changed name in 1990 from The Ghetto Boys to The Geto Boys. Shaw, a Jamaican-born dwarf, lost his right eye in a shooting on 5/10/91.	
7/27/91	**24**	16	▲ 1. We Can't Be Stopped	Rap-A-Lot 57161
3/27/93	**11**	8	● 2. Till Death Do Us Part	Rap-A-Lot 57191
			GETZ, Stan	
			Born Stan Gayetsky on 2/2/27 in Philadelphia. Died of liver cancer on 6/6/91. Jazz tenor saxophonist. With Stan Kenton (1944-45), Jimmy Dorsey (1945-46), Benny Goodman (1946) and Woody Herman (1947-49). Seventeen-time winner of *Down Beat* polls as top tenor saxophonist. Leader of the bossa nova movement of the '60s.	
10/13/62	**1**(1)	44	**1. Jazz Samba** [I]	Verve 8432
			STAN GETZ/CHARLIE BYRD M (guitar)	
1/5/63	**13**	20	2. Big Band Bossa Nova [I]	Verve 8494
			with The Gary McFarland Orchestra	
6/20/64	**2**(2)	50	● **3. Getz/Gilberto**	Verve 8545
			STAN GETZ/JOAO GILBERTO M (Brazilian singer/guitarist; married to Astrud Gilberto); 1964 Album of the Year Grammy Award *The Girl From Ipanema* (5-vocal by Astrud Gilberto)	
2/13/65	**24**	17	4. Getz Au Go Go [L]	Verve 8600
			THE NEW STAN GETZ QUARTET featuring ASTRUD GILBERTO	
			GIBB, Andy	
			Born Andrew Roy Gibb on 3/5/58 in Manchester, England. Died on 3/10/88 of an inflammatory heart virus in Oxford, England. Moved to Australia when six months old, then back to England at age nine. Youngest brother of Barry, Robin and Maurice Gibb, The Bee Gees. Hosted TV's "Solid Gold" from 1981-82.	
8/27/77	**19**	18	▲ 1. Flowing Rivers	RSO 3019
			I Just Want To Be Your Everything (1)/ *(Love Is) Thicker Than Water* (1)	
6/24/78	**7**	15	▲ **2. Shadow Dancing**	RSO 3034
			Shadow Dancing (1)/*An Everlasting Love* (5)/ *(Our Love) Don't Throw It All Away* (9)	
3/8/80	**21**	7	● 3. After Dark	RSO 3069
			Desire (4)	
			GIBSON, Debbie	
			Born on 8/31/70 in Long Island, New York. Singer/songwriter/pianist. Playing piano since age five and songwriting since age six. In 1991, played Eponine in *Les Miserables* on Broadway.	
12/19/87	**7**	45	▲³ **1. Out Of The Blue**	Atlantic 81780
			Only In My Dreams (4)/*Shake Your Love* (4)/*Out Of The Blue* (3)/*Foolish Beat* (1)	
2/18/89	**1**(5)	25	▲² **2. Electric Youth**	Atlantic 81932
			Lost In Your Eyes (1)	
			GILBERTO, Astrud — see GETZ, Stan	
			GILBERTO, Joao — see GETZ, Stan	

DATE	POS	WKS	ARTIST—RECORD TITLE	LABEL & NO.
			GILDER, Nick	
			Born on 11/7/51 in London. Moved to Vancouver, Canada, at age 10. Founding member of rock band Sweeney Todd.	
11/11/78	33	5	City Nights	Chrysalis 1202
			Hot Child In The City (1)	
			GILL, Johnny	
			Born on 5/22/66 in Washington, D.C. Sang in family gospel group, Wings of Faith, from age five. Joined New Edition in 1988. His brother Randy and cousin Jermaine Mickey are members of II D Extreme.	
5/12/90	8	25	▲² **1. Johnny Gill**	Motown 6283
			Rub You The Right Way (3)/*My, My, My* (10)	
6/26/93	14	4	● 2. Provocative	Motown 6355
			GILL, Vince	
			Born on 4/12/57 in Norman, Oklahoma. Country singer/guitarist. Member of Pure Prairie League from 1979-83. Married to Janis Oliver of The Sweethearts of the Rodeo.	
12/21/91	37	4	▲² 1. Pocket Full Of Gold	MCA 10140
9/19/92	10	25	▲³ **2. I Still Believe In You**	MCA 10630
12/4/93	14	6	▲ 3. Let There Be Peace On Earth [X]	MCA 10877
			Christmas charts: 1/'93, 6/'94	
6/25/94	6	14	▲ **4. When Love Finds You**	MCA 11047
			GILMER, Jimmy, & The Fireballs	
			Rock-and-roll band formed while high-school students in Raton, New Mexico. Lead vocalist Chuck Tharp was replaced in 1960 by Jimmy Gilmer, who was introduced to group by producer Norman Petty at his famed Clovis, New Mexico, studio.	
11/30/63	26	5	Sugar Shack	Dot 25545
			Sugar Shack (1)	
			GILMOUR, David	
			Born on 3/6/47 in Cambridge, England. Guitarist/vocalist with Pink Floyd.	
8/5/78	29	6	1. David Gilmour	Columbia 35388
4/21/84	32	10	2. About Face	Columbia 39296
			GIN BLOSSOMS	
			Tempe, Arizona, outfit: Robin Wilson (vocals), Jesse Valenzuela, Bill Leen, Scott Johnson and Phillip Rhodes. Early guitarist Doug Hopkins, writer of "Hey Jealousy" and "Found Out About You," died of self-inflicted bullet wound on 12/5/93 (age 32).	
8/28/93	30	17	▲² New Miserable Experience	A&M 5403
			2 covers released	
			GIUFFRIA	
			California-based rock quintet led by Gregg Giuffria (keyboardist with Angel) and David Glen Eisley. Gregg and member Chuck Wright joined House of Lords in 1988.	
1/26/85	26	7	Giuffria	MCA 5524
			GLASER, Tompall — see CONCEPT ALBUMS	
			GLASS TIGER	
			Canadian rock quintet: Alan Frew (vocals), Sam Reid (keyboards), Al Connelly (guitar), Wayne Parker (bass) and Michael Hanson (drums).	
10/4/86	27	28	● The Thin Red Line	Manhattan 53032
			Don't Forget Me (When I'm Gone) (2)/*Someday* (7)	

DATE	POS	WKS	ARTIST—RECORD TITLE	LABEL & NO.

GLEASON, Jackie

Born Herbert John Gleason on 2/26/16 in Brooklyn; died of cancer on 6/24/87. Star of stage and screen before enormous popularity on TV's "The Honeymooners," 1955-56, and his own CBS-TV variety series. From 1953-56, had 11 consecutive Top 10 hit albums of lushly recorded orchestral "mood music." His daughter is actress Linda Miller, whose son is actor Jason Patric. His albums featured dreamy "mood music" played by studio orchestras, conducted by Gleason with trumpet solos by Bobby Hackett and Pee Wee Erwin; Gleason wrote much of the music.

DATE	POS	WKS	ARTIST—RECORD TITLE	LABEL & NO.
3/5/55	**5**	16	**1. Music To Remember Her** [I]	Capitol 570
6/25/55	**1**(2)	23	**2. Lonesome Echo** [I]	Capitol 627
11/12/55	**2**(2)	11	**3. Romantic Jazz** [I]	Capitol 568
1/28/56	**7**	7	**4. Music For Lovers Only/Music To Make You Misty** [I-R]	Capitol 475 [2]
			reissue of albums from 1953 and 1954	
2/25/56	**8**	5	**5. Music To Change Her Mind** [I]	Capitol 632
6/9/56	**10**	10	**6. Night Winds** [I]	Capitol 717
12/8/56	**16**	3	7. Merry Christmas [X-I]	Capitol 758
			Christmas charts: 25/'63, 70/'66, 32/'67	
8/26/57	**13**	2	● 8. Music For The Love Hours [I]	Capitol 816
9/9/57	**16**	10	9. Velvet Brass [I]	Capitol 859
12/9/57	**14**	4	10. Jackie Gleason presents "Oooo!" [I]	Capitol 905

GODFREY, Arthur — see QUINN, Carmel

GODLEY & CREME

Kevin Godley (born 10/7/45, Manchester, England) and Lol Creme (born 9/19/47, Manchester, England) formed duo after leaving British group 10cc. Before 10cc, both were with Hotlegs.

DATE	POS	WKS	ARTIST—RECORD TITLE	LABEL & NO.
9/28/85	**37**	3	The History Mix Volume 1	Polydor 825981

GO-GO'S

Female rock group formed in 1978 in Los Angeles, consisting of Belinda Carlisle (vocals), Jane Wiedlin (guitar), Charlotte Caffey (guitar), Kathy Valentine (bass) and Gina Schock (drums). Disbanded in 1984. Reunion tour in 1990. Caffey formed The Graces in 1989.

DATE	POS	WKS	ARTIST—RECORD TITLE	LABEL & NO.
9/26/81	**1**(6)	38	▲² **1. Beauty And The Beat**	I.R.S. 70021
			We Got The Beat (2)	
8/21/82	**8**	10	● **2. Vacation**	I.R.S. 70031
			Vacation (8)	
4/21/84	**18**	18	3. Talk Show	I.R.S. 70041

GOLD, Marty, and His Orchestra

Born on 12/26/15 in New York City. Composer/conductor/pianist.

DATE	POS	WKS	ARTIST—RECORD TITLE	LABEL & NO.
4/27/63	**10**	11	**Soundpower!** [I]	RCA 2620

GOLDEN EARRING

Rock band from The Netherlands: Barry Hay (vocals), George Kooymans (guitars, vocals), Cesar Zuiderwijk (drums) and Rinus Gerritsen (bass, keyboards). Supported by keyboardist/arranger Robert Jan Stips through 1982.

DATE	POS	WKS	ARTIST—RECORD TITLE	LABEL & NO.
6/15/74	**12**	13	● 1. Moontan	Track 396
2/26/83	**24**	12	2. Cut	21 Records 9004
			Twilight Zone (10)	

DATE	POS	WKS	ARTIST—RECORD TITLE	LABEL & NO.
			GOLDSBORO, Bobby	
			Born on 1/18/41 in Marianna, Florida. Singer/songwriter/guitarist. To Dothan, Alabama, in 1956. Toured with Roy Orbison, 1962-64. Own syndicated TV show from 1972-75, "The Bobby Goldsboro Show."	
5/4/68	5	22	● **Honey**	United Art. 6642
			Honey (1)	
			GOODMAN, Benny	
			Born on 5/30/09 in Chicago. Died on 6/13/86 of an apparent heart attack. Nicknamed "King of Swing." Clarinetist/big band leader since the '30s. Fletcher Henderson arranged many of his early '30s hits. Won 1986 Lifetime Achievement Grammy Award.	
3/19/55	7	16	**1. B.G. In Hi-Fi** [I]	Capitol 565
3/24/56	4	10	**2. The Benny Goodman Story** [S-I]	Decca 8252/3 [2]
			Steve Allen portrays Goodman in the movie, although Goodman and his musicians play the music	
			GORE, Lesley	
			Born on 5/2/46 in New York City; raised in Tenafly, New Jersey. Discovered by Quincy Jones while singing at a hotel in Manhattan. In the movies *Girls on the Beach*, *Ski Party* and *The T.A.M.I. Show*.	
7/27/63	24	7	**I'll Cry If I Want To**	Mercury 60805
			It's My Party (1)/*Judy's Turn To Cry* (5)	
			GORME, Eydie	
			Born on 8/16/31 in New York City. Vocalist with the big bands of Tommy Tucker and Tex Beneke in the late '40s. Featured on Steve Allen's "The Tonight Show" from 1953. Married Steve Lawrence on 12/29/57. They recorded as the duo Parker & Penny in 1979.	
5/6/57	14	10	1. Eydie Gorme	ABC-Para. 150
10/28/57	19	4	2. Eydie Swings The Blues	ABC-Para. 192
3/31/58	19	4	3. Eydie Gorme Vamps The Roaring 20's	ABC-Para. 218
11/3/58	20	1	4. Eydie In Love ...	ABC-Para. 246
4/27/63	22	9	5. Blame It On The Bossa Nova	Columbia 8812
			Blame It On The Bossa Nova (7)	
6/4/66	22	9	6. Don't Go To Strangers	Columbia 9276
			GOULD, Morton, And His Orchestra	
			Born on 12/10/13 in Long Island, New York. Composer os semi-classical music; co-wrote two Broadway musicals. Conductor/arranger on NBC radio for years.	
11/9/59	5	33	**1. Tchaikovsky: 1812 Overture/Ravel: Bolero** [I]	RCA 2345
7/18/60	3	25	**2. Grofe: Grand Canyon Suite/Beethoven:**	RCA 2433
			Wellington's Victory [I]	
			GOULET, Robert	
			Born on 11/26/33 in Lawrence, Massachusetts. Began concert career in Edmonton, Canada. Broadway/movie/TV actor. Launched career as Sir Lancelot in hit Broadway musical *Camelot*. Won 1962 Best New Artist Grammy Award.	
11/10/62	20	14	1. Two Of Us	Columbia 8626
1/12/63	9	27	**2. Sincerely Yours ...**	Columbia 8731
5/4/63	11	14	3. The Wonderful World Of Love	Columbia 8793
11/9/63	16	10	4. Robert Goulet In Person [L]	Columbia 8888
			recorded at the Chicago Opera House	

DATE	POS	WKS	ARTIST—RECORD TITLE	LABEL & NO.
6/27/64	**31**	7	5. Manhattan Tower/The Man Who Loves Manhattan composed and conducted by Gordon Jenkins	Columbia 2450
1/23/65	**5**	18	• **6. My Love Forgive Me**	Columbia 9096
10/9/65	**31**	5	7. Summer Sounds	Columbia 9180
1/29/66	**33**	4	8. Robert Goulet On Broadway	Columbia 9218
			GQ	
			Bronx soul group: Emmanuel Rahiem LeBlanc (lead singer), Keith Crier, Herb Lane and Paul Service. Group became a trio with the departure of Service in 1980.	
4/21/79	**13**	19	▲ Disco Nights	Arista 4225
			GRAHAM, Larry	
			Born on 8/14/46 in Beaumont, Texas. To Oakland at the age of two. Bass player with Sly & The Family Stone from 1966-72. In 1973, formed Hot Chocolate (not to be confused with English group of the same name); band later renamed Graham Central Station. Consisted of Graham (lead), Hershall Kennedy and Robert Sam (keyboards), Willie Sparks and Patrice Banks (percussion), and David Vega (guitar). Graham went solo in 1980.	
8/30/75	**22**	6	• 1. Ain't No 'Bout-A-Doubt It **GRAHAM CENTRAL STATION**	Warner 2876
8/2/80	**26**	9	• 2. One In A Million You *One In A Million You* (9)	Warner 3447
			GRAMM, Lou	
			Born on 5/2/50 in Rochester, New York. Lead singer of Foreigner. Member of rock group Black Sheep, 1970-75. Left Foreigner in 1991 to form Shadow King; returned in 1992.	
3/28/87	**27**	7	Ready Or Not *Midnight Blue* (5)	Atlantic 81728
			GRAND FUNK RAILROAD	
			Hard-rock band formed in Flint, Michigan, in 1968. Consisted of Mark Farner (guitar), Mel Schacher (bass) and Don Brewer (drums). Band name inspired by Michigan landmark, the Grand Trunk Railroad. Brewer and Farner had been in Terry Knight & The Pack; Schacher was bassist with ? & The Mysterians. Knight became producer/manager for Grand Funk; fired in March 1972. Craig Frost (keyboards) added in 1973. Disbanded in 1976. Re-formed in 1981 with Farner, Brewer and Dennis Bellinger (bass); disbanded again shortly thereafter. Farner recorded contemporary Christian music.	
11/8/69	**27**	8	• 1. On Time	Capitol 307
2/7/70	**11**	15	▲ 2. Grand Funk	Capitol 406
7/11/70	**6**	24	▲² **3. Closer To Home**	Capitol 471
12/5/70	**5**	25	▲² **4. Live Album** [L]	Capitol 633 [2]
5/1/71	**6**	21	▲ 5. Survival	Capitol 764
12/4/71	**5**	15	▲ **6. E Pluribus Funk** circular, silver album cover is an imitation of a U.S. coin	Capitol 853
5/20/72	**17**	9	• 7. Mark, Don & Mel 1969-71 [K]	Capitol 11042 [2]
10/21/72	**7**	13	• **8. Phoenix**	Capitol 11099
8/18/73	**2**(2)	17	▲ **9. We're An American Band** * *We're An American Band* (1)	Capitol 11207
4/6/74	**5**	21	• **10. Shinin' On** * *The Loco-Motion* (1)	Capitol 11278
1/4/75	**10**	10	• **11. All The Girls In The World Beware!!!** * ***GRAND FUNK** *Some Kind Of Wonderful* (3)/*Bad Time* (4)	Capitol 11356

DATE	POS	WKS	ARTIST—RECORD TITLE	LABEL & NO.
9/27/75	21	5	12. Caught In The Act [L]	Capitol 11445 [2]
			GRAND PUBA	
			Maxwell Dixon, former member of rap group Brand Nubian. Born in New Rochelle, New York.	
11/7/92	28	2	Reel To Reel CD includes 2 bonus tracks	Elektra 61314
			GRANT, Amy	
			Born on 11/25/60 in Augusta, Georgia. The first lady of contemporary Christian music. Married to singer/songwriter Gary Chapman. Her pop-charted, non-holiday albums have all been #1 on the Inspirational charts for 29 weeks or more.	
8/24/85	35	4	▲ 1. Unguarded	A&M 5060
4/13/91	10	61	▲⁴ 2. Heart In Motion *Baby Baby* (1)/*Every Heartbeat* (2)/*That's What Love Is For* (7)/ *Good For Me* (8)	A&M 5321
11/21/92	2(1)	8	▲ 3. Home For Christmas [X] Christmas charts: 1/'92, 6/'93, 7/'94	A&M 31454
9/10/94	13	6	▲ 4. House Of Love	A&M 0230
			GRANT, Earl	
			Born in Oklahoma City in 1931; died in an automobile accident on 6/10/70. Organist/pianist/vocalist. First recorded for Decca in 1957. In the movies *Tender Is the Night*, *Imitation of Life* and *Tokyo Night*.	
8/28/61	7	32	● 1. Ebb Tide [I]	Decca 74165
7/14/62	17	13	2. Beyond The Reef [I]	Decca 74231
			GRANT, Eddy	
			Born Edmond Montague Grant on 3/5/48 in Plaisance, Guyana. Moved to London in 1960. Formed grou The Equals in London in 1967. Moved to Barbados in 1982.	
5/21/83	10	15	● Killer On The Rampage *Electric Avenue* (2)	Portrait 38554
			GRANT, Gogi — see SOUNDTRACK (*The Helen Morgan Story*)	
			GRASS ROOTS, The	
			Rock group formed in San Francisco in 1964 by drummer Joel Larson and lead singer Bill Fulton. Originally called The Bedouins. New group recruited in 1967 by pop producer Lou Adler and songwriters Steve Barri and P.F. Sloan (known as The Fantastic Baggies). Consisted of Rob Grill (lead singer, bass), Warren Entner and Creed Bratton (guitars), and Rick Coonce (drums). New lineup in 1971 included Entner, Grill, guitarists Reed Kailing and Virgil Webber, and Joel Larson (drums).	
1/25/69	25	6	● 1. Golden Grass [G] *Midnight Confessions* (5)	Dunhill 50047
12/20/69	36	6	2. Leaving It All Behind	Dunhill 50067

DATE	POS	WKS	ARTIST—RECORD TITLE	LABEL & NO.
			GRATEFUL DEAD	
			Legendary psychedelic-rock band formed in San Francisco in 1966. Consisted of Jerry Garcia (lead guitar), Bob Weir (rhythm guitar), Ron "Pigpen" McKernan (organ, harmonica), Phil Lesh (bass) and Bill Kreutzmann (drums). Mickey Hart (second drummer) and Tom Constanten (keyboards) added in 1968. Constanten left in 1970; Hart in 1971. Keith Godchaux (piano) and his wife, Donna (vocals), joined in 1972. Pigpen died of liver ailment on 3/8/73. Hart returned in 1975. Brent Mydland (keyboards) added in 1979, replacing Keith and Donna Godchaux. Mydland was a member of Silver. Keith Godchaux died on 7/23/80 from injuries suffered in a motorcycle accident. Mydland died on 7/26/90 (age 37) of a drug overdose. Tubes keyboardist Vince Welnick replaced Mydland. Incessant touring band with faithful followers known as "Deadheads." Inducted into the Rock and Roll Hall of Fame in 1994. Also see Benefit Recordings (*Deadicated*).	
7/11/70	27	10	▲ 1. Workingman's Dead	Warner 1869
12/26/70	30	6	▲ 2. American Beauty	Warner 1893
10/16/71	25	6	3. Grateful Dead [L]	Warner 1935 [2]
1/6/73	24	8	● 4. Europe '72 [L]	Warner 2668 [3]
11/17/73	18	6	5. Wake Of The Flood	Grateful Dead 01
7/20/74	16	9	6. Grateful Dead From The Mars Hotel	Grateful Dead 102
9/20/75	12	9	7. Blues For Allah	Grateful Dead 494
9/10/77	28	4	● 8. Terrapin Station	Arista 7001
5/24/80	23	8	9. Go To Heaven	Arista 9508
10/3/81	29	3	10. Dead Set [L]	Arista 8606 [2]
			recorded in New York City and San Francisco in 1980	
8/1/87	**6**	17	▲ **11. In The Dark**	Arista 8452
			Touch Of Grey (9)	
2/25/89	37	3	12. Dylan & The Dead [L]	Columbia 45056
			BOB DYLAN & GRATEFUL DEAD	
			recordings from 6 concert dates in July 1987	
11/25/89	27	3	● 13. Built To Last	Arista 8575
			GRAVEDIGGAZ	
			Male rap foursome: Prince Rakeem (aka The Rzarector; also of Wu-Tang Clan); Poetic (aka The Grym Reaper), and Stetsasonic's Prince Paul (aka The Undertaker; real name: Paul Huston) and Fruitkwan (aka The Gatekeeper; real name: Arnold Hamilton). Prince Paul also produced De La Soul.	
8/27/94	36	1	6 Feet Deep	Gee Street 524016
			GRAY, Glen, and the Casa Loma Orchestra	
			Born Glen Gray Knoblaugh on 6/7/06; died on 8/23/63. Alto saxophonist/bandleader. Led The Casa Loma Orchestra swing band.	
2/23/57	18	9	1. Casa Loma In Hi-Fi! [I]	Capitol 747
6/29/59	28	2	2. Sounds Of The Great Bands! [I]	Capitol 1022
			GREAN, Charles Randolph, Sounde	
			Grean (born 10/1/13, New York City) is former A&R director at RCA and Dot Records. Married singer Betty Johnson.	
8/16/69	23	5	Quentin's Theme [I]	Ranwood 8055
			title cut is from TV's "Dark Shadows"	

DATE	POS	WKS	ARTIST—RECORD TITLE	LABEL & NO.
			GREAT WHITE	
			Los Angeles hard-rock quintet led by vocalist Jack Russell and guitarist Mark Kendall. Lineup included Lorne Black (bass) and Garry Holland (drums). Audie Desbrow replaced Holland by 1986. Keyboardist Michael Lardie joined by 1987. Tony Montana replaced Black in 1987; left in 1992.	
9/12/87	23	18	▲ 1. Once Bitten	Capitol 12565
5/13/89	9	26	▲² **2. Twice Shy**	Capitol 90640
			Once Bitten Twice Shy (5)	
3/23/91	18	9	● 3. Hooked	Capitol 95330
			GREELEY, George	
			Guest pianist with the Warner Bros. Orchestra.	
6/19/61	29	5	1. The Best Of The Popular Piano Concertos [I-K]	Warner 1410
			GREEN, Al	
			Born on 4/13/46 in Forest City, Arkansas. Soul singer/songwriter. With gospel group The Greene Brothers. To Grand Rapids, Michigan, in 1959. First recorded for Fargo in 1960. In group The Creations from 1964-67. Sang with his brother, Robert Green, and Lee Virgins in the group Soul Mates from 1967-68. Went solo in 1969. Wrote most of his songs. Returned to gospel music in 1980. Inducted into the Rock and Roll Hall of Fame in 1995.	
2/26/72	8	20	● **1. Let's Stay Together**	Hi 32070
			Let's Stay Together (1)	
11/4/72	4	26	● **2. I'm Still In Love With You**	Hi 32074
			Look What You Done For Me (4)/ *I'm Still In Love With You* (3)	
2/3/73	19	11	3. Green Is Blues [E]	Hi 32055
			Green's first album on the Hi label	
5/26/73	10	20	● **4. Call Me**	Hi 32077
			You Ought To Be With Me (3)/*Call Me (Come Back Home)* (10)/ *Here I Am (Come And Take Me)* (10)	
1/19/74	24	8	● 5. Livin' For You	Hi 32082
12/7/74	15	16	● 6. Al Green Explores Your Mind	Hi 32087
			Sha-La-La (Make Me Happy) (7)	
3/22/75	17	8	7. Al Green/Greatest Hits [G]	Hi 32089
10/11/75	28	6	8. Al Green Is Love	Hi 32092
			GREENBAUM, Norman	
			Born on 11/20/42 in Malden, Massachusetts. Moved to the West Coast in 1965; formed the psychedelic jug band Dr. West's Medicine Show & Junk Band.	
4/18/70	23	5	Spirit In The Sky	Reprise 6365
			Spirit In The Sky (3)	
			GREEN DAY	
			Punk trio formed by Rodeo, California, natives Billie Joe (vocals, guitar; real last name: Armstrong) and Mike Dirnt (bass; real last name: Pritchard) with Tre Cool (drums; from Mendocino, California).	
5/14/94	2 (2)	42 +	▲⁶ **Dookie**	Reprise 45529
			GREENE, Lorne	
			Born on 2/12/14 in Ottawa, Canada; died on 9/11/87 of cardiac arrest. Chief newscaster for CBC radio, 1940-43. Acted in the movies *The Silver Chalice* and *Tight Spot*; starred in TV's "Bonanza" and "Battlestar Galactica."	
1/16/65	35	4	Welcome To The Ponderosa	RCA 2843
			Ringo (1)	

DATE	POS	WKS	ARTIST—RECORD TITLE	LABEL & NO.
			GREEN JELLY	
			Comical 12-member rock outfit formed in Kenmore, New York, in 1981. Revolving lineup led by Bill Manspeaker (aka Marshall "Duh" Staxx and Moronic Dicktator); has hosted 74 members. Video-only band until its surge in video popularity in 1993 led to release of group's recordings. Originally known as Green Jello.	
5/1/93	**23**	9	● Cereal Killer Soundtrack	Zoo 11038
			originally released with artist name Green Jello	
			GREGORY, Dick	
			Born on 10/12/32 in St. Louis. Black comedian/civil-rights activist. Became a diet guru in the '80s.	
7/24/61	**23**	5	In Living Black & White [C]	Colpix 417
			GROSS, Henry	
			Born on 4/1/51. Rock singer from Brooklyn. Original lead guitarist of Sha-Na-Na. Toured with The Beach Boys and Aerosmith.	
4/12/75	**26**	3	Plug Me Into Something	A&M 4502
			GTR	
			British hard-rock quintet featuring superstar guitarists Steve Hackett (Genesis) and Steve Howe (Yes; Asia), and vocalist Max Bacon.	
5/31/86	**11**	17	● GTR	Arista 8400
			GUARALDI, Vince, Trio	
			Guaraldi was born on 7/17/32 in San Francisco; died of a heart attack on 2/6/76. Pianist/leader of own jazz trio. Formerly with Woody Herman and Cal Tjader. Wrote the music for the "Peanuts" TV specials.	
4/13/63	**24**	7	Jazz Impressions of Black Orpheus [I]	Fantasy 3337
			features Guaraldi's interpretations of 4 songs from the movie *Black Orpheus*	
			GUESS WHO, The	
			Rock group formed in Winnipeg, Canada, in 1963. Consisted of Allan "Chad Allan" Kobel (guitar, vocals), Randy Bachman (lead guitar), Garry Peterson (drums), Bob Ashley (piano) and Jim Kale (bass). Recorded as The Reflections, and Chad Allan & The Expressions. Ashley replaced by new lead singer Burton Cummings in 1966. Allan left shortly thereafter. Bachman left in 1970 to form Bachman-Turner Overdrive; replaced by Kurt Winter and Greg Leskiw. Leskiw and Kale left in 1972; replaced by Don McDougall and Bill Wallace. Domenic Troiano replaced both Winter and McDougall in 1974. Group disbanded in 1975; several reunions since then.	
3/7/70	**9**	23	● 1. American Woman	RCA 4266
			No Time (5)/*American Woman* (1)	
10/17/70	**14**	11	● 2. Share The Land	RCA 4359
			Share The Land (10)	
4/24/71	**12**	23	● 3. The Best of The Guess Who [G]	RCA 1004
10/14/72	**39**	1	4. Live At The Paramount (Seattle) [L]	RCA 4779

DATE	POS	WKS	ARTIST—RECORD TITLE	LABEL & NO.
			GUNS N' ROSES	
			Los Angeles-based, hard-rock band: lead singer W. Axl Rose (born 1962, Indiana; real name is William Bailey; natural father's surname is Rose) with bassist Michael "Duff" McKagan, guitarists Izzy Stradlin' (Jeffrey Isbell) and Slash (Saul Hudson), and drummer Steven Adler. Rose married Erin Everly (daughter of Don Everly of The Everly Brothers) on 4/27/90; she filed for divorce three weeks later. Adler left in 1990; replaced by former Cult drummer Matt Sorum. Keyboardist Dizzy Reed joined in 1990. Stradlin' left in late 1991; replaced by Gilby Clarke (of Kill For Thrills). Slash married model Renee Surran in November 1992. Clarke left band in January 1995.	
1/30/88	1(5)	78	▲¹³ 1. **Appetite For Destruction** *Sweet Child O' Mine* (1)/*Welcome To The Jungle* (7)/ *Paradise City* (5)	Geffen 24148
12/24/88	2(1)	33	▲⁵ 2. **G N' R Lies** side A: reissue of band's 1986 4-song EP, *Live Like A Suicide*; side B: 4 tracks recorded in 1988 *Patience* (4)	Geffen 24198
10/5/91	1(2)	30	▲⁶ 3. **Use Your Illusion II**	Geffen 24420
10/5/91	2(2)	43	▲⁶ 4. **Use Your Illusion I** *Don't Cry* (10)/*November Rain* (3)	Geffen 24415
12/11/93	4	9	▲ 5. **The Spaghetti Incident?** includes uncredited 13th track, "Look At Your Game Girl," written by convicted mass murderer Charles Manson	Geffen 24617
			GUTHRIE, Arlo	
			Born on 7/10/47 in Coney Island, New York. Son of legendary folk singer Woody Guthrie. Starred as himself in the 1969 movie *Alice's Restaurant*, which was based on his 1967 song "Alice's Restaurant Massacree." Often performed in concert with Pete Seeger.	
1/27/68	17	23	▲ 1. **Alice's Restaurant** side 1 is the 18-minute tale of "Alice's Restaurant Massacree"	Reprise 6267
11/28/70	33	3	2. **Washington County**	Reprise 6411
			GUY	
			New York City R&B trio formed and fronted by Teddy Riley. Includes brothers Damion and Aaron Hall. By age 20, in 1988, Riley (ex-member of R&B group Kids At Work) was already a renowned producer. Trio disbanded in 1991. Riley formed Blackstreet in 1993.	
4/8/89	27	13	▲² 1. **Guy**	Uptown 42176
12/8/90	16	23	▲ 2. **The Future**	MCA 10115
			# H	
			HAGAR, Sammy	
			Born on 10/13/47 in Monterey, California. Rock singer/songwriter/guitarist. Lead singer of Montrose (1973-75). Replaced David Lee Roth as lead singer of Van Halen in 1985.	
2/20/82	28	14	▲ 1. **Standing Hampton**	Geffen 2006
1/29/83	17	14	● 2. **Three Lock Box**	Geffen 2021
11/3/84	32	9	▲ 3. **VOA**	Geffen 24043
7/25/87	14	11	4. **Sammy Hagar** as a result of an MTV contest, album title changed to *I Never Said Goodbye*; however, no vinyl copies were pressed with the new title	Geffen 24144

DATE	POS	WKS	ARTIST—RECORD TITLE	LABEL & NO.
			HAGGARD, Merle	
			Born on 4/6/37 in Bakersfield, California. Country singer/songwriter/guitarist. Served nearly three years in San Quentin prison on a burglary charge, 1957-60. Signed to Capitol Records in 1965 and then formed backing band, The Strangers. One of the top male vocalists of the country charts with 38 #1 country singles.	
8/20/83	37	1	▲ Poncho & Lefty **MERLE HAGGARD/WILLIE NELSON**	Epic 37958
			HAIRCUT ONE HUNDRED	
			British pop-rock sextet founded by vocalist Nick Heyward. Disbanded in 1983.	
7/10/82	31	7	Pelican West	Arista 6600
			HALEY, Bill, And His Comets	
			Born William John Clifton Haley, Jr., on 7/6/25 in Highland Park, Michigan; died on 2/9/81 of a heart attack. Began career as singer with New England country band, The Down Homers. The original Comets band that backed Haley on "Rock Around The Clock," recorded on 4/12/54, were Danny Cedrone (died 7/10/54 of a heart attack; lead guitar), Joey D'Ambrose (sax), Billy Williamson (steel guitar), Johnny Grande (piano), Marshall Lytle (bass) and Billy Guesack (session drums; Dick Richards was group's live drummer). D'Ambrose, Richards and Lytle left in September 1955 to form The Jodimars. Comets lineup on subsequent recordings included Williamson, Grande, Rudy Pompilli (died 2/5/76 [age 47]; sax), Al Rex (born Al Piccarelli; bass), Ralph Jones (drums) and Frank Beecher (lead guitar). Inducted into the Rock and Roll Hall of Fame in 1987.	
1/28/56	12	4	1. Rock Around The Clock [G] *Shake, Rattle And Roll* (7-'54)/*Rock Around The Clock* (1)/ *Burn That Candle* (9)	Decca 8225
10/13/56	18	5	2. Rock 'n Roll Stage Show	Decca 8345
			HALL, Daryl	
			Born Daryl Franklin Hohl on 10/11/48 in Philadelphia. Half of Hall & Oates duo.	
9/20/86	29	6	Three Hearts in the Happy Ending Machine *Dreamtime* (5)	RCA 7196
			HALL, Daryl, & John Oates	
			Daryl Hall (see previous entry) and John Oates (born 4/7/49, New York City) met while students at Temple University in 1967. Hall sang backup for many top soul groups before teaming up with Oates in 1972. In late '80s, they passed The Everly Brothers as the #1 charting duo of the rock era.	
5/22/76	17	11	● 1. Daryl Hall & John Oates *Sara Smile* (4)	RCA 1144
9/18/76	13	35	● 2. Bigger Than Both Of Us *Rich Girl* (1)	RCA 1467
10/30/76	33	4	● 3. Abandoned Luncheonette *She's Gone* (7)	Atlantic 7269
9/24/77	30	5	● 4. Beauty On A Back Street	RCA 2300
10/7/78	27	6	● 5. Along The Red Ledge	RCA 2804
11/24/79	33	6	6. X-Static	RCA 3494
8/30/80	17	35	▲ 7. Voices *Kiss On My List* (1)/*You Make My Dreams* (5)	RCA 3646
9/26/81	5	32	▲ **8. Private Eyes** *Private Eyes* (1)/*I Can't Go For That* (1)/ *Did It In A Minute* (9)	RCA 4028
11/6/82	3	46	▲² **9. H2O** *Maneater* (1)/*One On One* (7)/*Family Man* (6)	RCA 4383

DATE	POS	WKS	ARTIST—RECORD TITLE	LABEL & NO.
11/19/83	7	28	▲² **10. Rock 'N Soul, Part 1** [G]	RCA 4858
			Say It Isn't So (2)/*Adult Education* (8)	
10/27/84	5	31	▲² **11. Big Bam Boom**	RCA 5309
			Out Of Touch (1)/*Method Of Modern Love* (5)	
10/5/85	21	8	● 12. Live At The Apollo with David Ruffin & Eddie Kendrick [L]	RCA 7035
			recorded at the re-opening of New York's Apollo Theater; side 1 features guest vocalists Ruffin and Kendrick	
5/28/88	24	7	▲ **13. ooh yeah!**	Arista 8539
			Everything Your Heart Desires (3)	

HAMLISCH, Marvin

Born on 6/2/44 in New York City. Pianist/composer/conductor for numerous soundtracks. Won 1973 Best Song Academy Award and Grammy Award for "The Way We Were" and 1974 Best New Artist Grammy Award.

DATE	POS	WKS	ARTIST—RECORD TITLE	LABEL & NO.
3/2/74	1 (5)	23	● **The Sting** [S-I]	MCA 390
			The Entertainer (3)	

HAMMER

Born Stanley Kirk Burrell on 3/30/63 in Oakland. Rapper/producer/founder/leader of The Posse, an eight-member group of dancers, DJs and singers. Burrell was an Oakland A's batboy in the '70s; his nickname "The Little Hammer" stemmed from his resemblance to baseball great "Hammerin'" Hank Aaron. Oaktown's 3-5-7 and Ace Juice are members of The Posse. Billed as M.C. Hammer from 1988-91.

M.C. HAMMER:

DATE	POS	WKS	ARTIST—RECORD TITLE	LABEL & NO.
5/6/89	30	23	▲² 1. Let's Get It Started	Capitol 90924
3/17/90	1 (21)	70	▲¹⁰ **2. Please Hammer Don't Hurt 'Em**	Capitol 92857
			U Can't Touch This (8)/*Have You Seen Her* (4)/*Pray* (2)	
			HAMMER:	
11/16/91	2 (2)	29	▲³ **3. Too Legit To Quit**	Capitol 98151
			cassette includes bonus track, *Addams Groove* (7), not on CD *2 Legit 2 Quit* (5)	
3/19/94	12	12	▲ 4. The Funky Headhunter	Giant 24545

HANCOCK, Herbie

Born on 4/12/40 in Chicago. Jazz electronic keyboardist. Pianist with The Miles Davis Band, 1963-68. Won 1987 Academy Award for his *Round Midnight* movie score. Also scored the 1988 movie *Colors*.

DATE	POS	WKS	ARTIST—RECORD TITLE	LABEL & NO.
2/16/74	13	21	▲ 1. Head Hunters [I]	Columbia 32731
10/12/74	13	9	2. Thrust [I]	Columbia 32965
11/8/75	21	4	3. Man-Child [I]	Columbia 33812
4/21/79	38	3	4. Feets Don't Fail Me Now	Columbia 35764

HARMONICATS

Harmonica trio formed in 1944: Jerry Murad (born in Turkey), Al Fiore and Don Les (d: 8/25/94 [age 79]).

DATE	POS	WKS	ARTIST—RECORD TITLE	LABEL & NO.
3/20/61	17	1	Cherry Pink And Apple Blossom White [I]	Columbia 8356
			Jerry Murad's "Fabulous" HARMONICATS	

HARNELL, Joe, His Piano And Orchestra

Harnell was born on 8/2/24 in the Bronx. Conductor/arranger for Frank Sinatra, Peggy Lee and others. Musical director for many TV shows, including "The Mike Douglas Show."

DATE	POS	WKS	ARTIST—RECORD TITLE	LABEL & NO.
1/26/63	3	27	**Fly Me To The Moon and the Bossa Nova Pops** [I]	Kapp 3318

DATE	POS	WKS	ARTIST—RECORD TITLE	LABEL & NO.
			HARRIS, Eddie	
			Born on 10/20/36 in Chicago. Jazz tenor saxophonist/vocalist. Noted for experimentation with electronic reed instruments.	
6/19/61	**2**(1)	22	**1. Exodus To Jazz** [I]	Vee-Jay 3016
9/7/68	**36**	1	2. The Electrifying Eddie Harris [I]	Atlantic 1495
1/31/70	**29**	5	3. Swiss Movement [I-L]	Atlantic 1537
			LES McCANN & EDDIE HARRIS	
			recorded at The Montreux Jazz Festival, Switzerland	
			HARRIS, Emmylou	
			Born on 4/2/47 in Birmingham, Alabama. Contemporary country vocalist. Sang backup with Gram Parsons until his death in 1973. Own band from 1975.	
2/7/76	**25**	8	● 1. Elite Hotel	Reprise 2236
2/5/77	**21**	8	● 2. Luxury Liner	Warner 3115
2/25/78	**29**	5	● 3. Quarter Moon In A Ten Cent Town	Warner 3141
6/7/80	**26**	11	● 4. Roses In The Snow	Warner 3422
2/28/81	**22**	9	● 5. Evangeline	Warner 3508
3/28/87	**6**	14	▲ **6. Trio**	Warner 25491
			DOLLY PARTON, LINDA RONSTADT, EMMYLOU HARRIS	
			HARRIS, Major	
			Born on 2/9/47 in Richmond, Virginia. Soul singer. With The Jarmels in the early '60s. With The Delfonics from 1971-74.	
6/28/75	**28**	3	My Way	Atlantic 18119
			Love Won't Let Me Wait (5)	
			HARRIS, Richard	
			Born on 10/1/30 in Limerick, Ireland. Began prolific acting career in 1958. Portrayed King Arthur in the long-running stage production and movie version of *Camelot*.	
6/1/68	**4**	16	**1. A Tramp Shining**	Dunhill 50032
			MacArthur Park (2)	
12/14/68	**27**	6	2. The Yard Went On Forever ...	Dunhill 50042
11/10/73	**25**	9	3. Jonathan Livingston Seagull [T]	Dunhill 50160
			narration from the book; music composed by Terry James	
1/25/75	**29**	5	4. The Prophet by Kahlil Gibran [T]	Atlantic 18120
			Harris recites Gibran's classic work	
			HARRIS, Rolf	
			Born in Perth, Australia, on 3/30/30. Played piano from age nine. Moved to England in the mid-1950s. Developed his unique "wobble board sound" out of a sheet of masonite. Had own BBC-TV series from 1970.	
8/17/63	**29**	4	Tie Me Kangaroo Down, Sport & Sun Arise [N]	Epic 26053
			Tie Me Kangaroo Down, Sport (3)	
			HARRIS, Sam	
			Winner of TV's "Star Search" 1984 male vocalist category.	
11/17/84	**35**	3	● Sam Harris	Motown 6103

DATE	POS	WKS	ARTIST—RECORD TITLE	LABEL & NO.
			HARRISON, George	
			Born on 2/25/43 in Liverpool, England. Formed his first group, The Rebels, at age 13. Joined John Lennon and Paul McCartney in The Quarrymen in 1958; group later evolved into The Beatles, with Harrison as lead guitarist. Organized the Bangladesh benefit concerts at Madison Square Garden in 1971. Member of the 1988 supergroup Traveling Wilburys. In 1992, became first recipient of The Century Award, *Billboard's* honor for distinguished creative achievement.	
12/19/70	**1**(7)	22	▲² **1. All Things Must Pass**	Apple 639 [3]
			My Sweet Lord (1)/*What Is Life* (10)	
1/8/72	**2**(6)	23	● **2. The Concert For Bangla Desh** [L]	Apple 3385 [3]
			1972 Album of the Year Grammy Award; Madison Square Garden benefit concert on 8/1/71; with guests Bob Dylan, Eric Clapton, Ringo Starr, Billy Preston and Leon Russell	
6/16/73	**1**(5)	15	● **3. Living In The Material World**	Apple 3410
			Give Me Love (Give Me Peace On Earth) (1)	
1/4/75	**4**	9	● **4. Dark Horse**	Apple 3418
10/11/75	**8**	7	● **5. Extra Texture (Read All About It)**	Apple 3420
12/11/76	**31**	3	● **6. The Best of George Harrison** [G]	Capitol 11578
			side 1: hits while with The Beatles; side 2: solo hits	
12/18/76	**11**	8	● **7. Thirty-Three & 1/3**	Dark Horse 3005
			33 1/3: record playing speed and George's age	
3/17/79	**14**	9	● **8. George Harrison**	Dark Horse 3255
6/20/81	**11**	7	**9. Somewhere In England**	Dark Horse 3492
			All Those Years Ago (2)	
11/28/87	**8**	22	▲ **10. Cloud Nine**	Dark Horse 25643
			co-producer: Jeff Lynne (Electric Light Orchestra) *Got My Mind Set On You* (1)	
			HARRY, Debbie	
			Born on 7/1/45 in New York City. Lead singer of Blondie. In the movies *Roadie, Union City, Videodrome, Tales from the Darkside-The Movie* and *Hairspray.* Appeared in several episodes of TV's "Wiseguy."	
9/5/81	**25**	4	● KooKoo	Chrysalis 1347
			HART, Corey	
			Born in Montreal, Canada; raised in Spain and Mexico. Singer/songwriter/keyboardist.	
9/1/84	**31**	6	● **1. First Offense**	EMI America 17117
			Sunglasses At Night (7)	
8/3/85	**20**	15	● **2. Boy In The Box**	EMI America 17161
			Never Surrender (3)	
			HART, Freddie	
			Born Fred Segrest on 12/21/26 in Lochapoka, Alabama. Country singer/songwriter/guitarist.	
11/27/71	**37**	4	● Easy Loving	Capitol 838
			HATHAWAY, Donny	
			Born on 10/1/45 in Chicago; raised in St. Louis. Committed suicide by jumping from 15th floor of New York City's Essex House Hotel on 1/13/79. R&B singer/songwriter/keyboardist/producer/arranger. Gospel singer since age three. Attended Washington, D.C.'s Howard University on a fine-arts scholarship; classmate of Roberta Flack. Sang the theme of TV show "Maude." His wife, Eulalah, was a classical singer. Their daughter Lalah Hathaway began her solo recording career in 1990. Also see Roberta Flack.	
3/25/72	**18**	23	● **1. Donny Hathaway Live** [L]	Atco 386

DATE	POS	WKS	ARTIST—RECORD TITLE	LABEL & NO.
5/20/72	3	21	● **2. Roberta Flack & Donny Hathaway** **ROBERTA FLACK & DONNY HATHAWAY** *Where Is The Love* (5)	Atlantic 7216
			HAVENS, Richie	
			Born on 1/21/41 in Brooklyn. Black folk singer/guitarist. Opening act of 1969 Woodstock concert.	
5/15/71	29	7	Alarm Clock	Stormy F. 6005
			HAWKINS, Edwin, Singers	
			Hawkins (born August 1943) formed gospel group with Betty Watson in Oakland in 1967 as the Northern California State Youth Choir. Member Dorothy Morrison went on to solo career.	
5/17/69	15	8	Let Us Go Into The House Of The Lord *Oh Happy Day* (4)	Pavilion 10001
			HAYES, Isaac	
			Born on 8/20/42 in Covington, Tennessee. Soul singer/songwriter/keyboardist/producer/actor. Session musician for Otis Redding and other artists on the Stax label. Teamed with songwriter David Porter to compose "Soul Man," "Hold On! I'm A Comin'" and many other songs. Composed movie scores for *Shaft, Tough Guys, Truck Turner* and *Robin Hood: Men in Tights.*	
8/2/69	8	36	● **1. Hot Buttered Soul**	Enterprise 1001
5/2/70	8	28	**2. The Isaac Hayes Movement**	Enterprise 1010
12/5/70	11	20	3. To Be Continued	Enterprise 1014
8/28/71	1(1)	30	**4. Shaft** [S-I] 3 of 15 tracks feature vocals *Theme From Shaft* (1)	Enterprise 5002 [2]
12/18/71	10	15	**5. Black Moses**	Enterprise 5003 [2]
6/2/73	14	11	● 6. Live At The Sahara Tahoe [L]	Enterprise 5005 [2]
11/17/73	16	14	● 7. Joy	Enterprise 5007
7/5/75	18	9	● 8. Chocolate Chip	HBS 874
1/19/80	39	1	● 9. Don't Let Go	Polydor 6224
			HAYWARD, Justin	
			Born on 10/14/46 in Swindon, England. Lead singer/guitarist of The Moody Blues.	
4/19/75	16	8	1. Blue Jays **JUSTIN HAYWARD/JOHN LODGE** album title also refers to the name of the duo	Threshold 14
5/7/77	37	3	2. Songwriter	Deram 18073
			HAZLEWOOD, Lee — see SINATRA, Nancy	
			HEALEY, Jeff, Band	
			Toronto-based blues-rock trio: vocalist/guitarist Healey with drummer Tom Stephen and bassist Joe Rockman. Healey, blind since age one and guitarist since three, appeared in the 1989 movie *Road House*.	
9/2/89	22	8	▲ 1. See The Light *Angel Eyes* (5)	Arista 8553
6/23/90	27	12	● 2. Hell To Pay	Arista 8632

DATE	POS	WKS	ARTIST—RECORD TITLE	LABEL & NO.
			HEART	
			Rock band formed in Seattle in 1973. Originally known as The Army, then White Heart; shortened name to Heart in 1974. Group features Ann Wilson (lead singer) and her sister Nancy (guitar, keyboards). Band moved to Vancouver in 1975 when manager Mike Fisher was drafted; signed with new Mushroom label. When amnesty was declared, group returned to Seattle and signed with CBS Portrait label in 1976. Joining the Wilsons were guitarists Howard Leese and Roger Fisher (brother of Mike), bassist Steve Fossen and drummer Michael DeRosier. The Fishers left the band in 1979; Roger joined Alias in 1990. Fossen and DeRosier left by 1982; replaced by bassist Mark Andes (ex-Spirit; Jo Jo Gunne; Firefall) and drummer Denny Carmassi (ex-Gamma). Andes left by 1993. Carmassi left in 1994 to join Whitesnake. Nancy married movie director Cameron Crowe.	
8/7/76	7	21	▲ **1. Dreamboat Annie**	Mushroom 5005
			Magic Man (9)	
6/4/77	9	22	▲³ **2. Little Queen**	Portrait 34799
4/29/78	17	7	▲ 3. Magazine	Mushroom 5008
			recorded in 1976, but not released until 1978 because of legal battle	
10/14/78	17	22	▲² 4. Dog & Butterfly	Portrait 35555
3/8/80	5	13	● **5. Bebe Le Strange**	Epic 36371
12/6/80	13	12	▲² 6. Greatest Hits/Live　　　　　　　　[G-L]	Epic 36888 [2]
			6 of 18 tracks are live	
			Tell It Like It Is (8)	
6/19/82	25	4	7. Private Audition	Epic 38049
10/15/83	39	2	8. Passionworks	Epic 38800
7/27/85	1(1)	58	▲⁵ 9. Heart	Capitol 12410
			What About Love? (10)/*Never* (4)/*These Dreams* (1)/ *Nothin' At All* (10)	
6/13/87	2(3)	36	▲³ **10. Bad Animals**	Capitol 12546
			Alone (1)/*Who Will You Run To* (7)	
4/28/90	3	22	▲² **11. Brigade**	Capitol 91820
			All I Wanna Do Is Make Love To You (2)	
			HEATH, Ted, And His Music	
			Born Edward Heath on 3/30/1900 in London; died on 11/18/69. Trombonist/ leader of own band from 1945 until his death.	
10/16/61	28	8	1. Big Band Percussion　　　　　　　　　[I]	London P. 4 44002
9/15/62	36	2	2. Big Band Bash　　　　　　　　　　　　[I]	London P. 4 44017
			HEATWAVE	
			Multi-national, interracial group formed in Germany by brothers Johnnie and Keith Wilder of Dayton, Ohio. Johnnie became a paraplegic due to 1979 car accident.	
9/17/77	11	12	▲ 1. Too Hot To Handle	Epic 34761
			Boogie Nights (2)	
5/6/78	10	12	▲ **2. Central Heating**	Epic 35260
			The Groove Line (7)	
6/9/79	38	3	● 3. Hot Property	Epic 35970
			HEAVY D. & THE BOYZ	
			Rap group from Mount Vernon, New York: leader Heavy D. (Dwight Meyers), G. Whiz (Glen Parrish), Trouble T-Roy (Troy Dixon) and DJ Eddie F (Edward Ferrell). Dixon died on 7/15/90 (age 22) from an accidental fall in Indianapolis. Heavy D. appeared in the movie *Who's the Man?*	
7/22/89	19	14	▲ 1. Big Tyme	MCA/Uptown 42302

DATE	POS	WKS	ARTIST—RECORD TITLE	LABEL & NO.
7/20/91	**21**	10	▲ 2. Peaceful Journey CD includes bonus track	MCA/Uptown 10289
2/6/93	**40**	1	● 3. Blue Funk	MCA/Uptown 10734
6/11/94	**11**	5	● 4. Nuttin' But Love	MCA/Uptown 10998
			HEFTI, Neal, And His Orchestra	
			Born on 10/29/22 in Hastings, Nebraska. Trumpeter. Gained fame as arranger for Woody Herman (1944-46), Harry James and Count Basie, then as composer of TV themes.	
2/5/55	**8**	2	**Music Of Rudolf Friml** **[I]** 10" album	"X" 3021
			HEIGHTS, The — see TELEVISION SHOWS	
			HEINDORF, Ray/Matty Matlock	
			Heindorf was born on 8/25/08 in Haverstraw, New York; died on 2/3/80. Longtime musical director for the Warner Bros. Orchestra. Julian "Matty" Matlock was born on 4/27/07 in Paducah, Kentucky; died on 6/14/78. Clarinet player with numerous TV and radio appearances.	
9/3/55	**9**	6	**Pete Kelly's Blues** **[I]** songs from the movie; also see vocal recording by Peggy Lee & Ella Fitzgerald, and narrated recording by Jack Webb	Columbia 690
			HENDERSON, Michael	
			Born in 1951 in Yazoo City, Mississippi. Soul singer/bass player. To Detroit in the early '60s. Worked as session musician. Toured with Stevie Wonder and Aretha Franklin. Featured vocalist on Norman Connors's records.	
9/23/78	**38**	2	● 1. In The Night-Time	Buddah 5712
10/11/80	**35**	5	2. Wide Receiver	Buddah 6001
			HENDRIX, Jimi	
			Born on 11/27/42 in Seattle. Died of a drug overdose in London on 9/18/70. Legendary psychedelic-blues guitarist. Began career as a studio guitarist. In 1965, formed own band, Jimmy James & The Blue Flames. In 1966, discovered by The Animals' bassist Chas Chandler at New York City's Cafe Wha? who invited Hendrix to London, where he created The Jimi Hendrix Experience with Noel Redding (bass) and Mitch Mitchell (drums). Formed new group in 1969, Band of Gypsys, with Buddy Miles (drums) and Billy Cox (bass). The Jimi Hendrix Experience was inducted into the Rock and Roll Hall of Fame in 1992. Won 1992 Lifetime Achievement Grammy Award.	
9/16/67	**5**	77	▲² **1. Are You Experienced? ***	Reprise 6261
2/17/68	**3**	13	▲ **2. Axis: Bold As Love ***	Reprise 6281
11/2/68	**1**(2)	17	▲ **3. Electric Ladyland ***	Reprise 6307 [2]
8/9/69	**6**	17	▲² **4. Smash Hits *** **[G]** ***THE JIMI HENDRIX EXPERIENCE**	Reprise 2025
5/2/70	**5**	23	▲ **5. Band Of Gypsys** **[L]** with Buddy Miles (drums) and Billy Cox (bass); recorded New Year's Eve in 1969 at New York's Fillmore East	Capitol 472
9/26/70	**16**	8	● 6. Monterey International Pop Festival **[S-L]** **OTIS REDDING/THE JIMI HENDRIX EXPERIENCE** recorded June 1967 and featured in the movie *Monterey Pop*	Reprise 2029
3/6/71	**3**	17	● **7. The Cry Of Love** Hendrix's last self-authorized album	Reprise 2034
10/16/71	**15**	9	● 8. Rainbow Bridge **[S]** recordings from 1968-70	Reprise 2040
3/11/72	**12**	9	● 9. Hendrix In The West **[K-L]**	Reprise 2049
3/29/75	**5**	9	● **10. Crash Landing** **[K]**	Reprise 2204

DATE	POS	WKS	ARTIST—RECORD TITLE	LABEL & NO.
8/20/94	37	2	11. Jimi Hendrix: Woodstock [L] Hendrix's performance at the legendary 1969 rock festival	MCA 11063
			HENLEY, Don Born on 7/22/47 in Gilmer, Texas. Singer/songwriter/drummer. Own band, Shiloh, in the early '70s. Worked with Glenn Frey in Linda Ronstadt's backup band; the two then formed The Eagles with Randy Meisner and Bernie Leadon. Went solo in 1982.	
9/25/82	24	20	● 1. I Can't Stand Still *Dirty Laundry* (3)	Asylum 60048
12/22/84	13	30	▲³ 2. Building The Perfect Beast CD and cassette include bonus cut *The Boys Of Summer* (5)/*All She Wants To Do Is Dance* (9)	Geffen 24026
7/29/89	8	58	▲⁵ 3. The End Of The Innocence *The End Of The Innocence* (8)	Geffen 24217
			HERMAN, Woody, and his Orchestra Born Woodrow Charles Herman on 5/16/13 in Milwaukee. Died on 10/29/87 of cardiac arrest. Saxophonist/ clarinetist of dance bands beginning in 1929. Formed own band in 1936. Won 1987 Lifetime Achievement Grammy Award. One of the most innovative and contemporary of all big band leaders.	
2/19/55	11	2	The 3 Herds [K-I] recordings from 1945-54	Columbia 592
			HERMAN'S HERMITS Formed in Manchester, England, in 1964. Name derived from cartoon character Sherman of TV's "The Bullwinkle Show." Consisted of Peter "Herman" Noone (born 11/5/47; vocals), Derek Leckenby and Keith Hopwood (guitars), Karl Green (bass) and Barry Whitwam (drums). First called The Heartbeats. Noone left in 1972 for solo career; formed Los Angeles-based group The Tremblers in late '70s. Hosts own show on music video TV channel VH-1. Leckenby died of non-Hodgkins lymphoma on 6/4/94 (age 48).	
3/27/65	2(4)	26	● **1. Introducing Herman's Hermits** *Mrs. Brown You've Got A Lovely Daughter* (1)	MGM 4282
6/26/65	2(6)	24	● **2. Herman's Hermits On Tour** *Can't You Hear My Heartbeat* (2)/*Silhouettes* (5)/ *I'm Henry VIII, I Am* (1)	MGM 4295
11/27/65	5	27	● **3. The Best Of Herman's Hermits** [G] *Wonderful World* (4)/*Just A Little Bit Better* (7)	MGM 4315
4/30/66	14	7	4. Hold On! [S] group stars in the movie *A Must To Avoid* (8)/*Leaning On A Lamp Post* (9)	MGM 4342
1/7/67	20	7	● 5. The Best Of Herman's Hermits, Volume 2 [G] *Listen People* (3)/*Dandy* (5)	MGM 4416
3/25/67	13	13	● 6. There's A Kind Of Hush All Over The World *There's A Kind Of Hush* (4)	MGM 4438
			HEYWOOD, Eddie Born on 12/4/15 in Atlanta. Died on 1/2/89. Black jazz pianist/composer/ arranger. Played professionally by age 14. Own band in New York City in 1941. Worked with Billie Holiday. To the West Coast in 1947, with own trio. Active into the '70s.	
5/25/59	16	4	Canadian Sunset [I] title song written by Heywood; not the same version as with Hugo Winterhalter in 1956	RCA 1529

DATE	POS	WKS	ARTIST—RECORD TITLE	LABEL & NO.
			HIBBLER, Al	
			Born on 8/16/15 in Little Rock, Arkansas. Blind since birth; studied voice at Little Rock's Conservatory for the Blind. First recorded with Jay McShann for Decca in 1942. With Duke Ellington, 1943-51. Also recorded with Harry Carney, Tab Smith, Mercer Ellington and Billy Strayhorn.	
8/4/56	20	2	Starring Al Hibbler	Decca 8328
			HI-FIVE	
			R&B teen vocal quintet from Waco, Texas, and Oklahoma City: Tony Thompson, Roderick Clark, Russell Neal, Marcus Sanders and Toriano Easley (left after release of first album; replaced by Treston Irby). Clark and Neal left by 1993; Shannon and Terrance joined.	
5/4/91	38	3	● Hi-Five	Jive 1328
			I Like The Way (The Kissing Game) (1)/ *I Can't Wait Another Minute* (8)	
			HIGGINS, Bertie	
			Born Elbert Higgins on 12/8/44 in Tarpon Springs, Florida. Singer/songwriter. First recorded for ABC in 1964. Worked as drummer with The Roemans from 1964-66.	
6/12/82	38	3	Just Another Day In Paradise	Kat Family 37901
			Key Largo (8)	
			HIGH INERGY	
			Female soul group from Pasadena, California: sisters Barbara and Vernessa Mitchell, Linda Howard and Michelle Rumph. Vernessa left in 1978; group continued as a trio.	
12/10/77	28	7	Turnin' On	Gordy 978
			HILL, Dan	
			Born on 6/3/54 in Toronto. Author/singer/songwriter.	
2/11/78	21	8	● Longer Fuse	20th Century 547
			Sometimes When We Touch (3)	
			HI-LO'S, The	
			Vocal quartet formed in 1953: Gene Puerling, Clark Burroughs, Bob Morse and Bob Strasen. Numerous appearances on Rosemary Clooney's television show.	
4/13/57	13	3	1. Suddenly It's The Hi-Lo's	Columbia 952
7/22/57	14	7	2. Ring Around Rosie	Columbia 1006
			ROSEMARY CLOONEY AND THE HI-LO'S	
10/14/57	19	4	3. Now Hear This	Columbia 1023
			HIRT, Al	
			Born Alois Maxwell Hirt on 11/7/22 in New Orleans. Trumpet virtuoso. Toured with Jimmy and Tommy Dorsey, Ray McKinley and Horace Heidt. Formed own Dixieland combo (with Pete Fountain) in the late '50s.	
8/14/61	21	11	1. The Greatest Horn In The World [I]	RCA 2366
3/10/62	24	5	2. Horn A-Plenty [I]	RCA 2446
12/28/63	3	66	● 3. Honey In The Horn	RCA 2733
			Anita Kerr Singers do background vocals on some tracks *Java* (4)	
6/6/64	6	38	● 4. Cotton Candy [I]	RCA 2917
9/19/64	9	20	● 5. Sugar Lips	RCA 2965
11/7/64	18	12	6. "Pops" Goes The Trumpet [I]	RCA 2729
			AL HIRT/BOSTON POPS/ARTHUR FIEDLER	
2/13/65	13	26	● 7. The Best Of Al Hirt [G-I]	RCA 3309

DATE	POS	WKS	ARTIST—RECORD TITLE	LABEL & NO.
4/17/65	**28**	10	8. That Honey Horn Sound	RCA 3337
4/23/66	**39**	3	9. They're Playing Our Song [I]	RCA 3492

HO, Don, and the Aliis

Ho was born on 8/13/30 in Oahu, Hawaii. Nightclub singer/actor.

DATE	POS	WKS	ARTIST—RECORD TITLE	LABEL & NO.
3/4/67	**15**	8	Tiny Bubbles	Reprise 6232

HOLLIDAY, Jennifer

Born on 10/19/60 in Riverside, Texas. Won 1982 Best Actress Tony Award for Broadway's *Dreamgirls*. Also in Broadway's *Your Arm's Too Short to Box with God* (1978) and *Sing, Mahalia Sing* (1985).

DATE	POS	WKS	ARTIST—RECORD TITLE	LABEL & NO.
11/5/83	**31**	5	Feel My Soul	Geffen 4014

HOLLIES, The

Formed in Manchester, England, in 1962. Consisted of Allan Clarke (lead vocals), Graham Nash and Tony Hicks (guitars), Eric Haydock (bass) and Don Rathbone (drums). Clarke and Nash had worked as a duo, The Guytones; added other members, became The Fourtones, Deltas, then The Hollies. First recorded for Parlophone in 1963. Rathbone left in 1963; replaced by Bobby Elliott. Haydock left in 1966; replaced by Bernie Calvert (first heard on "Bus Stop"). Nash left in December 1968 to join David Crosby and Stephen Stills in new trio; replaced by Terry Sylvester, formerly in The Swinging Blue Jeans. Shuffling personnel since then. Clarke, Nash, Hicks and Elliott re-grouped briefly in 1983.

DATE	POS	WKS	ARTIST—RECORD TITLE	LABEL & NO.
7/1/67	**11**	12	1. The Hollies' Greatest Hits [G]	Imperial 12350
4/11/70	**32**	4	2. He Ain't Heavy, He's My Brother	Epic 26538
			He Ain't Heavy, He's My Brother (7)	
8/26/72	**21**	5	3. Distant Light	Epic 30958
			Long Cool Woman (In A Black Dress) (2)	
8/10/74	**28**	2	● 4. Hollies	Epic 32574
			The Air That I Breathe (6)	

HOLLY, Buddy/The Crickets

Born Charles Hardin Holley on 9/7/36 in Lubbock, Texas. One of rock and roll's most original and innovative performers. Began recording western and bop demos with Bob Montgomery in 1954. Signed to Decca label in January 1956 and recorded in Nashville as Buddy Holly & The Three Tunes (Sonny Curtis, lead guitar; Don Guess, bass; and Jerry Ivan Allison, drums). In February 1957, Holly assembled his backing group, The Crickets (Allison; Niki Sullivan, rhythm guitar; and Joe B. Mauldin, bass), for recordings at Norman Petty's studio in Clovis, New Mexico. Signed to Brunswick and Coral labels (subsidiaries of Decca Records). Because of contract arrangements, all Brunswick records were released as The Crickets, and all Coral records were released as Buddy Holly. Holly split from The Crickets in Fall 1958. Holly (age 22), Ritchie Valens and The Big Bopper were killed in a plane crash near Mason City, Iowa, on 2/3/59. Holly was inducted into the Rock and Roll Hall of Fame in 1986.

DATE	POS	WKS	ARTIST—RECORD TITLE	LABEL & NO.
4/27/59	**11**	22	● 1. The Buddy Holly Story [G]	Coral 57279
			includes 4 songs with The Crickets	
			That'll Be The Day (1)/*Peggy Sue* (3)/*Oh, Boy!* (10)	
4/20/63	**40**	1	2. Reminiscing [K]	Coral 57426
			BUDDY HOLLY	
			instrumental backing by The Fireballs dubbed in (1962)	

HOLLYRIDGE STRINGS, The

Arranged and conducted by Stu Phillips, later of The Golden Gate Strings.

DATE	POS	WKS	ARTIST—RECORD TITLE	LABEL & NO.
7/25/64	**15**	9	The Beatles Song Book [I]	Capitol 2116

HOLLYWOOD BOWL SYMPHONY ORCHESTRA
— see PENNARIO, Leonard

Judy Garland's bestselling album, *Judy At Carnegie Hall*, took the No. 1 slot for 13 weeks in 1961 and won the 1961 Album of the Year Grammy Award. In 1994, Garland's earlier recordings for Decca were compiled in a deluxe 4-CD box set released by MCA.

Marvin Gaye's 1969 album, M.P.G., featured a portrait likely to make his female fans swoon. Bolstered by the presence of the Top 10 singles "Too Busy Thinking About My Baby" and "That's the Way Love Is," the album rose to No. 33, his highest showing on the album charts until 1971's *What's Going On*.

The Grateful Dead's eponymous 1967 debut typified the new sounds emanating from San Francisco during the fabled "Summer of Love." Peaking at No. 73, the album wasn't an instant sales smash, but it was certified gold. The band didn't repeat this achievement until 1970's country-rockish *Workingman's Dead*.

Daryl Hall and John Oates's 1977 Top 30 entry, *Beauty On A Back Street*, came a few months after the duo's first No. 1 single, "Rich Girl." In 1985, the Philly-bred, blue-eyed soul singers later realized a longtime ambition by recording a live album featuring Temptations vocalists David Ruffin and Eddie Kendricks.

Jimi Hendrix recorded only five "official" albums in his lifetime, but a flurry of albums featuring the guitarist before his days in The Jimi Hendrix Experience flooded the market during the '60s and '70s. *Rare Hendrix*, recorded with singer Lonnie Youngblood in 1966, was one of them. Released in 1972, the disc reached No. 82.

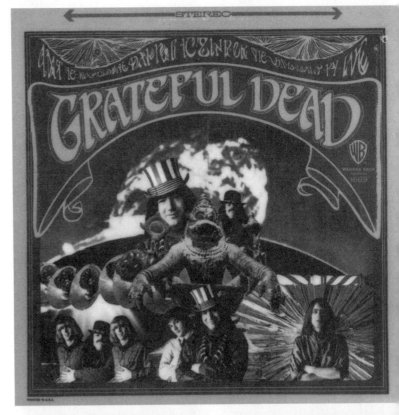

Al Hirt's Dixieland trumpet sound was a fixture of the '60s pop scene. *They're Playing Our Song*, released in 1966 by RCA, was the instrumentalist's last Top 40 album.

Whitney Houston's superstar presence was doubly felt in the 1992 movie *The Bodyguard*. Her music dominated the massively successful soundtrack, which by the end of 1994 had sold more than 13 million copies, and her acting debut with co-star Kevin Costner garnered significant praise from critics.

Alan Jackson became a certified country superstar with 1992's *A Lot About Livin' (And A Little 'Bout Love)*. The album reached No. 13, went quadruple platinum, and remained on the charts through late 1994.

Janet Jackson's hefty deal with Virgin Records was questioned by some in the early '90s, but her resulting debut for the label, 1993's *Janet*, swiftly went to No. 1, and by 1994 had sold more than 6 million copies.

DATE	POS	WKS	ARTIST—RECORD TITLE	LABEL & NO.
			HOLLYWOOD STUDIO ORCHESTRA, The	
3/27/61	**23**	1	Conducted by Mitchell Powell. Exodus [I] not the original soundtrack album	United Art. 6123
			HOLMES, Rupert	
1/5/80	**33**	12	Born on 2/24/47 in Cheshire, England. Moved to New York at age six. Member of the studio group Street People. Wrote and arranged for The Drifters, The Platters and Gene Pitney. Arranged/produced for Barbra Streisand. Wrote The Buoys' hit "Timothy" and the Broadway musical *Drood*. ● Partners In Crime *Escape (The Pina Colada Song)* (1)/*Him* (6)	Infinity 9020
			HONEYDRIPPERS, The	
11/3/84	**4**	18	A rock-superstar gathering: vocalist Robert Plant (Led Zeppelin), with guitarists Jimmy Page (The Yardbirds; Led Zeppelin; The Firm), Jeff Beck (The Yardbirds) and Nile Rodgers (Chic). ▲ **Volume One** [M] *Sea Of Love* (3)	Es Paranza 90220
			HOOTERS	
9/28/85 8/22/87	**12** **27**	30 5	Philadelphia rock band led by Rob Hyman and Eric Bazilian (arrangers/musicians/backing vocalists on Cyndi Lauper's album *She's So Unusual*). Hooter: nickname of their keyboard-harmonica. ▲² 1. Nervous Night ● 2. One Way Home	Columbia 39912 Columbia 40659
			HOPKIN, Mary	
4/12/69	**28**	7	Born on 5/3/50 in Pontardawe, Wales. Discovered by the model Twiggy. Married to producer Tony Visconti (worked with David Bowie) from 1971-81. Post Card produced by Paul McCartney *Those Were The Days* (2)	Apple 3351
			HOPKINS, Nicky	
2/19/72	**33**	3	Born on 2/24/44 in London. Died of stomach illness on 9/6/94. Session pianist for The Rolling Stones, The Who, The Kinks and others. Jamming With Edward! [I] jam session with Ry Cooder, Mick Jagger, Bill Wyman and Charlie Watts	Rolling S. 39100
			HORNE, Lena	
9/16/57 11/17/58 6/22/59	**24** **20** **13**	2 1 19	Born on 6/30/17 in Brooklyn. Broadway and movie musical star. Long-married to bandleader Lennie Hayton. Her career reached a new peak in early '80s with her one-woman Broadway show. Won 1989 Lifetime Achievement Grammy Award. 1. Lena Horne at the Waldorf Astoria [L] 2. Give The Lady What She Wants 3. Porgy & Bess **LENA HORNE/HARRY BELAFONTE**	RCA 1028 RCA 1879 RCA 1507

DATE	POS	WKS	ARTIST—RECORD TITLE	LABEL & NO.
			### HORNSBY, Bruce, And The Range	
			Hornsby was born on 11/23/54 in Williamsburg, Virginia. Singer/pianist/ songwriter/leader of jazz- influenced quintet The Range. Moved to Los Angeles in 1980. Backing pianist for Sheena Easton's touring band, 1983. Formed The Range in 1984 with Joe Puerta (bass), John Molo (drums), guitarists George Marinelli and David Mansfield (replaced by Peter Harris, who left by 1990). Won 1986 Best New Artist Grammy Award.	
10/25/86	3	42	▲³ **1. The Way It Is** originally released on RCA 8058 (with different cover) *The Way It Is* (1)/*Mandolin Rain* (4)	RCA 5904
5/28/88	5	19	▲ **2. scenes from the southside** *The Valley Road* (5)	RCA 6686
7/14/90	20	11	● 3. A Night On The Town	RCA 2041
			### HOROWITZ, Vladimir	
			Born Vladimir Gorowicz on 10/3/03 in Kiev, Russia; died of a heart attack on 11/5/89. Classical pianist. In 1925, left the U.S.S.R. Changed his name in 1926. Moved to the U.S. in 1928. Married for 56 years (until his death) to Wanda, the daughter of famed conductor Arturo Toscanini. His last public performance was in 1987. Won 1990 Lifetime Achievement Grammy Award and 23 other Grammy Awards.	
11/17/62	14	11	1. Vladimir Horowitz (Chopin, Schumann, Rachmaninoff, Liszt) [I]	Columbia 6371
8/28/65	22	8	2. Horowitz at Carnegie Hall — An Historic Return [I-L]	Columbia 728 [2]
			### HORTON, Johnny	
			Born on 4/30/25 in Los Angeles; raised in Tyler, Texas. Died in an auto accident on 11/5/60. Country singer. Married to Billie Jean Jones, widow of country-music superstar Hank Williams.	
2/27/61	8	14	▲ **Johnny Horton's Greatest Hits** [G] *The Battle Of New Orleans* (1)/*Sink The Bismarck* (3)/ *North To Alaska* (4)	Columbia 8396
			### HOT CHOCOLATE	
			Interracial rock-soul group formed in England by lead singer Errol Brown in 1970.	
2/17/79	31	4	Every 1's A Winner *Every 1's A Winner* (6)	Infinity 9002
			### HOT TUNA	
			Formed by Jefferson Airplane members Jorma Kaukonen (guitar) and Jack Casady (bass). Various personnel included harmonica player Will Scarlett (1970-71), violinist Papa John Creach (1971-72; later with Jefferson Starship), drummers Sammy Piazza (1971-74) and Bob Steeler (1975-78), and keyboardist Nick Buck (1978).	
8/15/70	30	5	Hot Tuna [L]	RCA 4353
			### HOUSE OF PAIN	
			Los Angeles-based rap outfit: Erik "Everlast" Schrody, "Danny Boy" O'Connor and Leor "DJ Lethal" DiMant. Met at Taft High School in Woodland Hills, California. Both Schrody and O'Connor were born in the U.S. of Irish parentage. DiMant was born in Latvia.	
8/15/92	14	19	▲ 1. House Of Pain *Jump Around* (3)	Tommy Boy 1056
7/16/94	12	7	● 2. Same As It Ever Was	Tommy Boy 1089

DATE	POS	WKS	ARTIST—RECORD TITLE	LABEL & NO.
			HOUSTON, Thelma	
			Born on 5/7/46. Soul singer/actress from Leland, Mississippi. In the movies *Norman ... Is That You?*, *Death Scream* and *The Seventh Dwarf*.	
2/26/77	**11**	16	Any Way You Like It	Tamla 345
			Don't Leave Me This Way (1)	
			HOUSTON, Whitney	
			Born on 8/9/63 in Newark, New Jersey. Daughter of Cissy Houston and cousin of Dionne Warwick. Began singing career at age 11 with the gospel group New Hope Baptist Junior Choir. As a teen, worked as a backing vocalist for Chaka Khan and Lou Rawls. Pursued modeling career in 1981, appearing in *Glamour* magazine and on the cover of *Seventeen*. Married Bobby Brown on 7/18/92. Starred in the movie *The Bodyguard*.	
6/15/85	**1**(14)	78	▲[11] **1. Whitney Houston**	Arista 8212
			You Give Good Love (3)/*Saving All My Love For You* (1)/ *How Will I Know* (1)/*Greatest Love Of All* (1)	
6/27/87	**1**(11)	51	▲[8] **2. Whitney**	Arista 8405
			I Wanna Dance With Somebody (Who Loves Me) (1)/ *Didn't We Almost Have It All* (1)/*So Emotional* (1)/ *Where Do Broken Hearts Go* (1)/*Love Will Save The Day* (9)	
11/24/90	**3**	31	▲[3] **3. I'm Your Baby Tonight**	Arista 8616
			I'm Your Baby Tonight (1)/*Miracle* (9)	
12/5/92	**1**(20)	76	▲[13] **4. The Bodyguard** [S]	Arista 18699
			6 of the 12 tracks are by Whitney Houston; other artists include Joe Cocker, Kenny G & Aaron Neville, Lisa Stansfield and more *I Will Always Love You* (1)/*I'm Every Woman* (4)/ *I Have Nothing* (4) 1993 Album of the Year Grammy Award	
			H-TOWN	
			Houston R&B vocal trio: brothers Shazam and John "Dino" Conner with Darryl "GI" Jackson.	
5/15/93	**16**	12	▲ Fever For Da Flavor	Luke 126
			Knockin' Da Boots (3)	
			HUDSON and LANDRY	
			Los Angeles DJs Bob Hudson and Ron Landry. Split up in 1976.	
6/12/71	**30**	4	1. Hanging In There [C]	Dore 324
1/1/72	**33**	4	2. Losing Their Heads [C]	Dore 326
			HUES CORPORATION, The	
			Black vocal trio formed in Los Angeles in 1969: Bernard Henderson, Fleming Williams and H. Ann Kelley. Williams replaced by Tommy Brown after "Rock The Boat." Brown replaced by Karl Russell in 1975.	
7/20/74	**20**	7	Freedom For The Stallion	RCA 0323
			Rock The Boat (1)	
			HUGO & LUIGI	
			Producers/songwriters/label executives Hugo Peretti (born 12/6/16) and Luigi Creatore (born 12/21/20; died 5/1/86). Owned record labels Roulette and Avco/Embassy.	
5/11/63	**14**	8	The Cascading Voices of the Hugo & Luigi Chorus	RCA 2641

DATE	POS	WKS	ARTIST—RECORD TITLE	LABEL & NO.
			HUMAN LEAGUE, The	
			Electro-pop band formed in 1977 in Sheffield, England, by synthesists Martyn Ware and Ian Craig Marsh and lead singer/synthesist Philip Oakey. Vocalists Joanne Catherall and Susanne Sulley joined in October 1980 when Ware and Marsh left to form Heaven 17.	
4/3/82	3	20	● **1. Dare**	A&M 4892
			Don't You Want Me (1)	
7/16/83	22	8	2. Fascination! [M]	A&M 12501
			(Keep Feeling) Fascination (8)	
11/1/86	24	12	3. Crash	A&M 5129
			Human (1)	
			HUMBLE PIE	
			Hard-rock band formed in late 1968 in Essex, England. Consisted of Peter Frampton (guitar, vocals; The Herd), Steve Marriott (died 4/20/91 [age 44]; vocals, guitar; Small Faces), Greg Ridley (bass; Spooky Tooth) and Jerry Shirley (drums). Frampton left in October 1971; replaced by Clem Clempson. Disbanded in 1975. Reunited from 1980-81 with Marriott, Shirley, Bobby Tench (guitar) and Anthony Jones (bass).	
11/13/71	21	8	● 1. Performance-Rockin' The Fillmore [L]	A&M 3506 [2]
4/1/72	6	14	● **2. Smokin'**	A&M 4342
11/18/72	37	4	3. Lost And Found [E-R]	A&M 3513 [2]
			re-issue of group's first 2 albums *Town And Country* and *As Safe As Yesterday Is*	
4/14/73	13	7	4. Eat It	A&M 3701 [2]
			side 4 recorded "live" in Glasgow, Scotland	
			HUMPERDINCK, Engelbert	
			Born Arnold George Dorsey on 5/2/36 in Madras, India. To Leicester, England, in 1947. First recorded for Decca in 1958. Met Tom Jones's manager, Gordon Mills, in 1965, who suggested his name change to Engelbert Humperdinck (a famous German opera composer). Starred in his own musical variety TV series in 1970.	
7/1/67	7	31	● **1. Release Me**	Parrot 71012
			Release Me (4)	
1/6/68	10	11	● **2. The Last Waltz**	Parrot 71015
9/21/68	12	19	● 3. A Man Without Love	Parrot 71022
4/5/69	12	11	● 4. Engelbert	Parrot 71026
1/3/70	5	19	● **5. Engelbert Humperdinck**	Parrot 71030
7/18/70	19	8	● 6. We Made It Happen	Parrot 71038
2/27/71	22	8	● 7. Sweetheart	Parrot 71043
9/18/71	25	5	● 8. Another Time, Another Place	Parrot 71048
12/25/76	17	8	▲² 9. After The Lovin'	Epic 34381
			After The Lovin' (8)	
			HUMPHREY, Bobbi	
			Born Barbara Ann Humphrey on 4/25/50 in Dallas. Jazz flutist. Studied at Southern Methodist and Texas Southern University. First recorded for Blue Note in 1971. Cousin of former Duke Ellington trumpet player Eddie Preston.	
2/22/75	30	4	Satin Doll	Blue Note 344
			HUNTER, Ian	
			Born on 6/3/46 in Shrewsbury, England. Singer/guitarist. Leader of Mott The Hoople from 1969-74.	
6/2/79	35	6	You're Never Alone With A Schizophrenic	Chrysalis 1214

DATE	POS	WKS	ARTIST—RECORD TITLE	LABEL & NO.
			HYMAN, Dick	
			Born on 3/8/27 in New York City. Piano-playing composer/conductor/ arranger who toured Europe with Benny Goodman in 1950. Staff pianist at WMCA and WNBC-New York from 1951-57. Music director of "Arthur Godfrey And His Friends" from 1958-62.	
11/25/57	**21**	2	1. 60 Great All Time Songs, Vol. 3 [I]	MGM 3537
			groups of medleys played by Hyman on the piano	
6/21/69	**30**	8	2. Moog — The Electric Eclectics of Dick Hyman [I]	Command 938
			synthesized songs on the Moog	
			I	
			IAN, Janis	
			Born Janis Eddy Fink on 4/7/51 in New York City. Singer/songwriter/pianist/ guitarist. Adopted the last name Ian (her brother's middle name) while studying at Manhattan's High School of Music and Art. Retired from performing from 1968-71.	
8/19/67	**29**	4	1. Janis Ian	Verve F. 3017
6/21/75	**1**(1)	24	▲ **2. Between The Lines**	Columbia 33394
			At Seventeen (3)	
1/31/76	**12**	10	3. Aftertones	Columbia 33919
			ICE CUBE	
			Los Angeles native O'Shea Jackson. Former lyricist of Los Angeles rap group N.W.A. Acted in the movies *Boyz N the Hood* and *Trespass*. His cousin is Del Tha Funkee Homosapien.	
6/16/90	**19**	12	▲ 1. AmeriKKKa's Most Wanted	Priority 57120
1/26/91	**34**	3	▲¹ 2. Kill At Will [M]	Priority 7230
11/16/91	**2**(1)	15	▲ **3. Death Certificate**	Priority 57155
12/5/92	**1**(1)	19	▲ **4. The Predator**	Priority 57185
12/25/93	**5**	14	▲ **5. Lethal Injection**	Priority 53876
12/10/94	**19**	2	● 6. Bootlegs & B-Sides [K]	Priority 53921
			remixes, flip sides and 3 new tracks	
			ICE-T	
			Los Angeles-based rapper Tracy Morrow. In the movies *Breakin'*, *Breakin' II*, *New Jack City*, *Who's the Man?* and *Trespass*. Formed his own Rhyme Syndicate label in 1988. Formed controversial speed-metal band Body Count in 1992.	
10/22/88	**35**	5	● 1. Power	Sire 25765
			cover features his common-law wife, Darlene	
11/4/89	**37**	3	● 2. Freedom Of Speech ... Just Watch What You Say	Sire 26028
			ICE-T The Iceberg	
6/1/91	**15**	8	● 3. O.G. Original Gangster	Sire 26492
4/10/93	**14**	3	● 4. Home Invasion	Rhyme Synd. 53858
			ICICLE WORKS	
			Liverpool rock trio: Robert Ian McNabb (vocals), Chris Layhe and Chris Sharrock.	
6/30/84	**40**	2	Icicle Works	Arista 8202

DATE	POS	WKS	ARTIST—RECORD TITLE	LABEL & NO.
			IDOL, Billy	
			Born William Broad on 11/30/55 in London. Leader of the London punk band Generation X from 1977-81. Suffered serious leg injuries in motorcycle crash on 2/6/90. Appeared in 1991 movie *The Doors*.	
2/25/84	6	38	▲² **1. Rebel Yell**	Chrysalis 41450
			Eyes Without A Face (4)	
11/8/86	6	21	▲ **2. Whiplash Smile**	Chrysalis 41514
			To Be A Lover (6)	
10/17/87	10	18	▲ 3. Vital Idol [K]	Chrysalis 41620
			remix versions of 8 of Idol's hits	
5/26/90	11	19	▲ 4. Charmed Life	Chrysalis 21735
			Cradle Of Love (2)	
			IGLESIAS, Julio	
			Born on 9/23/43 in Madrid. Spanish singer, immensely popular worldwide. Soccer goalie for the pro Real Madrid team until temporary paralysis from car crash. Won 1984 Country Music Association Vocal Duo of the Year Award (with Willie Nelson).	
4/30/83	32	9	▲² 1. Julio [F]	Columbia 38640
9/8/84	5	21	▲⁴ **2. 1100 Bel Air Place**	Columbia 39157
			To All The Girls I've Loved Before (5-with Willie Nelson)	
1/5/91	37	1	● 3. Starry Night	Columbia 46857
6/4/94	30	2	● 4. Crazy	Columbia 57584
			IMPRESSIONS, The	
			Soul group formed in Chicago in 1957; originally known as The Roosters. Consisted of Jerry Butler, Curtis Mayfield, Sam Gooden and brothers Arthur and Richard Brooks. Butler left for solo career in 1958; replaced by Fred Cash. The Brooks brothers left in 1962, leaving Mayfield as trio's leader. Mayfield left in 1970 for solo career; replaced by Leroy Hutson. In 1973, Hutson was replaced by Reggie Torian and Ralph Johnson. Johnson joined Mystique in 1976. Group did movie soundtrack for *Three the Hard Way* (1974). Butler, Mayfield, Gooden and Cash reunited for 1983 tour. Group inducted into the Rock and Roll Hall of Fame in 1991.	
9/12/64	8	21	**1. Keep On Pushing**	ABC-Para. 493
			Keep On Pushing (10)/*Amen* (7)	
4/17/65	23	9	2. People Get Ready	ABC-Para. 505
5/4/68	35	5	3. We're A Winner	ABC 635
			INDIGO GIRLS	
			Folk-pop duo of singers/songwriters/guitarists Amy Ray and Emily Saliers from Decatur, Georgia.	
7/29/89	22	11	▲ 1. Indigo Girls	Epic 45044
5/30/92	21	6	▲ 2. Rites Of Passage	Epic 48865
5/28/94	9	5	● **3. Swamp Ophelia**	Epic 57621
			INFORMATION SOCIETY	
			Techno-dance outfit formed in Minneapolis in 1985: Paul Robb (songwriter), Kurt Valaquen (vocals), Amanda Kramer (keyboards) and James Cassidy (bass). Reduced to trio in 1990 with departure of Kramer.	
10/8/88	25	9	● Information Society	Tommy Boy 25691
			What's On Your Mind (Pure Energy) (3)/*Walking Away* (9)	

DATE	POS	WKS	ARTIST—RECORD TITLE	LABEL & NO.
			INGRAM, Luther	
			Born on 11/30/44 in Jackson, Tennessee. Soul singer/songwriter. Sang in gospel group with his brothers. First recorded for Smash in 1965. In the movie *Wattstax*.	
12/9/72	**39**	3	If Loving You Is Wrong I Don't Want To Be Right	Koko 2202
			(If Loving You Is Wrong) I Don't Want To Be Right (3)	
			INSTANT FUNK	
			Large funk ensemble formed in Philadelphia in 1977. Led by singer/percussionist James Carmichael. Former backup band for Bunny Sigler.	
3/10/79	**12**	13	● Instant Funk	Salsoul 8513
			INXS	
			Rock sextet formed in Sydney, Australia, as The Farris Brothers. Members since group's formation in 1977: Michael Hutchence (lead singer), Kirk Pengilly (guitar), Garry Beers (bass), and brothers Tim (guitar), Andy (keyboards, guitar) and Jon (drums) Farriss. Hutchence, who starred in the movies *Dogs in Space* and *Frankenstein Unbound*, also co-founded the band Max Q. Jon Farriss married actress Leslie Bega.	
2/22/86	**11**	16	▲ 1. Listen Like Thieves	Atlantic 81277
			What You Need (5)	
11/21/87	**3**	65	▲⁴ **2. Kick**	Atlantic 81796
			Need You Tonight (1)/*Devil Inside* (2)/*New Sensation* (3)/ *Never Tear Us Apart* (7)	
10/13/90	**5**	29	▲ 3. X	Atlantic 82140
			Suicide Blonde (9)/*Disappear* (8)	
8/22/92	**16**	6	● 4. Welcome To Wherever You Are	Atlantic 82394
			IRISH ROVERS, The	
			Irish-born folk quintet formed in Alberta, Canada, in 1964. Brothers Will (vocals) and George Millar, their cousin Joe Millar, Jimmy Ferguson and Wilcil McDowell.	
5/25/68	**24**	11	The Unicorn	Decca 74951
			The Unicorn (7)	
			IRON BUTTERFLY	
			San Diego heavy-metal band: Doug Ingle (vocals, keyboards), Erik Braunn (guitar), Lee Dorman (bass) and Ron Bushy (drums). Braunn left in late 1969; replaced by Mike Pinera (leader of Blues Image) and Larry Reinhardt. Split in mid-1971. Braunn and Bushy regrouped in early '75 with Phil Kramer and Howard Reitzes.	
9/7/68	**4**	87	▲⁴ **1. In-A-Gadda-Da-Vida**	Atco 250
			translation of title: in the garden of life	
2/22/69	**3**	19	● **2. Ball**	Atco 280
5/23/70	**20**	6	3. Iron Butterfly Live [L]	Atco 318
			side 2 is a 19-minute version of "In-A-Gadda-Da-Vida"	
9/19/70	**16**	7	4. Metamorphosis	Atco 339
			IRON MAIDEN	
			Heavy-metal quintet from London. 1981 lineup: Paul Di'anno (lead vocals), Clive Burr, Dave Murray, Steve Harris and Adrian Smith. Burr and Di'anno left in 1982; replaced by Bruce Dickinson (lead vocals) and Nicko McBrain. 1990 lineup: Dickinson, Murray, Harris, McBrain and Janick Gers. Dickinson, the cousin of Rob Dickinson of Catherine Wheel, left band in September 1993; replaced by Blaze Bayley.	
5/22/82	**33**	5	▲ 1. The Number Of The Beast	Harvest 12202
			features new lead singer Bruce Dickinson	

DATE	POS	WKS	ARTIST—RECORD TITLE	LABEL & NO.
6/18/83	**14**	14	▲ 2. Piece Of Mind	Capitol 12274
10/6/84	**21**	7	▲ 3. Powerslave	Capitol 12321
11/23/85	**19**	10	▲ 4. Live After Death [L]	Capitol 12441 [2]
10/18/86	**11**	18	▲ 5. Somewhere In Time	Capitol 12524
5/7/88	**12**	11	● 6. Seventh Son Of A Seventh Son	Capitol 90258
10/27/90	**17**	5	● 7. No Prayer For The Dying	Epic 46905
5/30/92	**12**	2	8. Fear Of The Dark	Epic 48993
			ISAAK, Chris	
			Born on 6/26/56 in Stockton, California. San Francisco-based rockabilly singer/songwriter/guitarist. Attended college in Japan. Cameo appearances in the movies *Married to the Mob*, *The Silence of the Lambs*, and others, and starred in *Little Buddha*.	
2/2/91	**7**	21	▲ **1. Heart Shaped World**	Reprise 25837
			Wicked Game (6)	
5/1/93	**35**	5	● 2. San Francisco Days	Reprise 45116
			ISLEY BROTHERS, The	
			R&B trio of brothers from Cincinnati. Formed in early '50s as gospel group. Consisted of O'Kelly, Ronald and Rudolph Isley. Moved to New York in 1957 and first recorded for Teenage Records. Trio added their younger brothers Ernie (guitar, drums) and Marvin (bass, percussion) Isley and brother-in-law Chris Jasper (keyboards) in September 1969. Formed own T-Neck label the same year. Ernie, Marvin and Chris began recording as the trio Isley, Jasper, Isley in 1984. O'Kelly died of a heart attack on 3/31/86 (age 48); Ronald and Rudolph continued as The Isley Brothers through 1989. Ernie, Marvin and Ronald reunited as The Isley Brothers in late 1990. Ronald married Angela Winbush on 6/26/93.	
5/17/69	**22**	7	1. It's Our Thing	T-Neck 3001
			It's Your Thing (2)	
9/9/72	**29**	8	2. Brother, Brother, Brother	T-Neck 3009
9/22/73	**8**	13	▲ 3. 3 + 3	T-Neck 32453
			That Lady (6)	
10/5/74	**14**	9	● 4. Live It Up	T-Neck 33070
6/21/75	**1**(1)	21	▲ **5. The Heat Is On**	T-Neck 33536
			Fight The Power (4)	
6/5/76	**9**	14	● **6. Harvest For The World**	T-Neck 33809
4/23/77	**6**	14	▲ **7. Go For Your Guns**	T-Neck 34432
4/22/78	**4**	14	▲ **8. Showdown**	T-Neck 34930
6/23/79	**14**	7	● 9. Winner Takes All	T-Neck 36077 [2]
4/19/80	**8**	13	▲ **10. Go All The Way**	T-Neck 36305
4/11/81	**28**	5	● 11. Grand Slam	T-Neck 37080
6/18/83	**19**	9	● 12. Between The Sheets	T-Neck 38674
			IT'S A BEAUTIFUL DAY	
			San Francisco-based folk-rock group led by electric violinist/vocalist David LaFlamme.	
7/18/70	**28**	5	Marrying Maiden	Columbia 1058

DATE	POS	WKS	ARTIST—RECORD TITLE	LABEL & NO.
			IVES, Burl	
			Born on 6/14/09 in Huntington Township, Illinois. Actor/author/singer. Played semi-pro football. Began Broadway career in the late '30s. Own CBS network radio show *The Wayfaring Stranger* in 1944. Appeared in many movies, including *East of Eden* and *Cat on a Hot Tin Roof*. Narrated the children's TV classic "Rudolph the Red-Nosed Reindeer." Worked on TV series "The Bold Ones" in the early '70s.	
3/31/62	**35**	5	1. The Versatile Burl Ives!	Decca 4152
			A Little Bitty Tear (9)	
6/30/62	**24**	4	2. It's Just My Funny Way Of Laughin'	Decca 4279
			Funny Way Of Laughin' (10)	
			J	
			JACKSON, Alan	
			Born on 10/17/58 in Newnan, Georgia. Country singer.	
6/8/91	**17**	13	▲³ 1. Don't Rock The Jukebox	Arista 8681
10/31/92	**13**	45	▲ 2. A Lot About Livin' (And A Little 'Bout Love)	Arista 18711
7/16/94	**5**	19	▲² 3. Who I Am	Arista 18759
			JACKSON, Freddie	
			Born on 10/2/56 and raised in Harlem. Soul singer/songwriter. Backup singer for Melba Moore, Evelyn King and others. Member of R&B group Mystic Merlin. Since 1985, Jackson has had 10 #1 R&B hits.	
7/13/85	**10**	36	▲ 1. **Rock Me Tonight**	Capitol 12404
11/22/86	**23**	26	▲ 2. Just Like The First Time	Capitol 12495
			JACKSON, Janet	
			Born on 5/16/66 in Gary, Indiana. Sister of The Jacksons (youngest of nine children). Debuted at age seven at the MGM Grand in Las Vegas with her brothers. At age 10, she played Penny Gordon Woods in the TV series "Good Times" (1977-79); in the cast of "Diff'rent Strokes" (1981-82) and later "Fame." Married James DeBarge of DeBarge in August 1984; marriage annulled in March 1985. Signed a $32 million contract with Virgin Records in 1991. Starred in the 1993 movie *Poetic Justice*.	
3/29/86	**1**(2)	77	▲⁵ 1. **Control**	A&M 5106
			What Have You Done For Me Lately (4)/*Nasty* (3)/ *When I Think Of You* (1)/*Control* (5)/*Let's Wait Awhile* (2)	
10/7/89	**1**(4)	77	▲⁶ 2. **Janet Jackson's Rhythm Nation 1814**	A&M 3920
			"1814" refers to the year that Francis Scott Key wrote America's national anthem *Miss You Much* (1)/*Rhythm Nation* (2)/*Escapade* (1)/*Alright* (4)/ *Come Back To Me* (2)/*Black Cat* (1)/ *Love Will Never Do (Without You)* (1)	
6/5/93	**1**(6)	52	▲⁶ 3. **janet.**	Virgin 87825
			That's The Way Love Goes (1)/*If* (4)/*Again* (1)/ *Because Of Love* (10)/*Any Time, Any Place* (2)/*You Want This* (8)	
			JACKSON, Jermaine	
			Born on 12/11/54 in Gary, Indiana. Fourth oldest of the Jackson family. Vocalist/bassist of The Jackson 5 until group left Motown in 1976. Married Hazel Joy Gordy, daughter of Berry Gordy, Jr., on 12/15/73; later divorced. Rejoined The Jacksons in 1984 for their *Victory* album and tour.	
9/23/72	**27**	8	1. Jermaine	Motown 752
			Daddy's Home (9)	

DATE	POS	WKS	ARTIST—RECORD TITLE	LABEL & NO.
5/3/80	6	17	● 2. Let's Get Serious *Let's Get Serious* (9)	Motown 928
5/26/84	19	16	● 3. Jermaine Jackson	Arista 8203
			JACKSON, Joe	
			Born on 8/11/55 in Burton-on-Trent, England. Singer/songwriter/pianist, featuring an ever-changing music style. Moved to New York City in 1982.	
6/2/79	20	11	● 1. Look Sharp!	A&M 4743
11/10/79	22	8	2. I'm The Man	A&M 4794
9/18/82	4	30	● 3. Night And Day *Steppin' Out* (6)	A&M 4906
4/21/84	20	16	4. Body and Soul	A&M 5000
5/3/86	34	8	5. Big World [L]	A&M 6021 [2]
			3-sided album from a special "live"-concert set; includes an 8-page booklet with lyrics in 6 different languages	
			JACKSON, Michael	
			Born on 8/29/58 in Gary, Indiana. The seventh of nine children. Became lead singer of his brothers' group, The Jackson 5 (later known as The Jacksons), at age five. Played the Scarecrow in the 1978 movie musical *The Wiz*. His 1982 *Thriller* album, with sales of over 40 million copies, is the best-selling album in history. Starred in the 15-minute movie *Captain Eo*, which was shown exclusively at Disneyland and Disneyworld. His 1988 autobiography, *Moonwalker*, became a movie the same year. Winner of 12 Grammy Awards; awarded 1993 Living Legends Grammy Award. Jackson signed a $1 billion multimedia contract with Sony Software on 3/20/91. On 1/25/94, settled out of court for $15 million- $20 million after child sexual-molestation allegations. Jackson married Elvis Presley's daughter, Lisa Marie, on 5/26/94.	
2/26/72	14	12	1. Got To Be There *Got To Be There* (4)/*Rockin' Robin* (2)	Motown 747
9/23/72	5	15	**2. Ben** *Ben* (1)	Motown 755
9/8/79	3	52	▲⁶ **3. Off The Wall** *Don't Stop 'Til You Get Enough* (1)/*Rock With You* (1)/ *Off The Wall* (10)/*She's Out Of My Life* (10)	Epic 35745
12/25/82	1(37)	91	▲²⁴ **4. Thriller** best-selling album in history; produced by Quincy Jones; 1983 Album of the Year Grammy Award *The Girl Is Mine* (2-with Paul McCartney)/*Billie Jean* (1)/ *Beat It* (1)/*Wanna Be Startin' Somethin'* (5)/*Human Nature* (7)/ *P.Y.T. (Pretty Young Thing)* (10)/*Thriller* (4)	Epic 38112
9/26/87	1(6)	54	▲⁸ **5. Bad** *I Just Can't Stop Loving You* (1)/*Bad* (1)/ *The Way You Make Me Feel* (1)/*Man In The Mirror* (1)/ *Dirty Diana* (1)/*Smooth Criminal* (7)	Epic 40600
12/14/91	1(4)	47	▲⁶ **6. Dangerous** *Black Or White* (1)/*Remember The Time* (2)/*In The Closet* (6)/ *Will You Be There* (7)	Epic 45400
			JACKSON, Millie	
			Born on 7/15/44 in Thompson, Georgia. Soul singer/songwriter. To Newark, New Jersey, in 1958. Worked as model in New York City. Professional singing debut at Club Zanzibar in Hoboken, New Jersey, in 1964. First recorded for MGM in 1970.	
12/7/74	21	12	● 1. Caught Up	Spring 6703
12/17/77	34	7	● 2. Feelin' Bitchy	Spring 6715

DATE	POS	WKS	ARTIST—RECORD TITLE	LABEL & NO.
			JACKSON 5/JACKSONS	
			Quintet of brothers formed and managed by their father beginning in 1966 in Gary, Indiana. Consisted of Sigmund "Jackie" (born 5/4/51), Toriano "Tito" (born 10/15/53), Jermaine (born 12/11/54), Marlon (born 3/12/57) and lead singer Michael (born 8/29/58). First recorded for Steeltown in 1968. Known as The Jackson 5 from 1968-75. Jermaine replaced by Randy (born 10/29/61) in 1976. Jermaine rejoined group for 1984's highly publicized *Victory* album and tour. Marlon left for solo career in 1987. Their sisters Rebbie, La Toya and Janet backed the group; each had solo hits. Michael and Janet emerged with superstar solo careers in the '80s. Group lineup since 1989: Jackie, Tito, Jermaine and Randy.	
			THE JACKSON 5:	
1/31/70	5	21	**1. Diana Ross Presents The Jackson 5**	Motown 700
			I Want You Back (1)	
6/6/70	4	21	**2. ABC**	Motown 709
			ABC (1)/*The Love You Save* (1)	
9/26/70	4	23	**3. Third Album**	Motown 718
			I'll Be There (1)/*Mama's Pearl* (2)	
5/8/71	11	14	4. Maybe Tomorrow	Motown 735
			Never Can Say Goodbye (2)	
10/16/71	16	11	5. Goin' Back To Indiana [TV]	Motown 742
			TV special with guests Bill Cosby and Tom Smothers	
1/8/72	12	15	6. Jackson 5 Greatest Hits [G]	Motown 741
			Sugar Daddy (10)	
6/17/72	7	17	**7. Lookin' Through The Windows**	Motown 750
11/2/74	16	7	8. Dancing Machine	Motown 780
			Dancing Machine (2)	
8/2/75	36	3	9. Moving Violation	Motown 829
			THE JACKSONS:	
1/29/77	36	3	● 10. The Jacksons	Epic 34229
			Enjoy Yourself (6)	
3/10/79	11	15	▲ 11. Destiny	Epic 35552
			Shake Your Body (Down To The Ground) (7)	
10/18/80	10	18	▲ **12. Triumph**	Epic 36424
12/12/81	30	8	13. Jacksons Live [L]	Epic 37545 [2]
7/21/84	4	15	▲² **14. Victory**	Epic 38946
			State Of Shock (3)	
			JAGGER, Mick	
			Born Michael Phillip Jagger on 7/26/43 in Dartford, England. Lead singer of The Rolling Stones. Starred in 1970 movie *Ned Kelly*. Also in 1992 movie *Freejack*. Married to Nicaraguan model Bianca Peres Norena de Macias from 1971-80. Married actress/model Jerry Hall on 11/24/90.	
3/16/85	13	12	▲ 1. She's The Boss	Columbia 39940
2/27/93	11	4	● 2. Wandering Spirit	Atlantic 82436
			JAMAL, Ahmad	
			Born Fritz Jones on 7/2/30 in Pittsburgh. Jazz pianist/leader. Formed own trio, The Three Strings, with Ray Crawford (guitar) and Eddie Calhoun (bass). Recorded for Okeh in 1951.	
9/22/58	3	52	**1. But Not For Me/Ahmad Jamal at the Pershing** [I-L]	Argo 628
11/17/58	11	16	2. Ahmad Jamal, Volume IV [I-L]	Argo 636
2/1/60	32	7	3. Jamal At The Penthouse [I]	Argo 646

DATE	POS	WKS	ARTIST—RECORD TITLE	LABEL & NO.
			JAMES, Bob	
			Born on 12/25/39 in Marshall, Missouri. Jazz-fusion keyboardist. Discovered by Quincy Jones in 1962. Was Sarah Vaughan's musical director for four years. In 1973, became arranger of CTI records. In 1976, appointed director of progressive A&R at CBS Records. Formed own label, Tappan Zee, in 1977. Wrote/ performed theme for the TV show "Taxi." Joined the jazz quartet Fourplay in 1991.	
5/7/77	38	2	1. BJ4 [I]	CTI 7074
2/24/79	37	2	● 2. Touchdown [I]	Tappan Zee 35594
12/1/79	23	13	● 3. One On One [I]	Tappan Zee 36241
			BOB JAMES AND EARL KLUGH	
			JAMES, Harry	
			Born on 3/15/16 in Albany, Georgia; died on 7/5/83. Star trumpet player/ bandleader. Achieved fame playing with Benny Goodman in the late '30s. James's own band was very popular during the '40s. Married to movie star Betty Grable from 1943-65.	
11/12/55	10	2	**Harry James in Hi-Fi** [I]	Capitol 654
			5 of 15 tracks feature vocals (4 by Helen Forrest, 1 by Bob Marlo)	
			JAMES, Rick	
			Born James Johnson on 2/1/52 in Buffalo. Funk-rock singer/songwriter/ guitarist. In The Mynah Birds with Neil Young in the late '60s. To London; formed the band Main Line. Returned to the U.S. and formed Stone City Band. Produced Teena Marie, Mary Jane Girls, Eddie Murphy and others. In mid-1994, sentenced to five years in prison for assaults on two women.	
7/22/78	13	16	● 1. Come Get It!	Gordy 981
2/17/79	16	16	2. Bustin' Out Of L Seven	Gordy 984
12/1/79	34	3	3. Fire It Up	Gordy 990
5/30/81	3	27	▲ 4. Street Songs	Gordy 1002
6/12/82	13	10	● 5. Throwin' Down	Gordy 6005
9/10/83	16	12	● 6. Cold Blooded	Gordy 6043
			JAMES, Tommy, And The Shondells	
			James was born Thomas Jackson on 4/29/47 in Dayton, Ohio. To Niles, Michigan, at age 11. Formed pop group The Shondells at age 12. Recorded "Hanky Panky" on the Snap label in 1963. James relocated to Pittsburgh in 1965 after a DJ there popularized "Hanky Panky." Original master was sold to Roulette, whereupon James recruited Pittsburgh group The Raconteurs to become the official Shondells. Consisted of Mike Vale (bass), Pete Lucia (drums), Eddie Gray (guitar) and Ronnie Rosman (organ). James began recording solo in 1970.	
2/8/69	8	14	**1. Crimson & Clover**	Roulette 42023
			Crimson And Clover (1)/Crystal Blue Persuasion (2)	
12/27/69	21	10	2. The Best Of Tommy James & The Shondells [G]	Roulette 42040
			JAMES GANG, The	
			Cleveland hard-rock band: Joe Walsh (guitar, keyboards, vocals), Jim Fox (drums) and Tom Kriss (bass; replaced by Dale Peters in 1970). Walsh left in late 1971; replaced by Dominic Troiano and Roy Kenner. Troiano left in 1973; replaced by Tommy Bolin (died 12/4/76 [age 25]). Many personnel changes from 1974 until group disbanded in 1976.	
8/29/70	20	12	● 1. James Gang Rides Again	ABC 711
5/8/71	27	16	● 2. Thirds	ABC 721
9/25/71	24	5	● 3. James Gang Live In Concert [L]	ABC 733

DATE	POS	WKS	ARTIST—RECORD TITLE	LABEL & NO.
			JAN & DEAN	
			Jan Berry (born 4/3/41) and Dean Torrence (born 3/10/40) formed group called The Barons while attending high school in Los Angeles. Jan & Dean and Barons' member Arnie Ginsburg recorded "Jennie Lee" in Berry's garage. Torrence left for six-month Army Reserve stint, whereupon Berry signed with Doris Day's label, Arwin; the record was released as by Jan & Arnie. Upon Torrence's return from the service, Arnie (not to be confused with the famed DJ of the same name) joined the Navy, and Jan & Dean signed with Herb Alpert's Dore label. Berry was critically injured in auto accident on 4/19/66. Duo made comeback in 1978, after their biographical movie "Dead Man's Curve" aired on TV.	
9/21/63	32	4	1. Surf City And Other Swingin' Cities	Liberty 7314
			Surf City (1)	
2/22/64	22	2	2. Drag City	Liberty 7339
			Drag City (10)	
1/16/65	40	1	3. The Little Old Lady From Pasadena	Liberty 7377
			The Little Old Lady (From Pasadena) (3)	
5/8/65	33	3	4. Command Performance/Live In Person　　　[L]	Liberty 7403
			JANE'S ADDICTION	
			Los Angeles metal/funk band led by vocalist Perry Farrell with Eric Avery, Stephen Perkins and Dave Navarro. Farrell and Perkins later formed Porno For Pyros. Navarro joined Red Hot Chili Peppers in 1993.	
9/8/90	19	25	▲　　Ritual de lo Habitual	Warner 25993
			JANKOWSKI, Horst	
			Born on 1/30/36 in Berlin. Jazz pianist.	
7/24/65	18	12	The Genius Of Jankowski!　　　[I]	Mercury 60993
			JARREAU, Al	
			Born on 3/12/40 in Milwaukee. Soul-jazz vocalist. Has Master's degree in psychology from the University of Iowa. Worked clubs in San Francisco with George Duke.	
8/2/80	27	5	●　　1. This Time	Warner 3434
8/29/81	9	20	▲　　**2. Breakin' Away**	Warner 3576
4/23/83	13	12	●　　3. Jarreau	Warner 23801
			JAY & THE AMERICANS	
			Group formed in late 1959 by New York University students as The Harbor-Lites: John "Jay" Traynor (an early member of The Mystics), Sandy Yaguda, Kenny Vance (later a Hollywood musical director) and Howie Kane. Guitarist Marty Sanders joined during production of the group's first album in 1961. Traynor left after the first hit; replaced by lead singer Jay Black (born David Blatt 11/2/38) in 1962.	
1/15/66	21	5	Jay & The Americans Greatest Hits!　　　[G]	United Art. 6453

DATE	POS	WKS	ARTIST—RECORD TITLE	LABEL & NO.
			JEFFERSON AIRPLANE/STARSHIP	
			Formed as Jefferson Airplane (slang for a split paper match used as a marijuana cigarette holder) in San Francisco, 1965. Consisted of Marty Balin and Signe Anderson (vocals), Paul Kantner (vocals, guitar), Jorma Kaukonen (guitar), Jack Casady (bass) and Alexander "Skip" Spence (drums). Grace Slick and Spencer Dryden joined in 1966, replacing Anderson and Spence. Slick had been in The Great Society. Spence then formed Moby Grape. Dryden replaced by Joey Covington in 1970. Casady and Kaukonen left by 1974 to go full time with Hot Tuna. Balin left in 1971; rejoined in 1975, by which time group was renamed Jefferson Starship and consisted of Slick, Kantner, Papa John Creach (died 2/22/94; violin; Hot Tuna), David Freiberg (bass), Craig Chaquico (pronounced chuck-ee-so; guitar), Pete Sears (bass) and John Barbata (drums). Slick left group from June 1978 to January 1981. In 1979, singer Mickey Thomas joined, replacing Balin, along with Aynsley Dunbar (John Mayall's Bluesbreakers; Mothers of Invention; Journey), who replaced Barbata. Don Baldwin (formerly with Snail) replaced Dunbar (later with Whitesnake) in 1982. Kantner left in 1984, and, due to legal difficulties, band's name was shortened to Starship, whose lineup included Slick, Thomas, Sears, Chaquico and Baldwin. Slick left in early 1988. In 1989, the original 1966 lineup—Balin, Slick, Kantner, Kaukonen and Casady—reunited as Jefferson Airplane with Kenny Aronoff (from John Cougar Mellencamp's band) replacing Dryden. Continuing as Starship were Thomas, Chaquico, Baldwin, Brett Bloomfield (bass) and Mark Morgan (keyboards). Starship disbanded in 1990.	
			JEFFERSON AIRPLANE:	
1/7/67	**17**	9	1. After Bathing At Baxter's	RCA 1511
5/6/67	**3**	29	● **2. Surrealistic Pillow**	RCA 3766
			Somebody To Love (5)/*White Rabbit* (8)	
9/21/68	**6**	12	● **3. Crown Of Creation**	RCA 4058
3/8/69	**17**	8	4. Bless Its Pointed Little Head [L]	RCA 4133
11/29/69	**13**	13	● 5. Volunteers	RCA 4238
12/12/70	**12**	14	● 6. The Worst Of Jefferson Airplane [G]	RCA 4459
12/26/70	**20**	11	● 7. Blows Against The Empire	RCA 4448
			PAUL KANTNER/JEFFERSON STARSHIP	
			with Grace Slick, Jerry Garcia, David Crosby and Graham Nash	
9/18/71	**11**	11	● 8. Bark	Grunt 1001
9/9/72	**20**	9	● 9. Long John Silver	Grunt 1007
			JEFFERSON STARSHIP:	
11/23/74	**11**	10	● 10. Dragon Fly	Grunt 0717
7/26/75	**1** (4)	32	● **11. Red Octopus**	Grunt 0999
			Miracles (3)	
7/24/76	**3**	16	▲ **12. Spitfire**	Grunt 1557
2/19/77	**37**	3	● 13. Flight Log (1966-1976) [K]	Grunt 1255 [2]
			anthology of Airplane, Starship, Hot Tuna, Slick and Kantner releases	
3/18/78	**5**	23	▲ **14. Earth**	Grunt 2515
			Count On Me (8)	
2/24/79	**20**	5	● 15. Gold [G]	Grunt 3247
12/8/79	**10**	17	● **16. Freedom At Point Zero**	Grunt 3452
5/9/81	**26**	16	● 17. Modern Times	Grunt 3848
11/13/82	**26**	11	18. Winds Of Change	Grunt 4372
7/7/84	**28**	8	● 19. Nuclear Furniture	Grunt 4921
			STARSHIP:	
10/26/85	**7**	33	▲ **20. Knee Deep In The Hoopla**	Grunt 5488
			We Built This City (1)/*Sara* (1)	

DATE	POS	WKS	ARTIST—RECORD TITLE	LABEL & NO.
8/1/87	12	9	● 21. No Protection *Nothing's Gonna Stop Us Now* (1)/ *It's Not Over ('Til It's Over)* (9)	Grunt 6413
11/24/56	13	4	**JENKINS, Gordon** Born on 5/12/10 in Webster Groves, Missouri; died on 5/1/84. Pianist/ arranger/composer ("This Is All I Ask," "P.S. I Love You") in the early '30s with Isham Jones, Benny Goodman and others. Musical director/ conductor for Decca Records beginning in 1945. Gordon Jenkins complete Manhattan Tower musical narrative Jenkins originally composed in 1945	Capitol 766
			JENNINGS, Waylon Born on 6/15/37 in Littlefield, Texas. While working as DJ in Lubbock, Texas, Jennings befriended Buddy Holly. Holly produced Jennings's first record "Jole Blon" in 1958. Jennings then joined Holly's backing band as bass guitarist on the fateful "Winter Dance Party" tour in 1959. Established himself in the mid-1970s as a leader of the "outlaw" movement in country music. Married to Jessi Colter since 1969. In the movies *Nashville Rebel* and *MacKintosh and T.J.* Narrator for TV's "The Dukes of Hazzard." Also see Concept Albums.	
8/21/76	34	2	● 1. Are You Ready For The Country	RCA 1816
5/28/77	15	12	▲ 2. Ol' Waylon	RCA 2317
2/18/78	12	9	▲² 3. Waylon & Willie **WAYLON JENNINGS & WILLIE NELSON**	RCA 2686
6/23/79	28	4	▲⁴ 4. Greatest Hits [G]	RCA 3378
7/5/80	36	3	● 5. Music Man	RCA 3602
4/24/82	39	2	6. Black On Black	RCA 4247
9/3/94	12	9	**JERKY BOYS, The** John Brennan, Lou Gitano and Kamal Ahmed. Male prank callers from New York who record their telephone conversations. Gitano left by 1994. Starred in the 1995 movie *The Jerky Boys*. ● The Jerky Boys 2 [C]	Select 92411
6/11/94	36	1	**JERU THE DAMAJA** Real name: Kendrick Jeru Davis. Male rapper from Brooklyn. Appeared on the Gang Starr albums *Daily Operation* and *Hard To Earn*. The Sun Rises In The East	PayDay/ffrr 124011
4/13/91	25	23	**JESUS JONES** London quintet: Mike Edwards (vocals, guitar), Jerry De Borg (guitar), Barry D (keyboards), Al Jaworski (bass) and Gen (drums). ▲ Doubt *Right Here, Right Now* (2)/*Real, Real, Real* (4)	SBK 95715
10/25/69	20	9	**JETHRO TULL** Progressive-rock group formed in 1968 in Blackpool, England. Consisted of Ian Anderson (born 8/10/47, Edinburgh, Scotland; lead singer, flutist), Mick Abrahams (guitar), Glenn Cornick (bass) and Clive Bunker (drums). Named band after 18th-century agriculturist/inventor of seed drill. Recorded several rock-opera/concept albums. Abrahams left after recording of first album (in 1968) to form Blodwyn Pig; replaced by Martin Barre. Added keyboardist John Evan in 1970. Cornick replaced by Jeffrey Hammond-Hammond in 1971. Bunker left in late 1971; replaced by Barriemore Barlow. John Glascock replaced Hammond-Hammond by 1976. Glascock died in 1979; replaced by bassist David Pegg. Since 1980, Anderson and Barre have fronted several lineups that have included Pegg and drummer Doane Perry (Maxus). ● 1. Stand Up	Reprise 6360

DATE	POS	WKS	ARTIST—RECORD TITLE	LABEL & NO.
5/16/70	**11**	17	● 2. Benefit	Reprise 6400
5/15/71	**7**	32	▲³ 3. Aqualung	Reprise 2035
5/20/72	**1**(2)	20	● 4. Thick As A Brick	Reprise 2072
11/18/72	**3**	21	● 5. Living In The Past **[K]**	Chrysalis 2106 [2]
			primarily features unreleased material (1968-71); side 3 recorded live in Carnegie Hall	
7/28/73	**1**(1)	14	● 6. A Passion Play	Chrysalis 1040
11/2/74	**2**(3)	23	● 7. War Child	Chrysalis 1067
10/4/75	**7**	8	● 8. Minstrel In The Gallery	Chrysalis 1082
1/31/76	**13**	9	▲ 9. M.U. — The Best Of Jethro Tull **[G]**	Chrysalis 1078
6/5/76	**14**	7	10. Too Old To Rock 'N' Roll: Too Young To Die!	Chrysalis 1111
3/12/77	**8**	14	● **11. Songs From The Wood**	Chrysalis 1132
5/6/78	**19**	8	● 12. Heavy Horses	Chrysalis 1175
10/28/78	**21**	8	● 13. Jethro Tull Live — Bursting Out **[L]**	Chrysalis 1201 [2]
10/13/79	**22**	5	● 14. Stormwatch	Chrysalis 1238
10/4/80	**30**	4	15. "A"	Chrysalis 1301
5/22/82	**19**	7	16. The Broadsword And The Beast	Chrysalis 1380
12/5/87	**32**	8	● 17. Crest Of A Knave	Chrysalis 41590
			JETS, The	
			Minneapolis-based family band consisting of eight brothers and sisters: Leroy, Eddie, Eugene, Haini, Rudy, Kathi, Elizabeth and Moana Wolfgramm. Their parents are from the South Pacific country of Tonga. All members play at least two instruments. Eugene left group and formed duo Boys Club in 1988.	
5/17/86	**21**	25	▲ 1. The Jets	MCA 5667
			Crush On You (3)/*You Got It All* (3)	
6/11/88	**35**	6	● 2. Magic	MCA 42085
			Cross My Broken Heart (7)/*Rocket 2 U* (6)/*Make It Real* (4)	
			JETT, Joan, & The Blackhearts	
			Born on 9/22/60 in Philadelphia. Played guitar with the Los Angeles female rock band The Runaways, 1975-78. Formed her backing band, The Blackhearts, in 1980. Starred in the 1987 movie *Light of Day* as the leader of a rock band called The Barbusters.	
2/6/82	**2**(3)	20	▲ **1. I Love Rock-n-Roll**	Boardwalk 33243
			I Love Rock 'N Roll (1)/*Crimson And Clover* (7)	
7/23/83	**20**	10	● 2. Album	Blackheart 5437
9/10/88	**19**	18	▲ 3. Up Your Alley	Blackheart 44146
			I Hate Myself For Loving You (8)	
2/24/90	**36**	3	4. The Hit List	Blackheart 45473
			JOAN JETT Jett's cover versions of rock classics of the last 3 decades	
			JIMENEZ, Jose	
			Born William Szarthmary on 10/5/24 in Quincy, Massachusetts. Stage name: Bill Dana. Head writer for TV's "The Steve Allen Show." Star of own TV series from 1963-65. Created the Latin American comic character Jose Jimenez for Allen's TV series.	
8/1/60	**15**	21	1. My Name ... Jose Jimenez **[C]**	Signature 1013
8/21/61	**5**	19	**2. Jose Jimenez — The Astronaut (The First Man In Space)** **[C]**	Kapp 1238
4/7/62	**32**	2	3. Jose Jimenez In Orbit/Bill Dana On Earth **[C]**	Kapp 1257
11/17/62	**16**	5	4. Jose Jimenez Talks To Teenagers Of All Ages **[C]**	Kapp 1304

DATE	POS	WKS	ARTIST—RECORD TITLE	LABEL & NO.
3/16/63	30	3	5. Jose Jimenez — Our Secret Weapon [C]	Kapp 1320
			JIVE BUNNY and the Mastermixers	
			British dance outfit: DJ Les Hemstock and mixers John and Andy Pickles and Ian Morgan.	
1/27/90	26	6	● The Album	Music Fac. 91322
			JOBIM, Antonio Carlos — see SINATRA, Frank	
			JODECI	
			Two pairs of brothers/vocalists from Tiny Grove, North Carolina: Joel "JoJo" and Gedric "K-Ci" Hailey, with Dalvin and Donald "DeVante Swing" DeGrate Jr. Group name pronounced joe-deh-see.	
11/2/91	18	38	▲² 1. Forever My Lady	Uptown 10198
1/8/94	3	19	▲ **2. Diary Of A Mad Band**	MCA/Uptown 10915
			CD includes bonus track	
			JOEL, Billy	
			Born William Martin Joel on 5/9/49 in Hicksville, Long Island, New York. Formed his first band, The Echoes, in 1964, which later became The Lost Souls. Member of Long Island group The Hassles in the late '60s. Later formed rock duo, Attila, with The Hassles' drummer, Jon Small. Signed solo to Columbia Records in 1973. Involved in serious motorcycle accident in Long Island in 1982. Married supermodel Christie Brinkley on 3/23/85; divorced in 1994. Toured and recorded in Russia in 1987. Won 1990 Living Legends Grammy Award.	
3/23/74	27	7	▲³ 1. Piano Man	Columbia 32544
12/21/74	35	2	● 2. Streetlife Serenade	Columbia 33146
11/12/77	2(6)	70	▲⁹ **3. The Stranger**	Columbia 34987
			Just The Way You Are (3)	
11/4/78	1(8)	34	▲⁷ **4. 52nd Street**	Columbia 35609
			1979 Album of the Year Grammy Award *My Life* (3)	
3/22/80	1(6)	35	▲⁷ **5. Glass Houses**	Columbia 36384
			You May Be Right (7)/*It's Still Rock And Roll To Me* (1)	
10/3/81	8	10	▲² **6. Songs In The Attic** [L]	Columbia 37461
			1980 concert tour recordings of pre-*Stranger* songs	
10/16/82	7	23	▲² **7. The Nylon Curtain**	Columbia 38200
8/20/83	4	62	▲⁷ **8. An Innocent Man**	Columbia 38837
			Tell Her About It (1)/*Uptown Girl* (3)/*An Innocent Man* (10)	
7/27/85	6	26	▲⁶ **9. Greatest Hits, Volume I & Volume II** [G]	Columbia 40121 [2]
			You're Only Human (Second Wind) (9)	
8/23/86	7	29	▲² **10. The Bridge**	Columbia 40402
			Modern Woman (10)/*A Matter Of Trust* (10)	
11/21/87	38	3	● 11. Концерт [L]	Columbia 40996 [2]
			recorded in Leningrad (St. Petersburg), Russia; title translates roughly to in concert	
11/11/89	1(1)	28	▲⁴ **12. Storm Front**	Columbia 44366
			We Didn't Start The Fire (1)/*I Go To Extremes* (6)	
8/28/93	1(3)	35	▲⁴ **13. River Of Dreams**	Columbia 53003
			jacket cover painted by Joel's then-wife, supermodel Christie Brinkley *The River Of Dreams* (3)	

DATE	POS	WKS	ARTIST—RECORD TITLE	LABEL & NO.
			JOHN, Elton	
			Born Reginald Kenneth Dwight on 3/25/47 in Pinner, Middlesex, England. Formed his first group Bluesology in 1966. Group backed visiting U.S. soul artists; later became Long John Baldry's backing band. Took the name of Elton John from the first names of Bluesology members Elton Dean and John Baldry. Teamed up with lyricist Bernie Taupin beginning in 1969. Formed Rocket Records in 1973. Played the Pinball Wizard in the movie version of *Tommy*. Was the #1 pop artist of the '70s. Inducted into the Rock and Roll Hall of Fame in 1994. Also see Concept Albums.	
10/31/70	4	28	● **1. Elton John**	Uni 73090
			Your Song (8)	
1/23/71	5	20	● **2. Tumbleweed Connection**	Uni 73096
4/17/71	36	4	● 3. "Friends" [S]	Paramount 6004
5/29/71	11	12	● 4. 11-17-70 [L]	Uni 93105
			title is date of John's New York City concert broadcast on WPLJ-FM	
12/4/71	8	25	▲ **5. Madman Across The Water**	Uni 93120
6/24/72	1(5)	25	● **6. Honky Chateau**	Uni 93135
			Rocket Man (6)/*Honky Cat* (8)	
2/17/73	1(2)	27	▲ **7. Don't Shoot Me I'm Only The Piano Player**	MCA 2100
			Crocodile Rock (1)/*Daniel* (2)	
10/20/73	1(8)	43	▲⁵ **8. Goodbye Yellow Brick Road**	MCA 10003 [2]
			Goodbye Yellow Brick Road (2)/*Bennie And The Jets* (1)	
7/6/74	1(4)	20	▲² **9. Caribou**	MCA 2116
			Don't Let The Sun Go Down On Me (2)/*The Bitch Is Back* (4)	
11/30/74	1(10)	20	▲¹¹ **10. Elton John — Greatest Hits** [G]	MCA 2128
2/8/75	6	8	**11. Empty Sky** [R]	MCA 2130
			John's first album; originally released in 1969	
6/7/75	1(7)	24	▲ **12. Captain Fantastic And The Brown Dirt Cowboy**	MCA 2142
			Someone Saved My Life Tonight (4)	
11/8/75	1(3)	9	▲ **13. Rock Of The Westies**	MCA 2163
			Island Girl (1)	
5/22/76	4	8	● **14. Here And There** [L]	MCA 2197
			side 1: live in London; side 2: live in New York (both 1974)	
11/13/76	3	12	▲ **15. Blue Moves**	MCA/Rocket 11004 [2]
			Sorry Seems To Be The Hardest Word (6)	
10/29/77	21	8	▲ **16. Elton John's Greatest Hits, Volume II** [G]	MCA 3027
			Lucy In The Sky With Diamonds (1)/*Philadelphia Freedom* (1)/ *Don't Go Breaking My Heart* (1-with Kiki Dee)	
11/18/78	15	7	▲ **17. A Single Man**	MCA 3065
11/10/79	35	4	18. Victim Of Love	MCA 5104
6/7/80	13	9	● 19. 21 At 33	MCA 5121
			his 21st album, released at age 33; his 20th album, *Lady Samantha*, a compilation of his DJM label recordings hit the U.K. charts but not the *Billboard* album charts *Little Jeannie* (3)	
6/13/81	21	5	20. The Fox	Geffen 2002
5/15/82	17	8	● 21. Jump Up!	Geffen 2013
6/25/83	25	13	● 22. Too Low For Zero	Geffen 4006
			I Guess That's Why They Call It The Blues (4)	
7/28/84	20	14	● 23. Breaking Hearts	Geffen 24031
			Sad Songs (Say So Much) (5)	

DATE	POS	WKS	ARTIST—RECORD TITLE	LABEL & NO.
1/9/88	24	8	● 24. Live In Australia [L] recorded 12/14/86 in Sydney with the Melbourne Symphony Orchestra *Candle In The Wind* (6)	MCA 8022 [2]
7/9/88	16	19	● 25. Reg Strikes Back *I Don't Wanna Go On With You Like That* (2)	MCA 6240
9/23/89	23	11	▲ 26. Sleeping With The Past	MCA 6321
7/11/92	8	26	▲² **27. The One** *The One* (9)	MCA 10614
12/11/93	25	5	▲ 28. Duets guest artists include k.d. lang, Little Richard, Don Henley, Paul Young, Bonnie Raitt, George Michael, P.M. Dawn and 8 others	MCA 10926
			JOHNNY AND THE HURRICANES Rock-and-roll instrumental band formed as The Orbits in Toledo in 1958: leader Johnny Pocisk "Paris" (saxophone), Paul Tesluk (organ), Dave Yorko (guitar), Lionel "Butch" Mattice (bass) and Tony Kaye (drums; replaced in late 1959 by Bo Savich). Paris had own Attila label from 1965-70.	
4/18/60	34	3	Stormsville [I]	Warwick 2010
			JOHNSON, Don Born on 12/15/49 in Flatt Creek, Missouri. Actor/singer. Played Sonny Crockett on TV's "Miami Vice." Starred in several movies. Remarried his ex-wife, actress Melanie Griffith, in 1989.	
9/20/86	17	11	● Heartbeat *Heartbeat* (5)	Epic 40366
			JOLI, France Born in 1963 in Montreal. French Canadian singer.	
10/13/79	26	6	France Joli	Prelude 12170
			JOLSON, Al Born Asa Yoelson in St. Petersburg, Russia on 3/26/1886 to a rabbi father; raised in Washington, D.C.; died on 10/23/50. One of the most popular entertainers of the 20th century. Broadway star of many musicals, beginning in 1911. Starred in historical part-sound movie *The Jazz Singer* in 1927. Provided vocals for autobiographical movies *The Jolson Story* (1946) and *Jolson Sings Again* (1949). Married to actress Ruby Keeler from 1928-39.	
6/22/63	40	1	The Best Of Jolson [G] Jolson's recordings for the soundtracks *The Jolson Story* and *Jolson Sings Again*	Decca 169 [2]
			JONES, Grace Born on 5/19/52 in Spanishtown, Jamaica. Model/movie actress/singer. Moved to Syracuse, New York, in 1964. Cover girl on *Vogue*, *Elle* and *Der Stern* magazines in the '70s. Appeared in the movies *Conan the Destroyer*, *A View to a Kill* and *Vamp*.	
7/11/81	32	4	Nightclubbing	Island 9624
			JONES, Howard Born on 2/23/55 in Southampton, England. Pop singer/songwriter/synth wizard.	
5/4/85	10	21	▲ **1. Dream Into Action** *Things Can Only Get Better* (5)	Elektra 60390
6/14/86	34	6	2. Action Replay [K-M] 6 tracks; includes 3 remixes and 2 previously unreleased songs *No One Is To Blame* (4)	Elektra 60466

DATE	POS	WKS	ARTIST—RECORD TITLE	LABEL & NO.
			JONES, Jack	
			Born on 1/14/38 in Los Angeles. One of the top Adult Contemporary singers of the '60s. Son of actress Irene Hervey and actor/singer Allan Jones, who had the #8 pop hit "The Donkey Serenade" the year Jack was born. First recorded for Capitol in 1959. Performed the theme for "The Love Boat" TV series. Once married to actress Jill St. John.	
2/8/64	**18**	24	1. Wives And Lovers	Kapp 3352
2/6/65	**11**	11	2. Dear Heart	Kapp 3415
7/3/65	**29**	6	3. My Kind Of Town	Kapp 3433
9/3/66	**9**	15	**4. The Impossible Dream**	Kapp 3486
4/29/67	**23**	6	5. Lady	Kapp 3511
			JONES, Jesus — see JESUS	
			JONES, Jonah	
			Born Robert Jones on 12/31/08 in Louisville, Kentucky. Jazz trumpet player. Worked with Jimmie Lunceford, Stuff Smith, Billie Holiday and Cab Calloway.	
3/10/58	**7**	17	**1. Muted Jazz** [I]	Capitol 839
			THE JONAH JONES QUARTET:	
4/28/58	**7**	19	**2. Swingin' On Broadway** [I]	Capitol 963
9/8/58	**14**	5	3. Jumpin' With Jonah [I]	Capitol 1039
			JONES, Quincy	
			Born Quincy Delight Jones, Jr., on 3/14/33 in Chicago; raised in Seattle. Composer/producer/conductor/ arranger. Began as jazz trumpeter with Lionel Hampton, 1950-53. Music director for Mercury Records in 1961; then vice president in 1964. Wrote scores for many movies, 1965-73. Scored TV series "Roots" in 1977. Arranger/producer for hundreds of successful singers and orchestras. Produced Michael Jackson's mega-albums *Off The Wall*, *Thriller* and *Bad*. Established own Qwest label in 1981. Line producer for the movie *The Color Purple*. Married to actress Peggy Lipton (TV's "Mod Squad") from 1974-89. Most nominated artist in Grammy history with 76 nominations and 25 wins. Won 1989 Trustees Grammy Award. Won 1990 Living Legends Grammy Award. His biographical movie *Listen Up: The Lives Of Quincy Jones* was released in 1990.	
6/22/74	**6**	22	● **1. Body Heat**	A&M 3617
9/6/75	**16**	11	2. Mellow Madness	A&M 4526
			introduces The Brothers Johnson	
3/5/77	**21**	6	● 3. Roots [TV]	A&M 4626
7/1/78	**15**	9	▲ 4. Sounds ... And Stuff Like That!!	A&M 4685
4/18/81	**10**	26	▲ **5. The Dude**	A&M 3721
			featuring James Ingram's vocals on "Just Once" and "One Hundred Ways"	
12/23/89	**9**	22	▲ **6. Back On The Block**	Qwest 26020
			vocals and instrumentation by many of the pop and jazz artists Jones has worked with, among them: Ray Charles, Miles Davis, Ella Fitzgerald, Dizzy Gillespie, Ice-T, Chaka Khan and Sarah Vaughan	
			JONES, Rickie Lee	
			Born on 11/8/54 in Chicago. Pop-jazz-styled singer/songwriter. Moved to Los Angeles in 1977. Won 1979 Best New Artist Grammy Award.	
4/28/79	**3**	24	▲ **1. Rickie Lee Jones**	Warner 3296
			Chuck E.'s In Love (4)	
8/8/81	**5**	15	● **2. Pirates**	Warner 3432
7/30/83	**39**	2	3. Girl At Her Volcano [M]	Warner 23805
			10" album; 2 of the 7 tracks are live performances	

DATE	POS	WKS	ARTIST—RECORD TITLE	LABEL & NO.
11/18/89	**39**	2	4. Flying Cowboys	Geffen 24246

JONES, Tom

Born Thomas Jones Woodward on 6/7/40 in Pontypridd, South Wales. Worked local clubs as Tommy Scott; formed own trio The Senators in 1963. Began solo career in London in 1964. Won 1965 Best New Artist Grammy Award. Host of own TV musical-variety series from 1969-71.

DATE	POS	WKS	ARTIST—RECORD TITLE	LABEL & NO.
2/8/69	**5**	25	● **1. Help Yourself**	Parrot 71025
4/19/69	**14**	13	● 2. The Tom Jones Fever Zone	Parrot 71019
4/26/69	**13**	21	● 3. Tom Jones Live! [L]	Parrot 71014
			originally recorded and released in 1967	
6/21/69	**4**	26	● **4. This Is Tom Jones**	Parrot 71028
11/15/69	**3**	26	● **5. Tom Jones Live In Las Vegas** [L]	Parrot 71031
5/16/70	**6**	13	● **6. Tom**	Parrot 71037
			Without Love (There Is Nothing) (5)	
12/5/70	**23**	3	● 7. I (Who Have Nothing)	Parrot 71039
5/29/71	**17**	9	● 8. She's A Lady	Parrot 71046
			She's A Lady (2)	

JOPLIN, Janis

Born on 1/19/43 in Port Arthur, Texas. White blues-rock singer. Nicknamed "Pearl." To San Francisco in 1966; joined Big Brother & The Holding Company. Left band to go solo in 1968. Died of heroin overdose in Hollywood on 10/4/70. The Bette Midler movie *The Rose* was inspired by Joplin's life. Inducted into the Rock and Roll Hall of Fame in 1995.

DATE	POS	WKS	ARTIST—RECORD TITLE	LABEL & NO.
10/18/69	**5**	16	● **1. I Got Dem Ol' Kozmic Blues Again Mama!**	Columbia 9913
2/6/71	**1** (9)	23	▲³ **2. Pearl**	Columbia 30322
			Me And Bobby McGee (1)	
5/20/72	**4**	16	● **3. Joplin In Concert** [L]	Columbia 31160 [2]
			side 1: with Big Brother & The Holding Company; side 2: with Full Tilt Boogie Band	
8/18/73	**37**	2	▲² 4. Janis Joplin's Greatest Hits [G]	Columbia 32168

JOURNEY

Rock group formed in San Francisco in 1973. Consisted of Neal Schon, George Tickner (guitars), Gregg Rolie (keyboards, vocals), Ross Valory (bass) and Aynsley Dunbar (drums; John Mayall; Mothers of Invention). Schon and Rolie had been in Santana. Tickner left in 1975. Steve Perry (lead vocals) added by 1978. In 1979, Steve Smith replaced Dunbar, who later joined Jefferson Starship, then Whitesnake. Jonathan Cain (ex-keyboardist of The Babys) added in 1981, replacing Rolie. In 1986 group pared down to three-man core: Perry, Schon and Cain. The latter two hooked up with Bad English in 1989. Smith, Valory and Rolie joined The Storm in 1991. Schon with Hardline in 1992.

DATE	POS	WKS	ARTIST—RECORD TITLE	LABEL & NO.
3/25/78	**21**	13	▲³ 1. Infinity	Columbia 34912
4/28/79	**20**	22	▲³ 2. Evolution	Columbia 35797
3/22/80	**8**	17	▲³ **3. Departure**	Columbia 36339
2/21/81	**9**	12	▲² **4. Captured** [L]	Columbia 37016 [2]
8/8/81	**1** (1)	58	▲⁹ **5. Escape**	Columbia 37408
			Who's Crying Now (4)/*Don't Stop Believin'* (9)/ *Open Arms* (2)	
2/19/83	**2** (9)	42	▲⁵ **6. Frontiers**	Columbia 38504
			Separate Ways (Worlds Apart) (8)	
5/10/86	**4**	28	▲² **7. Raised On Radio**	Columbia 39936
			Be Good To Yourself (9)	
12/17/88	**10**	16	▲⁷ **8. Greatest Hits** [G]	Columbia 44493

DATE	POS	WKS	ARTIST—RECORD TITLE	LABEL & NO.
			JUDAS PRIEST	
			Heavy-metal group formed in Birmingham, England in 1973: vocalist Rob Halford, guitarists K.K. Downing and Glenn Tipton, bassist Ian Hill and drummer Dave Holland (replaced by Scott Travis by 1990). Halford left band in mid-1992 to form the rock group Fight.	
7/5/80	34	3	▲ 1. British Steel	Columbia 36443
5/23/81	39	2	● 2. Point Of Entry	Columbia 37052
8/7/82	17	22	▲ 3. Screaming For Vengeance	Columbia 38160
2/11/84	18	12	▲ 4. Defenders Of The Faith	Columbia 39219
4/19/86	17	11	▲ 5. Turbo	Columbia 40158
7/4/87	38	3	6. Priest ... Live! [L]	Columbia 40794 [2]
6/18/88	31	6	● 7. Ram It Down	Columbia 44244
10/13/90	26	7	● 8. Painkiller	Columbia 46891
			JUDD, Wynonna	
			Born Christina Ciminella on 5/30/64 in Ashland, Kentucky. Country singer. Half of The Judds duo with her mother, Naomi, from 1983-91. Moved to Hollywood in 1968. Appeared in *More American Graffiti*. To Nashville in 1979. Her sister is actress Ashley Judd of the TV show "Sisters."	
4/18/92	4	42	▲⁴ 1. Wynonna	Curb/MCA 10529
5/29/93	5	14	▲ 2. Tell Me Why	Curb/MCA 10822
			# K	
			KAEMPFERT, Bert, And His Orchestra	
			Born on 10/16/23 in Hamburg, Germany; died on 6/21/80 in Switzerland. Multi-instrumentalist/bandleader/ producer/arranger for Polydor Records in Germany. Composed "Strangers in the Night" and "Spanish Eyes" among others. Produced first Beatles recording session.	
12/31/60	1 (5)	28	● **1. Wonderland By Night** [I]	Decca 74101
			Wonderland By Night (1)	
10/6/62	14	12	2. That Happy Feeling [I]	Decca 74305
2/27/65	5	27	● **3. Blue Midnight** [I]	Decca 74569
10/9/65	27	10	4. The Magic Music Of Far Away Places [I]	Decca 74616
9/3/66	39	2	5. Strangers In The Night [I]	Decca 74795
12/17/66	30	6	● 6. Bert Kaempfert's Greatest Hits [G-I]	Decca 74810
			KAJAGOOGOO	
			English pop-synth quintet led by Limahl (Chris Hamill), who left in late 1983; replaced by Nick Beggs.	
7/9/83	38	2	White Feathers	EMI America 17094
			Too Shy (5)	
			KANE, Big Daddy	
			Antonio M. Hardy from Brooklyn, New York. Rap lyricist for Cold Chillin' Records. Wrote songs for Roxanne Shante and Biz Markie. Toured as Shante's DJ in 1985. Kane is acronym for King Asiatic Nobody's Equal. Appeared in the movies *The Meteor Man* and *Posse*.	
10/14/89	33	4	● 1. It's A Big Daddy Thing	Cold Chill. 25941
11/24/90	37	1	2. Taste Of Chocolate	Cold Chill. 26303

DATE	POS	WKS	ARTIST—RECORD TITLE	LABEL & NO.
			KANSAS	
			Progressive-rock group formed in Topeka in 1970. Consisted of Steve Walsh (lead vocals, keyboards), Kerry Livgren (guitar, keyboards), Phil Ehart (drums), Robby Steinhardt (violin), Rich Williams (guitar) and Dave Hope (bass). Walsh left in 1981; replaced by John Elefante (later a prolific Christian rock producer). Livgren became a popular contemporary Christian artist in the '80s. Revised lineup in 1986: Walsh, Ehart, Williams, Steve Morse (guitarist from Dixie Dregs) and Billy Greer (bass).	
12/11/76	5	26	▲³ **1. Leftoverture**	Kirshner 34224
10/29/77	4	33	▲³ **2. Point Of Know Return**	Kirshner 34929
			Dust In The Wind (6)	
12/9/78	32	6	▲ 3. Two For The Show [L]	Kirshner 35660 [2]
6/16/79	10	9	● **4. Monolith**	Kirshner 36008
10/11/80	26	8	● 5. Audio-Visions	Kirshner 36588
6/26/82	16	6	6. Vinyl Confessions	Kirshner 38002
1/10/87	35	5	7. Power	MCA 5838
			KANTNER, Paul	
			Born on 3/12/42 in San Francisco. Original member of rock group Jefferson Airplane, later known as Jefferson Starship. Co-founder of KBC.	
12/26/70	20	11	● Blows Against The Empire	RCA 4448
			PAUL KANTNER/JEFFERSON STARSHIP	
			with Grace Slick, Jerry Garcia, David Crosby and Graham Nash	
			KAOMA	
			Paris-based, multi-national outfit of singers, musicians and dancers. Fronted by keyboardist/arranger Jean-Claude Bonaventure.	
3/31/90	40	2	● World Beat [F]	Epic 46010
			1 of 10 tracks sung in English	
			KATRINA And The WAVES	
			British-based, pop-rock quartet fronted by Kansas-born Katrina Leskanich, with American Vince de la Cruz (bass) and Britons Alex Cooper (drums) and Kimberley Rew (guitar; Soft Boys).	
5/25/85	25	9	Katrina And The Waves	Capitol 12400
			Walking On Sunshine (9)	
			KAYE, Sammy	
			Born on 3/13/10 in Rocky River, Ohio. Died on 6/2/87 of cancer. Durable leader of popular "sweet" dance band with the slogan "Swing and Sway with Sammy Kaye." Also played clarinet and alto sax. Charted over 100 songs from 1937-53.	
8/4/56	20	1	1. My Fair Lady (For Dancing) [I]	Columbia 885
11/17/56	19	1	2. What Makes Sammy Swing and Sway [I]	Columbia 891
			SAMMY KAYE and his Swinging and Swaying Strings	
			KC And The SUNSHINE BAND	
			Disco-R&B band formed in Florida in 1973 by lead singer/keyboardist Harry "KC" Casey (born 1/31/51, Hialeah, Florida) and bassist Richard Finch (born 1/25/54, Indianapolis). Interracial band contained from 7 to 11 members.	
9/6/75	4	22	**1. KC And The Sunshine Band**	TK 603
			Get Down Tonight (1)/*That's The Way (I Like It)* (1)	
10/23/76	13	26	2. Part 3	TK 605
			(Shake, Shake, Shake) Shake Your Booty (1)/ *I'm Your Boogie Man* (1)/*Keep It Comin' Love* (2)	
9/9/78	36	5	3. Who Do Ya (Love)	TK 607

DATE	POS	WKS	ARTIST—RECORD TITLE	LABEL & NO.
			KELLY, R.	
			Robert Kelly is a singer/multi-instrumentalist from Chicago. Married singer Aaliyah on 8/31/94.	
11/27/93	**2**(1)	36	▲³ **12 Play**	Jive 41527
			Bump N' Grind (1)	
			KENDRICKS, Eddie	
			Born on 12/17/39 in Union Springs, Alabama; raised in Birmingham; died of lung cancer on 10/5/92. Joined R&B group The Primes in Detroit in the late '50s. Group later evolved into The Temptations; Kendricks sang lead from 1960-71. Later dropped letter "s" from his last name. Also see Hall & Oates.	
9/29/73	**18**	8	1. Eddie Kendricks	Tamla 327
			Keep On Truckin' (1)	
4/6/74	**30**	4	2. Boogie Down!	Tamla 330
			Boogie Down (2)	
4/17/76	**38**	2	3. He's A Friend	Tamla 343
			KENNEDY, John Fitzgerald	
			Tributes to President Kennedy, who was born on 5/29/17 in Brookline, Massachusetts; assassinated in Dallas on 11/22/63.	
1/11/64	**8**	8	1. The Presidential Years 1960-1963 [T]	20th Century 3127
			narrated by David Teig	
1/25/64	**5**	8	2. That Was The Week That Was [T]	Decca 9116
			BBC telecast tribute to Kennedy on 11/23/63	
2/1/64	**18**	4	● 3. A Memorial Album [T]	Premier 2099
			narrated by Ed Brown; a broadcast by WMCA, New York on 11/22/63	
2/22/64	**29**	4	4. Four Days That Shocked The World [T]	Colpix 2500
			Reid Collins narrates the complete story of the events of Nov. 22-25, 1963	
			KENNY G	
			Born Kenny Gorelick on 7/6/56 in Seattle. Fusion saxophonist. Joined Barry White's Love Unlimited Orchestra at age 17. Graduated Phi Beta Kappa and magna cum laude from the University of Washington with an accounting degree. His non-instrumental albums include featured vocalists Freddie Jackson, Lillo Thomas, Kashif, Lenny Williams and others.	
5/9/87	**6**	41	▲⁴ 1. Duotones	Arista 8427
			Songbird (4)	
10/29/88	**8**	27	▲³ 2. Silhouette [I]	Arista 8457
12/23/89	**16**	21	▲³ 3. Live [L]	Arista 8613 [2]
			recorded August 26-27, 1989, in Seattle	
12/5/92	**2**(11)	66	▲⁷ 4. Breathless [I]	Arista 18646
			includes 2 vocal tracks by Peabo Bryson and Aaron Neville	
11/19/94	**1**(3)	10	▲³ 5. Miracles — The Holiday Album [X-I]	Arista 18767
			Christmas charts: 1/'94	
			KENTON, Stan	
			Born on 2/19/12 in Wichita, Kansas; died in Los Angeles on 8/25/79. Progressive jazz bandleader/pianist/ composer. Organized his first jazz band in 1941. Third person named to the Jazz Hall of Fame.	
9/8/56	**13**	2	1. Kenton in Hi-Fi [I]	Capitol 724
9/15/56	**17**	4	2. Cuban Fire! [I]	Capitol 731
11/18/61	**16**	7	3. Kenton's West Side Story [I]	Capitol 1609

Michael Jackson's extraordinary *Thriller*, released by Epic Records in 1982, remains the bestselling album of all time. At the end of 1994, the reclusive singer was reported to be working on new material for a long-awaited best-of compilation.

The Jackson 5's 1970 debut album, *Diana Ross Presents The Jackson 5*, started off young Michael Jackson's career with a bang. The disc rose to No. 5, significantly bolstered by the No. 1 pop smash, "I Want You Back."

Jan & Dean's first charting album, 1963's *Jan & Dean Take Linda Surfin'*, included the duo's hit version of "Linda" released the same year. The latter was actually Jan & Dean's fourth Top 30 single; as far back as 1958, the pair had scored a Top 10 hit with "Jennie Lee," recording under the name Jan & Arnie.

Jethro Tull's climb to '70s stardom was greatly helped via the group's third album, *Benefit*, which reached No. 11, went gold, and prepared the world for what was to come next: the 1971 classic Aqualung, the band's all-time best-seller.

Billy Joel couldn't have titled his 1985 greatest-hits compilation more accurately, despite its seemingly nervy name. The two-record set, billed as *Greatest Hits, Volume I & Volume II*, could barely accommodate the sheer volume of Top 40 singles (24 total) the singer had produced since 1974.

Elton John's 1974 *Greatest Hits* collection arrived in stores at the height of the singer's fame. His bestselling album ever, it was his fifth consecutive No. 1 album and held the top spot for 10 weeks. *Volume II* came in 1977, and *Volume III*, from his stint at Geffen Records, followed 10 years later.

Janis Joplin's solo-career high point, *Pearl*, issued three months after her tragic death from a heroin overdose, went triple platinum and stayed at No. 1 for nine weeks. Her entire career was well documented in 1993 via Columbia's 3-CD compilation, *Janis*.

Wynonna Judd dropped the "Judd" upon embarking on her post-Judds solo career in late 1991. One of country music's hottest female performers, Wynonna's debut went double platinum, a sizable achievement for a woman in that field.

Carole King's 1982 Atlantic debut, *One To One*, peaked at No. 119 and was the last charting album the distinguished voice behind *Tapestry* would produce in more than seven years. The singer signed to an independent label in 1993 with the release of *Colour Of Your Dreams*.

The Kingston Trio's enormous popularity helped ignite America's taste for folk music in the early '60s. Like its predecessor *The Kingston Trio At Large*, 1959's presciently titled *Here We Go Again!*, zoomed to No. 1, where it stayed a total of eight weeks.

DATE	POS	WKS	ARTIST—RECORD TITLE	LABEL & NO.
			KENTUCKY HEADHUNTERS, The	
			Rock-country quintet from Edmonton, Kentucky. Founded by brothers Richard (born 1/27/55) and Fred (born 7/8/58) Young with their cousin Greg Martin (born 3/31/54). Brothers Doug (born 2/16/60) and Ricky Lee (born 10/8/53) Phelps left in 1992 to form Brother Phelps; replaced by Mark Orr (born 11/16/49) and Anthony Kenney (born 10/8/53). Group hosted own show on WLOC-FM radio, *The Chitlin' Show*.	
5/11/91	29	4	● Electric Barnyard	Mercury 848054
			KESNER, Dick, & his Stradivarius Violin	
			Violin player. A regular on TV's "The Lawrence Welk Show" (1955-59).	
1/12/59	22	2	Lawrence Welk Presents Dick Kesner [I]	Brunswick 54044
			KHAN, Chaka	
			Born Yvette Marie Stevens on 3/23/53 in Great Lakes, Illinois. Became lead singer of Rufus in 1972. Rufus members Andre Fischer and Kevin Murphy were with The American Breed. Recorded solo and with Rufus since 1978. Sister of vocalists Taka Boom and Mark Stevens (Jamaica Boys). Khan's daughter Milini is a member of Pretty In Pink.	
11/18/78	12	8	● 1. Chaka	Warner 3245
5/16/81	17	9	● 2. What Cha' Gonna Do For Me	Warner 3526
11/3/84	14	16	▲ 3. I Feel For You	Warner 25162
			I Feel For You (3)	
			KIHN, Greg, Band	
			Kihn is a rock singer/songwriter/guitarist from Baltimore. Formed band in Berkeley, California, in 1975.	
8/1/81	32	5	1. Rockihnroll	Beserkley 10069
5/15/82	33	4	2. Kihntinued	Beserkley 60101
3/19/83	15	12	3. Kihnspiracy	Beserkley 60224
			Jeopardy (2)	
			KIM, Andy	
			Born Andrew Joachim on 12/5/46 in Montreal. His parents were from Lebanon. Pop singer/songwriter. Teamed with Jeff Barry to write "Sugar, Sugar."	
10/26/74	21	6	Andy Kim	Capitol 11318
			Rock Me Gently (1)	
			KING, B.B.	
			Born Riley B. King on 9/16/25 in Itta Bena, Mississippi. The most famous blues singer/guitarist in the world today. Moved to Memphis in 1946. Own radio show on WDIA-Memphis, 1949-50, where he was dubbed "The Beale Street Blues Boy," later shortened to "Blues Boy," then simply "B.B." First recorded for Bullet in 1949. Inducted into the Rock and Roll Hall of Fame in 1987. Won 1987 Lifetime Achievement Grammy Award. Appeared in the movies *Into the Night* (1985) and *Amazon Women on the Moon* (1987).	
4/4/70	38	3	1. Completely Well	BluesWay 6037
11/7/70	26	6	2. Indianola Mississippi Seeds	ABC 713
3/13/71	25	7	3. Live In Cook County Jail [L]	ABC 723
			KING, Ben E.	
			Born Benjamin Earl Nelson on 9/23/38 in Henderson, North Carolina. To New York in 1947. Worked with The Moonglows for six months while still in high school. Joined The Five Crowns in 1957, who became the new Drifters in 1959. Wrote lyrics to "There Goes My Baby," his first lead performance with The Drifters. Went solo in May 1960.	
6/28/75	39	1	1. Supernatural	Atlantic 18132
			Supernatural Thing (5)	

DATE	POS	WKS	ARTIST—RECORD TITLE	LABEL & NO.
8/20/77	**33**	5	2. Benny And Us **AVERAGE WHITE BAND & BEN E. KING**	Atlantic 19105
			KING, Carole	
			Born Carole Klein on 2/9/42 in Brooklyn. Singer/songwriter/pianist. Neil Sedaka wrote his 1959 hit "Oh! Carol" about her. Married lyricist Gerry Goffin in 1958; team wrote four #1 hits: "Will You Love Me Tomorrow," "Go Away Little Girl," "Take Good Care Of My Baby" and "The Loco-Motion." Divorced Goffin in 1968. First solo album in 1970. In 1971, won four Grammy Awards. King and Goffin's daughter, Louise Goffin, began solo career in 1979. King is one of the most successful female songwriters of the rock era. She and Goffin were inducted as a songwriting team into the Rock and Roll Hall of Fame in 1990.	

4/24/71	**1**(15)	68	▲² **1. Tapestry**
			      1971 Album of the Year Grammy Award
			      It's Too Late (1)
				Ode 77009

12/18/71	**1**(3)	20	● **2. Music** *Sweet Seasons* (9)	Ode 77013
11/11/72	**2**(5)	20	● **3. Rhymes & Reasons**	Ode 77016
6/30/73	**6**	15	● **4. Fantasy**	Ode 77018
10/5/74	**1**(1)	13	● **5. Wrap Around Joy** *Jazzman* (2)/*Nightingale* (9)	Ode 77024
3/29/75	**20**	4	6. Really Rosie [TV] from the original animated TV soundtrack	Ode 77027
2/7/76	**3**	14	● **7. Thoroughbred**	Ode 77034
8/13/77	**17**	7	● **8. Simple Things**	Capitol 11667
			KING, Evelyn "Champagne"	
			Born on 6/29/60 in the Bronx. To Philadelphia in 1970. Employed as cleaning woman at Sigma Studios when discovered.	
7/22/78	**14**	13	● 1. Smooth Talk *Shame* (9)	RCA 2466
5/12/79	**35**	3	● 2. Music Box **EVELYN KING:**	RCA 3033
8/15/81	**28**	6	3. I'm In Love	RCA 3962
10/9/82	**27**	7	● 4. Get Loose	RCA 4337
			KING CRIMSON	
			English progressive-rock group formed in 1969 by eccentric guitarist Robert Fripp. Group featured an ever-changing lineup of top British artists, among them Ian McDonald (sax; Foreigner), Greg Lake (bass, vocals; Emerson, Lake & Palmer), Bill Bruford (drums; Yes), Boz Burrell (bass, vocals; Bad Company), John Wetton (bass, vocals; Uriah Heep; U.K.; Asia) and American Adrian Belew (vocals, guitar).	
2/28/70	**28**	6	● 1. In The Court Of The Crimson King — An Observation By King Crimson	Atlantic 8245
9/19/70	**31**	5	2. In The Wake Of Poseidon lead singer is Greg Lake on above 2	Atlantic 8266
			KINGDOM COME	
			Hard-rock quintet formed and fronted by Hamburg, Germany, native Lenny Wolf (vocals). In 1984, Wolf formed and fronted Stone Fury.	
3/26/88	**12**	12	● Kingdom Come	Polydor 835368

DATE	POS	WKS	ARTIST—RECORD TITLE	LABEL & NO.
			KING FAMILY	
			The daughters of William King Driggs, Sr., with their families, numbering nearly 40. The extended family had own variety TV series in 1965. Accompanied by The Alvino Rey Orchestra (the husband of Luise Driggs).	
7/31/65	**34**	4	The King Family Show!	Warner 1601
			KINGSMEN, The	
			Rock band formed in Portland, Oregon, in 1957. Consisted of Jack Ely (lead singer, guitar), Lynn Easton (drums), Mike Mitchell (guitar), Bob Nordby (bass) and Don Gallucci (keyboards). After release of "Louie Louie" (featuring lead vocal by Ely), Easton took over leadership of band and replaced Ely as lead singer. One of America's premier '60s garage rock bands.	
2/22/64	**20**	28	1. The Kingsmen In Person [L]	Wand 657
			Louie, Louie (2)	
10/17/64	**15**	9	2. The Kingsmen, Volume II [L]	Wand 659
4/10/65	**22**	7	3. The Kingsmen, Volume 3 [L]	Wand 662
			The Jolly Green Giant (4)	
			KINGSTON TRIO, The	
			Folk trio formed in San Francisco in 1957: Dave Guard (banjo), Bob Shane and Nick Reynolds (guitars). Five of the trio's first six albums hit #1 for a total of 46 weeks. Big break came at San Francisco's Purple Onion, where the group stayed for eight months. Guard left in 1961 to form The Whiskeyhill Singers; John Stewart replaced him. Disbanded in 1968. Shane formed The New Kingston Trio. Guard died on 3/22/91 (age 56) of lymphoma. Current trio consists of Shane, Reynolds and George Grove (joined group in 1972). Originators of the folk-music craze of the '60s.	
11/3/58	**1**(1)	114	● 1. The Kingston Trio	Capitol 996
			Tom Dooley (1)	
2/16/59	**2**(4)	47	● 2. From The Hungry i [L]	Capitol 1107
			The Hungry i is a nightclub in San Francisco	
6/22/59	**1**(15)	43	● 3. The Kingston Trio At Large	Capitol 1199
11/9/59	**1**(8)	40	● 4. Here We Go Again!	Capitol 1258
4/25/60	**1**(12)	42	● 5. Sold Out	Capitol 1352
8/15/60	**1**(10)	27	● 6. String Along	Capitol 1407
9/5/60	**15**	13	7. Stereo Concert [L]	Capitol 1183
			concert in Liberty Hall, El Paso, Texas	
12/5/60	**11**	4	8. The Last Month Of The Year [X]	Capitol 1446
2/27/61	**2**(1)	30	9. Make Way!	Capitol 1474
7/17/61	**3**	20	10. Goin' Places	Capitol 1564
10/16/61	**3**	24	11. Close-Up	Capitol 1642
			Stewart replaces Guard from here on	
3/17/62	**3**	26	12. College Concert [L]	Capitol 1658
			concert on the campus of UCLA	
6/23/62	**7**	48	● 13. The Best Of The Kingston Trio [G]	Capitol 1705
8/25/62	**7**	18	14. Something Special	Capitol 1747
			with orchestral and chorus background	
1/5/63	**16**	23	15. New Frontier	Capitol 1809
4/6/63	**4**	23	16. The Kingston Trio #16	Capitol 1871
			Reverend Mr. Black (8)	
8/31/63	**7**	13	17. Sunny Side!	Capitol 1935
2/22/64	**18**	7	18. Time To Think	Capitol 2011
6/27/64	**22**	5	19. Back In Town [L]	Capitol 2081
			recorded at San Francisco's Hungry i nightclub	

DATE	POS	WKS	ARTIST—RECORD TITLE	LABEL & NO.
			KINKS, The	
			Rock group formed in London in 1963 by Ray Davies (lead singer, guitar) and his brother Dave (lead guitar, vocals). Original lineup also included Peter Quaife (bass) and Mike Avory (drums). Numerous personnel changes during the '70s. Ray appeared in the 1986 movie *Absolute Beginners*. 1987 lineup consisted of Ray and Dave Davies, Ian Gibbons (keyboards; left by 1989), Bob Henrit (drums) and Jim Rodford (bass). Henrit and Rodford were members of Argent. Group inducted into the Rock and Roll Hall of Fame in 1990.	
2/20/65	29	5	1. You Really Got Me	Reprise 6143
			You Really Got Me (7)	
5/1/65	13	11	2. Kinks-Size	Reprise 6158
			All Day And All Of The Night (7)/ *Tired Of Waiting For You* (6)	
9/17/66	9	15	● 3. The Kinks Greatest Hits! [G]	Reprise 6217
1/9/71	35	3	4. Lola Versus Powerman and The Moneygoround, Part One	Reprise 6423
			Lola (9)	
3/19/77	21	8	5. Sleepwalker	Arista 4106
7/15/78	40	1	6. Misfits	Arista 4167
8/4/79	11	10	● 7. Low Budget	Arista 4240
7/5/80	14	14	● 8. One For The Road [L]	Arista 8401 [2]
9/26/81	15	9	● 9. Give The People What They Want	Arista 9567
6/25/83	12	12	10. State of Confusion	Arista 8018
			Come Dancing (6)	
			KISS	
			Hard-rock band formed in New York City in 1973. Consisted of Gene Simmons (bass), Paul Stanley (guitar), Ace Frehley (lead guitar) and Peter Criss (drums). Noted for elaborate makeup and highly theatrical stage shows; Simmons was made up as "The Bat Lizard," Stanley as "Star Child," Frehley as "Space Man" and Criss as "The Cat." Criss replaced by Eric Carr in 1981. Frehley replaced by Vinnie Vincent in 1982. Group appeared without makeup for the first time in 1983 on album cover *Lick It Up*. Mark St. John replaced Vincent in 1984. Bruce Kulick, brother of Bob Kulick of Balance, replaced St. John in 1985. Carr died of cancer on 11/25/91 (age 41). Drummer Eric Singer joined in 1991.	
6/7/75	32	3	● 1. Dressed To Kill	Casablanca 7016
11/1/75	9	17	● 2. Alive! [L]	Casablanca 7020 [2]
4/10/76	11	14	▲ 3. Destroyer	Casablanca 7025
			Beth (7)	
9/18/76	36	3	4. The Originals [R]	Casablanca 7032 [3]
			reissue of the band's first 3 albums (*Kiss*, *Hotter Than Hell* and *Dressed To Kill*)	
11/20/76	11	26	▲ 5. Rock And Roll Over	Casablanca 7037
7/9/77	4	4	▲ 6. Love Gun	Casablanca 7057
11/26/77	7	14	▲ 7. Alive II [L]	Casablanca 7076 [2]
6/10/78	22	5	▲ 8. Double Platinum [G]	Casablanca 7100 [2]
			during October 1978, each member of Kiss issued solo album; all but Peter Criss's made the Top 40	
6/23/79	9	11	▲ 9. Dynasty	Casablanca 7152
7/12/80	35	4	● 10. Kiss Unmasked	Casablanca 7225
10/29/83	24	7	▲ 11. Lick It Up	Mercury 814297
			group shown unmasked for the first time	
10/20/84	19	17	▲ 12. Animalize	Mercury 822495

DATE	POS	WKS	ARTIST—RECORD TITLE		LABEL & NO.
10/12/85	**20**	16	● 13. Asylum		Mercury 826099
10/17/87	**18**	17	▲ 14. Crazy Nights		Mercury 832626
12/10/88	**21**	11	▲ 15. Smashes, Thrashes & Hits	[G]	Mercury 836427
11/11/89	**29**	5	● 16. Hot In The Shade		Mercury 838913
			Forever (8)		
6/6/92	**6**	3	● **17. Revenge**		Mercury 848037
6/5/93	**9**	3	● **18. Alive III**	[L]	Mercury 514777
			recorded in 1992 in Cleveland, Detroit and Indianapolis		
			KLAATU		
			Canadian rock trio: Terry Draper, Dee Long and John Woloschuck. Anonymous first release led to speculation that they were The Beatles. Name taken from alien character in the classic 1951 sci-fi movie *The Day the Earth Stood Still.*		
4/30/77	**32**	3	Klaatu		Capitol 11542
			KLF, The		
			British duo previously known as The Timelords: Bill Drummond (founding member of Big In Japan/former manager of Echo & The Bunnymen and Teardrop Explodes) and Jimmy Cauty (formerly with Zodiac Mindwarp). KLF stands for Kopyright Liberation Front.		
9/14/91	**39**	1	● The White Room	[K]	Arista 8657
			tracks written and recorded from 1987-91		
			3 A.M. Eternal (5)		
			KLUGH, Earl		
			Born on 9/16/53 in Detroit. Jazz acoustic guitarist/pianist. Taught guitar from age 15. Worked Baker's Keyboard Lounge. Toured with Chick Corea's Return to Forever and George Benson. First solo recording for Blue Note in 1976. The Earl Klugh Trio includes Ray Armstrong and Gene Dunlap.		
12/1/79	**23**	13	● 1. One On One	[I]	Tappan Zee 36241
			BOB JAMES AND EARL KLUGH		
6/11/83	**38**	3	2. Low Ride	[I]	Capitol 12253
			KLYMAXX		
			Black female band founded by drummer/producer Bernadette Cooper in Los Angeles in 1979. Lead vocals by Lorena Porter Shelby and Joyce "Fenderella" Irby. Pared down to trio of Shelby, Cheryl Cooley (guitar) and Robbin Grider (keyboards) in 1990.		
12/14/85	**18**	15	● Meeting In The Ladies Room		Constellation 5529
			I Miss You (5)		
			KNACK, The		
			Rock group formed in Los Angeles in 1978. Consisted of Doug Fieger (lead singer, guitar), Berton Averre (lead guitar), Bruce Gary (drums) and Prescott Niles (bass). Disbanded in 1982. All members but Gary reunited in 1986; replaced by drummer Billy Ward. Fieger was a member of the Detroit rock trio Sky.		
7/14/79	**1** (5)	22	▲² **1. Get The Knack**		Capitol 11948
			My Sharona (1)		
3/8/80	**15**	9	● 2. But The Little Girls Understand		Capitol 12045

DATE	POS	WKS	ARTIST—RECORD TITLE	LABEL & NO.

KNIGHT, Gladys, & The Pips

R&B family group from Atlanta. Formed in 1952 when lead singer Gladys was eight years old. Consisted of Gladys (born 5/28/44, Atlanta), her brother Merald "Bubba" Knight and sister Brenda, and cousins William and Eleanor Guest. Named "Pips" for their manager, cousin James "Pip" Woods. First recorded for Brunswick in 1958. Brenda and Eleanor replaced by cousins Edward Patten and Langston George in 1959. Langston left group in 1962. Group has remained a quartet with the same members ever since. Because of legal problems, Gladys couldn't record with The Pips from 1977-80. Gladys was a cast member of the 1985 TV series "Charlie & Co."

DATE	POS	WKS	ARTIST—RECORD TITLE	LABEL & NO.
8/7/71	35	2	1. If I Were Your Woman *If I Were Your Woman (9)*	Soul 731
3/31/73	9	10	**2. Neither One Of Us** *Neither One Of Us (Wants To Be The First To Say Goodbye) (2)*	Soul 737
11/10/73	9	33	● 3. Imagination *Midnight Train To Georgia (1)/* *I've Got To Use My Imagination (4)/* *Best Thing That Ever Happened To Me (3)*	Buddah 5141
7/13/74	35	3	● 4. Claudine [S] *On And On (5)*	Buddah 5602
12/7/74	17	13	● 5. I Feel A Song	Buddah 5612
11/22/75	24	4	● 6. 2nd Anniversary title refers to the group's signing with Buddah Records	Buddah 5639
3/20/76	36	4	7. The Best Of Gladys Knight & The Pips [G]	Buddah 5653
6/18/83	34	6	● 8. Visions	Columbia 38205
3/5/88	39	3	● 9. All Our Love	MCA 42004

KOOL & THE GANG

R&B group formed in Jersey City, New Jersey, in 1964 by bass player Robert "Kool" Bell as The Jazziacs. Session work in New York City, 1964-68. First recorded for De-Lite in 1969. Added lead singer James "J.T." Taylor in 1979. Current lineup consists of brothers Robert and Ronald Bell (sax, keyboards), George Brown (drums), Curtis "Fitz" Williams (keyboards) and Charles Smith (guitar). Taylor left in 1988; replaced by lead singers Gary Brown, Odeen Mays and former Dazz Band lead vocalist Skip Martin. Brown left by 1990.

DATE	POS	WKS	ARTIST—RECORD TITLE	LABEL & NO.
2/23/74	33	4	● 1. Wild And Peaceful *Jungle Boogie (4)/Hollywood Swinging (6)*	De-Lite 2013
10/20/79	13	28	▲ 2. Ladies' Night *Ladies Night (8)/Too Hot (5)*	De-Lite 9513
11/22/80	10	24	▲ **3. Celebrate!** *Celebration (1)*	De-Lite 9518
10/24/81	12	30	▲ 4. Something Special *Get Down On It (10)*	De-Lite 8502
10/23/82	29	12	● 5. As One	De-Lite 8505
1/21/84	29	11	● 6. In The Heart 73 De-Lite 8508 *Joanna (2)*	
2/16/85	13	51	▲ 7. Emergency *Misled (10)/Fresh (9)/Cherish (2)*	De-Lite 822943
12/20/86	25	9	● 8. Forever *Victory (10)/Stone Love (10)*	Mercury 830398

DATE	POS	WKS	ARTIST—RECORD TITLE	LABEL & NO.
			KOOL MOE DEE	
			Rapper from Harlem. Real name: Mohandas DeWese. Formerly with The Treacherous Three.	
5/7/88	**35**	4	▲ 1. How Ya Like Me Now	Jive 1079
7/1/89	**25**	8	● 2. Knowledge Is King	Jive 1182
			KOOPER, AI	
			Born on 2/5/44 in Brooklyn. Top session keyboardist/guitarist/vocalist. Founded Blood, Sweat & Tears in 1968; left in 1969. Member of The Royal Teens in 1959. Founded The Blues Project in 1967.	
10/5/68	**12**	10	● 1. Super Session **MIKE BLOOMFIELD/AL KOOPER/STEVE STILLS**	Columbia 9701
2/15/69	**18**	10	2. The Live Adventures Of Mike Bloomfield And Al Kooper [L] **MIKE BLOOMFIELD & AL KOOPER**	Columbia 6 [2]
			KOSTELANETZ, Andre, and his Orchestra	
			Born on 12/23/01 in St. Petersburg, Russia; died on 1/13/80. Conductor/arranger on radio and records from the '30s to the '70s.	
10/1/55	**4**	11	**Meet Andre Kostelanetz** [K-I]	Columbia KZ 1
			KRAFTWERK	
			Synthesizer band formed in 1970 in Dusseldorf, Germany, by Ralf Hutter and Florian Schneider. Kraftwerk is German for power station.	
3/8/75	**5**	11	**Autobahn** [I]	Vertigo 2003
			KRAVITZ, Lenny	
			Singer/songwriter/multi-instrumentalist raised in New York City and later Los Angeles. Three-year member of the California Boys Choir. Married for a time to actress Lisa Bonet. Son of actress Roxie Roker (played Helen Willis on TV's "The Jeffersons").	
8/24/91	**39**	2	● 1. Mama Said *It Ain't Over 'Til It's Over* (2)	Virgin 91610
3/27/93	**12**	31	▲² 2. Are You Gonna Go My Way	Virgin 86984
			KRIS KROSS	
			Rap duo of Atlanta junior-high-school students: Chris "Mack Daddy" Kelly (born 5/1/78) and Chris "Daddy Mack" Smith (born 1/10/79). Appeared in the movie *Who's the Man?*	
4/18/92	**1**(2)	45	▲⁴ **1. Totally Krossed Out** *Jump* (1)	Ruffhouse 48710
8/21/93	**13**	7	▲ 2. Da Bomb	Ruffhouse 57278
			KRISTOFFERSON, Kris	
			Born on 6/22/36 in Brownsville, Texas. Singer/songwriter/actor. Attended England's Oxford University on a Rhodes scholarship. Married to singer Rita Coolidge from 1973-80. Wrote "Me And Bobby McGee," "For The Good Times" and "Help Me Make It Through The Night." Has starred in many movies since 1972.	
8/21/71	**21**	14	● 1. The Silver Tongued Devil And I	Monument 30679
9/22/73	**31**	4	● 2. Jesus Was A Capricorn	Monument 31909
10/13/73	**26**	6	● 3. Full Moon **KRIS KRISTOFFERSON & RITA COOLIDGE**	A&M 4403
			KROKUS	
			Heavy-metal band from Zurich, Switzerland. Led by Marc Storace (vocals) and Fernando Von Arb (guitar).	
6/11/83	**25**	8	● 1. Headhunter	Arista 9623

DATE	POS	WKS	ARTIST—RECORD TITLE	LABEL & NO.
9/29/84	**31**	6	● 2. The Blitz	Arista 8243
			KRS-ONE	
			Rapper Kris Parker, co-founder of Boogie Down Productions. Brother-in-law of female rapper Harmony.	
10/16/93	**37**	1	Return Of The Boom Bap	Jive 41517

L

DATE	POS	WKS	ARTIST—RECORD TITLE	LABEL & NO.
			LaBELLE, Patti	
			Born Patricia Holt on 5/24/44 in Philadelphia. Began singing career as leader of The Ordettes, which evolved into The Blue Belles. The quartet, formed in Philadelphia in 1962, included Nona Hendryx, Sarah Dash and Cindy Birdsong. Birdsong left in 1967 to join The Supremes. Group continued as a trio. In 1971, the group shortened its name to LaBelle. Trio disbanded in 1977.	
2/15/75	**7**	11	● **1. Nightbirds**	Epic 33075
			LaBELLE	
			Lady Marmalade (1)	
3/3/84	**40**	2	● 2. I'm In Love Again	Phil. Int. 38539
5/24/86	**1**(1)	19	▲ **3. Winner In You**	MCA 5737
			On My Own (1-with Michael McDonald)	
			L.A. GUNS	
			Hollywood male hard-rock group founded by guitarist Tracii Guns and led by vocalist Philip Lewis. Includes Mick Cripps, Kelly Nickels and Steve Riley. Guns was also a member of Contraband in 1991.	
7/7/90	**38**	1	● Cocked & Loaded	Vertigo 838592
			LAINE, Frankie	
			Born Frank Paul LoVecchio on 3/30/13 in Chicago. To Los Angeles in the early '40s. First recorded for Exclusive in 1945. With Johnny Moore's Three Blazers. Signed to the Mercury label in 1947. Dynamic singer whose popularity lasted well into the rock era.	
4/20/57	**13**	12	1. Rockin'	Columbia 975
6/17/67	**16**	9	2. I'll Take Care Of Your Cares	ABC 604
			LAKESIDE	
			Nine-man funk aggregation from Dayton, Ohio, formed in 1969. Consisted of Tiemeyer McCain, Thomas Oliver Shelby, Otis Stokes and Mark Wood (vocals), Steve Shockley (guitar), Norman Beavers (keyboards), Marvin Craig (bass), Fred Alexander, Jr. (drums) and Fred Lewis (percussion).	
1/10/81	**16**	12	● Fantastic Voyage	Solar 3720
			LANG, k.d.	
			Born Kathryn Dawn Lang on 11/2/61 in Consort, Alberta, Canada. Named her group The Reclines, in honor of Patsy Cline. Left country music in 1992.	
3/13/93	**18**	3	▲ Ingenue	Sire 26840
			LANIN, Lester, And His Orchestra	
			Born on 8/26/11; raised in Philadelphia. Leader of society dance bands. First five albums below contain medleys of 25-50 songs with a party-atmosphere background.	
6/24/57	**7**	10	**1. Dance To The Music Of Lester Lanin** [I]	Epic 3340
11/11/57	**18**	2	2. Lester Lanin And His Orchestra [I]	Epic 3242

DATE	POS	WKS	ARTIST—RECORD TITLE		LABEL & NO.
2/3/58	17	2	3. Lester Lanin At The Tiffany Ball	[I]	Epic 3410
6/9/58	19	3	4. Lester Lanin Goes To College	[I]	Epic 3474
11/17/58	12	4	5. Have Band, Will Travel	[I]	Epic 3520
2/10/62	37	1	6. Twistin' in High Society!	[I]	Epic 3825

LANZA, Mario

Born Alfredo Cocozza on 1/31/21 in Philadelphia; died on 10/7/59. Became the most popular operatic tenor since Enrico Caruso, with his voice featured in seven movies, though no theatrical operas.

DATE	POS	WKS	ARTIST—RECORD TITLE		LABEL & NO.
4/28/56	9	6	1. Serenade	[S]	RCA 1996
3/17/58	7	8	2. Seven Hills Of Rome	[S]	RCA 2211
			side 1: soundtrack; side 2: various Lanza recordings		
11/2/59	5	30	3. For The First Time	[S]	RCA 2338
			Mario sings and stars in the above 3 movies		
12/14/59	4	4	4. Lanza Sings Christmas Carols	[X]	RCA 2333
5/16/60	4	32	5. Mario Lanza Sings Caruso Favorites	[F]	RCA 2393
			recorded in Rome, June 1959		

LARSON, Nicolette

Born on 7/17/52 in Helena, Montana; raised in Kansas City. To San Francisco in 1974. Session vocalist with Neil Young, Linda Ronstadt, Van Halen and many others.

DATE	POS	WKS	ARTIST—RECORD TITLE	LABEL & NO.
1/20/79	15	12	● Nicolette	Warner 3243
			Lotta Love (8)	

LAST POETS, The

Black protest quartet: Abiodun Oyewole, Alafia Pudim, Omar Ben Hassen and Nilaja. Oyewole left after first album.

DATE	POS	WKS	ARTIST—RECORD TITLE	LABEL & NO.
8/29/70	29	7	The Last Poets	Douglas 3

LAUPER, Cyndi

Born on 6/20/53 in Queens, New York. Recorded an album for Polydor Records in 1980 with the group Blue Angel. Supported by The Hooters, 1983-84. Won 1984 Best New Artist Grammy Award. In the movies *Vibes* and *Life with Mikey*. Married actor David Thornton on 11/24/91.

DATE	POS	WKS	ARTIST—RECORD TITLE	LABEL & NO.
2/11/84	4	62	▲5 1. She's So Unusual	Portrait 38930
			Girls Just Want To Have Fun (2)/*Time After Time* (1)/	
			She Bop (3)/*All Through The Night* (5)	
10/11/86	4	23	▲2 2. True Colors	Portrait 40313
			True Colors (1)/*Change Of Heart* (3)	
6/24/89	37	4	3. A Night To Remember	Epic 44318
			I Drove All Night (6)	

LAWRENCE, Steve

Born Sidney Leibowitz on 7/8/35 in Brooklyn. Regular performer on Steve Allen's "The Tonight Show" for five years. First recorded for King in 1952. Married singer Eydie Gorme on 12/29/57; they recorded as Parker & Penny in 1979. Steve and Eydie remain a durable nightclub act.

DATE	POS	WKS	ARTIST—RECORD TITLE	LABEL & NO.
6/2/58	19	2	1. Here's Steve Lawrence	Coral 57204
3/2/63	27	7	2. Winners!	Columbia 8753
			Go Away Little Girl (1)	

LAWRENCE, Tracy

Born on 1/27/68 in Atlanta, Texas; raised in Foreman, Arkansas. Male country singer. In May 1991, he was shot four times in an attempted holdup in Nashville; fully recovered.

DATE	POS	WKS	ARTIST—RECORD TITLE	LABEL & NO.
3/27/93	25	12	▲ 1. Alibis	Atlantic 82483

DATE	POS	WKS	ARTIST—RECORD TITLE	LABEL & NO.
10/8/94	**28**	3	● 2. I See It Now	Atlantic 82656

LAWS, Ronnie

Born on 10/3/50 in Houston. R&B-jazz saxophonist. Brother of Debra, Eloise and Hubert Laws. With Earth, Wind & Fire from 1972-73.

DATE	POS	WKS	ARTIST—RECORD TITLE	LABEL & NO.
6/18/77	**37**	2	● 1. Friends And Strangers [I]	Blue Note 730
3/8/80	**24**	6	2. Every Generation	United Art. 1001

LED ZEPPELIN

British heavy-metal rock supergroup formed in October 1968. Consisted of Robert Plant (lead singer), Jimmy Page (lead guitar), John Paul Jones (bass, keyboards) and John Bonham (drums). First known as The New Yardbirds. Page had been in The Yardbirds, 1966-68. Plant and Bonham had been in a group called Band Of Joy. Led Zeppelin's U.S. tour in 1973 broke many box-office records. Formed own Swan Song label in 1974. Plant seriously injured in an auto accident in Greece on 8/4/75. In concert movie *The Song Remains the Same* in 1976. Bonham died on 9/25/80 (age 33) of asphyxiation. Group disbanded in December 1980. Plant and Page formed The Honeydrippers in 1984. Page also with The Firm (1984-86). "Bonham" is the name of group formed by Jason Bonham, John's son, in 1989. Led Zeppelin's most famous recording, "Stairway To Heaven" (on album *Led Zeppelin IV*), was never released as a commercial single. Group inducted into the Rock and Roll Hall of Fame in 1995.

DATE	POS	WKS	ARTIST—RECORD TITLE	LABEL & NO.
2/22/69	**10**	50	▲^{4} **1. Led Zeppelin**	Atlantic 8216
11/15/69	**1**(7)	29	▲^{6} **2. Led Zeppelin II**	Atlantic 8236
			Whole Lotta Love (4)	
10/24/70	**1**(4)	19	▲^{3} **3. Led Zeppelin III**	Atlantic 7201
11/27/71	**2**(4)	24	▲^{11} **4. Led Zeppelin IV (untitled)**	Atlantic 7208
4/21/73	**1**(2)	39	▲^{6} **5. Houses Of The Holy**	Atlantic 7255
3/15/75	**1**(6)	15	▲^{4} **6. Physical Graffiti**	Swan Song 200 [2]
4/24/76	**1**(2)	13	▲^{2} **7. Presence**	Swan Song 8416
11/6/76	**2**(3)	12	▲ **8. The Soundtrack From The Film** *The Song Remains The Same* [S-L]	Swan Song 201 [2]
			soundtrack recorded at Madison Square Garden	
9/8/79	**1**(7)	28	▲^{5} **9. In Through The Out Door**	Swan Song 16002
			6 versions of cover released depicting same bar scene photographed at 6 different angles	
12/18/82	**6**	9	▲ **10. Coda** [K]	Swan Song 90051
			previously unreleased recordings from 1969-78	
11/10/90	**18**	11	▲^{4} **11. Led Zeppelin** [K]	Atlantic 82144 [4]
			54 tracks recorded from 1968-78; includes a 36-page booklet	

LEE, Brenda

Born Brenda Mae Tarpley on 12/11/44 in Lithonia, Georgia. Professional singer since age six. Signed to Decca Records in 1956. Became known as "Little Miss Dynamite." Successful country singer from 1971-85. Lee ranks as the #1 female singer of the '60s (as designated in *Joel Whitburn's Pop Singles Annual 1955-1994*).

DATE	POS	WKS	ARTIST—RECORD TITLE	LABEL & NO.
8/22/60	**5**	20	**1. Brenda Lee**	Decca 74039
			Sweet Nothin's (4)/*I'm Sorry* (1)/ *That's All You Gotta Do* (6)	
11/21/60	**4**	9	**2. This Is ..... Brenda**	Decca 74082
			I Want To Be Wanted (1)	
4/10/61	**24**	11	3. Emotions	Decca 74104
			Emotions (7)	
9/11/61	**17**	10	4. All The Way	Decca 74176
			Dum Dum (4)	

DATE	POS	WKS	ARTIST—RECORD TITLE	LABEL & NO.
4/21/62	29	3	5. Sincerely	Decca 74216
11/17/62	20	4	6. Brenda, That's All	Decca 74326
			You Can Depend On Me (6)/*Fool #1* (3)	
3/23/63	25	8	7. All Alone Am I	Decca 74370
			All Alone Am I (3)	
1/25/64	39	1	8. Let Me Sing	Decca 74439
			Break It To Me Gently (4)/*Losing You* (6)	
11/13/65	36	2	9. Too Many Rivers	Decca 74684

LEE, Peggy

Born Norma Jean Egstrom on 5/26/20 in Jamestown, North Dakota. Jazz singer with Jack Wardlow band (1936-40), Will Osborne (1940-41) and Benny Goodman (1941-43). Went solo in March 1943. In movies *Mister Music* (1950), *The Jazz Singer* (1953) and *Pete Kelly's Blues* (1955). Co-wrote many songs with husband Dave Barbour (married, 1943-52). Awarded nearly $4 million in court for her singing in the animated movie *Lady and The Tramp*.

DATE	POS	WKS	ARTIST—RECORD TITLE	LABEL & NO.
9/17/55	7	10	**1. Songs from Pete Kelly's Blues**	Decca 8166
			PEGGY LEE and ELLA FITZGERALD songs from the movie in which Lee and Fitzgerald had supporting roles; also see Ray Heindorf and Jack Webb	
9/23/57	20	1	2. The Man I Love	Capitol 864
			orchestra conducted by Frank Sinatra	
7/14/58	15	2	3. Jump For Joy	Capitol 979
12/8/58	16	1	4. Things Are Swingin'	Capitol 1049
4/11/60	11	34	5. Latin ala Lee!	Capitol 1290
2/9/63	40	1	6. Sugar 'N' Spice	Capitol 1772
5/4/63	18	9	7. I'm A Woman	Capitol 1857

LeGRAND, Michel, And His Orchestra

Born on 2/24/32 in Paris. Pianist/composer/conductor/arranger. Scored over 50 motion pictures, including *Summer of '42* and *The Thomas Crown Affair*.

DATE	POS	WKS	ARTIST—RECORD TITLE	LABEL & NO.
5/28/55	5	16	**1. Holiday In Rome** [I]	Columbia 647
9/17/55	13	2	2. Vienna Holiday [I]	Columbia 706
6/30/56	9	4	**3. Castles In Spain** [I]	Columbia 888

LEHRER, Tom

Born on 4/9/28 in New York City. Satirist (in song) who performed on the TV show "That Was the Week That Was." Alumnus of Harvard, where he also taught mathematics.

DATE	POS	WKS	ARTIST—RECORD TITLE	LABEL & NO.
12/11/65	18	19	That Was The Year That Was [C]	Reprise 6179

LENNON, John

Born on 10/9/40 in Liverpool, England. Shot to death on 12/8/80 in New York City. Founding member of The Beatles. Married Cynthia Powell on 8/23/62; had son Julian Lennon. Divorced Powell on 11/8/68. Met Yoko Ono in 1966; married her on 3/20/69. Formed Plastic Ono Band in 1969. To New York City in 1971. Fought deportation from the U.S., 1972-76, until he was granted a permanent visa. Won 1991 Lifetime Achievement Grammy Award. Inducted into the Rock and Roll Hall of Fame in 1994.

DATE	POS	WKS	ARTIST—RECORD TITLE	LABEL & NO.
1/24/70	10	13	● **1. The Plastic Ono Band — Live Peace In Toronto 1969** [L]	Apple 3362
			THE PLASTIC ONO BAND 9/13/69 concert featuring Eric Clapton on guitar	
12/26/70	6	12	● **2. John Lennon/Plastic Ono Band** *	Apple 3372
			Plastic Ono Band: John's backing musicians	
10/2/71	1(1)	17	● **3. Imagine** *	Apple 3379

DATE	POS	WKS	ARTIST—RECORD TITLE	LABEL & NO.
			Imagine (3)	
11/24/73	**9**	11	● 4. **Mind Games**	Apple 3414
10/19/74	**1**(1)	11	● 5. **Walls And Bridges**	Apple 3416
			Whatever Gets You Thru The Night (1)/*#9 Dream* (9)	
3/15/75	**6**	9	● 6. **Rock 'N' Roll**	Apple 3419
11/15/75	**12**	6	▲ 7. Shaved Fish * [G]	Apple 3421
			***JOHN LENNON/PLASTIC ONO BAND**	
			Instant Karma (3-'70)	
12/6/80	**1**(8)	27	▲³ 8. **Double Fantasy **	Geffen 2001
			7 songs by Lennon; 7 by Ono; 1981 Album of the Year Grammy Award	
			(Just Like) Starting Over (1)/*Woman* (2)/	
			Watching The Wheels (10)	
12/11/82	**33**	8	9. The John Lennon Collection [G]	Geffen 2023
2/11/84	**11**	10	● 10. Milk and Honey **	Polydor 817160
			6 songs by Lennon; 6 by Ono; recorded in 1980	
			****JOHN LENNON & YOKO ONO**	
			Nobody Told Me (5)	
11/5/88	**31**	5	▲² 11. Imagine: John Lennon [S]	Capitol 90803 [2]
			from the movie documentary of Lennon's life; includes 9 cuts by The Beatles	
			LENNON, Julian	
			Born John Charles Julian Lennon on 4/8/63. Son of Cynthia and John Lennon. First child born to any of The Beatles.	
11/24/84	**17**	28	● 1. Valotte	Atlantic 80184
			title refers to the French studio where album was recorded	
			Valotte (9)/*Too Late For Goodbyes* (5)	
4/19/86	**32**	5	● 2. The Secret Value of DayDreaming	Atlantic 81640
			LENNOX, Annie	
			Born on 12/25/54 in Aberdeen, Scotland. Lead singer of The Eurythmics. Appeared in the movie *Edward II*.	
5/30/92	**23**	35	▲ Diva	Arista 18704
			CD includes a bonus track; also available as Arista 18709, a limited edition CD that includes an interview	
			LETTERMEN, The	
			Harmonic vocal group formed in Los Angeles in 1960. Consisted of Tony Butala (born 11/20/40), Jim Pike (born 11/6/38) and Bob Engemann (born 2/19/36). First recorded for Warner Bros. Engemann replaced by Gary Pike (Jim's brother) in 1968. The #1 Adult Contemporary vocal group of the '60s.	
3/10/62	**6**	25	1. **A Song For Young Love**	Capitol 1669
			When I Fall In Love (7)	
7/21/62	**30**	2	2. Once Upon A Time	Capitol 1711
3/14/64	**31**	3	3. A Lettermen Kind Of Love	Capitol 2013
4/17/65	**27**	5	4. Portrait Of My Love	Capitol 2270
9/18/65	**13**	10	5. The Hit Sounds Of The Lettermen	Capitol 2359
11/19/66	**17**	11	● 6. The Best Of The Lettermen [G]	Capitol 2554
8/5/67	**31**	4	7. Spring!	Capitol 2711
1/27/68	**10**	16	● 8. **The Lettermen!!! ... and "Live!"** [L]	Capitol 2758
			Goin' Out Of My Head/Can't Take My Eyes Off You (7)	
4/20/68	**13**	14	● 9. Goin' Out Of My Head	Capitol 2865
9/20/69	**17**	11	● 10. Hurt So Bad	Capitol 269

DATE	POS	WKS	ARTIST—RECORD TITLE	LABEL & NO.
			LEVEL 42	
			Band from Manchester, England: Mark King (lead vocals), Mike Lindup, and brothers Phil and Boon Gould. The brothers left the band in October 1987; replaced by Alan Murphy (guitar) and Gary Husband (drums). Murphy died on 10/19/89 of AIDS. Alan Holdsworth joined in 1991.	
5/10/86	**18**	13	1. World Machine	Polydor 827487
			Something About You (7)	
6/20/87	**23**	10	2. Running In The Family	Polydor 831593
			LEVERT	
			Soul trio from Ohio: Sean and Gerald Levert (sons of The O'Jays' Eddie Levert), and Marc Gordon. Gerald discovered the group Troop.	
10/3/87	**32**	7	● 1. The Big Throwdown	Atlantic 81773
			Casanova (5)	
4/10/93	**35**	5	● 2. For Real Tho'	Atlantic 82462
			LEVERT, Gerald	
			Lead singer of the Ohio trio Levert. Son of The O'Jays' Eddie Levert. Also discovered Troop.	
9/24/94	**18**	6	● groove On	EastWest 92416
			CD includes bonus track	
			LEWIS, Gary, And The Playboys	
			Pop group formed in Los Angeles in 1964: Lewis (vocals, drums), Al Ramsey, John West (guitars), David Walker (keyboards) and David Costell (bass). Lewis (born Cary Levitch on 7/31/45; name changed at age two) is the son of comedian Jerry Lewis. Group worked regularly at Disneyland in 1964. Lewis inducted into the Army on New Year's Day in 1967; resumed career after discharge in 1968.	
5/8/65	**26**	5	1. This Diamond Ring	Liberty 7408
			This Diamond Ring (1)	
10/30/65	**18**	5	2. A Session With Gary Lewis And The Playboys	Liberty 7419
			Count Me In (2)/*Save Your Heart For Me* (2)	
11/19/66	**10**	13	● **3. Golden Greats** [G]	Liberty 7468
			LEWIS, Huey, and the News	
			Born Hugh Cregg, III, on 7/5/50 in New York City. Joined the country-rock band Clover in the late '70s. Formed his six-man, pop-rock band, The News, in San Francisco in 1980: Huey (lead singer), Chris Hayes (lead guitar), Mario Cipollina (bass; brother of Quicksilver Messenger Service guitarist John Cipollina), Bill Gibson (drums), Sean Hopper (keyboards) and Johnny Colla (sax, guitar). Lewis acted in the movie *Short Cuts*.	
4/10/82	**13**	14	● 1. Picture This	Chrysalis 1340
			Do You Believe In Love (7)	
11/5/83	**1**(1)	71	▲⁷ **2. Sports**	Chrysalis 41412
			Heart And Soul (8)/*I Want A New Drug* (6)/ *The Heart Of Rock & Roll* (6)/*If This Is It* (6)	
9/20/86	**1**(1)	41	▲³ **3. Fore!**	Chrysalis 41534
			Stuck With You (1)/*Hip To Be Square* (3)/*Jacob's Ladder* (1) *I Know What I Like* (9)/*Doing It All For My Baby* (6)	
8/20/88	**11**	12	▲ 4. Small World	Chrysalis 41622
			Perfect World (3)	
5/25/91	**27**	3	● 5. Hard At Play	EMI 93355

DATE	POS	WKS	ARTIST—RECORD TITLE	LABEL & NO.
			LEWIS, Jerry	
			Born Joseph Levitch on 3/16/25 in Newark, New Jersey. Comedian/actor. Formed comedy duo with Dean Martin in 1946, in Atlantic City, that lasted 16 movies and 10 years. Movie debut in 1949 in *My Friend Irma*. His son Gary Lewis was a '60s pop star. National chairman in campaign against muscular dystrophy.	
12/22/56	**3**	19	**Jerry Lewis Just Sings** *Rock-A-Bye Your Baby With A Dixie Melody* (10)	Decca 8410
			LEWIS, Jerry Lee	
			Born on 9/29/35 in Ferriday, Louisiana. Played piano since age nine, professionally since age 15. First recorded for Sun in 1956. Appeared in the movie *Jamboree!* in 1957. Career waned in 1958 after marriage to 13-year-old cousin, Myra Gale Brown, daughter of his bass player. Made comeback in country music beginning in 1968. Nicknamed "The Killer," Lewis has been surrounded by personal tragedies in the past two decades; also survived several serious illnesses. Cousin of both country singer Mickey Gilley and TV evangelist Jimmy Swaggart. Inducted into the Rock and Roll Hall of Fame in 1986. Lewis's early career is documented in the 1989 movie *Great Balls of Fire* starring Dennis Quaid.	
5/19/73	**37**	3	The Session recorded in London with Peter Frampton, Rory Gallagher, Albert & Alvin Lee and others	Mercury 803 [2]
			LEWIS, Ramsey	
			Ramsey (born 5/27/35, Chicago; piano) formed The Gentlemen Of Swing, a jazz-oriented trio, in 1956 in Chicago. Consisted of Ramsey, Eldee Young (bass) and Isaac "Red" Holt (drums). All had been in The Clefs in the early '50s. First recorded for Chess/Argo in 1956. Disbanded in 1965. Young and Holt then formed The Young-Holt Trio. Lewis re-formed his trio with Cleveland Eaton (bass) and Maurice White (drums; later with Earth, Wind & Fire). Reunited with Young and Holt in 1983.	
			THE RAMSEY LEWIS TRIO:	
9/11/65	**2**(1)	33	1. The In Crowd　　　　　　　　　　　　[I-L] *The "In" Crowd* (5)	Argo 757
3/12/66	**15**	15	2. Hang On Ramsey!　　　　　　　　　　[I-L] above albums are by the original trio	Cadet 761
			RAMSEY LEWIS:	
10/8/66	**16**	13	3. Wade In The Water　　　　　　　　　　[I]	Cadet 774
2/8/75	**12**	14	● 4. Sun Goddess with Earth, Wind & Fire on 2 of 6 cuts	Columbia 33194
			LIGHT, Enoch, & The Light Brigade	
			Light was born on 8/18/07 in Canton, Ohio. Died in New York City on 7/31/78. Conductor of own orchestra, The Light Brigade, since 1935. President of Grand Award label and managing director for Command Records, for whom he produced a long string of hit stereo percussion albums in the '60s. Light's studio musicians variously billed as Terry Snyder and The All-Stars (Snyder died on 3/15/63 [age 47]), and The Command All-Stars. Also see Charleston City All-Stars, Los Admiradores, and Tony Mottola.	
6/15/59	**38**	2	1. I Want To Be Happy Cha Cha's　　　　[I]	Grand Award 388
1/25/60	**1**(13)	105	● 2. Persuasive Percussion　　　　　　　[I]	Command 800
1/25/60	**2**(5)	69	3. Provocative Percussion　　　　　　　[I]	Command 806
8/22/60	**3**	36	4. Persuasive Percussion, Volume 2　　　[I]	Command 808
9/19/60	**4**	31	5. Provocative Percussion, Volume 2　　　[I]	Command 810
5/1/61	**3**	15	6. Persuasive Percussion, Volume 3　　　[I]	Command 817
10/9/61	**1**(7)	57	7. Stereo 35/MM　　　　　　　　　　　[I] 35/MM: magnetic film used in recording process	Command 826

DATE	POS	WKS	ARTIST—RECORD TITLE	LABEL & NO.
2/17/62	**8**	22	**8. Stereo 35/MM, Volume Two** [I]	Command 831
3/3/62	**34**	5	9. Persuasive Percussion, Volume 4 [I]	Command 830
4/21/62	**27**	12	10. Great Themes From Hit Films [I]	Command 835
12/22/62	**8**	29	**11. Big Band Bossa Nova** [I]	Command 844
			LIGHTFOOT, Gordon	
			Born on 11/17/38 in Orillia, Ontario, Canada. Folk-pop-country singer/ songwriter/guitarist. Worked on "Country Hoedown," CBC-TV series. Teamed with Jim Whalen as The Two Tones in the mid-1960s. Wrote hit "Early Mornin' Rain" for Peter, Paul and Mary. First recorded for Chateau in 1965.	
1/30/71	**12**	12	● 1. Sit Down Young Stranger	Reprise 6392
			later reissued as *If You Could Read My Mind*	
			If You Could Read My Mind (5)	
7/3/71	**38**	3	2. Summer Side Of Life	Reprise 2037
3/16/74	**1** (2)	23	▲ **3. Sundown**	Reprise 2177
			Sundown (1)/*Carefree Highway* (10)	
3/15/75	**10**	9	**4. Cold On The Shoulder**	Reprise 2206
1/3/76	**34**	4	▲² 5. Gord's Gold [G]	Reprise 2237 [2]
			first record features re-recordings of his '60s songs	
7/17/76	**12**	26	▲ 6. Summertime Dream	Reprise 2246
			The Wreck Of The Edmund Fitzgerald (2)	
2/11/78	**22**	7	● 7. Endless Wire	Warner 3149
			LIMELITERS, The	
			Folk trio formed in Hollywood in 1959. Consisted of Glen Yarbrough (tenor), Lou Gottlieb (bass) and Alex Hassilev (baritone). Yarbrough went solo in 1963.	
2/27/61	**5**	42	**1. Tonight: In Person** [L]	RCA 2272
			recorded at the Ash Grove in Hollywood	
10/2/61	**40**	2	2. The Limeliters	Elektra 7180
10/9/61	**8**	22	**3. The Slightly Fabulous Limeliters** [L]	RCA 2393
2/17/62	**14**	21	4. Sing Out!	RCA 2445
6/16/62	**25**	11	5. Through Children's Eyes [L]	RCA 2512
			featuring 70 children from Berkeley, California	
10/13/62	**21**	6	6. Folk Matinee	RCA 2547
3/9/63	**37**	2	7. Our Men In San Francisco [L]	RCA 2609
			LINDSAY, Mark	
			Born on 3/9/42 in Cambridge, Idaho. Lead singer/saxophonist of Paul Revere & The Raiders. Also recorded with Raider, Keith Allison, and Steve Alaimo as The Unknowns.	
3/28/70	**36**	4	Arizona	Columbia 9986
			Arizona (10)	
			LIPPS, INC.	
			Funk project from Minneapolis formed by producer/songwriter/multi-instrumentalist Steven Greenberg (pronounced lip-synch). Vocals by Cynthia Johnson, Miss Black Minnesota U.S.A. of 1976.	
5/3/80	**5**	13	● **Mouth To Mouth**	Casablanca 7197
			Funkytown (1)	

DATE	POS	WKS	ARTIST—RECORD TITLE	LABEL & NO.
			LISA LISA AND CULT JAM	
			Harlem trio: Lisa Velez (born 1/15/67; lead vocals), Mike Hughes and Alex "Spanador" Moseley. Assembled and produced by Full Force.	
5/16/87	7	29	▲ **Spanish Fly**	Columbia 40477
			all songs written, arranged and produced by Full Force *Head To Toe* (1)/*Lost In Emotion* (1)	
			LITTLE, Rich	
			Born on 11/26/38 in Ottawa, Canada. Comedian/impressionist. Made first U.S. television appearance on "The Judy Garland Show" in 1964.	
2/27/82	29	6	The First Family Rides Again [C]	Boardwalk 33248
			with Melanie Chartoff, Michael Richards, Shelley Hack, Jenilee Harrison, Earle Doud (producer) and Vaughn Meader	
			LITTLE FEAT	
			Los Angeles seminal rock band formed in 1969, fronted by guitarist Paul Barrere and vocalist Lowell George (ex-Mothers Of Invention) with Bill Payne, Richie Hayward, Kenny Gradney and Sam Clayton. Frank Zappa named group after George's shoe size. George died on 6/29/79 (age 34) of drug-related heart failure. Reunited briefly in 1985. Re-grouped in 1988 with Craig Fuller (vocals, guitar; formerly with Pure Prairie League); Fred Tackett also added to lineup.	
11/16/74	36	2	● 1. Feats Don't Fail Me Now	Warner 2784
12/6/75	36	3	2. The Last Record Album	Warner 2884
6/4/77	34	4	● 3. Time Loves A Hero	Warner 3015
3/25/78	18	11	▲ 4. Waiting For Columbus [L]	Warner 3140 [2]
12/15/79	29	7	5. Down On The Farm	Warner 3345
9/19/81	39	2	6. Hoy-Hoy! [K]	Warner 3538 [2]
10/1/88	36	4	● 7. Let It Roll	Warner 25750
			LITTLE RICHARD	
			Born Richard Wayne Penniman on 12/5/32 in Macon, Georgia. R&B/rock-and-roll singer/pianist. Talent contest win led to first recordings for RCA-Victor in 1951. Worked with The Tempo Toppers, 1953-55. Appeared in three early rock-and-roll movies: *Don't Knock the Rock*, *The Girl Can't Help It* and *Mister Rock 'n' Roll* and the 1986 comedy *Down And Out In Beverly Hills*. Earned theology degree in 1961 and was ordained a minister. Left R&B for gospel music, 1959-62, and again in the mid-1970s. One of the key figures in the transition from R&B to rock and roll. Inducted into the Rock and Roll Hall of Fame in 1986. Won 1993 Lifetime Achievement Grammy Award.	
8/5/57	13	5	Here's Little Richard [G]	Specialty 2100
			Long Tall Sally (6)/*Jenny, Jenny* (10)	
			LITTLE RIVER BAND	
			Pop-rock group formed in Australia in 1975. Consisted of Glenn Shorrock (lead singer), Rick Formosa, Beeb Birtles and Graham Goble (guitars), Roger McLachlan (bass) and Derek Pellicci (drums). McLachlan replaced by George McArdle in 1977; Formosa replaced by David Briggs in 1978. American bassist Wayne Nelson replaced McLachlan in 1980. In 1983, Shorrock replaced by John Farnham; Briggs replaced by Steve Housden. By 1985, Pellicci replaced by Steven Prestwich; Birtles had left and keyboardist David Hirschfelder joined. Pellicci and Shorrock returned in 1987. By 1992, Goble had left; Peter Beckett, ex-leader of Player, had joined. Band named after a resort town near Melbourne.	
8/26/78	16	12	▲ 1. Sleeper Catcher	Harvest 11783
			Reminiscing (3)/*Lady* (10)	
8/18/79	10	15	▲ **2. First Under The Wire**	Capitol 11954
			Lonesome Loser (6)/*Cool Change* (10)	

DATE	POS	WKS	ARTIST—RECORD TITLE	LABEL & NO.
10/3/81	21	9	● 3. Time Exposure *The Night Owls* (6)/*Take It Easy On Me* (10)	Capitol 12163
1/8/83	33	12	▲² 4. Greatest Hits [G]	Capitol 12247
			LIVE Rock quartet from York, Pennsylvania: Edward Kowalczyk (vocals), Chad Taylor, Patrick Dalheimer and Chad Gracey.	
5/14/94	12+	6+	● Throwing Copper *co-produced by Jerry Harrison (Talking Heads)*	Radioactive 10997
			LIVING COLOUR Black rock quartet from New York City: London-born, Brooklyn-raised lead guitarist/songwriter Vernon Reid with vocalist Corey Glover (appeared in the movie *Platoon*), bassist Muzz Skillings and drummer William Calhoun. Skillings left in early 1992; replaced by Doug Wimbush (ex-Tackhead; former member of Sugarhill Records band; backed George Clinton and James Brown). Glover is currently a VJ for VH-1.	
2/4/89	6	39	▲² **1. Vivid**	Epic 44099
9/22/90	13	7	● 2. Time's Up	Epic 46202
3/20/93	26	1	3. Stain	Epic 52780
			LIVING STRINGS European orchestra.	
2/27/61	26	1	Living Strings Play All The Music From Camelot [I] *arranged and conducted by Hill Bowen*	RCA Camden 657
			L.L. COOL J Real name: James Todd Smith. Rapper from Queens, New York. Stage name is abbreviation for Ladies Love Cool James. Appeared in the movies *Krush Groove*, *The Hard Way* and *Toys*.	
6/27/87	3	23	▲² **1. Bigger And Deffer**	Def Jam 40793
7/8/89	6	14	▲ **2. Walking With A Panther** *album features 16 tracks, 18 on the CD and 20 on the cassette*	Def Jam 45172
10/13/90	16	36	▲² 3. Mama Said Knock You Out *Around The Way Girl* (9)	Def Jam 46888
4/17/93	5	6	● **4. 14 Shots To The Dome**	Def Jam 53325
			LOBO Born Roland Kent Lavoie on 7/31/43 in Tallahassee, Florida. Pop singer/songwriter/guitarist. Played with The Legends in Tampa in 1961. The Legends included Jim Stafford, Gerald Chambers, Gram Parsons and Jon Corneal. Lavoie formed own publishing company, Boo Publishing, in 1974. Lobo is Spanish for wolf.	

12/16/72	37	7	Of A Simple Man
			      I'd Love You To Want Me (2)/
			      Don't Expect Me To Be Your Friend (8)
				Big Tree 2013

			LODGE, John — see HAYWARD, Justin	
			LOFGREN, Nils Born in 1952 in Chicago; raised in Maryland. Pop-rock singer/guitarist/pianist. Leader of Grin (1969-1974). Member of Bruce Springsteen's E Street Band, 1984-85.	
5/22/76	32	3	1. Cry Tough	A&M 4573
4/23/77	36	2	2. I Came To Dance	A&M 4628

DATE	POS	WKS	ARTIST—RECORD TITLE	LABEL & NO.
			LOGGINS, Kenny	
			Born on 1/7/47 in Everett, Washington; raised in Alhambra, California. Pop-rock singer/songwriter/ guitarist. Cousin of singer Dave Loggins. In band Gator Creek with producer Michael Omartian (later with Rhythm Heritage); later in Second Helping. Worked as songwriter for Wingate Music; wrote Nitty Gritty Dirt Band's "House At Pooh Corner." Signed as solo artist with Columbia in 1971 where he met and recorded with Jim Messina from 1972-76 (as Loggins & Messina).	
6/11/77	27	7	▲ 1. Celebrate Me Home	Columbia 34655
8/5/78	7	17	▲ **2. Nightwatch**	Columbia 35387
			Whenever I Call You "Friend" (5)	
10/27/79	16	24	▲ 3. Keep The Fire	Columbia 36172
10/11/80	11	11	● 4. Kenny Loggins Alive [L]	Columbia 36738 [2]
9/25/82	13	9	● 5. High Adventure	Columbia 38127
			LOGGINS & MESSINA	
			Duo of Kenny Loggins and Jim Messina. Messina (Buffalo Springfield; Poco) was originally hired as a producer for Loggins; however, they formed a partnership that lasted five years.	
12/30/72	16	13	▲ 1. Loggins And Messina	Columbia 31748
			Your Mama Don't Dance (4)	
11/24/73	10	17	▲ **2. Full Sail**	Columbia 32540
5/25/74	5	16	▲ **3. On Stage** [L]	Columbia 32848 [2]
11/23/74	8	12	● **4. Mother Lode**	Columbia 33175
9/20/75	21	8	5. So Fine	Columbia 33810
			featuring popular '50s tunes	
2/7/76	16	9	● 6. Native Sons	Columbia 33578
			LOMBARDO, Guy, And His Royal Canadians	
			Born on 6/19/02 in London, Ontario, Canada; died on 11/5/77. Leader of the #1 dance band of the '30s and '40s. Known for his classic theme "Auld Lang Syne," which he traditionally played to climax his annual New Year's Eve broadcasts.	
1/19/57	18	2	1. Your Guy Lombardo Medley [I]	Capitol 739
			medley of 40 tunes	
7/28/58	12	4	2. Berlin By Lombardo [I]	Capitol 1019
			medley of 40 Irving Berlin songs	
			LONDON, Julie	
			Born on 9/26/26 in Santa Rosa, California. Singer/actress. Played Dixie McCall on the TV series "Emergency." Married to Jack Webb, 1945-53.	
1/28/56	2(2)	14	**1. Julie Is Her Name**	Liberty 3006
			Cry Me A River (9)	
8/11/56	16	8	2. Lonely Girl	Liberty 3012
12/15/56	18	6	3. Calendar Girl	Liberty 9002
7/22/57	15	4	4. About The Blues	Liberty 3043
			LONDONBEAT	
			Britain-based soul outfit. Vocal trio of Americans Jimmy Helms and George Chandler, with Trinidad native Jimmy Chambers. Backed by British producer/ multi-instrumentalist Willy M.	
4/13/91	21	6	● In The Blood	Radioactive 10192
			CD includes bonus track	
			I've Been Thinking About You (1)	
			LONG, Loretta — see CHILDREN'S ALBUMS	

DATE	POS	WKS	ARTIST—RECORD TITLE	LABEL & NO.
			LONGET, Claudine	
			Born on 1/29/42 in France. Singer/actress. Formerly married to singer Andy Williams. Jailed, for a time, for fatally shooting skier Spider Savich.	
6/3/67	**11**	22	● 1. Claudine	A&M 4121
11/25/67	**33**	6	2. The Look Of Love	A&M 4129
6/1/68	**29**	5	3. Love Is Blue	A&M 4142
			LOPEZ, Trini	
			Born Trinidad Lopez, III, on 5/15/37 in Dallas. Pop-folk singer/guitarist. Discovered by Don Costa while performing at PJ's nightclub in Los Angeles. Portrayed Pedro Jiminez in the movie *The Dirty Dozen*.	
8/3/63	**2**(6)	48	● **1. Trini Lopez At PJ'S** [L]	Reprise 6093
			If I Had A Hammer (3)	
12/21/63	**11**	8	2. More Trini Lopez At PJ'S [L]	Reprise 6103
7/11/64	**32**	2	3. On The Move [L]	Reprise 6112
9/19/64	**18**	11	4. The Latin Album [F]	Reprise 6125
11/28/64	**30**	7	5. Live At Basin St. East [L]	Reprise 6134
2/27/65	**18**	9	6. The Folk Album	Reprise 6147
7/24/65	**32**	3	7. The Love Album	Reprise 6165
			LOS ADMIRADORES	
			Percussion group produced by Enoch Light.	
8/29/60	**2**(1)	34	**1. Bongos Bongos Bongos** [I]	Command 809
10/24/60	**3**	16	**2. Bongos/Flutes/Guitars** [I]	Command 812
			LOS INDIOS TABAJARAS	
			Brazilian Indian brothers: Natalicio and Antenor Lima.	
11/30/63	**7**	11	**Maria Elena** [I]	RCA 2822
			Maria Elena (6)	
			LOS LOBOS	
			Hispanic American rock quintet formed in East Los Angeles in 1973 by David Hidalgo (lead vocals), Cesar Rosas, Conrad Lozano and Louie Perez. Steve Berlin, former Blasters' saxophonist, joined in 1983.	
8/8/87	**1**(2)	19	▲² **La Bamba** [S]	Slash 25605
			movie based on the life of Ritchie Valens; 8 cuts by Los Lobos, plus 4 by other artists *La Bamba* (1)	
			LOVE AND ROCKETS	
			British trio: Daniel Ash (guitar, vocals), Kevin Haskins (drums) and David J. (bass). All were members of Bauhaus, 1979-83. Band name taken from the title of an underground comic book. Ash went solo in 1991.	
6/10/89	**14**	17	● Love And Rockets	Begr. B. 9715
			So Alive (3)	
			LOVERBOY	
			Rock quintet formed in Vancouver, Canada in 1978: Mike Reno (lead singer), Paul Dean (lead guitar), Scott Smith (bass), Matt Frenette (drums) and Doug Johnson (keyboards; left by 1989).	
3/28/81	**13**	17	▲² 1. Loverboy	Columbia 36762
12/5/81	**7**	51	▲⁴ **2. Get Lucky**	Columbia 37638
7/2/83	**7**	22	▲² **3. Keep It Up**	Columbia 38703
9/21/85	**13**	22	▲² 4. Lovin' Every Minute Of It	Columbia 39953
			Lovin' Every Minute Of It (9)/*This Could Be The Night* (10)	

DATE	POS	WKS	ARTIST—RECORD TITLE	LABEL & NO.
			LOVETT, Lyle	
			Country singer born on 11/1/56 in Houston; raised in Klein, Texas. Graduate of Texas A&M University with degrees in German and journalism. Acted in the movie *The Player*. Married actress Julia Roberts on 6/26/93.	
10/15/94	26	3	I Love Everybody	Curb/MCA 10808
			LOVE UNLIMITED	
			Female soul trio from San Pedro, California: sisters Glodean and Linda James, and Diane Taylor. Barry White, who married Glodean on 7/4/74, was the group's manager and producer.	
12/8/73	3	17	● **Under The Influence Of ...**	20th Century 414
			LOVE UNLIMITED ORCHESTRA	
			Forty-piece studio orchestra conducted and arranged by Barry White. Formed to back Love Unlimited, also heard on some of White's solo hits. Kenny G was a member at age 17.	
2/23/74	8	11	● **1. Rhapsody In White** [I]	20th Century 433
			Love's Theme (1)	
12/28/74	28	2	● 2. White Gold [I]	20th Century 458
			LOVIN' SPOONFUL, The	
			Jug-band rock group formed in New York City in 1965. Consisted of John Sebastian (lead vocals, songwriter, guitarist, harmonica), Zal Yanovsky (lead guitar), Steve Boone (bass) and Joe Butler (drums). Sebastian had been with The Even Dozen Jug Band; did session work at Elektra. Yanovsky and Sebastian were members of The Mugwumps with Mama Cass Elliot and Denny Doherty (later with The Mamas & The Papas). Yanovsky replaced by Jerry Yester (keyboards) in 1967. Disbanded in 1968.	
5/7/66	10	11	**1. Daydream**	Kama Sutra 8051
			You Didn't Have To Be So Nice (10)/*Daydream* (2)	
7/16/66	32	7	2. Do You Believe In Magic	Kama Sutra 8050
			Do You Believe In Magic (9)/ *Did You Ever Have To Make Up Your Mind* (2)	
1/21/67	14	8	3. Hums Of The Lovin' Spoonful	Kama Sutra 8054
			Summer In The City (1)/*Rain On The Roof* (10)/ *Nashville Cats* (8)	
3/25/67	3	26	● **4. The Best Of The Lovin' Spoonful** [G]	Kama Sutra 8056
			LOWE, Nick	
			Born on 3/25/49 in Woodbridge, Suffolk, England. With Brinsley Schwarz (1970-75) and Rockpile. Married Carlene Carter on 8/18/79; later divorced. Produced albums for Elvis Costello, Graham Parker & The Rumour and others. Co-founder of Little Village.	
9/8/79	31	7	Labour Of Lust	Columbia 36087
			L.T.D.	
			Ten-man, R&B-funk band from Greensboro, North Carolina. Jeffrey Osborne, lead singer. Osborne left in 1980; replaced by Leslie Wilson and Andre Ray. L.T.D. stands for Love, Togetherness and Devotion.	
9/10/77	21	14	● 1. Something To Love	A&M 4646
			(Every Time I Turn Around) Back In Love Again (4)	
7/22/78	18	11	▲ 2. Togetherness	A&M 4705
8/4/79	29	5	● 3. Devotion	A&M 4771
9/20/80	28	8	4. Shine On	A&M 4819

DATE	POS	WKS	ARTIST—RECORD TITLE	LABEL & NO.
			LUBOFF, Norman, Choir	
			Born on 5/14/17 in Chicago; died of cancer on 9/22/87. Composer/ conductor; formed own choral group.	
10/15/55	15	3	1. Songs Of The West	Columbia 657
7/14/56	19	2	2. Songs Of The South	Columbia 860
5/27/57	19	4	3. Calypso Holiday	Columbia 1000
1/13/58	22	1	4. Songs Of Christmas [X]	Columbia 926
			Christmas charts: 57/'65, 44/'66	
			LULU	
			Born Marie Lawrie on 11/3/48 near Glasgow, Scotland. Married to Maurice Gibb (Bee Gees) from 1969-73. Appeared in the 1967 movie *To Sir With Love*. Hosted own U.K. TV show in 1968.	
12/2/67	24	10	To Sir With Love	Epic 26339
			also see soundtrack of same title	
			To Sir With Love (1)	
			LYMAN, Arthur	
			Born on the island of Kauai, Hawaii, on 2/2/32. Plays vibraphone, guitar, piano and drums. Formerly with Martin Denny.	
5/12/58	6	39	**1. Taboo** [I]	HiFi 806
7/24/61	10	18	**2. Yellow Bird** [I]	HiFi 1004
			Yellow Bird (4)	
4/6/63	36	1	3. I Wish You Love [I]	HiFi 1009
			LYMON, Frankie, and The Teenagers	
			R&B group formed as The Premiers in the Bronx in 1955. Lead singer Lymon was born on 9/30/42 in New York City; died of a drug overdose on 2/28/68. Other members included Herman Santiago and Jimmy Merchant (tenors), Joe Negroni (died 9/5/78; baritone) and Sherman Garnes (died 2/26/77; bass). Group appeared in the movies *Rock, Rock, Rock* and *Mister Rock 'n' Roll*. Inducted into the Rock and Roll Hall of Fame in 1993.	
1/19/57	19	1	The Teenagers featuring Frankie Lymon	Gee 701
			Why Do Fools Fall In Love (6)	
			LYNN, Cheryl	
			Born on 3/11/57 in Los Angeles. Soul singer. Discovered on TV's "Gong Show." Cousin of soul singer D'La Vance.	
1/27/79	23	6	● Cheryl Lynn	Columbia 35486
			LYNNE, Gloria	
			Born on 11/23/31 in New York City. Jazz-styled vocalist.	
3/16/63	39	4	1. Gloria Lynne at the Las Vegas Thunderbird [L]	Everest 5208
			with the Herman Foster Trio	
4/18/64	27	10	2. Gloria, Marty & Strings	Everest 5220
			arranged and conducted by Marty Paich (Emmy-Award-winning songwriter; father of Toto's David Paich)	

DATE	POS	WKS	ARTIST—RECORD TITLE		LABEL & NO.
			LYNYRD SKYNYRD		
			Southern-rock band formed by Ronnie Van Zant (born 1/15/49; lead singer), Gary Rossington (guitar) and Allen Collins (guitar) while they were in junior high school in Jacksonville, Florida, in 1965. Named after their gym teacher Leonard Skinner. Changing lineup featured drummers Bob Burns, Rick Medlocke (later of Blackfoot) and Artimus Pyle; bassists Larry Junstrom (later of 38 Special), Greg Walker (later of Blackfoot), Leon Wilkeson and Ed King (ex-Strawberry Alarm Clock); pianist Billy Powell; and guitarist Steve Gaines. Plane crash on 10/20/77 in Gillsburg, Mississippi, killed Van Zant and members Steve and his sister Cassie Gaines (vocals). Rossington and Collins formed The Rossington Collins Band in 1980; split in 1982. Rossington and vocalist Johnny Van Zant (the younger brother of Ronnie and Donnie [lead singer of 38 Special] Van Zant) re-grouped with old and new band members for the 1987 Lynyrd Skynyrd Tribute Tour. Collins (paralyzed in a car accident in 1986) died of pneumonia on 1/23/90 (age 37). Rossington, Van Zant, Pyle, Wilkeson, King, Powell re-grouped in 1991 with Randall Hall (guitar) and Custer (drums). Pyle left by 1993.		
5/25/74	**12**	19	▲² 1. Second Helping		MCA/Sounds 413
			Sweet Home Alabama (8)		
2/15/75	**27**	4	▲ 2. Lynyrd Skynyrd (pronounced leh-nerd skin-nerd)		MCA/Sounds 363
4/19/75	**9**	10	▲ **3. Nuthin' Fancy**		MCA 2137
3/13/76	**20**	5	● 4. Gimme Back My Bullets		MCA 2170
10/16/76	**9**	15	▲³ **5. One More From The Road**	[L]	MCA 6001 [2]
11/19/77	**5**	15	▲² **6. Street Survivors**		MCA 3029
			album released 3 days before the plane crash; original cover pictured the group engulfed in flames; after the crash, MCA issued a new cover omitting the flames		
9/30/78	**15**	7	▲ 7. Skynyrd's First And ... Last	[E]	MCA 3047
			recordings from 1970-72		
1/5/80	**12**	11	▲³ 8. Gold & Platinum	[G]	MCA 11008 [2]

M

DATE	POS	WKS	ARTIST—RECORD TITLE		LABEL & NO.
			MABLEY, Moms		
			Born Loretta Mary Aiken on 3/19/1894 in Brevard, North Carolina; died on 5/23/75. Bawdy comedienne/ actress. In the movies *Boarding House Blues*, *Emperor Jones* and *Amazing Grace*.		
5/29/61	**16**	11	1. Moms Mabley At The "UN"	[C]	Chess 1452
12/11/61	**39**	1	2. Moms Mabley at The Playboy Club	[C]	Chess 1460
4/28/62	**28**	6	3. Moms Mabley At Geneva Conference	[C]	Chess 1463
9/29/62	**27**	4	4. Moms Mabley Breaks It Up	[C]	Chess 1472
3/2/63	**19**	5	5. Young Men, Si — Old Men, No	[C]	Chess 1477
			MacDONALD, Jeanette, & Nelson Eddy		
			MacDonald was born on 6/18/01 in Philadelphia; died on 1/14/65. Eddy was born on 6/29/01 in Providence, Rhode Island; died on 3/6/67. Top movie duo of the '30s.		
5/25/59	**40**	1	● Favorites In Hi-Fi		RCA 1738
			MacGREGOR, Mary		
			Born on 5/6/48 in St. Paul, Minnesota. Pop singer.		
2/19/77	**17**	7	Torn Between Two Lovers		Ariola Am. 50015
			Torn Between Two Lovers (1)		

The Kinks remain highly regarded as one of England's finest pop bands of the '60s. Continuing in the tradition of such previous titles as *Kinda Kinks* and *Kinks Kinkdom*, 1966's *The Kink Kontroversy* entered the Top 100 and now stands as a valued collectible.

Kiss's painted faces and loud, roaring rock and roll, amply displayed on the band's 1974 Casablanca debut, attracted a young but loyal audience in the mid-1970s. In 1994, the clearly proud-of-itself group crafted its own tribute album and invited other artists to participate in its making.

Gladys Knight & the Pips, one of R&B's most cherished and prolific acts, produced 25 charting albums together between 1967–87. In 1985, Knight, along with Elton John, Stevie Wonder and Dionne Warwick, among others, made "That's What Friends Are For," Dionne & Friends' No. 1 smash.

Led Zeppelin's second album, *Led Zeppelin II,* was released in 1969, stayed at No. 1 for seven weeks and stands as the band's highest-charting record ever. The group's bestseller, however, came two years later with its famously untitled fourth album, often referred to as *Zoso*.

John Lennon's last live performance, in Madison Square Garden in 1972, was posthumously released by Capitol in 1986, six years after his tragic death. *Live In New York City*, which featured The Plastic Ono Elephants Memory Band as backing band, peaked at No. 41.

The Lettermen's *A Song For Young Love* was the group's highest-charting album, reaching No. 6 in 1962; it was also the trio's first showing in the Top 20. Helping the album make its climb was the inclusion of the group's first three Top 10 singles.

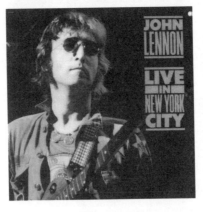

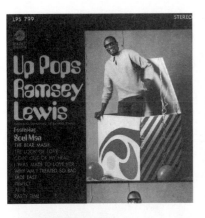

Ramsey Lewis was one of jazz's earliest crossover artists, scoring a No. 2 album with his 1965 set, *The In Crowd* (recorded with his famous trio), and going gold a decade later with his Top 20 *Sun Goddess* set. The Chicago-born pianist inked a deal with the GRP label in the '90s.

Henry Mancini's 1962 soundtrack for *Breakfast at Tiffany's* spent 12 full weeks at the top of the charts and included the much-loved standard "Moon River." Among those who have felt that song's influence is British singer Morrissey, who recorded a cover version in 1994.

Barry Manilow's 1978 *Greatest Hits* collection was the fifth of his seven Top 10 albums to see release between 1974–79. Although this album was certified triple platinum, a second volume of hits, released by Arista in 1983, managed to reach only the gold mark.

Mantovani's smooth orchestral sounds made an enormous chart impact in the late '50s and early '60s. Between 1955 and 1966, the Italian-born orchestra leader produced 30 albums that reached the Top 40. *Mr. Music . . . Mantovani*, released in the fall of 1966, peaked at No. 27 and was his last Top 40 showing.

Bob Marley & The Wailers' classic *Rastaman Vibration* represented an all-time chart high for the group, reaching No. 8 in 1976. *Legend*, a compilation of Marley's recordings released three years after his 1981 death, has since gone well past triple platinum in sales and now stands as the reggae star's bestseller.

DATE	POS	WKS	ARTIST—RECORD TITLE	LABEL & NO.
			MACK, Craig	
			Rapper from Long Island, New York. Was a roadie for EPMD. Discovered by producer Sean "Puffy" Combs.	
10/8/94	**21**	3	● Project: Funk Da World	Bad Boy 73001
			Flava In Ya Ear (9)	
			MADONNA	
			Born Madonna Louise Ciccone on 8/16/58 in Bay City, Michigan. To New York in the late '70s; performed with the Alvin Ailey dance troupe. Short-lived member of The Breakfast Club, early '80s. Married to actor Sean Penn from 1985-89. Acted in the movies *Desperately Seeking Susan*, *Dick Tracy*, *A League of Their Own* and *Body of Evidence*, among others. Appeared in Broadway's *Speed-The-Plow*. Released concert-tour documentary movie *Truth or Dare* in 1991. Released adults-only picture book *Sex* in 1992. The top female performer of the past decade.	
2/18/84	**8**	36	▲⁴ 1. Madonna	Sire 23867
			Borderline (10)/*Lucky Star* (4)	
12/8/84	**1**(3)	52	▲⁹ 2. Like A Virgin	Sire 25157
			Like A Virgin (1)/*Material Girl* (2)/*Angel* (5)/ *Dress You Up* (5)	
7/19/86	**1**(5)	52	▲⁷ 3. True Blue	Sire 25442
			Live To Tell (1)/*Papa Don't Preach* (1)/*True Blue* (3)/ *Open Your Heart* (1)/*La Isla Bonita* (4)	
8/22/87	**7**	13	▲ 4. Who's That Girl [S]	Sire 25611
			4 of 9 cuts are by Madonna *Who's That Girl* (1)/*Causing A Commotion* (2)	
12/12/87	**14**	12	▲ 5. You Can Dance [K]	Sire 25535
			features 7 extended remixes of Madonna's dance hits	
4/8/89	**1**(6)	31	▲³ 6. Like A Prayer	Sire 25844
			Like A Prayer (1)/*Express Yourself* (2)/*Cherish* (2)/ *Keep It Together* (8)	
6/16/90	**2**(3)	16	▲² 7. I'm Breathless [S]	Sire 26209
			songs from and songs inspired by the movie *Dick Tracy* *Vogue* (1)/*Hanky Panky* (10)	
12/1/90	**2**(2)	33	▲⁴ 8. The Immaculate Collection [G]	Sire 26440
			Justify My Love (1)/*Rescue Me* (9)	
11/7/92	**2**(1)	15	▲² 9. Erotica	Maverick 45154
			Erotica (3)/*Deeper And Deeper* (7)	
11/12/94	**3**	16+	▲² 10. Bedtime Stories	Maverick/Sire 45767
			Secret (3)/*Take A Bow* (1)	
			MAHARIS, George	
			Born on 9/1/28 in New York City. Movie/TV actor. Played Buz Murdock on TV's "Route 66."	
7/14/62	**10**	8	1. George Maharis Sings!	Epic 26001
9/15/62	**32**	3	2. Portrait In Music	Epic 26021
			MAHAVISHNU ORCHESTRA — see McLAUGHLIN, John	
			MALMSTEEN('S), Yngwie J., Rising Force	
			Swedish; former lead guitarist of Alcatrazz. Backed by his band, Rising Force: Anders Johansson, Joe Lynn Turner (vocals) and Jens Johansson.	
5/14/88	**40**	2	Odyssey	Polydor 835451

DATE	POS	WKS	ARTIST—RECORD TITLE	LABEL & NO.
			MALO	
			Latin-rock band formed by Jorge Santana (brother of Carlos Santana). Malo is Spanish for bad.	
3/18/72	**14**	14	Malo	Warner 2584
			MAMAS & THE PAPAS, The	
			Quartet formed in New York City in 1963. Consisted of John Phillips (born 8/30/35, Paris Island, South Carolina); Holly Michelle Gilliam Phillips (born 6/4/45, Long Beach, California); Dennis Doherty (born 11/29/41, Halifax, Nova Scotia, Canada) and Cass Elliot (born 9/19/41, Baltimore; died 7/29/74). John had been in The Journeymen; married Michelle in 1962. Elliot had been in The Mugwumps with Doherty and future Lovin' Spoonful member Zal Yanovsky. Group moved to Los Angeles in 1964. Disbanded in 1968; reunited briefly in 1971. Michelle acted in the movies *Dillinger* and *Valentino*, and was a cast member of TV's "Knots Landing"; married for eight days to actor Dennis Hopper in 1970. New Mamas & Papas group formed in 1982: John and daughter, actress MacKenzie Phillips, Dennis Doherty and Spanky McFarlane of Spanky & Our Gang. Michelle and John's daughter, Chynna, is a member of the trio Wilson Phillips.	
4/23/66	**1**(1)	34	● 1. **If You Can Believe Your Eyes And Ears** *California Dreamin'* (4)/*Monday, Monday* (1)	Dunhill 50006
10/8/66	**4**	32	● 2. **The Mamas & The Papas** *I Saw Her Again* (5)/*Words Of Love* (5)	Dunhill 50010
3/25/67	**2**(7)	25	● 3. **The Mamas & The Papas Deliver** *Dedicated To The One I Love* (2)/*Creeque Alley* (5)	Dunhill 50014
11/25/67	**5**	18	● 4. **Farewell To The First Golden Era** [G]	Dunhill 50025
6/22/68	**15**	11	5. The Papas & The Mamas	Dunhill 50031
			MANASSAS — see STILLS, Stephen	
			MANCHESTER, Melissa	
			Born on 2/15/51 in the Bronx. Vocalist/pianist/composer. Father is a bassoon player with the New York Metropolitan Opera Orchestra. She studied songwriting under Paul Simon at the University School of the Arts in the early '70s. Former backup singer for Bette Midler.	
7/19/75	**12**	11	● 1. Melissa *Midnight Blue* (6)	Arista 4031
2/28/76	**24**	8	2. Better Days & Happy Endings	Arista 4067
3/17/79	**33**	3	3. Don't Cry Out Loud *Don't Cry Out Loud* (10)	Arista 4186
8/28/82	**19**	8	4. Hey Ricky *You Should Hear How She Talks About You* (5)	Arista 9574
			MANCINI, Henry	
			Born on 4/16/24 in Cleveland; raised in Aliquippa, Pennsylvania. Died of cancer on 6/14/94. Leading movie and TV composer/arranger/conductor. Staff composer for Universal Pictures, 1952-58. Winner of four Academy Awards and 20 Grammy Awards. Married Ginny O'Connor, an original member of Mel Torme's Mel-Tones.	
2/9/59	**1**(10)	47	● 1. **The Music From Peter Gunn** [TV-I] *1958 Album of the Year Grammy Award*	RCA 1956
6/29/59	**7**	28	2. **More Music From Peter Gunn** [TV-I]	RCA 2040
3/28/60	**2**(1)	35	3. **Music From Mr. Lucky** [TV-I]	RCA 2198
5/8/61	**28**	10	4. Mr. Lucky Goes Latin [I]	RCA 2360
10/9/61	**1**(12)	69	● 5. **Breakfast At Tiffany's** [S-I]	RCA 2362
3/10/62	**28**	7	6. Combo! [I] *recorded June 1960*	RCA 2258

DATE	POS	WKS	ARTIST—RECORD TITLE		LABEL & NO.
6/30/62	37	1	7. Experiment In Terror	[S-I]	RCA 2442
7/28/62	4	35	**8. Hatari!**	[S-I]	RCA 2559
2/23/63	12	23	9. Our Man In Hollywood		RCA 2604
7/6/63	5	11	**10. Uniquely Mancini**	[I]	RCA 2692
2/1/64	6	18	**11. Charade**	[S-I]	RCA 2755
4/25/64	8	41	● **12. The Pink Panther**	[S-I]	RCA 2795
8/15/64	15	7	13. The Concert Sound of Henry Mancini	[I]	RCA 2897
			medleys of 30 tunes; with a 70-piece orchestra		
2/20/65	11	11	14. Dear Heart And Other Songs About Love		RCA 2990
6/7/69	5	19	● **15. A Warm Shade Of Ivory**	[I]	RCA 4140
			Love Theme From Romeo & Juliet (1)		
3/6/71	26	4	16. Mancini plays the Theme From Love Story		RCA 4466
			MANDELL, Steve — see WEISSBERG, Eric		
			MANDRILL		
			Brooklyn Latin jazz-rock septet formed in 1968 by the Wilson brothers: Louis "Sweet Lou," Richard "Dr. Ric" and Carlos "Mad Dog." Included Omar, Mesa, Claude "Coffee" Cave, Charlie Pardo and Fudgie Kae.		
5/12/73	28	8	Composite Truth		Polydor 5043
			MANFRED MANN — see MANN, Manfred		
			MANGIONE, Chuck		
			Born on 11/29/40 in Rochester, New York. Flugelhorn player/bandleader/composer. Recorded with older brother Gaspare ("Gap") as The Jazz Brothers for Riverside in 1960. To New York City in 1965; played with Maynard Ferguson, Kai Winding and Art Blakey's Jazz Messengers.		
2/18/78	2 (2)	28	▲² **1. Feels So Good**	[I]	A&M 4658
			Feels So Good (4)		
9/30/78	14	10	● 2. Children of Sanchez	[S-I]	A&M 6700 [2]
7/28/79	27	6	3. An Evening Of Magic — Chuck Mangione Live At The Hollywood Bowl	[I-L]	A&M 6701 [2]
3/1/80	8	11	● **4. Fun and Games**	[I]	A&M 3715
			MANHATTANS, The		
			Soul vocal group from Jersey City, New Jersey. Consisted of George "Smitty" Smith (died 1970, spinal meningitis; lead vocals), Winfred "Blue" Lovett (bass), Edward "Sonny" Bivins and Kenneth "Wally" Kelly (tenors) and Richard Taylor (baritone). Smith replaced by Gerald Alston in 1971. First recorded for Piney in 1962. Taylor (aka Abdul Rashid Talhah) left in 1976; died on 12/7/87 (age 47) following lengthy illness. Featured female vocalist Regina Belle began solo career in 1987. Alston went solo in 1988.		
6/19/76	16	12	● 1. The Manhattans		Columbia 33820
			Kiss And Say Goodbye (1)		
6/7/80	24	10	● 2. After Midnight		Columbia 36411
			Shining Star (5)		
			MANHATTAN TRANSFER, The		
			Versatile vocal-harmony quartet formed in New York City in 1972: Tim Hauser, Alan Paul, Janis Siegel and Cheryl Bentyne (replaced Laurel Masse in 1979).		
6/28/75	33	4	● 1. The Manhattan Transfer		Atlantic 18133
7/4/81	22	13	2. Mecca For Moderns		Atlantic 16036
			Boy From New York City (7)		

DATE	POS	WKS	ARTIST—RECORD TITLE	LABEL & NO.
			MANILOW, Barry	
			Born Barry Alan Pincus on 6/17/46 in Brooklyn. Vocalist/pianist/composer. Studied at New York's Juilliard School. Music director for the WCBS-TV series "Callback." Worked at New York's Continental Baths bathhouse/ nightclub in New York as Bette Midler's accompanist in 1972; later produced her first two albums. First recorded solo as Featherbed. Wrote jingles for Dr. Pepper, Pepsi, State Farm Insurance, Band-Aids and McDonald's ("You Deserve A Break Today," which he also sang).	
1/11/75	9	11	▲ 1. Barry Manilow II [R] first released on Bell 1314 in 1973 *Mandy* (1)	Arista 4016
10/4/75	28	6	● 2. Barry Manilow I [R] first released on Bell 1129 in 1972 *Could It Be Magic* (6)	Arista 4007
11/29/75	5	15	▲² 3. Tryin' To Get The Feeling *I Write The Songs* (1)/*Tryin' To Get The Feeling Again* (10)	Arista 4060
8/21/76	6	27	▲² 4. This One's For You *Weekend In New England* (10)/*Looks Like We Made It* (1)	Arista 4090
5/28/77	1(1)	26	▲³ 5. Barry Manilow/Live [L]	Arista 8500 [2]
3/4/78	3	28	▲³ 6. Even Now *Can't Smile Without You* (3)/*Copacabana (At The Copa)* (8)/ *Somewhere In The Night* (9)	Arista 4164
12/2/78	7	16	▲³ 7. Greatest Hits [G]	Arista 8601 [2]
10/20/79	9	15	▲ 8. One Voice *Ships* (9)	Arista 9505
12/20/80	15	9	▲ 9. Barry *I Made It Through The Rain* (10)	Arista 9537
10/24/81	14	11	● 10. If I Should Love Again	Arista 9573
1/8/83	32	6	● 11. Here Comes The Night	Arista 9610
12/17/83	30	7	● 12. Barry Manilow/Greatest Hits, Vol. II [G]	Arista 8102
1/5/85	28	6	● 13. 2:00 AM Paradise Cafe with jazz greats Sarah Vaughan, Gerry Mulligan and Mel Torme	Arista 8254
12/22/90	40	2	● 14. Because It's Christmas [X] Christmas charts: 1/'90, 8/'91, 28/'92	Arista 8644
			MANN, Herbie	
			Born Herbert Jay Solomon on 4/16/30 in Brooklyn. Renowned jazz flutist. First recorded with The Mat Mathews Quintet for Brunswick in 1953. First recorded as a solo for Bethlehem in 1954.	
11/3/62	30	11	1. Herbie Mann at the Village Gate [I-L]	Atlantic 1380
6/21/69	20	17	2. Memphis Underground [I] with Roy Ayers (vibes) and Larry Coryell (guitar)	Atlantic 1522
6/7/75	27	3	3. Discotheque [I]	Atlantic 1670
			MANN, Manfred	
			Rock group formed in England in 1964: Manfred Mann (born Michael Lubowitz, 10/21/40 in Johannesburg, South Africa; keyboards), Paul Jones (vocals), Mike Hugg (drums), Michael Vickers (guitar) and Tom McGuinness (bass). Manfred Mann formed his new Earth Band in 1971, featuring Mick Rogers (vocals), Colin Pattenden (bass) and Chris Slade (drums). Rogers replaced by Chris Thompson (vocals, guitar) in 1976. Thompson also recorded with own group Night in 1979. McGuinness left to form McGuinness Flint in 1970.	
1/23/65	35	4	1. the Manfred Mann album *Do Wah Diddy Diddy* (1)	Ascot 16015

DATE	POS	WKS	ARTIST—RECORD TITLE	LABEL & NO.
			MANFRED MANN'S EARTH BAND:	
1/22/77	**10**	11	● **2. The Roaring Silence**	Warner 2965
			Blinded By The Light (1)	
3/24/84	**40**	2	3. Somewhere In Afrika	Arista 8194
			MANNA, Charlie	
			Comedian from New York.	
9/11/61	**27**	1	Manna Overboard!! [C]	Decca 4159
			MANNHEIM STEAMROLLER	
			Classical-rock group from Omaha, Nebraska. Best known for its Fresh Aire albums. Under the direction of composer/producer/drummer Chip Davis, who founded American Gramaphone Records in 1974. Gained recognition through performance on a series of "Old Home Bread" TV commercials. Davis wrote C.W. McCall's "Convoy." Group's personnel fluctuated; named after Europe's mid-18th century Mannheim School.	
12/17/88	**36**	4	▲⁴ A Fresh Aire Christmas [X-I]	American G. 1988
			Christmas charts: 1/'88, 2/'89, 3/'90, 1/'91, 5/'92, 2/'93, 3/'94	
			MANTOVANI	
			Born Annunzio Paolo Mantovani on 11/15/05 in Venice, Italy. Died on 3/29/80. Played classical violin in England before forming his own orchestra in the early '30s. Had first U.S. chart hit in 1935, "Red Sails In The Sunset." Achieved international fame 20 years later with his 40-piece orchestra and distinctive "cascading strings" sound. His arrangements of favorite classical and pop tunes made him America's favorite orchestra conductor from 1952-72.	
2/19/55	**13**	2	1. The Music Of Rudolf Friml [I]	London 1150
3/19/55	**14**	2	2. Waltz Time [I]	London 1094
7/9/55	**8**	8	● **3. Song Hits From Theatreland** [I]	London 1219
5/26/56	**12**	7	4. Waltzes Of Irving Berlin [I]	London 1452
5/27/57	**1**(1)	113	● **5. Film Encores** [I]	London 1700
3/24/58	**22**	1	6. Mantovani Plays Tangos * [I]	London 768
5/19/58	**5**	56	● **7. Gems Forever ...** [I]	London 3032
11/24/58	**7**	24	● **8. Strauss Waltzes *** [I]	London 685
			*released in 1953	
2/16/59	**13**	31	9. Continental Encores [I]	London 3095
6/1/59	**6**	11	**10. Mantovani Stereo Showcase** [K-I]	London SS1
6/22/59	**14**	15	11. Film Encores, Vol. 2 [I]	London 3117
1/4/60	**8**	18	**12. All-American Showcase** [K-I]	London 3122 [2]
			one side each: Sigmund Romberg/Victor Herbert/Irving Berlin/ Rudolf Friml	
3/28/60	**11**	30	13. The American Scene [I]	London 3136
			side 1 features the music of Stephen Foster	
7/25/60	**21**	18	14. Songs To Remember [I]	London 3149
12/5/60	**2**(5)	44	● **15. Mantovani plays music from Exodus and other great themes** [I]	London 3231
2/20/61	**22**	1	16. Operetta Memories [I]	London 3181
6/26/61	**8**	15	**17. Italia Mia** [I]	London 3239
8/21/61	**29**	5	18. Themes From Broadway [I]	London 3250
6/16/62	**8**	19	**19. American Waltzes** [I]	London 248
11/3/62	**24**	8	20. Moon River and other great film themes [I]	London 249
6/1/63	**10**	13	**21. Latin Rendezvous** [I]	London 295
12/19/64	**37**	3	22. The Incomparable Mantovani [I]	London 392

DATE	POS	WKS	ARTIST—RECORD TITLE	LABEL & NO.
5/1/65	26	8	23. The Mantovani Sound — Big Hits From Broadway And Hollywood [I]	London 419
4/16/66	23	8	24. Mantovani Magic [I]	London 448
11/26/66	27	7	25. Mr. Music ... Mantovani [I]	London 474
			CHRISTMAS ALBUM:	
12/9/57	4	6	● **26. Christmas Carols** [X-I] originally released in 1953	London 913
12/22/58	3	3	**27. Christmas Carols** [X-I-R]	London 913
12/21/59	16	3	28. Christmas Carols [X-I-R]	London 913
12/19/60	8	3	**29. Christmas Carols** [X-I-R]	London 913
1/6/62	36	2	30. Christmas Carols [X-I-R]	London 913
			MARIE, Teena	
			Born Mary Christine Brockert in Santa Monica in 1957; raised in Venice, California. White-funk singer/ composer/keyboardist/guitarist/producer/ actress. Produced the group Ozone.	
11/22/80	38	3	1. Irons In The Fire	Gordy 997
7/18/81	23	9	● 2. It Must Be Magic	Gordy 1004
3/2/85	31	9	● 3. Starchild *Lovergirl* (4)	Epic 39528
			MARKETTS, The	
			Hollywood instrumental surf quintet led by Tommy Tedesco.	
3/14/64	37	2	Out Of Limits! [I] *Out Of Limits* (3)	Warner 1537
			MARKY MARK And The Funky Bunch	
			Mark was born Mark Wahlberg on 6/5/71 in Boston. Younger brother of Donnie Wahlberg of New Kids on the Block. The Funky Bunch is DJ Terry Yancey and three male and two female dancers.	
9/7/91	21	20	▲ Music For The People *Good Vibrations* (1)/*Wildside* (10)	Interscope 91737
			MARLEY, Bob, & The Wailers	
			Born on 2/6/45 in Rhoden Hall, Jamaica. Died of brain cancer on 5/11/81. Singer/guitarist. Celebrated as the master of reggae music. The Wailers included Peter Tosh and Bunny Wailer; both left in 1974. Wrote Eric Clapton's hit "I Shot The Sheriff." Father of Ziggy Marley and Rohan Marley (football linebacker for the University of Miami Hurricanes). Inducted into the Rock and Roll Hall of Fame in 1994.	
5/15/76	8	14	**1. Rastaman Vibration**	Island 9383
7/9/77	20	11	2. Exodus	Island 9498
			MARLEY, Ziggy, And The Melody Makers	
			Kingston, Jamaica, family reggae group. Children of the late reggae master Bob Marley: David ("Ziggy"), Stephen, Cedella and Sharon Marley.	
5/14/88	23	16	▲ 1. Conscious Party	Virgin 90878
8/26/89	26	8	2. One Bright Day	Virgin 91256
			MARSHALL TUCKER BAND, The	
			Southern rock band formed in South Carolina in 1971: Doug Gray (lead singer), brothers Toy (lead guitarist; died 2/25/93 of respiratory failure [age 45]) and Tommy Caldwell, (died 4/28/80 in auto accident [age 30]; replaced by Franklin Wilkie; bass), George McCorkle (rhythm guitar), Paul Riddle (drums) and Jerry Eubanks (sax, flute). Caldwell left band in 1984. Marshall Tucker was the owner of the band's rehearsal hall.	
10/6/73	29	8	● 1. The Marshall Tucker Band	Capricorn 0112

DATE	POS	WKS	ARTIST—RECORD TITLE	LABEL & NO.
3/30/74	37	3	● 2. A New Life	Capricorn 0124
10/11/75	15	8	● 3. Searchin' For A Rainbow	Capricorn 0161
7/24/76	32	5	4. Long Hard Ride	Capricorn 0170
4/2/77	23	15	▲ 5. Carolina Dreams	Capricorn 0180
6/3/78	22	5	● 6. Together Forever	Capricorn 0205
6/2/79	30	3	7. Running Like The Wind	Warner 3317
4/5/80	32	5	8. Tenth	Warner 3410

MARTIKA

Born Marta Marrera on 5/18/69. Los Angeles-based, Cuban American singer/writer/actress/dancer. Starred in the TV program "Kids, Incorporated." Appeared in the 1982 movie musical *Annie*.

DATE	POS	WKS	ARTIST—RECORD TITLE	LABEL & NO.
7/22/89	15	12	● Martika *Toy Soldiers* (1)	Columbia 44290

MARTIN, Dean

Born Dino Crocetti on 6/7/17 in Steubenville, Ohio. Vocalist/actor. To California in 1937; worked local clubs. Teamed with comedian Jerry Lewis in Atlantic City in 1946. First movie, *My Friend Irma*, in 1949. Team broke up after 16th movie, *Hollywood or Bust*, in 1956. Appeared in many movies since then; own TV series from 1965-74. First recorded for Diamond Records in 1946.

DATE	POS	WKS	ARTIST—RECORD TITLE	LABEL & NO.
8/22/64	2 (4)	32	● **1. Everybody Loves Somebody** *Everybody Loves Somebody* (1)	Reprise 6130
10/10/64	15	9	● 2. Dream With Dean	Reprise 6123
11/28/64	9	15	● **3. The Door Is Still Open To My Heart** *The Door Is Still Open To My Heart* (6)	Reprise 6140
3/13/65	13	9	● 4. Dean Martin Hits Again	Reprise 6146
10/2/65	12	16	● 5. (Remember Me) I'm The One Who Loves You	Reprise 6170
12/4/65	11	17	● 6. Houston *I Will* (10)	Reprise 6181
5/14/66	40	2	● 7. Somewhere There's A Someone	Reprise 6201
1/21/67	34	3	8. The Dean Martin TV Show	Reprise 6233
9/16/67	20	16	● 9. Welcome To My World	Reprise 6250
7/13/68	26	12	● 10. Dean Martin's Greatest Hits! Vol. 1 [G]	Reprise 6301
2/8/69	14	9	● 11. Gentle On My Mind	Reprise 6330

MARTIN, Steve

Born on 6/8/45 in Waco, Texas; raised in California. Popular TV and movie comedian. Comedy writer for "The Smothers Brothers Comedy Hour" TV show and others; frequent appearances on "Saturday Night Live," '70s and '80s. Movies include *The Jerk, All of Me, Roxanne, Planes, Trains and Automobiles, L.A. Story* and *Leap of Faith*, among many others. Married actress Victoria Tennant; divorced in 1992.

DATE	POS	WKS	ARTIST—RECORD TITLE	LABEL & NO.
10/15/77	10	12	▲ **1. Let's Get Small** [C]	Warner 3090
11/11/78	2 (6)	18	▲ **2. A Wild And Crazy Guy** [C]	Warner 3238
10/20/79	25	5	● 3. Comedy Is Not Pretty! [C]	Warner 3392

MARTINO, Al

Born Alfred Cini on 10/7/27 in Philadelphia. Encouraged by success of boyhood friend Mario Lanza. Winner on "Arthur Godfrey's Talent Scouts" TV show in 1952. Portrayed singer Johnny Fontane in the 1972 movie *The Godfather*.

DATE	POS	WKS	ARTIST—RECORD TITLE	LABEL & NO.
6/29/63	7	13	**1. I Love You Because** *I Love You Because* (3)	Capitol 1914

DATE	POS	WKS	ARTIST—RECORD TITLE	LABEL & NO.
10/26/63	9	21	**2. Painted, Tainted Rose**	Capitol 1975
2/29/64	13	10	3. Living A Lie	Capitol 2040
8/15/64	31	6	4. I Love You More And More Every Day/ Tears And Roses *I Love You More And More Every Day* (9)	Capitol 2107
2/12/66	19	8	5. My Cherie	Capitol 2362
3/12/66	8	26	● **6. Spanish Eyes**	Capitol 2435
8/12/67	23	4	7. Daddy's Little Girl	Capitol 2733
			MARX, Richard	
			Born on 9/16/63 in Chicago. Pop-rock singer/songwriter. Professional jingle singer since age five. Backing singer for Lionel Richie. Co-wrote Kenny Rogers's hit "What About Me." On 1/8/89, married Cynthia Rhodes, lead singer of Animotion.	
8/15/87	8	63	▲³ **1. Richard Marx** *Don't Mean Nothing* (3)/*Should've Known Better* (3)/ *Endless Summer Nights* (2)/*Hold On To The Nights* (1)	EMI-Man. 53049
5/27/89	1(1)	47	▲³ **2. Repeat Offender** *Satisfied* (1)/*Right Here Waiting* (1)/*Angelia* (4)	EMI 90380
11/23/91	35	5	▲ 3. Rush Street *Hazard* (9)	Capitol 95874
3/5/94	37	2	▲ 4. Paid Vacation *Now and Forever* (7)	Capitol 81232
			MARY JANE GIRLS	
			Female "funk & roll" quartet: Joanne McDuffie, Candice Ghant, Kim Wuletich and Yvette Marina. Formed and produced by Rick James. Marina is the daughter of disco singer Pattie Brooks.	
5/25/85	18	11	Only Four You *In My House* (7)	Gordy 6092
			MASEKELA, Hugh	
			Born Hugh Ramapolo Masekela on 4/4/39 in Wilbank, South Africa. Trumpeter/bandleader/arranger. Played trumpet since age 14. To England in 1959; to New York City in 1960. Formed own band in 1964. Married to Miriam Makeba from 1964-66.	
7/20/68	17	10	The Promise of a Future *Grazing In The Grass* (1)	Uni 73028
			MASON, Dave	
			Born on 5/10/46 in Worcester, England. Vocalist/composer/guitarist. Original member of Traffic from March through December 1967 and from June 1968 on. Joined Delaney & Bonnie for a short time in 1970. Joined Fleetwood Mac in 1993.	
7/11/70	22	10	● 1. Alone Together with guests Leon Russell, Jim Capaldi, Rita Coolidge and Delaney & Bonnie	Blue Thumb 19
11/30/74	25	4	● 2. Dave Mason	Columbia 33096
11/1/75	27	6	3. Split Coconut with guests The Manhattan Transfer, David Crosby and Graham Nash	Columbia 33698
5/28/77	37	2	● 4. Let It Flow	Columbia 34680

DATE	POS	WKS	ARTIST—RECORD TITLE		LABEL & NO.
			MATHIS, Johnny		
			Born on 9/30/35 in San Francisco. Studied opera from age 13. Track scholarship at San Francisco State College. Invited to Olympic tryouts; chose singing career instead. Discovered by George Avakian of Columbia Records. To New York City in 1956. Initially recorded as jazz-styled singer. Columbia A&R executive Mitch Miller switched him to singing pop ballads; he subsequently became young America's favorite MOR male vocalist.		
9/9/57	4	26	**1. Wonderful Wonderful**		Columbia 1028
			the title song is not included on the album		
12/23/57	2(4)	50	● **2. Warm**		Columbia 1078
4/7/58	10	12	**3. Good Night, Dear Lord**		Columbia 1119
4/14/58	1(3)	178	▲ **4. Johnny's Greatest Hits**	[G]	Columbia 1133
			It's Not For Me To Say (5)/*Chances Are* (1)/ *The Twelfth Of Never* (9)		
9/8/58	6	16	● **5. Swing Softly**		Columbia 1165
2/9/59	4	74	● **6. Open Fire, Two Guitars**		Columbia 1270
7/27/59	2(2)	39	● **7. More Johnny's Greatest Hits**	[G]	Columbia 1344
9/21/59	1(5)	40	▲ **8. Heavenly**		Columbia 1351
1/18/60	2(1)	39	● **9. Faithfully**		Columbia 8219
8/29/60	4	21	**10. Johnny's Mood**		Columbia 8326
10/3/60	6	13	**11. The Rhythms And Ballads Of Broadway**		Columbia 803 [2]
7/17/61	38	1	12. I'll Buy You A Star		Columbia 8423
9/4/61	2(7)	28	**13. Portrait Of Johnny**	[G]	Columbia 8444
3/24/62	14	12	14. Live It Up!		Columbia 8511
11/3/62	12	14	15. Rapture		Columbia 8715
4/27/63	6	17	**16. Johnny's Newest Hits**	[G]	Columbia 8816
			Gina (6)/*What Will Mary Say* (9)		
9/21/63	20	9	17. Johnny		Columbia 8844
1/25/64	23	7	18. Romantically		Columbia 8898
2/29/64	13	16	19. Tender Is The Night		Mercury 60890
6/27/64	35	4	20. I'll Search My Heart and Other Great Hits	[K]	Columbia 8943
12/26/64	40	1	21. This Is Love		Mercury 60942
5/14/66	9	16	**22. The Shadow Of Your Smile**		Mercury 61073
6/8/68	26	6	23. Love Is Blue		Columbia 9637
5/9/70	38	2	24. Raindrops Keep Fallin' On My Head		Columbia 1005
4/22/78	9	11	▲ **25. You Light Up My Life**		Columbia 35259
			Too Much, Too Little, Too Late (1-with Deniece Williams)		
7/29/78	19	8	● 26. That's What Friends Are For		Columbia 35435
			JOHNNY MATHIS & DENIECE WILLIAMS		
			CHRISTMAS ALBUM:		
12/15/58	3	4	▲² **27. Merry Christmas**	[X]	Columbia 1195
12/28/59	10	2	**28. Merry Christmas**	[X-R]	Columbia 1195
12/31/60	10	2	**29. Merry Christmas**	[X-R]	Columbia 8021
1/6/62	31	2	30. Merry Christmas	[X-R]	Columbia 8021
12/22/62	12	2	31. Merry Christmas	[X-R]	Columbia 8021
			Christmas charts: 2/'63, 2/'64, 7/'65, 2/'66, 2/'67, 5/'68, 15/'69, 3/'73, 18/'88, 20/'89, 16/'90, 17/'91, 12/'92, 21/'93, 35/'94		
			MATLOCK, Matty — see HEINDORF, Ray, and WEBB, Jack		

DATE	POS	WKS	ARTIST—RECORD TITLE	LABEL & NO.
			MATTHEWS, Dave, Band	
			Jazz group led by South African native Dave Matthews (vocals, guitar), with Stefan Lessard, Leroi Moor, Boyd Tinsley and Carter Beauford.	RCA 66449
10/15/94	**34**	1	Under The Table And Dreaming	
			MAURIAT, Paul	
			Born in 1925. French conductor/arranger. Moved to Paris at age 10. Formed own touring orchestra at 17.	Philips 248
2/10/68	**1**(5)	25	● **Blooming Hits** [I]	
			Love Is Blue (1)	
			MAXWELL, Robert, His Harp and Orchestra	
			Born on 4/19/21 in New York City. Jazz harpist/composer. With NBC Symphony under Toscanini at age 17. Also recorded as Mickey Mozart.	Decca 74421
5/23/64	**17**	12	Shangri-La [I]	
			MAY, Billy, And His Orchestra	
			Born on 1/10/16 in Pittsburgh. Arranger/conductor/sideman for many of the big bands. After leading his own band in early '50s, May went on to arrange/conduct for Frank Sinatra and compose movie scores.	Capitol 562
3/5/55	**7**	6	**Sorta-May** [I]	
			MAYALL, John	
			Born on 11/29/33 in Macclesfield, Cheshire, England. Bluesman John Mayall & his Bluesbreakers band spawned many of Britain's leading rock musicians.	
11/8/69	**32**	2	● 1. The Turning Point [L]	Polydor 4004
			featuring Jon Mark and Johnny Almond	
4/11/70	**33**	4	2. Empty Rooms	Polydor 4010
10/31/70	**22**	5	3. USA Union	Polydor 4022
			featuring Harvey Mandel and other American artists	
			MAYFIELD, Curtis	
			Born on 6/3/42 in Chicago. Soul singer/songwriter/producer. With Jerry Butler in the gospel group Northern Jubilee Singers. Joined The Impressions in 1957. Wrote most of the hits for The Impressions, Jerry Butler and himself. Own labels: Windy C, Mayfield and Curtom. Went solo in 1970. Scored movies *Superfly*, *Claudine*, *A Piece of the Action* and *Short Eyes*. Appeared in *Short Eyes*. Paralyzed from the chest down when a stage lighting tower fell on him before a concert on 8/13/90.	
10/24/70	**19**	18	● 1. Curtis	Curtom 8005
6/12/71	**21**	11	2. Curtis/Live! [L]	Curtom 8008 [2]
12/11/71	**40**	1	3. Roots	Curtom 8009
9/16/72	**1**(4)	30	● 4. Superfly [S]	Curtom 8014
			Freddie's Dead (4)/*Superfly* (8)	
6/23/73	**16**	10	● 5. Back To The World	Curtom 8015
7/6/74	**39**	1	6. Sweet Exorcist	Curtom 8601
			MAZE Featuring Frankie Beverly	
			Soul group formed in Philadelphia as The Butlers (later, Raw Soul); moved to San Francisco in 1972. Nucleus consisted of Frankie Beverly (vocals), Wayne Thomas, Sam Porter, Robin Duhe, Roame Lowry and McKinley Williams.	
3/4/78	**27**	5	● 1. Golden Time Of Day	Capitol 11710
5/12/79	**33**	3	● 2. Inspiration	Capitol 11912
9/13/80	**31**	4	● 3. Joy And Pain	Capitol 12087
8/8/81	**34**	4	● 4. Live In New Orleans [L]	Capitol 12156 [2]
			side 4 contains new studio recordings	

DATE	POS	WKS	ARTIST—RECORD TITLE	LABEL & NO.
6/4/83	**25**	5	5. We Are One	Capitol 12262
10/7/89	**37**	3	● 6. Silky Soul	Warner 25802
9/11/93	**37**	2	● 7. Back To Basics	Warner 45297

MAZZY STAR

California duo of songwriter/guitarist David Roback and vocalist Hope Sandoval. Roback was a member of Rain Parade and Opal.

9/24/94	**36**	3	● So Tonight That I Might See	Capitol 98253

McCALL, C.W.

Born William Fries on 11/15/28 in Audubon, Iowa. The character "C.W. McCall" was created for the Mertz Bread Company. Fries was its advertising man. Elected mayor of Ouray, Colorado, in the early '80s.

1/10/76	**12**	8	● Black Bear Road *Convoy* (1)	MGM 5008

McCALLUM, David

Born on 9/19/33 in Glasgow, Scotland. Studio orchestra conductor. Son of a concert violinist. Portrayed secret agent Illya Kuryakin on TV's "The Man from U.N.C.L.E."

4/16/66	**27**	8	Music — A Part Of Me [I] McCallum conducts a studio orchestra	Capitol 2432

McCANN, Les

Born on 9/23/35 in Lexington, Kentucky. Jazz keyboardist/vocalist. First recorded with Leroy Vinnegar (bass) and Ron Jefferson (drums), as Les McCann Ltd., for Pacific Jazz in 1959.

1/31/70	**29**	5	Swiss Movement [I-L] **LES McCANN & EDDIE HARRIS** recorded at the Montreux Jazz Festival, Switzerland	Atlantic 1537

McCARTNEY, Paul/Wings

Born James Paul McCartney on 6/18/42 in Liverpool, England. Writer of over 50 Top 10 singles. Founding member/bass guitarist of The Beatles. Married Linda Eastman on 3/12/69. First solo album in 1970. Formed group Wings in 1971 with Linda (keyboards, backing vocals), Denny Laine (guitar; ex-Moody Blues) and Denny Seiwell (drums). Henry McCullough (guitar) joined in 1972. Seiwell and McCullough left in 1973. In 1975, Joe English (drums) and ex-Thunderclap Newman guitarist Jimmy McCulloch (died 9/27/79 [age 26] of heart failure) joined; both left in 1977. Wings officially disbanded in April 1981. McCartney starred in own movie *Give My Regards to Broad Street* (1984). Won 1990 Lifetime Achievement Grammy Award.

PAUL McCARTNEY:

5/9/70	**1**(3)	20	▲² 1. McCartney recorded at home by Paul as a one-man band	Apple 3363

PAUL AND LINDA McCARTNEY:

6/5/71	**2**(2)	28	▲ 2. RAM *Uncle Albert/Admiral Halsey* (1)	Apple 3375

WINGS:

12/25/71	**10**	10	● 3. Wild Life	Apple 3386
5/19/73	**1**(3)	16	● 4. Red Rose Speedway **PAUL McCARTNEY & WINGS** *My Love* (1)	Apple 3409
12/22/73	**1**(4)	40	▲³ 5. Band On The Run **PAUL McCARTNEY & WINGS** *Helen Wheels* (10)/*Jet* (7)/*Band On The Run* (1)	Apple 3415
6/14/75	**1**(1)	17	▲ 6. Venus And Mars *Listen To What The Man Said* (1)	Capitol 11419

DATE	POS	WKS	ARTIST—RECORD TITLE	LABEL & NO.
4/10/76	**1**(7)	27	▲ **7. Wings At The Speed Of Sound** *Silly Love Songs* (1)/*Let 'Em In* (3)	Capitol 11525
12/25/76	**1**(1)	18	▲ **8. Wings Over America** **[L]** 30 tracks from the group's 1976 U.S. tour *Maybe I'm Amazed* (10)	Capitol 11593 [3]
4/15/78	**2**(6)	16	▲ **9. London Town** *With A Little Luck* (1)	Capitol 11777
1/6/79	**29**	5	▲ **10. Wings Greatest** **[G]** *Another Day* (5-'71)/*Hi, Hi, Hi* (10-'73)/ *Live And Let Die* (2-'73)/*Junior's Farm* (3-'75)	Capitol 11905
7/7/79	**8**	11	▲ **11. Back To The Egg** **PAUL McCARTNEY:**	Columbia 36057
6/14/80	**3**	12	● **12. McCartney II** recorded solely by Paul at his home	Columbia 36511
5/15/82	**1**(3)	18	▲ **13. Tug Of War** *Ebony And Ivory* (1-with Stevie Wonder)/*Take It Away* (10)	Columbia 37462
11/26/83	**15**	12	▲ **14. Pipes Of Peace** above 2 produced by George Martin *Say Say Say* (1-with Michael Jackson)	Columbia 39149
11/10/84	**21**	10	● **15. Give my regards to Broad Street** **[S]** 13 of 16 cuts are re-recordings of Beatles/McCartney hits *No More Lonely Nights* (6)	Columbia 39613
9/27/86	**30**	5	16. Press To Play	Capitol 12475
7/1/89	**21**	6	● 17. Flowers In The Dirt	Capitol 91653
12/1/90	**26**	6	18. Tripping The Live Fantastic **[L]** 30 Beatles, Wings and solo McCartney songs performed during 1989-90 world tour	Capitol 94778 [2]
6/22/91	**14**	3	19. Unplugged (The Official Bootleg) **[L]** acoustic music from the MTV program "Unplugged," recorded at Limehouse Studios in Wembley, London, on 1/25/91; features Linda, Paul "Wix" Wickens, Blair Cunningham, Hamish Stuart and Robbie McIntosh	Capitol 96413
2/27/93	**17**	2	● 20. Off The Ground	Capitol 80362
			McCLINTON, Delbert Born on 11/4/40 in Lubbock, Texas. Played harmonica on Bruce Channel's hit "Hey Baby." Leader of The Ron-Dels.	
2/21/81	**34**	4	The Jealous Kind *Giving It Up For Your Love* (8)	Capitol 12115
			McCOO, Marilyn, & Billy Davis, Jr. McCoo (born 9/30/43, Jersey City, New Jersey) and husband Davis (born 6/26/39, St. Louis, Missouri) were members of The 5th Dimension. Duo hosted own summer variety TV series in 1977. McCoo co-hosted TV's "Solid Gold" from 1981-84.	
12/18/76	**30**	7	● I Hope We Get To Love In Time *You Don't Have To Be A Star (To Be In My Show)* (1)	ABC 952
			McCOY, Van, & The Soul City Symphony Born on 1/6/44 in Washington, D.C.; died on 7/6/79 of a heart attack. Pianist/ producer/songwriter/ singer. Formed own Rock'N label in 1960. A&R man at Scepter/Wand from 1961-64. Own MAXX label, mid-1960s. Produced The Shirelles, Gladys Knight, The Stylistics and Brenda & The Tabulations.	
6/14/75	**12**	9	Disco Baby *The Hustle* (1)	Avco 69006

DATE	POS	WKS	ARTIST—RECORD TITLE	LABEL & NO.
			McCRAE, George	
			Born on 10/19/44 in West Palm Beach, Florida. Duets with wife Gwen McCrae; became her manager.	
9/7/74	**38**	2	Rock Your Baby *Rock Your Baby* (1)	TK 501
			McDONALD, Country Joe — see COUNTRY JOE	
			McDONALD, Michael	
			Born on 12/2/52 in St. Louis, Missouri. Vocalist/keyboardist. First recorded for RCA in 1972. Formerly with Steely Dan and The Doobie Brothers. Married to singer Amy Holland.	
9/11/82	**6**	11	● **If That's What It Takes** *I Keep Forgettin'* (4)	Warner 23703
			MC EIHT Featuring CMW	
			Leader of rap group Compton's Most Wanted. EIHT stands for Experienced In Hardcore-Thumpin'.	
8/6/94	**5**	8	● **We Come Strapped**	Epic Street 57696
			McENTIRE, Reba	
			Born on 3/28/54 in Chockie, Oklahoma. Country singer. Sang with older brother Pake and younger sister Susie at rodeos as The Singing McEntires while a teenager. Competed in rodeos as a horseback barrel rider. Discovered by country singer Red Steagall when she sang the national anthem at the National Rodeo Finals in Oklahoma City in 1974. Married rodeo champion Charlie Battles on 6/21/76; divorced in 1987. Married her manager, Narvel Blackstock, in 1989. First worked on the *Grand Ole Opry* in 1977; became member in 1985. Acted in the movie *Tremors* and several TV movies.	
5/25/91	**39**	1	▲² 1. Rumor Has It	MCA 10016
10/19/91	**13**	29	▲² 2. For My Broken Heart	MCA 10400
1/2/93	**8**	26	▲³ 3. It's Your Call	MCA 10673
10/16/93	**5**	23	▲³ 4. Greatest Hits Volume Two [G]	MCA 10906
5/14/94	**2**(1)	15	▲² **5. Read My Mind**	MCA 10994
			McFADDEN & WHITEHEAD	
			R&B duo of Gene McFadden and John Whitehead from Philadelphia. Wrote songs for many Philadelphia soul acts; defined "The Sound Of Philadelphia." Whitehead recorded solo in 1988. John's sons, Kenny and Johnny, charted as The Whitehead Brothers.	
6/9/79	**23**	8	● McFadden & Whitehead	Phil. Int. 35800
			McFERRIN, Bobby	
			Born on 3/11/50 in New York City. Unaccompanied, jazz-styled improvisation vocalist. Sang 1987 theme for "The Cosby Show" and the Levis 501 Blues jingle. Father was a baritone with the New York Metropolitan Opera.	
9/3/88	**5**	16	▲ **Simple Pleasures** *Don't Worry Be Happy* (1)	EMI-Man. 48059
			MC5	
			Detroit hard-rock quintet: Rob Tyner, lead singer (born Robert Derminer; died 9/17/91 [age 46] from a heart attack). Guitarist Fred "Sonic" Smith (died 11/4/94 [age 45] from a heart attack) married Patti Smith in 1980. MC5 is short for Motor City Five.	
5/10/69	**30**	3	Kick Out The Jams [L]	Elektra 74042
			McGRATH, Bob — see CHILDREN'S ALBUMS	

DATE	POS	WKS	ARTIST—RECORD TITLE	LABEL & NO.
			McGRAW, Tim	
			Born on 5/1/67 in Delhi, Louisiana; raised in Start, Louisiana. Country singer. His father, Tug McGraw, was a professional baseball player from 1964-84. Tim attended Northeast Louisiana University on several sports scholarships.	
4/9/94	**1**(2)	47+	▲³ Not A Moment Too Soon	Curb 77659
			McGRIFF, Jimmy	
			Born on 4/3/36 in Philadelphia. Jazz-R&B organist/multi-instrumentalist.	
12/29/62	**22**	14	I've Got A Woman [I]	Sue 1012
			McGUINN, CLARK & HILLMAN	
			Roger McGuinn (born 7/13/42; vocals, guitar), Gene Clark (born 11/17/44; died 5/24/91; guitar) and Chris Hillman (born 6/4/42; bass). All were founding members of The Byrds.	
4/28/79	**39**	2	McGuinn, Clark & Hillman	Capitol 11910
			McGUIRE, Barry	
			Born on 10/15/37 in Oklahoma City. Member of The New Christy Minstrels (1962-65). Currently records contemporary Christian music.	
11/27/65	**37**	3	Eve Of Destruction *Eve Of Destruction* (1)	Dunhill 50003
			McGUIRE SISTERS, The	
			Sisters Phyllis (born 2/14/31), Christine (born 7/30/29) and Dorothy (born 2/13/30) from Middletown, Ohio. Replaced The Chordettes on the "Arthur Godfrey and His Friends" TV show in 1953. Phyllis went solo in 1964. Reunited in 1986.	
3/5/55	**11**	6	By Request ... [M] 10" album of 8 songs *Sincerely* (1)	Coral 56123
			M.C. HAMMER — see HAMMER	
			McKENZIE, Bob & Doug	
			Canadian comedians Rick Moranis and Dave Thomas of "SCTV." Both featured in the movie *Strange Brew*. Moranis later starred in *Ghostbusters*, *Spaceballs*, *Honey, I Shrunk The Kids* and many others. Thomas, the brother of singer Ian Thomas, hosted own CBS-TV series in 1990 and is a cast member of TV's "Grace Under Fire."	
2/6/82	**8**	13	● Great White North [C]	Mercury 4034
			McKINLEY, Ray — see MILLER, Glenn	
			McLAUGHLIN, John	
			Born on 1/4/42 in Yorkshire, England. Jazz-fusion guitar virtuoso. Formed his Mahavishnu Orchestra in 1971 with Billy Cobham, Jan Hammer, Rick Laird and Jerry Goodman. Original group disbanded in 1973.	
3/10/73	**15**	11	● 1. Birds Of Fire [I] **MAHAVISHNU ORCHESTRA**	Columbia 31996
7/21/73	**14**	7	● 2. Love Devotion Surrender [I] **CARLOS SANTANA/MAHAVISHNU JOHN McLAUGHLIN**	Columbia 32034
			McLEAN, Don	
			Born on 10/2/45 in New Rochelle, New York. Singer/songwriter/poet. Inspired the hit "Killing Me Softly."	
12/11/71	**1**(7)	26	● 1. American Pie *American Pie* (1)	United Art. 5535
2/3/73	**23**	7	2. Don McLean	United Art. 5651

DATE	POS	WKS	ARTIST—RECORD TITLE	LABEL & NO.
3/21/81	28	6	3. Chain Lightning *Crying* (5)	Millennium 7756
			MC REN Rapper Lorenzo Patterson, former member of N.W.A.	
7/18/92	12	4	▲ 1. Kizz My Black Azz	Ruthless 53802
12/4/93	22	1	2. Shock Of The Hour	Ruthless 5505
			McVIE, Christine Born Christine Perfect on 7/12/43 in Birmingham, England. Vocalist/keyboardist with Fleetwood Mac since 1970. Married to Fleetwood Mac bassist John McVie, 1968-77. Stopped touring with group after 1990.	
3/3/84	26	7	Christine McVie *Got A Hold On Me* (10)	Warner 25059
			MEADER, Vaughn Born on 3/20/36 in Boston.. President John F. Kennedy impersonator.	
12/8/62	1 (12)	26	● 1. The First Family　　　　　　[C] 1962 Album of the Year Grammy Award	Cadence 3060
6/1/63	4	11	2. The First Family, volume two　　[C] above albums feature Naomi Brossart as Jackie Kennedy	Cadence 3065
			MEAT LOAF Born Marvin Lee Aday on 9/27/51 in Dallas. Rock singer. Sang lead vocals on Ted Nugent's 1976 *Free-For- All* album. Played Eddie in the Los Angeles production and movie of *The Rocky Horror Picture Show*. Appeared in movies *Americathon, Roadie, Out of Bounds, The Squeeze* and *Leap of Faith*.	
5/13/78	14	28	▲^{12} 1. Bat Out Of Hell	Cleve. I. 34974
10/2/93	1 (1)	33	▲^{4} 2. Bat Out Of Hell II: Back Into Hell *I'd Do Anything For Love (But I Won't Do That)* (1)	MCA 10699
			MECO Disco producer Meco Monardo, born on 11/29/39 in Johnsonburg, Pennsylvania. Played trombone in Cadet Band at West Point. Later moved to New York; became a session musician and arranger. Co-produced Gloria Gaynor's hit "Never Can Say Goodbye."	
9/10/77	13	9	▲ Star Wars And Other Galactic Funk　[I] *Star Wars Theme/Cantina Band* (1)	Millennium 8001
			MEGADETH Heavy-metal group formed in Southern California by Dave Mustaine (vocals, guitar; former guitarist of Metallica) and Dave Ellefson (bass).	
2/13/88	28	6	● 1. so far, so good ... so what!	Capitol 48148
10/27/90	23	5	▲ 2. Rust In Peace	Capitol 91935
8/1/92	2 (1)	13	▲^{2} 3. Countdown To Extinction	Capitol 98531
11/19/94	4	3	▲ 4. Youthanasia	Capitol 29004
			MEHTA, Zubin — see CARRERAS, Jose	
			MELACHRINO, George, And His Orchestra Born on 5/1/09 in London of Greek parentage; died on 6/18/65. Multi-instrumentalist. First to use masses of strings to produce sentimental mood music.	
1/8/55	10	2	1. Christmas in High Fidelity　　[X-I]	RCA 1045
5/25/59	30	1	2. Under Western Skies　　　　　[I]	RCA 1676

DATE	POS	WKS	ARTIST—RECORD TITLE	LABEL & NO.
			MELANIE	
			Born Melanie Safka on 2/3/47 in Queens, New York. Neighborhood Records formed by Safka and her husband/ producer, Peter Schekeryk. Wrote The New Seekers' hit "Look What They've Done To My Song Ma."	
6/13/70	**17**	11	● 1. Candles In The Rain	Buddah 5060
			Lay Down (Candles In The Rain) (6-with The Edwin Hawkins Singers)	
9/26/70	**33**	4	2. Leftover Wine [L]	Buddah 5066
12/11/71	**15**	14	● 3. Gather Me	Neighbor. 47001
			Brand New Key (1)	
			MELLENCAMP, John Cougar	
			Born on 10/7/51 in Seymour, Indiana. Rock singer/songwriter/producer. Worked outside of music until 1975. Given name Johnny Cougar by David Bowie's manager, Tony DeFries. First recorded for MCA in 1976. Directed and starred in the 1992 movie *Falling from Grace*; leader of The Buzzin' Cousins group that appeared in the movie. Married model Elaine Irwin on 9/5/92.	
			JOHN COUGAR:	
5/16/81	**37**	3	● 1. Nothin' Matters And What If It Did	Riva 7403
5/29/82	**1**(9)	40	▲⁴ 2. American Fool	Riva 7501
			Hurts So Good (2)/*Jack & Diane* (1)	
			JOHN COUGAR MELLENCAMP:	
11/12/83	**9**	36	▲³ 3. Uh-Huh	Riva 7504
			Crumblin' Down (9)/*Pink Houses* (8)	
9/21/85	**2**(3)	48	▲⁴ 4. Scarecrow	Riva 824865
			Lonely Ol' Night (6)/*Small Town* (6)/ *R.O.C.K. In The U.S.A.* (2)	
9/19/87	**6**	37	▲³ 5. The Lonesome Jubilee	Mercury 832465
			Paper In Fire (9)/*Cherry Bomb* (8)	
6/3/89	**7**	15	▲ 6. Big Daddy	Mercury 838220
			JOHN MELLENCAMP:	
10/26/91	**17**	7	▲ 7. Whenever We Wanted	Mercury 510151
9/25/93	**7**	9	▲ 8. Human Wheels	Mercury 518088
7/9/94	**13**	10	▲ 9. Dance Naked	Mercury 522428
			Wild Night (3-with Me'Shell Ndegeocello)	
			MELVIN, Harold, And The Blue Notes	
			Philadelphia soul group, The Blue Notes, formed in 1954: Harold Melvin, Bernard Williams, Jesse Gillis, Jr., Franklin Peaker and Roosevelt Brodie. First recorded for Josie in 1956. Numerous personnel changes until 1970, when Teddy Pendergrass joined as drummer and lead singer. Pendergrass went solo in 1976; replaced by David Ebo.	
5/3/75	**26**	12	● 1. To Be True	Phil. Int. 33148
12/27/75	**9**	12	● 2. Wake Up Everybody	Phil. Int. 33808
			MEN AT WORK	
			Melbourne, Australia, rock quintet formed in 1979: Colin James Hay (lead singer, guitar), Ron Strykert (lead guitar), Greg Ham (sax, keyboards), Jerry Speiser (drums) and John Rees (bass). Won 1982 Best New Artist Grammy Award. Speiser and Rees left in 1984.	
8/28/82	**1**(15)	48	▲⁶ 1. Business As Usual	Columbia 37978
			Who Can It Be Now? (1)/*Down Under* (1)	
5/7/83	**3**	23	▲³ 2. Cargo	Columbia 38660
			Overkill (3)/*It's A Mistake* (6)	

DATE	POS	WKS	ARTIST—RECORD TITLE	LABEL & NO.
			MENDES, Sergio, & Brasil '66	
			Mendes was born on 2/11/41 in Niteroi, Brazil. Pianist/leader of Latin-styled group originating from Brazil. Member Lani Hall (vocals) married Herb Alpert.	
10/15/66	7	30	● **1. Sergio Mendes & Brasil '66**	A&M 4116
5/20/67	24	6	● 2. Equinox	A&M 4122
4/6/68	5	33	● **3. Look Around**	A&M 4137
			The Look Of Love (4)	
12/21/68	3	16	● **4. Fool On The Hill**	A&M 4160
			The Fool On The Hill (6)	
9/27/69	33	2	5. Crystal Illusions	A&M 4197
6/11/83	27	10	6. Sergio Mendes	A&M 4937
			SERGIO MENDES	
			Never Gonna Let You Go (4)	
			MEN WITHOUT HATS	
			Nucleus of techno-rock band from Montreal consists of Ivan Doroschuk (singer/songwriter) with his brother Stefan (guitar). Fluctuating personnel included their brother Colin (1983-84).	
8/20/83	13	14	● Rhythm Of Youth	Backstreet 39002
			The Safety Dance (3)	
			MERCY, The	
			Florida group led by Jack Sigler, Jr.	
7/12/69	38	3	The Mercy & Love (Can Make You Happy)	Sundi 803
			Love (Can Make You Happy) (2)	
			METALLICA	
			Speed-metal quartet formed by Lars Ulrich (drums) and James Hetfield (vocals) in Los Angeles in 1981. Early rhythm guitarist Dave Mustaine (now the leader of Megadeth) was replaced by Kirk Hammett in 1982. Bassist Cliff Burton was killed in a bus crash in Sweden on 9/27/86 (age 24); replaced by Jason Newsted.	
4/12/86	29	7	▲^{3} 1. Master Of Puppets	Elektra 60439
9/26/87	28	8	▲ 2. The $5.98 E.P.: Garage Days Re-Revisited [M]	Elektra 60757
9/24/88	6	34	▲^{3} 3. ... And Justice For All	Elektra 60812 [2]
8/31/91	1 (4)	85	▲^{8} **4. Metallica**	Elektra 61113
12/11/93	26	1	5. Live Shit: Binge & Purge [L]	Elektra 61594 [3]
			recorded at Mexico City's Sports Palace, 2/25-27/93 and 3/1-2/93; includes 3 videocassettes of concerts in San Diego (1992) and Seattle (1989) plus a 72-page booklet and a "scary guy" stencil; packaged in a cardboard touring-trunk replica	
			METHOD MAN	
			Born Clifford Smith in Staten Island, New York. Male rapper. Member of Wu-Tang Clan.	
12/3/94	4	2	● **Tical**	Def Jam 523839
			produced by Prince Rakeem (Wu-Tang Clan)	
			MFSB	
			Large interracial studio band formed by producers Kenny Gamble and Leon Huff. Also recorded as The James Boys; Family. Name means "Mother, Father, Sister, Brother."	
3/9/74	4	14	● **1. Love Is The Message** [I]	Phil. Int. 32707
			TSOP (The Sound Of Philadelphia) (1)	
1/10/76	39	2	2. Philadelphia Freedom [I]	Phil. Int. 33845

DATE	POS	WKS	ARTIST—RECORD TITLE	LABEL & NO.
			MIAMI SOUND MACHINE — see ESTEFAN, Gloria	
			MICHAEL, George/Wham!	
			Born Georgios Kyriacos Panayiotou on 6/26/63 in Bushey, England. Wham!, formed in early '80s, centered around Michael's vocals and songwriting, and included Andrew Ridgeley (born 1/26/63, Bushey, England) on guitar. Their association ended in 1986. Ridgeley pursued race-car driving, then solo career in 1990. **WHAM!:**	
11/17/84	**1**(3)	56	▲⁶ **1. Make It Big** *Wake Me Up Before You Go-Go* (1)/*Careless Whisper* (1)/ *Everything She Wants* (1)/*Freedom* (3)	Columbia 39595
7/26/86	**10**	11	▲ **2. Music From The Edge Of Heaven** *I'm Your Man* (3)/*A Different Corner* (7-George Michael)/ *The Edge Of Heaven* (10) **GEORGE MICHAEL:**	Columbia 40285
11/28/87	**1**(12)	69	▲⁹ **3. Faith** *1988 Album of the Year Grammy Award* *I Want Your Sex* (2)/*Faith* (1)/*Father Figure* (1)/ *One More Try* (1)/*Monkey* (1)/*Kissing A Fool* (5)	Columbia 40867
9/29/90	**2**(1)	27	▲² **4. Listen Without Prejudice** *Praying For Time* (1)/*Freedom* (8)	Columbia 46898
			MICHAELS, Lee	
			Born on 11/24/45 in Los Angeles. Rock organist/vocalist.	
9/11/71	**16**	12	"5th" *Do You Know What I Mean* (6)	A&M 4302
			MICHEL'Le	
			Michel'le (pronounced mee-shell-LAY) Toussant is an 18-year-old (in 1990) singer from Los Angeles. Former backing singer of the World Class Wreckin Cru.	
3/17/90	**35**	6	● Michel'le *No More Lies* (7)	Ruthless 91282
			MIDLER, Bette	
			Born on 12/1/45 in Paterson, New Jersey; raised in Hawaii. Vocalist/actress. In the Broadway show *Fiddler on the Roof* for three years. Won 1973 Best New Artist Grammy Award. Barry Manilow was her arranger/accompanist in early years. Nominated for an Academy Award for her performance in *The Rose* (1979). Also in movies *Down and Out in Beverly Hills*, *Ruthless People*, *Beaches*, *For the Boys* and others.	
1/13/73	**9**	23	▲ **1. The Divine Miss M** *Boogie Woogie Bugle Boy* (8)	Atlantic 7238
12/22/73	**6**	11	● **2. Bette Midler** above 2 co-produced by Barry Manilow	Atlantic 7270
2/7/76	**27**	6	3. Songs For The New Depression	Atlantic 18155
1/12/80	**12**	23	▲² 4. The Rose [S-L] *The Rose* (3)	Atlantic 16010
12/13/80	**34**	4	5. Divine Madness [S-L] the movie captures a concert at the Pasadena Civic Auditorium	Atlantic 16022
2/25/89	**2**(3)	33	▲³ **6. Beaches** [S] *Wind Beneath My Wings* (1)	Atlantic 81933
10/27/90	**6**	29	▲² **7. Some People's Lives** [S] *From A Distance* (2)	Atlantic 82129
12/7/91	**22**	6	● 8. For The Boys [S]	Atlantic 82329

DATE	POS	WKS	ARTIST—RECORD TITLE	LABEL & NO.
			MIDNIGHT OIL	
			Australian rock quintet: Peter Garrett (lead vocals), Peter Gifford, Martin Rotsey, James Moginie and Rob Hirst (replaced by bassist Bones Hillman in 1987). Garrett ran for the Australian Senate in 1984.	
4/30/88	21	26	▲ 1. Diesel And Dust	Columbia 40967
3/24/90	20	14	● 2. Blue Sky Mining	Columbia 45398
			MIDNIGHT STAR	
			R&B-funk group formed in 1976 at Kentucky State University. Lead vocals by Belinda Lipscomb. Until 1988, band led by brothers Reggie (trumpet) and Vincent (trombone) Calloway. They produced many artists in the mid-1980s; formed own duo Calloway in 1988.	
9/17/83	27	30	▲^{2} 1. No Parking On The Dance Floor	Solar 60241
1/19/85	32	7	● 2. Planetary Invasion	Solar 60384
			MIDNIGHT STRING QUARTET	
			A Snuff Garrett production (The Renaissance).	
2/11/67	17	12	Rhapsodies For Young Lovers [I]	Viva 6001
			MIGUEL, Luis	
			Born in April 1970. Native of Mexico. Popular singer in Hispanic music world. Acted in movies *Nunca Mas* (1982) and *Fiebre De Amor* (1984).	
9/17/94	29	2	● Segundo Romance [F]	WEA Latina 97234
			MIKE + THE MECHANICS	
			Rock quintet: bassist Mike Rutherford (Genesis), vocalists Paul Carrack (Ace; Squeeze) and Paul Young (Sad Cafe), drummer Peter Van Hooke (Van Morrison) and keyboardist Adrian Lee.	
2/8/86	26	21	● 1. Mike + The Mechanics	Atlantic 81287
			Silent Running (6)/*All I Need Is A Miracle* (5)	
2/25/89	13	13	● 2. Living Years	Atlantic 81923
			The Living Years (1)	
			MILES, Buddy	
			Born George Miles on 9/5/46 in Omaha. R&B vocalist/drummer. Prominent session musician. Lead singer of The Fidelity's in 1958. Worked as sideman in The Dick Clark Revue, 1963-64. With Wilson Pickett, 1965-66. In Michael Bloomfield's Electric Flag, 1967. In Jimi Hendrix's Band of Gypsys, 1969-70. In 1987, was the voice of The California Raisins, the claymation TV-ad characters.	
8/29/70	35	5	1. Them Changes	Mercury 61280
7/29/72	8	14	▲ 2. Carlos Santana & Buddy Miles! Live! [L]	Columbia 31308
			CARLOS SANTANA & BUDDY MILES	
			MILLER, Glenn	
			Born Alton Glenn Miller on 3/1/04 in Clarinda, Iowa. Leader of most popular big band of all time. Played trombone for Ben Pollack, Red Nichols, Benny Goodman and The Dorsey Brothers. Became de facto leader of Ray Noble's 1935 American band; did arrangements for Glen Gray and others before starting his own band in 1937. Miller disappeared on a plane flight from England to France on 12/15/44.	
9/16/57	16	6	1. Marvelous Miller Moods [E]	RCA 1494
			GLENN MILLER ARMY AIR FORCE BAND with Johnny Desmond (vocals); from radio broadcasts during 1943-44	
12/9/57	17	4	2. The New Glenn Miller Orchestra In Hi Fi	RCA 1522
			directed by Ray McKinley (leader of the orchestra after Miller's death)	

DATE	POS	WKS	ARTIST—RECORD TITLE	LABEL & NO.
2/24/58	**19**	3	3. The Glenn Miller Carnegie Hall Concert [E-L] recorded on 10/06/39	RCA 1506
			MILLER, Mitch, & The Gang	
			Born on 7/4/11 in Rochester, New York. Producer/conductor/arranger. Oboe soloist with the CBS Symphony from 1936-47. A&R executive for both Columbia and Mercury Records. Best known for his sing-along albums and TV show (1961-64).	
7/14/58	**1**(8)	128	● **1. Sing Along With Mitch**	Columbia 1160
11/10/58	**4**	117	● **2. More Sing Along With Mitch**	Columbia 1243
3/23/59	**4**	71	● **3. Still More! Sing Along With Mitch**	Columbia 1283
6/15/59	**11**	31	● 4. Folk Songs Sing Along With Mitch	Columbia 1316
8/31/59	**7**	66	● **5. Party Sing Along With Mitch**	Columbia 1331
1/4/60	**10**	30	6. Fireside Sing Along With Mitch	Columbia 1389
4/4/60	**8**	40	● **7. Saturday Night Sing Along With Mitch**	Columbia 1414
6/27/60	**5**	32	● **8. Sentimental Sing Along With Mitch**	Columbia 1457
10/10/60	**40**	1	9. March Along With Mitch [I]	Columbia 1475
10/31/60	**5**	25	● **10. Memories Sing Along With Mitch**	Columbia 8342
3/6/61	**9**	8	**11. Mitch's Greatest Hits** [G] *The Yellow Rose Of Texas* (1-'55)/ *Song For A Summer Night* (8-'56)	Columbia 8344
3/13/61	**5**	23	● **12. Happy Times! Sing Along With Mitch**	Columbia 8368
6/12/61	**3**	40	**13. TV Sing Along With Mitch**	Columbia 8428
10/2/61	**6**	23	**14. Your Request Sing Along With Mitch**	Columbia 8471
3/10/62	**21**	7	15. Rhythm Sing Along With Mitch	Columbia 8527
7/21/62	**27**	5	16. Family Sing Along With Mitch	Columbia 8573
			CHRISTMAS ALBUMS:	
12/29/58	**1**(2)	5	● **17. Christmas Sing-Along With Mitch** [X]	Columbia 1205
12/14/59	**8**	4	**18. Christmas Sing-Along With Mitch** [X-R]	Columbia 1205
12/19/60	**6**	3	**19. Christmas Sing-Along With Mitch** [X-R]	Columbia 8027
12/11/61	**9**	7	**20. Christmas Sing-Along With Mitch** [X-R]	Columbia 8027
12/29/62	**37**	1	21. Christmas Sing-Along With Mitch [X-R]	Columbia 8027
12/4/61	**1**(1)	13	● **22. Holiday Sing Along With Mitch** [X]	Columbia 8501
12/29/62	**33**	1	23. Holiday Sing Along With Mitch [X-R]	Columbia 8501
			Christmas charts: 9/'63, 15/'64, 22/'65, 14/'66, 17/'67, 37/'68	
			MILLER, Mrs.	
			Mrs. Elva Miller. Tone-deaf singer from Claremont, California.	
6/4/66	**15**	10	Mrs. Miller's Greatest Hits [N]	Capitol 2494
			MILLER, Roger	
			Born on 1/2/36 in Fort Worth, Texas; raised in Erick, Oklahoma; died of cancer on 10/25/92. Country vocalist/humorist/guitarist/composer. To Nashville in the mid-1950s; began songwriting career. Debuted on the country charts in 1960 on RCA. With Faron Young as writer/drummer in 1962. Won six Grammy Awards in 1965. Own TV show in 1966. Songwriter of 1985's Tony Award-winning Broadway musical *Big River*.	
12/12/64	**37**	2	● 1. Roger And Out [N] *Dang Me* (7)/*Chug-A-Lug* (9)	Smash 67049
3/13/65	**4**	29	● **2. The Return Of Roger Miller** *King Of The Road* (4)	Smash 67061
8/7/65	**13**	9	3. The 3rd Time Around *Engine Engine #9* (7)	Smash 67068

DATE	POS	WKS	ARTIST—RECORD TITLE	LABEL & NO.
12/11/65	6	21	● **4. Golden Hits** [G] *England Swings* (8)	Smash 67073

MILLER, Steve, Band

Miller was born on 10/5/43 in Milwaukee; moved to Dallas at age six. Blues-rock singer/songwriter/ guitarist. Formed band in high school, The Marksmen, which included Boz Scaggs. While at the University of Wisconsin-Madison, Miller led the blues-rock band The Ardells, later known as The Fabulous Night Trains, featuring Scaggs. After graduating, studied literature at the University of Copenhagen. To San Francisco in 1966; formed The Steve Miller Band, which featured a fluctuating lineup.

DATE	POS	WKS	ARTIST—RECORD TITLE	LABEL & NO.
11/16/68	24	8	1. Sailor	Capitol 2984
7/5/69	22	8	2. Brave New World	Capitol 184
12/27/69	38	5	3. Your Saving Grace	Capitol 331
8/15/70	23	7	4. Number 5	Capitol 436
11/3/73	2(1)	20	▲ **5. The Joker** *The Joker* (1)	Capitol 11235
6/12/76	3	48	▲⁴ **6. Fly Like An Eagle** *Rock'n Me* (1)/*Fly Like An Eagle* (2)	Capitol 11497
5/28/77	2(2)	27	▲³ **7. Book Of Dreams** *Jet Airliner* (8)	Capitol 11630
12/23/78	18	9	▲⁶ **8. Greatest Hits 1974-78** [G]	Capitol 11872
11/21/81	26	5	● 9. Circle Of Love	Capitol 12121
7/10/82	3	18	▲ **10. Abracadabra** *Abracadabra* (1)	Capitol 12216

MILLI VANILLI

Europop act formed in Germany by producer Frank Farian (creator of Boney M and Far Corporation). Milli Vanilli is Turkish for positive energy. Originally thought to be Rob Pilatus (from Germany) and Fabrice Morvan (from France). Duo was stripped of its 1989 Best New Artist Grammy Award when it was revealed that they didn't sing on their debut album. Actual vocalists are Charles Shaw, John Davis and Brad Howe.

DATE	POS	WKS	ARTIST—RECORD TITLE	LABEL & NO.
4/1/89	1(8)	61	▲⁶ **1. Girl You Know It's True** *Girl You Know It's True* (2)/*Baby Don't Forget My Number* (1)/ *Girl I'm Gonna Miss You* (1)/*Blame It On The Rain* (1)/ *All Or Nothing* (4)	Arista 8592
6/23/90	32	5	● 2. The Remix Album [K] 5 of 9 tracks are remixes of hits from the above album	Arista 8622

MILLS, Frank

Born in Toronto in 1943. Pianist/composer/producer/arranger.

DATE	POS	WKS	ARTIST—RECORD TITLE	LABEL & NO.
4/14/79	21	5	● Music Box Dancer [I] *Music Box Dancer* (3)	Polydor 6192

MILLS, Stephanie

Born on 3/26/56 in Brooklyn. In 1967, appeared for four weeks at the Apollo Theater with The Isley Brothers. At age 15, won starring role of Dorothy in the hit Broadway musical *The Wiz*. Played role for four years. Briefly married to Jeffrey Daniels of Shalamar in 1980.

DATE	POS	WKS	ARTIST—RECORD TITLE	LABEL & NO.
8/18/79	22	9	● 1. Whatcha Gonna Do ... With My Lovin'?	20th Century 583
5/10/80	16	22	● 2. Sweet Sensation *Never Knew Love Like This Before* (6)	20th Century 603
6/6/81	30	5	● 3. Stephanie	20th Century 700
8/15/87	30	9	● 4. If I Were Your Woman	MCA 5996

DATE	POS	WKS	ARTIST—RECORD TITLE	LABEL & NO.
			MILLS BROTHERS, The	
			Legendary family vocal group from Piqua, Ohio. Consisted of John, Jr. (born 1911; died 1936), Herbert (born 1912; died 4/12/89), Harry (born 1913; died 6/28/82) and Donald (born 1915). Originally featured unusual vocal style of imitating instruments. Achieved national fame via radio broadcasts and appearances in movies. Father, John, Sr., joined group in 1936; replaced John, Jr.; remained in group until 1956 (died 12/8/67). Group continued as a trio until 1982. Donald and his son John, III, continued singing as a duo.	
4/13/68	21	10	Fortuosity	Dot 25809
			MILSAP, Ronnie	
			Born on 1/16/46 in Robbinsville, North Carolina. Country singer/pianist/guitarist. Blind since birth; multi-instrumentalist by age 12. With J.J. Cale band; own band from 1965. First charted (Bubbling Under) in 1965 on Scepter Records.	
2/14/81	36	4	▲² 1. Greatest Hits [G]	RCA 3772
10/3/81	31	3	● 2. There's No Gettin' Over Me	RCA 4060
			(There's) No Gettin' Over Me (5)	
6/11/83	36	3	3. Keyed Up	RCA 4670
			MINISTRY	
			An assemblage of musicians spearheaded by Chicago-based producers/performers Alain Jourgensen and Paul Barker. Formed by Jourgensen in 1981. Barker joined Ministry in 1986. Varying personnel are members of The Tribe, an affiliation of musicians from various groups.	
8/1/92	27	1	● Psalm 69	Sire 26727
			MINNELLI, Liza	
			Born on 3/12/46 in Los Angeles. Singer and Broadway/movie actress. Daughter of legendary singer/actress Judy Garland and movie director Vincente Minnelli. Starred in many movies (*Arthur*, among them) and in Broadway productions. Won 1972 Best Actress Academy Award for *Cabaret*. Winner of three Tony Awards. Married to Peter Allen from 1967-73. Married movie producer Jack Haley, Jr., on 9/15/74; later divorced. Won 1989 Living Legends Grammy Award.	
10/21/72	19	11	1. Liza With A "Z" [TV-L]	Columbia 31762
5/5/73	38	2	2. Liza Minnelli The Singer	Columbia 32149
			MIRACLES, The	
			R&B group formed at Northern High School in Detroit in 1955. Consisted of William "Smokey" Robinson (lead), Emerson and Bobby Rogers (tenors), Ronnie White (baritone) and Warren "Pete" Moore (bass). Emerson left in 1956 for U.S. Army; replaced by Claudette Rogers, Robinson's future wife. First recorded for End in 1958. Claudette retired in 1964. Bobby married Wanda Young of The Marvelettes. Robinson wrote many hit songs for the group and other Motown artists. Robinson went solo in 1972; replaced by William Griffin.	
5/29/65	21	14	1. Greatest Hits From The Beginning [G]	Tamla 254 [2]
			Shop Around (2-'61)	
			SMOKEY ROBINSON & THE MIRACLES:	
1/1/66	8	19	**2. Going To A Go-Go**	Tamla 267
11/11/67	28	7	3. Make It Happen	Tamla 276
			The Tears Of A Clown (1-'70)	
3/2/68	7	11	**4. Greatest Hits, Vol. 2** [G]	Tamla 280
			I Second That Emotion (4)	
8/16/69	25	8	5. Time Out for Smokey Robinson & The Miracles	Tamla 295
			Baby, Baby Don't Cry (8)	
			THE MIRACLES:	
1/3/76	33	10	6. City Of Angels	Tamla 339
			Love Machine (1)	

Dean Martin's many Reprise albums were strong sellers during the mid-1960s. *Gentle On My Mind* entered the charts in early 1969 and became the Italian-American star's final Top 20 album, as well as his last to be certified gold.

Al Martino's first Top 10 album, and his highest-charting ever, was 1963's *I Love You Because*, which featured the No. 3 hit single of the same name. Although *Spanish Eyes*, his 1966 Capitol album, didn't chart as high, peaking at No. 8, it sold longer and became the Italian singer's sole gold album.

Johnny Mathis's 1957 *Wonderful Wonderful* was his first of 16 Top 10 albums recorded for Columbia between 1957–78. *Johnny's Greatest Hits*, released less than a year later, spent an astounding total of 490 weeks on the album chart before finally dropping off.

Paul McCartney's two greatest-hits compilations have fared poorly on the charts in comparison to the performances of his regular albums. 1978's *Wings Greatest* compilation was his first-ever non-Top 10 release, peaking at No. 29, and 1987's two-LP *All The Best* reached only No. 62.

MC Hammer's 1990 smash, *Please Hammer Don't Hurt 'Em*, was an across-the-boards phenomenon that sold over 10 million copies and stayed on the charts for more than two years. Unfortunately for rapper Stanley Burrell, his career soon nose-dived, and his success was short-lived.

Vaughn Meader's skill at impersonating President John F. Kennedy helped push his 1962 comedy set, *The First Family*, to the top of the charts for 12 weeks and win the Album of the Year Grammy Award. The demand for Kennedy impersonators decreased significantly, however, following the president's 1963 assassination.

John Cougar Mellencamp's career breakthrough came via 1982's captivating *American Fool*, a No. 1 record for 12 weeks. The triple-platinum set, which contained the huge hits "Hurts So Good" and "Jack & Diane," marked the last time the Indiana-born singer refrained from using Mellencamp, his real surname.

George Michael's 1987 solo smash, *Faith*, established him as one of the world's biggest superstars. Winner of the 1988 Album of the Year Grammy Award, the hit-packed collection featured six Top 5 songs, four of which reached No. 1. The British-born singer spent much of the early '90s enmeshed in a contractual dispute with Sony Music.

Mitch Miller and his popular singalong albums were a constant presence on the charts during the late '50s and early '60s. From 1958's original *Sing Along With Mitch* through 1962's *Family Sing Along With Mitch*, Miller and his "gang" placed 16 albums in the Top 40.

Steve Miller ended his 18-album, 20-year affiliation with Capitol Records following the release of his 1988 jazz/blues set, *Born 2B Blue*. A hugely popular live attraction, the singer/guitarist then signed with PolyGram and released *Wide River* in 1993.

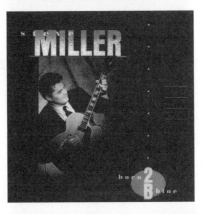

DATE	POS	WKS	ARTIST—RECORD TITLE	LABEL & NO.
			MISSING PERSONS	
			New-wave quintet formed in Los Angeles in 1980: Dale Bozzio (lead singer; former Playboy bunny from Boston), her then-husband Terry Bozzio (drummer; Roxy Music; U.K.), Warren Cuccurullo (joined Duran Duran in 1990), Patrick O'Hearn and Chuck Wild. All but Wild were with Frank Zappa's band. Disbanded in 1986. Terry worked with Jeff Beck in 1989.	
11/13/82	**17**	26	● Spring Session M title is an anagram of group's name	Capitol 12228
			MR. BIG	
			Rock quartet: Eric Martin (vocals), Pat Torpey (former drummer of Ted Nugent's band; Impellitteri), Billy Sheehan (bass) and Paul Gilbert (guitar). Group took its name from the title of a song by Free.	
2/15/92	**15**	14	▲ Lean Into It *To Be With You* (1)	Atlantic 82209
			MR. MISTER	
			Los Angeles-based, pop-rock quartet: Richard Page (vocals), Steve George, Pat Mastelotto and Steve Farris (left in 1989; replaced by Buzz Feiten, ex-guitarist of Paul Butterfield Blues Band; Stevie Wonder's band; The Larsen-Feiten Band). Page later joined Patick Leonard 3rd Matinee, which evolved from Toy Matinee.	
11/2/85	**1**(1)	34	▲ **Welcome To The Real World** *Broken Wings* (1)/*Kyrie* (1)/*Is It Love* (8)	RCA 8045
			MITCHELL, Chad, Trio	
			Mitchell was leader of folk-pop trio that included Mike Kobluk and Joe Frazier. Group formed while sophomores at Gonzaga University in Spokane, Washington. John Denver replaced Mitchell after he went solo in 1965; group renamed The Mitchell Trio.	
6/2/62	**39**	1	1. Mighty Day On Campus [L] Jim McGuinn (Byrds), guitarist	Kapp 3262
12/21/63	**39**	1	2. Singin' Our Mind	Mercury 60838
4/11/64	**29**	4	3. Reflecting	Mercury 60891
			MITCHELL, Joni	
			Born Roberta Joan Anderson on 11/7/43 in Fort McLeod, Alberta, Canada; raised in Saskatoon, Saskatchewan. Singer/songwriter/guitarist/pianist. Moved to New York in 1966. Wrote the hits "Both Sides Now" and "Woodstock." Married her producer/bassist, Larry Klein, in 1982.	
6/21/69	**31**	6	1. Clouds	Reprise 6341
4/25/70	**27**	9	▲ 2. Ladies Of The Canyon	Reprise 6376
7/10/71	**15**	12	▲ 3. Blue	Reprise 2038
12/30/72	**11**	12	● 4. For The Roses	Asylum 5057
2/9/74	**2**(4)	31	● **5. Court And Spark** *Help Me* (7)	Asylum 1001
12/21/74	**2**(1)	14	● **6. Miles Of Aisles** [L] with Tom Scott & The L.A. Express	Asylum 202
12/13/75	**4**	10	● **7. The Hissing Of Summer Lawns**	Asylum 1051
12/18/76	**13**	8	● 8. Hejira	Asylum 1087
1/14/78	**25**	4	● 9. Don Juan's Reckless Daughter	Asylum 701 [2]

7/14/79	**17**	9	10. Mingus
			     music composed by Charles Mingus
			     (jazz pianist; died 1/5/79 [age 56])
				Asylum 505

10/18/80	**38**	3	11. Shadows And Light [L] with guests Pat Metheny, Michael Brecker and Jaco Pastorius	Asylum 704 [2]

DATE	POS	WKS	ARTIST—RECORD TITLE	LABEL & NO.
12/4/82	25	5	12. Wild Things Run Fast	Geffen 2019
			MOBY GRAPE	
			Rock group from San Francisco. Original lineup: Bob Mosley, Jerry Miller, Don Stevenson, Peter Lewis and Alexander "Skip" Spence (guitarist/lead vocalist; ex-drummer of Jefferson Airplane).	
7/29/67	24	7	1. Moby Grape	Columbia 9498
			10 of 13 cuts released simultaneously on 45s	
5/18/68	20	6	2. Wow	Columbia 9613 [2]
			includes bonus LP titled *Grape Jam* (jam sessions with Al Kooper and Mike Bloomfield)	
			MODUGNO, Domenico	
			Born on 1/9/28 in Polignano a Mare, Italy; died of a heart attack on 8/6/94. Singer/actor.	
9/15/58	8	6	**Nel Blu Dipinto Di Blu (Volare) and other Italian favorites** **[F]**	Decca 8808
			Nel Blu Dipinto Di Blu (1)	
			MOLLY HATCHET	
			Southern hard-rock sextet from Jacksonville, Florida. Original lineup: Danny Joe Brown (lead singer), Bruce Crump, Bonner Thomas, Duane Roland, Dave Hlubek and Steve Holland. Jimmy Farrar replaced Brown in 1980; Brown returned and replaced Farrar in 1983.	
10/6/79	19	18	▲² 1. Flirtin' With Disaster	Epic 36110
10/4/80	25	6	● 2. Beatin' The Odds	Epic 36572
12/26/81	36	4	3. Take No Prisoners	Epic 37480
			MOMENTS, The — see RAY, GOODMAN & BROWN	
			MONEY, Eddie	
			Born Edward Mahoney on 3/2/49 in Brooklyn, New York. Rock singer discovered and subsequently managed by the late West Coast promoter Bill Graham. Formerly an officer with the New York Police Department.	
4/22/78	37	2	▲² 1. Eddie Money	Columbia 34909
2/3/79	17	10	▲ 2. Life For The Taking	Columbia 35598
9/6/80	35	5	3. Playing For Keeps	Columbia 36514
8/21/82	20	13	▲ 4. No Control	Columbia 37960
10/18/86	20	21	▲ 5. Can't Hold Back	Columbia 40096
			Take Me Home Tonight (4)	
			MONKEES, The	
			Formed in Los Angeles in 1965. Chosen from over 400 applicants for new Columbia TV series. Consisted of Davy Jones (born 12/30/45, Manchester, England; vocals), Michael Nesmith (born 12/30/42, Houston; guitar, vocals), Peter Tork (born 2/13/44, Washington, D.C.; bass, vocals) and Micky Dolenz (born 3/8/45, Tarzana, California; drums, vocals). Dolenz had appeared in TV series "Circus Boy," using the name Mickey Braddock in 1956. Jones had been a racehorse jockey; appeared in London musicals *Oliver* and *Pickwick*. Tork had been in The Phoenix Singers; Nesmith had done session work for Stax/Volt. Group starred in the movie *Head* (1968). TV show dropped after 58 episodes, 1966-68. Tork left in 1968. Group disbanded in 1969; re-formed (minus Nesmith) in 1986.	
10/15/66	1(13)	49	▲⁵ **1. The Monkees**	Colgems 101
			Last Train To Clarksville (1)	
2/11/67	1(18)	45	▲⁵ **2. More Of The Monkees**	Colgems 102
			I'm A Believer (1)	

DATE	POS	WKS	ARTIST—RECORD TITLE	LABEL & NO.
6/17/67	**1**(1)	41	▲² **3. Headquarters**	Colgems 103
11/25/67	**1**(5)	19	▲ **4. Pisces, Aquarius, Capricorn & Jones Ltd.**	Colgems 104
			Pleasant Valley Sunday (3)	
5/18/68	**3**	15	▲ **5. The Birds, The Bees & The Monkees**	Colgems 109
			Daydream Believer (1)/*Valleri* (3)	
3/22/69	**32**	5	6. Instant Replay	Colgems 113
8/16/86	**21**	12	▲ **7. Then & Now ... The Best Of The Monkees** [G]	Arista 8432
			includes 3 new songs by Dolenz and Tork	
			MONTE, Lou	
			Born on 4/2/17 in Lyndhurst, New Jersey. Vocalist/guitarist.	
1/5/63	**9**	18	**Pepino The Italian Mouse & Other Italian Fun Songs** [N]	Reprise 6058
			Pepino The Italian Mouse (5)	
			MONTENEGRO, Hugo, And His Orchestra	
			Born in 1925; raised in New York City; died on 2/6/81. Conductor/composer. Composed and conducted the movie soundtrack of *Hurry Sundown*.	
4/13/68	**9**	17	● **Music From "A Fistful Of Dollars" & "For A Few Dollars More" & "The Good, The Bad And The Ugly"** [I]	RCA 3927
			The Good, The Bad And The Ugly (2)	
			MONTEZ, Chris	
			Born Ezekiel Christopher Montanez on 1/17/43 in Los Angeles. Protege of Ritchie Valens.	
9/3/66	**33**	4	The More I See You/Call Me	A&M 4115
			MONTGOMERY, John Michael	
			Born on 1/20/65 in Danville, Kentucky. Country singer/guitarist.	
5/8/93	**27**	8	▲² 1. Life's A Dance	Atlantic 82420
2/12/94	**1**(1)	33	▲³ **2. Kickin' It Up**	Atlantic 82559
			MONTGOMERY, Wes	
			Born John Leslie Montgomery on 3/6/25 in Indianapolis; died on 6/15/68. Jazz guitarist. His brother Monk played bass; brother Buddy played piano.	
11/11/67	**13**	23	● 1. A Day In The Life [I]	A&M 3001
8/31/68	**38**	1	2. Down Here On The Ground [I]	A&M 3006
			MOODY BLUES, The	
			Formed in Birmingham, England, in 1964. Consisted of Denny Laine (guitar, vocals), Ray Thomas (flute, vocals), Mike Pinder (keyboards, vocals), Clint Warwick (bass) and Graeme Edge (drums). Laine and Warwick left in the summer of 1966; replaced by Justin Hayward (lead vocals, lead guitar) and John Lodge (vocals, bass). Laine joined Wings in 1971. Switzerland-born Patrick Moraz (former keyboardist of Yes) replaced Pinder in 1978; left group in early 1992.	
9/28/68	**3**	23	▲ **1. Days Of Future Passed**	Deram 18012
			with The London Festival Orchestra	
			Nights In White Satin (2-'72)	
10/12/68	**23**	11	● 2. In Search Of The Lost Chord	Deram 18017
6/7/69	**20**	13	● 3. On The Threshold Of A Dream	Deram 18025
1/31/70	**14**	12	● 4. To Our Children's Children's Children	Threshold 1
9/19/70	**3**	17	▲ **5. A Question Of Balance**	Threshold 3
8/21/71	**2**(3)	21	● **6. Every Good Boy Deserves Favour**	Threshold 5
			title's initials, EGBDF, refers to music's treble clef	

DATE	POS	WKS	ARTIST—RECORD TITLE	LABEL & NO.
11/25/72	**1**(5)	23	● **7. Seventh Sojourn**	Threshold 7
12/7/74	**11**	9	● 8. This Is The Moody Blues [G]	Threshold 12/13 [2]
7/2/77	**26**	5	9. Caught Live +5 [L]	London 690/1 [2]
			first 3 sides recorded "live" at the Royal Albert Hall in 1969; side 4: previously unreleased studio recordings	
7/8/78	**13**	9	▲ 10. Octave	London 708
6/20/81	**1**(3)	23	▲ **11. Long Distance Voyager**	Threshold 2901
9/24/83	**26**	6	12. The Present	Threshold 2902
5/17/86	**9**	22	▲ **13. The Other Side Of Life**	Threshold 829179
			Your Wildest Dreams (9)	
7/9/88	**38**	5	14. Sur la mer	Polydor 835756
			title is French for on the sea	
			MOORE, Bob, and His Orchestra	
			Born on 11/30/32 in Nashville. Top session bass player. Led the band on Roy Orbison's sessions for Monument Records. Also worked as sideman for Elvis Presley, Brenda Lee, Pat Boone and others.	
11/20/61	**33**	2	Mexico and Other Great Hits! [I]	Monument 4005
			Mexico (7)	
			MOORE, Dorothy	
			Born in Jackson, Mississippi, in 1946. Lead singer of The Poppies. Also a popular gospel artist.	
6/26/76	**29**	7	Misty Blue	Malaco 6351
			Misty Blue (3)	
			MORGAN, Jane	
			Born Jane Currier in Boston; raised in Florida. Popular singer in France before achieving U.S. fame via TV and nightclub entertaining.	
12/9/57	**13**	3	Fascination	Kapp 1066
			JANE MORGAN and THE TROUBADORS *Fascination* (7)	
			MORGAN, Lee	
			Born on 7/10/38 in Philadelphia; fatally shot on 2/19/72. Jazz trumpeter.	
12/26/64	**25**	7	The Sidewinder [I]	Blue Note 84157
			MORMON TABERNACLE CHOIR, The	
			375-voice choir directed by Richard P. Condie (died 12/22/85).	
10/19/59	**1**(1)	38	● **1. The Lord's Prayer**	Columbia 6068
			features Eugene Ormandy conducting The Philharmonic Orchestra	
12/28/59	**5**	2	**2. The Spirit Of Christmas** [X]	Columbia 6100
			MORRISON, Van	
			Born George Ivan on 8/31/45 in Belfast, Ireland. Blue-eyed soul singer/ songwriter. Leader of Them. Wrote the classic hit "Gloria." Inducted into the Rock and Roll Hall of Fame in 1993.	
5/30/70	**29**	3	▲ 1. Moondance	Warner 1835
12/26/70	**32**	5	2. His Band And The Street Choir	Warner 1884
			Domino (9)	
11/13/71	**27**	6	● 3. Tupelo Honey	Warner 1950
9/2/72	**15**	12	4. Saint Dominic's Preview	Warner 2633
8/25/73	**27**	6	5. Hard Nose The Highway	Warner 2712
11/18/78	**28**	5	6. Wavelength	Warner 3212

DATE	POS	WKS	ARTIST—RECORD TITLE	LABEL & NO.
6/26/93	29	2	7. Too Long In Exile	Polydor 519219
			MORRISSEY	
			Born Stephen Morrissey on 5/22/59 in Manchester, England. Former lead singer/songwriter of The Smiths.	
8/15/92	21	1	1. Your Arsenal	Sire 26994
			produced by Mick Ronson	
4/9/94	18	1	2. Vauxhall And I	Sire/Reprise 45451
			MOTELS, The	
			Los Angeles-based quintet led by vocalist Martha Davis. Formed in Berkeley. To Los Angeles in the early '70s. Re-formed in 1978; signed to Capitol in 1979. Disbanded in 1987.	
5/29/82	16	15	● 1. All Four One	Capitol 12177
			Only The Lonely (9)	
10/22/83	22	8	● 2. Little Robbers	Capitol 12288
			Suddenly Last Summer (9)	
9/21/85	36	2	3. Shock	Capitol 12378
			MOTHERS OF INVENTION, The — see ZAPPA, Frank	
			MOTLEY CRUE	
			Los Angeles-based, hard-rock band: "Vince Neil" Wharton (lead vocals), Mick Mars (real name: Bob Deal; guitar), Nikki Sixx (Frank Ferranno; bass) and "Tommy Lee" Bass (drums; married to actress Heather Locklear until 1993; married actress Pamela Anderson on 2/19/95). Sixx married *Playboy* playmate Brandi Brandt. Neil married mud wrestler Sharisse Rudell; left band in February 1992, replaced by John Corabi (ex-Scream).	
12/3/83	17	28	▲³ 1. Shout At The Devil	Elektra 60289
7/20/85	6	18	▲² **2. Theatre Of Pain**	Elektra 60418
6/13/87	2(1)	26	▲² **3. Girls, Girls, Girls**	Elektra 60725
9/23/89	1(2)	55	▲⁴ **4. Dr. Feelgood**	Elektra 60829
			Dr. Feelgood (6)/Without You (8)	
10/19/91	2(1)	17	▲ **5. Decade Of Decadence — '81-'91** [G]	Elektra 61204
4/2/94	7	3	● **6. Motley Crue**	Elektra 61534
			MOTTOLA, Tony	
			Born on 4/18/18 in Kearney, New Jersey. Latin-style guitarist. Produced by Enoch Light.	
4/14/62	26	10	Roman Guitar [I]	Command 816
			MOTT THE HOOPLE	
			British glitter-rock group led by vocalist Ian Hunter. Group name taken from a Willard Manus novel. Various personnel included guitarist Mick Ralphs (left in 1973 to form Bad Company). Hunter left in 1976; members Pete "Overend" Watts, Morgan Fisher and Dale "Buffin" Griffin formed The British Lions.	
10/13/73	35	4	1. Mott	Columbia 32425
5/18/74	28	7	2. The Hoople	Columbia 32871
1/4/75	23	4	3. Mott The Hoople Live [L]	Columbia 33282
			MOUNTAIN	
			New York power-rock group led by Leslie West (born Leslie Weinstein, 10/22/45, New York City) and Felix Pappalardi (born 1939, the Bronx; fatally shot on 4/17/83 [age 44] in New York City). Also see West, Bruce & Laing.	
4/11/70	17	21	● 1. Mountain Climbing!	Windfall 4501

DATE	POS	WKS	ARTIST—RECORD TITLE	LABEL & NO.
2/13/71	16	7	● 2. Nantucket Sleighride	Windfall 5500
1/15/72	35	4	3. Flowers Of Evil	Windfall 5501
			MTUME	
			Progressive funk band led by Philadelphian James Mtume (pronounced EM-too-may), featuring female vocalist Tawatha Agee. Mtume (keyboards, vocals) was a percussionist with Miles Davis in the early '70s.	
6/18/83	26	7	Juicy Fruit	Epic 38588
			MULDAUR, Maria	
			Born Maria D'Amato on 9/12/43 in New York City. Member of Jim Kweskin's Jug Band with former husband Geoff Muldaur (divorced in 1972). Maria later became an Inspirational recording artist.	
3/16/74	3	21	● **1. Maria Muldaur**	Reprise 2148
			Midnight At The Oasis (6)	
12/7/74	23	6	2. Waitress In The Donut Shop	Reprise 2194
			MULLIGAN('S), Gerry, Jazz Combo	
			Mulligan was born on 4/6/27 in New York City. West Coast-based jazz baritone saxophonist. Teamed with trumpeter Chet Baker in 1951. Combo included Shelly Manne (drums), Art Farmer (trumpet), Bud Shank (sax), Frank Rosolino (trombone), Pete Jolly (piano) and Red Mitchell (bass).	
5/25/59	39	2	I Want To Live! [S-I]	United Art. 5006
			arranged and composed by Johnny Mandel	
			MUNCH, Charles — see BOSTON SYMPHONY ORCHESTRA	
			MUPPETS — see CHILDREN'S ALBUMS	
			MURAD, Jerry — see HARMONICATS	
			MURPHEY, Michael	
			Born Michael Martin Murphey on 5/5/38 in Dallas. Progressive country singer/songwriter. Toured as Travis Lewis of The Lewis & Clarke Expedition in 1967. Worked as staff writer for Screen Gems. Lived in Austin from 1971-74; Colorado from 1974-79. Based in Taos, New Mexico, since 1979.	
5/3/75	18	13	● Blue Sky-Night Thunder	Epic 33290
			Wildfire (3)	
			MURPHY, Eddie	
			Born on 4/3/61 in Hempstead, New York. Comedian/actor. Former cast member of TV's "Saturday Night Live." Starred in the movies *Beverly Hills Cop (I, II & III)*, *Trading Places*, *48 Hrs.*, *Coming to America*, *Boomerang* and many others. Married model Nicole Mitchell on 3/18/93.	
1/14/84	35	3	▲² 1. Eddie Murphy: Comedian [C]	Columbia 39005
12/7/85	26	10	2. How Could It Be	Columbia 39952
			Party All The Time (2)	
			MURPHY, Walter, Band	
			Born in 1952 in New York City. Studied classical and jazz piano at the Manhattan School of Music. Former arranger for Doc Severinsen and "The Tonight Show" orchestra.	
10/2/76	15	6	● A Fifth Of Beethoven	Private S. 2015
			A Fifth Of Beethoven (1)	

DATE	POS	WKS	ARTIST—RECORD TITLE	LABEL & NO.
			MURRAY, Anne	
			Born Morna Anne Murray on 6/20/45 in Springhill, Nova Scotia. High-school teacher for one year after college. With CBC-TV show "Sing Along Jubilee." First recorded for ARC in 1969. Regular on Glen Campbell's "Goodtime Hour" TV series. Currently resides in Toronto.	
6/2/73	**39**	2	1. Danny's Song	Capitol 11172
			Danny's Song (7)	
7/13/74	**24**	6	2. Love Song	Capitol 11266
			You Won't See Me (8)	
10/19/74	**32**	2	● 3. Country [K]	Capitol 11324
10/14/78	**12**	8	▲ 4. Let's Keep It That Way	Capitol 11743
			You Needed Me (1)	
3/10/79	**23**	6	▲ 5. New Kind Of Feeling	Capitol 11849
12/8/79	**24**	9	● 6. I'll Always Love You	Capitol 12012
11/1/80	**16**	17	▲⁴ 7. Anne Murray's Greatest Hits [G]	Capitol 12110
			MURRAY, Keith	
			Rapper born in 1972 in Long Island, New York.	
11/26/94	**34**	1	The Most Beautifullest Thing In This World	Jive 41555
			CD includes bonus track	
			MURRAY THE "K" — see COMPILATIONS BY DISC JOCKEYS	
			MUSICAL YOUTH	
			Five schoolboys (ages 11 to 16 in 1983) from Birmingham, England: Dennis Seaton (lead), with brothers Kelvin (guitar) & Michael (keyboards) Grant, and Patrick (bass) & Junior Waite (drums).	
2/5/83	**23**	8	The Youth Of Today	MCA 5389
			Pass The Dutchie (10)	
			MYLES, Alannah	
			Born in Toronto; raised in Buckhorn, Canada. Rock singer.	
2/17/90	**5**	19	▲ **Alannah Myles**	Atlantic 81956
			Black Velvet (1)	

N

DATE	POS	WKS	ARTIST—RECORD TITLE	LABEL & NO.
			NABORS, Jim	
			Born on 6/12/32 in Sylacauga, Alabama. Gomer Pyle on TV's "The Andy Griffith Show" (1963-64) and "Gomer Pyle-U.S.M.C." (1964-69). Own TV variety series, "The Jim Nabors Hour" (1969-71).	
12/3/66	**24**	7	● 1. Jim Nabors Sings Love Me With All Your Heart	Columbia 9358
7/4/70	**34**	3	2. The Jim Nabors Hour	Columbia 1020
			NAKED EYES	
			English duo: Pete Byrne (vocals) and Rob Fisher (keyboards, synthesizer). Split in 1984. Fisher later in duo Climie Fisher.	
6/4/83	**32**	4	Naked Eyes	EMI America 17089
			Always Something There To Remind Me (8)	

DATE	POS	WKS	ARTIST—RECORD TITLE	LABEL & NO.
			NAS	
			Nasir Jones, male rapper. Native of Long Island City, New York. Nas pronounced nos.	
5/7/94	12	2	Illmatic	Columbia 57684
			NASH, Graham	
			Born on 2/2/42 in Blackpool, England. Co-founding member/guitarist of The Hollies. Formed Crosby, Stills & Nash in 1970.	
6/19/71	15	11	● 1. Songs For Beginners	Atlantic 7204
4/29/72	4	14	● **2. Graham Nash/David Crosby ***	Atlantic 7220
2/23/74	34	3	3. Wild Tales	Atlantic 7288
10/25/75	6	12	● **4. Wind On The Water ***	ABC 902
8/21/76	26	6	● 5. Whistling Down The Wire *	ABC 956
			*DAVID CROSBY/GRAHAM NASH	
			NASH, Johnny	
			Born on 8/19/40 in Houston. Vocalist/guitarist/actor. Appeared on local TV from age 13. With Arthur Godfrey's TV and radio shows from 1956-63. In the movie *Take a Giant Step* in 1959. Own JoDa label in 1965. Began recording in Jamaica in the late '60s.	
11/18/72	23	8	I Can See Clearly Now	Epic 31607
			I Can See Clearly Now (1)	
			NAUGHTY BY NATURE	
			Rap trio from East Orange, New Jersey: Anthony "Treach" Criss, Vincent Brown and Kier "dj KG" Gist. Appeared in the movies *The Meteor Man* and *Who's the Man?*	
9/21/91	16	30	▲ 1. Naughty By Nature	Tommy Boy 1044
			O.P.P. (6)	
3/13/93	3	13	▲ **2. 19 Naughty III**	Tommy Boy 1069
			Hip Hop Hooray (8)	
			NAZARETH	
			Hard-rock group formed in Scotland in 1969: Dan McCafferty (lead singer), Manny Charlton (lead guitar), Pete Agnew (bass) and Darrell Sweet (drums). Billy Rankin (lead guitar) and John Locke (keyboards) added in 1981.	
2/14/76	17	9	▲ 1. Hair Of The Dog	A&M 4511
			Love Hurts (8)	
5/8/76	24	7	2. Close Enough For Rock 'N' Roll	A&M 4562
			NEIL, Vince	
			Born Vincent Neil Wharton on 2/8/61 in Hollywood. Former lead vocalist of Motley Crue. Married mud wrestler Sharisse Rudell on 6/16/88. Backing band features guitarist Steve Stevens and drummer Vik Foxx (Enuff Z'nuff).	
5/15/93	13	3	Exposed	Warner 45260
			NEKTAR	
			English art-rock quartet based in Germany. Roye Albrighton, lead singer.	
10/26/74	19	6	1. Remember The Future	Passport 98002
4/12/75	32	3	2. Down To Earth	Passport 98005

DATE	POS	WKS	ARTIST—RECORD TITLE	LABEL & NO.
			NELSON	
			Gunnar (vocals, bass) and Matthew Nelson (vocals, rhythm guitar), the identical twin sons (born 9/20/67) of the late Ricky Nelson. Their sister is actress Tracy Nelson of TV's "Father Dowling Mysteries."	
8/18/90	**17**	41	▲ After The Rain	DGC 24290
			(Can't Live Without Your) Love And Affection (1)/ *After The Rain* (6)	
			NELSON, Ricky	
			Born Eric Hilliard Nelson on 5/8/40 in Teaneck, New Jersey; died on 12/31/85 in a plane crash in DeKalb, Texas. Son of bandleader Ozzie Nelson and vocalist Harriet Hilliard. Rick and brother David appeared on Nelson's radio show from March 1949; later on TV, 1952-66. Formed The Stone Canyon Band in 1969. In movies *Rio Bravo*, *The Wackiest Ship in the Army* and *Love and Kisses*. Married Kristin Harmon (sister of actor Mark Harmon) in 1963; divorced in 1982. Their daughter Tracy is a movie/TV actress. Their twin sons began recording as Nelson in 1990. Ricky was one of the first teen idols of the rock era. Inducted into the Rock and Roll Hall of Fame in 1987.	
11/11/57	**1**(2)	33	**1. Ricky**	Imperial 9048
			Be-Bop Baby (3)	
7/28/58	**7**	9	**2. Ricky Nelson**	Imperial 9050
			Poor Little Fool (1)	
2/2/59	**14**	19	3. Ricky Sings Again	Imperial 9061
			Believe What You Say (4)/*Lonesome Town* (7)/ *Never Be Anyone Else But You* (6)/*It's Late* (9)	
10/5/59	**22**	24	4. Songs By Ricky	Imperial 9082
			Just A Little Too Much (9)/*Sweeter Than You* (9)	
8/29/60	**18**	11	5. More Songs By Ricky	Imperial 9122
			RICK NELSON:	
6/26/61	**8**	17	**6. Rick Is 21**	Imperial 9152
			Travelin' Man (1)/*Hello Mary Lou* (9)	
6/2/62	**27**	6	7. Album Seven By Rick	Imperial 9167
6/22/63	**20**	5	8. For Your Sweet Love	Decca 74419
1/18/64	**14**	12	9. Rick Nelson sings "For You"	Decca 74479
			For You (6)	
1/20/73	**32**	5	10. Garden Party	Decca 75391
			RICK NELSON And The Stone Canyon Band *Garden Party* (6)	
			NELSON, Sandy	
			Born Sander Nelson on 12/1/38 in Santa Monica, California. Rock 'n' roll drummer. Became prominent studio musician. Heard on "Alley Oop," "To Know Him Is To Love Him," "A Thousand Stars" and many others. Lost portion of right leg in a motorcycle accident in 1963. Returned to performing in 1964.	
2/3/62	**6**	21	**1. Let There Be Drums** [I]	Imperial 9159
			Let There Be Drums (7)	
5/26/62	**29**	3	2. Drums Are My Beat! [I]	Imperial 9168

DATE	POS	WKS	ARTIST—RECORD TITLE	LABEL & NO.
			NELSON, Willie	
			Born on 4/30/33 in Ft. Worth, Texas; raised in Abbott, Texas. Prolific country singer/songwriter (writer of Patsy Cline's "Crazy" and Faron Young's "Hello Walls"). Played bass for Ray Price. Moved to Nashville in 1960; moved back to Texas in 1970. Pioneered the "outlaw" country movement. Appeared in several movies including *The Electric Horseman* (1979), *Honeysuckle Rose* (1980) and *Barbarosa* (1982). Won 1989 Living Legends Grammy Award. Elected to the Country Music Hall of Fame in 1993. Also see Concept Albums.	
11/15/75	28	4	▲² 1. Red Headed Stranger	Columbia 33482
2/18/78	12	9	▲ 2. Waylon & Willie	RCA 2686
			WAYLON JENNINGS & WILLIE NELSON	
6/17/78	30	3	▲⁴ 3. Stardust	Columbia 35305
			an album of pop standards from 1926-55 (produced by Booker T. Jones)	
1/13/79	32	4	▲² 4. Willie and Family Live [L]	Columbia 35642 [2]
			recorded at Harrah's, Lake Tahoe, Nevada	
7/7/79	25	5	● 5. One For The Road	Columbia 36064 [2]
			WILLIE NELSON AND LEON RUSSELL	
9/13/80	11	13	▲² 6. Honeysuckle Rose [S-L]	Columbia 36752 [2]
			WILLIE NELSON & FAMILY	
3/21/81	31	6	▲ 7. Somewhere Over The Rainbow	Columbia 36883
10/3/81	27	6	▲ 8. Willie Nelson's Greatest Hits (& Some That Will Be) [G]	Columbia 37542 [2]
3/27/82	2(4)	28	▲⁴ **9. Always On My Mind**	Columbia 37951
			Always On My Mind (5)	
5/21/83	39	1	10. Tougher Than Leather	Columbia 38248
8/20/83	37	1	▲ 11. Poncho & Lefty	Epic 37958
			MERLE HAGGARD/WILLIE NELSON	
			NENA	
			Gabriele "Nena" Kerner (born 3/26/60) with four-member backup group from Hagen, Germany.	
3/31/84	27	6	99 Luftballons	Epic 39294
			99 Luftballons (2)	
			NERO, Peter	
			Born on 5/22/34 in Brooklyn. Pop-jazz-classical pianist. Won 1961 Best New Artist Grammy Award.	
8/7/61	34	5	1. Piano Forte [I]	RCA 2334
10/2/61	32	3	2. New Piano In Town [I]	RCA 2383
4/14/62	22	9	3. Young And Warm And Wonderful [I]	RCA 2484
8/11/62	16	12	4. For The Nero-Minded [I]	RCA 2536
3/30/63	40	1	5. The Colorful Peter Nero [I]	RCA 2618
4/13/63	5	18	**6. Hail The Conquering Nero** [I]	RCA 2638
11/16/63	31	3	7. Peter Nero In Person [I-L]	RCA 2710
6/27/64	38	2	8. Reflections [I]	RCA 2853
12/25/71	23	10	● 9. Summer of '42 [I]	Columbia 31105
			NEVIL, Robbie	
			Pop singer/songwriter/guitarist from Los Angeles.	
1/31/87	37	3	Robbie Nevil	Manhattan 53006
			C'est La Vie (2)/*Wot's It To Ya* (10)	

DATE	POS	WKS	ARTIST—RECORD TITLE	LABEL & NO.
			NEVILLE, Aaron	
			Born on 1/24/41 in New Orleans. Member of New Orleans family group The Neville Brothers. Brother Art was keyboardist of The Meters. Bassist/singer Ivan Neville is his son. Also see Linda Ronstadt.	
9/25/93	37	2	▲ 1. The Grand Tour	A&M 0086
12/25/93	36	2	2. Aaron Neville's Soulful Christmas [X]	A&M 0127
			Christmas charts: 8/'93, 16/'94	
			NEW BIRTH, The	
			R&B vocal group portion of New Birth, Inc. Original group consisted of vocalists Londee Loren, Bobby Downs, Melvin Wilson, Leslie Wilson, Ann Bogan and soloist Alan Frye, with instrumental backing by The Nite-Liters. Melvin, Leslie and Ann recorded as Love, Peace & Happiness in 1972.	
5/26/73	31	4	Birth Day	RCA 4797
			NEW CHRISTY MINSTRELS, The	
			Folk/balladeer troupe named after The Christy Minstrels (formed in 1842 by Edwin "Pop" Christy). Group founded and led by Randy Sparks; featured Barry McGuire, Kenny Rogers (in 1966) and Kim Carnes (in the late '60s).	
10/27/62	19	8	1. The New Christy Minstrels	Columbia 8672
3/2/63	30	4	2. The New Christy Minstrels In Person [L]	Columbia 8741
6/29/63	20	7	3. Tall Tales! Legends & Nonsense	Columbia 8817
9/14/63	15	23	● 4. Ramblin' featuring Green, Green	Columbia 8855
5/16/64	9	20	**5. Today** [S]	Columbia 8959
			featuring songs from the movie *Advance to the Rear*	
7/31/65	22	8	6. Chim Chim Cher-ee	Columbia 9169
			NEW EDITION	
			Boston R&B teen vocal quintet (ages 13 to 15 in 1983): Ralph Tresvant, Ronald DeVoe, Michael Bivins, Ricky Bell and Bobby Brown. Formed in 1982 by future New Kids on the Block and Perfect Gentlemen producer Maurice Starr. Brown left for solo career in 1986; replaced by Johnny Gill in 1988. Bell, Bivins and DeVoe recorded as Bell Biv DeVoe in 1990. Tresvant and Gill recorded solo in the '90s.	
11/17/84	6	29	▲ **1. New Edition**	MCA 5515
			Cool It Now (4)	
1/11/86	32	15	▲ 2. All For Love	MCA 5679
7/23/88	12	37	▲² 3. Heart Break	MCA 42207
			If It Isn't Love (7)	
			NEWHART, Bob	
			Born on 9/5/29 in Oak Park, Illinois. Enduring deadpan comedian/TV actor. Newhart starred in three TV situation comedies: "The Bob Newhart Show" (1972-78), "Newhart" (1982-90) and "Bob" (1992-93). Won 1960 Best New Artist Grammy Award.	
5/16/60	1(14)	67	● **1. The Button-Down Mind Of Bob Newhart** [C]	Warner 1379
			1960 Album of the Year Grammy Award	
11/14/60	1(1)	31	● **2. The Button-Down Mind Strikes Back!** [C]	Warner 1393
11/6/61	10	11	**3. Behind The Button-Down Mind Of Bob Newhart** [C]	Warner 1417
10/27/62	28	3	4. The Button-Down Mind On TV [C]	Warner 1467
			Newhart hosted a comedy variety show from 1961-62	

DATE	POS	WKS	ARTIST—RECORD TITLE	LABEL & NO.
			NEW KIDS ON THE BLOCK	
			Boston teen vocal quintet: Joe McIntyre (born 12/31/72), Donnie Wahlberg (born 8/17/69), Danny Wood (born 5/14/69), and brothers Jordan (born 5/17/70) and Jon Knight (born 11/29/68). Formed in the summer of 1984 by New Edition's founder/producer, Maurice Starr. Wahlberg is older brother of Marky Mark.	
2/11/89	**1**(2)	71	▲⁸ **1. Hangin' Tough** *Please Don't Go Girl* (10)/*You Got It (The Right Stuff)* (3)/ *I'll Be Loving You (Forever)* (1)/*Hangin' Tough* (1)/ *Cover Girl* (2)	Columbia 40985
10/14/89	**25**	18	▲³ 2. New Kids On The Block [E] the group's first album, originally released in 1987 *Didn't I (Blow Your Mind)* (8)	Columbia 40475
10/21/89	**9**	14	▲² **3. Merry, Merry Christmas** [X] Christmas charts: 1/'89, 4/'90 *This One's For The Children* (7)	Columbia 45280
6/23/90	**1**(1)	27	▲³ **4. Step By Step** *Step By Step* (1)/*Tonight* (7)	Columbia 45129
12/15/90	**19**	12	● 5. No More Games/The Remix Album [K] remixes of the group's hits; all of above produced by Maurice Starr	Columbia 46959
2/12/94	**37**	1	6. Face The Music **NKOTB**	Columbia 52969
			NEWMAN, Randy	
			Born on 11/28/43 in New Orleans. Singer/composer/pianist. Nephew of composers Alfred, Emil and Lionel Newman. Scored the movies *Ragtime*, *The Natural* and *Avalon*.	
11/30/74	**36**	2	1. Good Old Boys background vocals by The Eagles' Glenn Frey and Don Henley	Reprise 2193
11/19/77	**9**	18	● **2. Little Criminals** guest appearances by members of The Eagles *Short People* (2)	Warner 3079
			NEW ORDER	
			Techno-dance quartet from Manchester, England. Evolved from the industrial-rock group Warsaw, formed in April 1977. Changed name to Joy Division. After suicide of vocalist Ian Curtis (May 1980), name changed to New Order. Lineup since 1986: Bernard Sumner, Stephen Morris, Peter Hook and Gillian Gilbert. Sumner was also a member of Electronic; Hook, with Revenge. Morris and Gilbert also recorded as The Other Two.	
10/17/87	**36**	4	▲ 1. Substance [G]	Qwest 25621 [2]
2/25/89	**32**	6	● 2. Technique	Qwest 25845
5/29/93	**11**	4	● 3. Republic	Qwest 45250
			NEW RIDERS OF THE PURPLE SAGE	
			San Francisco country-rock band formed in 1969 by Jerry Garcia as an offshoot of The Grateful Dead. Garcia left after first album in 1971.	
10/30/71	**39**	2	1. New Riders Of The Purple Sage	Columbia 30888
6/17/72	**33**	6	2. Powerglide	Columbia 31284
			NEW SEEKERS, The	
			British-Australian group formed by former Seekers member Keith Potger after The Seekers disbanded in 1969. Consisted of Eve Graham, Lyn Paul, Peter Doyle, Marty Kristian and Paul Layton.	
1/29/72	**37**	2	We'd Like To Teach The World To Sing *I'd Like To Teach The World To Sing (In Perfect Harmony)* (7)	Elektra 74115

DATE	POS	WKS	ARTIST—RECORD TITLE	LABEL & NO.
			NEWTON, Juice	
			Born Judy Kay Newton on 2/18/52 in New Jersey; raised in Virginia Beach. Pop/country singer. Performed folk music from age 13. Moved to Los Angeles with own Silver Spur band in 1974; recorded for RCA in 1975. Group disbanded in 1978. Newton is an accomplished equestrienne.	
4/25/81	22	34	▲ 1. Juice	Capitol 12136
			Angel Of The Morning (4)/*Queen Of Hearts* (2)/ *The Sweetest Thing (I've Ever Known)* (7)	
6/5/82	20	8	● 2. Quiet Lies	Capitol 12210
			Love's Been A Little Bit Hard On Me (7)	
			NEWTON, Wayne	
			Born on 4/3/42 in Roanoke, Virginia. Singer/multi-instrumentalist. Top Las Vegas entertainer. Began singing career with regular appearances on Jackie Gleason's TV variety show in 1962. Appeared in the 1989 James Bond movie *License to Kill* and the 1990 movie *The Adventures of Ford Fairlane*.	
6/5/65	17	8	1. Red Roses For A Blue Lady	Capitol 2335
8/19/72	34	5	2. Daddy Don't You Walk So Fast	Chelsea 1001
			Daddy Don't You Walk So Fast (4)	
			NEWTON-JOHN, Olivia	
			Born on 9/26/48 in Cambridge, England. To Australia in 1953. At age 16, won talent-contest trip to England; sang with Pat Carroll as Pat & Olivia. With the group Toomorrow, in British movie of the same name. Granddaughter of Nobel Prize-winning German physicist Max Born. In movies *Grease*, *Xanadu* and *Two of a Kind*. Married actor Matt Lattanzi in 1984. Opened own chain of clothing boutiques (Koala Blue) in 1984. Battled breast cancer in 1992.	
6/29/74	1(1)	20	● **1. If You Love Me, Let Me Know**	MCA 411
			If You Love Me (Let Me Know) (5)/*I Honestly Love You* (1)	
3/1/75	1(1)	17	● **2. Have You Never Been Mellow**	MCA 2133
			Have You Never Been Mellow (1)/*Please Mr. Please* (3)	
10/18/75	12	6	● 3. Clearly Love	MCA 2148
3/27/76	13	10	● 4. Come On Over	MCA 2186
11/27/76	30	4	● 5. Don't Stop Believin'	MCA 2223
8/27/77	34	4	6. Making A Good Thing Better	MCA 2280
11/12/77	13	13	▲² 7. Olivia Newton-John's Greatest Hits [G]	MCA 3028
1/13/79	7	16	▲ **8. Totally Hot**	MCA 3067
			A Little More Love (3)	
8/9/80	4	15	▲² **9. Xanadu** [S]	MCA 6100
			side 1: Olivia; side 2: Electric Light Orchestra *Magic* (1)/*Xanadu* (8-with Electric Light Orchestra)	
11/7/81	6	27	▲² **10. Physical**	MCA 5229
			Physical (1)/*Make A Move On Me* (5)	
10/16/82	16	21	▲² 11. Olivia's Greatest Hits, Vol. 2 [G]	MCA 5347
			Heart Attack (3)	
11/16/85	29	5	● 12. Soul Kiss	MCA 6151
			NEW VAUDEVILLE BAND, The	
			Creation of British composer/record producer Geoff Stephens (born 10/1/34, London).	
12/17/66	5	17	● **Winchester Cathedral**	Fontana 27560
			Winchester Cathedral (1)	
			NEW WORLD THEATRE ORCHESTRA, The — see SOUNDTRACKS (*Around the World in 80 Days*)	

DATE	POS	WKS	ARTIST—RECORD TITLE	LABEL & NO.
			NEW YORK PHILHARMONIC — see BERNSTEIN, Leonard	
			NICHOLS, Mike, & Elaine May	
			Improvisational comedy team. Nichols (born Michael Peschkowsky on 11/6/31, Berlin) is a premier Broadway/movie director. Movies: *The Graduate*, *Catch-22*, *Silkwood* and others. Married to network newscaster Diane Sawyer. May (born 4/21/32, Pennsylvania) is a movie writer/director/actress. Wrote screenplay for *California Suite* and *Heaven Can Wait*.	
7/13/59	39	1	1. Improvisations To Music [C] with Marty Rubenstein at the piano	Mercury 20376
1/23/61	10	8	**2. An evening with Mike Nichols and Elaine May** **[OC-C]** opened on Broadway on 10/8/60	Mercury 2200
3/24/62	17	9	3. Mike Nichols & Elaine May Examine Doctors [C]	Mercury 20680
			NICKS, Stevie	
			Born Stephanie Nicks on 5/26/48 in Phoenix; raised in California. Became vocalist of Bay-area group Fritz and subsequently met guitarist Lindsey Buckingham. Teamed up and recorded album *Buckingham- Nicks* in 1973. Joined Fleetwood Mac in January 1975 as vocalist. Stopped touring with band after 1990; left in January 1993.	
8/15/81	1(1)	45	▲⁴ **1. Bella Donna** *Stop Draggin' My Heart Around* (3-with Tom Petty)/ *Leather And Lace* (6-with Don Henley)	Modern 139
7/9/83	5	22	▲² **2. The Wild Heart** *Stand Back* (5)	Modern 90048
12/21/85	12	17	▲ 3. Rock A Little *Talk To Me* (4)	Modern 90479
6/17/89	10	11	● **4. The Other Side Of The Mirror**	Modern 91245
9/21/91	30	2	● 5. TimeSpace — The Best Of Stevie Nicks [G]	Modern 91711
			NIGHT RANGER	
			Rock group from California: lead singers Kelly Keagy (drums) and Jack Blades (bass), with guitarists Jeff Watson and Brad Gillis, and keyboardist Alan "Fitz" Gerald. Blades and Gillis were members of Rubicon. Gerald left in 1988; band split up in early 1989. Blades joined supergroup Damn Yankees.	
3/5/83	38	8	1. Dawn Patrol	Boardwalk 33259
5/5/84	15	29	▲ 2. Midnight Madness *Sister Christian* (5)	MCA 5456
6/15/85	10	25	▲ **3. 7 Wishes** *Sentimental Street* (8)	MCA/Camel 5593
5/2/87	28	3	● 4. Big Life	MCA 5839
			NILSSON	
			Born Harry Edward Nelson, III, on 6/15/41 in Brooklyn; died on 1/15/94 of a heart attack. Wrote Three Dog Night's hit "One"; scored the movie *Skidoo*, the animated TV movie *The Point* and TV's "The Courtship of Eddie's Father." Close friend of John Lennon and Ringo Starr.	
4/10/71	25	8	1. The Point! [TV] songs and narration from his animated TV special	RCA 1003
2/5/72	3	19	● **2. Nilsson Schmilsson** *Without You* (1)/*Coconut* (8)	RCA 4515
8/5/72	12	13	● 3. Son Of Schmilsson	RCA 4717

DATE	POS	WKS	ARTIST—RECORD TITLE	LABEL & NO.
			NINE INCH NAILS	
			Industrial-rock band spearheaded by Trent Reznor. A native of Mercer, Pennsylvania, and a classically trained pianist.	
10/10/92	**7**	3	▲ **1. Broken**	Nothing/TVT 92213
			includes a mini CD with 2 tracks	
3/26/94	**2**(1)	18	▲ **2. The Downward Spiral**	Nothing/TVT 92346
			NIRVANA	
			Grunge-rock trio from Aberdeen, Washington: Kurt Cobain (vocals), Chris Novoselic (bass) and Dave Grohl (drums). Early lineup: Cobain, Novoselic, Jason Everman (guitar) and Chad Channing (drums). Everman left in mid-1989. In September 1990, Dan Peters (later of Mudhoney) briefly replaced Channing; Grohl joined later the same month. Cobain married Courtney Love, lead singer of rock group Hole, on 2/24/92. Cobain was found dead of a self-inflicted gunshot wound on 4/8/94.	
11/2/91	**1**(2)	50	▲^{7} **1. Nevermind**	DGC 24425
			an uncredited track, "Endless Nameless," is hidden at the end of the CD; produced by Butch Vig (Firetown)	
			Smells Like Teen Spirit (6)	
1/16/93	**39**	1	● 2. Incesticide [K]	DGC 24504
			early recordings on independent labels, unreleased demos and performances on British radio broadcasts; cover art by Kurt Cobain	
10/9/93	**1**(1)	29	▲^{4} **3. In Utero**	DGC 24607
11/19/94	**1**(1)	15+	▲^{3} **4. MTV Unplugged In New York** [L]	DGC 24727
			band's performance on the MTV program "Unplugged" on 11/18/93	
			NITTY GRITTY DIRT BAND	
			Country-folk-rock group from Long Beach, California. Led by Jeff Hanna (born 7/11/47; vocals, guitar) and John McEuen (born 12/19/45; banjo, mandolin). Changed name to Dirt Band in 1976; resumed using Nitty Gritty Dirt Band name in 1982. Various members included ex-Eagle Bernie Leadon, who replaced McEuen briefly in early 1987. Revamped quartet since late 1987: Hanna, Jimmy Ibbotson, Bob Carpenter and Jimmie Fadden. In the movies *For Singles Only* and *Paint Your Wagon*.	
9/14/74	**28**	6	Stars & Stripes Forever [L]	United Art. 184 [2]
			NKOTB — see NEW KIDS ON THE BLOCK	
			NOTORIOUS B.I.G., The	
			Chris Wallace; Brooklyn-born rapper. Rapped on remixes of Mary J. Blige's "Real Love" and "What's The 411?" Also known as Biggie Smalls.	
10/1/94	**15**	8+	● Ready To Die	Bad Boy 73000
			NOVA, Aldo	
			Born Aldo Scarporuscio in Montreal. Rock singer/songwriter/guitarist/keyboardist.	
4/3/82	**8**	16	▲^{2} Aldo Nova	Portrait 37498
			NUGENT, Ted	
			Born on 12/13/48 in Detroit. Heavy-metal rock guitarist; leader of The Amboy Dukes. Currently a member of the supergroup Damn Yankees.	
3/13/76	**28**	6	▲^{2} 1. Ted Nugent	Epic 33692
10/16/76	**24**	8	▲^{2} 2. Free-For-All	Epic 34121
			featuring vocals by Meat Loaf	
7/2/77	**17**	19	▲^{2} 3. Cat Scratch Fever	Epic 34700
2/25/78	**13**	8	▲ 4. Double Live Gonzo! [L]	Epic 35069 [2]
11/18/78	**24**	10	▲ 5. Weekend Warriors	Epic 35551

DATE	POS	WKS	ARTIST—RECORD TITLE	LABEL & NO.
6/9/79	**18**	6	● 6. State Of Shock	Epic 36000
6/7/80	**13**	9	● 7. Scream Dream	Epic 36404
			NUMAN, Gary	
			Born Gary Webb on 3/8/58 in Hammersmith, England. Synthesized techno-rock artist.	
3/29/80	**16**	14	The Pleasure Principle	Atco 120
			Cars (9)	
			NU SHOOZ	
			Portland, Oregon, R&B group centered around husband-and-wife team of guitarist/songwriter John Smith and lead singer Valerie Day.	
6/21/86	**27**	8	● Poolside	Atlantic 81647
			I Can't Wait (3)	
			N.W.A.	
			Los Angeles-based rap outfit: Eric "Eazy-E" Wright, Lorenzo "M.C. Ren" Patterson, Andre "Dr. Dre" Young, O'Shea "Ice Cube" Jackson (left by 1990) and DJ Antoine "Yella" Carraby. N.W.A. stands for Niggas With Attitude. Eazy-E, M.C. Ren, Dr. Dre and Ice Cube went on to platinum solo careers. Young and Carraby were also members of World Class Wreckin Cru and produced others.	
4/8/89	**37**	9	▲² 1. Straight Outta Compton	Ruthless 57102
9/15/90	**27**	7	▲ 2. 100 Miles And Runnin' [M]	Ruthless 7224
6/15/91	**1**(1)	18	▲ **3. EFIL4ZAGGIN**	Ruthless 57126
			title actually appears on album as an inverse image of NIGGAZ4LIFE	
			NYRO, Laura	
			Born Laura Nigro on 10/18/47 in the Bronx, New York. White soul-gospel singer/songwriter. Wrote "Stoned Soul Picnic," "Wedding Bell Blues," "And When I Die" and "Stoney End."	
11/22/69	**32**	3	New York Tendaberry	Columbia 9737

O

DATE	POS	WKS	ARTIST—RECORD TITLE	LABEL & NO.
			OAK RIDGE BOYS	
			Country-pop vocal group's roots go back to early '40s when they were formed as a gospel quartet in Oak Ridge, Tennessee. Fluctuating lineup of over 40 members has survived two disbandonments in 1946 and 1956. Consistent lineup from 1973-1987: Duane Allen (lead), Joe Bonsall (tenor), Richard Sterban (bass) and Bill Golden (baritone). Steve Sanders, group's guitarist, replaced Golden in 1987.	
7/4/81	**14**	10	▲² 1. Fancy Free	MCA 5209
			Elvira (5)	
3/6/82	**20**	9	● 2. Bobbie Sue	MCA 5294
			OCASEK, Ric	
			Born Richard Otcasek on 3/23/49 in Baltimore. Lead singer/guitarist/songwriter of The Cars. Appeared in the 1987 movie *Made in Heaven.* Married supermodel/actress Paulina Porizkova in 1989. His son, Christopher Otcasek, is leader of Glamour Camp.	
2/5/83	**28**	9	1. Beatitude	Geffen 2022
11/1/86	**31**	5	2. This Side Of Paradise	Geffen 24098

DATE	POS	WKS	ARTIST—RECORD TITLE	LABEL & NO.
			OCEAN, Billy	
			Born Leslie Sebastian Charles on 1/21/50 in Trinidad; raised in England. Worked as a tailor. Did session work in London. Moved to the U.S. in the late '70s.	
9/22/84	9	57	▲² **1. Suddenly**	Jive 8213
			Caribbean Queen (No More Love On The Run) (1)/ *Loverboy* (2)/*Suddenly* (4)	
5/24/86	6	30	▲² **2. Love Zone**	Jive 8409
			There'll Be Sad Songs (To Make You Cry) (1)/*Love Zone* (10)	
4/2/88	18	11	▲ 3. Tear Down These Walls	Jive 8495
			Get Outta My Dreams, Get Into My Car (1)	
			O'CONNOR, Sinead	
			Born on 12/8/67 in Dublin, Ireland. Female singer/songwriter. Pronounced shin-NAYD.	
4/9/88	36	5	● 1. The Lion And The Cobra	Chrysalis 41612
4/7/90	1(6)	27	▲² **2. I Do Not Want What I Haven't Got**	Ensign 21759
			Nothing Compares 2 U (1)	
10/10/92	27	2	3. Am I Not Your Girl?	Ensign 21952
10/1/94	36	1	4. Universal Mother	Ensign 30549
			ODYSSEY	
			New York soul-disco trio: Manila-born Tony Reynolds, and sisters Lillian and Louise Lopez, originally from the Virgin Islands.	
12/3/77	36	5	Odyssey	RCA 2204
			OFFSPRING	
			Punk rock group from California: Brian "Dexter" Holland (lead singer), Kevin "Noodles" Wasserman (guitar), Greg Kriesel (bass) and Ron Welty (drums).	
7/16/94	4	33+	▲³ **Smash**	Epitaph 86432
			OHIO PLAYERS	
			Originally an R&B instrumental group called The Ohio Untouchables, formed in Dayton in 1959. Backup on The Falcons' records. First recorded for LuPine in 1962. Members during prime (1974-79): Marshall Jones, Clarence "Satch" Satchell, Jimmy "Diamond" Williams, Marvin "Merv" Pierce, Billy Beck, Ralph "Pee Wee" Middlebrook and Leroy "Sugarfoot" Bonner.	
6/8/74	11	22	● 1. Skin Tight	Mercury 705
11/30/74	1(1)	19	● **2. Fire**	Mercury 1013
			Fire (1)	
8/23/75	2(1)	24	● **3. Honey**	Mercury 1038
			Love Rollercoaster (1)	
6/19/76	12	9	● 4. Contradiction	Mercury 1088
11/27/76	31	4	● 5. Ohio Players Gold [G]	Mercury 1122
			O'JAYS, The	
			R&B group from Canton, Ohio, formed in 1958 as the Triumphs. Consisted of Eddie Levert, Walter Williams, William Powell, Bobby Massey and Bill Isles. Recorded as The Mascots for the King label in 1961. Renamed by Cleveland DJ, Eddie O'Jay. Isles left in 1965. Massey left to become a record producer in 1971; Levert, Williams and Powell continued as a trio. Powell retired from touring due to illness in late 1975 (died 5/26/77); replaced by Sammy Strain, formerly with Little Anthony & The Imperials. Strain returned to his former group by 1993; replaced by Nathaniel Best. Levert's sons Gerald and Sean are members of the trio Levert.	
10/7/72	10	11	● **1. Back Stabbers**	Phil. Int. 31712
			Back Stabbers (3)/*Love Train* (1)	

DATE	POS	WKS	ARTIST—RECORD TITLE	LABEL & NO.
1/12/74	**11**	19	▲ 2. Ship Ahoy	Phil. Int. 32408
			Put Your Hands Together (10)/*For The Love Of Money* (9)	
8/10/74	**17**	7	● 3. The O'Jays Live In London [L]	Phil. Int. 32953
5/17/75	**11**	14	● 4. Survival	Phil. Int. 33150
12/6/75	**7**	17	▲ **5. Family Reunion**	Phil. Int. 33807
			I Love Music (5)	
10/16/76	**20**	6	● 6. Message In The Music	Phil. Int. 34245
6/11/77	**27**	5	● 7. Travelin' At The Speed Of Thought	Phil. Int. 34684
5/13/78	**6**	13	▲ **8. So Full Of Love**	Phil. Int. 35355
			Use Ta Be My Girl (4)	
9/22/79	**16**	8	▲ 9. Identify Yourself	Phil. Int. 36027
9/27/80	**36**	3	10. The Year 2000	TSOP 36416
			OLDFIELD, Mike	
			Born on 5/15/53 in Reading, England. Classical-rock, multi-instrumentalist/composer.	
1/26/74	**3**	23	● **Tubular Bells** [I]	Virgin 105
			Tubular Bells (7); one 49-minute recording (excerpts used in movie *The Exorcist*)	
			OLIVER	
			Born William Oliver Swofford on 2/22/45 in North Wilkesboro, North Carolina.	
9/6/69	**19**	10	Good Morning Starshine	Crewe 1333
			Good Morning Starshine (3)/*Jean* (2)	
			O'NEAL, Alexander	
			Born on 11/15/53 in Natchez, Mississippi. Minneapolis-based R&B vocalist. Own band, Alexander, in the late '70s. Lead singer of Flyte Tyme, which included Jimmy "Jam" Harris, Terry Lewis and Monte Moir and later evolved into The Time. Went solo in 1980. Co-producer of Janet Jackson's hit "Control."	
9/5/87	**29**	8	● Hearsay	Tabu 40320
			O'NEAL, Shaquille	
			Born on 3/6/72 in Newark, New Jersey. All-star center with the NBA's Orlando Magic. Stands 7 feet, 1-inch tall. Starred in the 1994 movie *Blue Chips*.	
11/13/93	**25**	3	▲ Shaq Diesel	Jive 41529
			101 STRINGS	
			European orchestra under the direction of D.L. Miller.	
5/25/59	**9**	32	**1. The Soul of Spain** [I]	Somerset 6600
			this album was #1 for 46 of the 47 weeks that *Billboard* published a special Best Selling Low Price LP's chart (2/19/60-1/8/61)	
1/9/61	**21**	4	2. The Soul of Spain, Volume II [I]	Somerset 9900
			ONO, Yoko	
			Born in Tokyo on 2/18/33. Moved to New York at age 14. Avant-garde artist/poet in the late '60s. Married John Lennon (died 12/8/80) in Gibraltar on 3/20/69.	
12/6/80	**1(8)**	27	▲³ **1. Double Fantasy**	Geffen 2001
			JOHN LENNON & YOKO ONO	
			7 songs by Lennon, 7 by Ono; 1981 Album of the Year Grammy Award	
			(Just Like) Starting Over (1)/*Woman* (2)/	
			Watching The Wheels (10)	

DATE	POS	WKS	ARTIST—RECORD TITLE	LABEL & NO.
2/11/84	11	10	● 2. Milk and Honey **JOHN LENNON & YOKO ONO** 6 songs by Lennon, 6 by Ono; recorded in 1980 *Nobody Told Me* (5)	Polydor 817160
			ONYX Rap foursome based in Jamaica, New York: Sticky Fingaz, Big D.S., Fredro Star and Suave Sonny Caesar.	
4/17/93	17	20	▲ Bacdafucup *Slam* (4)	RAL/Chaos 53302
			ORBISON, Roy Born on 4/23/36 in Vernon, Texas; died of a heart attack on 12/6/88 in Madison, Tennessee. Had own band, The Wink Westerners, in 1952. Attended North Texas State University with Pat Boone. First recorded for Je-Wel in early 1956 as leader of The Teen Kings. Toured with Sun Records shows to 1958. Toured with The Beatles in 1963. Wife Claudette killed in a motorcycle accident on 6/7/66; two sons died in a fire in 1968. Resurgence in career beginning in 1985. Inducted into the Rock and Roll Hall of Fame in 1987. Member of the supergroup Traveling Wilburys in 1988.	
6/9/62	21	7	1. Crying *Running Scared* (1)/*Crying* (2)	Monument 4007
9/15/62	13	48	● 2. Roy Orbison's Greatest Hits [G] *Only The Only* (2)/*Blue Angel* (9)/*Dream Baby* (4)	Monument 4009
10/26/63	35	2	● 3. In Dreams *In Dreams* (7)	Monument 18003
10/3/64	19	16	4. More Of Roy Orbison's Greatest Hits [G] *It's Over* (9)/*Mean Woman Blues* (5)	Monument 18024
2/25/89	**5**	16	▲ **5. Mystery Girl** *You Got It* (9)	Virgin 91058
			ORCHESTRAL MANOEUVRES IN THE DARK English electro-pop quartet: keyboardists/vocalists Paul Humphreys and Andrew McCluskey, with drummer Malcolm Holmes and multi-instrumentalist Martin Cooper. Humphreys left band in 1991.	
11/2/85	38	5	Crush	A&M 5077
			ORLANDO, Tony — see DAWN	
			ORLEANS Rock group founded in New York City by John Hall with the Hoppen brothers (Lawrence and Lance), Wells Kelly and Jerry Marotta. Hall and Marotta left in 1977; replaced by Bob Leinbach and R.A. Martin.	
10/11/75	33	5	1. Let There Be Music *Dance With Me* (6)	Asylum 1029
10/2/76	30	5	2. Waking And Dreaming *Still The One* (5)	Asylum 1070
			ORMANDY, Eugene — see PHILADELPHIA ORCHESTRA	
			OSBORNE, Jeffrey Born on 3/9/48 in Providence, Rhode Island. Soul singer/songwriter/drummer. Lead singer of L.T.D. until 1980.	
9/3/83	25	23	● 1. Stay With Me Tonight	A&M 4940
11/24/84	39	4	● 2. Don't Stop	A&M 5017
7/12/86	26	11	● 3. Emotional	A&M 5103

DATE	POS	WKS	ARTIST—RECORD TITLE	LABEL & NO.
			OSBOURNE, Ozzy	
			Born John Michael Osbourne on 12/3/48 in Birmingham, England. Heavy-metal artist; former lead singer of Black Sabbath. Appeared in the 1986 movie *Trick or Treat*.	
5/23/81	**21**	16	▲³ 1. Blizzard Of Ozz	Jet 36812
11/28/81	**16**	23	▲³ 2. Diary Of A Madman	Jet 37492
12/18/82	**14**	10	▲ 3. Speak Of The Devil [L]	Jet 38350 [2]
			recorded at The Ritz, New York	
12/17/83	**19**	11	▲² 4. Bark At The Moon	CBS Assoc. 38987
2/22/86	**6**	17	▲² **5. The Ultimate Sin**	CBS Assoc. 40026
5/16/87	**6**	14	▲ **6. Tribute** [L]	CBS Assoc. 40714 [2]
			OZZY OSBOURNE/RANDY RHOADS	
			"live" recordings from 1981 featuring Osbourne's guitarist, Randy Rhoads, who was killed in an airplane crash on 3/19/82 (age 25)	
10/29/88	**13**	13	▲ 7. No Rest For The Wicked	CBS Assoc. 44245
10/5/91	**7**	29	▲³ **8. No More Tears**	Epic 46795
7/3/93	**22**	2	● 9. Live & Loud [L]	Epic Assc. 48973 [2]
			recorded on Osbourne's 1991-92 world tour; includes a 24-page booklet and 2 tattoos	
			OSKAR, Lee	
			Born on 3/24/48 in Copenhagen, Denmark. Harmonica player. Studio musician in Los Angeles. Original member of War.	
6/19/76	**29**	4	Lee Oskar [I]	United Art. 594
			includes 2 vocal tracks	
			OSMOND, Donny	
			Born on 12/9/57 in Ogden, Utah. Seventh son of George and Olive Osmond, Donny became a member of The Osmonds in 1963. Owner of production company Night Star.	
7/24/71	**13**	18	● 1. The Donny Osmond Album	MGM 4782
			Sweet And Innocent (7)	
11/13/71	**12**	14	● 2. To You With Love, Donny	MGM 4797
			Go Away Little Girl (1)	
6/10/72	**6**	10	● **3. Portrait Of Donny**	MGM 4820
			Hey Girl (9)/*Puppy Love* (3)	
8/5/72	**11**	14	● 4. Too Young	MGM 4854
1/6/73	**29**	6	● 5. My Best To You [G]	MGM 4872
4/14/73	**26**	7	6. Alone Together	MGM 4886
			The Twelfth Of Never (8)	
			OSMOND, Donny And Marie	
			Brother-and-sister co-hosts of own musical/variety TV series from 1976-78. Starred in the movie *Goin' Coconuts*. Marie was born on 10/13/59 in Ogden, Utah.	
11/2/74	**35**	4	● I'm Leaving It All Up To You	MGM 4968
			I'm Leaving It (All) Up To You (4)/ *Morning Side Of The Mountain* (8)	

DATE	POS	WKS	ARTIST—RECORD TITLE	LABEL & NO.
			OSMONDS, The	
			Family group from Ogden, Utah. Alan (born 6/22/49), Wayne (born 8/28/51), Merrill (born 4/30/53), Jay (born 3/2/55) and Donny Osmond (born 12/9/57). Began as a quartet in 1959, singing religious and barbershop-quartet songs. Regulars on Andy Williams's TV show from 1962-67. Alan, Wayne, Merrill and Jay turned to country music as The Osmond Brothers in the early '80s.	
2/6/71	**14**	10	● 1. Osmonds	MGM 4724
			One Bad Apple (1)	
7/3/71	**22**	10	● 2. Homemade	MGM 4770
2/5/72	**10**	13	● **3. Phase-III**	MGM 4796
			Yo-Yo (3)/*Down By The Lazy River* (4)	
7/1/72	**13**	15	● 4. The Osmonds "Live" [L]	MGM 4826 [2]
11/4/72	**14**	11	● 5. Crazy Horses	MGM 4851
			O'SULLIVAN, Gilbert	
			Born Raymond O'Sullivan on 12/1/46 in Waterford, Ireland.	
8/19/72	**9**	14	**Gilbert O'Sullivan-Himself**	MAM 4
			Alone Again (Naturally) (1)	
			OUTFIELD, The	
			British pop-rock trio: Tony Lewis (lead singer; bass), John Spinks (guitar, keyboards, vocals) and Alan Jackman (drums). Jackman left by 1990; Lewis and Spinks continued as a duo.	
3/29/86	**9**	29	▲² **1. Play Deep**	Columbia 40027
			Your Love (6)	
7/18/87	**18**	11	● 2. Bangin'	Columbia 40619
			OUTKAST	
			Atlanta-based male rap duo: Andre "Dre" Benjamin and Antoine "Big Boi" Patton. Both were 18 years old in 1994.	
5/14/94	**20**	9	● Southernplayalisticadillacmuzik	LaFace 26010
			OUTLAWS	
			Southern-rock band formed in Tampa in 1974. Consisted of guitarists Hughie Thomasson, Billy Jones and Henry Paul, with drummer Monte Yoho and bassist Frank O'Keefe (replaced by Harvey Arnold in 1977). Paul, Yoho and Arnold left by 1980. Paul was a member of the country trio BlackHawk by 1993.	
9/20/75	**13**	7	● 1. Outlaws	Arista 4042
5/15/76	**36**	2	2. Lady In Waiting	Arista 4070
4/15/78	**29**	4	● 3. Bring It Back Alive [L]	Arista 8300 [2]
2/7/81	**25**	7	● 4. Ghost Riders	Arista 9542
			OUTSIDERS, The	
			Cleveland rock quintet: Sonny Geraci (lead singer), Tom King (guitar), Bill Bruno (lead guitar), Mert Madsen (bass) and Rick Baker (drums). Geraci later led band Climax.	
7/16/66	**37**	3	Time Won't Let Me	Capitol 2501
			Time Won't Let Me (5)	
			OZARK MOUNTAIN DAREDEVILS	
			Country-rock group from Springfield, Missouri. Nucleus: Larry Lee (keyboards, guitar), Steve Cash (harp), John Dillon (guitar) and Michael Granda (bass).	
6/22/74	**26**	5	● 1. The Ozark Mountain Daredevils	A&M 4411
2/8/75	**19**	7	2. It'll Shine When It Shines	A&M 3654
			Jackie Blue (3)	

DATE	POS	WKS	ARTIST—RECORD TITLE	LABEL & NO.

P

PABLO CRUISE

San Francisco pop-rock quartet formed in 1973: Dave Jenkins (vocals, guitar), Bud Cockrell (vocals, bass; member of It's A Beautiful Day), Cory Lerios (keyboards) and Stephen Price (drums). Cockrell replaced by Bruce Day in 1977. John Pierce replaced Day. Guitarist Angelo Rossi joined in 1980.

DATE	POS	WKS	ARTIST—RECORD TITLE	LABEL & NO.
7/2/77	19	17	▲ 1. A Place In The Sun *Whatcha Gonna Do?* (6)	A&M 4625
7/15/78	6	14	▲ **2. Worlds Away** *Love Will Find A Way* (6)	A&M 4697
12/8/79	39	2	3. Part Of The Game	A&M 3712
8/22/81	34	5	4. Reflector	A&M 3726

PAGE, Jimmy

Born on 1/9/44 in London. Prominent guitarist. Member of The Yardbirds, 1966 to July 1968. In October 1968, formed The New Yardbirds, which evolved into rock supergroup Led Zeppelin. Page produced all of the group's music. Joined The Honeydrippers in 1984. Also co-founded The Firm with vocalist Paul Rodgers.

DATE	POS	WKS	ARTIST—RECORD TITLE	LABEL & NO.
7/16/88	26	6	● 1. Outrider vocals by Chris Farlowe, Robert Plant and John Miles	Geffen 24188
11/26/94	4	5	▲ **2. No Quarter** **JIMMY PAGE & ROBERT PLANT UNLEDDED** all but 3 of the 13 new recordings are Led Zeppelin songs	Atlantic 82706

PAGE, Patti

Born Clara Ann Fowler on 11/8/27 in Muskogee, Oklahoma. One of 11 children. Raised in Tulsa. Performed on radio KTUL with Al Klauser & His Oklahomans as Ann Fowler in the late '40s. Another singer was billed as "Patti Page" for the Page Milk Company show on KTUL. When she left, Fowler took her place and name. With The Jimmy Joy Band in 1947. On *Breakfast Club*, Chicago radio in 1947; signed by Mercury Records. Used multi-voice effect on records from 1947. Own TV series "The Patti Page Show," 1955-58, and "The Big Record," 1957-58. In the 1960 movie *Elmer Gantry*.

DATE	POS	WKS	ARTIST—RECORD TITLE	LABEL & NO.
11/24/56	18	2	1. Manhattan Tower a version of Gordon Jenkins's musical narrative	Mercury 20226
6/26/65	27	7	2. Hush, Hush, Sweet Charlotte *Hush, Hush, Sweet Charlotte* (8)	Columbia 9153

PAGE, Tommy

Born on 5/24/69 in West Caldwell, New Jersey.

DATE	POS	WKS	ARTIST—RECORD TITLE	LABEL & NO.
4/28/90	38	2	Paintings In My Mind *I'll Be Your Everything* (1)	Sire 26148

PALMER, Robert

Born Alan Palmer on 1/19/49 in Batley, England, and raised on the Mediterranean island of Malta. Formed first band, Mandrake Paddle Steamer, in 1969. Lead singer of short-lived supergroup The Power Station.

DATE	POS	WKS	ARTIST—RECORD TITLE	LABEL & NO.
8/25/79	19	8	1. Secrets	Island 9544
3/22/86	8	35	▲ **2. Riptide** *Addicted To Love* (1)/*I Didn't Mean To Turn You On* (2)	Island 90471
7/30/88	13	20	▲ 3. Heavy Nova *Simply Irresistible* (2)	EMI-Man. 48057

DATE	POS	WKS	ARTIST—RECORD TITLE	LABEL & NO.
			PANTERA	
			Heavy-metal band: Philip Anselmo (vocals), Diamond Darrell (guitar), Rex (bass) and Vinnie Paul (drums). Darrell and Paul are brothers. Darrell changed his first name to Dimebag in 1994. Group name is Spanish for panther.	
4/9/94	**1**(1)	7	● **Far Beyond Driven**	EastWest 92302
			PARAMOR, Norrie, His Strings and Orchestra	
			Born in England in 1914; died on 9/9/79 (age 65). Conductor/composer/arranger. A&R man for EMI Columbia; guided the careers of Cliff Richard, Frank Ifield and many others.	
9/8/56	**18**	3	In London, In Love ... [I]	Capitol Int. 10025
			PARKER, Graham, & The Rumour	
			Born on 11/18/50 in East London. Pub-rock vocalist/guitarist/songwriter. The Rumour featured guitarists Brinsley Schwarz and Martin Belmont, bassist Andrew Bodnar, keyboardist Bob Andrews (left by 1980) and drummer Stephen Goulding.	
5/26/79	**40**	2	1. Squeezing Out Sparks	Arista 4223
7/5/80	**40**	1	2. The Up Escalator	Arista 9517
			Bruce Springsteen sings on one track	
			PARKER, Ray Jr./Raydio	
			Born on 5/1/54 in Detroit. Prominent session guitarist in California; worked with Stevie Wonder, Barry White and others. Formed band Raydio in 1977 with Arnell Carmichael, Jerry Knight, Larry Tolbert, Darren Carmichael and Charles Fearing. Parker went solo in 1982. Knight later recorded in duo Ollie & Jerry.	
			RAYDIO:	
3/18/78	**27**	9	● 1. Raydio	Arista 4163
			Jack And Jill (8)	
			RAY PARKER JR. & RAYDIO:	
5/10/80	**33**	5	● 2. Two Places At The Same Time	Arista 9515
5/2/81	**13**	16	● 3. A Woman Needs Love	Arista 9543
			A Woman Needs Love (Just Like You Do) (4)	
			RAY PARKER JR.:	
5/8/82	**11**	12	● 4. The Other Woman	Arista 9590
			The Other Woman (4)	
			PARKS, Michael	
			Born on 4/4/38 in Corona, California. Portrayed Jim Bronson on TV's "Then Came Bronson."	
2/28/70	**35**	5	1. Closing The Gap	MGM 4646
5/30/70	**24**	6	2. Long Lonesome Highway	MGM 4662
			PARLIAMENT	
			Funk aggregation that evolved from The Parliaments. Spearheaded by George Clinton, part of his "A Parliafunkadelicament Thang" corporation. The group's nearly 40 members also recorded under the names Funkadelic; P. Funk All Stars; and Parlet, among others.	
4/10/76	**13**	17	▲ 1. Mothership Connection	Casablanca 7022
10/23/76	**20**	8	● 2. The Clones Of Dr. Funkenstein	Casablanca 7034
6/4/77	**29**	5	● 3. Parliament Live/P. Funk Earth Tour [L]	Casablanca 7053 [2]
1/21/78	**13**	19	▲ 4. Funkentelechy Vs. The Placebo Syndrome	Casablanca 7084
12/23/78	**23**	10	● 5. Motor-Booty Affair	Casablanca 7125

DATE	POS	WKS	ARTIST—RECORD TITLE	LABEL & NO.
			PARSONS, Alan, Project	
			Duo formed in London in 1975. Consisted of producer Alan Parsons (guitar, keyboards) and lyricist Eric Woolfson (vocals, keyboards). Both had worked at the Abbey Road Studios; Parsons was an engineer; Woolfson, a songwriter. Parsons engineered Pink Floyd's *Dark Side Of The Moon* and The Beatles' *Abbey Road* albums. Project features varying musicians and vocalists.	
7/4/76	38	4	1. Tales Of Mystery And Imagination — Edgar Allan Poe musical interpretation of Poe's most notable works	20th Century 508
8/6/77	9	19	▲ **2. I Robot**	Arista 7002
7/22/78	26	9	● 3. Pyramid	Arista 4180
9/22/79	13	12	● 4. Eve	Arista 9504
11/29/80	13	21	▲ 5. The Turn Of A Friendly Card	Arista 9518
7/10/82	7	21	▲ **6. Eye In The Sky** *Eye In The Sky* (3)	Arista 9599
3/24/84	15	13	● 7. Ammonia Avenue	Arista 8204
			PARTON, Dolly	
			Born on 1/19/46 in Sevier County, Tennessee. Leading female artist of the country charts. Worked on Knoxville radio show at age 11. First recorded for Gold Band in 1957. To Nashville in 1964. Replaced Norma Jean on Porter Wagoner's TV show, 1967-74. Joined the *Grand Ole Opry* in 1969. Starred in the movies *9 to 5*, *The Best Little Whorehouse in Texas*, *Steel Magnolias* and *Straight Talk*. Hosted own TV variety show in 1987.	
12/3/77	20	13	▲ 1. Here You Come Again *Here You Come Again* (3)	RCA 2544
9/16/78	27	8	● 2. Heartbreaker	RCA 2797
7/21/79	40	1	● 3. Great Balls Of Fire	RCA 3361
1/17/81	11	15	● 4. 9 to 5 and Odd Jobs *9 To 5* (1)	RCA 3852
12/22/84	31	4	▲² 5. Once Upon A Christmas [X] **KENNY ROGERS & DOLLY PARTON** Christmas charts: 1/'84, 4/'85, 10/'87, 16/'88, 15/'89, 14/'90, 14/'91, 19/'92, 25/'93	RCA 5307
3/28/87	6	14	▲ **6. Trio** **DOLLY PARTON, LINDA RONSTADT, EMMYLOU HARRIS**	Warner 25491
5/25/91	24	3	▲ 7. Eagle When She Flies	Columbia 46882
3/20/93	16	7	▲ 8. Slow Dancing With The Moon	Columbia 53199
			PARTRIDGE FAMILY, The	
			Popularized through "The Partridge Family" TV series, broadcast from 1970-74. Recordings by series stars David Cassidy (lead singer) and real-life stepmother Shirley Jones (backing vocals). Cassidy, son of actor Jack Cassidy, was born on 4/12/50 in New York City; raised in California. Jones, born on 3/31/34 in Smithton, Pennsylvania, starred in the movie musicals *Oklahoma!* and *The Music Man*; married Jack in 1956. **THE PARTRIDGE FAMILY Starring Shirley Jones Featuring David Cassidy:**	
11/7/70	4	36	● **1. The Partridge Family Album** *I Think I Love You* (1)	Bell 6050
4/3/71	3	23	● **2. Up To Date** *Doesn't Somebody Want To Be Wanted* (6)/ *I'll Meet You Halfway* (9)	Bell 6059
9/4/71	9	22	● **3. The Partridge Family Sound Magazine**	Bell 6064
4/1/72	18	7	● 4. The Partridge Family Shopping Bag	Bell 6072

DATE	POS	WKS	ARTIST—RECORD TITLE	LABEL & NO.
10/7/72	**21**	10	● 5. The Partridge Family at home with their Greatest Hits [G]	Bell 1107
1/6/73	**17**	9	**PAUL, Billy** Born Paul Williams on 12/1/34 in Philadelphia. Soul singer; sang on Philadelphia radio broadcasts at age 11. First recorded for Jubilee in 1952. ● 360 Degrees Of Billy Paul *Me And Mrs. Jones* (1)	Phil. Int. 31793
5/14/55	**15**	6	**PAUL, Les, and Mary Ford** Paul was born Lester Polsfuss on 6/9/16 in Waukesha, Wisconsin. Ford was born Colleen Summer on 7/7/28 in Pasadena; died on 9/30/77. Self-taught guitarist Paul is an innovator in electric guitar and multi- track recordings. Paul and vocalist Ford married on 12/29/49; divorced in 1963. Paul won the 1983 Trustees Grammy Award; was inducted into the Rock and Roll Hall of Fame in 1988. Les and Mary 10 songs feature Ford's vocals; 6 are instrumentals by Paul	Capitol 577
3/16/63	**9**	8	**PAUL & PAULA** Paul was born Ray Hildebrand on 12/21/40 in Joshua, Texas. Paula was born Jill Jackson on 5/20/42 in McCaney, Texas. Formed duo at Howard Payne College, Brownwood, Texas. Paul & Paula Sing For Young Lovers *Hey Paula* (1)/*Young Lovers* (6)	Philips 078
3/2/91	**35**	6	**PAVAROTTI, Luciano** Born on 10/12/35 in Modena, Italy. World-renowned operatic tenor. Former teacher and insurance salesperson. Operatic debut in 1961 in *La Boheme*. ▲ 1. CARRERAS DOMINGO PAVAROTTI in concert [L] **CARRERAS DOMINGO PAVAROTTI** concert on 7/7/90 of opera tenors: Jose Carreras, Placido Domingo, Luciano Pavarotti with orchestra conducted by Zubin Mehta at the Baths of Caracalla in Rome	London 460433
9/17/94	**4**	13	2. The 3 Tenors In Concert 1994 [L] **CARRERAS, DOMINGO, PAVAROTTI with MEHTA** concert on 7/16/94 of opera tenors Jose Carreras, Placido Domingo and Luciano Pavarotti with orchestra conducted by Zubin Mehta at Dodger Stadium in Los Angeles	Atlantic 82614
6/24/67	**30**	6	**PEACHES & HERB** Soul duo from Washington, D.C.: Herb Fame (born Herbert Feemster, 1942) and Francine Barker (born Francine Hurd, 1947). Fame had been recording solo; Barker sang in vocal group Sweet Things. Marlene Mack filled in for Barker from 1968-69. Re-formed with Fame and Linda Green in 1977. 1. Let's Fall In Love *Close Your Eyes* (8)	Date 4004
2/17/79	**2** (6)	23	▲ **2. 2 Hot!** *Shake Your Groove Thing* (5)/*Reunited* (1)	Polydor 6172
12/1/79	**31**	5	● 3. Twice The Fire	Polydor 6239

DATE	POS	WKS	ARTIST—RECORD TITLE	LABEL & NO.
			PEARL JAM	
			Seattle-based rock band: vocalist Eddie Vedder (born Eddie Mueller), guitarists Stone Gossard and Mike McCready, bassist Jeff Ament and drummer Dave Abbruzzese (replaced Dave Krusen who played on the album *Ten*). Gossard and Ament were members of Mother Love Bone. All except Krusen recorded with Temple Of The Dog. Band acted in the movie *Singles* as Matt Dillon's band, Citizen Dick. Abbruzzese left band in August 1994. Drummer Jack Irons (ex-Red Hot Chili Peppers) joined in late 1994.	
2/15/92	**2** (4)	100	▲8 **1. Ten**	Epic/Assc. 47857
11/6/93	**1** (5)	28	▲5 **2. Vs.**	Epic/Assc. 53136
12/24/94	**1** (1)	10+	▲4 **3. Vitalogy**	Epic 66900
			PEBBLES	
			Born Perri Alette McKissack. Native of Oakland. Nicknamed "Pebbles" by her family for her resemblance to cartoon character Pebbles Flintstone. Worked with Con Funk Shun in the early '80s while still a teenager. Married to singer/songwriter/producer L.A. Reid of The Deele. Her cousin is vocalist Cherrelle. Put together/managed the female rap group TLC.	
4/2/88	**14**	19	▲ 1. Pebbles	MCA 42094
			Girlfriend (5)/*Mercedes Boy* (2)	
11/3/90	**37**	4	● 2. Always	MCA 10025
			Giving You The Benefit (4)	
			PENDERGRASS, Teddy	
			Born on 3/26/50 in Philadelphia. Worked local clubs; became drummer for Harold Melvin's Blue Notes in 1969; lead singer with same group in 1970. Went solo in 1976. In the 1982 movie *Soup for One*. Auto accident on 3/18/82 left him partially paralyzed.	
4/9/77	**17**	11	▲ 1. Teddy Pendergrass	Phil. Int. 34390
7/8/78	**11**	15	▲ 2. Life Is A Song Worth Singing	Phil. Int. 35095
6/30/79	**5**	14	▲ **3. Teddy**	Phil. Int. 36003
1/26/80	**33**	4	● 4. Teddy Live! Coast To Coast [L]	Phil. Int. 36294 [2]
			side 4: interviews and new studio recordings	
8/23/80	**14**	16	▲ 5. TP	Phil. Int. 36745
10/10/81	**19**	7	● 6. It's Time For Love	Phil. Int. 37491
7/21/84	**38**	5	● 7. Love Language	Asylum 60317
			PENN, Michael	
			Los Angeles-based singer/songwriter. Older brother of actors Sean and Christopher Penn. Son of actor/ director Leo Penn and actress Eileen Ryan.	
3/10/90	**31**	8	March	RCA 9692
			PENNARIO, Leonard	
			Born on 7/9/24 in Buffalo, New York. Classical pianist. To Los Angeles at age 10 and appeared on Bing Crosby's *Kraft Music Hall*. Debuted at age 12 with the Dallas Symphony. Has performed with nearly every prestigious international orchestra.	
6/8/59	**29**	1	Concertos under the Stars [I]	Capitol 8326
			with the Hollywood Bowl Symphony Orchestra, conducted by Carmen Dragon	
			PERRY, Steve	
			Born on 1/22/49 in Hanford, California. Lead singer of Journey since 1978.	
5/5/84	**12**	18	▲2 1. Street Talk	Columbia 39334
			Oh Sherrie (3)	
8/6/94	**15**	4	● 2. For The Love Of Strange Medicine	Columbia 44287

The Miracles' extremely rare first album, *The Fabulous Miracles*, issued on Tamla in 1963, featured the classic "You've Really Got A Hold On Me." The disc also helped group leader Smokey Robinson establish himself as one of Motown's truly legendary figures.

The Monkees' *Headquarters* was the third of the group's four consecutive No. 1 albums. In late 1994, Rhino Records began an extensive reissue program, releasing that disc and all other Monkee works with previously unheard bonus tracks.

Anne Murray's 1970 album, *Snowbird*, included the Top 10 hit of the same name and launched the Canadian singer into the U.S. marketplace in fine style. Her 1980 *Anne Murray's Greatest Hits* compilation was a surprisingly strong seller that sold well over 4 million copies domestically.

Naughty By Nature's 1991 self-titled *Tommy Boy* debut was a clear indication that rap, more than most other musical genres, was a wide-open field for talented newcomers. The disc quickly went platinum and spent more than a year
on the charts.

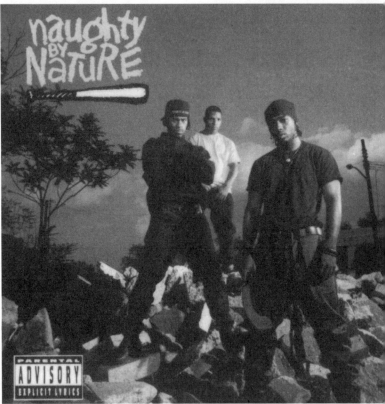

Ricky Nelson was, long before the dawn of MTV, the perfect example of the power of music video. His weekly appearances on TV's "The Adventures of Ozzie and Harriet" gave such discs as 1962's *Album Seven By Rick* an unprecedented promotional push to an audience of virtually millions.

Willie Nelson devoted an entire album to the songs of his friend on 1979's *Willie Nelson Sings Kristofferson*. The successful result became his fourth platinum release, and the pair went on to star together in the 1984 film *Song-Writer*.

Bob Newhart's comedy records were chart fixtures during the early '60s. With 1960's *The Button-Down Mind Of Bob Newhart*, the future television superstar scored a No. 1 record that held that slot for 14 weeks and remained on the album charts for more than two years.

Olivia Newton-John became one of the most popular female vocalists of the '70s via her string of highly successful recordings for MCA. *Don't Stop Believin'*, her sixth consecutive gold album, came two years before her appearance both in the 1978 film *Grease* and on its accompanying soundtrack.

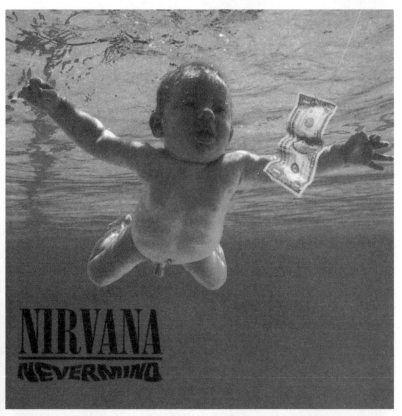

Nirvana's major-label debut album, 1991's *Nevermind*, became one of the most influential rock-and-roll releases of the decade. Containing the Top 10 hit "Smells Like Teen Spirit," the record was a cornerstone of the so-called "Seattle sound" further popularized by such bands as Pearl Jam and Soundgarden.

NWA's double-platinum 1989 debut, *Straight Outta Compton*, introduced Middle America to a cast of rappers who later became stars in their own right. The group included Andre "Dr. Dre" Young, Eric "Eazy-E" Wright and Oshea "Ice Cube" Jackson.

Roy Orbison's 1963 Monument album, *In Dreams*, became the Texan-born singer's second gold album. Its title track played an important role throughout his career, most notably when redone for *Blue Velvet*, David Lynch's 1988 film.

DATE	POS	WKS	ARTIST—RECORD TITLE	LABEL & NO.
			PETER AND GORDON	
			Pop duo formed in London in 1963: Peter Asher (born 6/22/44, London) and Gordon Waller (born 6/4/45, Braemar, Scotland). Asher's sister Jane was Paul McCartney's girlfriend; McCartney wrote the duo's first three chart hits. Toured the U.S. in 1964; appeared on "Shindig," "Hullabaloo" and "The Ed Sullivan Show." Disbanded in 1967. Asher went into production and management, including work with Linda Ronstadt, James Taylor and 10,000 Maniacs.	
7/25/64	21	5	A World Without Love *A World Without Love* (1)	Capitol 2115
			PETER, PAUL & MARY	
			Folk group formed in New York City in 1961. Consisted of Mary Travers (born 11/7/37, Louisville); Peter Yarrow (born 5/31/38, New York City); and Paul Stookey (born 12/30/37, Baltimore). Yarrow had worked the Newport Folk Festival in 1960. Stookey had done TV work, and Travers had been in the Broadway musical *The Next President*. Disbanded in 1971; reunited in 1978.	
6/2/62	1(7)	112	▲² 1. Peter, Paul and Mary *If I Had A Hammer* (10)	Warner 1449
1/26/63	2(9)	71	● 2. (Moving) *Puff (The Magic Dragon)* (2)	Warner 1473
10/26/63	1(5)	58	● 3. In The Wind *Blowin' In The Wind* (2)/ *Don't Think Twice, It's All Right* (9)	Warner 1507
8/29/64	4	25	● 4. Peter, Paul and Mary In Concert　　　　　[L]	Warner 1555 [2]
5/1/65	8	26	● 5. A Song Will Rise	Warner 1589
11/27/65	11	8	● 6. See What Tomorrow Brings	Warner 1615
9/17/66	22	9	7. Peter, Paul and Mary Album	Warner 1648
9/9/67	15	25	● 8. Album 1700 *I Dig Rock And Roll Music* (9)/*Leaving On A Jet Plane* (1-'69)	Warner 1700
10/12/68	14	12	9. Late Again	Warner 1751
6/21/69	12	9	● 10. Peter, Paul and Mommy	Warner 1785
6/27/70	15	11	▲ 11. 10 Years Together/The Best Of Peter, Paul and Mary　　　　　[G]	Warner 2552
			PET SHOP BOYS	
			British duo: Neil Tennant (vocals) and Chris Lowe (keyboards). Tennant was a writer for British fan magazine *Smash Hits*. In 1989, Tennant also recorded with the group Electronic.	
4/19/86	7	21	▲ 1. Please *West End Girls* (1)/*Opportunities* (10)	EMI America 17193
10/17/87	25	22	● 2. Pet Shop Boys, actually. *It's A Sin* (9)/ *What Have I Done To Deserve This?* (2-with Dusty Springfield)	EMI-Man. 46972
11/26/88	34	3	● 3. Introspective *Always On My Mind* (4)	EMI-Man. 90868
10/23/93	20	2	● 4. Very	EMI 89721

DATE	POS	WKS	ARTIST—RECORD TITLE	LABEL & NO.
			PETTY, Tom, And The Heartbreakers	
			Rock group formed in Los Angeles in 1975. Consisted of Petty (born 10/20/53, Gainesville, Florida; guitar, vocals), Mike Campbell (guitar), Benmont Tench (keyboards), Ron Blair (bass) and Stan Lynch (drums). Petty, Campbell and Tench had been in Florida group Mudcrutch in the early '70s. Backed Stevie Nicks on solo album *Bella Donna*. Blair left in 1982; replaced by Howard Epstein. Toured with Bob Dylan in 1986. Petty appeared in the 1987 movie *Made in Heaven*. Member of the supergroup Traveling Wilburys.	
7/1/78	23	8	● 1. You're Gonna Get It!	Shelter 52029
11/17/79	2 (7)	29	▲² **2. Damn The Torpedoes**	Backstreet 5105
			Don't Do Me Like That (10)	
5/23/81	5	17	▲ **3. Hard Promises**	Backstreet 5160
11/27/82	9	22	● **4. Long After Dark**	Backstreet 5360
4/13/85	7	18	▲ **5. Southern Accents**	MCA 5486
1/18/86	22	9	6. Pack Up The Plantation — Live! [L]	MCA 8021 [2]
5/23/87	20	13	● 7. Let Me Up (I've Had Enough)	MCA 5836
5/20/89	3	51	▲³ **8. Full Moon Fever**	MCA 6253
			TOM PETTY backing by all of The Heartbreakers except drummer Stan Lynch	
			Free Fallin' (7)	
7/20/91	13	16	▲ 9. Into The Great Wide Open	MCA 10317
			above 2 co-produced by Jeff Lynne	
12/4/93	5	27	▲³ **10. Greatest Hits** [G]	MCA 10813
11/19/94	8	15+	▲² **11. Wildflowers**	Warner 45759
			TOM PETTY backing by all of The Heartbreakers except drummer Stan Lynch	
			PHAIR, Liz	
			Born on 4/17/67 in New Haven, Connecticut. Rock singer/songwriter.	
10/8/94	27	1	Whip-Smart	Matador 92429
			PHILADELPHIA ORCHESTRA, The	
			Conducted by Eugene Ormandy (born 11/18/1899, Budapest, Hungary; died 3/12/85). Came to the U.S. in 1921; conducted orchestra from 1938-1980. Also see Mormon Tabernacle Choir.	
5/26/62	17	11	The Magnificent Sound Of The Philadelphia Orchestra [K-I]	Columbia 1 [2]
			compiled from 16 of their albums	
			PHILLIPS, Esther	
			Born Esther Mae Jones on 12/23/35 in Galveston, Texas. Bouts with drug addiction interrupted her career and led to her death on 8/7/84 (liver and kidney failure). One of the first female superstars of R&B. Vocalist/multi-instrumentalist. Moved to Los Angeles in 1940. Recorded and toured with The Johnny Otis Orchestra as "Little Esther," 1948-54; scored seven Top 10 hits on the R&B charts in 1950.	
9/20/75	32	6	What A Diff'rence A Day Makes	Kudu 23
			with jazz guitarist Joe Beck	
			PHISH	
			Burlington, Vermont, rock quartet: Page McConnell, Mike Gordon, Trey Anastasio and Jon "Tubbs" Fishman. The first three share vocals.	
4/16/94	34	1	(Hoist)	Elektra 61628

DATE	POS	WKS	ARTIST—RECORD TITLE	LABEL & NO.
			PICKETT, Bobby "Boris", And The Crypt-Kickers	
			Born on 2/11/40 in Somerville, Massachusetts. Began recording career in Hollywood while aspiring to be an actor. A member of The Stompers in early 1962. Leon Russell, Johnny MacCrae (Ronny & The Daytonas), Rickie Page (The Bermudas) and Gary Paxton (Hollywood Argyles) were Crypt-Kickers.	
12/15/62	**19**	3	The Original Monster Mash [N] *Monster Mash* (1)	Garpax 57001
			PICKETT, Wilson	
			Born on 3/18/41 in Prattville, Alabama. Soul singer/songwriter. Sang in local gospel groups. To Detroit in 1955. With The Falcons, 1961-63. Career took off after recording in Memphis with guitarist/producer Steve Cropper. Inducted into the Rock and Roll Hall of Fame in 1991. Sentenced to one year in jail for striking and injuring a pedestrian in New Jersey while driving drunk in 1992.	
10/15/66	**21**	7	1. The Exciting Wilson Pickett *Land Of 1000 Dances* (6)	Atlantic 8129
1/27/68	**35**	8	2. The Best Of Wilson Pickett [G]	Atlantic 8151
			PINK FLOYD	
			English progressive-rock band formed in 1965: David Gilmour (born 3/6/46; guitar; replaced Syd Barrett in 1968), Roger Waters (born 9/6/44; bass), Nick Mason (born 1/27/45; drums) and Rick Wright (born 7/28/45; keyboards). Wright left in early 1982; Waters went solo in 1984. Band inactive, 1984-86. Gilmour, Mason and Wright re-grouped in 1987. Group name taken from Georgia bluesmen Pink Anderson and Floyd Council.	
3/31/73	**1**(1)	63	▲13 **1. The Dark Side Of The Moon** charted a record 741 weeks on the *Top 200 Albums* chart; as of 1993, over 20 million units sold	Harvest 11163
1/26/74	**36**	4	● 2. A Nice Pair [E-R] reissue of the group's first 2 British albums *The Piper At The Gates Of Dawn* and *A Saucerful Of Secrets*	Harvest 11257 [2]
9/27/75	**1**(2)	15	▲4 **3. Wish You Were Here**	Columbia 33453
2/19/77	**3**	9	▲4 **4. Animals**	Columbia 34474
12/22/79	**1**(15)	35	▲8 **5. The Wall** concept album released as a movie in the early '80s *Another Brick In The Wall (Part II)* (1)	Columbia 36183 [2]
12/19/81	**31**	7	▲ 6. A Collection Of Great Dance Songs [G]	Columbia 37680
4/9/83	**6**	12	▲ **7. The Final Cut**	Columbia 38243
10/3/87	**3**	26	▲3 **8. A Momentary Lapse of Reason**	Columbia 40599
12/17/88	**11**	10	▲ 9. Delicate Sound Of Thunder [L] recorded in August 1988; CD contains bonus track	Columbia 44484 [2]
4/23/94	**1**(4)	20	▲2 **10. The Division Bell**	Columbia 64200
			PLANT, Robert	
			Born on 8/20/48 in West Bromwich, England. Lead singer of Led Zeppelin; The Honeydrippers.	
7/24/82	**5**	14	▲ **1. Pictures At Eleven**	Swan Song 8512
8/6/83	**8**	18	▲ **2. The Principle Of Moments**	Es Paranza 90101
6/22/85	**20**	8	● 3. Shaken 'N' Stirred	Es Paranza 90265
3/19/88	**6**	25	▲ **4. Now And Zen**	Es Paranza 90863
4/7/90	**13**	11	● 5. Manic Nirvana	Es Paranza 91336
6/19/93	**34**	1	● 6. Fate Of Nations	Es Paranza 92264

DATE	POS	WKS	ARTIST—RECORD TITLE	LABEL & NO.
11/26/94	4	5	▲ **7. No Quarter** **JIMMY PAGE & ROBERT PLANT** all but 3 of the 13 new recordings are Led Zeppelin songs	Atlantic 82706
			PLASTIC ONO BAND — see LENNON, John	
			PLATTERS, The	
			R&B group formed in Los Angeles in 1953. Consisted of Tony Williams (lead), David Lynch (tenor), Paul Robi (baritone), Herb Reed (bass) and Zola Taylor. Group first recorded for Federal in 1954, with Alex Hodge instead of Robi, and without Zola Taylor. Hit "Only You" was written by manager Buck Ram (died 1/1/91; age 83) and first recorded for Federal. To Mercury in 1955; re-recorded "Only You." Williams left to go solo; replaced by Sonny Turner in 1961. Taylor replaced by Sandra Dawn; Robi replaced by Nate Nelson (formerly in The Flamingos) in 1966. Lynch died of cancer on 1/2/81 (age 61). Nelson died of heart disease on 6/1/84 (age 52). Robi died of cancer on 2/1/89. Williams died on 8/14/92 of diabetes and emphysema. Group inducted into the Rock and Roll Hall of Fame in 1990. Several unrelated groups use The Platters' famous name today.	
7/14/56	7	26	**1. The Platters** *My Prayer* (1)	Mercury 20146
1/19/57	12	8	2. The Platters, Volume Two	Mercury 20216
3/30/59	15	6	3. Remember When? *Smoke Gets In Your Eyes* (1)	Mercury 20410
3/14/60	6	66	● **4. Encore Of Golden Hits** [G] *Only You (And You Alone)* (5)/*The Great Pretender* (1)/ *(You've Got) The Magic Touch* (4)/*Twilight Time* (1)	Mercury 20472
11/14/60	20	7	● 5. More Encore Of Golden Hits [G] *Harbor Lights* (8)	Mercury 20591
			PLAYER	
			Pop-rock group formed in Los Angeles: Peter Beckett (vocals, guitar), John Crowley (vocals, guitar), Ronn Moss (bass), John Friesen (drums) and Wayne Cooke (keyboards). Moss plays Ridge Forrester on the TV soap "The Bold & The Beautiful." Crowley began solo country career in 1988. Beckett joined Little River Band by 1992.	
1/28/78	26	6	● 1. Player *Baby Come Back* (1)/*This Time I'm In It For Love* (10)	RSO 3026
11/4/78	37	2	● 2. Danger Zone	RSO 3036
			PM DAWN	
			Jersey City, New Jersey, rap duo of brothers Attrell (born 5/15/70) and Jarrett (born 7/17/71) Cordes — nicknamed "Prince Be" and "DJ Minutemix." PM Dawn means "from the darkest hour comes the light."	
4/10/93	30	10	● The Bliss Album ... ? *I'd Die Without You* (3)/*Looking Through Patient Eyes* (6)	Gee Street 514517
			POCO	
			Country-rock band formed in Los Angeles by Rusty Young (pedal steel guitar) and Buffalo Springfield members Richie Furay (rhythm guitar) and Jim Messina (lead guitar). Randy Meisner (later of The Eagles) left in 1969; replaced by bassist Timothy B. Schmit. As of second album, group consisted of Furay, Messina, Young, Schmit and George Grantham (drums). Messina left in 1970; replaced by Paul Cotton. Furay left in 1973. Grantham and Schmit (joined The Eagles) left in 1977; replaced by Charlie Harrison, Kim Bullard and Steve Chapman. Disbanded in 1984. In 1989, Young, Furay, Messina, Grantham and Meisner reunited.	
2/13/71	26	6	1. Deliverin' [L]	Epic 30209
10/20/73	38	2	2. Crazy Eyes	Epic 32354
3/3/79	14	10	● 3. Legend	ABC 1099

DATE	POS	WKS	ARTIST—RECORD TITLE	LABEL & NO.
11/11/89	**40**	2	● 4. Legacy	RCA 9694
			POINTER SISTERS	
			Soul group formed in Oakland in 1971, consisting of sisters Ruth, Bonnie, June and Anita Pointer. Parents were ministers. Group was originally a trio; youngest sister, June, joined in the early '70s. First recorded for Atlantic in 1971. Backup work for Cold Blood, Elvin Bishop, Boz Scaggs, Grace Slick and many others. Sang in nostalgic '40s style, 1973-77. In the 1976 movie *Car Wash*. Bonnie went solo in 1978; group continued as trio in new musical style.	
8/25/73	**13**	13	● 1. The Pointer Sisters	Blue Thumb 48
8/9/75	**22**	7	2. Steppin	Blue Thumb 6021
2/3/79	**13**	10	● 3. Energy	Planet 1
			Fire (2)	
11/1/80	**34**	5	4. Special Things	Planet 9
			He's So Shy (3)	
7/18/81	**12**	14	● 5. Black & White	Planet 18
			Slow Hand (2)	
3/17/84	**8**	65	▲² **6. Break Out**	Planet 4705
			Automatic (5)/*Jump (For My Love)* (3)/*I'm So Excited* (9)/ *Neutron Dance* (6)	
4/20/85	**24**	17	▲ 7. Contact	RCA 5487
			POISON	
			Hard-rock quartet formed in Harrisburg, Pennsylvania: Bret Michaels (vocals), Bobby Dall (bass), Rikki Rockett (drums) and CC DeVille (guitar; left band in early 1992; replaced by Richie Kotzen).	
3/7/87	**3**	47	▲³ **1. Look What The Cat Dragged In**	Capitol 12523
			Talk Dirty To Me (9)	
5/21/88	**2**(1)	52	▲⁵ **2. Open Up and Say ... Ahh!**	Enigma 48493
			Nothin' But A Good Time (6)/*Every Rose Has Its Thorn* (1)/ *Your Mama Don't Dance* (10)	
7/28/90	**2**(1)	37	▲³ **3. Flesh & Blood**	Capitol 918132
			Unskinny Bop (3)/*Something To Believe In* (4)	
3/6/93	**16**	2	● 4. Native Tongue	Capitol 98961
			POLICE, The	
			Rock trio formed in England in 1977: Gordon "Sting" Sumner (born 10/2/51; vocals, bass), Andy Summers (born 12/31/42; guitar) and Stewart Copeland (born 7/16/52; drums). First guitarist was Henri Padovani; replaced by Summers in 1977. Copeland had been with Curved Air. Inactive as a group since appearance at "Amnesty '86." Sting began recording solo in 1985. Copeland formed group Animal Logic in 1989.	
3/31/79	**23**	11	▲ 1. Outlandos d'Amour	A&M 4753
11/17/79	**25**	8	● 2. Reggatta de Blanc	A&M 4792
11/1/80	**5**	31	▲ 3. Zenyatta Mondatta	A&M 4831
			De Do Do Do, De Da Da Da (10)/ *Don't Stand So Close To Me* (10)	
10/24/81	**2**(6)	30	▲² 4. Ghost In The Machine	A&M 3730
			Every Little Thing She Does Is Magic (3)	
7/2/83	**1**(17)	50	▲⁴ 5. Synchronicity	A&M 3735
			Every Breath You Take (1)/*King Of Pain* (3)/ *Wrapped Around Your Finger* (8)	
11/29/86	**7**	13	▲³ **6. Every Breath You Take — The Singles** [G]	A&M 3902

DATE	POS	WKS	ARTIST—RECORD TITLE	LABEL & NO.
			PONTY, Jean-Luc	
			Born on 9/29/42 in Normandy, France. Classically trained, jazz-rock violinist. First American appearance at the 1967 Monterey Jazz Festival. Worked with Frank Zappa and Elton John. Emigrated to the U.S. in 1973. Member of Mahavishnu Orchestra, 1973-75.	
10/29/77	**35**	3	1. Enigmatic Ocean [I]	Atlantic 19110
10/28/78	**36**	3	2. Cosmic Messenger [I]	Atlantic 19189
			PORNO FOR PYROS	
			Alternative-rock band formed by former Jane's Addiction members Perry Farrell (vocals) and Stephen Perkins (drums). Includes Peter DiStefano (guitar) and Martyn Le Noble (bass).	
5/15/93	**3**	7	● **Porno For Pyros**	Warner 45228
			POWER STATION, The	
			Superstar quartet: Robert Palmer (lead singer), Chic's Tony Thompson (drums) and Duran Duran's John Taylor (bass) and Andy Taylor (guitar). Formed as a one-album studio project. Michael Des Barres replaced Palmer for the group's 1985 concert tour.	
4/20/85	**6**	25	▲ **The Power Station** *Some Like It Hot* (6)/*Get It On* (9)	Capitol 12380
			PRADO, Perez	
			Born Damaso Perez Prado on 12/11/16 in Mantanzas, Cuba. "The King of Mambo" died on 9/14/89 after suffering a stroke in Colonia del Valle, Mexico. Bandleader/organist. Moved to Mexico City in 1949; formed a big band. Toured and worked in the U.S. beginning in 1954. In the movie *Underwater!*	
5/25/59	**22**	3	"Prez" [I]	RCA 1556
			PRESLEY, Elvis	
			Born on 1/8/35 in Tupelo, Mississippi; died at his Graceland mansion in Memphis on 8/16/77 (age 42) of heart failure caused by prescription drug abuse. "The King of Rock & Roll." Won talent contest at age eight, singing "Old Shep." Moved to Memphis in 1948. First recorded for Sun in 1954. Signed to RCA Records on 11/22/55. With his good looks, a passionate bluesy voice, a great band (Bill Black, bass; Scotty Moore, guitar; D.J. Fontana, drums), a smooth vocal quartet (The Jordanaires), and a shrewd manager (Tom Parker), Presley blazed his way to the #1 star of rock 'n roll, a position he hasn't relinquished yet. Made his nationwide TV debut on "Stage Show" on 1/28/56. Starred in 31 feature movies (beginning with *Love Me Tender* in 1956). In U.S. Army from 3/24/58 to 3/5/60. Married Priscilla Beaulieu on 5/1/67; divorced on 10/11/73. Priscilla pursued acting in the '80s, beginning with a role on TV's "Dallas." Their only child, Lisa Marie, was born on 2/1/68; married Michael Jackson on 5/26/94. Presley's last "live" performance was in Indianapolis on 6/26/77. Won 1971 Lifetime Achievement Grammy Award. Inducted into the Rock and Roll Hall of Fame in 1986. The first rock 'n' roll artist to be honored by the U.S. Postal Service with a commemorative stamp on 1/8/93.	
3/31/56	**1**(10)	48	● **1. Elvis Presley** includes 5 Sun studio recordings	RCA LPM-1254
11/10/56	**1**(5)	32	● **2. Elvis** *Love Me* (2)	RCA LPM-1382
5/13/57	**3**	9	▲ **3. Peace In The Valley** [EP] 7" EP of sacred songs	RCA EPA-4054
7/22/57	**1**(10)	29	● **4. Loving You** [S] only side 1 has the soundtrack recordings *(Let Me Be Your) Teddy Bear* (1)	RCA LPM-1515
9/2/57	**18**	1	▲ 5. Loving You, Vol. II [EP-S] 7" EP; 4 songs from the soundtrack of previous album	RCA EPA 2-1515

DATE	POS	WKS	ARTIST—RECORD TITLE	LABEL & NO.
9/2/57	**22**	1	▲ 6. Love Me Tender [EP-S]	RCA EPA-4006
			7" EP of songs from Presley's first movie *Love Me Tender* (1)	
9/30/57	**16**	1	7. Just For You [EP]	RCA EPA-4041
			7" EP; 3 of 4 songs from side 2 of *Loving You*; in addition to the above 4 charted EP's, 10 other Presley EP's made *Billboard*'s pop singles charts, including 5 from soundtracks: "Flaming Star," "Follow That Dream," "Kid Galahad," "Viva Las Vegas" and "Tickle Me"	
12/2/57	**1**(4)	7	▲² 8. Elvis' Christmas Album [X]	RCA LOC-1035
			gatefold with 10 pages of bound-in color photos of Presley; includes all 4 songs from *Peace In The Valley* EP; see special Christmas section for more details	
4/21/58	**3**	36	▲⁵ 9. Elvis' Golden Records [G]	RCA LPM-1707
			Heartbreak Hotel (1)/ *I Want You, I Need You, I Love You* (1)/ *Don't Be Cruel* (1)/*Hound Dog* (1)/*Too Much* (1)/ *All Shook Up* (1)/*Jailhouse Rock* (1)	
9/15/58	**2**(1)	15	**10. King Creole** [S]	RCA LPM-1884
			Hard Headed Woman (1)	
3/23/59	**19**	7	11. For LP Fans Only [E]	RCA LPM-1990
			includes 4 Sun studio recordings; others from 1956	
9/21/59	**32**	6	12. A Date With Elvis [E]	RCA LPM-2011
			includes 5 Sun studio recordings; others from 1956-57	
2/15/60	**31**	6	▲ 13. 50,000,000 Elvis Fans Can't Be Wrong — Elvis' Gold Records-Volume 2 [G]	RCA LPM-2075
			Don't (1)/*I Beg Of You* (8)/ *Wear My Ring Around Your Neck* (2)/*One Night* (4)/ *I Got Stung* (8)/*A Fool Such As I* (2)/ *I Need Your Love Tonight* (4)/*A Big Hunk O' Love* (1)	
5/9/60	**2**(3)	32	**14. Elvis Is Back!**	RCA LSP-2231
			recorded shortly after his March 5th release from the Army	
10/31/60	**1**(10)	46	▲ **15. G.I. Blues** [S]	RCA LSP-2256
12/31/60	**33**	1	16. Elvis' Christmas Album [X-R]	RCA LPM-1951
			repackage of LOC-1035 album (no gatefold or photos)	
1/9/61	**13**	9	▲ 17. His Hand in Mine	RCA LSP-2328
			Presley's first full album of sacred songs	
7/24/61	**1**(3)	17	**18. Something for Everybody**	RCA LSP-2370
10/30/61	**1**(20)	53	▲² **19. Blue Hawaii** [S]	RCA LSP-2426
			Can't Help Falling In Love (2)	
7/14/62	**4**	18	**20. Pot Luck**	RCA LSP-2523
12/8/62	**3**	21	● **21. Girls! Girls! Girls!** [S]	RCA LSP-2621
			Return To Sender (2)	
4/27/63	**4**	18	**22. It Happened At The World's Fair** [S]	RCA LSP-2697
9/28/63	**3**	20	▲ **23. Elvis' Golden Records, Volume 3** [G]	RCA LSP-2765
			Stuck On You (1)/*It's Now Or Never* (1)/ *Are You Lonesome To-night* (1)/*Surrender* (1)/ *I Feel So Bad* (5)/*Little Sister* (5)/ *(Marie's the Name) His Latest Flame* (4)/ *Good Luck Charm* (1)/*She's Not You* (5)	
1/4/64	**3**	16	**24. Fun in Acapulco** [S]	RCA LSP-2756
			includes 2 bonus songs not in the movie *Bossa Nova Baby* (8)	
4/18/64	**6**	15	**25. Kissin' Cousins** [S]	RCA LSP-2894
			includes 2 bonus songs not in the movie	

DATE	POS	WKS	ARTIST—RECORD TITLE	LABEL & NO.
11/28/64	**1**(1)	20	● **26. Roustabout** [S]	RCA LSP-2999
5/8/65	**8**	17	**27. Girl Happy** [S] includes one bonus song not in the movie	RCA LSP-3338
9/18/65	**10**	11	**28. Elvis For Everyone!** [K] recordings from 2/57 to 1/64 (plus one Sun studio recording)	RCA LSP-3450
11/27/65	**8**	11	**29. Harum Scarum** [S] includes 2 bonus songs not in the movie	RCA LSP-3468
5/14/66	**20**	9	30. Frankie And Johnny [S]	RCA LSP-3553
8/6/66	**15**	9	31. Paradise, Hawaiian Style [S] includes one bonus song not in the movie	RCA LSP-3643
12/3/66	**18**	10	32. Spinout [S] includes 3 bonus songs not in the movie	RCA LSP-3702
4/29/67	**18**	9	▲² 33. How Great Thou Art Presley's second full album of sacred songs *Crying In The Chapel* (3)	RCA LSP-3758
2/10/68	**40**	1	34. Clambake [S] includes 5 bonus songs not in the movie	RCA LSP-3893
5/11/68	**33**	4	● 35. Elvis' Gold Records, Volume 4 [G] *(You're the) Devil In Disguise* (3)	RCA LSP-3921
1/25/69	**8**	14	● **36. Elvis** [TV-L] NBC-TV special; Presley's first "live" album	RCA LPM-4088
6/14/69	**13**	15	● 37. From Elvis In Memphis first Memphis sessions since Presley's 1955 Sun recordings *In The Ghetto* (3)	RCA LSP-4155
11/29/69	**12**	12	● 38. From Memphis To Vegas/From Vegas To Memphis [L] record 1: Elvis in Person at the International Hotel, Las Vegas; record 2: Elvis Back in Memphis (studio)	RCA LSP-6020 [2]
6/20/70	**13**	11	● 39. On Stage-February, 1970 [L] recorded at the International Hotel, Las Vegas *The Wonder Of You* (9)	RCA LSP-4362
12/19/70	**21**	6	● 40. Elvis-That's The Way It Is [S-L] 5 of 12 songs are "live" (Las Vegas)	RCA LSP-4445
1/30/71	**12**	10	● 41. Elvis Country ("I'm 10,000 Years Old")	RCA LSP-4460
6/26/71	**33**	5	42. Love Letters from Elvis all songs recorded in Nashville during June 1970	RCA LSP-4530
7/15/72	**11**	18	▲ 43. Elvis As Recorded At Madison Square Garden [L] the entire show of 6/10/72	RCA LSP-4776
11/25/72	**22**	11	● 44. Burning Love and hits from his movies, volume 2 [K] featuring songs from 8 of Presley's movies (1960-67) *Burning Love* (2)	RCA Camden 2595
3/10/73	**1**(1)	19	▲² **45. Aloha from Hawaii via Satellite** [TV-L] RCA's first QuadraDisc; recorded on 1/14/73	RCA VPSX-6089 [2]
8/10/74	**33**	4	46. Elvis Recorded Live On Stage In Memphis [L]	RCA CPL-0606
7/30/77	**3**	17	▲² **47. Moody Blue** [K] recordings from 1974-77 (4 "live"; 6 recorded at Graceland); Presley's last album release before his death	RCA AFL-2428
10/29/77	**5**	7	▲ **48. Elvis In Concert** [TV-L] record 1: from the CBS-TV Special; record 2: from Presley's final tour, June 1977	RCA APL-2587 [2]

DATE	POS	WKS	ARTIST—RECORD TITLE	LABEL & NO.
8/30/80	27	5	▲ 49. Elvis Aron Presley [K] boxed set: 1: An Early Live Performance/Monolog; 2: An Early Benefit Performance; 3: Collectors' Gold From The Movie Years; 4: The TV Specials; 5: The Las Vegas Years; 6: Lost Singles; 7: Elvis At The Piano/The Concert Years-Part 1; 8: The Concert Years-Concluded	RCA CPL-3699 [8]
			PRESTON, Billy	
			Born on 9/9/46 in Houston. R&B vocalist/keyboardist. To Los Angeles at an early age. With Mahalia Jackson in 1956. Played piano in movie *St. Louis Blues*, 1958. Regular on "Shindig" TV show. Recorded with The Beatles on "Get Back" and "Let It Be"; worked Concert For Bangladesh in 1969. Prominent session man, played on Sly & The Family Stone hits. With The Rolling Stones U.S. tour in 1975.	
7/1/72	32	8	1. I Wrote A Simple Song *Outa-Space* (2)	A&M 3507
6/30/73	32	6	2. Music Is My Life *Will It Go Round In Circles* (1)	A&M 3516
10/12/74	17	6	3. The Kids & Me *Nothing From Nothing* (1)	A&M 3645
			PRETENDERS, The	
			Rock quartet featuring lead singer/songwriter/guitarist Chrissie Hynde (born 9/7/51, Akron, Ohio). Formed in 1978. Early British lineup included guitarist James Honeyman-Scott (died 6/16/82; replaced by Robbie MacIntosh), bassist Pete Farndon (died 4/14/83; replaced in 1982 by Malcolm Foster) and drummer Martin Chambers. Hynde was married to Jim Kerr of Simple Minds. With the exception of Hynde, numerous personnel changes since 1985. Chambers returned to lineup in 1994.	
3/15/80	9	17	▲ **1. Pretenders**	Sire 6083
5/2/81	27	4	2. Extended Play [M]	Sire 3563
8/29/81	10	9	**3. Pretenders II**	Sire 3572
2/4/84	5	22	▲ **4. Learning To Crawl** *Back On The Chain Gang* (5)	Sire 23980
11/15/86	25	14	● 5. Get Close *Don't Get Me Wrong* (10)	Sire 25488
			PREVIN, Andre	
			Born on 4/6/29 in Berlin. Pianist/conductor/arranger/composer. Became musical director for MGM movies by the age of 21. Composed and arranged background music for *Gigi* and many other movies. In the '70s, served as resident conductor of the London Symphony Orchestra. Married to actress Mia Farrow from 1970-79.	
6/29/59	16	13	1. Secret Songs For Young Lovers [I] with David Rose & His Orchestra	MGM 3716
7/4/60	25	6	2. Like Love [I]	Columbia 1437
			PRICE, Leontyne	
			Born on 2/10/27 in Laurel, Mississippi. One of the great sopranos of opera. Career took off after touring Europe in *Porgy and Bess* during the mid-1950s. Won 1989 Lifetime Achievement Grammy Award.	
5/18/63	29	9	Giacomo Puccini: Madama Butterfly [F] with Richard Tucker (tenor), Rosalind Elias (mezzo-soprano), Philip Maero (baritone) and Erich Leinsdorf (conductor)	RCA 6160 [3]
			PRICE, Ray	
			Born on 1/12/26 in Perryville, Texas; raised in Dallas. Country singer. Price charted over 80 Top 40 singles on *Billboard's* country charts. Known as "The Cherokee Cowboy."	
12/19/70	28	16	● For The Good Times	Columbia 30106

DATE	POS	WKS	ARTIST—RECORD TITLE	LABEL & NO.
			PRIDE, Charley	
			Born on 3/18/38 in Sledge, Mississippi. The most successful black country performer. Discovered by Red Sovine in 1963. Pride has charted 29 #1 singles on the country charts.	
11/22/69	**24**	16	● 1. The Best Of Charley Pride [G]	RCA 4223
3/14/70	**22**	7	● 2. Just Plain Charley	RCA 4290
9/12/70	**30**	2	● 3. Charley Pride's 10th Album	RCA 4367
1/15/72	**38**	2	● 4. Charley Pride Sings Heart Songs	RCA 4617
			PRIMA, Louis, & Keely Smith	
			Prima was born on 12/7/11 in New Orleans. Surgery for a brain tumor in 1975 left him in a coma until his death on 8/24/78. Vocalist/trumpeter/composer/leader. Prima was married to jazz-styled vocalist Dorothy "Keely" Smith (born 3/9/32, Norfolk, Virginia) from 1952-61. The popular Las Vegas duo was backed by Sam Butera & The Witnesses. Prima was the voice of King Louis in animated Disney movie *The Jungle Book*.	
6/23/58	**12**	4	1. Las Vegas Prima Style [L]	Capitol 1010
5/25/59	**37**	1	2. Hey Boy! Hey Girl! [S]	Capitol 1160
			Prima and Smith portray Las Vegas entertainers in the movie	
1/16/61	**9**	9	**3. Wonderland By Night** **[I]**	Dot 25352
			LOUIS PRIMA	
			PRIMUS	
			San Francisco thrash-jazz-rock trio: Les Claypool (vocals, bass), Larry LaLonde (guitar) and Tim Alexander (drums).	
5/8/93	**7**	5	● **Pork Soda**	Interscope 92257
			PRINCE	
			Born Prince Roger Nelson on 6/7/58 in Minneapolis. Vocalist/multi-instrumentalist/composer/producer. Named for The Prince Roger Trio, led by his father. Self-taught musician; own band, Grand Central, in junior high school. Self-produced first album in 1978. Starred in the movies *Purple Rain*, *Under the Cherry Moon*, *Sign 'O' the Times* and *Graffiti Bridge*. Founded own label, Paisley Park. The Revolution featured Lisa Coleman (keyboards), Wendy Melvoin (guitar), Bobby Z (percussion), Matt "Dr." Fink (keyboards), Eric Leeds (saxophone) and Andre Cymone (bass; replaced by Brownmark in 1981). Coleman and Melvoin formed duo Wendy & Lisa in 1987. Sheila E. (drums) joined Prince's band in 1986. Prince formed new band, New Power Generation (named for the oldest Prince fan club in Britain), in 1990, featured Levi Seacer, Jr. (guitar), Sonny T. (bass), Tommy Barbarella (keyboard), dancer/percussionists Kirk Johnson and Damon Dickson, Michael Bland (drums), rapper Tony M. and Rosie Gaines (keyboards, vocals; replaced by Mayte [pronounced my-tie] by 1992). Prince announced that he would no longer record on 4/27/93. Changed his name on 6/7/93 to a combination male/female symbol; announced his separation from New Power Generation. Revealed in September 1993 that he would be called "Victor." His music is featured in The Joffrey's 1993 rock ballet titled *Billboards*. By 1994 referred to as "The Artist Formerly Known As Prince."	
12/15/79	**22**	10	▲ 1. Prince	Warner 3366
11/14/81	**21**	5	▲ 2. Controversy	Warner 3601
11/27/82	**9**	57	▲³ **3. Prince **1999****	Warner 23720 [2]
			Little Red Corvette (6)/*Delirious* (8)	
			PRINCE and the REVOLUTION:	
7/14/84	**1 (24)**	42	▲¹¹ **4. Purple Rain** **[S]**	Warner 25110
			movie is a semi-autobiographical story about Prince's career	
			When Doves Cry (1)/*Let's Go Crazy* (1)/*Purple Rain* (2)/	
			I Would Die 4 U (8)	
5/11/85	**1 (3)**	27	▲² **5. Around the World in a Day**	Paisley P. 25286
			Raspberry Beret (2)/*Pop Life* (7)	

DATE	POS	WKS	ARTIST—RECORD TITLE	LABEL & NO.
4/19/86	3	17	▲ **6. Parade** [S] music from the movie *Under the Cherry Moon* *Kiss* (1) **PRINCE:**	Paisley P. 25395
4/18/87	6	12	▲ **7. Sign "O" The Times** *Sign 'O' The Times* (3)/*U Got The Look* (2)/ *I Could Never Take The Place Of Your Man* (10)	Paisley P. 25577 [2]
6/4/88	11	9	● 8. Lovesexy *Alphabet St.* (8)	Paisley P. 25720
7/8/89	1 (6)	17	▲² 9. Batman [S] *Batdance* (1)	Warner 25936
9/8/90	6	8	● 10. Graffiti Bridge [S] features performances by The Time, Tevin Campbell, George Clinton and Mavis Staples *Thieves In The Temple* (6) **PRINCE & THE NEW POWER GENERATION:**	Paisley P. 27493
10/19/91	3	26	▲² **11. Diamonds And Pearls** album cover is a hologram *Cream* (1)/*Diamonds And Pearls* (3)	Paisley P. 25379
10/31/92	5	6	▲ **12. (untitled)** released on Paisley Park 45123 with inexplicit edit of "Sexy M.F." *7* (7)	Paisley P. 45037
10/2/93	19	2	▲ 13. The Hits/The B-Sides [G] **PRINCE** of the 56 tracks, 6 are previously unreleased; 18 are rare B- sides	Paisley P. 45440 [3]
9/3/94	15	4	● 14. Come [E] **PRINCE (1958-1993)**	Warner 45700
			PROCLAIMERS, The Pop duo of twin brothers Craig and Charlie Reid (born 3/5/62) from Edinburgh, Scotland.	
8/7/93	31	3	● Sunshine On Leith originally charted for 11 weeks; peaked at position 125 on 5/6/89 for 2 weeks; re-entered on 6/5/93 on Chrysalis 21668 *I'm Gonna Be (500 Miles)* (3)	Chrysalis 41668
			PROCOL HARUM British rock group formed in 1967 by Gary Brooker (vocals, piano) and lyricist Keith Reid. Included Matthew Fisher (organ), Dave Knights (bass), Ray Royer (guitar) and Bobby Harrison (drums). Royer and Harrison left after recording of "Whiter Shade Of Pale"; replaced by Robin Trower and Barry J. Wilson (died 1989). Knights and Fisher left in early 1969; bassist Chris Copping added. Trower left in mid-1971; replaced by Dave Ball. Bassist Alan Cartright added while Copping switched to keyboards. Ball left in mid-1972; replaced by Mick Grabham (ex-Cochise). Cartright left in mid- 1976; Copping moved to bass; keyboardist Pete Solley joined. Band split up in 1977. Reunited in 1991 with Brooker, Reid, Fisher and Trower. In Latin "procol" means beyond these things.	
12/7/68	24	7	1. Shine On Brightly	A&M 4151
5/31/69	32	5	2. A Salty Dog	A&M 4179
8/1/70	34	6	3. Home	A&M 4261
5/22/71	32	5	4. Broken Barricades	A&M 4294
5/20/72	5	19	● **5. Procol Harum Live In Concert with the Edmonton Symphony Orchestra** [L]	A&M 4335
4/21/73	21	7	6. Grand Hotel	Chrysalis 1037

DATE	POS	WKS	ARTIST—RECORD TITLE	LABEL & NO.
			PROVINE, Dorothy	
			Born on 1/20/37 in Deadwood, South Dakota. Portrayed songstress Pinky Pinkham in the TV series "The Roaring Twenties" (1960-62).	
9/25/61	34	4	The Roaring 20's	Warner 1394
			medleys of 30 songs from the '20s	
			PRYOR, Richard	
			Born on 12/1/40 in Peoria, Illinois. Ribald comedian/actor. In movies *Stir Crazy*, *Silver Streak*, *Superman III* and many others. Diagnosed with multiple sclerosis in 1986.	
8/17/74	29	8	● 1. That Nigger's Crazy [C]	Partee 2404
9/6/75	12	8	▲ 2. Is It Something I Said? [C]	Reprise 2227
10/23/76	22	7	● 3. Bicentennial Nigger [C]	Warner 2960
2/10/79	32	3	● 4. Wanted [C]	Warner 3364 [2]
5/1/82	21	7	5. Richard Pryor Live On The Sunset Strip [C-S]	Warner 3660
			filmed "live" at the Hollywood Palladium	
			PSYCHEDELIC FURS	
			New York-based, British techno-rock group. Formed in 1978 by brothers Richard (vocals) and Tim Butler (bass), and John Ashton (guitar). Richard Butler formed Love Spit Love in 1994.	
3/28/87	29	11	Midnight To Midnight	Columbia 40466
			PUBLIC ENEMY	
			Rap group led by Chuck D. (Carlton Ridenhauer). Includes Flavor Flav (William Drayton), DJ Terminator X (Norman Rogers) and Professor Griff (Richard Griffin). Disbanded briefly in June 1989 due to controversy over anti-semitic remarks Griffin made. Griffin left band at end of 1989. Flavor Flav was arrested on 11/1/93 for a shooting incident in the Bronx.	
4/28/90	10	15	▲ **1. Fear Of A Black Planet**	Def Jam 45413
10/19/91	4	18	▲ **2. Apocalypse 91 ... The Enemy Strikes Black**	Def Jam 47374
10/3/92	13	3	● 3. Greatest Misses	Def Jam 53014
			CD includes bonus track	
9/10/94	14	2	● 4. Muse Sick-N-Hour Mess Age	Def Jam 523362
			PUCKETT, Gary, And The Union Gap	
			Singer/guitarist Gary Puckett (born 10/17/42, Hibbing, Minnesota) formed The Union Gap in San Diego in 1967; named after the town of Union Gap, Washington. Included Kerry Chater (bass), Paul Whitebread (drums), Dwight Bement (sax) and Gary Withem (keyboards).	
3/30/68	22	8	1. Woman, Woman	Columbia 9612
			THE UNION GAP Featuring Gary Puckett	
			Woman, Woman (4)	
6/29/68	21	11	● 2. Young Girl	Columbia 9664
			Young Girl (2)	
11/23/68	20	10	3. Incredible	Columbia 9715
			Lady Willpower (2)/*Over You* (7)	
			PURE PRAIRIE LEAGUE	
			Country-rock group formed in Cincinnati in 1971. Numerous personnel changes. Craig Fuller, guitarist/ vocalist from 1971-75; joined Little Feat by 1988. Country singer Vince Gill was lead singer from late 1979-83.	
5/17/75	34	3	● 1. Bustin' Out	RCA 4769
6/21/75	24	6	2. Two Lane Highway	RCA 0933
3/20/76	33	3	3. If The Shoe Fits	RCA 1247

DATE	POS	WKS	ARTIST—RECORD TITLE	LABEL & NO.
7/12/80	37	3	4. Firin' Up *Let Me Love You Tonight* (10)	Casablanca 7212
			PURSELL, Bill	

4/13/63	28	6	Pianist from Tulare, California. Appeared with the Nashville Symphony Orchestra. Taught musical composition at Vanderbilt University.
			Our Winter Love [I]
			    arrangements by Bill Justis; orchestra directed by Grady Martin
			    Our Winter Love (9)
				Columbia 1992

Q

DATE	POS	WKS	ARTIST—RECORD TITLE	LABEL & NO.
			QUARTERFLASH	
			Rock group from Portland, Oregon, led by the husband-and-wife team of Marv (guitar) and Rindy (vocals, saxophone) Ross. Originally known as Seafood Mama.	
12/12/81	8	21	▲ **1. Quarterflash** *Harden My Heart* (3)	Geffen 2003
8/6/83	34	4	2. Take Another Picture	Geffen 4011
			QUATRO, Suzi	
5/12/79	37	5	Rock singer born on 6/3/50 in Detroit. Moved to England in 1970; signed with Mickie Most's RAK label. Played Leather Tuscadero on TV's "Happy Days" in 1977. Her older sister Patti was a bassist with Fanny. If You Knew Suzi ... *Stumblin' In* (4-with Chris Norman)	RSO 3044
			QUEEN	
			Rock group formed in England in 1972: Freddie Mercury (born Fred Bulsara on 9/5/46 in Zanzibar; died on 11/24/91 of AIDS; vocals), Brian May (guitar), John Deacon (bass) and Roger Taylor (drums). May and Taylor had been in the group Smile. Mercury had recorded as Larry Lurex.	
4/5/75	12	10	● 1. Sheer Heart Attack	Elektra 1026
1/24/76	4	28	● **2. A Night At The Opera** *Bohemian Rhapsody* (9)	Elektra 1053
1/15/77	5	8	● **3. A Day At The Races**	Elektra 101
12/3/77	3	21	▲ **4. News Of The World** *We Are The Champions* (4)	Elektra 112
12/9/78	6	11	▲ **5. Jazz**	Elektra 166
7/14/79	16	7	● 6. Queen Live Killers [L]	Elektra 702 [2]

7/19/80	1 (5)	31	▲ **7. The Game**
			    Crazy Little Thing Called Love (1)/
			    Another One Bites The Dust (1)
				Elektra 513

1/10/81	23	7	8. Flash Gordon [S]	Elektra 518
11/14/81	14	13	▲ 9. Greatest Hits [G]	Elektra 564
6/5/82	22	5	● 10. Hot Space	Elektra 60128
3/24/84	23	9	● 11. The Works	Capitol 12322
7/1/89	24	4	12. The Miracle CD includes 3 bonus tracks	Capitol 92357
3/2/91	30	5	● 13. Innuendo	Hollywood 61020

DATE	POS	WKS	ARTIST—RECORD TITLE	LABEL & NO.
3/28/92	4	20	▲² **14. Classic Queen** [G] U.S. version of the U.K. release *Greatest Hits II* *Bohemian Rhapsody* (2)	Hollywood 61311
10/3/92	11	10	▲ 15. Greatest Hits [G]	Hollywood 61265
			QUEENSRYCHE	
			Heavy-metal quintet formed in 1981, in Bellevue, Washington, by high-school classmates: Geoff Tate (vocals), Chris DeGarmo, Michael Wilton, Eddie Jackson and Scott Rockenfield.	
9/22/90	7	48	▲³ **1. Empire** *Silent Lucidity* (9)	EMI 92806
11/23/91	38	1	2. Operation:livecrime [L] package includes CD, a one-hour video and a 44-page booklet; *Operation:mindcrime* performances filmed on location in Wisconsin	EMI 97048
11/5/94	3	3	▲ **3. Promised Land**	EMI 30711
			QUICKSILVER MESSENGER SERVICE	
			San Francisco acid-rock group featuring guitarist John Cipollina (brother of Huey Lewis & The News' bassist Mario Cipollina; died 5/29/89 [age 45] of emphysema) and bassist David Freiberg (joined Jefferson Starship in 1973). Many personnel changes. One-time lead singer Dino Valenti died on 11/16/94 (age 57).	
4/26/69	27	6	● 1. Happy Trails [L] includes several studio tracks	Capitol 120
2/7/70	25	5	2. Shady Grove	Capitol 391
9/5/70	27	8	3. Just For Love	Capitol 498
1/30/71	26	4	4. What About Me	Capitol 630
			QUIET RIOT	
			Heavy-metal rock quartet from Los Angeles: Kevin DuBrow (lead singer), Carlos Cavazo (guitar), Frankie Banali (drums) and Rudy Sarzo (bass; replaced by Chuck Wright in 1985). DuBrow and Wright left group in 1987; replaced by Paul Shortino (vocals) and Sean McNabb (bass).	
7/16/83	1(1)	36	▲⁴ **1. Metal Health** *Cum On Feel The Noize* (5)	Pasha 38443
8/11/84	15	10	▲ 2. Condition Critical	Pasha 39516
9/6/86	31	9	3. QR III	Pasha 40321
			QUINN, Carmel	
			Born in 1931 in Dublin, Ireland. Female singer.	
4/2/55	4	10	**Arthur Godfrey presents Carmel Quinn**	Columbia 629
			# R	
			RABBITT, Eddie	
			Born Edward Thomas Rabbitt on 11/27/44 in Brooklyn; raised in East Orange, New Jersey. Country singer/ songwriter/guitarist. First recorded for 20th Century in 1964. Moved to Nashville in 1968. Became established after Elvis Presley recorded his song "Kentucky Rain."	
9/27/80	19	15	▲ 1. Horizon *Drivin' My Life Away* (5)/*I Love A Rainy Night* (1)	Elektra 276
9/12/81	23	8	● 2. Step By Step *Step By Step* (5)	Elektra 532

DATE	POS	WKS	ARTIST—RECORD TITLE	LABEL & NO.
1/22/83	**31**	7	3. Radio Romance *You And I* (7-with Crystal Gayle)	Elektra 60160
8/7/93	**32**	7	**RADIOHEAD** Rock quintet from Oxford, England: Thom E. Yorke (vocals), brothers Jonny and Colin Greenwood, Ed O'Brien and Phil Selway. ● Pablo Honey	Capitol 81409
6/3/78	**1**(1)	23	**RAFFERTY, Gerry** Born on 4/16/47 in Paisley, Scotland. Singer/songwriter/guitarist. Co-leader of Stealers Wheel. ▲ **1. City to City** *Baker Street* (2)	United Art. 840
6/23/79	**29**	6	● 2. Night Owl	United Art. 958
			RAIDERS — see REVERE, Paul	
10/4/75	**30**	4	**RAINBOW** Hard-rock band led by British guitarist Ritchie Blackmore and bassist Roger Glover, both members of Deep Purple. Fluctuating lineup included vocalists Ronnie James Dio and Joe Lynn Turner, keyboardist Tony Carey and drummer Cozy Powell. Group split up upon re-formation of Deep Purple in 1984. Turner joined Deep Purple in 1990. 1. Ritchie Blackmore's R-A-I-N-B-O-W **BLACKMORE'S RAINBOW**	Oyster 6049
5/29/82	**30**	5	2. Straight Between The Eyes	Mercury 4041
10/29/83	**34**	4	3. Bent Out Of Shape	Mercury 815305
5/14/77	**25**	4	**RAITT, Bonnie** Born on 11/8/49 in Burbank, California. Veteran blues-rock singer/guitarist. Daughter of Broadway actor/singer John Raitt. Winner of four 1989 Grammy Awards for her album *Nick Of Time*. Married actor Michael O'Keefe (*Caddyshack* movie and TV's "Against The Law") on 4/28/91. ● 1. Sweet Forgiveness	Warner 2990
11/10/79	**30**	5	2. The Glow	Warner 3369
4/3/82	**38**	3	3. Green Light	Warner 3630
5/13/89	**1**(3)	40	▲⁴ **4. Nick Of Time** 1989 Album of the Year Grammy Award	Capitol 91268
7/13/91	**2**(2)	58	▲⁴ **5. Luck Of The Draw** *Something To Talk About* (5)	Capitol 96111
4/9/94	**1**(1)	13	▲² **6. Longing In Their Hearts**	Capitol 81427
5/25/63	**34**	4	**RAMIN, Sid, and Orchestra** Born on 1/22/24 in Boston. Conductor/composer/arranger. Won 1961 Academy Award for collaboration on *West Side Story* soundtrack. Music director for TV's "The Patty Duke Show," "The Milton Berle Show" and "Candid Camera." New Thresholds in Sound [I]	RCA 2658
10/15/77	**34**	4	**RAM JAM** East Coast rock quartet led by Bill Bartlett (lead guitarist of The Lemon Pipers). Member Howie Blauvelt played bass in Billy Joel's group, The Hassles; died of a heart attack on 10/25/93 (age 44). Ram Jam	Epic 34885

DATE	POS	WKS	ARTIST—RECORD TITLE	LABEL & NO.
			RANDOLPH, Boots	
			Born Homer Louis Randolph, III, on 6/3/27 in Paducah, Kentucky. Premier Nashville session saxophonist.	
4/22/67	36	4	● Boots with Strings [I]	Monument 18066
			RARE EARTH	
			Nucleus of Detroit rock group: Gil Bridges (saxophone, flute), John Persh (trombone, bass) and Pete Rivera (born Pete Hoorelbeke; drums). Worked as The Sunliners in the '60s. In 1970, added Ed Guzman (percussion) and Ray Monette (replaced guitarist Rob Richards). Mark Olson replaced Kenneth James (keyboards) in 1971. Many changes thereafter. Persh died in 1979 of a staph virus. Olson died of alcohol-related complications in 1982. Guzman died on 7/29/93 (age 49).	
3/14/70	12	28	1. Get Ready	Rare Earth 507
			side 2 is a 21 1/2-minute version of the title song *Get Ready* (4)	
7/18/70	15	18	2. Ecology	Rare Earth 514
			(I Know) I'm Losing You (7)	
8/14/71	28	11	3. One World	Rare Earth 520
			I Just Want To Celebrate (7)	
1/29/72	29	4	4. Rare Earth In Concert [L]	Rare Earth 534 [2]
			RASCALS, The	
			Blue-eyed, soul-pop quartet formed in New York City in 1964. Consisted of Felix Cavaliere, Dino Danelli, Eddie Brigati and Gene Cornish. All except Danelli had been in Joey Dee's Starliters. Brigati and Cornish left in 1971; replaced by Robert Popwell, Buzzy Feiten and Ann Sutton. Group disbanded in 1972. Cavaliere, Cornish and Danelli reunited in June 1988.	
			THE YOUNG RASCALS:	
6/11/66	15	14	● 1. The Young Rascals	Atlantic 8123
			Good Lovin' (1)	
3/18/67	14	24	● 2. Collections	Atlantic 8134
8/19/67	5	21	● **3. Groovin'**	Atlantic 8148
			Groovin' (1)/*A Girl Like You* (10)/*How Can I Be Sure* (4)	
			THE RASCALS:	
3/9/68	9	12	**4. Once Upon A Dream**	Atlantic 8169
7/27/68	1(1)	32	● **5. Time Peace/The Rascals' Greatest Hits** [G]	Atlantic 8190
			A Beautiful Morning (3)	
4/5/69	17	6	● 6. Freedom Suite	Atlantic 901 [2]
			record 2, entitled *Music Music*, is all instrumental *People Got To Be Free* (1)	
			RASPBERRIES	
			Pop-rock band formed in Mentor, Ohio, in 1971: Eric Carmen (lead singer, guitar), Wally Bryson (lead guitar), David Smalley (bass) and Jim Bonfanti (drums). Smalley and Bonfanti replaced by Scott McCarl and Michael McBride in 1974. Carmen went solo in 1975.	
1/20/73	36	4	Fresh	Capitol 11123
			RATT	
			Los Angeles hard-rock quintet: Stephen Pearcy (lead singer), Warren DeMartini (guitar), Robbin Crosby (guitar), Juan Croucier (bass) and Bobby Blotzer (drums; also a member of Contraband in 1991). Pearcy left band in early 1992; formed Arcade.	
6/16/84	7	26	▲³ **1. Out Of The Cellar**	Atlantic 80143
6/29/85	7	18	▲ **2. Invasion Of Your Privacy**	Atlantic 81257
11/1/86	26	7	▲ 3. Dancin' Undercover	Atlantic 81683

DATE	POS	WKS	ARTIST—RECORD TITLE	LABEL & NO.
11/26/88	**17**	13	▲ 4. Reach For The Sky	Atlantic 81929
9/15/90	**23**	6	● 5. Detonator	Atlantic 82127
			RAWLS, Lou	
			Born on 12/1/35 in Chicago. With The Pilgrim Travelers gospel group, 1957-59. Summer replacement TV show "Lou Rawls & The Golddiggers" in 1969. In the movies *Angel Angel, Down We Go* and *Believe In Me*. Voice of many Budweiser beer ads and featured singer in the "Garfield" TV specials.	
5/27/57	**18**	14	1. Too Much!	Capitol 2713
6/18/66	**4**	38	● **2. Lou Rawls Live!** [L]	Capitol 2459
10/8/66	**7**	22	● **3. Lou Rawls Soulin'**	Capitol 2566
3/4/67	**20**	10	4. Lou Rawls Carryin' On!	Capitol 2632
9/9/67	**29**	2	5. That's Lou	Capitol 2756
7/31/76	**7**	12	▲ **6. All Things In Time**	Phil. Int. 33957
			You'll Never Find Another Love Like Mine (2)	
			RAY, Johnnie	
			Born on 1/10/27 in Dallas, Oregon. Died on 2/25/90 of liver failure. Wore hearing aid since age 14. First recorded for Okeh in 1951. Famous for emotion-packed delivery, with R&B influences. Appeared in three movies.	
3/2/57	**19**	2	The Big Beat	Columbia 961
			RAYDIO — see PARKER, Ray Jr.	
			RAY, GOODMAN & BROWN	
			Soul group consisting of Harry Ray (died 10/1/92 [age 45] of a stroke; tenor), Al Goodman (bass) and Billy Brown (falsetto). Formerly known as The Moments.	
3/1/80	**17**	11	● Ray, Goodman & Brown	Polydor 6240
			Special Lady (5)	
			READY FOR THE WORLD	
			Black sextet from Flint, Michigan, formed in 1982: Melvin Riley, Jr. (lead singer), Gordon Strozier, Gregory Potts, Willie Triplett, John Eaton and Gerald Valentine.	
8/31/85	**17**	30	▲ 1. Ready For The World	MCA 5594
			Oh Sheila (1)	
2/14/87	**32**	5	● 2. Long Time Coming	MCA 5829
			Love You Down (9)	
			REDBONE, Leon	
			Blues and ragtime-styled vocalist. Rose to fame in the mid-1970s with appearances on TV's "Saturday Night Live." Baritone voice of several TV commercials.	
2/26/77	**38**	4	Double Time	Warner 2971
			REDDING, Otis	
			Born on 9/9/41 in Dawson, Georgia. Killed in a plane crash in Lake Monona in Madison, Wisconsin, on 12/10/67. Soul singer/songwriter/producer/pianist. First recorded with Johnny Jenkins & The Pinetoppers on Confederate in 1960. Own label, Jotis. Plane crash also killed four members of The Bar-Kays. Inducted into the Rock and Roll Hall of Fame in 1989.	
7/22/67	**36**	3	1. King & Queen	Stax 716
			OTIS REDDING & CARLA THOMAS	
9/9/67	**32**	4	2. Otis Redding Live In Europe [L]	Volt 416
1/27/68	**9**	19	**3. History Of Otis Redding** [G]	Volt 418
3/30/68	**4**	20	**4. The Dock Of The Bay**	Volt 419
			(Sittin' On) The Dock Of The Bay (1)	

DATE	POS	WKS	ARTIST—RECORD TITLE	LABEL & NO.
9/26/70	**16**	8	● 5. Monterey International Pop Festival [S-L] **OTIS REDDING/THE JIMI HENDRIX EXPERIENCE** recorded June 1967; featured in the movie *Monterey Pop*	Reprise 2029
			REDDY, Helen	
			Born on 10/25/41 in Melbourne, Australia. Family was in show business; Reddy made stage debut at age four. Own TV series in the early '60s. Migrated to New York in 1966. To Los Angeles in 1968. Acted in the movies *Airport 1975*, *Pete's Dragon* and *Sgt. Pepper's Lonely Hearts Club Band*.	
1/6/73	**14**	17	▲ 1. I Am Woman *I Am Woman* (1)	Capitol 11068
8/25/73	**8**	15	● **2. Long Hard Climb** *Delta Dawn* (1)/*Leave Me Alone (Ruby Red Dress)* (3)	Capitol 11213
5/4/74	**11**	14	● 3. Love Song For Jeffrey *You And Me Against The World* (9)	Capitol 11284
11/23/74	**8**	16	● **4. Free And Easy** *Angie Baby* (1)	Capitol 11348
8/9/75	**11**	10	● 5. No Way To Treat A Lady *Ain't No Way To Treat A Lady* (8)	Capitol 11418
12/20/75	**5**	11	▲² **6. Helen Reddy's Greatest Hits** [G]	Capitol 11467
8/14/76	**16**	8	● 7. Music, Music	Capitol 11547
			RED HOT CHILI PEPPERS	
			Los Angeles-based, rap-styled rock foursome: Anthony Kiedis (vocals), Michael "Flea" Balzary (bass), Hillel Slovak (guitar) and Jack Irons (drums). Slovak died of a heroin overdose on 6/25/88 (age 26); replaced by John Frusciante. Irons left in 1988 and later joined Eleven; replaced by Chad Smith. Frusciante left in May 1992; replaced by Zander Schloss (Thelonious Monster), then by Arik Marshall, then by Jesse Tobias and finally by Dave Navarro (Jane's Addiction) in September 1993. Kiedis appeared in the movie *Point Break*.	
10/12/91	**3**	46	▲³ **1. Blood Sugar Sex Magik** *Under The Bridge* (2)	Warner 26681
10/17/92	**22**	5	▲ 2. What Hits!? [K]	EMI 94762
			REDMAN	
			Rapper from Newark, New Jersey. Discovered by Erick Sermon of EPMD.	
12/10/94	**13**	1	● Dare Iz A Darkside	RAL 523846
			REED, Lou	
			Born Louis Firbank on 3/2/42 in Freeport, Long Island, New York. Lead singer/songwriter of the New York seminal-rock band, Velvet Underground. Appeared in the movie *One Trick Pony*.	
3/24/73	**29**	9	1. Transformer produced by David Bowie	RCA 4807
10/19/74	**10**	7	**2. Sally Can't Dance**	RCA 0611
4/8/89	**40**	1	3. New York	Sire 25829
			REESE, Della	
			Born Delloreese Patricia Early on 7/6/31 in Detroit. With Mahalia Jackson gospel troupe from 1945-49; with Erskine Hawkins in the early '50s. Solo since 1957. Actress/singer on many TV shows. Appeared in the 1958 movie *Let's Rock* and the 1989 movie *Harlem Nights*. Own series "Della" in 1970. Played Della Rogers on the TV series "Chico & The Man" from 1976-78. On TV's "The Royal Family."	
3/7/60	**35**	2	Della	RCA 2157

DATE	POS	WKS	ARTIST—RECORD TITLE		LABEL & NO.
			REEVES, Jim		
			Born James Travis Reeves on 8/20/24 in Panola County, Texas; killed in a plane crash on 7/31/64. Prominent country singer. Joined the *Grand Ole Opry* in 1955. Own TV series in 1957. In the movie *Kimberly Jim* in 1963. Posthumously continued to have country hits into the '80s.		
5/23/60	**18**	13	1. He'll Have To Go		RCA 2223
			He'll Have To Go (2)		
9/5/64	**30**	2	2. Moonlight and Roses		RCA 2854
9/19/64	**9**	18	● 3. **The Best Of Jim Reeves**	**[G]**	RCA 2890
7/16/66	**21**	10	● 4. **Distant Drums**	**[K]**	RCA 3542
			R.E.M.		
			Athens, Georgia, rock quartet formed in 1980: Michael Stipe (vocals), Peter Buck (guitar), Mike Mills (bass) and Bill Berry (drums). R.E.M. is abbreviation for Rapid Eye Movement, the dream stage of sleep. Developed huge following with college audiences in the early '80s as one of the first "alternative-rock" bands. Buck, Mills and Berry recorded with Warren Zevon as The Hindu Love Gods in 1990.		
7/30/83	**36**	3	● 1. Murmur		I.R.S. 70604
5/26/84	**27**	6	● 2. Reckoning		I.R.S. 70044
7/6/85	**28**	14	● 3. Fables Of The Reconstruction		I.R.S. 5592
9/6/86	**21**	12	● 4. Lifes Rich Pageant		I.R.S. 5783
10/3/87	**10**	20	▲ 5. **R.E.M. No. 5: Document**		I.R.S. 42059
			The One I Love (9)		
11/26/88	**12**	27	▲^{2} 6. Green		Warner 25795
			Stand (6)		
3/30/91	**1**(2)	48	▲^{4} 7. **Out Of Time**		Warner 26496
			Losing My Religion (4)/*Shiny Happy People* (10)		
10/24/92	**2**(2)	24	▲^{4} 8. **Automatic For The People**		Warner 45138
			jewel box-only CD and cassette catalog number is 45055		
10/15/94	**1**(2)	20+	▲^{2} 9. **Monster**		Warner 45740
			REO SPEEDWAGON		
			Rock quintet from Champaign, Illinois: Kevin Cronin (lead vocals, rhythm guitar), Gary Richrath (lead guitar), Neal Doughty (keyboards), Bruce Hall (bass) and Alan Gratzer (drums). Gratzer left in 1988; replaced by former Santana drummer Graham Lear. 1990 lineup: Cronin, Doughty and Hall, joined by new members Bryan Hitt, Dave Amato and Jesse Harms (left by 1991). Group named after a 1911 fire truck.		
6/3/78	**29**	5	▲ 1. You can Tune a piano, but you can't Tuna fish		Epic 35082
9/8/79	**33**	5	● 2. Nine Lives		Epic 35988
12/27/80	**1**(15)	50	▲^{7} 3. **Hi Infidelity**		Epic 36844
			Keep On Loving You (1)/*Take It On The Run* (5)		
7/10/82	**7**	16	▲ 4. **Good Trouble**		Epic 38100
			Keep The Fire Burnin' (7)		
2/2/85	**7**	21	▲^{2} 5. **Wheels are turnin'**		Epic 39593
			Can't Fight This Feeling (1)		
3/14/87	**28**	7	● 6. Life As We Know It		Epic 40444
			RETURN TO FOREVER		
			Jazz-rock band: Chick Corea (keyboards), Stanley Clarke (bass), Lenny White (drums) and Al DiMeola (guitar).		
11/23/74	**32**	4	1. Where Have I Known You Before	[I]	Polydor 6509
4/5/75	**39**	2	2. No Mystery	[I]	Polydor 6512
5/22/76	**35**	3	● 3. Romantic Warrior	[I]	Columbia 34076

DATE	POS	WKS	ARTIST—RECORD TITLE	LABEL & NO.
5/14/77	38	2	4. Musicmagic	Columbia 34682

REVERE, Paul, And The Raiders

Pop-rock group formed in Portland, Oregon, in 1960. Group featured Paul Revere (born 1/7/42, Boise, Idaho; keyboards) and Mark Lindsay (lead singer). To Los Angeles in 1965. On daily ABC-TV show "Where The Action Is" in 1965. Own TV show "Happening" in 1968. Lindsay and Raider member, Keith Allison, recorded with Steve Alaimo as The Unknowns in 1966. Country star Freddy Weller with group, 1967-71. Group had many personnel changes.

DATE	POS	WKS	ARTIST—RECORD TITLE	LABEL & NO.
3/12/66	5	19	● 1. Just Like Us!	Columbia 9251
7/2/66	9	15	● 2. Midnight Ride	Columbia 9308
			Kicks (4)	
1/14/67	9	17	● 3. The Spirit Of '67	Columbia 9395
			Hungry (6)/Good Thing (4)	
5/27/67	9	19	● 4. Greatest Hits [G]	Columbia 9462
9/23/67	25	7	5. Revolution!	Columbia 9521
			Weller joins group as lead guitarist	
			Him or Me-What's It Gonna Be? (5)	
7/3/71	19	11	6. Indian Reservation	Columbia 30768
			RAIDERS	
			Indian Reservation (1)	

REYNOLDS, Debbie

Born Mary Reynolds on 4/1/32 in El Paso, Texas. Leading lady of '50s musicals; later in comedies. Married Eddie Fisher on 9/26/55; divorced in 1959. Mother of actress/author Carrie Fisher.

DATE	POS	WKS	ARTIST—RECORD TITLE	LABEL & NO.
6/11/66	23	4	The Singing Nun [S]	MGM 7
			movie is a fictionalized story about the late Soeur Sourire	

RHEIMS, Robert

Los Angeles-based arranger/conductor.

DATE	POS	WKS	ARTIST—RECORD TITLE	LABEL & NO.
1/5/59	25	1	1. Merry Christmas in Carols [X-I]	Rheims 6006
			Christmas charts: 16/'63, 67/'66, 23/'67	
1/4/60	39	1	2. We Wish You A Merry Christmas [X]	Rheims 6008
			The ROBERT RHEIMS Choraliers	

RHODES, Emitt

Born in 1949 in Hawthorne, California. Lead singer of The Merry-Go-Round.

DATE	POS	WKS	ARTIST—RECORD TITLE	LABEL & NO.
1/9/71	29	7	Emitt Rhodes	Dunhill 50089

RHYTHM HERITAGE

Los Angeles studio group assembled by prolific producers Steve Barri and Michael Omartian (keyboards). Vocals by Oren and Luther Waters. Omartian was in the band Gator Creek with Kenny Loggins.

DATE	POS	WKS	ARTIST—RECORD TITLE	LABEL & NO.
4/24/76	40	2	Disco-Fied [I]	ABC 934
			Theme From S.W.A.T. (1)	

RICH, Charlie

Born on 12/14/32 in Colt, Arkansas. Rockabilly-country singer/pianist/songwriter. First played jazz and blues. Own jazz group, The Velvetones, mid-1950s, while in U.S. Air Force. Session work with Sun Records in 1958. Known as the "Silver Fox."

DATE	POS	WKS	ARTIST—RECORD TITLE	LABEL & NO.
12/8/73	8	32	▲ 1. Behind Closed Doors	Epic 32247
			The Most Beautiful Girl (1)	
3/30/74	36	2	● 2. There Won't Be Anymore [E]	RCA 0433
4/6/74	24	11	● 3. Very Special Love Songs	Epic 32531

DATE	POS	WKS	ARTIST—RECORD TITLE	LABEL & NO.
12/28/74	**25**	9	4. The Silver Fox	Epic 33250
			RICHARDS, Keith	
			Born on 12/18/43 in Dartford, England. Lead guitarist of The Rolling Stones. Dropped the "s" from his last name in the '60s and '70s. Married model Patti Hansen on 12/18/83.	
10/29/88	**24**	7	● Talk Is Cheap	Virgin 90973
			RICHIE, Lionel	
			Born on 6/20/49 in Tuskegee, Alabama. Grew up on the campus of Tuskegee Institute where his grandfather worked. Former lead singer of The Commodores. Appeared in the movie *Thank God It's Friday* (1978).	
10/30/82	**3**	39	▲⁴ **1. Lionel Richie**	Motown 6007
			Truly (1)/*You Are* (4)/*My Love* (5)	
11/12/83	**1**(3)	78	▲¹⁰ **2. Can't Slow Down**	Motown 6059
			1984 Album of the Year Grammy Award	
			All Night Long (All Night) (1)/*Running With The Night* (7)/ *Hello* (1)/*Stuck On You* (3)/*Penny Lover* (8)	
8/30/86	**1**(2)	38	▲⁴ **3. Dancing On The Ceiling**	Motown 6158
			Dancing On The Ceiling (2)/*Love Will Conquer All* (9)/ *Ballerina Girl* (7)	
5/23/92	**19**	9	▲ 4. Back To Front [G]	Motown 6338
			includes 4 hits Richie recorded while with The Commodores	
			RICHTER, Sviatoslav	
			Born in Zhitomir, Ukraine, Russia, in 1915. Classical pianist.	
12/12/60	**5**	20	**Brahms: Piano Concerto No. 2** [I]	RCA 2466
			with the Chicago Symphony Orchestra conducted by Erich Leinsdorf	
			RIDDLE, Nelson	
			Born on 6/1/21 in Oradell, New Jersey; died on 10/6/85. Trombonist/arranger with Charlie Spivak and Tommy Dorsey in the '40s. One of the most in-demand of all arranger/conductors for many top artists, including Frank Sinatra (several classic '50s albums), Nat King Cole, Ella Mae Morse, and more recently, Linda Ronstadt. Also arranger/musical director for many movies.	
5/27/57	**20**	1	1. Hey ... Let Yourself Go! [I]	Capitol 814
2/17/58	**20**	1	2. C'mon ... Get Happy! [I]	Capitol 893
			RIGHTEOUS BROTHERS, The	
			Blue-eyed soul duo: Bill Medley (born 9/19/40, Santa Ana, California; baritone) and Bobby Hatfield (born 8/10/40, Beaver Dam, Wisconsin; tenor). Formed duo in 1962. First recorded as The Paramours for Smash in 1962. On "Hullabaloo" and "Shindig" TV shows. Split up from 1968-74. Medley went solo; replaced by Jimmy Walker (The Knickerbockers); rejoined Hatfield in 1974.	
2/6/65	**4**	19	**1. You've Lost That Lovin' Feelin'**	Philles 4007
			You've Lost That Lovin' Feelin' (1)	
2/6/65	**11**	9	2. Right Now! [E]	Moonglow 1001
2/6/65	**14**	10	3. Some Blue-Eyed Soul [E]	Moonglow 1002
7/17/65	**9**	18	**4. Just Once In My Life...**	Philles 4008
			Just Once In My Life (9)/*Unchained Melody* (4)	
8/7/65	**39**	1	5. This Is New! [E]	Moonglow 1003
2/5/66	**16**	11	6. Back To Back	Philles 4009
			Ebb Tide (5)	
5/7/66	**7**	19	● **7. Soul & Inspiration**	Verve 5001
			(You're My) Soul And Inspiration (1)	

DATE	POS	WKS	ARTIST—RECORD TITLE	LABEL & NO.
10/15/66	32	6	8. Go Ahead And Cry	Verve 5004
11/11/67	21	5	● 9. Greatest Hits [G]	Verve 5020
			Philles and Moonglow label hits; a CD reissue of album, with 10 additional cuts on Verve 823119, re-entered chart in 1990	
9/28/74	27	8	10. Give It To The People	Haven 9201
			Rock And Roll Heaven (3)	
9/29/90	31	7	11. Greatest Hits [G-R]	Verve 823119
			contains the duo's entire 1967 Greatest Hits album plus 10 more songs	
			RILEY, Jeannie C.	
			Born Jeanne Carolyn Stephenson on 10/19/45 in Anson, Texas. Country singer.	
11/2/68	12	12	● Harper Valley P.T.A.	Plantation 1
			all songs about characters mentioned in the title song	
			Harper Valley P.T.A. (1)	
			RIPERTON, Minnie	
			Born on 11/8/47 in Chicago; died of cancer on 7/12/79 in Los Angeles. Recorded as Andrea Davis on Chess in 1966. Lead singer of the rock-R&B sextet Rotary Connection from 1967-70. In Stevie Wonder's backup group Wonderlove in 1973.	
10/26/74	4	18	● **1. Perfect Angel**	Epic 32561
			Lovin' You (1)	
6/14/75	18	8	2. Adventures In Paradise	Epic 33454
8/25/79	29	4	3. Minnie	Capitol 11936
9/27/80	35	4	4. Love Lives Forever	Capitol 12097
			recordings from 1978 with new accompaniment featuring George Benson, Peabo Bryson, Roberta Flack, Michael Jackson, Patrice Rushen, Stevie Wonder and many others	
			RITCHARD, Cyril — see CHILDREN'S ALBUMS	
			RITCHIE FAMILY, The	
			Philadelphia disco group named for arranger/producer Ritchie Rome. Group featured various session singers and musicians.	
10/2/76	30	7	Arabian Nights	Marlin 2201
			RITENOUR, Lee	
			Born on 1/11/52 in Los Angeles. Guitarist/composer/arranger. Top session guitarist. Has appeared on more than 200 albums. Nicknamed "Captain Fingers." Member of jazz outfits Brass Fever and Fourplay.	
6/13/81	26	7	"Rit"	Elektra 331
			5 of 10 tracks feature vocals	
			RIVERS, Joan	
			Born on 6/8/33 in New York City. Popular comedienne. Guest host for Johnny Carson, 1983-86; host of "The Late Show," 1986-87. Currently hosts own TV talk show. Directed the 1978 movie Rabbit Test.	
5/14/83	22	6	What Becomes A Semi-Legend Most? [C]	Geffen 4007
			RIVERS, Johnny	
			Born John Ramistella on 11/7/42 in New York City; raised in Baton Rouge. Rock-and-roll singer/guitarist/ songwriter/producer. Recorded with The Spades for Suede in 1957. Named Johnny Rivers by DJ Alan Freed in 1958. To Los Angeles in 1961. Rivers recorded for 12 different labels (1958-64) before his smash debut on Imperial. Began own Soul City label in 1966. Recorded Christian music in the early '80s.	
7/11/64	12	20	1. Johnny Rivers At The Whisky a Go Go [L]	Imperial 12264
			Memphis (2)	

DATE	POS	WKS	ARTIST—RECORD TITLE	LABEL & NO.
12/12/64	**38**	1	2. Here We a Go Go Again! [L]	Imperial 12274
7/31/65	**21**	6	3. Meanwhile Back At The Whisky a Go Go [L]	Imperial 12284
			Seventh Son (7)	
2/4/66	**33**	5	4. Changes	Imperial 12334
			Poor Side Of Town (1)	
11/5/66	**29**	9	● 5. Johnny Rivers' Golden Hits [G]	Imperial 12324
7/8/67	**14**	8	6. Rewind	Imperial 12341
			Baby I Need Your Lovin' (3)/*The Tracks Of My Tears* (10)	
7/27/68	**5**	16	● **7. Realization**	Imperial 12372
7/12/69	**26**	10	● 8. A Touch Of Gold [G]	Imperial 12427
			ROB BASE & D.J. E-Z ROCK	
			Harlem rap duo: Robert Ginyard with DJ Rodney "Skip" Bryce.	
11/12/88	**31**	8	▲ It Takes Two	Profile 1267
			ROBBINS, Marty	
			Born Martin David Robinson on 9/26/25 in Glendale, Arizona; died of a heart attack on 12/8/82. Country singer/guitarist/songwriter. Own radio show with K-Bar Cowboys, late '40s. Own TV show, "Western Caravan," KPHO-Phoenix, 1951. First recorded for Columbia in 1952. Regular on the *Grand Ole Opry* since 1953. Own Robbins label in 1958. Raced stock cars. Movies: *Road to Nashville* and *Guns of a Stranger*. Robbins, Eddy Arnold, Jim Reeves and Johnny Cash were the first major country stars to have a big impact on the pop charts.	
12/28/59	**6**	36	▲ **1. Gunfighter Ballads and Trail Songs**	Columbia 1349
			El Paso (1)	
1/9/61	**21**	2	2. More Gunfighter Ballads and Trail Songs	Columbia 1481
1/12/63	**35**	1	3. Devil Woman	Columbia 1918
			ROBERTSON, Robbie	
			Born Jaime Robbie Robertson on 7/5/44 in Toronto. Vocalist/bassist/composer/producer. Joined Ronnie Hawkins's Hawks in 1960, which evolved into The Band in 1967. Group disbanded Thanksgiving Day, 1976. Produced movie soundtracks. Appeared in the movie *Carny*. Wrote Joan Baez's 1971 hit "The Night They Drove Old Dixie Down."	
12/19/87	**38**	3	● Robbie Robertson	Geffen 24160
			guest musicians: BoDeans, Peter Gabriel, Maria McKee (Lone Justice) and U2	
			ROBINSON, Smokey	
			Born William Robinson on 2/19/40 in Detroit. Formed The Miracles (then called The Matadors) at Northern High School in 1955. First recorded for End in 1958. Married Miracles member Claudette Rogers in 1963; later divorced. Left The Miracles on 1/29/72. Wrote dozens of hit songs for Motown artists. Vice President of Motown Records, 1985-88. Inducted into the Rock and Roll Hall of Fame in 1987. Won 1989 Living Legends Grammy Award.	
6/14/75	**36**	3	1. A Quiet Storm	Tamla 337
1/5/80	**17**	11	2. Where There's Smoke..	Tamla 366
			Cruisin' (4)	
4/5/80	**14**	12	3. Warm Thoughts	Tamla 367
4/4/81	**10**	17	● **4. Being With You**	Tamla 375
			Being With You (2)	
3/13/82	**33**	4	5. Yes It's You Lady	Tamla 6001
5/23/87	**26**	17	● 6. One Heartbeat	Motown 6226
			Just To See Her (8)/*One Heartbeat* (10)	

DATE	POS	WKS	ARTIST—RECORD TITLE	LABEL & NO.
11/29/80	27	10	**ROCKPILE** British pop-rock quartet: Dave Edmunds, Nick Lowe, Billy Bremner, Terry Williams. Seconds Of Pleasure *includes a 7" EP of Edmunds and Lowe singing 4 Everly Brothers tunes*	Columbia 36886
3/3/84	15	12	**ROCKWELL** Born Kennedy Gordy on 3/15/64 in Detroit. Son of Motown chairman, Berry Gordy, Jr. ● Somebody's Watching Me *Somebody's Watching Me (2)*	Motown 6052
12/16/57	15	3	**RODGERS, Jimmie** Born James Frederick Rodgers on 9/18/33 in Camas, Washington. Vocalist/guitarist/pianist. Formed first group while in the Air Force. Own NBC-TV variety series in 1959. Career hampered following mysterious assault on the San Diego Freeway on 12/1/67, which left him with a fractured skull. Returned to performing a year later. Starred in movies *The Little Shepherd of Kingdom Come* and *Back Door to Hell.* Jimmie Rodgers *Honeycomb (1)/Kisses Sweeter Than Wine (3)*	Roulette 25020
4/26/69 1/17/70	25 21	8 13	**ROE, Tommy** Born on 5/9/42 in Atlanta. Pop-rock singer/guitarist/composer. Formed band The Satins at Brown High School; worked local dances in the late '50s. Group recorded for Judd in 1960. Moved to Britain in the mid-1960s; returned in 1969. 1. Dizzy *Dizzy (1)* 2. 12 In A Roe/A Collection of Tommy Roe's Greatest Hits [G] *Jam Up Jelly Tight (8)*	 ABC 683 ABC 700
10/24/81 1/23/88 11/13/93	26 35 39	6 5 1	**ROGER** Born Roger Troutman in Hamilton, Ohio. Leader of the family funk group Zapp (Roger, Lester, Tony and Larry). Worked with Sly Stone and George Clinton. Father of male singer Lynch. ● 1. The Many Facets Of Roger ● 2. Unlimited! *I Want To Be Your Man (3)* ● 3. All The Greatest Hits [G] **ZAPP & ROGER**	Warner 3594 Reprise 25496 Reprise 45143
12/4/61	37	3	**ROGERS, Eric, and his Orchestra** Born on 9/25/21 in Halifax, Yorkshire, England. The Percussive Twenties [I]	London P. 4 44006

Pearl Jam's powerful 1993 set, *Vs.*, reached No. 1 and sold more than 5 million copies in a little over a year. The Seattle group daringly opted to release the album without any accompanying music videos, a nearly unheard-of practice in the MTV-dominated '90s.

Peter, Paul & Mary's fifth and final album to reach the Top 10 was 1965's *A Song Will Rise*. The much-loved folk trio temporarily disbanded in the early '70s to pursue solo careers but reunited by 1978. In 1987, the trio released *No Easy Walk to Freedom* on the baby-boomer-conscious Gold Castle label.

Pink Floyd's 1967 debut album, *The Piper At The Gates Of Dawn*, (titled simply *Pink Floyd* in the U.S.) was the group's only album to fully feature the singing and playing of band founder Syd Barrett. The enormously popular group replaced him with guitarist David Gilmour in 1968 and continued to enjoy great success. Barrett was the subject of "Shine On You Crazy Diamond" from 1975's *Wish You Were Here*.

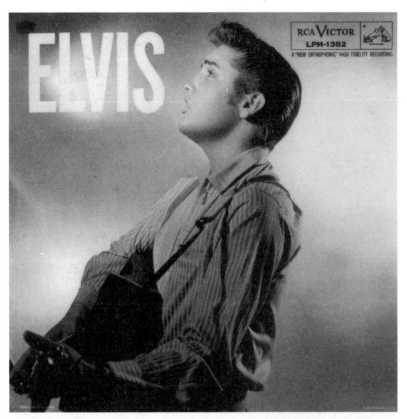

Elvis Presley's second album, released in 1956 and simply titled *Elvis*, followed the lead of its predecessor and climbed to the No. 1 spot, where it stayed for five weeks. Included on it was his No. 2 hit "Love Me." The disc was digitally remastered and restored to mono by RCA in 1984.

Prince's resounding success with the 1984 film *Purple Rain* and its sound-track resulted in several other similar projects, including 1986's *Parade* (featuring music from the film *Under the Cherry Moon*) and 1990's *Graffiti Bridge*.

Queen's entire catalog of albums was reissued on compact disc by the Disney-owned Hollywood Records label in the early '90s. Colorful lead singer Freddie Mercury, whose vocals brought the quartet 13 Top 40 hits between 1975–84, died of AIDS in 1992.

Kenny Rogers's follow-up to his 1978 album, *Love Or Something Like It*, was *The Gambler*. The title track on this later album provided him with a Top 20 hit and a new career as an actor in the film *The Gambler* and its two sequels.

DATE	POS	WKS	ARTIST—RECORD TITLE		LABEL & NO.
			ROGERS, Kenny		
			Born Kenneth Donald Rogers on 8/21/38 in Houston. With high-school band The Scholars in 1958. Bass player of jazz group The Bobby Doyle Trio; recorded for Columbia. First recorded for Carlton in 1958. In Kirby Stone Four and The New Christy Minstrels, mid-1960s. Formed and fronted The First Edition in 1967. Original lineup included Thelma Camacho, Mike Settle, Terry Williams and Mickey Jones. All but Jones were members of The New Christy Minstrels. Group hosted own syndicated TV variety show "Rollin" in 1972. Rogers split from group in 1973. Starred in movies *The Gambler I, II & III, Coward of the County* and *Six Pack*. Married Marianne Gordon of TV's "Hee Haw" in 1977.		
5/2/70	26	6	1. Something's Burning		Reprise 6385
			KENNY ROGERS AND THE FIRST EDITION		
6/11/77	30	4	● 2. Kenny Rogers		United Art. 689
			Lucille (5)		
9/24/77	39	2	● 3. Daytime Friends		United Art. 754
3/18/78	33	4	▲ 4. Ten Years Of Gold	[G]	United Art. 835
			side 1: new versions of his First Edition hits		
2/24/79	12	21	▲ 5. The Gambler		United Art. 934
			She Believes In Me (5)		
10/6/79	5	26	▲ **6. Kenny**		United Art. 979
			You Decorated My Life (7)/*Coward Of The County* (3)		
4/26/80	12	11	▲ 7. Gideon		United Art. 1035
			Don't Fall In Love With A Dreamer (4-with Kim Carnes)		
10/18/80	1 (2)	36	▲ **8. Kenny Rogers' Greatest Hits**	**[G]**	Liberty 1072
			Lady (1)		
7/11/81	6	13	▲ **9. Share Your Love**		Liberty 1108
			produced by Lionel Richie		
			I Don't Need You (3)		
12/26/81	34	3	▲ 10. Christmas	[X]	Liberty 51115
8/14/82	34	7	● 11. Love Will Turn You Around		Liberty 51124
3/12/83	18	12	● 12. We've Got Tonight		Liberty 51143
			We've Got Tonight (6-with Sheena Easton)		
10/1/83	6	24	▲ **13. Eyes That See In The Dark**		RCA 4697
			produced by Barry Gibb		
			Islands In The Stream (1-with Dolly Parton)		
11/26/83	22	11	▲ 14. Twenty Greatest Hits	[G]	Liberty 51152
10/13/84	31	8	▲ 15. What About Me?		RCA 5043
12/22/84	31	4	▲² 16. Once Upon A Christmas	[X]	RCA 5307
			KENNY ROGERS & DOLLY PARTON		
			Christmas charts: 1/'84, 4/'85, 10/'87, 16/'88, 15/'89, 14/'90, 14/'91, 19/'92, 25/'93		

DATE	POS	WKS	ARTIST—RECORD TITLE	LABEL & NO.
			ROLLING STONES, The	
			British R&B-influenced rock group formed in London in January 1963. Consisted of Mick Jagger (born 7/26/43; vocals), Keith Richards (born 12/18/43; lead guitar), Brian Jones (born 2/28/42; died 7/3/69; guitar), Bill Wyman (born 10/24/36; bass) and Charlie Watts (born 6/2/41; drums). Jagger was lead singer of Blues, Inc. Group took its name from a Muddy Waters song. Promoted as the bad boys in contrast to The Beatles. First U.K. tour, with The Ronettes, in 1964. Jones left group shortly before drowning; replaced by Mick Taylor (born 1/17/48). In 1975, Ron Wood (ex-Jeff Beck Group; ex-Faces) replaced Taylor. Movie *Gimme Shelter* is a documentary of the Stones' controversial Altamont concert on 12/6/69 at which a concertgoer was murdered by a member of the Hell's Angels. Won 1986 Lifetime Achievement Grammy Award. Inducted into the Rock and Roll Hall of Fame in 1989. Wyman left band in late 1992. Bassist Darryl Jones (billed as a "side musician") played on the 1994 *Voodoo Lounge* album and tour. Considered by many to be the world's all-time greatest rock-and-roll band.	
7/25/64	**11**	12	● 1. England's Newest Hit Makers/The Rolling Stones	London 375
11/28/64	3	20	● 2. 12 x 5	London 402
			Time Is On My Side (6)	
4/10/65	5	29	● 3. The Rolling Stones, Now!	London 420
8/14/65	1(3)	35	▲ 4. Out Of Our Heads	London 429
			The Last Time (9)/*(I Can't Get No) Satisfaction* (1)	
12/18/65	4	22	● 5. December's Children (and everybody's)	London 451
			Get Off Of My Cloud (1)/*As Tears Go By* (6)	
4/23/66	3	35	▲² 6. Big Hits (High Tide And Green Grass) [G]	London 1
			19th Nervous Breakdown (2)	
7/16/66	2(2)	26	▲ 7. Aftermath	London 476
			Paint It, Black (1)	
12/31/66	6	11	● 8. got Live if you want it! [L]	London 493
			recorded at the Royal Albert Hall, London	
2/25/67	2(4)	19	● 9. Between The Buttons	London 499
			Ruby Tuesday (1)	
7/29/67	3	18	● 10. Flowers [G]	London 509
			Mothers Little Helper (8)/ *Have You Seen Your Mother, Baby, Standing In The Shadow?* (9)	
12/23/67	2(6)	13	● 11. Their Satanic Majesties Request	London 2
12/21/68	5	13	▲ 12. Beggars Banquet	London 539
9/20/69	2(2)	16	▲ 13. Through The Past, Darkly (Big Hits Vol. 2) [G]	London 3
			Jumpin' Jack Flash (3)/*Honky Tonk Women* (1)	
12/13/69	3	19	▲² 14. Let It Bleed	London 4
			Jones's last appearance; Taylor's first with band	
10/17/70	6	10	▲ 15. 'Get Yer Ya-Ya's Out!' [L]	London 5
			recorded at New York's Madison Square Garden, November 1969	
5/15/71	1(4)	26	● 16. Sticky Fingers	Rolling S. 59100
			Brown Sugar (1)	
1/8/72	4	30	▲⁶ 17. Hot Rocks 1964-1971 [G]	London 606/7 [2]
			reissued on CD on Abkco 6667 during its chart run in 1989	
6/10/72	1(4)	17	● 18. Exile On Main St.	Rolling S. 2900 [2]
			Tumbling Dice (7)	
1/20/73	9	12	● 19. More Hot Rocks (big hits & fazed cookies) [G]	London 626/7 [2]
9/29/73	1(4)	19	● 20. Goats Head Soup	Rolling S. 59101
			Angie (1)	

DATE	POS	WKS	ARTIST—RECORD TITLE	LABEL & NO.
11/9/74	**1**(1)	11	● **21. It's Only Rock 'N Roll**	Rolling S. 79101
6/21/75	**8**	8	**22. Metamorphosis** [K]	Abkco 1
			collection of old and new songs	
6/28/75	**6**	9	● **23. Made In The Shade** [G]	Rolling S. 79102
5/8/76	**1**(4)	14	▲ **24. Black And Blue**	Rolling S. 79104
			Wood's first appearance with band	
			Fool To Cry (10)	
10/15/77	**5**	7	● **25. Love You Live** [L]	Rolling S. 9001 [2]
6/24/78	**1**(2)	32	▲⁴ **26. Some Girls**	Rolling S. 39108
			Miss You (1)/*Beast Of Burden* (8)	
7/19/80	**1**(7)	20	▲ **27. Emotional Rescue**	Rolling S. 16015
			Emotional Rescue (3)	
4/4/81	**15**	6	● **28. Sucking In The Seventies** [G]	Rolling S. 16028
9/12/81	**1**(9)	30	▲³ **29. Tattoo You**	Rolling S. 16052
			Start Me Up (2)	
7/3/82	**5**	10	● **30. "Still Life" (American Concert 1981)** [L]	Rolling S. 39113
11/26/83	**4**	12	▲ **31. Undercover**	Rolling S. 90120
			Undercover Of The Night (9)	
4/12/86	**4**	15	▲ **32. Dirty Work**	Rolling S. 40250
			Harlem Shuffle (5)	
9/23/89	**3**	27	▲² **33. Steel Wheels**	Rolling S. 45333
			Mixed Emotion (5)	
4/20/91	**16**	5	● **34. Flashpoint** [L]	Rolling S. 47456
			recorded during the 1989-90 Steel Wheels/Urban Jungle World Tour	
7/30/94	**2**(1)	17	▲² **35. Voodoo Lounge**	Virgin 39782

ROLLINS BAND

Henry Rollins (born 2/13/61, Washington, D.C.) was lead singer of hard-core punk band Black Flag from July 1981 to July 1986. Formed Rollins Band in April 1987 with guitarist Chris Haskett, bassist Andrew Weiss, drummer Sim Cain and soundman Theo Van Rock. By 1994, Melvin Gibbs replaced Weiss. An accomplished poet, Rollins has toured as a spoken-word performer since 1983. Acted in the movie *The Chase*.

DATE	POS	WKS	ARTIST—RECORD TITLE	LABEL & NO.
4/30/94	**33**	1	Weight	Imago 21034

ROMANTICS, The

Rock quartet from Detroit formed in 1977. Original lineup: Wally Palmar (lead singer, guitar), Mike Skill (lead guitar), Richard Cole (bass) and Jimmy Marinos (drums).

DATE	POS	WKS	ARTIST—RECORD TITLE	LABEL & NO.
12/17/83	**14**	15	● In Heat	Nemperor 38880
			Talking In Your Sleep (3)	

RONSTADT, Linda

Born on 7/15/46 in Tucson, Arizona. While in high school formed folk trio The Three Ronstadts (with sister and brother). To Los Angeles in 1964. Formed The Stone Poneys with Bobby Kimmel (guitar) and Ken Edwards (keyboards); recorded for Sidewalk in 1966. Went solo in 1968. In 1971 formed backing band with Glenn Frey, Don Henley, Randy Meisner and Bernie Leadon (later became The Eagles). In *Pirates of Penzance* operetta in New York City in 1980; also in the movie version in 1983.

DATE	POS	WKS	ARTIST—RECORD TITLE	LABEL & NO.
12/14/74	**1**(1)	19	▲² **1. Heart Like A Wheel**	Capitol 11358
			You're No Good (1)/*When Will I Be Loved* (2)	
10/11/75	**4**	10	▲ **2. Prisoner In Disguise**	Asylum 1045
			Heat Wave (5)	
9/4/76	**3**	15	▲ **3. Hasten Down The Wind**	Asylum 1072

DATE	POS	WKS	ARTIST—RECORD TITLE	LABEL & NO.
12/18/76	6	15	▲⁵ 4. Greatest Hits [G] includes her hits on Capitol	Asylum 1092
10/1/77	1(5)	23	▲³ 5. Simple Dreams *Blue Bayou* (3)/*It's So Easy* (5)	Asylum 104
10/7/78	1(1)	17	▲ 6. Living In The USA *Ooh Baby Baby* (7)	Asylum 155
3/15/80	3	17	▲ 7. Mad Love *How Do I Make You* (10)/*Hurt So Bad* (8)	Asylum 510
11/15/80	26	10	▲ 8. Greatest Hits, Volume Two [G]	Asylum 516
10/30/82	31	6	● 9. Get Closer	Asylum 60185
10/8/83	3	25	▲³ 10. What's New	Asylum 60260
12/15/84	13	11	▲ 11. Lush Life above 2 arranged and conducted by Nelson Riddle	Asylum 60387
3/28/87	6	14	▲ 12. Trio **DOLLY PARTON, LINDA RONSTADT, EMMYLOU HARRIS**	Warner 25491
10/28/89	7	37	▲ 13. Cry Like A Rainstorm — Howl Like The Wind **LINDA RONSTADT featuring Aaron Neville** includes 4 duets with Neville *Don't Know Much* (2-with Neville)	Elektra 60872
			ROOFTOP SINGERS, The Folk trio from New York City: Erik Darling, Willard Svanoe and Lynne Taylor (died 1982). Disbanded in 1967. Darling was a member of The Tarriers in 1956 and The Weavers, 1958-62. Taylor was a vocalist with Benny Goodman and Buddy Rich.	
3/2/63	15	7	Walk Right In! *Walk Right In* (1)	Vanguard 9123
			ROS, Edmundo Born on 12/7/10 in Venezuela. London-based bandleader/drummer.	
5/25/59	28	2	1. Hollywood Cha Cha Cha [I]	London 152
9/22/62	31	5	2. Dance Again [I]	London P. 4 44015
			ROSE, David, And His Orchestra Born on 6/15/10 in London. Died on 8/23/90 of heart disease. Moved to Chicago at an early age. Conductor/composer/arranger for numerous movies. Scored many TV series, such as "The Red Skelton Show," "Bonanza" and "Little House on the Prairie." Married to Martha Raye (1938-41) and Judy Garland (1941-43).	
7/7/62	3	28	● The Stripper and other fun Songs for the family [I] *The Stripper* (1)	MGM 4062
			ROSE ROYCE Eight-member backing band formed in Los Angeles in the early '70s. Backed Edwin Starr as Total Concept Unlimited in 1973. Backed The Temptations; became regular band for Undisputed Truth. Lead vocalist Gwen Dickey added and name changed to Rose Royce in 1976.	
12/18/76	14	13	● 1. Car Wash [S] *Car Wash* (1)/*I Wanna Get Next To You* (10)	MCA 6000 [2]
9/17/77	9	14	▲ 2. Rose Royce II/In Full Bloom	Whitfield 3074
9/23/78	28	6	● 3. Rose Royce III/Strikes Again!	Whitfield 3227

DATE	POS	WKS	ARTIST—RECORD TITLE	LABEL & NO.
			ROSS, Diana	
			Born Diane Earle on 3/26/44 in Detroit. In vocal group The Primettes; first recorded for LuPine in 1960. Lead singer of The Supremes from 1961-69. Went solo in late 1969. Oscar nominee for the 1972 movie *Lady Sings the Blues*. Also appeared in the movies *Mahogany* and *The Wiz*. Own Broadway show *An Evening with Diana Ross*, 1976. Married Norwegian shipping magnate Arne Naess in 1986. Ross would rank among the Top 5 artists of the rock era if her solo and Supremes' hits were combined.	
7/18/70	19	14	1. Diana Ross	Motown 711
			Ain't No Mountain High Enough (1)	
12/23/72	1(2)	24	**2. Lady Sings The Blues** [S]	Motown 758 [2]
			Ross portrayed Billie Holiday in the movie	
7/28/73	5	15	**3. Touch Me In The Morning**	Motown 772
			Touch Me In The Morning (1)	
12/8/73	26	5	4. Diana & Marvin	Motown 803
			DIANA ROSS & MARVIN GAYE	
3/27/76	5	18	**5. Diana Ross**	Motown 861
			Love Hangover (1)	
8/14/76	13	14	6. Diana Ross' Greatest Hits [G]	Motown 869
3/19/77	29	3	7. An Evening With Diana Ross [L]	Motown 877 [2]
			recorded at the Ahmanson Theatre, Los Angeles	
10/22/77	18	13	8. Baby It's Me	Motown 890
7/7/79	14	17	● 9. The Boss	Motown 923
6/21/80	2(2)	34	▲ **10. Diana**	Motown 936
			Upside Down (1)/*I'm Coming Out* (5)	
3/28/81	32	4	11. To Love Again [K]	Motown 951
			It's My Turn (9)	
11/14/81	15	20	▲ 12. Why Do Fools Fall In Love	RCA 4153
			Why Do Fools Fall In Love (7)/*Mirror, Mirror* (8)	
11/21/81	37	3	● 13. All The Great Hits [G]	Motown 960 [2]
			includes medleys with The Supremes	
			Endless Love (1-with Lionel Richie)	
10/30/82	27	7	● 14. Silk Electric	RCA 4384
			Muscles (10)	
8/6/83	32	4	15. Ross	RCA 4677
10/6/84	26	18	● 16. Swept Away	RCA 5009
			Missing You (10)	
			ROSSINGTON COLLINS BAND	
			Band formed by four surviving members of Lynyrd Skynyrd, featuring Gary Rossington and Allen Collins (paralyzed in a 1986 car crash). Disbanded in 1982. Rossington and wife Dale Krantz-Rossington (vocals), Jay Johnson, Tim Lindsey, Ronnie Eades, Tim Sharpton and Mitch Rigel recorded as The Rossington Band in 1988. Collins died of pneumonia on 1/23/90 (age 37).	
7/19/80	13	13	● 1. Anytime, Anyplace, Anywhere	MCA 5130
10/17/81	24	5	2. This Is The Way	MCA 5207
			ROTARY CONNECTION	
			Canadian rock-R&B sextet. Minnie Riperton, lead singer.	
5/4/68	37	4	Rotary Connection	Cadet Concept 312
			ROTH, David Lee	
			Born on 10/10/55 in Bloomington, Indiana. Former lead singer of Van Halen.	
2/23/85	15	20	▲ 1. Crazy From The Heat [M]	Warner 25222
			California Girls (3)	

DATE	POS	WKS	ARTIST—RECORD TITLE	LABEL & NO.
7/26/86	4	21	▲ **2. Eat 'Em And Smile** also released as a Spanish version *Sonrisa Salvaje*	Warner 25470
2/13/88	6	16	▲ **3. Skyscraper** *Just Like Paradise* (6)	Warner 25671
2/9/91	18	5	● 4. A Little Ain't Enough	Warner 26477
			ROXETTE Male/female Swedish pop-rock duo: Marie Fredriksson (born 5/30/58; vocals) and Per Gessle (born 6/12/59; songwriter).	
4/29/89	23	21	▲ 1. Look Sharp! *The Look* (1)/*Listen To Your Heart* (1)/*Dangerous* (2)	EMI 91098
4/27/91	12	20	▲ 2. Joyride *Joyride* (1)/*Fading Like A Flower (Every Time You Leave)* (2)	EMI 94435
			ROXY MUSIC English art-rock band. Nucleus consisted of Bryan Ferry (vocals, keyboards), Phil Manzanera (guitar) and Andy MacKay (horns).	
3/8/75	37	3	1. Country Life	Atco 106
4/14/79	23	8	2. Manifesto	Atco 114
8/9/80	35	3	3. Flesh + Blood	Atco 102
			ROYAL PHILHARMONIC ORCHESTRA, The British orchestra. Louis Clark, conductor (born in Birmingham, England; arranger for ELO).	
12/12/81	4	22	▲ **1. Hooked On Classics** [I] *Hooked On Classics* (10)	RCA 4194
9/18/82	33	7	● 2. Hooked On Classics II (Can't Stop the Classics) [I]	RCA 4373
			ROYAL SCOTS DRAGOON GUARDS, The The military band of Scotland's armored regiment. Led by bagpipe soloist Major Tony Crease.	
7/22/72	34	5	Amazing Grace [I]	RCA 4744
			RUBINSTEIN, Arthur Born on 1/28/1887 in Lodz, Poland; died on 12/20/82. Classical pianist. Father of Broadway/TV actor John Rubinstein.	
2/13/61	30	1	Heart of the Piano Concerto [I] favorite movements from 6 piano concertos	RCA 2495
			RUDY, Ed — see BEATLES, The	
			RUFFIN, David Born Davis Eli Ruffin on 1/18/41 in Meridian, Mississippi. Died of a drug overdose on 6/1/91. Brother of Jimmy Ruffin. With The Dixie Nightingales gospel group. Recorded for Anna in 1960. Co-lead singer of The Temptations from 1963-68. Also see Hall & Oates.	
6/28/69	31	7	1. My Whole World Ended *My Whole World Ended (The Moment You Left Me)* (9)	Motown 685
1/17/76	31	6	2. Who I Am *Walk Away From Love* (9)	Motown 849

DATE	POS	WKS	ARTIST—RECORD TITLE	LABEL & NO.
			RUFUS Featuring Chaka Khan	
			Soul group from Chicago. First known as Smoke, then Ask Rufus. Varying membership included Chaka Khan (vocals), Tony Maiden (guitar), Nate Morgan, Kevin Murphy (keyboards), Bobby Watson (bass), Andre Fischer (drums; ex-American Breed; later married to Natalie Cole) and Moon Calhoun. Khan has been recording solo and with Rufus since 1978. After 1978, Maiden and David Wolinski also sang lead.	
8/3/74	4	11	● **1. Rags To Rufus** **RUFUS** *Tell Me Something Good* (3)	ABC 809
1/25/75	7	12	● **2. Rufusized** *Once You Get Started* (10)	ABC 837
12/6/75	7	24	● **3. Rufus featuring Chaka Khan** *Sweet Thing* (5)	ABC 909
2/12/77	12	10	▲ 4. Ask Rufus	ABC 975
2/25/78	14	14	● 5. Street Player	ABC 1049
11/24/79	14	16	● 6. Masterjam	MCA 5103
			RUNDGREN, Todd	
			Born on 6/22/48 in Upper Darby, Pennsylvania. Virtuoso musician/ songwriter/producer/engineer. Leader of groups Nazz and Utopia. Produced Meat Loaf's *Bat Out Of Hell* album. Also produced albums for Badfinger, Grand Funk Railroad, The Tubes, XTC, Patti Smith and many others.	
12/15/73	29	8	● 1. Something/Anything? side 4: an impromptu operetta cut live with his band in the studio *Hello It's Me* (5)	Bearsville 2066 [2]
6/17/78	36	2	2. Hermit Of Mink Hollow	Bearsville 6981
			RUN-D.M.C.	
			Rap trio from Queens, New York: rappers Joseph Simmons (Run), Darryl McDaniels (DMC), with DJ Jason Mizell (Jam Master Jay). In movies *Krush Groove* and *Tougher than Leather*.	
6/21/86	3	49	▲³ **1. Raising Hell** *Walk This Way* (4)	Profile 1217
6/4/88	9	14	▲ **2. Tougher Than Leather**	Profile 1265
5/22/93	7	4	● **3. Down With The King**	Profile 1440
			RUSH	
			Canadian power-rock trio formed in Toronto in 1969: Geddy Lee (born 7/29/53; vocals, bass), Alex Lifeson (born 8/27/53; guitar) and John Rutsey (drums). Neil Peart (born 9/12/52) replaced Rutsey after first album.	
11/20/76	40	2	▲ 1. All The World's A Stage	[L]	Mercury 7508 [2]
10/8/77	33	5	▲ 2. A Farewell To Kings	Mercury 1184
2/9/80	4	15	▲ **3. Permanent Waves**	Mercury 4001
3/7/81	3	29	▲⁴ **4. Moving Pictures**	Mercury 4013
11/14/81	10	14	▲ **5. Exit ... Stage Left**	[L]	Mercury 7001 [2]
10/2/82	10	11	▲ **6. Signals**	Mercury 4063
5/5/84	10	12	▲ **7. Grace Under Pressure**	Mercury 818476
11/2/85	10	14	▲ **8. Power Windows**	Mercury 826098
10/3/87	13	14	● 9. Hold Your Fire	Mercury 832464
2/4/89	21	5	● 10. A Show Of Hands	[L]	Mercury 836346 [2]
			recorded during the trio's 1986 and 1988 world tours	
12/9/89	16	11	● 11. Presto	Atlantic 82040
9/21/91	3	5	● **12. Roll The Bones**	Atlantic 82293

DATE	POS	WKS	ARTIST—RECORD TITLE	LABEL & NO.
11/6/93	2(1)	3	● 13. Counterparts	Atlantic 82528
			RUSHEN, Patrice	
			Born on 9/30/54 in Los Angeles. Jazz-soul vocalist/pianist/songwriter. Much session work with Jean Luc-Ponty, Lee Ritenour and Stanley Turrentine.	
3/1/80	39	2	1. Pizzazz	Elektra 243
5/15/82	14	8	2. Straight From The Heart	Elektra 60015
7/28/84	40	3	3. Now	Elektra 60360
			RUSSELL, Leon	
			Born on 4/2/41 in Lawton, Oklahoma. Rock singer/songwriter/multi-instrumentalist sessionman. Known as Russell Bridges early in session career. Regular with Phil Spector's "Wall of Sound" session group. Formed Shelter Records with British producer Denny Cordell in 1970. Recorded as Hank Wilson in 1973. Married Mary McCreary (vocalist with Little Sister; part of Sly Stone's "family") in 1976. Formed Paradise label in 1976. Wrote "Superstar" and "This Masquerade." Also see Joe Cocker.	
6/12/71	17	10	● 1. Leon Russell & The Shelter People	Shelter 8903
			LEON RUSSELL & THE SHELTER PEOPLE	
7/29/72	2(4)	20	● 2. Carney	Shelter 8911
7/14/73	9	12	● 3. Leon Live [L]	Shelter 8917 [3]
			recorded at the Long Beach Arena, Long Beach, California	
9/29/73	28	6	4. Hank Wilson's Back, Vol. I	Shelter 8923
			HANK WILSON	
7/13/74	34	3	5. Stop All That Jazz	Shelter 2108
5/31/75	30	7	● 6. Will O' The Wisp	Shelter 2138
6/12/76	34	4	7. Wedding Album	Paradise 2943
			LEON & MARY RUSSELL	
12/4/76	40	1	● 8. Best Of Leon [G]	Shelter 52004
7/7/79	25	5	● 9. One For The Road	Columbia 36064 [2]
			WILLIE NELSON AND LEON RUSSELL	
			RYDELL, Bobby	
			Born Robert Ridarelli on 4/26/42 in Philadelphia. Regular on Paul Whiteman's amateur TV show, 1951-54. Drummer with Rocco & His Saints, which included Frankie Avalon on trumpet in 1956. First recorded for Veko in 1957. In the movies *Bye Bye Birdie* and *That Lady from Peking*.	
2/27/61	12	8	1. Bobby's Biggest Hits [G]	Cameo 1009
			We Got Love (6)/*Wild One* (2)/*Swingin' School* (5)/ *Volare* (4)	
12/25/61	7	11	2. Bobby Rydell/Chubby Checker	Cameo 1013
			BOBBY RYDELL/CHUBBY CHECKER	
			RYDER, Mitch, And The Detroit Wheels	
			Born William Levise, Jr., on 2/26/45 in Detroit. Leader of white soul-rock group The Detroit Wheels. Group was originally known as Billy Lee & The Rivieras. Renamed by its producer Bob Crewe. Ryder went solo in 1967. Formed new rock group, Detroit, in 1971.	
2/25/67	23	7	1. Breakout ... !!!	New Voice 2002
			Devil With A Blue Dress On & Good Golly Miss Molly (4)	
5/6/67	34	3	2. Sock It To Me!	New Voice 2003
			Sock It To Me-Baby! (6)	
1/20/68	37	4	3. All Mitch Ryder Hits! [G]	New Voice 2004

DATE	POS	WKS	ARTIST—RECORD TITLE	LABEL & NO.

S

SADE

Born Helen Folasade Adu on 1/16/59 in Ibadan, Nigeria; moved to London at age four. Pronounced SHAH-day. Appeared in the 1986 movie *Absolute Beginners*. Former designer of menswear. Won 1985 Best New Artist Grammy Award.

DATE	POS	WKS	ARTIST—RECORD TITLE	LABEL & NO.
3/9/85	5	27	▲⁴ 1. Diamond Life *Smooth Operator* (5)	Portrait 39581
12/21/85	1(2)	27	▲³ 2. Promise *The Sweetest Taboo* (5)	Portrait 40263
6/11/88	7	21	▲³ 3. Stronger Than Pride	Epic 44210
11/21/92	3	38	▲⁴ 4. Love Deluxe	Epic 53178
11/26/94	9	14+	▲ 5. Best Of Sade [G]	Epic 66686

SADLER, SSgt Barry

Born on 11/1/40 in Carlsbad, New Mexico. Died of heart failure on 11/5/89 in Tennessee. Staff Sergeant of U.S. Army Special Forces (aka Green Berets). Served in Vietnam until injuring leg in booby trap. Shot in the head during a 1988 robbery attempt at his Guatemala home; suffered brain damage.

DATE	POS	WKS	ARTIST—RECORD TITLE	LABEL & NO.
3/12/66	1(5)	20	● **Ballads of the Green Berets** *The Ballad Of The Green Berets* (1)	RCA 3547

SAGA

Toronto-based rock quintet: Michael Sadler, brothers Jim and Ian Crichton, Jim Gilmour and Steve Negus.

DATE	POS	WKS	ARTIST—RECORD TITLE	LABEL & NO.
1/8/83	29	13	● Worlds Apart	Portrait 38246

SAHL, Mort

Born on 5/11/27 in Montreal. Topical satirist/actor. Own one-man Broadway show, *Mort Sahl on Broadway!*

DATE	POS	WKS	ARTIST—RECORD TITLE	LABEL & NO.
10/24/60	22	4	Mort Sahl At The Hungry i [C] recorded at the Hungry i nightclub in San Francisco	Verve 15012

SAILCAT

Country-rock duo: Court Pickett and John Wyker.

DATE	POS	WKS	ARTIST—RECORD TITLE	LABEL & NO.
10/7/72	38	2	Motorcycle Mama	Elektra 75029

SAKAMOTO, Kyu

Native of Kawasaki, Japan. Kyu (pronounced: cue) was one of 520 people killed in the crash of the Japan Airlines 747 near Tokyo on 8/12/85 (age 43).

DATE	POS	WKS	ARTIST—RECORD TITLE	LABEL & NO.
7/6/63	14	8	Sukiyaki and other Japanese hits [F] *Sukiyaki* (1)	Capitol 10349

SALSOUL ORCHESTRA

Disco orchestra conducted by Philadelphia producer/arranger Vincent Montana, Jr. Vocalists included Phyllis Rhodes, Ronni Tyson, Carl Helm, Philip Hurt and Jocelyn Brown.

DATE	POS	WKS	ARTIST—RECORD TITLE	LABEL & NO.
2/7/76	14	14	The Salsoul Orchestra [I]	Salsoul 5501

DATE	POS	WKS	ARTIST—RECORD TITLE	LABEL & NO.
			SALT-N-PEPA	
			Queens-based female rap trio: Cheryl "Salt" James, Sandra "Pepa" Denton (from Kingston, Jamaica) and Dee Dee "DJ Spinderella LaToya" Roper. James and Denton recorded earlier as Super Nature. Took a line from their Super Nature recording "Showstopper" and changed name to Salt-N-Pepa. Appeared in the movie *Who's the Man?*	
2/6/88	26	14	▲ 1. Hot, Cool & Vicious	Next Plat. 1007
9/3/88	38	4	● 2. A Salt With A Deadly Pepa	Next Plat. 1011
4/28/90	38	2	▲ 3. Blacks' Magic	Next Plat. 1019
11/13/93	4	29	▲³ **4. Very Necessary**	Next Plat. 828392
			Shoop (4)/*Whatta Man* (3-with En Vogue)	
			SAMBORA, Richie	
			Born on 7/11/59 in Passaic, New Jersey. Guitarist of Bon Jovi.	
9/21/91	36	1	Stranger In This Town	Mercury 848895
			SAM THE SHAM and The PHARAOHS	
			Dallas rock-and-roll group formed in the early '60s, featuring lead singer Domingo "Sam" Samudio (born 1940, Dallas). Included Ray Stinnet, David Martin, Jerry Patterson and Butch Gibson. First recorded for Tupelo in 1963. Samudio went solo in 1970. Formed new band in 1974. On the 1982 movie soundtrack *The Border*. Samudio later became a street preacher in Memphis.	
8/14/65	26	5	Wooly Bully	MGM 4297
			Wooly Bully (2)	
			SANDPIPERS, The	
			Los Angeles-based trio: Jim Brady (born 8/24/44), Michael Piano (born 10/26/44) and Richard Shoff (born 4/30/44); met while in The Mitchell Boys Choir.	
11/26/66	13	10	● Guantanamera	A&M 4117
			Guantanamera (9)	
			SANDS, Tommy	
			Born on 8/27/37 in Chicago. Pop singer/actor. Mother was a vocalist with Art Kassel's band. Married Nancy Sinatra in 1960; divorced in 1965. In the movies *Sing Boy Sing, Mardi Gras, Babes in Toyland* and *The Longest Day.*	
5/6/57	4	18	**1. Steady Date with Tommy Sands**	Capitol 848
2/24/58	17	4	2. Sing Boy Sing [S]	Capitol 929
			Sands portrays fictional singer Virgil Walker in the movie	
			SANG, Samantha	
			Born Cheryl Gray on 8/5/53 in Melbourne, Australia. Began career on Melbourne radio at age eight.	
4/8/78	29	3	● Emotion	Private S. 7009
			Emotion (3)	
			SAN SEBASTIAN STRINGS, The	
			Music composed by Anita Kerr (with sound effects), featuring narration of the poetry of Rod McKuen.	
2/1/69	20	4	Home To The Sea [I-T]	Warner 1764
			SANTA ESMERALDA	
			Spanish-flavored disco studio project produced by Nicolas Skorsky and Jean-Manuel de Scarano.	
1/14/78	25	8	● Don't Let Me Be Misunderstood	Casablanca 7080
			vocals by Leroy Gomez	

DATE	POS	WKS	ARTIST—RECORD TITLE	LABEL & NO.
			SANTANA	
			Latin-rock group formed in San Francisco in 1966. Consisted of Devadip Carlos Santana (born 7/20/47, Autlan de Navarro, Mexico; vocals, guitar), Gregg Rolie (keyboards) and David Brown (bass). Added percussionists Michael Carabello, Jose Chepitos Areas and Michael Shrieve in 1969. Worked Fillmore West and Woodstock in 1969. Neal Schon (guitar) added in 1971. Santana began solo work in 1972. Schon and Rolie formed Journey in 1973. Shrieve left in 1975 to form Automatic Man.	
9/27/69	4	42	▲² 1. Santana	Columbia 9781
			Evil Ways (9)	
10/10/70	1 (6)	40	▲⁴ 2. Abraxas	Columbia 30130
			Black Magic Woman (4)	
10/16/71	1 (5)	22	▲² 3. Santana III	Columbia 30595
11/11/72	8	17	▲ 4. Caravanserai	Columbia 31610
12/15/73	25	9	● 5. Welcome	Columbia 32445
8/24/74	17	11	▲² 6. Santana's Greatest Hits [G]	Columbia 33050
11/23/74	20	5	● 7. Borboletta	Columbia 33135
4/17/76	10	11	● 8. Amigos	Columbia 33576
			title is Spanish for friends	
1/29/77	27	4	● 9. Festival	Columbia 34423
11/12/77	10	9	▲ 10. Moonflower [L]	Columbia 34914 [2]
11/11/78	27	5	● 11. Inner Secrets	Columbia 35600
11/3/79	25	6	● 12. Marathon	Columbia 36154
5/2/81	9	21	● 13. Zebop!	Columbia 37158
9/11/82	22	10	14. Shango	Columbia 38122
			title is Spanish for monkey	
			SANTANA, Carlos	
			Mexican-born rock and jazz-fusion guitarist. Leader of Santana. Added 'Devadip' (which means 'the light of the lamp of the Supreme') to his name after becoming a disciple of guru Sri Chinmoy.	
7/29/72	8	14	▲ 1. Carlos Santana & Buddy Miles! Live! [L]	Columbia 31308
			CARLOS SANTANA & BUDDY MILES	
			recorded in Hawaii's Diamond Head volcano crater	
7/21/73	14	7	● 2. Love Devotion Surrender [I]	Columbia 32034
			CARLOS SANTANA/MAHAVISHNU JOHN McLAUGHLIN	
5/14/83	31	4	3. Havana Moon	Columbia 38642
			with guests Willie Nelson, Booker T. Jones and The Fabulous Thunderbirds	
			SANTO & JOHNNY	
			Brooklyn-born guitar duo: Santo Farina (born 10/24/37; steel guitar) and his brother Johnny (born 4/30/41; rhythm guitar). Sister Ann Farina helped with songwriting.	
1/18/60	20	24	1. Santo & Johnny [I]	Canadian-Am. 1001
			Sleep Walk (1)	
9/26/60	11	9	2. Encore [I]	Canadian-Am. 1002
			SATRIANI, Joe	
			Berkeley-based rock guitarist raised in Carle Place, Long Island. Former guitar teacher of Steve Vai (with David Lee Roth and Whitesnake) and Kirk Hammett (Metallica).	
4/9/88	29	9	▲ 1. Surfing With The Alien [I]	Relativity 8193
11/25/89	23	14	● 2. Flying In A Blue Dream	Relativity 1015
			6 of 18 cuts feature Satriani's vocals	

DATE	POS	WKS	ARTIST—RECORD TITLE	LABEL & NO.
8/8/92	22	3	● 3. The Extremist [I]	Relativity 1053

SAVOY BROWN

British blues-rock band formed in 1966 by guitarist Kim Simmonds. Many personnel changes. Members Dave Peverett, Roger Earl and Tony Stevens left in 1971 to form Foghat.

DATE	POS	WKS	ARTIST—RECORD TITLE	LABEL & NO.
11/21/70	39	1	1. Looking In	Parrot 71042
4/15/72	34	7	2. Hellbound Train	Parrot 71052

SAYER, Leo

Born Gerard Sayer on 5/21/48 in Shoreham, England. With Patches in the early '70s. Songwriting team with David Courtney, 1972-75. Own British TV show in 1978 and again in 1983.

DATE	POS	WKS	ARTIST—RECORD TITLE	LABEL & NO.
4/19/75	16	7	1. Just A Boy	Warner 2836
			Long Tall Glasses (I Can Dance) (9)	
1/22/77	10	14	▲ **2. Endless Flight**	Warner 2962
			You Make Me Feel Like Dancing (1)/*When I Need You* (1)	
11/5/77	37	2	3. Thunder In My Heart	Warner 3089
12/27/80	36	6	4. Living In A Fantasy	Warner 3483
			More Than I Can Say (2)	

SCAGGS, Boz

Born William Royce Scaggs on 6/8/44 in Ohio; raised in Texas. Joined Steve Miller's band, The Marksmen, in 1959 in Dallas. Hooked up with Miller at the University of Wisconsin in The Ardells; later known as The Fabulous Night Trains. Joined R&B band The Wigs in 1963. To Europe in 1964; toured as folk singer. Re-joined Miller in 1967; solo since 1969. Retired from music and opened a restaurant in San Francisco, 1983-87. Made comeback in 1988.

DATE	POS	WKS	ARTIST—RECORD TITLE	LABEL & NO.
5/1/76	2 (5)	53	▲⁵ **1. Silk Degrees**	Columbia 33920
			Lowdown (3)	
12/10/77	11	14	▲ 2. Down Two Then Left	Columbia 34729
4/19/80	8	21	▲ **3. Middle Man**	Columbia 36106
12/6/80	24	14	▲ 4. Hits! [G]	Columbia 36841

SCANDAL

New York-based rock band led by Patty Smyth and Zack Smith.

DATE	POS	WKS	ARTIST—RECORD TITLE	LABEL & NO.
5/28/83	39	3	● 1. Scandal [M]	Columbia 38194
8/18/84	17	14	▲ 2. Warrior	Columbia 39173
			SCANDAL FEATURING PATTY SMYTH	
			The Warrior (7)	

SCARFACE

Brad Jordan, member of the Houston-based rap group The Geto Boys.

DATE	POS	WKS	ARTIST—RECORD TITLE	LABEL & NO.
9/4/93	7	6	● **1. The World Is Yours**	Rap-A-Lot 53861
11/5/94	2 (1)	5	▲ **2. The Diary**	Rap-A-Lot 39946

SCHAFER, Kermit

Collection of bloopers by radio and TV producer Kermit Schafer. Died on 3/8/79.

DATE	POS	WKS	ARTIST—RECORD TITLE	LABEL & NO.
1/27/58	17	1	Pardon My Blooper! Volume 6 [C]	Jubilee 6
			narrated by George de Holczer	

SCHIFRIN, Lalo

Born Boris Schifrin on 6/21/32 in Buenos Aires, Argentina. Pianist/conductor/composer. To the U.S. in 1958. Scored movies *Bullitt*, *Dirty Harry*, *Brubaker* and many others.

DATE	POS	WKS	ARTIST—RECORD TITLE	LABEL & NO.
12/29/62	35	2	Bossa Nova — New Brazilian Jazz [I]	Audio Fidel. 1981

DATE	POS	WKS	ARTIST—RECORD TITLE	LABEL & NO.
			SCHNEIDER, John	
			Born on 4/8/59 in Mount Kisco, New York. Moved to Atlanta at age 14. Country singer/actor. Played "Bo Duke" on TV's "The Dukes of Hazzard." Appeared in many TV movies. Scriptwriter/director.	
8/8/81	37	3	Now Or Never	Scotti Br. 37400
			SCHORY, Dick	
			Born on 12/13/31 in Chicago; raised in Ames, Iowa. Percussionist. Vice president of Ludwig drum company, 1957-70. Owner of Ovation Records, 1970-82. Currently runs Chicago marketing firm.	
6/29/59	11	26	1. Music For Bang, Baa-room and Harp [I]	RCA 1866
			DICK SCHORY'S New Percussion Ensemble	
5/11/63	13	9	2. Supercussion [I]	RCA 2613
			DICK SCHORY'S Percussion Pops Orchestra	
			SCORPIONS	
			German heavy-metal rock quintet: Rudolf Schenker (Michael Schenker's brother; lead guitar), Klaus Meine (lead singer), Matthias Jabs (guitar), Francis Buchholz (bass) and Herman Rarebell (drums). Buchholz left band in 1992; replaced by Ralph Rieckermann.	
4/10/82	10	18	▲ **1. Blackout**	Mercury 4039
3/24/84	6	27	▲² **2. Love At First Sting**	Mercury 814981
7/20/85	14	16	▲ 3. World Wide Live [L]	Mercury 824344 [2]
5/7/88	5	22	▲ **4. Savage Amusement**	Mercury 832963
12/1/90	21	23	▲ 5. Crazy World	Mercury 846908
			Wind Of Change (4)	
10/9/93	24	1	6. Face The Heat	Mercury 518258
			SCOTT, Tom, & The L.A. Express	
			Born on 5/19/48 in Los Angeles. Pop-jazz-fusion saxophonist. Did session work for Joni Mitchell, Steely Dan, Carole King and others. Composer of movie and TV scores. Led the house band for TV's "The Pat Sajak Show." Son of Nathan Scott, a composer of TV scores for "Dragnet," "Wagon Train," "My Three Sons" and others.	
5/3/75	18	8	Tom Cat [I]	Ode 77029
			SCOTT-HERON, Gil, And Brian Jackson	
			Keyboard duo: Scott-Heron (born 4/1/49, Chicago) is the lyricist; Jackson composes the music.	
3/22/75	30	3	The First Minute Of A New Day	Arista 4030
			featuring backup group The Midnight Band	
			SEAL	
			Born Sealhenry Samuel in Paddington, England, of Nigerian/Brazilian descent. Male singer.	
8/24/91	24	7	▲ 1. Seal	Sire 26627
			Crazy (7)	
6/18/94	20	13	▲ 2. Seal	ZTT/Sire 45415
			SEA LEVEL	
			Seven-man, jazzy blues-rock band formed by three members of The Allman Brothers Band (Jai Johnny Johanson, Chuck Leavell and Lamar Williams).	
3/4/78	31	3	Cats On The Coast	Capricorn 0198

DATE	POS	WKS	ARTIST—RECORD TITLE	LABEL & NO.
			SEALS & CROFTS	
			Pop duo: Jim Seals (born 10/17/41, Sidney, Texas; guitar, fiddle, saxophone) and Dash Crofts (born 8/14/40, Cisco, Texas; drums, mandolin, keyboards, guitar). With Dean Beard, recorded for Edmoral and Atlantic in 1957. To Los Angeles in 1958. With The Champs from 1958-65. Own group, The Dawnbreakers, in the late '60s; entire band converted to Baha'i faith in 1969. Seals is the brother of "England" Dan Seals and the cousin of country singers Troy Seals (Jo Ann and Troy), Brady Seals (Little Texas) and Johnny Duncan.	
10/14/72	7	33	● **1. Summer Breeze**	Warner 2629
			Summer Breeze (6)	
5/5/73	4	31	● **2. Diamond Girl**	Warner 2699
			Diamond Girl (6)	
3/23/74	14	16	● 3. Unborn Child	Warner 2761
5/3/75	30	5	● 4. I'll Play For You	Warner 2848
11/22/75	11	11	▲² 5. Greatest Hits [G]	Warner 2886
5/29/76	37	10	● 6. Get Closer	Warner 2907
			Get Closer (6)	
			SEARCHERS, The	
			Liverpool, England, rock quartet formed in 1960: Mike Pender and John McNally (vocals, guitars), Tony Jackson (vocals, bass) and Chris Curtis (drums). Worked as backup band for Johnny Sandon; toured England and worked Star Club in Hamburg, Germany. Left Sandon in 1962. Jackson replaced by Frank Allen in 1965. Curtis replaced by John Blunt in 1966. Blunt replaced by Billy Adamson in 1969. Pender left in 1985; formed own Searchers group; replaced by Spencer James.	
6/13/64	22	8	Meet The Searchers/Needles & Pins	Kapp 3363
			SEBASTIAN, John	
			Born on 3/17/44 in New York City. Played with The Even Dozen Jug Band as "John Benson" in 1964. Did session work for Elektra Records; toured with Mississippi John Hurt. Formed The Lovin' Spoonful in 1965. Went solo in 1968. Continues to write and perform into the '90s.	
4/18/70	20	7	John B. Sebastian	MGM 4654
			album also released on Reprise 6379	
			SECADA, Jon	
			Cuban-born, Miami-raised singer/songwriter. Left Cuba in 1971 at age eight. Earned a Master's degree in jazz at the University of Miami. Co-wrote six songs on Gloria Estefan's album *Into The Light*; backing vocalist for that tour. Legally changed first name from Juan to Jon in 1990.	
8/8/92	15	31	▲³ 1. Jon Secada	SBK 98845
			Just Another Day (5)	
6/11/94	21	9	▲ 2. Heart, Soul & A Voice	SBK 29272
			If You Go (10)	
			SEDAKA, Neil	
			Born on 3/13/39 in Brooklyn. Pop singer/songwriter/pianist. Studied piano since elementary school. Formed songwriting team with lyricist Howard Greenfield while attending Lincoln High School (partnership lasted over 20 years). Recorded with The Tokens on Melba in 1956. Attended Juilliard School for classical piano. Prolific hit songwriter. Career revived in 1974 after signing with Elton John's new Rocket label.	
2/8/75	23	8	● 1. Sedaka's Back [K]	Rocket 463
			compilation of cuts from 3 albums made in Britain	
			Laughter In The Rain (1)	
11/8/75	16	10	● 2. The Hungry Years	Rocket 2157
			Bad Blood (1)/*Breaking Up Is Hard To Do* (8)	

DATE	POS	WKS	ARTIST—RECORD TITLE	LABEL & NO.
5/15/76	**26**	5	3. Steppin' Out	Rocket 2195
			SEDUCTION	
			Female vocal trio from New York: Idalis Leon, April Harris and Michelle Visage. Leon left in 1990; replaced by Sinoa Loren. Visage was a member of The S.O.U.L. S.Y.S.T.E.M. by 1992. Leon is currently a VJ for MTV.	
2/17/90	**36**	7	● Nothing Matters Without Love *Two To Make It Right* (2)	A&M 5280
			SEEKERS, The	
			Australian-born, pop-folk quartet: Judith Durham (born 7/3/43; lead singer), Keith Potger (guitar), Bruce Woodley (Spanish guitar) and Athol Guy (standup bass). Potger formed The New Seekers in 1970.	
3/25/67	**10**	12	**Georgy Girl** *Georgy Girl* (2)	Capitol 2431
			SEGER, Bob, & The Silver Bullet Band	
			Born on 5/6/45 in Dearborn, Michigan; raised in Detroit. Rock singer/songwriter/guitarist. First recorded in 1966; formed the System in 1968. Left music to attend college in 1969; returned in 1970. Formed own backing group The Silver Bullet Band in 1976: Alto Reed (horns), Robyn Robbins (keyboards), Drew Abbott (guitar), Chris Campbell (bass) and Charlie Allen Martin (drums). Various personnel changes since then; Campbell is the only remaining original member.	
6/12/76	**34**	2	▲⁴ 1. 'Live' Bullet [L] *recorded at Cobo Hall, Detroit*	Capitol 11523 [2]
1/8/77	**8**	23	▲⁵ 2. Night Moves *Night Moves* (4)	Capitol 11557
6/3/78	**4**	33	▲⁵ 3. Stranger in Town *Still The Same* (4)	Capitol 11698
3/15/80	**1**(6)	43	▲⁴ 4. Against The Wind *Fire Lake* (6)/*Against The Wind* (5)	Capitol 12041
9/26/81	**3**	21	▲³ 5. Nine Tonight [L] *Tryin' To Live My Life Without You* (5)	Capitol 12182 [2]
1/15/83	**5**	23	▲ 6. The Distance *Shame On The Moon* (2)	Capitol 12254
4/26/86	**3**	28	▲ 7. Like A Rock	Capitol 12398
9/14/91	**7**	14	▲ 8. The Fire Inside	Capitol 91134
11/12/94	**8**	16+	▲ 9. Greatest Hits [G]	Capitol 30334
			SEPULTURA	
			Speed-metal band from Belo Horizonte, Brazil: brothers Max (vocals) and Igor Cavalera with Andreas Kisser and Paulo Jr. Sepultura is Portuguese for grave.	
11/6/93	**32**	1	Chaos A.D.	Roadrunner 57458
			SERENDIPITY SINGERS, The	
			Nine-member, pop-folk group organized at the University of Colorado.	
4/11/64	**11**	18	The Serendipity Singers *Don't Let The Rain Come Down (Crooked Little Man)* (6)	Philips 115
			SERMON, Erick	
			Erick is the 'E' in the Long Island rap duo EPMD.	
11/6/93	**16**	2	No Pressure *CD includes bonus track*	Def Jam 57460
			SESAME STREET — see CHILDREN'S ALBUMS	

DATE	POS	WKS	ARTIST—RECORD TITLE	LABEL & NO.
			SEXTON, Charlie	
			Austin, Texas, rock singer/guitarist. Lead guitarist for Joe Ely's band at age 13 in 1982. Co-founder of The Arc Angels. Appeared in the movie *Thelma & Louise*.	
2/15/86	**15**	13	Pictures For Pleasure	MCA 5629
			SHAI	
			A cappella quartet formed at Howard University in Washington, D.C. Consists of Garfield A. Bright, Marc Gay, Carl "Groove" Martin and Darnell Van Rensalier. Group name pronounced shy.	
1/9/93	**6**	19	▲² **... If I Ever Fall In Love**	Gasoline A. 10762
			If I Ever Fall In Love (2)/*Comforter* (10)/*Baby I'm Yours* (10)	
			SHALAMAR	
			Black vocal trio formed in 1978 by Don Cornelius, producer/host of TV's "Soul Train." Consisted of vocalists/dancers Jody Watley and Jeffrey Daniels with Gerald Brown. Howard Hewett replaced Brown in early 1979. Watley and Daniels (former husband of Stephanie Mills) pursued solo careers in 1984; replaced by Delisa Davis (former Miss Teenage Georgia and Miss Tennessee State) and Micki Free. Hewett left in 1985; replaced by Sydney Justin (former football defensive back with the Los Angeles Rams).	
2/9/80	**23**	11	● 1. Big Fun	Solar 3479
			The Second Time Around (8)	
3/28/81	**40**	2	● 2. Three For Love	Solar 3577
5/8/82	**35**	3	● 3. Friends	Solar 28
9/17/83	**38**	2	4. The Look	Solar 60239
			SHA NA NA	
			Fifties rock-and-roll specialists led by John "Bowzer" Baumann (born 9/14/47, Queens, New York). Formed at Columbia University in 1969. Own syndicated variety TV show, 1977-81. Henry Gross was a member; left in 1970. Many personnel changes.	
6/9/73	**38**	2	● The Golden Age Of Rock 'N' Roll [L]	Kama Sutra 2073 [2]
			SHANNON	
			Brenda Shannon Greene from Washington, D.C. Began singing career at York University.	
3/10/84	**32**	4	● Let The Music Play	Mirage 90134
			Let The Music Play (8)	
			SHANNON, Del	
			Born Charles Westover on 12/30/34 in Coopersville, Michigan. Died on 2/8/90 of a self-inflicted gunshot wound. With U.S. Army *Get Up And Go* radio show in Germany. Discovered by Ann Arbor DJ/producer Ollie McLaughlin. Formed own Berlee label in 1963. Wrote "I Go To Pieces" for Peter & Gordon. To Los Angeles in 1966; production work.	
7/6/63	**12**	9	Little Town Flirt	Big Top 1308
			Runaway (1)/*Hats Off To Larry* (5)	
			SHARPLES, Bob	
			Bandleader from Bury, Lancashire, England.	
10/16/61	**11**	20	Pass In Review [I]	London P. 4 44001
			SHAW, Robert, Chorale	
			Born on 4/30/16 in Red Bluff, California. Conductor/music director. Led The Fred Waring Glee Clubs, 1938-45; organized own singing group in 1948. Music director of the Atlanta Symphony Orchestra and Chorus, 1967-87.	
12/23/57	**5**	4	● **1. Christmas Hymns And Carols** [X]	RCA 1711
12/22/58	**13**	3	2. Christmas Hymns And Carols [X-R]	RCA 1711
			Christmas charts: 9/'63, 31/'64, 41/'66, 28/'67	

DATE	POS	WKS	ARTIST—RECORD TITLE	LABEL & NO.
5/25/59	21	1	3. Deep River and Other Spirituals	RCA 2247
6/8/63	27	7	4. America, The Beautiful	RCA 2662
			with the RCA Victor Symphony Orchestra	
			SHAW, Roland, Orchestra	
			English conductor.	
6/19/65	38	1	Themes From The James Bond Thrillers [I]	London 412
			SHEARING, George, Quintet	
			Shearing was born on 8/13/19 in London. Piano stylist; blind since birth. Moved to the U.S. in 1947.	
10/6/56	20	1	1. Velvet Carpet [I]	Capitol 720
10/7/57	13	3	2. Black Satin [I]	Capitol 858
8/25/58	17	2	3. Burnished Brass [I]	Capitol 1038
7/25/60	11	23	4. White Satin	Capitol 1334
5/12/62	27	9	5. Nat King Cole sings/George Shearing plays	Capitol 1675
			SHEILA E.	
			Born Sheila Escovedo on 12/12/59 in San Francisco. Singer/percussionist. With father Pete Escovedo in the band Azteca in the mid-1970s. Toured with Lionel Richie; since 1986, toured and recorded with Prince. Brother Peto was in Con Funk Shun. Uncle Coke Escovedo is a noted percussionist.	
9/1/84	28	9	● Sheila E. in The Glamorous Life	Warner 25107
			The Glamorous Life (7)	
			SHELTON, Ricky Van	
			Born on 1/12/52 in Danville, Virginia; raised in Grit, Virginia. Country singer.	
6/22/91	23	8	▲ Backroads	Columbia 46855
			SHERMAN, Allan	
			Born Allan Copelon on 11/30/24 in Chicago; died on 11/21/73. Began as professional comedy writer for Jackie Gleason, Joe E. Lewis and others. Creator/producer of TV's "I've Got A Secret."	
11/10/62	1(2)	29	● **1. My Son, The Folk Singer** [C]	Warner 1475
1/26/63	1(1)	19	**2. My Son, The Celebrity** [C]	Warner 1487
8/24/63	1(8)	24	**3. My Son, The Nut** [C]	Warner 1501
			Hello Mudduh, Hello Fadduh! (2)	
5/16/64	25	6	4. Allan In Wonderland [C]	Warner 1539
1/2/65	32	5	5. For Swingin' Livers Only! [C]	Warner 1569
			SHERMAN, Bobby	
			Born on 7/18/43 in Santa Monica, California. Regular on TV's "Shindig"; played Jeremy Bolt on TV's "Here Come the Brides." First recorded for Starcrest in 1962. Currently involved in TV production.	
11/22/69	11	15	● 1. Bobby Sherman	Metromedia 1014
			Little Woman (3)	
4/18/70	10	12	● **2. Here Comes Bobby**	Metromedia 1028
			La La La (If I Had You) (9)/*Easy Come, Easy Go* (9)	
10/24/70	20	8	● 3. With Love, Bobby	Metromedia 1032
			Julie, Do Ya Love Me (5)	

DATE	POS	WKS	ARTIST—RECORD TITLE	LABEL & NO.
			SHIRELLES, The	
			R&B vocal trio from Passaic, New Jersey: Shirley Owens Alston, Beverly Lee, Doris Kenner and Addie "Micki" Harris (died 6/10/82 [age 42]). Formed in junior high school as The Poquellos. Kenner left group in 1968; returned in 1975. Alston left for solo career in 1975; recorded as Lady Rose.	
2/9/63	**19**	18	The Shirelles Greatest Hits　　　　　　　[G]	Scepter 507
			Will You Love Me Tomorrow (1)/ *Dedicated To The One I Love* (3)/*Mama Said* (4)	
			SHIRLEY, Donald	
			Born on 1/27/27 in Kingston, Jamaica. Pianist/organist.	
4/2/55	**14**	4	Tonal Expressions　　　　　　　　　　[I]	Cadence 1001
			SHOCKING BLUE, The	
			Dutch rock quartet: Mariska Veres (lead singer), Robbie van Leeuwen (guitar), Cor van Beek (drums) and Klaasje van der Wal (bass). Disbanded in 1974.	
3/7/70	**31**	3	The Shocking Blue	Colossus 1000
			Venus (1)	
			SILK	
			Atlanta R&B male vocal quintet: Timothy Cameron, Jimmy Gates, Jr., Jonathan Rasboro, Gary Jenkins and Gary Glenn. Discovered by Keith Sweat. Not to be confused with the Philadelphia R&B band from 1977.	
2/6/93	**7**	26	▲　　**Lose Control**	Keia 61394
			Freak Me (1)	
			SILVER CONVENTION	
			German studio disco act assembled by producer Michael Kunze and writer/arranger Silvester Levay. Female vocal trio formed in 1976 consisting of Penny McLean, Ramona Wolf and Linda Thompson.	
10/25/75	**10**	10	●　　**1. Save Me**	Midland Int. 1129
			Fly, Robin, Fly (1)	
5/1/76	**13**	10	2. Silver Convention	Midland Int. 1369
			Get Up And Boogie (That's Right) (2)	
			SIMMONS, Gene	
			Born Gene Klein on 8/25/49 in Haifa, Israel. Bass guitarist of Kiss. Appeared in the movies *Runaway* (1984) and *Trick Or Treat* (1986).	
11/11/78	**22**	12	▲　　Gene Simmons	Casablanca 7120
			SIMON, Carly	
			Born on 6/25/45 in New York City. Pop vocalist/songwriter. Father is co-founder of Simon & Schuster publishing company. Folk duo with sister Lucy (The Simon Sisters), mid-1960s. Won 1971 Best New Artist Grammy Award. Married James Taylor on 11/3/72; divorced in 1983.	
7/3/71	**30**	7	1. Carly Simon	Elektra 74082
			That's The Way I've Always Heard It Should Be (10)	
2/12/72	**30**	5	●　　2. Anticipation	Elektra 75016
12/23/72	**1**(5)	23	●　　**3. No Secrets**	Elektra 75049
			You're So Vain (1)	
2/9/74	**3**	16	●　　**4. Hotcakes**	Elektra 1002
			Mockingbird (5-with James Taylor)	
5/10/75	**10**	9	**5. Playing Possum**	Elektra 1033
12/20/75	**17**	9	●　　6. The Best Of Carly Simon　　　[G]	Elektra 1048
7/4/76	**29**	4	7. Another Passenger	Elektra 1064
5/13/78	**10**	17	▲　　**8. Boys In The Trees**	Elektra 128
			You Belong To Me (6)	

DATE	POS	WKS	ARTIST—RECORD TITLE	LABEL & NO.
11/1/80	36	4	9. Come Upstairs	Warner 3443
8/29/87	25	10	▲ 10. Coming Around Again	Arista 8443

SIMON, Paul

Born on 10/13/42 in Newark, New Jersey; raised in Queens, New York. Vocalist/composer/guitarist. Met Art Garfunkel in high school; recorded together as Tom & Jerry in 1957. Worked as Jerry Landis, Tico and The Triumphs, Paul Kane, Harrison Gregory and True Taylor in the early '60s. To England from 1963-64. Returned to the U.S.; recorded first album with Garfunkel in 1965. Went solo in 1971. Married to actress Carrie Fisher from 1983-85. Married singer Edie Brickell on 5/30/92. In the movies *Annie Hall* and *One-Trick Pony*. Winner of 12 Grammy Awards.

DATE	POS	WKS	ARTIST—RECORD TITLE	LABEL & NO.
2/19/72	4	18	▲ **1. Paul Simon** *Mother And Child Reunion* (4)	Columbia 30750
6/9/73	2 (2)	24	▲ **2. There Goes Rhymin' Simon** *Kodachrome* (2)/*Loves Me Like A Rock* (2)	Columbia 32280
4/13/74	33	3	● 3. Paul Simon In Concert/Live Rhymin' [L]	Columbia 32855
11/1/75	1 (1)	29	● **4. Still Crazy After All These Years** 1975 Album of the Year Grammy Award *My Little Town* (9-Simon & Garfunkel)/ *50 Ways To Leave Your Lover* (1)	Columbia 33540
12/17/77	18	9	▲ **5. Greatest Hits, Etc.** [G] *Slip Slidin' Away* (5)	Columbia 35032
9/6/80	12	13	● **6. One-Trick Pony** [S] Simon starred in the movie *Late In The Evening* (6)	Warner 3472
12/3/83	35	8	7. Hearts And Bones	Warner 23942
9/27/86	3	52	▲⁵ **8. Graceland** 1986 Album of the Year Grammy Award; South African-flavored tunes written by Simon; backed by a South African ensemble	Warner 25447
11/3/90	4	26	▲² **9. The Rhythm Of The Saints** partially recorded in Rio de Janeiro, Brazil; incorporates the rhythmic sounds native to South America	Warner 26098

SIMON & GARFUNKEL

Folk-rock duo from New York City: Paul Simon and Art Garfunkel. Recorded as Tom & Jerry in 1957. Duo split in 1964; Simon was working solo in England; Garfunkel was in graduate school. They re-formed in 1965; stayed together until 1971. Reunited briefly in 1981 for national tour. Inducted into the Rock and Roll Hall of Fame in 1990.

DATE	POS	WKS	ARTIST—RECORD TITLE	LABEL & NO.
2/12/66	30	3	● 1. Wednesday Morning, 3 AM contains original unmixed version of "The Sounds Of Silence"	Columbia 9049
4/9/66	21	34	▲² 2. Sounds of Silence *The Sounds Of Silence* (1)/*I Am A Rock* (3)	Columbia 9269
11/19/66	4	60	▲³ **3. Parsley, Sage, Rosemary and Thyme** *Homeward Bound* (5)	Columbia 9363
3/23/68	1 (9)	47	● **4. The Graduate** [S] includes 4 previously released Simon & Garfunkel songs; the 2 "Mrs. Robinson" cuts are not the hit versions	Columbia 3180
5/4/68	1 (7)	40	▲² **5. Bookends** side 2: hit singles previously unavailable on an album *Mrs. Robinson* (1)	Columbia 9529
2/28/70	1 (10)	24	▲⁵ **6. Bridge Over Troubled Water** 1970 Grammy winner: Album of the Year *The Boxer* (7)/*Bridge Over Troubled Water* (1)/*Cecilia* (4)	Columbia 9914
7/8/72	5	22	▲⁶ **7. Simon And Garfunkel's Greatest Hits** [G]	Columbia 31350

DATE	POS	WKS	ARTIST—RECORD TITLE	LABEL & NO.
3/13/82	6	11	▲ **8. The Concert In Central Park** [L] recorded in New York City's Central Park on 9/19/81	Warner 3654 [2]
			SIMONE, Nina	
			Born Eunice Waymon on 2/21/33 in Tryon, South Carolina. Jazz-influenced vocalist/pianist/composer. Attended the Juilliard School of Music in New York City. Devoted more time to political activism in the '70s; infrequent recording.	
3/6/61	23	1	Nina At Newport [L]	Colpix 412
			SIMPLE MINDS	
			Scottish rock group. Nucleus of band: Jim Kerr (lead singer; formerly married to Chrissie Hynde of The Pretenders; later married Patsy Kensit of Eighth Wonder), Michael MacNeil (keyboards), Charles Burchill (keyboards), Mel Gaynor (drums) and John Giblin (bass). MacNeil left in 1989.	
11/16/85	10	27	● **Once Upon A Time** Alive & Kicking (3)	A&M 5092
			SIMPLY RED	
			Manchester, England, group: vocalist Mick "Red" Hucknall (born 6/8/60), keyboardists Fritz McIntyre & Tim Kellett, Tony Bowers (bass), Chris Joyce (drums) and Sylvan Richardson (guitar). 1991 lineup: Hucknall, McIntyre, Kellett, saxophonist Ian Kirkham, Brazilian guitarist Heitor T.P. and Japanese drummer Gota.	
5/31/86	16	28	▲ 1. Picture Book Holding Back The Years (1)	Elektra 60452
4/18/87	31	5	2. Men And Women	Elektra 60727
6/17/89	22	14	● 3. A New Flame If You Don't Know Me By Now (1)	Elektra 60828
			SIMPSONS, The	
			The voices of the Fox network's animated TV series. Nancy Cartwright is Bart; Dan Castellaneta is Homer; Julie Kavner is Marge; Yeardley Smith is Lisa; and the show's creator, Matt Groening, is Maggie.	
1/5/91	3	21	▲² **The Simpsons Sing The Blues** [N] guest appearance by Buster Poindexter	Geffen 24308
			SINATRA, Frank	
			Born Francis Albert Sinatra on 12/12/15 in Hoboken, New Jersey. With Harry James from 1939-40; first recorded for Brunswick in 1939; with Tommy Dorsey, 1940-42. Went solo in late 1942; charted 40 Top 10 hits through 1954. Appeared in many movies from 1941 on. Won an Academy Award for the movie *From Here to Eternity* in 1953. Own TV show in 1957. Own Reprise record company in 1961; sold to Warner Bros. in 1963. Won 1965 Lifetime Achievement Grammy Award. Married to actress Ava Gardner from 1951-57. Married to actress Mia Farrow from 1966-68. Announced his retirement in 1970, but made comeback in 1973. Regarded by many as the greatest popular singer of the 20th century.	
5/28/55	2 (18)	33	**1. in the Wee Small Hours**	Capitol 581
3/31/56	2 (1)	50	● **2. songs for Swingin' Lovers!**	Capitol 653
12/22/56	8	17	● **3. This is Sinatra!** [G] Young At Heart (2-'54)/Three Coins In The Fountain (7-'54)/ Learnin' The Blues (1)/Love And Marriage (5)/ (Love Is) The Tender Trap (7)	Capitol 768
3/2/57	5	14	**4. Close To You** featuring The Hollywood String Quartet	Capitol 789
5/27/57	2 (1)	36	**5. a Swingin' Affair!**	Capitol 803
9/23/57	3	21	**6. Where are you?**	Capitol 855
11/11/57	2 (1)	27	**7. Pal Joey** [S]	Capitol 912

DATE	POS	WKS	ARTIST—RECORD TITLE	LABEL & NO.
			Sinatra plays Joey Evans and sings on 6 of the tracks, including "The Lady Is A Tramp"; orchestra numbers conducted by Morris Stoloff	
12/30/57	18	2	▲ 8. a Jolly Christmas from Frank Sinatra [X]	Capitol 894
2/3/58	1 (5)	50	**9. Come fly with me**	Capitol 920
4/28/58	8	7	**10. This Is Sinatra, Volume Two** [G]	Capitol 982
			Hey! Jealous Lover (3)	
6/2/58	12	1	11. The Frank Sinatra Story [K]	Columbia 6 [2]
9/29/58	1 (5)	55	● **12. Frank Sinatra sings for Only The Lonely**	Capitol 1053
2/9/59	2 (5)	52	● **13. Come Dance With Me!**	Capitol 1069
			1959 Album of the Year Grammy Award	
6/1/59	8	11	**14. Look to Your Heart** [K]	Capitol 1164
8/31/59	2 (2)	34	**15. No One Cares**	Capitol 1221
8/22/60	1 (9)	35	● **16. Nice 'n' Easy**	Capitol 1417
2/13/61	3	22	**17. Sinatra's Swingin' Session!!!**	Capitol 1491
4/10/61	4	27	**18. All The Way** [G]	Capitol 1538
			All The Way (2)/*Witchcraft* (6)	
5/8/61	4	20	**19. Ring-A-Ding Ding!**	Reprise 1001
			the first album for Sinatra's own record company	
8/21/61	8	12	**20. Come Swing With Me!**	Capitol 1594
8/28/61	6	18	**21. Sinatra Swings**	Reprise 1002
11/20/61	3	23	**22. I Remember Tommy ...**	Reprise 1003
			songs popularized by Tommy Dorsey	
3/17/62	8	20	**23. Sinatra & Strings**	Reprise 1004
5/5/62	19	23	24. Point Of No Return	Capitol 1676
8/25/62	15	9	25. Sinatra Sings ... of love and things [K]	Capitol 1729
9/15/62	18	8	26. Sinatra and Swingin' Brass	Reprise 1005
11/24/62	25	8	27. All Alone	Reprise 1007
2/9/63	5	22	**28. Sinatra-Basie** *	Reprise 1008
7/6/63	6	11	**29. The Concert Sinatra**	Reprise 1009
10/19/63	8	17	● **30. Sinatra's Sinatra**	Reprise 1010
			newly recorded Sinatra favorites	
4/25/64	10	16	**31. Days Of Wine And Roses, Moon River, and other academy award winners**	Reprise 1011
9/12/64	13	15	32. It Might As Well Be Swing *	Reprise 1012
			***FRANK SINATRA/COUNT BASIE**	
2/6/65	19	12	33. Softly, As I Leave You	Reprise 1013
7/17/65	9	32	**34. Sinatra '65**	Reprise 6167
9/25/65	5	46	● **35. September Of My Years**	Reprise 1014
			1965 Album of the Year Grammy Award	
1/15/66	9	20	● **36. A Man And His Music** [K]	Reprise 1016 [2]
			1966 Album of the Year Grammy Award; an anthology of Sinatra's career, narrated and sung by him	
2/19/66	30	3	37. My Kind Of Broadway	Reprise 1015
6/18/66	34	2	38. Moonlight Sinatra	Reprise 1018
7/2/66	1 (1)	43	▲ **39. Strangers In The Night**	Reprise 1017
			Strangers In The Night (1)	
9/10/66	9	15	● **40. Sinatra At The Sands** [L]	Reprise 1019 [2]
			with Count Basie & The Orchestra	

DATE	POS	WKS	ARTIST—RECORD TITLE	LABEL & NO.
1/21/67	6	22	● **41. That's Life** *That's Life* (4)	Reprise 1020
5/13/67	19	6	42. Francis Albert Sinatra & Antonio Carlos Jobim _{Jobim is a Brazilian songwriter/guitarist/vocalist (died 12/8/94)}	Reprise 1021
9/30/67	24	9	43. Frank Sinatra *Somethin' Stupid* (1-with Nancy Sinatra)	Reprise 1022
1/18/69	18	7	● 44. Cycles	Reprise 1027
5/17/69	11	8	● 45. My Way	Reprise 1029
9/27/69	30	5	46. A Man Alone & Other Songs of Rod McKuen	Reprise 1030
11/17/73	13	10	● 47. Ol' Blue Eyes Is Back	Reprise 2155
1/4/75	37	2	48. Sinatra — The Main Event Live [L] _{recorded at New York's Madison Square Garden; with Woody Herman & The Young Thundering Herd}	Reprise 2207
5/3/80	17	12	● 49. Trilogy: Past, Present, Future	Reprise 2300 [3]
11/20/93	2 (3)	17	▲² **50. Duets** _{collection of standards with duet partners Charles Aznavour, Anita Baker, Tony Bennett, Bono (of U2), Natalie Cole, Gloria Estefan, Aretha Franklin, Julio Iglesias, Kenny G, Liza Minnelli, Carly Simon, Barbra Streisand and Luther Vandross}	Capitol 89611
12/3/94	9	6	**51. Duets II** _{collection of standards with duet partners Jimmy Buffett, Neil Diamond, Lena Horne, Chrissie Hynde (The Pretenders), Antonio Carlos Jobim, Gladys Knight & Stevie Wonder, Patti LaBelle, Steve Lawrence & Eydie Gorme, Luis Miguel, Lorrie Morgan, Willie Nelson, Linda Ronstadt, Jon Secada and Frank Sinatra, Jr.}	Capitol 28103
			SINATRA, Nancy _{Born on 6/8/40 in Jersey City, New Jersey. First child of Nancy and Frank Sinatra. Moved to Los Angeles while a child. Made national TV debut with father and Elvis Presley in 1959. Married to singer/ actor Tommy Sands, 1960-65. Appeared on "Hullabaloo," "American Bandstand" and own specials in the mid-1960s. In movies *For Those Who Think Young*, *Get Yourself a College Girl*, *The Oscar* and *Speedway* (with Elvis Presley).}	
3/26/66	5	24	● **1. Boots** *These Boots Are Made For Walkin'* (1)	Reprise 6202
3/18/67	18	6	2. Sugar *Sugar Town* (5)	Reprise 6239
3/16/68	37	4	3. Movin' With Nancy [TV] _{guests: Frank Sinatra, Dean Martin and Lee Hazlewood}	Reprise 6277
5/25/68	13	18	● 4. Nancy & Lee **NANCY SINATRA & LEE HAZLEWOOD**	Reprise 6273
			SINGING NUN, The _{Sister Luc-Gabrielle (real name: Jeanine Deckers) from the Fichermont, Belgium, convent. Recorded under the name Soeur Sourire ("Sister Smile"). Committed suicide on 3/31/85 (age 52).}	
11/23/63	1 (10)	22	● **The Singing Nun** [F] *Dominique* (1)	Philips 203
			SIR MIX-A-LOT _{Seattle rapper Anthony Ray. Appears as the host of the anthology TV series "The Watcher."}	
2/22/92	9	28	▲ **Mack Daddy** *Baby Got Back* (1)	Def Amer. 26765

DATE	POS	WKS	ARTIST—RECORD TITLE	LABEL & NO.
			SISTER SLEDGE	
			Sisters Debra, Joni, Kim and Kathy Sledge from North Philadelphia. First recorded as Sisters Sledge for Money Back label in 1971. Worked as backup vocalists. Began producing their own albums in 1981.	
3/24/79	3	19	▲ **1. We Are Family**	Cotillion 5209
			He's The Greatest Dancer (9)/We Are Family (2)	
3/29/80	31	5	2. Love Somebody Today	Cotillion 16012
			SKID ROW	
			New York hard-rock quintet: Toronto native Sebastian "Bach" Bierk (vocals), Rachel Bolan (bass), Dave Sabo (guitar), Scott Hill (guitar) and Rob Affuso (drums).	
3/18/89	6	57	▲³ **1. Skid Row**	Atlantic 81936
			18 And Life (4)/I Remember You (6)	
6/29/91	1(1)	15	▲ **2. Slave To The Grind**	Atlantic 82278
			SKYY	
			Brooklyn R&B-pop-funk octet. Vocals by sisters Denise, Delores and Bonnie Dunning. Organized by Randy Muller, former leader of Brass Construction.	
2/6/82	18	11	● Skyy Line	Salsoul 8548
			SLADE	
			English hard-rock quartet: Noddy Holder (born 6/15/50; lead singer), David Hill (guitar), Jim Lea (bass, keyboards) and Don Powell (drums).	
6/16/84	33	4	Keep Your Hands Off My Power Supply	CBS Assoc. 39336
			SLATKIN, Felix	
			St. Louis native. Died on 2/9/63 (age 47). Virtuoso violinist/conductor/composer/arranger. Worked with many movie and record companies.	
5/11/63	20	7	Our Winter Love [I]	Liberty 7287
			SLAUGHTER	
			Las Vegas hard-rock quartet led by vocalist Mark Slaughter, who, with bandmate Dana Strum (bass), was a member of The Vinnie Vincent Invasion. Includes guitarist Tim Kelly and drummer Blas Elias.	
4/14/90	18	41	▲² 1. Stick It To Ya	Chrysalis 21702
5/9/92	8	8	● **2. The Wild Life**	Chrysalis 21911
			SLAVE	
			Funk band from Dayton, Ohio, formed by Steve Washington (trumpet) in 1975; left by 1981. Longtime members of group included Mark "The Hansolor" Adams (bass), Floyd Miller (vocals, horns) and Danny Webster (vocals, guitar). Studio vocalist Steve Arrington was a member from 1979-82.	
6/18/77	22	12	● Slave	Cotillion 9914
			SLAYER	
			Southern California heavy-metal band formed in 1982: Tom Araya (vocals), Jeff Hanneman, Kerry King and Dave Lombardo.	
11/3/90	40	1	● 1. Seasons In The Abyss	Def Amer. 24307
10/15/94	8	3	● **2. Divine Intervention**	American 45522
			SLEDGE, Percy	
			Born in 1941 in Leighton, Alabama. Worked local clubs with Esquires Combo until going solo. Pleaded guilty to tax evasion on 4/7/94.	
8/6/66	37	2	When A Man Loves A Woman	Atlantic 8125
			When A Man Loves A Woman (1)	

DATE	POS	WKS	ARTIST—RECORD TITLE	LABEL & NO.
			SLICK, Grace	
			Born Grace Wing on 10/30/39 in Chicago. Female lead singer of Jefferson Airplane/Starship. Before joining Jefferson Airplane, she was a member of The Great Society.	
4/26/80	32	4	Dreams	RCA 3544
			SLICK RICK	
			Ricky Walters, born to Jamaican parents in South Wimbledon, London. To the U.S. at age 14. Attended New York's High School of Music & Art. Teamed with Doug E. Fresh, 1984-85; known as "MC Ricky D." In 1991, sentenced to 3-10 years in prison for a shooting incident. Entered a work-release program in June 1993.	
5/27/89	31	5	▲ 1. The Great Adventures Of Slick Rick	Def Jam 40513
7/20/91	29	1	2. The Ruler's Back	Def Jam 47372
			SLY & THE FAMILY STONE	
			San Francisco interracial, psychedelic-soul group formed by Sylvester "Sly Stone" Stewart (born 3/15/44, Dallas; lead singer, keyboards), Stewart's brother Freddie Stone (guitar), Cynthia Robinson (trumpet), Jerry Martini (saxophone), Stewart's sister Rosie Stone (piano, vocals), Stewart's cousin Larry Graham (bass) and Gregg Errico (drums). Stewart recorded gospel at age four. Producer and writer for Bobby Freeman, The Mojo Men, The Beau Brummels. Formed own groups, The Stoners in 1966 and The Family Stone in 1967. Played Woodstock Festival in 1969. Career waned in the mid-1970s. Worked with George Clinton in 1982. Graham formed Graham Central Station in 1973. Group inducted into the Rock and Roll Hall of Fame in 1993.	
5/3/69	13	24	▲ 1. Stand!	Epic 26456
			Everyday People (1)	
11/14/70	2(1)	27	▲³ **2. Greatest Hits** [G]	Epic 30325
			Hot Fun In The Summertime (2)/ *Thank You (Falettinme Be Mice Elf Agin)* (1)	
11/13/71	1(2)	18	● **3. There's A Riot Goin' On**	Epic 30986
			Family Affair (1)	
7/7/73	7	16	● **4. Fresh**	Epic 32134
8/17/74	15	7	● 5. Small Talk	Epic 32930
			SLY FOX	
			Black-and-white duo: Gary "Mudbone" Cooper (P-Funk) and Michael Camacho.	
4/26/86	31	4	Let's Go All The Way	Capitol 12367
			Let's Go All The Way (7)	
			SMASHING PUMPKINS	
			Three-man, one-woman alternative band formed in Chicago by singer/guitarist Billy Corgan, James Iha (guitar), D'Arcy (bass) and Jimmy Chamberlain (drums). D'Arcy married Kerry Brown (drummer of Catherine) on 6/7/94.	
8/14/93	10	59	▲³ **1. Siamese Dream**	Virgin 88267
10/22/94	4	6	▲ **2. Pisces Iscariot** [K]	Virgin 39834
			B-sides and previously unavailable tracks	
			SMITH	
			Los Angeles-based rock quintet fronted by St. Louis blues rocker Gayle McCormick.	
11/1/69	17	11	a group called Smith	Dunhill 50056
			Baby It's You (5)	

The Rolling Stones' *Black And Blue* held the No. 1 slot for four weeks in 1976 and was the band's first album to feature former Faces guitarist Ronnie Wood on its cover. A notorious advertisement for the record drew the wrath of many women's groups of the era.

Linda Ronstadt's 1973 album, *Don't Cry Now*, marked her recording debut for David Geffen's Asylum Record label and was her first set to be certified gold. But *Heart Like A Wheel*, the album's 1974 follow-up released on Capitol by contractual obligation, was the bigger record, courtesy of the hits "You're No Good" and "When Will I Be Loved."

Diana Ross's 1976 greatest-hits compilation was the former Supremes singer's third Top 5 album as a solo artist. With her former band, she had scored a grand total of seven between 1964–68.

Run-D.M.C.'s 1988 platinum set, *Tougher Than Leather*, was the pioneering rap group's second Top 10 album. It shared its title with a film that also starred the Queens-based trio.

Rush's *Fly By Night* was the hard-rocking Canadian trio's second album. The 1975 release marked the debut of longtime Rush drummer Neil Peart, whose style both musically and lyrically has brought the group more than 20 years of chart fame.

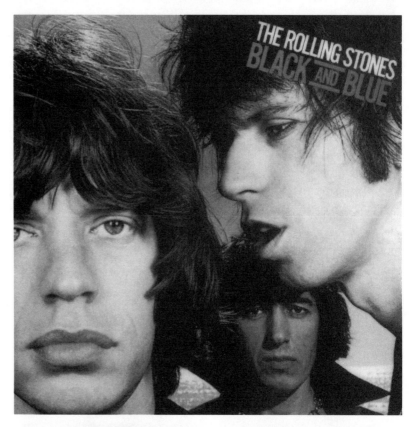

Salt 'N' Pepa's 1993 album, *Very Necessary*, was a triple-platinum smash that entered the Top 5 and became the Queens-based rap trio's most popular effort to date.

Santana's *Freedom*, which peaked at No. 95 in 1987, was the legendary San Franciscan band's sixteenth charting album recorded for Columbia. In 1992, after 23 years with the label, bandleader Carlos Santana departed and released *Milagro* on Polydor.

Allan Sherman's unique style of comedy was everpresent in the early '60s. *My Son, the Nut* was No. 1 for eight weeks in 1963. Sherman's work was later collected and reissued by longtime fans at Rhino Records.

Simon & Garfunkel's 1970 No. 1 smash, *Bridge Over Troubled Water*, was the last album the duo recorded while officially together. The pair later reunited many times for special concerts, as documented on 1982's platinum *The Concert In Central Park* album.

Frank Sinatra's presence on the *Billboard* pop albums chart has been felt since its 1955 inception. Well into the '90s, the singer released a set of very popular duet albums, each of which entered the Top 10 and made headlines the world over.

DATE	POS	WKS	ARTIST—RECORD TITLE	LABEL & NO.
			SMITH, Jimmy	
			Born on 12/8/25 in Norristown, Pennsylvania. Pioneer jazz organist. Won Major Bowes Amateur Show in 1934. With father (James, Sr.) in song-and-dance team, 1942. With Don Gardner & The Sonotones; recorded for Bruce in 1953. Smith first recorded with own trio for Blue Note in 1956.	
4/21/62	28	5	1. Midnight Special [I]	Blue Note 84078
			with Stanley Turrentine (sax) and Kenny Burrell (guitar)	
7/21/62	10	20	**2. Bashin'** [I]	Verve 8474
3/23/63	14	8	3. Back At The Chicken Shack [I]	Blue Note 84117
			with Stanley Turrentine and Kenny Burrell	
5/25/63	11	15	4. Hobo Flats [I]	Verve 8544
11/30/63	25	7	5. Any Number Can Win [I]	Verve 8552
5/23/64	16	15	6. Who's Afraid Of Virginia Woolf? [I]	Verve 8583
10/31/64	12	13	7. The Cat [I]	Verve 8587
7/10/65	35	4	8. Monster [I]	Verve 8618
10/30/65	15	10	9. Organ Grinder Swing [I]	Verve 8628
			featuring Kenny Burrell (guitar) and Grady Tate (drums)	
5/28/66	28	10	10. Got My Mojo Workin' [I]	Verve 8641
			SMITH, Kate	
			Born on 5/1/07 in Greenville, Virginia; died on 6/17/86. Tremendously popular soprano who was for years one of the most listened to of all radio singers. Later hosted own TV variety series, 1951-52, 1960. Smith introduced the classic Irving Berlin hit "God Bless America."	
4/16/66	36	5	How Great Thou Art	RCA 3445
			SMITH, Keely	
			Born Dorothy Smith on 3/9/32 in Norfolk, Virginia. Jazz-styled vocalist. Married to singer/trumpeter/ bandleader Louis Prima, 1952-61; they recorded as a successful duo. Also see Louis Prima.	
10/20/58	14	8	1. Politely!	Capitol 1073
5/25/59	23	4	2. Swingin' Pretty	Capitol 1145
1/4/60	40	1	3. Be My Love	Dot 3241
			SMITH, O.C.	
			Born Ocie Lee Smith on 6/21/36 in Mansfield, Louisiana. To Los Angeles in 1939. Sang while in U.S. Air Force from 1953-57. First recorded for Cadence in 1956. With Count Basie from 1961-63.	
11/23/68	19	10	Hickory Holler Revisited	Columbia 9680
			Little Green Apples (2)	
			SMITH, Patti, Group	
			Smith was born on 12/31/46 in Chicago; raised in New Jersey. Poet-turned-punk rocker. As a freelance rock journalist, wrote articles for *Rolling Stone*, *Crawdaddy* and *Creem*. Has published several books of poetry. Married to Fred "Sonic" Smith of the MC5 from 1980 until his death in 1994. Left music industry from September of 1979 to 1988 to raise a family. Band included Lenny Kaye, Richard Sohl, Jay Dee Daughtery and Ivan Kral. Not to be confused with Patty Smyth of Scandal.	
5/27/78	20	8	1. Easter	Arista 4171
5/26/79	18	7	2. Wave	Arista 4221
			produced by Todd Rundgren	

DATE	POS	WKS	ARTIST—RECORD TITLE	LABEL & NO.
			SMITH, Rex	Columbia 35813
			Born on 9/19/56 in Jacksonville, Florida. Vocalist/actor. Starred in several Broadway musicals and in the TV movie *Sooner or Later*. Appeared in movies *The Pirates of Penzance* and *Streethawk*. Younger brother of Starz's lead singer, Michael Lee Smith.	
5/12/79	**19**	8	● Sooner Or Later	
			You Take My Breath Away (10)	
			SMITH, Sammi	Mega 1000
			Born on 8/5/43 in Orange, California; raised in Oklahoma. Female country singer. Moved to Nashville in 1967.	
3/27/71	**33**	4	Help Me Make It Through The Night	
			Help Me Make It Through The Night (8)	
			SMOTHERS BROTHERS, The	
			Comedians Tom (born 2/2/37; guitar) and Dick Smothers (born 11/20/39; standup bass), both born in York City. Hosts of their own TV comedy variety series from 1967-69. Own summer variety series, 1970; 1988-89.	
11/24/62	**26**	11	● 1. The Two Sides Of The Smothers Brothers [C]	Mercury 20675
			side 1: comedy; side 2: serious singing	
5/4/63	**27**	22	● 2. (Think Ethnic!) [C]	Mercury 20777
1/4/64	**13**	10	3. Curb Your Tongue, Knave! [C]	Mercury 20862
6/20/64	**23**	7	4. It Must Have Been Something I Said! [C]	Mercury 20904
1/29/66	**39**	2	5. Mom Always Liked You Best! [C]	Mercury 21051
			SNAP!	Arista 8536
			German studio group assembled by producers Michael Muenzing and Luca Anzilotti. Group includes a revolving lineup of lead singers including Turbo B, Jackie Harris, Penny Ford, Thea Austin, Niki Harris and Summer (real name: Paula Brown).	
8/11/90	**30**	9	● World Power	
			The Power (2)	
			SNIFF 'n' the TEARS	Atlantic 19242
			British rock group led by Paul Roberts (vocals) and Loz Netto (guitar). Roberts joined The Stranglers in 1991.	
10/6/79	**35**	3	Fickle Heart	
			SNOOP DOGGY DOGG	Death Row 92279
			Calvin Broadus, rapper with Dr. Dre. Native of Long Beach, California. Childhood friend of Dr. Dre and Warren G. & Nate Dogg. Arrested in connection with a drive-by shooting in Los Angeles on 8/25/93.	
12/11/93	**1**(3)	31	▲⁴ **Doggy Style**	
			produced by Dr. Dre	
			What's My Name? (8)/*Gin & Juice* (8)	
			SNOW	EastWest 92207
			Born Darren O'Brien on 10/30/69. White male reggae singer from Toronto.	
3/6/93	**5**	22	▲ **12 Inches Of Snow**	
			CD includes 2 bonus tracks	
			Informer (1)	
			SNOW, Phoebe	Shelter 2109
			Born Phoebe Laub on 7/17/52 in New York City; raised in New Jersey. Vocalist/guitarist/songwriter. Began performing in Greenwich Village in the early '70s.	
11/16/74	**4**	22	● **1. Phoebe Snow**	
			Poetry Man (5)	

DATE	POS	WKS	ARTIST—RECORD TITLE	LABEL & NO.
2/21/76	**13**	10	● 2. Second Childhood	Columbia 33952
11/27/76	**29**	7	3. It Looks Like Snow [C]	Columbia 34387
			SNYDER, Terry — see LIGHT, Enoch	
			SOFT CELL	
			British electro-rock duo: Marc Almond (vocals) and David Ball (synthesizer). Almond began solo career in late 1988.	
3/20/82	**22**	18	Non-Stop Erotic Cabaret	Sire 3647
			Tainted Love (8)	
			SONIC YOUTH	
			Post-punk band based in New York City and formed in 1981: guitarists Thurston Moore and Lee Ranaldo, Kim Gordon (bass) and Steve Shelley (drums). All share vocals. Moore and Gordon are married.	
5/28/94	**34**	1	Experimental Jet Set, Trash And No Star	DGC 24632
			SONNY & CHER	
			Husband-and-wife duo: Cher (born 5/20/46) and Sonny Bono (born 2/16/35). Began career as session singers for Phil Spector. First recorded as Caesar & Cleo for Vault in 1963. Married in 1963; divorced in 1974. In the movies *Good Times* (1966) and *Chastity* (1968). Own CBS-TV variety series from 1971-74. Brief TV reunion in 1975. Bono was mayor of Palm Springs, California from 1988-92; elected to Congress in 1994.	
9/4/65	**2**(8)	25	● **1. Look At Us**	Atco 177
			I Got You Babe (1)	
6/4/66	**34**	6	2. The Wondrous World Of Sonny & Cher	Atco 183
9/2/67	**23**	10	3. The Best of Sonny & Cher [G]	Atco 219
12/4/71	**35**	2	● 4. Sonny & Cher Live [L]	Kapp 3654
3/11/72	**14**	15	● 5. All I Ever Need Is You	Kapp 3660
			All I Ever Need Is You (7)/*A Cowboys Work Is Never Done* (8)	
			S.O.S. BAND, The	
			Funk-R&B band from Atlanta. Lead singer/keyboardist Mary Davis went solo in 1986; various personnel changes since. Name means "Sounds Of Success."	
7/12/80	**12**	11	● S.O.S.	Tabu 36332
			Take Your Time (Do It Right) (3)	
			SOUL, David	
			Born David Solberg on 8/28/43 in Chicago. Played Ken Hutchinson on TV's "Starsky & Hutch" (1975-79). Began career as a folk singer and appeared several times on "The Merv Griffin Show" as "The Covered Man" (wore a ski mask).	
4/23/77	**40**	1	David Soul	Private S. 2019
			Don't Give Up On Us (1)	
			SOUL ASYLUM	
			Rock band formed in Minneapolis in 1983: Dave Pirner (vocals), Daniel Murphy, Karl Mueller and Grant Young. Pirner appeared in the movie *Reality Bites*.	
7/3/93	**11**	18	▲² Grave Dancers Union	Columbia 48898
			Runaway Train (5)	

DATE	POS	WKS	ARTIST—RECORD TITLE	LABEL & NO.
			SOUL II SOUL	
			South London soul outfit led by the duo of Beresford "Jazzie B." Romeo and Nellee Hooper. Features female vocalists Caron Wheeler, Do'Reen and Rose Windross. Musical backing by the Reggae Philharmonic Orchestra. Wheeler left in 1990.	
7/29/89	**14**	36	▲² 1. Keep On Movin' *Back To Life* (4)	Virgin 91267
6/23/90	**21**	8	● 2. Vol II — 1990 — A New Decade	Virgin 91367
			SOUNDGARDEN	
			Seattle-based, metal-punk band: Chris Cornell (vocals), Kim Thayil (guitar), Hiro Yamamoto (bass; replaced by Hunter "Ben" Shepherd in 1991) and Matt Cameron (drums). Cornell and Cameron also recorded with Temple Of The Dog. Cornell is married to band's manager, Susan Silver.	
2/29/92	**39**	1	▲ 1. Badmotorfinger	A&M 5374
3/26/94	**1**(1)	35	▲³ **2. Superunknown**	A&M 0198
			SOUNDS ORCHESTRAL	
			British studio project produced by John Schroeder. Included arranger/producer Johnny Pearson on piano.	
6/19/65	**11**	9	Cast Your Fate To The Wind [I] *Cast Your Fate To The Wind* (10)	Parkway 7046
			SOUTH CENTRAL CARTEL	
			Rap outfit: Havoc da Mouthpiece (son of an original member of The Chi-Lites), Prodeje, Havikk da Rymeson, L.V. da voice, Kaos #1 and Gripp.	
5/28/94	**32**	2	'N Gatz We Truss *CD includes 2 bonus tracks*	GWK 57294
			SOUTHER, HILLMAN, FURAY BAND, The	
			Country-rock sextet formed as supergroup featuring J.D. Souther, Chris Hillman (The Byrds; The Flying Burrito Brothers; The Desert Rose Band) and Richie Furay (Buffalo Springfield; Poco).	
8/3/74	**11**	11	● 1. The Souther, Hillman, Furay Band	Asylum 1006
7/26/75	**39**	1	2. Trouble In Paradise	Asylum 1036
			SPANDAU BALLET	
			English quintet: Tony Hadley (lead singer), Steve Norman, John Keeble, and brothers Gary and Martin Kemp. The Kemps starred in the 1990 movie *The Krays*. Gary, later in *The Bodyguard*, married actress Sadie Frost (of the 1992 movie *Bram Stoker's Dracula*).	
10/8/83	**19**	8	True *True* (4)	Chrysalis 41403
			SPICE 1	
			Rapper born in Byron, Texas; raised in Hayward and Oakland, California. Discovered by Too $hort.	
10/16/93	**10**	4	● **1. 187 He Wrote** *187 is slang for murder*	Jive 41513
12/10/94	**22**	2	● 2. AmeriKKKa's Nightmare	Jive 41547
			SPIN DOCTORS	
			Rock quartet formed at New York's New School of Jazz: Christopher Barron (vocals), Eric Schenkman, Mark White and Aaron Comess.	
9/19/92	**3**	52	▲⁴ **1. Pocket Full Of Kryptonite** *Two Princes* (7)	Epic/Assc. 47461
7/2/94	**28**	3	● 2. Turn It Upside Down	Epic 52907

DATE	POS	WKS	ARTIST—RECORD TITLE	LABEL & NO.
			SPINNERS	
			R&B vocal group from Ferndale High School near Detroit. Originally known as The Domingoes. Discovered by Harvey Fuqua, producer/lead singer of The Moonglows; became The Spinners in 1961. First recorded on Fuqua's Tri-Phi label. Many personnel changes. G.C. Cameron was lead singer from 1968-72. 1972 hit lineup included Phillippe Wynne (tenor; died 7/14/84), Bobbie Smith (tenor), Billy Henderson (tenor), Henry Fambrough (baritone) and Pervis Jackson (bass). Wynne left group in 1977; toured with Parliament/ Funkadelic; replaced by John Edwards.	
5/12/73	**14**	11	● 1. Spinners	Atlantic 7256
			I'll Be Around (3)/Could It Be I'm Falling In Love (4)	
4/6/74	**16**	14	● 2. Mighty Love	Atlantic 7296
12/28/74	**9**	14	● **3. New And Improved**	Atlantic 18118
			Then Came You (1-with Dionne Warwick)	
8/16/75	**8**	16	● **4. Pick Of The Litter**	Atlantic 18141
			They Just Can't Stop It (The Games People Play) (5)	
1/17/76	**20**	9	5. Spinners Live! [L]	Atlantic 910 [2]
8/14/76	**25**	9	● 6. Happiness Is Being With The Detroit Spinners	Atlantic 18181
			The Rubberband Man (2)	
4/9/77	**26**	4	7. Yesterday, Today & Tomorrow	Atlantic 19100
3/22/80	**32**	4	8. Dancin' And Lovin'	Atlantic 19256
			Working My Way Back To You/Forgive Me, Girl (2)	
			SPIRIT	
			Los Angeles eclectic rock group: Jay Ferguson (lead singer), Mark Andes (bass), Ed Cassidy (drums), Randy California (guitar) and John Locke (keyboards). Ferguson and Andes left to form Jo Jo Gunne in mid-1971. Andes became an original member of Firefall in 1975; joined Heart in 1983.	
8/31/68	**31**	16	1. Spirit	Ode 44004
2/8/69	**22**	12	2. The Family That Plays Together	Ode 44014
			SPLIT ENZ	
			Sextet from New Zealand led by brothers Tim and Neil Finn. The Finns and drummer Paul Hester were later members of Crowded House. Tim Finn married actress Greta Scacchi in 1985.	
11/15/80	**40**	2	True Colours	A&M 4822
			record pressed in laser-etched vinyl	
			SPRINGFIELD, Rick	
			Born on 8/23/49 in Sydney, Australia. Singer/actor/songwriter. With top Australian teen-idol band Zoot before going solo in 1972. Turned to acting in the late '70s; played Noah Drake on the TV soap opera "General Hospital" in the early '80s. Starred in the movie *Hard to Hold* in 1984.	
9/30/72	**35**	4	1. Beginnings	Capitol 11047
6/27/81	**7**	38	▲ **2. Working Class Dog**	RCA 3697
			Jessie's Girl (1)/I've Done Everything For You (8)	
4/3/82	**2** (3)	15	▲ **3. Success Hasn't Spoiled Me Yet**	RCA 4125
			Don't Talk To Strangers (2)	
5/7/83	**12**	24	▲ 4. Living in Oz	RCA 4660
			Affair Of The Heart (9)	
4/21/84	**16**	9	▲ 5. Hard To Hold [S]	RCA 4935
			Springfield starred in the movie Love Somebody (5)	
5/11/85	**21**	11	● 6. Tao	RCA 5370

DATE	POS	WKS	ARTIST—RECORD TITLE	LABEL & NO.
			SPRINGSTEEN, Bruce	
			Born on 9/23/49 in Freehold, New Jersey. Rock singer/songwriter/guitarist. Worked local clubs in New Jersey and Greenwich Village, mid-1960s. Own E-Street Band in 1973; consisted of Clarence Clemons (saxophone), David Sancious and Danny Federici (keyboards), Gary Tallent (bass) and Vini Lopez (drums). Sancious and Lopez replaced by Roy Bittan and Max Weinberg (became musical director for TV's "Late Night with Conan O'Brien" in 1993). Miami Steve Van Zandt (guitar) joined group in 1975. Springsteen wrote Manfred Mann's Earth Band's "Blinded By The Light" and The Pointer Sisters' "Fire." After *Born To Run*, a court injunction prevented the release of any new albums until 1978. Married to model/actress Julianne Phillips from 1985-89. Appeared in the 1987 movie *Hail! Hail! Rock 'N' Roll*. Split from the E-Street Band in November 1989. Married Patti Scialfa, former singer with the E-Street Band, on 6/8/91.	
9/20/75	3	12	▲⁴ **1. Born To Run**	Columbia 33795
6/17/78	5	17	▲² **2. Darkness on the Edge of Town**	Columbia 35318
11/1/80	1(4)	22	▲³ **3. The River**	Columbia 36854 [2]
			Hungry Heart (5)	
10/9/82	3	11	▲ **4. Nebraska**	Columbia 38358
			recorded on a 4-track cassette recorder at home	
6/23/84	1(7)	96	▲¹⁴ **5. Born In The U.S.A.**	Columbia 38653
			Dancing In The Dark (2)/*Cover Me* (7)/ *Born In The U.S.A.* (9)/*I'm On Fire* (6)/*Glory Days* (5)/ *I'm Goin' Down* (9)/*My Hometown* (6)	
11/29/86	1(7)	15	▲ **6. Bruce Springsteen & The E Street Band Live/1975-85** [L]	Columbia 40558 [5]
			BRUCE SPRINGSTEEN & THE E STREET BAND contains 40 songs and a 36-page color booklet with lyrics *War* (8)	
10/24/87	1(1)	33	▲³ **7. Tunnel of Love**	Columbia 40999
			Brilliant Disguise (5)/*Tunnel Of Love* (9)	
4/18/92	2(2)	10	▲ **8. Human Touch**	Columbia 53000
4/18/92	3	7	▲ **9. Lucky Town**	Columbia 53001
			SPYRO GYRA	
			Jazz-pop band formed in 1975 in Buffalo, New York. Led by saxophonist Jay Beckenstein (born 5/14/51).	
6/9/79	27	11	▲ 1. Morning Dance [I]	Infinity 9004
4/5/80	19	8	● 2. Catching The Sun [I]	MCA 5108
			SQUEEZE	
			English pop-rock group led by vocalists/guitarists Chris Difford and Glenn Tilbrook. Originally known as UK Squeeze due to confusion with American band Tight Squeeze. Paul Carrack (Ace; Mike + The Mechanics) was keyboardist/vocalist of fluctuating lineup in 1981; re-joined in 1993.	
6/26/82	32	4	1. Sweets From A Stranger	A&M 4899
11/21/87	36	7	2. Babylon And On	A&M 5161
			SQUIER, Billy	
			Born on 5/12/50 in Wellesley Hills, Massachusetts. Hard-rock singer/ songwriter/guitarist.	
6/20/81	5	38	▲³ **1. Don't Say No**	Capitol 12146
8/21/82	5	29	▲² **2. Emotions in Motion**	Capitol 12217
8/11/84	11	14	▲ 3. Signs of Life	Capitol 12361

DATE	POS	WKS	ARTIST—RECORD TITLE	LABEL & NO.
			STAFFORD, Jo	
			Born on 11/12/20 in Coalinga, California. Member of Tommy Dorsey's vocal group The Pied Pipers, 1940-43. Married to orchestra leader Paul Weston; recorded together as the novelty duo, Jonathan & Darlene Edwards. Stafford also recorded as the hillbilly Cinderella G. Stump in 1947. Stafford and Dinah Shore rank as the top 2 female vocalists of the pre-rock era.	
12/29/56	**13**	8	Ski Trails	Columbia 910
			with husband Paul Weston (conductor) and The Norman Luboff Choir	
			STANLEY, Paul	
			Born Paul Stanley Eisen on 1/20/52 in Queens, New York. Rhythm guitarist of Kiss. Married model Pamela Bowen on 7/26/92.	
12/16/78	**40**	3	▲ Paul Stanley	Casablanca 7123
			STANSFIELD, Lisa	
			Born on 4/11/66. Lead singer of Blue Zone U.K. from Roachdale, England. Vocalist on Coldcut's 1989 club hit "People Hold On."	
3/17/90	**9**	25	▲ **Affection**	Arista 8554
			CD and cassette include bonus track *All Around The World* (3)	
			STAPLE SINGERS, The	
			Family soul group consisting of Roebuck "Pop" Staples (born 12/28/15, Winoma, Mississippi), with his son Pervis (who left in 1971) and daughters Cleotha, Yvonne and lead singer Mavis Staples. Roebuck was a blues guitarist in his teens; later with The Golden Trumpets gospel group. Moved to Chicago in 1935. Formed own gospel group in early '50s. First recorded for United in 1953. Mavis recorded solo in 1970.	
4/15/72	**19**	12	1. Bealtitude: Respect Yourself	Stax 3002
			I'll Take You There (1)	
11/29/75	**20**	8	2. Let's Do It Again [S]	Curtom 5005
			Let's Do It Again (1)	
			STARGARD	
			Disco trio: Rochelle Runnells, Debra Anderson and Janice Williams. Appeared as The Diamonds in the movie *Sgt. Pepper's Lonely Hearts Club Band.*	
3/18/78	**26**	6	Stargard	MCA 2321
			STARLAND VOCAL BAND	
			Washington, D.C.-based pop quartet: Bill and wife Taffy Danoff, and John Carroll and future wife Margot Chapman. Bill and Taffy had fronted the folk quintet Fat City. Bill co-wrote "Take Me Home, Country Roads" with friend John Denver. Denver owned Windsong record label. Won 1976 Best New Artist Grammy Award.	
7/10/76	**20**	10	Starland Vocal Band	Windsong 1351
			Afternoon Delight (1)	
			STARR, Ringo	
			Born Richard Starkey on 7/7/40 in Liverpool, England. Played with Rory Storm and The Hurricanes before joining The Beatles following ousting of drummer Pete Best in 1962. First solo album in 1970. Acted in many movies including *The Magic Christian, 200 Motels* and *Cave Man.* Played Mr. Conductor on PBS-TV's "Shining Time Station" from 1989-91.	
5/23/70	**22**	6	1. Sentimental Journey	Apple 3365
11/17/73	**2**(2)	19	▲ **2. Ringo**	Apple 3413
			featuring backing by the other 3 Beatles *Photograph* (1)/*You're Sixteen* (1)/*Oh My My* (5)	

DATE	POS	WKS	ARTIST—RECORD TITLE	LABEL & NO.
12/7/74	8	12	● **3. Goodnight Vienna** guests: John Lennon and Elton John *Only You* (6)/*No No Song* (3)	Apple 3417
12/27/75	30	5	4. Blast From Your Past　　　　　　　[G] *It Don't Come Easy* (4)/*Back Off Boogaloo* (9)	Apple 3422
10/23/76	28	6	5. Ringo's Rotogravure guests: Paul McCartney, John Lennon, Eric Clapton & Peter Frampton	Atlantic 18193
			STARS ON Dutch session vocalists and musicians assembled by producer Jaap Eggermont. Group's albums are composed of medleys.	
6/20/81	9	8	● **Stars On Long Play** side 1: medley of Beatles songs	Radio 16044
			STATON, Dakota Born Aliyah Rabia on 6/3/31 in Pittsburgh. Jazz stylist.	
2/24/58	4	41	**1. The Late, Late Show**	Capitol 876
10/27/58	22	1	2. Dynamic!	Capitol 1054
6/8/59	23	6	3. Crazy He Calls Me	Capitol 1170
			STEELHEART Hard-rock group from Norwalk, Connecticut: Michael Matijevic (vocals), Chris Risola, Frank Dicostanzo, Jimmy Ward and John Fowler.	
7/13/91	40	1	● Steelheart	MCA 6368
			STEELY DAN Los Angeles-based, pop/jazz-styled group formed by Donald Fagen (born 1/10/48, Passaic, New Jersey; keyboards, vocals) and Walter Becker (born 2/20/50, New York City; bass, vocals). Group, primarily known as a studio unit, featured Fagen and Becker with various studio musicians. Actor/comedian Chevy Chase was the band's drummer in its formative years. Fagen and Becker went their separate ways in 1981. Drummer Jimmy Hodder drowned on 6/5/90 (age 42). Fagen and Becker reunited for concert tour in 1993.	
2/10/73	17	17	▲ 1. Can't Buy A Thrill *Do It Again* (6)	ABC 758
9/15/73	35	3	● 2. Countdown To Ecstasy	ABC 779
5/4/74	8	19	▲ **3. Pretzel Logic** *Rikki Don't Lose That Number* (4)	ABC 808
4/19/75	13	9	▲ 4. Katy Lied	ABC 846
5/29/76	15	9	▲ 5. The Royal Scam	ABC 931
10/15/77	3	52	▲² **6. Aja**	ABC 1006
12/9/78	30	9	▲ 7. Greatest Hits　　　　　　　[G]	ABC 1107 [2]
12/13/80	9	19	▲ **8. Gaucho** *Hey Nineteen* (10)	MCA 6102
			STEPPENWOLF Hard-rock quintet formed in Los Angeles in 1967. Original lineup: John Kay (born Joachim Krauledat on 4/12/44 in Tilsit, East Germany; vocals, guitar) Michael Monarch (guitar), Goldy McJohn (keyboards), Nick St. Nicholas (bass), Mars Bonfire (born Dennis Edmonton; guitar) and brother Jerry Edmonton (drums; died 11/28/93 in a car crash). All but Monarch were members of Canadian group Sparrow. Many personnel changes except for Kay. Group named after a Herman Hesse novel.	
7/27/68	6	25	● **1. Steppenwolf** *Born To Be Wild* (2)	Dunhill 50029

DATE	POS	WKS	ARTIST—RECORD TITLE	LABEL & NO.
10/19/68	3	24	● 2. The Second	Dunhill 50037
			Magic Carpet Ride (3)	
3/29/69	7	11	3. At Your Birthday Party	Dunhill 50053
			Rock Me (10)	
8/2/69	29	6	4. Early Steppenwolf [E-L]	Dunhill 50060
			recorded in 1967 when band was known as Sparrow; side 2 is a 21 1/2-minute version of "The Pusher"	
12/6/69	17	16	● 5. Monster	Dunhill 50066
4/25/70	7	15	● 6. Steppenwolf 'Live' [L]	Dunhill 50075 [2]
11/21/70	19	7	● 7. Steppenwolf 7	Dunhill 50090
3/13/71	24	9	● 8. Steppenwolf Gold/Their Great Hits [G]	Dunhill 50099

STEVENS, Cat

Born Steven Georgiou on 7/21/47 in London. Began career playing folk music at Hammersmith College in 1966. Contracted tuberculosis in 1968 and spent over a year recuperating. Adopted new style when he re-emerged. Lived in Brazil in the mid-1970s. Converted to Muslim religion in 1979; took name Yusef Islam.

DATE	POS	WKS	ARTIST—RECORD TITLE	LABEL & NO.
2/13/71	8	44	● 1. Tea for the Tillerman	A&M 4280
10/16/71	2(1)	37	● 2. Teaser And The Firecat	A&M 4313
			Peace Train (7)/*Morning Has Broken* (6)	
10/28/72	1(3)	26	● 3. Catch Bull At Four	A&M 4365
8/4/73	3	15	● 4. Foreigner	A&M 4391
4/20/74	2(3)	25	● 5. Buddha And The Chocolate Box	A&M 3623
			Oh Very Young (10)	
7/26/75	6	12	▲³ 6. Greatest Hits [G]	A&M 4519
			Another Saturday Night (6)	
12/13/75	13	13	● 7. Numbers	A&M 4555
5/28/77	7	12	● 8. Izitso	A&M 4702
1/20/79	33	4	9. Back To Earth	A&M 4735

STEVENS, Ray

Born Ray Ragsdale on 1/24/39 in Clarkdale, Georgia. Attended Georgia State University; studied music theory and composition. First recorded for Prep Records in 1957. Production work in the mid-1960s. Numerous appearances on Andy Williams's TV show in the late '60s. Own TV show in summer of 1970. Featured on "Music Country" TV show, 1973-74. The #1 novelty recording artist of the past 35 years.

DATE	POS	WKS	ARTIST—RECORD TITLE	LABEL & NO.
7/4/70	35	3	Everything Is Beautiful	Barnaby 35005
			Everything Is Beautiful (1)	

STEWART, Al

Born on 9/5/45 in Glasgow, Scotland. Pop-rock singer/composer/guitarist.

DATE	POS	WKS	ARTIST—RECORD TITLE	LABEL & NO.
4/12/75	30	3	1. Modern Times	Janus 7012
11/20/76	5	21	▲ 2. Year Of The Cat	Janus 7022
			Year Of The Cat (8)	
10/14/78	10	14	▲ 3. Time Passages	Arista 4190
			above 3 albums produced by Alan Parsons	
			Time Passages (7)	
10/4/80	37	4	4. 24 Carrots	Arista 9520

DATE	POS	WKS	ARTIST—RECORD TITLE	LABEL & NO.
			STEWART, Amii	
			Born in Washington, D.C. in 1956. Disco singer/dancer/actress. In the Broadway musical *Bubbling Brown Sugar*. Her niece is singer Sinitta.	
3/31/79	19	9	● Knock On Wood	Ariola 50054
			Knock On Wood (1)	
			STEWART, Jermaine	
			Chicago-bred singer. Dancer on TV's "Soul Train." Worked as backup vocalist for Shalamar and Boy George.	
8/16/86	32	5	Frantic Romantic	Arista 8395
			We Don't Have To Take Our Clothes Off (5)	
			STEWART, John	
			Born on 9/5/39 in San Diego. Member of The Kingston Trio from 1961-67. Wrote "Daydream Believer."	
6/16/79	10	14	**Bombs Away Dream Babies**	RSO 3051
			Gold (5)	
			STEWART, Rod	
			Born Roderick Stewart on 1/10/45 in London. Worked as a folksinger in Europe in the early '60s. Recorded for English Decca in 1964. With The Hoochie Coochie Men, Steampacket and Shotgun Express. Joined Jeff Beck Group, 1967-69. With Faces from 1969-75; also recorded solo during this time. Left Faces in December 1975. Won 1989 Living Legends Grammy Award. Married to actress Alana Hamilton from 1979-84. Married supermodel Rachel Hunter on 12/15/90. Inducted into the Rock and Roll Hall of Fame in 1994. Into his third decade as one of rock music's leading hit-makers.	
7/11/70	27	7	1. Gasoline Alley	Mercury 61264
6/26/71	1(4)	35	▲ **2. Every Picture Tells A Story**	Mercury 609
			Maggie May (1)	
8/12/72	2(3)	21	● **3. Never A Dull Moment**	Mercury 646
8/11/73	31	3	● 4. Sing It Again Rod [G]	Mercury 680
11/9/74	13	5	5. Smiler	Mercury 1017
			all Mercury albums feature members of Faces	
9/20/75	9	10	● **6. Atlantic Crossing**	Warner 2875
7/31/76	2(5)	30	▲² **7. A Night On The Town**	Warner 2938
			Tonight's The Night (Gonna Be Alright) (1)	
11/26/77	2(6)	27	▲³ **8. Foot Loose & Fancy Free**	Warner 3092
			You're In My Heart (The Final Acclaim) (4)	
1/6/79	1(3)	24	▲⁴ **9. Blondes Have More Fun**	Warner 3261
			Da Ya Think I'm Sexy? (1)	
12/1/79	22	7	▲³ 10. Rod Stewart Greatest Hits [G]	Warner 3373
12/6/80	12	15	▲ 11. Foolish Behaviour	Warner 3485
			Passion (5)	
11/28/81	11	20	▲ 12. Tonight I'm Yours	Warner 3602
			Young Turks (5)	
7/9/83	30	4	13. Body Wishes	Warner 23877
7/7/84	18	19	● 14. Camouflage	Warner 25095
			Infatuation (6)/*Some Guys Have All The Luck* (10)	
7/26/86	28	7	15. Rod Stewart	Warner 25446
			Love Touch (6)	
6/18/88	20	46	▲² 16. Out Of Order	Warner 25684
			My Heart Can't Tell You No (4)	

DATE	POS	WKS	ARTIST—RECORD TITLE	LABEL & NO.
4/7/90	**20**	12	▲ 17. Downtown Train: Selections From The Storyteller Anthology [G] most of these 12 tracks are Stewart's hits of the last 15 years *Downtown Train* (3)/*This Old Heart Of Mine* (10-with Ronald Isley)	Warner 26158
4/20/91	**10**	20	▲ 18. Vagabond Heart *Rhythm Of My Heart* (5)/*The Motown Song* (10)	Warner 26300
6/12/93	**2**(5)	37	▲² 19. Unplugged ... And Seated [L] recorded on the MTV program "Unplugged"; with special guest Ronnie Wood (guitar) *Have I Told You Lately* (5)	Warner 45289
			STILLS, Stephen	
			Born on 1/3/45 in Dallas. Member of Buffalo Springfield and Crosby, Stills & Nash. Group Manassas included Chris Hillman (The Byrds), Dallas Taylor, Fuzzy Samuels, Paul Harris, Al Perkins and Joe Lala.	
10/5/68	**12**	10	● 1. Super Session **MIKE BLOOMFIELD/AL KOOPER/STEVE STILLS**	Columbia 9701
12/5/70	**3**	16	● 2. Stephen Stills guests: Jimi Hendrix, Eric Clapton, David Crosby, Graham Nash	Atlantic 7202
7/24/71	**8**	9	● 3. Stephen Stills 2	Atlantic 7206
5/6/72	**4**	15	● 4. Manassas	Atlantic 903 [2]
6/2/73	**26**	6	5. Down The Road **STEPHEN STILLS & MANASSAS** *M* (above 2)	Atlantic 7250
7/12/75	**19**	6	6. Stills	Columbia 33575
6/19/76	**31**	3	7. Illegal Stills	Columbia 34148
10/30/76	**26**	6	● 8. Long May You Run **STILLS-YOUNG BAND** *M* (Neil Young)	Reprise 2253
			STING	
			Born Gordon Sumner on 10/2/51 in Wallsend, England. Lead singer/bass guitarist of The Police. In the movies *Quadrophenia*, *Dune*, *The Bride*, *Plenty* and others. Married actress/producer Trudie Styler in early 1992. Nicknamed "Sting" because of a yellow and black jersey he liked to wear.	
7/20/85	**2**(6)	37	▲³ 1. The Dream Of The Blue Turtles backed by jazz musicians Wynton and Branford Marsalis, Kenny Kirkland and Omar Hakim *If You Love Somebody Set Them Free* (3)/ *Fortress Around Your Heart* (8)	A&M 3750
11/7/87	**9**	26	▲² 2. ... Nothing Like The Sun *We'll Be Together* (7)	A&M 6402 [2]
2/9/91	**2**(1)	15	▲ 3. The Soul Cages *All This Time* (5)	A&M 6405
3/27/93	**2**(1)	30	▲³ 4. Ten Summoner's Tales	A&M 0070
11/26/94	**7**	12	5. Fields Of Gold — The Best Of Sting 1984-1994 [G]	A&M 0269
			STONE, Kirby, Four	
			Stone was born on 4/27/18 in New York City. His quartet includes Eddie Hall, Larry Foster and Mike Gardner. Stone was musical director for various TV shows.	
8/25/58	**13**	9	Baubles, Bangles And Beads	Columbia 1211
			STONE TEMPLE PILOTS	
			Alternative-metal band based in Los Angeles: Scott Weiland (vocals), brothers Robert and Dean DeLeo, and Eric Kretz.	
4/10/93	**3**	50	▲³ 1. Core	Atlantic 82418

DATE	POS	WKS	ARTIST—RECORD TITLE	LABEL & NO.
6/25/94	**1** (3)	36	▲³ **2. Purple**	Atlantic 82607
			STORIES	
			New York rock quartet: Ian Lloyd (lead singer, bass), Michael Brown (keyboards; founding member of Left Banke), Steve Love (guitar) and Bryan Madey (drums). Brown left group in 1973; replaced by Ken Aaronson (bass; later charted with Sammy Hagar) and Ken Bichel (keyboards).	
9/1/73	**29**	6	About Us	Kama Sutra 2068
			Brother Louie (1)	
			STRAIT, George	
			Born on 5/18/52 in Poteet, Texas. Country singer. Starred in the movie *Pure Country*.	
6/16/90	**35**	3	▲ 1. Livin' It Up	MCA 6415
5/16/92	**33**	1	● 2. Holding My Own	MCA 10532
10/10/92	**6**	40	▲³ **3. Pure Country** [S]	MCA 10651
10/16/93	**5**	14	▲² **4. Easy Come, Easy Go**	MCA 10907
11/26/94	**26**	3	▲ 5. Lead On	MCA 11092
			STRAWBERRY ALARM CLOCK, The	
			West Coast psychedelic-rock sextet: Ed King (lead guitar), Mark Weitz (keyboards), Lee Freeman (guitar), Gary Lovetro (bass), George Bunnel (bass) and Randy Seol (drums). King joined Lynyrd Skynyrd, 1973-75. Originally known as Thee Sixpence.	
12/2/67	**11**	13	Incense And Peppermints	Uni 73014
			Incense And Peppermints (1)	
			STRAY CATS	
			Long Island, New York rockabilly trio: Brian Setzer (born 4/10/60; lead singer, guitar), Lee Rocker (born Leon Drucher; string bass) and Slim Jim Phantom (born Jim McDonell; drums). Recorded two albums in Britain in 1981 and 1982. Group disbanded in 1984; reunited in 1988. Phantom and Rocker formed trio Phantom, Rocker & Slick in 1985. Setzer portrayed Eddie Cochran in the movie *La Bamba*. Phantom portrayed Charlie Parker's drummer in the movie *Bird*. Phantom married to actress Britt Ekland, 1984-93.	
9/4/82	**2** (15)	37	▲ **1. Built For Speed**	EMI America 17070
			Rock This Town (9)/*Stray Cat Strut* (3)	
9/17/83	**14**	10	● 2. Rant n' Rave with the Stray Cats	EMI America 17102
			(She's) Sexy + 17 (5)	
			STREISAND, Barbra	
			Born Barbara Joan Streisand on 4/24/42 in Brooklyn. Made Broadway debut in *I Can Get It for You Wholesale*, 1962. Lead role in Broadway's *Funny Girl*, 1964. Movie debut in *Funny Girl* in 1968 (tied with Katharine Hepburn for Best Actress Academy Award); also starred in *A Star Is Born, Hello Dolly, Funny Lady, The Way We Were* and many others. Produced/directed/starred in the movies *Yentl* and *Prince of Tides*. Married to actor Elliott Gould from 1963-71.	
5/4/63	**8**	78	● **1. The Barbra Streisand Album**	Columbia 8807
			1963 Album of the Year Grammy Award	
9/28/63	**2** (3)	47	● **2. The Second Barbra Streisand Album**	Columbia 8854
3/14/64	**5**	42	● **3. The Third Album**	Columbia 8954
5/2/64	**2** (3)	40	● **4. Funny Girl** [OC]	Capitol 2059
			based on the early life of Fanny Brice	
10/10/64	**1** (5)	48	● **5. People**	Columbia 9015
			People (5)	
5/29/65	**2** (3)	46	● **6. My Name Is Barbra** [TV]	Columbia 9136
			Streisand's first TV special (4/28/65)	

DATE	POS	WKS	ARTIST—RECORD TITLE	LABEL & NO.
11/13/65	2(3)	31	▲ 7. My Name Is Barbra, Two ...	Columbia 9209
4/23/66	3	22	● 8. Color Me Barbra [TV]	Columbia 9278
			Streisand's second TV special (3/30/66)	
12/3/66	5	13	9. Je m'appelle Barbra	Columbia 9347
			je m'appelle is French for my name is	
12/2/67	12	12	10. Simply Streisand	Columbia 9482
11/9/68	12	31	▲ 11. Funny Girl [S]	Columbia 3220
			screen version of the Broadway musical	
11/9/68	30	13	● 12. A Happening In Central Park [L]	Columbia 9710
			recorded on 6/17/67; broadcast on TV on 9/15/68	
9/20/69	31	4	13. What About Today?	Columbia 9816
3/21/70	32	2	▲² 14. Barbra Streisand's Greatest Hits [G]	Columbia 9968
2/27/71	10	11	▲ 15. Stoney End	Columbia 30378
			Stoney End (6)	
9/25/71	11	15	● 16. Barbra Joan Streisand	Columbia 30792
12/16/72	19	8	▲ 17. Live Concert At The Forum [L]	Columbia 31760
2/23/74	1(2)	12	▲ 18. The Way We Were	Columbia 32801
			not the soundtrack album (see Soundtracks)	
			The Way We Were (1)	
11/30/74	13	11	● 19. ButterFly	Columbia 33095
4/12/75	6	9	● 20. Funny Lady [S]	Arista 9004
			movie is the sequel to Funny Girl	
11/15/75	12	10	● 21. Lazy Afternoon	Columbia 33815
12/25/76	1(6)	28	▲⁴ 22. A Star Is Born [S-L]	Columbia 34403
			Kris Kristofferson sings on 5 of the 12 tracks (all but 4 tracks are "live"); third version of the 1937 movie classic	
			Evergreen (1)	
7/2/77	3	14	▲² 23. Streisand Superman	Columbia 34830
			My Heart Belongs To Me (4)	
6/24/78	12	13	▲ 24. Songbird	Columbia 35375
12/2/78	1(3)	17	▲ 25. Barbra Streisand's Greatest Hits, Volume 2 [G]	Columbia 35679
			You Don't Bring Me Flowers (1-with Neil Diamond)	
7/21/79	20	9	● 26. The Main Event [S]	Columbia 36115
			3 versions of title song; others by various artists	
			Main Event/Fight (3)	
11/10/79	7	14	▲ 27. Wet	Columbia 36258
			No More Tears (Enough Is Enough) (1-with Donna Summer)	
10/11/80	1(3)	33	▲⁵ 28. Guilty	Columbia 36750
			produced by Barry Gibb	
			Woman In Love (1)/Guilty (3-with Barry Gibb/	
			What Kind Of Fool (10-with Barry Gibb)	
12/12/81	10	15	▲⁴ 29. Memories [K]	Columbia 37678
12/3/83	9	13	▲ 30. Yentl [S]	Columbia 39152
			Streisand is the first woman to produce, direct, write and perform a movie's title role	
11/3/84	19	11	▲ 31. Emotion	Columbia 39480
11/30/85	1(3)	24	▲⁴ 32. The Broadway Album	Columbia 40092
			Streisand sings 14 of her favorite Broadway tunes	
5/16/87	9	12	▲ 33. One Voice [L]	Columbia 40788
			recorded at her Malibu ranch for an audience of 500 invited guests	
11/19/88	10	14	▲ 34. Till I Loved You	Columbia 40880

DATE	POS	WKS	ARTIST—RECORD TITLE	LABEL & NO.
10/28/89	26	12	▲ 35. A Collection Greatest Hits ... And More [G]	Columbia 45369
10/12/91	38	1	▲ 36. Just For The Record [K]	Columbia 44111 [4]
			spans 30 years of unreleased studio & live tracks; original demos; TV, nightclub & award-show appearances; includes 92-page booklet	
7/17/93	1(1)	12	▲² 37. **Back To Broadway**	Columbia 44189
			Streisand sings 12 of her favorite Broadway tunes; 2 duets: one with Michael Crawford; the other with Johnny Mathis	
10/15/94	10	9	▲ 38. **The Concert** [L]	Columbia 66109 [2]
			recorded at Madison Square Garden in New York City, June 1994	
			STRYPER	
			Christian heavy-metal band from Orange County, California: brothers Michael (vocals) and Robert (drums) Sweet, with Oz Fox (guitar) and Tim Gaines (bass). Michael left in mid-1992.	
11/29/86	32	12	▲ 1. To Hell With The Devil	Enigma 73237
7/23/88	32	5	● 2. In God We Trust	Enigma 73317
9/15/90	39	2	3. Against The Law	Enigma 73527
			STYLISTICS, The	
			Soul group from Philadelphia formed in 1968. Consisted of Russell Thompkins, Jr. (born 3/21/51; lead), Airrion Love, James Smith, James Dunn and Herbie Murrell. Thompkins, Love and Smith sang with The Percussions; Murrell and Dunn with The Monarchs from 1965-68. First recorded for Sebring in 1969.	
1/15/72	23	18	● 1. The Stylistics	Avco 33023
			You Are Everything (9)/*Betcha By Golly, Wow* (3)	
1/27/73	32	9	● 2. Round 2: The Stylistics	Avco 11006
			I'm Stone In Love With You (10)/*Break Up To Make Up* (5)	
6/22/74	14	8	● 3. Let's Put It All Together	Avco 69001
			STYX	
			Chicago-based rock quintet: Dennis DeYoung (vocals, keyboards), Tommy Shaw (lead guitar), James Young (guitar), and twin brothers John (drums) and Chuck Panozzo (bass). Band earlier known as TW4. Shaw replaced John Curulewski in 1976. Most songs written by Dennis DeYoung and/or Tommy Shaw. Band broke up when DeYoung and Shaw went solo in 1984. Reunited in 1990 with guitarist Glen Burtnick replacing Shaw, who joined Damn Yankees. In Greek mythology, Styx is a river in Hades.	
2/22/75	20	6	● 1. Styx II [R]	Wooden N. 1012
			originally released in 1973 (*Styx I* didn't chart) *Lady* (6)	
9/3/77	6	37	▲³ 2. **The Grand Illusion**	A&M 4637
			Come Sail Away (8)	
10/7/78	6	28	▲³ 3. **Pieces of Eight**	A&M 4724
10/13/79	2(1)	26	▲² 4. **Cornerstone**	A&M 3711
			Babe (1)	
1/31/81	1(3)	35	▲³ 5. **Paradise Theater**	A&M 3719
			The Best Of Times (3)/*Too Much Time On My Hands* (9)	
3/19/83	3	22	▲ 6. **Kilroy Was Here**	A&M 3734
			Mr. Roboto (3)/*Don't Let It End* (6)	
5/5/84	31	6	7. Caught In The Act — Live [L]	A&M 6514 [2]

DATE	POS	WKS	ARTIST—RECORD TITLE	LABEL & NO.
			SUGARLOAF	
			Rock quartet from Denver: Jerry Corbetta (lead singer, keyboards), Bob Webber (guitar), Bob Raymond (bass) and Bob MacVittie (drums). Robert Yeazel (guitar, vocals) joined in 1971. By 1974, Myron Pollock replaced MacVittie; Yeazel had left.	
10/3/70	24	10	Sugarloaf	Liberty 7640
			Green-Eyed Lady (3)	
			SUMMER, Donna	
			Born Adrian Donna Gaines on 12/31/48 in Boston. With group Crow, played local clubs. In German production of *Hair*, European productions of *Godspell*, *The Me Nobody Knows* and *Porgy and Bess*. Settled in Germany, where she recorded "Love To Love You Baby." In the movie *Thank God It's Friday* in 1979. Married Bruce Sudano (Alive & Kicking; Brooklyn Dreams) in 1980. Dubbed "The Queen of Disco."	
12/13/75	11	13	● 1. Love To Love You Baby	Oasis 5003
			Love To Love You Baby (2)	
5/1/76	21	9	● 2. A Love Trilogy	Oasis 5004
11/20/76	29	5	● 3. Four Seasons Of Love	Casablanca 7038
6/18/77	18	18	● 4. I Remember Yesterday	Casablanca 7056
			I Feel Love (6)	
12/3/77	26	10	● 5. Once Upon A Time ...	Casablanca 7078 [2]
9/16/78	1 (1)	32	▲ 6. Live And More [L]	Casablanca 7119 [2]
			one of 4 sides is a studio recording	
			MacArthur Park (1)/*Heaven Knows* (4)	
5/12/79	1 (6)	26	▲² 7. Bad Girls	Casablanca 7150 [2]
			Hot Stuff (1)/*Bad Girls* (1)/*Dim All The Lights* (2)	
11/10/79	1 (1)	23	▲ 8. On The Radio-Greatest Hits-Volumes I & II [G]	Casablanca 7191 [2]
			Last Dance (3)/*No More Tears (Enough Is Enough)* (1-with Barbra Streisand)/*On The Radio* (5)	
11/8/80	13	9	● 9. The Wanderer	Geffen 2000
			The Wanderer (3)	
8/21/82	20	9	● 10. Donna Summer	Geffen 2005
			Love Is In Control (Finger On The Trigger) (10)	
7/23/83	9	15	● **11. She Works Hard For The Money**	Mercury 812265
			She Works Hard For The Money (3)	
10/13/84	40	2	12. Cats Without Claws	Geffen 24040
			SUNDAYS, The	
			British alternative-pop group: Harriet Wheeler (vocals), Dave Gavurin, Paul Brindley and Pat Hannan.	
8/11/90	39	4	● Reading, Writing And Arithmetic	DGC 24277
			SUPERTRAMP	
			British rock quintet: Roger Hodgson (vocals, guitar), Rick Davies (vocals, keyboards), John Helliwell (sax), Dougie Thomson (bass) and Bob Siebenberg (drums). Hodgson went solo in 1983.	
5/17/75	38	3	● 1. Crime Of The Century	A&M 3647
5/14/77	16	17	● 2. Even In The Quietest Moments ...	A&M 4634
4/7/79	1 (6)	48	▲⁴ 3. Breakfast In America	A&M 3708
			The Logical Song (6)/*Take The Long Way Home* (10)	
10/11/80	8	11	● 4. Paris [L]	A&M 6702 [2]
			recorded at the Paris Pavillon on 11/29/79	
11/13/82	5	17	● 5. ... famous last words ...	A&M 3732
6/15/85	21	10	6. Brother Where You Bound	A&M 5014

DATE	POS	WKS	ARTIST—RECORD TITLE	LABEL & NO.
			SUPREMES, The	
			R&B vocal group from Detroit, formed as The Primettes in 1959. Consisted of lead singer Diana Ross (born 3/26/44), Mary Wilson (born 3/6/44), Florence Ballard (born 6/30/43; died 2/22/76 of cardiac arrest) and Barbara Martin. Recorded for LuPine in 1960. Signed to Motown's Tamla label in 1960. Changed name to The Supremes in 1961; Martin left shortly thereafter. Worked as backing vocalists for Motown until 1964. Backed Marvin Gaye on "Can I Get A Witness." Ballard discharged from group in 1967; replaced by Cindy Birdsong, formerly with Patti LaBelle's Blue Belles. Ross left in 1969 for solo career; replaced by Jean Terrell. Birdsong left in 1972; replaced by Lynda Lawrence. Terrell and Lawrence left in 1973. Wilson re-formed group with Scherrie Payne (sister of Freda Payne) and Birdsong. Birdsong left again in 1976; replaced by Susaye Greene. In 1978, Wilson toured England with Karen Ragland and Karen Jackson, but lost rights to the name "Supremes" thereafter. Inducted into the Rock and Roll Hall of Fame in 1988.	
10/31/64	2 (4)	48	**1. Where Did Our Love Go** *Where Did Our Love Go* (1)/*Baby Love* (1)/ *Come See About Me* (1)	Motown 621
1/23/65	21	8	2. A Bit Of Liverpool	Motown 623
9/11/65	6	17	**3. More Hits By The Supremes** *Stop! In The Name Of Love* (1)/*Back In My Arms Again* (1)	Motown 627
12/4/65	11	24	4. The Supremes at the Copa [L]	Motown 636
4/2/66	8	14	**5. I Hear A Symphony** *I Hear A Symphony* (1)/*My World Is Empty Without You* (5)	Motown 643
10/8/66	1 (2)	31	**6. The Supremes A' Go-Go** *Love Is Like An Itching In My Heart* (9)/ *You Can't Hurry Love* (1)	Motown 649
2/25/67	6	17	**7. The Supremes sing Holland-Dozier-Holland** songs written by Brian Holland, Lamont Dozier, Eddie Holland *You Keep Me Hangin' On* (1)/ *Love Is Here And Now You're Gone* (1)	Motown 650
7/1/67	20	7	8. The Supremes Sing Rodgers & Hart songwriting team: Richard Rodgers and Lorenz Hart **DIANA ROSS & THE SUPREMES:**	Motown 659
10/7/67	1 (5)	49	**9. Diana Ross and the Supremes Greatest Hits** [G] *The Happening* (1)	Motown 663 [2]
5/11/68	18	9	10. Reflections *Reflections* (2)/*In And Out Of Love* (9)	Motown 665
12/21/68	2 (1)	14	**11. Diana Ross & the Supremes Join the Temptations *** *I'm Gonna Make You Love Me* (2)	Motown 679
12/28/68	14	7	12. Love Child *Love Child* (1)	Motown 670
1/11/69	1 (1)	19	**13. TCB *** [TV]	Motown 682
7/5/69	24	6	14. Let The Sunshine In *I'm Livin' In Shame* (10)	Motown 689
11/15/69	28	3	15. Together *	Motown 692
12/20/69	33	7	16. Cream Of The Crop *Someday We'll Be Together* (1)	Motown 694
12/20/69	38	2	17. On Broadway * [TV] ***DIANA ROSS & THE SUPREMES with THE TEMPTATIONS**	Motown 699
1/31/70	31	6	18. Diana Ross & the Supremes Greatest Hits, Volume 3 [G]	Motown 702

DATE	POS	WKS	ARTIST—RECORD TITLE	LABEL & NO.
6/6/70	**25**	6	19. Right On **THE SUPREMES** *Up The Ladder To The Roof* (10)	Motown 705
			SURFARIS, The	
			Teenage surf band from Glendora, California: Ron Wilson (died of an aneurysm, May 1989; drummer), Jim Fuller (lead guitar), Bob Berryhill (rhythm guitar), Pat Connolly (bass) and Jim Pash (sax, clarinet).	
9/7/63	**15**	16	Wipe Out [I] *Wipe Out* (2)	Dot 25535
			SURVIVOR	
			Midwest rock group: Dave Bickler (lead singer), Jim Peterik (keyboards; former lead singer of Ides Of March), Frankie Sullivan (guitar), Gary Smith (drums) and Dennis Johnson (bass). Smith and Johnson replaced by Marc Droubay and Stephan Ellis in 1981. Bickler replaced by Jimi Jamison in 1984. Droubay and Ellis left in 1988.	
7/3/82	**2** (4)	19	▲ 1. Eye Of The Tiger *Eye Of The Tiger* (1)	Scotti Br. 38062
3/9/85	**16**	27	▲ 2. Vital Signs *High On You* (8)/*The Search Is Over* (4)	Scotti Br. 39578
			SWAN, Billy	
			Born on 5/12/42 in Cape Girardeau, Missouri. Singer/songwriter/keyboardist/ guitarist. Wrote "Lover Please" for Clyde McPhatter. Produced Tony Joe White's first three albums. Toured with Kris Kristofferson from the early '70s. Formed band Black Tie with Randy Meisner in 1986.	
1/4/75	**21**	7	I Can Help *I Can Help* (1)	Monument 33279
			SWEAT, Keith	
			Born and raised in Harlem. Soul singer/songwriter. Worked as a commodities broker on Wall Street.	
2/20/88	**15**	27	▲³ 1. Make It Last Forever *I Want Her* (5)	Vintertn. 60763
6/30/90	**6**	24	▲² **2. I'll Give All My Love To You** *I'll Give All My Love To You* (7)	Vintertn. 60861
12/14/91	**19**	12	▲ 3. Keep It Comin'	Elektra 61216
7/16/94	**8**	8	▲ **4. Get Up On It**	Elektra 61550
			SWEET	
			English rock band: Brian Connolly (lead singer), Steve Priest (bass, vocals), Andy Scott (guitar, keyboards) and Mick Tucker (drums).	
9/27/75	**25**	6	● 1. Desolation Boulevard *Ballroom Blitz* (5)/*Fox On The Run* (5)	Capitol 11395
3/20/76	**27**	7	2. Give Us A Wink	Capitol 11496
			SWINGLE SINGERS, The	
			Ward Swingle (born 9/21/27, Mobile, Alabama; piano, sax) and his scat-singing French singers. Swingle moved to Paris in 1956. Won 1963 Best New Artist Grammy Award.	
11/23/63	**15**	24	Bach's Greatest Hits [I]	Philips 097
			SWING OUT SISTER	
			British jazz-pop trio: Corinne Drewery (vocals), Andy Connell and Martin Jackson. Drewery was a fashion designer. Reduced to a duo in 1989 with departure of Jackson.	
2/27/88	**40**	1	● It's Better To Travel *Breakout* (6)	Mercury 832213

DATE	POS	WKS	ARTIST—RECORD TITLE	LABEL & NO.
			SWITCH	
			Soul-funk sextet from Mansfield, Ohio: Bobby DeBarge, Phillip Ingram (lead vocals), Greg Williams, Tommy DeBarge, Eddie Fluellen and Jody Sims. Discovered by Jermaine Jackson. DeBarge brothers were later in family group DeBarge.	
11/18/78	37	4	1. Switch	Gordy 980
8/11/79	37	4	2. Switch II	Gordy 988
			SWV (Sisters With Voices)	
			New York female vocal trio: Cheryl "Coko" Gamble, Tamara "Taj" Johnson and Leanne "Lelee" Lyons.	
3/27/93	8	33	▲² **It's About Time**	RCA 66074
			I'm So Into You (6)/*Weak* (1)	
			SYLVESTER	
			Born Sylvester James in Los Angeles. Died on 12/16/88 (age 41) of AIDS-related complications. Moved to San Francisco in 1967. With vocal group The Cockettes. In movie *The Rose*. Backing vocals by Martha Wash, Izora Rhodes (later known as Two Tons O' Fun; The Weather Girls) and Jeanie Tracy.	
9/30/78	28	6	● Step II	Fantasy 9556

T

DATE	POS	WKS	ARTIST—RECORD TITLE	LABEL & NO.
			TACO	
			Born Taco Ockerse in 1955 to Dutch parents in Jaharta, Indonesia. German-based singer.	
8/6/83	23	11	After Eight	RCA 4818
			Puttin' On The Ritz (4)	
			TAG TEAM	
			Hip-hop duo based in Atlanta: Cecil Glenn ("D.C. The Brain Supreme") and Steve Gibson ("Steve Rollin"). High-school classmates in Denver.	
8/21/93	39	1	● Whoomp! (There It Is)	Life 78000
			Whoomp! (There It Is) (2)	
			TALKING HEADS	
			New York City-based, new-wave quartet: David Byrne (lead singer, guitar), Jerry Harrison (keyboards, guitar), Tina Weymouth (bass) and husband Chris Frantz (drums). Formed as a trio of Byrne, Weymouth and Frantz at the Rhode Island School of Design. Harrison was a member of The Modern Lovers. Disbanded in late 1991. Also see Tom Tom Club.	
10/28/78	29	5	● 1. More Songs About Buildings And Food	Sire 6058
9/15/79	21	10	● 2. Fear Of Music	Sire 6076
11/15/80	19	9	● 3. Remain In Light	Sire 6095
			above 3 albums produced by Brian Eno	
5/8/82	31	4	4. The Name Of This Band Is Talking Heads [L]	Sire 3590 [2]
7/2/83	15	25	▲ 5. Speaking In Tongues	Sire 23883
			Burning Down The House (9)	
7/6/85	20	24	▲² 6. Little Creatures	Sire 25305
10/18/86	17	16	● 7. True Stories	Sire 25512
			contains group's versions of songs featured in the movie *True Stories*	
4/9/88	19	10	● 8. Naked	Sire 25654

DATE	POS	WKS	ARTIST—RECORD TITLE	LABEL & NO.
			TASTE OF HONEY, A	
			Soul-disco quartet, formed in Los Angeles in 1972. Consisted of Janice Marie Johnson (vocals, guitar), Hazel Payne (vocals, bass), Perry Kimble (keyboards) and Donald Johnson (drums). Re-formed in 1980 with Janice Johnson and Hazel Payne. Won 1978 Best New Artist Grammy Award.	
7/29/78	6	14	▲ **1. A Taste of Honey**	Capitol 11754
			Boogie Oogie Oogie (1)	
5/23/81	36	4	2. Twice As Sweet	Capitol 12089
			Sukiyaki (3)	
			TAVARES	
			Family R&B group from New Bedford, Massachusetts. Consisted of brothers Ralph, Antone "Chubby," Feliciano "Butch," Arthur "Pooch" and Perry Lee "Tiny" Tavares. Worked as Chubby & The Turnpikes from 1964-69. Butch was married to Lola Falana.	
9/27/75	26	5	1. In The City	Capitol 11396
			It Only Takes A Minute (10)	
7/24/76	24	11	2. Sky High!	Capitol 11533
			TAYLOR, James	
			Born on 3/12/48 in Boston. Singer/songwriter/guitarist. With older brother Alex in The Fabulous Corsairs in 1964. In New York group The Flying Machine in 1967, with friend Danny Kortchmar. Moved to England in 1968; recorded for Peter Asher. Married Carly Simon on 11/3/72; divorced in 1983. In movie *Two Lane Blacktop* with Dennis Wilson in 1973. Sister Kate and brothers Alex (died 3/12/93) and Livingston Taylor also recorded. Their father, Isaac, was the dean of the University of North Carolina medical school until 1971.	
4/18/70	3	54	▲³ **1. Sweet Baby James**	Warner 1843
			Fire And Rain (3)	
5/8/71	2 (4)	31	▲² **2. Mud Slide Slim And The Blue Horizon**	Warner 2561
			You've Got A Friend (1)	
12/16/72	4	12	● **3. One Man Dog**	Warner 2660
7/27/74	13	10	4. Walking Man	Warner 2794
6/14/75	6	15	● **5. Gorilla**	Warner 2866
			How Sweet It Is (To Be Loved By You) (5)	
7/10/76	16	14	● 6. In The Pocket	Warner 2912
12/18/76	23	7	▲⁷ 7. Greatest Hits [G]	Warner 2979
7/16/77	4	24	▲² **8. JT**	Columbia 34811
			Handy Man (4)	
5/19/79	10	10	▲ **9. Flag**	Columbia 36058
3/21/81	10	12	● **10. Dad Loves His Work**	Columbia 37009
12/7/85	34	8	▲ 11. That's Why I'm Here	Columbia 40052
2/27/88	25	11	▲ 12. Never Die Young	Columbia 40851
10/19/91	37	5	▲ 13. New Moon Shine	Columbia 46038
8/28/93	20	5	▲ 14. (Live) [L]	Columbia 47056 [2]
			TAYLOR, Johnnie	
			Born on 5/5/38 in Crawfordsville, Arkansas. With gospel group The Highway QC's in Chicago, early '50s. In vocal group The Five Echoes; recorded for Sabre in 1954. In The Soul Stirrers gospel group before going solo. First solo recording for SAR in 1961. Known as The Soul Philosopher.	
3/27/76	5	11	● **Eargasm**	Columbia 33951
			Disco Lady (1)	

DATE	POS	WKS	ARTIST—RECORD TITLE	LABEL & NO.
			TCHAIKOVSKY, Bram — see BRAM TCHAIKOVSKY	
			TEARS FOR FEARS	
			British duo: Roland Orzabal (born 8/22/61; vocals, guitar, keyboards) and Curt Smith (born 6/24/61; vocals, bass). Adopted name from Arthur Janev's book *Prisoners of Pain*. Assisted by Manny Elias (drums) and Ian Stanley (keyboards). Smith left duo by 1992.	
4/20/85	**1**(5)	55	▲⁴ **1. Songs From The Big Chair**	Mercury 824300
			Everybody Wants To Rule The World (1)/*Shout* (1)/ *Head Over Heels* (3)	
10/14/89	**8**	17	▲ **2. The Seeds Of Love**	Fontana 838730
			Sowing The Seeds Of Love (2)	
			TECHNOTRONIC	
			Dance outfit created by Belgian DJ/producer Thomas DeQuincey (real name: Jo Bogaert) and female rapper Ya Kid K (of Hi Tek 3). Nonvocalist Felly, a model from Zaire, fronted the group for videos.	
1/20/90	**10**	22	▲ **Pump Up The Jam — The Album**	SBK 93422
			Pump Up The Jam (2)/*Get Up! (Before The Night Over)* (7)/ *Move This* (6)	
			TEENAGERS, The — see LYMON, Frankie	
			TEMPLE OF THE DOG	
			Gathering of Seattle musicians in tribute to Andrew Wood, lead singer of Mother Love Bone, who died of a heroin overdose in 1990. Features Stone Gossard, Jeff Ament, Eddie Vedder and Mike McCready of Pearl Jam with Chris Cornell and Matt Cameron of Soundgarden. Gossard and Ament were members of Mother Love Bone.	
7/18/92	**5**	15	▲ **Temple Of The Dog**	A&M 5350
			TEMPTATIONS, The	
			Detroit soul group formed in 1960. Consisted of Eddie Kendricks (died 10/5/92 of lung cancer [age 52]), Paul Williams (died 8/17/73), Melvin Franklin, Otis Williams (not to be confused with the same-named member of The Charms) and Elbridge Bryant, who was replaced by David Ruffin in 1964. Originally called The Primes and Elgins; first recorded for Miracle in 1961. Ruffin (died 6/1/91 of drug overdose [age 50]; cousin of Billy Stewart) replaced by Dennis Edwards (ex-Contours) in 1968. Kendricks and Paul Williams left in 1971; replaced by Ricky Owens (ex-Vibrations) and Richard Street. Owens was replaced by Damon Harris. Harris left in 1975; replaced by Glenn Leonard. Edwards left group, 1977-79; replaced by Louis Price. Ali Ollie Woodson replaced Edwards from 1984-87. 1988 lineup: Otis Williams, Franklin, Street, Edwards and Ron Tyson. Recognized as America's all-time favorite soul group. Inducted into the Rock and Roll Hall of Fame in 1989.	
5/29/65	**35**	3	1. The Temptations Sing Smokey	Gordy 912
			tribute to songwriter/producer Smokey Robinson *My Girl* (1)	
1/1/66	**11**	19	2. Temptin' Temptations	Gordy 914
8/13/66	**12**	18	3. Gettin' Ready	Gordy 918
1/14/67	**5**	65	**4. The Temptations Greatest Hits** [G]	Gordy 919
			Beauty Is Only Skin Deep (3)	
4/15/67	**10**	18	**5. Temptations Live!** [L]	Gordy 921
8/19/67	**7**	18	**6. With A Lot O' Soul**	Gordy 922
			(I Know) I'm Losing You (8)/*All I Need* (8)/ *You're My Everything* (6)	
1/27/68	**13**	14	7. The Temptations in a Mellow Mood	Gordy 924
6/22/68	**13**	14	8. Wish It Would Rain	Gordy 927
			I Wish It Would Rain (4)	

DATE	POS	WKS	ARTIST—RECORD TITLE	LABEL & NO.
12/21/68	**2**(1)	14	**9. Diana Ross & the Supremes Join the Temptations ***	Motown 679
			I'm Gonna Make You Love Me (2)	
1/11/69	**1**(1)	19	**10. TCB *** [TV]	Motown 682
2/1/69	**15**	9	11. Live At The Copa [L]	Gordy 938
3/22/69	**4**	26	**12. Cloud Nine**	Gordy 939
			Cloud Nine (6)/*Run Away Child, Running Wild* (6)	
8/16/69	**24**	10	13. The Temptations Show [TV]	Gordy 933
			with guests Kaye Stevens and George Kirby	
10/25/69	**5**	19	**14. Puzzle People**	Gordy 949
			I Can't Get Next To You (1)	
11/15/69	**28**	3	15. Together *	Motown 692
12/27/69	**38**	2	16. On Broadway * [TV]	Motown 699
			*DIANA ROSS & THE SUPREMES with THE TEMPTATIONS	
4/11/70	**9**	18	**17. Psychedelic Shack**	Gordy 947
			Psychedelic Shack (7)	
9/5/70	**21**	6	18. Live at London's Talk of The Town [L]	Gordy 953
10/10/70	**15**	12	19. Temptations Greatest Hits II [G]	Gordy 954
			Ball Of Confusion (That's What The World Is Today) (3)	
5/22/71	**16**	15	20. Sky's The Limit	Gordy 957
			Just My Imagination (Running Away With Me) (1)	
2/19/72	**24**	8	21. Solid Rock	Gordy 961
9/16/72	**2**(2)	25	**22. All Directions**	Gordy 962
			Papa Was A Rollin' Stone (1)	
3/24/73	**7**	14	**23. Masterpiece**	Gordy 965
			Masterpiece (7)	
1/26/74	**19**	8	24. 1990	Gordy 966
3/22/75	**13**	16	25. A Song For You	Gordy 969
12/20/75	**40**	2	26. House Party	Gordy 973
5/15/76	**29**	6	27. Wings Of Love	Gordy 971
6/5/82	**37**	2	28. Reunion	Gordy 6008
			Ruffin and Kendricks return for this album	
			10cc	
			English art-rock group that evolved from Hotlegs. Consisted of Eric Stewart (guitar), Graham Gouldman (bass), Lol Creme (guitar, keyboards) and Kevin Godley (drums). Stewart and Gouldman were members of The Mindbenders. Godley & Creme left in 1976; replaced by drummer Paul Burgess. Added members Rick Fenn, Stuart Tosh and Duncan MacKay in 1978. Gouldman later in duo Wax.	
6/28/75	**15**	10	1. The Original Soundtrack	Mercury 1029
			I'm Not In Love (2)	
5/28/77	**31**	5	2. Deceptive Bends	Mercury 3702
			The Things We Do For Love (5)	
			10,000 MANIACS	
			Jamestown, New York, group formed in 1981: Natalie Merchant (vocals), Robert Buck (guitar), Dennis Drew (keyboards), Steven Gustafson (bass), Jerome Augustyniak (drums) and John Lombardo (guitar). Lombardo left in July 1986. Merchant left the band in August 1993.	
5/14/88	**37**	2	▲ 1. In My Tribe	Elektra 60738
6/10/89	**13**	19	● 2. Blind Man's Zoo	Elektra 60815
			above 2 produced by Peter Asher (Peter & Gordon)	

DATE	POS	WKS	ARTIST—RECORD TITLE	LABEL & NO.
10/17/92	28	9	▲ 3. Our Time In Eden	Elektra 61385
11/13/93	13	18	▲ 4. MTV Unplugged [L]	Elektra 61569
			recorded on the MTV program "Unplugged"	
			TEN YEARS AFTER	
			British blues-rock quartet formed in 1967: Alvin Lee (born 12/19/44, Nottingham, England; vocals, guitar), Leo Lyons (bass), Chick Churchill (keyboards) and Ric Lee (drums). Inactive as band from 1975-87.	
9/13/69	20	7	1. SSSSH	Deram 18029
4/25/70	14	8	2. Cricklewood Green	Deram 18038
12/19/70	21	8	3. Watt	Deram 18050
9/11/71	17	10	▲ 4. A Space In Time	Columbia 30801
7/28/73	39	2	5. Recorded Live [L]	Columbia 32290 [2]
			TESLA	
			Sacramento hard-rock quintet: Jeff Keith (vocals), Frank Hannon, Tommy Skeoch, Brian Wheat and Troy Luccketta. Band named after Nikola Tesla, the inventor of radio.	
3/14/87	32	8	▲ 1. Mechanical Resonance	Geffen 24120
2/25/89	18	17	▲ 2. The Great Radio Controversy	Geffen 24224
			Love Song (10)	
12/8/90	12	27	▲ 3. Five Man Acoustical Jam [L]	Geffen 24311
			recorded July 2, 1990, at the Trocadero in Philadelphia; title is a pun on Five Man Electrical Band who hit #3 with "Signs" in 1971	
			Signs (8)	
9/28/91	13	5	▲ 4. Psychotic Supper	Geffen 24424
9/10/94	20	2	5. Bust A Nut	Geffen 24713
			TEX, Joe	
			Born Joseph Arrington, Jr., on 8/8/33 in Rogers, Texas; died of a heart attack on 8/13/82. Sang with local gospel groups. Won recording contract during Apollo Theater talent contest in 1954. First recorded for King in 1955. Converted to the Muslim faith; changed name to "Joseph Hazziez" in July 1972.	
5/6/72	17	11	I Gotcha	Dial 6002
			I Gotcha (2)	
			THIN LIZZY	
			Rock quartet formed by Dublin, Ireland, natives Phil Lynott (born 8/20/51; died 1/4/86; vocals, bass) and Brian Downey (drums). Gary Moore was lead guitarist in early 1974, then 1978-79. Added guitarists Brian Robertson (from Glasgow) and Scott Gorham (from California) in June 1974. Robertson left in 1977 (later joined Motorhead); replaced by various guitarists. Keyboardist Darren Wharton joined in 1983.	
6/5/76	18	10	● 1. Jailbreak	Mercury 1081
10/29/77	39	2	2. Bad Reputation	Mercury 1186
			3RD BASS	
			White rappers from Queens, New York: Prime Minister Pete Nice (Pete Nash) and MC Serch (Michael Berrin). Supported by black DJ Richie Rich (Richard Lawson). Disbanded in early 1992. Nash and Lawson continued as duo: Prime Minister Pete Nice and DJ Daddy Rich; Berrin went solo.	
7/6/91	19	11	● Derelicts Of Dialect	Def Jam 47369

DATE	POS	WKS	ARTIST—RECORD TITLE	LABEL & NO.
			38 SPECIAL	
			Florida-based Southern rock sextet: Donnie Van Zant (lead singer; younger brother of Lynyrd Skynyrd's Ronnie Van Zant), Don Barnes, Jeff Carlisi, Steve Brookins, Jack Grondin and Larry Jungstrom (ex-Lynyrd Skynyrd; replaced Ken Lyons in 1979). By 1988, Barnes and Brookins replaced by Danny Chauncey and Max Carl. Barnes returned in 1992 to replace Carl.	
3/14/81	18	18	▲ 1. Wild-Eyed Southern Boys	A&M 4835
6/5/82	10	11	▲ 2. Special Forces	A&M 4888
			Caught Up In You (10)	
12/10/83	22	20	▲ 3. Tour De Force	A&M 4971
5/24/86	17	20	● 4. Strength In Numbers	A&M 5115
9/19/87	35	3	● 5. Flashback [G]	A&M 3910
			includes a bonus 4-song live EP	
			THOMAS, B.J.	
			Born Billy Joe Thomas on 8/7/42 in Hugo, Oklahoma; raised in Rosenberg, Texas. Sang in church choir as a teenager. Joined band, The Triumphs, while in high school. Thomas has featured gospel music since 1976.	
1/31/70	12	23	● Raindrops Keep Fallin' On My Head	Scepter 580
			Raindrops Keep Fallin' On My Head (1)	
			THOMAS, Carla — see REDDING, Otis	
			THOMPSON TWINS	
			British trio: Tom Bailey (born 1/18/56, England; lead singer, synthesizer), Alannah Currie (born 9/28/57, New Zealand; xylophone, percussion) and Joe Leeway (born 11/15/57, London; conga, synthesizer). Leeway left in 1986.	
3/26/83	34	4	1. Side Kicks	Arista 6607
3/31/84	10	24	▲ 2. Into The Gap	Arista 8200
			Hold Me Now (3)	
10/26/85	20	24	● 3. Here's To Future Days	Arista 8276
			Lay Your Hands On Me (6)/*King For A Day* (8)	
			THOROGOOD, George, & The Destroyers	
			Thorogood is the leader of the Delaware rock & blues band The Destroyers. Lineup since 1980: Thorogood (born Wilmington, Delaware; vocals, guitar), Billy Blough (bass), Jeff Simon (drums) and Hank Carter (sax). Added guitarist Steve Chrismar in 1986.	
3/31/79	33	7	● 1. Move It On Over	Rounder 3024
4/6/85	32	15	● 2. Maverick	EMI America 17145
9/20/86	33	4	● 3. Live [L]	EMI America 17214
2/20/88	32	10	● 4. Born To Be Bad	EMI-Man. 46973
			THORPE, Billy	
			English-born singer/guitarist; raised in Australia. Superstar artist in Australia. Member of The Zoo.	
9/29/79	39	1	Children Of The Sun	Polydor 6228
			originally released on Capricorn 0221	
			THREE DEGREES, The	
			Philadelphia R&B trio discovered by Richard Barrett. Originally consisted of Fayette Pinkney, Linda Turner and Shirley Porter. Turner and Porter replaced by Sheila Ferguson and Valerie Holiday in 1966.	
1/18/75	28	5	The Three Degrees	Phil. Int. 32406
			When Will I See You Again (2)	

DATE	POS	WKS	ARTIST—RECORD TITLE	LABEL & NO.
			THREE DOG NIGHT	
			Los Angeles pop-rock group formed in 1968 featuring lead singers Danny Hutton (born 9/10/42), Cory Wells (born 2/5/42) and Chuck Negron (born 6/8/42). Disbanded in the mid-1970s. Re-formed in the mid-1980s.	
4/5/69	11	26	● 1. Three Dog Night	Dunhill 50048
			One (5)	
7/26/69	16	27	● 2. Suitable for Framing	Dunhill 50058
			Easy To Be Hard (4)/*Eli's Coming* (10)	
12/6/69	6	24	● 3. Captured Live At The Forum [L]	Dunhill 50068
5/9/70	8	20	● 4. It Ain't Easy	Dunhill 50078
			Mama Told Me (Not To Come) (1)	
12/19/70	14	22	● 5. Naturally	Dunhill 50088
			Joy To The World (1)/*Liar* (7)	
3/6/71	5	30	● 6. Golden Bisquits [G]	Dunhill 50098
10/23/71	8	21	● 7. Harmony	Dunhill 50108
			An Old Fashioned Love Song (4)/*Never Been To Spain* (5)	
8/12/72	6	19	● 8. Seven Separate Fools	Dunhill 50118
			Black & White (1)	
3/31/73	18	9	● 9. Around The World With Three Dog Night [L]	Dunhill 50138 [2]
11/10/73	26	6	● 10. Cyan	Dunhill 50158
			Shambala (3)	
4/27/74	20	8	● 11. Hard Labor	Dunhill 50168
			The Show Must Go On (4)	
1/11/75	15	8	● 12. Joy To The World-Their Greatest Hits [G]	Dunhill 50178
			THREE SUNS, The	
			Instrumental trio from Philadelphia: brothers Al (died 1965; guitar) and Morty Nevins (died 7/20/90 of cancer; accordion), with cousin Artie Dunn (died 1989; organ). Al Nevins founded, with Don Kirshner, Aldon Music, the famed publishing company largely responsible for the "Brill Building" rock-and-roll sound.	
5/28/55	13	9	1. Soft and Sweet [I]	RCA 1041
8/18/56	19	1	2. High Fi and Wide [I]	RCA 1249
1/26/57	16	6	3. Midnight For Two [I]	RCA 1333
			TIERRA	
			East Los Angeles group formed in 1972. Band led by the Salas brothers: Steve (trombone, timbales) and Rudy (guitar); both formerly with El Chicano.	
3/7/81	38	4	City Nights	Boardwalk 36995
			TIFFANY	
			Born Tiffany Darwisch on 10/2/71. California pop singer originally from Oklahoma.	
11/7/87	1(2)	35	▲⁴ 1. Tiffany	MCA 5793
			I Think We're Alone Now (1)/*Could've Been* (1)/ *I Saw Him Standing There* (7)	
12/17/88	17	19	▲ 2. Hold An Old Friend's Hand	MCA 6267
			All This Time (6)	
			TILLOTSON, Johnny	
			Born on 4/20/39 in Jacksonville, Florida; raised in Palatka, Florida. On local radio *Young Folks Revue* from age nine. DJ on WWPF. Appeared on the "Toby Dowdy" TV show in Jacksonville; then own show. Signed by Cadence Records in 1958. In the movie *Just for Fun*.	
8/25/62	8	10	It Keeps Right On A-Hurtin'	Cadence 3058
			It Keeps Right On A-Hurtin' (3)	

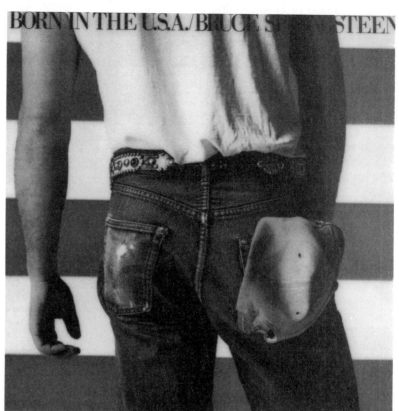

The Singing Nun's unexpected 1963 hit, "Dominique," made her one of the most unusual pop stars of the era. The track pushed *The Singing Nun* to the top of the charts for 10 weeks during 1963–64.

Jimmy Smith's deeply influential jazz-organ style appealed to many pop fans during the '60s. The prolific stylist lodged 21 discs in the pop charts between 1962–69, highlighted by 1962's Top 10 *Bashin'*. Oliver Nelson's arrangements were heard on 1966's *Hoochie Coochie Man*.

Bruce Springsteen's career zoomed upward during the '70s, but it was 1984's *Born In The U.S.A.* that capped his career. Staying at No. 1 for 12 weeks, the powerful set yielded an amazing total of seven Top 10 hits.

Rod Stewart's 1976 album, *A Night On The Town*, marked his first time out as a solo artist following the disbanding of Faces, his group, in 1975. A big success, the record boasted Stewart's longest-ever No. 1 hit, "Tonight's The Night (Gonna Be Alright)."

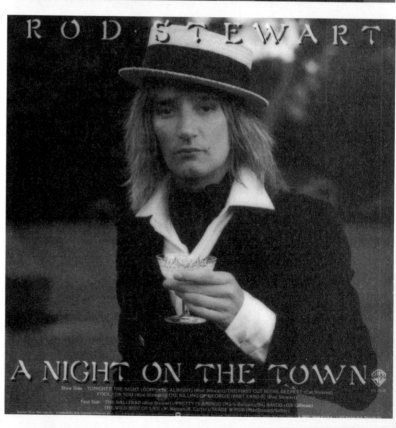

Barbra Streisand's vast commercial appeal was apparent from the beginning of her recording career. Starting with *The Barbra Streisand Album*, which won 1963's Album of the Year Grammy Award, she chalked up nine Top 10 albums in a row.

SWV's *It's About Time* climbed to No. 8 in 1993 and became one of RCA's biggest sellers of the year. The label responded by issuing a special EP of album-track remixes the next year.

The Temptations' 1965 album, *Temptin' Temptations*, was briefly the highest-charting album of the group's career. Within a year, it was eclipsed by *The Temptations Greatest Hits*; this collection reached No. 5.

U2's acclaimed classic, *The Joshua Tree*, won the 1987 Album of the Year Grammy Award and lingered in the No. 1 slot for a total of nine weeks. The set contained both of the Irish band's biggest hits, each of which reached No. 1, "With Or Without You" and "I Still Haven't Found What I'm Looking For."

Vanilla Ice's *To The Extreme* lived up to its title upon its 1990 release. The disc stayed at No. 1 for 16 weeks and sold more than 7 million copies. The Miami-born rapper had nowhere to go but down after that, which, sadly, is what happened.

DATE	POS	WKS	ARTIST—RECORD TITLE	LABEL & NO.
			'TIL TUESDAY	
			Boston pop quartet: Aimee Mann (lead singer, bass), Michael Hausmann (drums), Robert Holmes (guitar) and Joey Pesce (keyboards; replaced by Michael Montes in 1988).	
6/1/85	19	12	● Voices Carry	Epic 39458
			Voices Carry (8)	
			TIME, The	
			Funk group formed in Minneapolis by Prince and Morris Day in 1981. Original lineup: Morris Day (lead singer), Terry Lewis, Jimmy "Jam" Harris, Monte Moir, Jesse Johnson and Jellybean Johnson. Lewis, Harris and Moir left before band's featured role in movie *Purple Rain*. Paul "St. Paul" Peterson and Lewis's half-brother, Jerome Benton, joined in 1984; group disbanded later that year. Day and Jesse Johnson went solo; Lewis and Harris became highly successful songwriting/producing team. Lewis married singer Karyn White. Original lineup plus Benton re-grouped in 1990.	
10/2/82	26	8	● 1. What Time Is It?	Warner 23701
8/25/84	24	34	▲ 2. Ice Cream Castle	Warner 25109
8/4/90	18	8	● 3. Pandemonium	Paisley P. 27490
			Jerk Out (9)	
			TIN MACHINE	
			Quartet of David Bowie (vocals), Reeves Gabrels (guitar; ex-Rubber Rodeo), Hunt (drums; ex-Utopia; ex-Paris) and Tony Sales (bass; ex-Utopia; ex-Chequered Past). The Sales brothers are the sons of television comedian Soupy Sales. Tony acted in the movie *Hard to Hold* and appeared in Budweiser commercials.	
6/17/89	28	5	Tin Machine	EMI 91990
			TINY TIM	
			Born Herbert Khaury on 4/12/30 in New York City. Novelty singer/ukulele player. Shot to national attention with appearances on TV's "Rowan & Martin's Laugh-In." Married "Miss Vicki" on Johnny Carson's "The Tonight Show" 12/18/69; divorced in 1977.	
6/8/68	7	10	**God Bless Tiny Tim** **[N]**	Reprise 6292
			TLC	
			Atlanta-based teenage female rap trio: Tionne "T-Boz" Watkins, Lisa "Left Eye" Lopes and Rozonda "Chilli" Thomas. Founded and managed by Pebbles. Lopes was charged with felony arson for setting fire to the house of her boyfriend, Andre Rison, a receiver for the Atlanta Falcons football team, on 6/9/94.	
7/4/92	14	37	▲² 1. Oooooooohhh ... On The TLC Tip	LaFace 26003
			Ain't 2 Proud 2 Beg (6)/*Baby-Baby-Baby* (2)/ *What About Your Friends* (7)	
12/3/94	7	13+	▲² 2. CrazySexyCool	LaFace 26009
			Creep (1)	
			TOAD THE WET SPROCKET	
			Pop quartet from Santa Barbara, California: Glen Phillips (vocals), Todd Nichols (guitar), Dean Dinning (bass) and Randy Guss (drums). Name taken from a Monty Python skit.	
6/11/94	34	1	● Dulcinea	Columbia 57744
			TOBY BEAU	
			Texas pop quintet: Balde Silva (vocals), Danny McKenna, Rob Young, Steve Zipper and Ron Rose.	
9/2/78	40	1	Toby Beau	RCA 2771

DATE	POS	WKS	ARTIST—RECORD TITLE	LABEL & NO.
			TOMLIN, Lily	
			Born on 9/1/39 in Detroit. TV and movie actress/comedienne. Member of TV's "Rowan & Martin's Laugh-In" series (1970-73). In movies *9 to 5*, *All of Me*, *Big Business* and others. In Broadway's *The Search for Signs of Intelligent Life in the Universe*.	
4/10/71	**15**	11	This is a Recording　　　　　　　　[C]	Polydor 4055
			TOMMY TUTONE	
			San Francisco rock band led by Tommy Heath (vocals) and Jim Keller (lead guitar).	
4/17/82	**20**	8	Tommy Tutone-2	Columbia 37401
			867-5309/Jenny (4)	
			TOM TOM CLUB	
			Studio project formed by Talking Heads members Chris Frantz and wife Tina Weymouth. Production work for Ziggy Marley & The Melody Makers, Happy Mondays and others.	
2/20/82	**23**	10	● 　Tom Tom Club	Sire 3628
			TONE LOC	
			Los Angeles-based rapper, Anthony Smith. Stage name pronounced tone loke; derived from his Spanish nickname "Antonio Loco." Contributed voice to animated movie *Bebe's Kids* and appeared in *Surf Ninjas*, *Posse* and *Ace Ventura — Pet Detective*.	
2/25/89	**1**(1)	23	▲² 　**Loc-ed After Dark**	Delicious V. 3000
			Wild Thing (2)/*Funky Cold Medina* (3)	
			TONY! TONI! TONE!	
			R&B-funk trio from Oakland, California. Brothers Dwayne and Raphael Wiggins, with cousin Timothy Christian. Appeared in the movie *House Party 2*. Dwayne assembled Simple E.	
6/23/90	**34**	5	▲ 　1. The Revival	Wing 841902
			Feels Good (9)	
7/10/93	**24**	18	▲ 　2. Sons Of Soul	Wing 514933
			TONY TONI TONE	
			If I Had No Loot (7)/*Anniversary* (10)	
			TOO $HORT	
			Born Todd Shaw on 4/28/66 in Los Angeles. Oakland-based 5'7" rapper.	
4/29/89	**37**	8	▲ 　1. Life Is ... Too $hort	Dangerous 1149
10/6/90	**20**	10	▲ 　2. Short Dog's In The House	Jive 1348
8/1/92	**6**	6	● 　**3. Shorty The Pimp**	Jive 41467
11/13/93	**4**	5	▲ 　**4. Get In Where You Fit In**	Jive 41526
			TOTO	
			Pop-rock group formed in Los Angeles in 1978. Consisted of Bobby Kimball (vocals; his real last name is not Toteaux as widely rumored), Steve Lukather (guitar), David Paich and Steve Porcaro (keyboards), David Hungate (bass) and Jeff Porcaro (died 8/5/92 [age 38]; drums). Prominent session musicians, most notably behind Boz Scaggs in the late '70s. Hungate was replaced by Mike Porcaro in 1983. (The Porcaros are brothers.) Kimball replaced by Fergie Fredericksen in 1984; Fredericksen replaced by Joseph Williams (conductor John's son) in 1986. Steve Porcaro left in 1988. South African native Jean-Michel Byron replaced Frederiksen in 1990. Paich and his father, Marty, won an Emmy Award for writing the theme for the TV series "Ironside."	
12/9/78	**9**	20	▲² 　**1. Toto**	Columbia 35317
			Hold The Line (5)	
12/15/79	**37**	3	● 　2. Hydra	Columbia 36229

DATE	POS	WKS	ARTIST—RECORD TITLE	LABEL & NO.
5/8/82	4	42	▲³ **3. Toto IV** [C]	Columbia 37728
			1982 Album of the Year Grammy Award	
			Rosanna (2)/*Africa* (1)/*I Won't Hold You Back* (10)	
11/29/86	40	2	● 4. Fahrenheit	Columbia 40273
			TOWER OF POWER	
			Interracial Oakland-based, R&B-funk band formed by sax player Emilio "Mimi" Castillo in the late '60s. Originally known as The Motowns. Lenny Williams sang lead from 1972-75.	
7/28/73	15	8	● 1. Tower Of Power	Warner 2681
4/6/74	26	5	2. Back to Oakland [C]	Warner 2749
2/22/75	22	5	3. Urban Renewal [C]	Warner 2834
			TOWNSHEND, Pete	
			Born on 5/19/45 in London. Lead guitarist/songwriter of The Who. First solo album *Who Came First*, 1972. Own publishing house, Eel Pie Press, mid-1970s. Currently plagued by a significant hearing loss.	
5/24/80	5	19	● **1. Empty Glass**	Atco 100
			Let My Love Open The Door (9)	
7/24/82	26	9	2. All The Best Cowboys Have Chinese Eyes	Atco 149
4/9/83	35	4	3. Scoop [K]	Atco 90063 [2]
			primarily a collection of Townshend's demo recordings	
12/28/85	26	11	● 4. White City — A Novel	Atco 90473
			T'PAU	
			Group from Shrewsbury, England: Carol Decker, lead singer. Band named after a Vulcan princess in an episode of the TV series "Star Trek."	
8/22/87	31	3	T'Pau	Virgin 90595
			Heart And Soul (4)	
			TRACTORS, The	
			Country-rock band formed in Tulsa, Oklahoma of veteran sidemen: Steve Ripley (guitar), Walt Richmond (keyboards), Ron Getman (guitar), Casey Van Beek (vocals) and Jamie Oldaker (drums).	
10/29/94	19	16	▲ The Tractors	Arista 18728
			TRAFFIC	
			British rock band. Original lineup: Steve Winwood (keyboards, guitar), Dave Mason (guitar), Jim Capaldi (drums) and Chris Wood (died 7/12/83; flute, sax). Many personnel changes until the group disbanded in 1974. Winwood and Capaldi reunited in 1994.	
12/21/68	17	8	1. Traffic	United Art. 6676
5/24/69	19	7	2. Last Exit	United Art. 6702
7/25/70	5	16	● **3. John Barleycorn Must Die**	United Art. 5504
10/16/71	26	7	4. Welcome To The Canteen [L]	United Art. 5550
			TRAFFIC, ETC.	
12/18/71	7	20	● **5. The Low Spark Of High Heeled Boys**	Island 9306
2/17/73	6	12	● **6. Shoot Out At The Fantasy Factory**	Island 9323
11/24/73	29	5	7. Traffic-On The Road [L]	Island 9336 [2]
10/5/74	9	10	● **8. When The Eagle Flies**	Asylum 1020
5/21/94	33	1	9. Far From Home	Virgin 39490

DATE	POS	WKS	ARTIST—RECORD TITLE	LABEL & NO.
			TRAVELING WILBURYS	
			Supergroup masquerading as a band of brothers. Spearheaded by Nelson (George Harrison), with Lucky (Bob Dylan), Otis (Jeff Lynne of ELO), Lefty (Roy Orbison) and Charlie T. Junior (Tom Petty) Wilbury. Orbison died on 12/6/88 (age 52). For their second album, *Vol. 3*, the brothers' names have changed to Spike (Harrison), Muddy (Petty), Clayton (Lynne) and Boo (Dylan).	
11/19/88	3	32	▲³ **1. Volume One**	Wilbury 25796
11/17/90	11	12	▲ 2. Vol. 3 [L]	Wilbury 26324
			TRAVERS, Pat	
			Born in Toronto in 1954. Blues-rock guitarist/vocalist.	
9/1/79	29	4	1. Pat Travers Band Live! Go For What You Know [L]	Polydor 6202
4/12/80	20	12	2. Crash And Burn	Polydor 6262
			PAT TRAVERS BAND *M* (above 2)	
4/25/81	37	2	3. Radio Active	Polydor 6313
			TRAVIS, Randy	
			Born Randy Bruce Traywick in Marshville, North Carolina, on 5/4/59. Country singer/guitarist. Moved to Nashville in 1981; worked as singer/dishwasher/cook at Lib Hatcher's Nashville Palace. Recorded as Randy Traywick and Randy Ray before adopting stage name, Randy Travis, in 1985. Married Hatcher, his longtime manager, on 5/31/91. The youngest male inducted into the *Grand Ole Opry*.	
6/6/87	19	21	▲⁴ 1. Always & Forever	Warner 25568
8/13/88	35	6	▲ 2. Old 8x10	Warner 25738
10/28/89	33	3	▲ 3. No Holdin' Back	Warner 25988
10/20/90	31	5	▲ 4. Heroes And Friends	Warner 26310
			Travis sings duets with Dolly Parton, Willie Nelson, Merle Haggard, Vern Gosdin, Loretta Lynn, B.B. King, George Jones, Kris Kristofferson, Tammy Wynette, Clint Eastwood, Conway Twitty and Roy Rogers; Chet Atkins appears on the Parton duet	
			TRAVOLTA, John	
			Born on 2/18/54 in Englewood, New Jersey. Actor/singer. Played Vinnie Barbarino on the TV series "Welcome Back Kotter." Starred in the movies *Saturday Night Fever*, *Grease*, *Urban Cowboy*, *Look Who's Talking*, *Pulp Fiction* and others. Married actress Kelly Preston on 9/5/91.	
7/17/76	39	4	John Travolta *Let Her In* (10)	Midland Int. 1563
			TRESVANT, Ralph	
			Born on 5/16/68; raised in Roxbury, Massachusetts. Member of New Edition. Appeared in the movie *House Party 2*.	
12/15/90	17	15	▲ Ralph Tresvant CD includes 2 bonus tracks *Sensitivity* (4)	MCA 10116
			T. REX	
			British rock group led by Marc Bolan (born Marc Feld on 7/30/47 in London; killed in an auto accident on 9/16/77. Guitarist Jack Green joined in 1973; left a year later to join Pretty Things.	
3/18/72	32	5	1. Electric Warrior *Bang A Gong (Get It On)* (10)	Reprise 6466
10/7/72	17	11	2. The Slider	Reprise 2095

DATE	POS	WKS	ARTIST—RECORD TITLE	LABEL & NO.
			TRIBE CALLED QUEST, A	
			New York rap outfit: Q-Tip, Ali Shaheed Muhammad and Phife. Jarobi was a member for first album.	
11/27/93	8	3	▲ **Midnight Marauders**	Jive 41490
			TRITT, Travis	
			Born on 2/9/63 in Marietta, Georgia. Country singer.	
6/29/91	22	36	▲² 1. It's All About To Change	Warner 26589
9/5/92	27	6	▲ 2. T-R-O-U-B-L-E	Warner 45048
			with guests Brooks & Dunn, George Jones, Gary Rossington, Tanya Tucker and Billy Joe Walker, Jr.	
5/28/94	20	4	▲ 3. Ten Feet Tall And Bulletproof	Warner 45603
			TRIUMPH	
			Canadian hard-rock trio formed in Toronto in 1975. Consisted of Rik Emmett (guitar, vocals), Gil Moore (drums, vocals) and Mike Levine (keyboards, bass). Emmett went solo in 1988.	
4/19/80	32	6	1. Progressions Of Power	RCA 3524
10/17/81	23	9	● 2. Allied Forces	RCA 3902
2/12/83	26	12	● 3. Never Surrender	RCA 4382
2/2/85	35	7	4. Thunder Seven	MCA 5537
10/25/86	33	5	5. The Sport Of Kings	MCA 5786
			TRIUMVIRAT	
			German synthesized rock group: Helmut Kollen (guitar, vocals), Hans Bathelt (drums) and Jurgen Fritz (keyboards). Kollen replaced by Barry Palmer (vocals) and Dick Frangenberg (bass) in 1976.	
7/26/75	27	5	Spartacus	Capitol 11392
			TRIXTER	
			Rock quartet from Paramus, New Jersey: Peter Loran (vocals), Steve Brown, P.J. Farley and Mark "Gus" Scott.	
1/26/91	28	13	● Trixter	MCA 6389
			TROWER, Robin	
			Born on 3/9/45 in London. Rock guitarist. Original member of Procol Harum, 1967-72. James Dewar, vocalist (except on *B.L.T.* album).	
5/11/74	7	21	● **1. Bridge Of Sighs**	Chrysalis 1057
3/8/75	5	9	● **2. For Earth Below**	Chrysalis 1073
4/3/76	10	8	**3. Robin Trower Live!** **[L]**	Chrysalis 1089
10/16/76	24	6	● 4. Long Misty Days	Chrysalis 1107
10/22/77	25	6	● 5. In City Dreams	Chrysalis 1148
10/7/78	37	4	6. Caravan To Midnight	Chrysalis 1189
4/5/80	34	3	7. Victims Of The Fury	Chrysalis 1215
4/25/81	37	3	8. B.L.T.	Chrysalis 1324
			B.L.T.: Jack Bruce, Bill Lordan, Robin Trower	
			TUBES, The	
			San Francisco theater-rock troupe led by vocalist Fee Waybill (born John Waldo on 9/17/50 in Omaha, Nebraska). Group appeared in movie musical *Xanadu* with Olivia Newton-John in 1980.	
7/18/81	36	4	1. The Completion Backward Principle	Capitol 12151
4/30/83	18	14	2. Outside Inside	Capitol 12260
			She's A Beauty (10)	

DATE	POS	WKS	ARTIST—RECORD TITLE	LABEL & NO.
			### TURNER, Ike & Tina	
			Husband-and-wife duo: guitarist Ike Turner (born 11/5/31, Clarksdale, Mississippi) and vocalist Tina Turner (born Anna Mae Bullock on 11/26/38, Brownsville, Tennessee). Married from 1958-76. At age 11, Ike was backing pianist for bluesmen Sonny Boy Williamson (Aleck Ford) and Robert Nighthawk (of The Nighthawks). Formed own band, The Kings of Rhythm, while in high school; backed Jackie Brenston's hit "Rocket '88'." Prolific session, production and guitar work during the '50s. In 1960, developed a dynamic stage show around Tina; "The Ike & Tina Turner Revue" featuring her backing vocalists, The Ikettes, and Ike's Kings Of Rhythm. Disbanded in 1974. In the mid-1980s, Tina emerged as a successful solo artist. Duet inducted into the Rock and Roll Hall of Fame in 1991.	
3/13/71	25	8	1. Workin' Together *Proud Mary* (4)	Liberty 7650
7/31/71	25	11	● 2. Live At Carnegie Hall/What You Hear Is What You Get [L]	United Art. 9953 [2]
			### TURNER, Tina	
			Born Anna Mae Bullock on 11/26/38 in Brownsville, Tennessee. R&B-rock vocalist/actress. Half of Ike & Tina Turner duo when married to Ike from 1958-76. In movies *Tommy* (1975) and *Mad Max-Beyond Thunderdome* (1985). With Ike, inducted into the Rock and Roll Hall of Fame in 1991.	
6/30/84	3	71	▲⁵ **1. Private Dancer** *What's Love Got To Do With It* (1)/*Better Be Good To Me* (5)/ *Private Dancer* (7)	Capitol 12330
10/4/86	4	17	▲ **2. Break Every Rule** *Typical Male* (2)	Capitol 12530
10/14/89	31	5	● 3. Foreign Affair	Capitol 91873
7/3/93	17	11	▲ 4. What's Love Got To Do With It [S] *I Don't Wanna Fight* (9)	Virgin 88189
			### TURTLES, The	
			Pop-folk-rock group formed at Westchester High School in Los Angeles in 1961. Led by Mark Volman (born 4/19/47, Los Angeles) and Howard Kaylan (born Howard Kaplan on 6/22/47, New York City). First called The Nightriders; then The Crossfires. Recorded for Capco in 1963. Name changed to The Turtles in 1965. Many personnel changes except for Volman and Kaylan. Group disbanded in 1970. Volman and Kaylan joined The Mothers of Invention. Went out as a duo in 1972 and recorded as Phlorescent Leech & Eddie and later as Flo & Eddie. Did soundtrack for the movie *Strawberry Shortcake*. Toured again as The Turtles in 1985.	
5/20/67	25	7	1. Happy Together *Happy Together* (1)/*She'd Rather Be With Me* (3)	White Whale 7114
12/16/67	7	16	● **2. The Turtles! Golden Hits** [G]	White Whale 7115
			### TUTONE, Tommy — see TOMMY	
			### TWILLEY, Dwight	
			Born on 6/6/51 in Tulsa, Oklahoma. Rock singer/songwriter/pianist. Formed The Dwight Twilley Band with Phil Seymour (died 8/17/93 [age 41] of lymphoma; bass, drums) in 1974.	
4/14/84	39	3	Jungle	EMI America 17107
			### TWISTED SISTER	
			Long Island, New York, heavy-metal quintet led by Dee Snider (born 3/15/55, Massapequa, Long Island, New York). Included Jay French (guitar), Eddie Ojeda (guitar), Mark Mendosa (bass) and A.J. Pero (drums). Pero replaced by Joey Franco in 1987. Disbanded in late 1987.	
8/4/84	15	26	▲² Stay Hungry	Atlantic 80156

DATE	POS	WKS	ARTIST—RECORD TITLE	LABEL & NO.
			2 LIVE CREW, The	
			Miami-based rap quartet: David "Mr. Mix" Hobbs, Chris "Kid-Ice" Wong Won, Mark "Brother Marquis" Ross and Luther "Luke Skyywalker" Campbell (owner of Luke Records). Group's obscenity arrests sparked national censorship controversy in 1990. By 1994, group consisted of Campbell, Won and Larry "Verb" Dobson, with special appearances by Rudy Ray "Dolomite" Moore; changed its name to The New 2 Live Crew.	
9/2/89	**29**	31	▲ 1. As Nasty As They Wanna Be	Luke Sky. 107 [2]
			also released alternate single album version, As Clean As They Wanna Be	
8/18/90	**21**	7	● 2. Banned In The U.S.A.	Luke 91424
			LUKE Featuring THE 2 LIVE CREW	
10/26/91	**22**	4	● 3. Sports Weekend (As Nasty As They Wanna Be Part II)	Luke 91720
			also released alternate version, Sports Weekend (As Clean As They Wanna Be Part II)	
			2 PAC	
			Rapper/actor Tupac Amaru Shakur. Member of Digital Underground in 1991. Appeared in the movies *Nothing But Trouble, Juice* and *Poetic Justice*. Numerous run-ins with the law. Found guilty on 2/10/94 of the 1993 assault and battery of *Menace II Society* co-director Allen Hughes. Shot five times during a robbery in Manhattan on 11/29/94. Sentenced for up to four years in prison on 2/7/95 for a 1993 sexual assault.	
3/6/93	**24**	2	● Strictly 4 My N.I.G.G.A.Z...	Interscope 92209
			TYLER, Bonnie	
			Born Gaynor Hopkins on 6/8/53 in Swansea, Wales. Worked local clubs until the mid-1970s. Distinctive raspy vocals caused by operation to remove throat nodules in 1976.	
6/10/78	**16**	8	● 1. It's A Heartache	RCA 2821
			It's A Heartache (3)	
9/10/83	**4**	18	▲ **2. Faster Than The Speed Of Night**	Columbia 38710
			Total Eclipse Of The Heart (1)	
			TYMES, The	
			Soul group formed in Philadelphia in 1956. Consisted of George Williams (lead), George Hilliard, Donald Banks, Albert Berry and Norman Burnett. First called The Latineers.	
8/24/63	**15**	9	So Much In Love	Parkway 7032
			So Much In Love (1)/*Wonderful! Wonderful!* (7)	

U

DATE	POS	WKS	ARTIST—RECORD TITLE	LABEL & NO.
			UB40	
			British interracial reggae octet formed in 1978: Ali Campbell (born 2/15/59, Birmingham, England), lead singer. UB40 stands for Unemployment Benefits, form 40. Members include Campbell's brother Robin Campbell, Earl Falconer, Michael Virtue, Astro, Norman Hassan, Brian Travers and James Brown.	
4/14/84	**14**	15	▲ 1. Labour of Love	A&M 4980
			originally peaked at POS 39 in 1984; re-entered and reached new peak in 1988	
			Red Red Wine (1)	
10/5/85	**40**	3	2. Little Baggariddim [M]	A&M 5090

DATE	POS	WKS	ARTIST—RECORD TITLE	LABEL & NO.
7/20/91	30	5	▲ 3. Labour Of Love II *The Way You Do The Things You Do* (6)/ *Here I Am (Come And Take Me)* (7)	Virgin 91324
8/14/93	6	13	▲ **4. Promises and Lies** *Can't Help Falling In Love* (1)	Virgin 88229
			UFO	
			British hard-rock group led by Phil Mogg (vocals) and Michael Schenker (guitar; left by 1980 to form own group). Numerous personnel changes.	
7/23/77	23	12	Lights Out	Chrysalis 1127
			UGLY KID JOE	
			Thrash-metal band from Isla Vista, California: Whitfield Crane (vocals), Klaus Eichstadt, Roger Lahr, Cordell Crockett and Mark Davis. Lahr replaced by guitarist Dave Fortman by 1992.	
3/7/92	4	14	▲¹ **1. As Ugly As They Want To Be** [M] the first multi-platinum, short-form LP certified by RIAA since the category was introduced in 1991 *Everything About You* (9)	Stardog 868823
9/26/92	27	12	▲ 2. America's Least Wanted *Cats In The Cradle* (6)	Stardog 512571
			ULLMAN, Tracey	
			Born on 12/30/59 in Buckinghamshire, England. Actress/singer/comedienne. Own variety-style TV show on Fox network, 1987-90. In the movies *I Love You to Death*, *Plenty* and *Give My Regards to Broad Street*.	
4/28/84	34	5	You Broke My Heart In 17 Places *They Don't Know* (8)	MCA 5471
			ULTIMATE SPINACH	
			Psychedelic-rock quintet from Boston: Ian Bruce-Douglas, Barbara Hudson, Keith Lahteinen, Richard Nese and Geoffrey Winthrop.	
4/20/68	34	4	Ultimate Spinach	MGM 4518
			UNION GAP, The — see PUCKETT, Gary	
			UNITED STATES MARINE BAND, The	
			Directed by Lieutenant Colonel Albert F. Schoepper. Formed in 1798 at the direction of President Adams.	
6/22/63	22	6	The United States Marine Band [I] proceeds from this album and the Navy album below donated to fund-raising project for The National Cultural Center in Washington, D.C.	RCA 2687
			UNITED STATES NAVY BAND, The	
			Directed by Commander Anthony A. Mitchell. Formed in 1925 at the direction of President Coolidge.	
6/22/63	38	1	The United States Navy Band with The Sea Chanters on 2 tracks	RCA 2688
			URIAH HEEP	
			British hard-rock band. Key members: David Byron (lead singer), Mick Box (lead guitar) and Ken Hensley (keyboards; later with Blackfoot). John Lawton replaced Byron in 1977. Peter Goalby replaced Lawton in 1982.	
8/26/72	23	13	● 1. Demons And Wizards	Mercury 630
1/6/73	31	8	● 2. The Magician's Birthday	Mercury 652
6/9/73	37	5	● 3. Uriah Heep Live [L]	Mercury 7503 [2]
11/3/73	33	3	● 4. Sweet Freedom	Warner 2724

DATE	POS	WKS	ARTIST—RECORD TITLE	LABEL & NO.
8/24/74	**38**	2	5. Wonderworld	Warner 2800

USA for AFRICA

USA stands for United Support of Artists. A group of 46 major artists joined to help the suffering people of Africa and the U.S.

DATE	POS	WKS	ARTIST—RECORD TITLE	LABEL & NO.
4/20/85	**1**(3)	11	▲³ **We Are The World** tracks contributed by Northern Lights (Canada's superstar artists), Bruce Springsteen, Prince, Huey Lewis, Chicago, Tina Turner, The Pointer Sisters, Kenny Rogers, Steve Perry *We Are The World* (1-featuring 46 major recording artists)	Columbia 40043

US3

Jazz/rap collaboration by London producers Mel Simpson (keyboards) and Geoff Wilkinson (samples). Samples of recordings on the Blue Note jazz record label serve as the backdrop for new rap solos and jazz playing by some of Britain's top players. US3 pronounced us three.

DATE	POS	WKS	ARTIST—RECORD TITLE	LABEL & NO.
2/12/94	**31**	8	● Hand On The Torch *Cantaloop* (9)	Blue Note 80883

UTOPIA

Veteran pop-rock group: Todd Rundgren (guitar), Kasim Sulton (bass), Roger Powell (keyboards) and Willie Wilcox (drums). Built own recording studio near Woodstock, New York.

DATE	POS	WKS	ARTIST—RECORD TITLE	LABEL & NO.
12/14/74	**34**	2	1. Todd Rundgren's Utopia **TODD RUNDGREN'S UTOPIA**	Bearsville 6954
2/16/80	**32**	5	2. Adventures In Utopia	Bearsville 6991

U2

Rock band formed in Dublin, Ireland, in 1976. Consists of Paul "Bono" Hewson (vocals), Dave "The Edge" Evans (guitar), Adam Clayton (bass) and Larry Mullen, Jr. (drums). Emerged in 1987 as leading rock act. Released concert tour documentary movie *Rattle and Hum* in 1988.

DATE	POS	WKS	ARTIST—RECORD TITLE	LABEL & NO.
4/2/83	**12**	16	▲ 1. War	Island 90067
1/7/84	**28**	13	▲³ 2. Under A Blood Red Sky [M-L] recorded in the summer of 1983 in Germany and Boston, and at the Red Rocks festival in Colorado	Island 90127
10/27/84	**12**	22	▲² 3. The Unforgettable Fire	Island 90231
6/29/85	**37**	1	▲¹ 4. Wide Awake In America [M-L] side A: "live"; side B: outtakes from *The Unforgettable Fire* album; album dropped by *Billboard* after charting for one week because it was only a 4-cut album that listed for less than $5.98	Island 90279
4/4/87	**1**(9)	58	▲⁵ 5. The Joshua Tree 1987 Album of the Year Grammy Award *With Or Without You* (1)/ *I Still Haven't Found What I'm Looking For* (1)	Island 90581
10/29/88	**1**(6)	23	▲³ 6. Rattle And Hum [S] music from the band's 1988 concert/documentary movie *Desire* (3)	Island 91003 [2]
12/7/91	**1**(1)	47	▲⁵ 7. Achtung Baby title taken from a line in the Mel Brooks movie *The Producers* *Mysterious Ways* (9)/*One* (10)	Island 10347
7/24/93	**1**(2)	15	▲² 8. Zooropa	Island 518047

DATE	POS	WKS	ARTIST—RECORD TITLE	LABEL & NO.
			# V	
			VAI, Steve	
			Born on 6/6/60 in Long Island, New York. Rock guitarist. With Frank Zappa's band (1979-84); Alcatrazz (1985); David Lee Roth's band (1986-88); and Whitesnake (1989). Formed Vai in 1992, which featured vocalist Devin Townsend and fluctuating band members. Former guitar student of Joe Satriani.	
6/16/90	18	13	● Passion and Warfare [I] includes spoken introductions to songs	Relativity 1037
			VALE, Jerry	
			Born Genaro Vitaliano on 7/8/32 in the Bronx. Pop-ballad singer. Frequently sang in Italian.	
4/13/63	34	4	1. Arrivederci, Roma	Columbia 8755
10/26/63	22	6	2. The Language Of Love	Columbia 8843
3/21/64	28	6	3. Till The End Of Time songs based on famous classical melodies	Columbia 8916
10/17/64	26	6	4. Be My Love	Columbia 8981
4/24/65	30	5	5. Have You Looked Into Your Heart	Columbia 9113
4/30/66	38	1	6. It's Magic	Columbia 9244
			VALENS, Ritchie	
			Born Richard Valenzuela on 5/13/41 in Pacoima, California. Latin rock-and-roll singer/songwriter/ guitarist. Killed in the plane crash that also took the lives of Buddy Holly and the Big Bopper on 2/3/59. In the movie *Go Johnny Go*. The 1987 movie *La Bamba* was based on his life.	
4/6/59	23	5	Ritchie Valens *Donna* (2)	Del-Fi 1201
			VALLI, Frankie	
			Born Francis Castellucio on 5/3/37 in Newark, New Jersey. Recorded his first solo single in 1953 as Frank Valley on the Corona label. Formed own group, The Variatones, in 1955 and changed its name to The Four Lovers in 1956, which evolved into The 4 Seasons by 1961. Began solo work in 1965. Suffered from a disease that caused hearing loss in the late '70s; corrected by surgery.	
8/26/67	34	2	Frankie Valli-Solo *Can't Take My Eyes Off You* (2)	Philips 247
			VANDROSS, Luther	
			Born on 4/20/51 in New York City. Soul singer/producer/songwriter. Commercial jingle singer; then top session vocalist/arranger. Sang lead on a few of Change's early albums. Appeared in the movie *The Meteor Man*.	
10/10/81	19	10	▲ 1. Never Too Much	Epic 37451
10/30/82	20	12	▲ 2. Forever, For Always, For Love	Epic 38235
1/28/84	32	9	▲ 3. Busy Body	Epic 39196
4/20/85	19	15	▲² 4. The Night I Fell In Love	Epic 39882
11/8/86	14	32	▲² 5. Give Me The Reason	Epic 40415
10/29/88	9	16	▲ **6. Any Love**	Epic 44308
11/25/89	26	22	▲ 7. The Best Of Luther Vandross...The Best Of Love [G] Vandross's hits from 1980-89 *Here And Now* (6)	Epic 45320 [2]

DATE	POS	WKS	ARTIST—RECORD TITLE	LABEL & NO.
5/25/91	7	22	▲² **8. Power Of Love**	Epic 46789
			Power Of Love/Love Power (4)/*Don't Want To Be A Fool* (9)	
6/19/93	6	9	▲ **9. Never Let Me Go**	Epic 53231
10/8/94	5	9	▲ **10. Songs**	LV 57775
			Endless Love (2-with Mariah Carey)	
			VANGELIS	
			Born Evangelos Papathanassiou on 3/29/43 in Valos, Greece. Keyboardist/ composer. Moved to Paris during the late '60s; moved to London in the mid-1970s. Formed rock band Aphrodite's Child in France with Demis Roussos, 1968-early '70s.	
2/20/82	**1**(4)	20	▲ **Chariots Of Fire** [S-I]	Polydor 6335
			movie is based on the true story of 2 members of Britain's 1924 Olympic team	
			Chariots Of Fire-Titles (1)	
			VAN HALEN	
			Hard-rock band formed in Pasadena, California, in 1974. Consisted of David Lee Roth (born 10/10/55; vocals), Eddie Van Halen (born 1/26/57; guitar), Michael Anthony (born 6/20/55; bass) and Alex Van Halen (born 5/8/55; drums). The Van Halen brothers were born in Nijmegen, The Netherlands, and moved to Pasadena in 1968. Sammy Hagar replaced Roth as lead singer in 1985. Eddie married actress Valerie Bertinelli on 4/11/81.	
4/15/78	19	12	▲⁸ **1. Van Halen**	Warner 3075
4/21/79	6	18	▲⁴ **2. Van Halen II**	Warner 3312
4/19/80	6	13	▲³ **3. Women and Children First**	Warner 3415
5/30/81	5	12	▲² **4. Fair Warning**	Warner 3540
5/8/82	3	16	▲³ **5. Diver Down**	Warner 3677
1/28/84	**2**(5)	52	▲⁷ **6. 1984 (MCMLXXXIV)**	Warner 23985
			Jump (1)	
4/12/86	**1**(3)	32	▲⁵ **7. 5150**	Warner 25394
			5150: New York Police code for the criminally insane; also the name of Eddie Van Halen's recording studio	
			Why Can't This Be Love (3)	
6/18/88	**1**(4)	35	▲³ **8. OU812**	Warner 25732
			When It's Love (5)	
7/6/91	**1**(3)	26	▲³ **9. For Unlawful Carnal Knowledge**	Warner 26594
3/13/93	5	4	▲² **10. LIVE: Right here, right now.** [L]	Warner 45198 [2]
			VANILLA FUDGE	
			Psychedelic-rock quartet formed in New York in 1966. Consisted of Mark Stein (lead singer, keyboards), Vinnie Martell (guitar), Tim Bogert (bassist with Cactus; Rod Stewart; Jeff Beck) and Carmine Appice (drummer with Cactus; Jeff Beck; Rod Stewart; KGB; Blue Murder).	
9/23/67	6	39	● **1. Vanilla Fudge**	Atco 224
			You Keep Me Hangin' On (6)	
3/9/68	17	9	**2. The Beat Goes On**	Atco 237
8/10/68	20	9	**3. Renaissance**	Atco 244
3/15/69	16	9	**4. Near the Beginning** [L]	Atco 278
			side 2: live	
11/1/69	34	4	**5. Rock & Roll**	Atco 303

DATE	POS	WKS	ARTIST—RECORD TITLE	LABEL & NO.
			VANILLA ICE	
			Born Robert Van Winkle on 10/31/68 in Miami Lakes, Florida. Dallas-based white rapper. Starred in the movie *Cool as Ice*.	
10/6/90	1 (16)	39	▲⁷ **1. To The Extreme**	SBK 95325
			originally released as *Hooked* on Ultra Records and distributed by Ichiban Records	
			Ice Ice Baby (1)/*Play That Funky Music* (4)	
6/29/91	30	4	● 2. Extremely Live [L]	SBK 96648
			recorded January through March 1991	
			VANNELLI, Gino	
			Born on 6/16/52 in Montreal. Pop singer/songwriter. His brother Ross produced Earth, Wind & Fire; Howard Hewett; The California Raisins.	
9/11/76	32	5	1. The Gist of The Gemini	A&M 4596
1/7/78	33	4	2. A Pauper In Paradise	A&M 4664
			side 2: with the Royal Philharmonic Orchestra	
11/4/78	13	11	▲ 3. Brother To Brother	A&M 4722
			I Just Wanna Stop (4)	
4/25/81	15	15	4. Nightwalker	Arista 9539
			Living Inside Myself (6)	
			VAUGHAN, Sarah	
			Born on 3/27/24 in Newark, New Jersey; died of lung cancer on 4/3/90. Jazz singer dubbed "The Divine One." Apollo Theater amateur contest win in 1942 led to her joining Earl Hines's band as vocalist/second pianist. With Billy Eckstine from 1944-45. Married manager/trumpeter George Treadwell in 1947. Later husbands included pro football player Clyde Atkins and trumpeter Waymon Reed. Performed into the '80s. Won 1989 Lifetime Achievement Grammy Award.	
11/24/56	20	2	1. Linger Awhile	Columbia 914
12/1/56	21	1	2. Sassy	EmArcy 36089
4/13/57	14	9	3. Great Songs From Hit Shows	Mercury 100 [2]
8/19/57	14	9	4. Sarah Vaughan sings George Gershwin	Mercury 101 [2]
			VAUGHAN, Stevie Ray, & Double Trouble	
			Vaughan was born on 10/3/54 in Dallas. Died in a helicopter crash on 8/27/90. Blues-rock guitarist. Leader of the Austin-based band Double Trouble. Lead guitarist on David Bowie's *Let's Dance* album. His brother is Jimmie Vaughan (The Fabulous Thunderbirds). Double Trouble was Jackie Newhouse (bass) and Chris Layton (drums).	
9/3/83	38	3	▲ 1. Texas Flood	Epic 38734
7/7/84	31	8	▲ 2. Couldn't Stand The Weather	Epic 39304
10/26/85	34	6	▲ 3. Soul To Soul	Epic 40036
8/12/89	33	6	▲ 4. In Step	Epic 45024
11/23/91	10	14	▲ **5. The Sky Is Crying** [K]	Epic 47390
			recordings from 1984-89	
			VAUGHAN BROTHERS, The	
			Blues-rock duo of Dallas-bred brothers Jimmie and Stevie Ray Vaughan. Jimmie was the lead guitarist of The Fabulous Thunderbirds. See above for Stevie's bio.	
10/13/90	7	16	▲ **Family Style**	Epic/Assc. 46225

DATE	POS	WKS	ARTIST—RECORD TITLE		LABEL & NO.
			VAUGHN, Billy		
			Born Richard Vaughn on 4/12/19 in Glasgow, Kentucky. Died on 9/26/91 of cancer. Organized The Hilltoppers vocal group in 1952. Music director for Dot Records. Arranger/conductor for Pat Boone, Gale Storm, The Fontane Sisters and many other Dot artists. Vaughn had more pop hits than any other orchestra leader during the rock era.		
4/21/58	5	44	● **1. Sail Along Silv'ry Moon**	[I]	Dot 3100
			Sail Along Silvery Moon (5)/*Raunchy* (10)		
10/13/58	15	41	2. Billy Vaughn Plays The Million Sellers	[I]	Dot 3119
5/4/59	20	3	3. Billy Vaughn Plays	[I]	Dot 3156
5/25/59	7	48	● **4. Blue Hawaii**	[I]	Dot 3165
1/18/60	36	1	5. Golden Saxophones	[I]	Dot 3205
3/21/60	1(2)	38	● **6. Theme from A Summer Place**	[I]	Dot 3276
8/15/60	5	21	**7. Look For A Star**	[I]	Dot 3322
12/19/60	5	13	**8. Theme from The Sundowners**	[I]	Dot 3349
5/8/61	11	20	9. Orange Blossom Special and Wheels	[I]	Dot 3366
10/9/61	17	9	10. Golden Waltzes	[I]	Dot 3280
12/4/61	20	15	11. Berlin Melody	[I]	Dot 3396
3/24/62	18	11	12. Greatest String Band Hits		Dot 3409
6/9/62	14	13	13. Chapel By The Sea	[I]	Dot 3424
10/6/62	10	10	**14. A Swingin' Safari**	[I]	Dot 3458
2/16/63	17	12	15. 1962's Greatest Hits	[I]	Dot 25497
7/6/63	15	6	16. Sukiyaki and 11 Hawaiian Hits	[I]	Dot 25523
3/6/65	18	9	17. Pearly Shells	[I]	Dot 25605
11/13/65	31	6	18. Moon Over Naples	[I]	Dot 25654
			VEE, Bobby		
			Born Robert Velline on 4/30/43 in Fargo, North Dakota. Formed The Shadows with his brother and a friend in 1959. After Buddy Holly's death in a plane crash, The Shadows filled in on Holly's next scheduled show in Fargo. First recorded for Soma in 1959. In the movies *Swingin' Along*, *It's Trad, Dad*, *Play It Cool*, *C'mon Let's Live a Little* and *Just for Fun*. Still performing on oldies tours.		
3/20/61	18	2	1. Bobby Vee		Liberty 7181
			Devil Or Angel (6)/*Rubber Ball* (6)		
12/1/62	24	9	2. Bobby Vee's Golden Greats	[G]	Liberty 7245
			VEGA, Suzanne		
			Born on 8/12/59 in New York City. Alternative singer/songwriter/guitarist.		
7/4/87	11	17	● Solitude Standing		A&M 5136
			Luka (3)		
			VENTURES, The		
			Guitar-based instrumental rock-and-roll band formed in the Seattle/Tacoma, Washington area. Consisted of guitarists Nokie Edwards (born 5/9/39; bass), Bob Bogle (born 1/16/37; lead) and Don Wilson (born 2/10/37; rhythm), and drummer Howie Johnson (died 1988). First recorded for own Blue Horizon label in 1959. Johnson was injured in an auto accident; replaced by Mel Taylor in 1961. Taylor formed Mel Taylor & The Dynamics in 1973; returned in 1978. Edwards left in 1967; replaced by Gerry McGee. Edwards returned in 1972; left again in 1985. Added keyboardist John Durrill in 1969. Latest recordings feature Bogle, Wilson, Taylor and McGee. Group still active into the '90s; extremely popular in Japan.		
12/5/60	11	9	1. Walk Don't Run	[I]	Dolton 8003
			Walk-Don't Run (2)		

DATE	POS	WKS	ARTIST—RECORD TITLE	LABEL & NO.
7/31/61	39	2	2. Another Smash!!! [I]	Dolton 8006
2/3/62	24	12	3. Twist With The Ventures [I]	Dolton 8010
5/19/62	40	1	4. The Ventures' Twist Party, Vol. 2 [I]	Dolton 8014
1/19/63	8	11	● **5. The Ventures play Telstar, The Lonely Bull** **[I]**	Dolton 8019
6/1/63	30	5	6. "Surfing" [I]	Dolton 8022
10/12/63	30	2	7. Let's Go! [I]	Dolton 8024
2/15/64	27	7	8. (The) Ventures In Space [I]	Dolton 8027
8/22/64	32	4	9. The Fabulous Ventures [I]	Dolton 8029
11/7/64	17	10	10. Walk, Don't Run, Vol. 2 [I]	Dolton 8031
			Walk-Don't Run '64 (8)	
4/10/65	31	5	11. The Ventures Knock Me Out! [I]	Dolton 8033
8/28/65	27	9	12. The Ventures On Stage [I-L]	Dolton 8035
10/23/65	16	20	13. The Ventures a go-go [I]	Dolton 8037
4/23/66	33	3	14. Where The Action Is [I]	Dolton 8040
8/20/66	39	2	15. Go With The Ventures! [I]	Dolton 8045
11/5/66	33	6	16. Wild Things! [I]	Dolton 8047
5/17/69	11	14	● 17. Hawaii Five-O [I]	Liberty 8061
			Hawaii Five-O (4)	
			VERA, Billy, & The Beaters	
			Vera was born William McCord on 5/28/44 in Riverside, California; raised in Westchester County, New York. Wrote hits for many pop, R&B and country artists. In the movies *Buckaroo Banzai* and *The Doors*, and the HBO movie *Baja Oklahoma*. Formed The Beaters (an R&B-based, 10-piece band) in Los Angeles in 1979.	
1/17/87	15	10	● By Request (The Best Of Billy Vera & The Beaters) [E-L] 7 of 9 tracks recorded at the Roxy in Hollywood in 1981 *At This Moment* (1)	Rhino 70858
			VILLAGE PEOPLE	
			Campy, New York City disco group formed by French producer Jacques Morali (died 11/15/91 [age 44] of AIDS). Consisted of Victor Willis (lead singer), Randy Jones, David Hodo, Felipe Rose, Glenn Hughes and Alexander Briley. Willis replaced by Ray Simpson (brother of Valerie Simpson of Ashford & Simpson) in late 1979. Group appeared in the movie *Can't Stop the Music* (1980).	
7/29/78	24	8	▲ 1. Macho Man	Casablanca 7096
11/11/78	3	26	▲ **2. Cruisin'** *Y.M.C.A.* (2)	Casablanca 7118
4/14/79	8	13	▲ **3. Go West** *In The Navy* (3)	Casablanca 7144
11/17/79	32	5	● 4. Live and Sleazy [L] record 1: "live"; record 2: studio	Casablanca 7183 [2]
			VILLAGE STOMPERS, The	
			Greenwich Village, New York, Dixieland-styled band.	
11/23/63	5	14	**Washington Square** [I] *Washington Square* (2)	Epic 26078

DATE	POS	WKS	ARTIST—RECORD TITLE	LABEL & NO.
			VINCENT, Gene, and His Blue Caps	
			Born Vincent Eugene Craddock on 2/11/35 in Norfolk, Virginia; died from an ulcer hemorrhage on 10/12/71. Innovative rock-and-roll singer/songwriter/ guitarist. Injured left leg in motorcycle accident in 1953; had to wear steel brace thereafter. Formed The Blue Caps in Norfolk in 1956. Appeared in the movies *The Girl Can't Help It* and *Hot Rod Gang*. To England from 1960-67. Injured in car crash that killed Eddie Cochran in England in 1960.	
9/29/56	16	2	Bluejean Bop!	Capitol 764
			VINTON, Bobby	
			Born Stanley Robert Vinton on 4/16/35 in Canonsburg, Pennsylvania. Father was a bandleader. Formed own band while in high school; toured as backing band for Dick Clark's "Caravan of Stars" in 1960. Left band for a singing career in 1962. Own musical variety TV series from 1975-78.	
8/18/62	5	14	**1. Roses Are Red**	Epic 26020
			Roses Are Red (My Love) (1)/*Mr. Lonely* (1-'64)	
9/7/63	10	18	**2. Blue Velvet**	Epic 26068
			Blue On Blue (3)/*Blue Velvet* (1)	
2/22/64	8	12	**3. There! I've Said It Again**	Epic 26081
			There! I've Said It Again (1)/ *My Heart Belongs To Only You* (9)	
8/22/64	31	4	4. Tell Me Why	Epic 26113
12/5/64	12	14	● 5. Bobby Vinton's Greatest Hits [G]	Epic 26098
1/30/65	18	7	6. Mr. Lonely	Epic 26136
2/1/69	21	6	7. I Love How You Love Me	Epic 26437
			I Love How You Love Me (9)	
12/21/74	16	7	● 8. Melodies Of Love	ABC 851
			My Melody Of Love (3)	
			VOGUES, The	
			Vocal group formed in Turtle Creek, Pennsylvania, in 1960. Consisted of Bill Burkette (lead), Hugh Geyer and Chuck Blasko (tenors) and Don Miller (baritone). Met in high school.	
12/7/68	29	4	1. Turn Around, Look At Me	Reprise 6314
			Turn Around, Look At Me (7)/*My Special Angel* (7)	
4/5/69	30	6	2. Till	Reprise 6326
			VOYAGE	
			European disco group. Sylvia Mason, lead singer.	
7/1/78	40	2	Voyage	Marlin 2213
			# W	
			WAILERS, The — see MARLEY, Bob	
			WAITE, John	
			Born on 7/4/55 in Lancashire, England. Lead singer of The Babys and Bad English.	
8/4/84	10	17	● **1. No Brakes**	EMI America 17124
			Missing You (1)	
10/5/85	36	3	2. Mask Of Smiles	EMI America 17164

DATE	POS	WKS	ARTIST—RECORD TITLE	LABEL & NO.
			WAKEMAN, Rick	
			Born on 5/18/49 in London. Former keyboardist of Strawbs and Yes. In 1989, joined group Anderson, Bruford, Wakeman, Howe, all formerly with Yes. Also a popular contemporary Christian rock artist.	
5/19/73	30	13	● 1. The Six Wives of Henry VIII [I]	A&M 4361
6/22/74	3	16	● **2. Journey To The Centre Of The Earth** [L]	A&M 3621
			with the London Symphony Orchestra	
5/3/75	21	6	3. The Myths and Legends of King Arthur and the Knights of the Round Table	A&M 4515
			with the English Chamber Choir and orchestra	
			WALSH, Joe	
			Born on 11/20/47 in Wichita, Kansas. Rock singer/songwriter/guitarist. Member of The James Gang (1969-71) and The Eagles (1975-82). Own band (1972-75), Barnstorm, which featured drummer Joe Vitale and bassist Kenny Passarelli.	
8/18/73	6	20	● **1. The Smoker You Drink, The Player You Get**	Dunhill 50140
2/1/75	11	10	● 2. So What	Dunhill 50171
4/17/76	20	9	3. You Can't Argue With A Sick Mind [L]	ABC 932
6/17/78	8	14	▲ **4. But Seriously, Folks ...**	Asylum 141
6/13/81	20	9	5. There Goes The Neighborhood	Asylum 523
			WANDERLEY, Walter	
			Brazilian organist/pianist/composer. Died of cancer on 9/4/86 (age 55).	
11/19/66	22	9	Rain Forest [I]	Verve 8658
			WANG CHUNG	
			British pop-rock group: Jack Hues (lead singer, guitar, keyboards), Nick Feldman (bass, keyboards) and Darren Costin (drums). Costin left in 1985. Originally known as Huang Chung.	
6/23/84	30	6	Points On The Curve	Geffen 4004
			WAR	
			Band formed in Long Beach, California, in 1969. Consisted of Lonnie Jordan (keyboards), Howard Scott (guitar), Charles Miller (saxophone; murdered in 1980), Morris "B.B." Dickerson (bass), Harold Brown and Thomas "Papa Dee" Allen (percussion; died 8/30/88 of a cerebral hemorrhage) and Lee Oskar (harmonica). Eric Burdon's backup band until 1971. Dickerson was replaced by Luther Rabb. Jordan and Oskar also recorded solo. Alice Tweed Smyth (vocals) added in 1978. Pat Rizzo (horns) and Ron Hammon (percussion; former member of Aalon) added in 1979. Smyth left group in 1982. Lineup by 1994: Jordan, Scott, Brown and Hammon with Rae Valentine, Charles Green, Kerry Campbell, Tetsuya Nakamura and Sal Rodriguez.	
7/11/70	18	13	1. Eric Burdon Declares "War"	MGM 4663
			ERIC BURDON AND WAR Spill The Wine (3)	
3/4/72	16	20	● 2. All Day Music	United Art. 5546
12/16/72	1(2)	25	● **3. The World Is A Ghetto**	United Art. 5652
			The World Is A Ghetto (7)/The Cisco Kid (2)	
9/8/73	6	14	● **4. Deliver The Word**	United Art. 128
			Gypsy Man (8)	
4/6/74	13	11	● 5. War Live! [L]	United Art. 193 [2]
7/12/75	8	19	● **6. Why Can't We Be Friends?**	United Art. 441
			Why Can't We Be Friends? (6)/Low Rider (7)	
9/4/76	6	13	▲ **7. Greatest Hits** [G]	United Art. 648
			Summer (7)	

DATE	POS	WKS	ARTIST—RECORD TITLE	LABEL & NO.
8/6/77	23	7	● 8. Platinum Jazz [K]	Blue Note 690 [2]
12/17/77	15	12	● 9. Galaxy	MCA 3030
			WARD, Anita	
			Born on 12/20/57 in Memphis. R&B-disco vocalist. Toured in Rust College female quartet.	
6/9/79	8	10	**Songs Of Love** *Ring My Bell* (1)	Juana 200,004
			WARING, Fred, And The Pennsylvanians	
			Born on 6/9/1900 in Tyrone, Pennsylvania; died on 7/29/84. Glee club/ bandleader from early '20s.	
9/9/57	25	1	1. Fred Waring And The Pennsylvanians In Hi-Fi	Capitol 845
12/23/57	6	3	**2. Now Is The Caroling Season** **[X]**	Capitol 896
12/22/58	19	3	3. Now Is The Caroling Season [X-R]	Capitol 896
			WARRANT	
			Los Angeles-based, hard-rock male band: Jani Lane (vocals), Erik Turner (guitar), Joey Allen (guitar), Jerry Dixon (bass) and Steven Sweet (drums). Lane married Bobbie Brown, spokesmodel champion on TV's "Star Search," on 7/27/91.	
4/15/89	10	33	▲² **1. Dirty Rotten Filthy Stinking Rich** *Heaven* (2)	Columbia 44383
9/29/90	7	37	▲² **2. Cherry Pie** *Cherry Pie* (10)/*I Saw Red* (10)	Columbia 45487
9/12/92	25	3	● 3. Dog Eat Dog	Columbia 52584
			WARREN, Rusty	
			Born Ilene Goldman in 1931 in New York; raised in Milton, Massachusetts. Singer/storyteller of adult comedy.	
11/7/60	8	98	**1. Knockers Up!** **[C]**	Jubilee 2029
5/29/61	21	12	2. Sin-Sational [C]	Jubilee 2034
2/10/62	31	5	3. Rusty Warren Bounces Back [C]	Jubilee 2039
12/1/62	22	11	4. Rusty Warren In Orbit [C]	Jubilee 2044
			WARREN G	
			Born Warren Griffin III in Long Beach, California. Rapper. Half-brother of Dr. Dre. Wrote, produced and performed on Mista Grimm's "Indo Smoke" and on Slick Rick's "Behind Bars." Childhood friend of Snoop Doggy Dogg.	
6/25/94	2 (1)	22	▲² **Regulate ... G Funk Era** *Regulate* (2)/*This DJ* (9)	Violator/RAL 523364
			WARWICK, Dionne	
			Born Marie Dionne Warwick on 12/12/40 in East Orange, New Jersey. In church choir from age six. With The Drinkard Singers gospel group. Formed trio, The Gospelaires, with sister Dee Dee Warwick and their aunt, Cissy Houston. (Dionne is cousin of Whitney Houston). Attended Hartt College of Music, Hartford, Connecticut. Much backup studio work in New York during the late '50s. Added an "e" to her last name for a time in the early '70s. She was Burt Bacharach and Hal David's main "voice" for the songs they composed. Co-hosted TV's "Solid Gold" 1980-81; 1985-86.	
7/1/67	18	15	● 1. Here Where There is Love	Scepter 555
11/11/67	22	6	2. The Windows of The World *I Say A Little Prayer* (4)	Scepter 563
12/2/67	10	23	**3. Dionne Warwick's Golden Hits, Part One** **[G]** *Anyone Who Had A Heart* (8-'64)	Scepter 565

DATE	POS	WKS	ARTIST—RECORD TITLE	LABEL & NO.
3/16/68	6	18	● **4. Valley of the Dolls** *(Theme From) Valley Of The Dolls* (2)/ *Do You Know The Way To San Jose* (10)	Scepter 568
1/18/69	18	11	5. Promises, Promises *This Girl's In Love With You* (7)	Scepter 571
4/19/69	11	9	6. Soulful	Scepter 573
9/20/69	31	5	● 7. Dionne Warwick's Greatest Motion Picture Hits [K]	Scepter 575
11/22/69	28	4	8. Dionne Warwick's Golden Hits, Part 2 [G] *Message To Michael* (8-'66)	Scepter 577
5/9/70	23	14	9. I'll Never Fall In Love Again *I'll Never Fall In Love Again* (6)	Scepter 581
1/9/71	37	4	10. Very Dionne	Scepter 587
8/18/79	12	13	▲ 11. Dionne produced by Barry Manilow *I'll Never Love This Way Again* (5)	Arista 4230
8/30/80	23	6	12. No Night So Long	Arista 9526
11/27/82	25	10	13. Heartbreaker produced by Barry Gibb *Heartbreaker* (10)	Arista 9609
1/11/86	12	13	● 14. Friends *That's What Friends Are For* (1-with Elton John, Stevie Wonder and Gladys Knight)	Arista 8398

WASHINGTON, Dinah

Born Ruth Lee Jones on 8/29/24 in Tuscaloosa, Alabama. Died on 12/14/63 (from an overdose of alcohol and pills). Jazz-blues vocalist/pianist. Moved to Chicago in 1927. With the Sallie Martin gospel singers, 1940-41; local club work in Chicago, 1941-43. With Lionel Hampton, 1943-46. First recorded for Keynote in 1943. Solo touring from 1946. Married seven times, once to singer Eddie Chamblee. Inducted into the Rock and Roll Hall of Fame in 1993 as an early influence.

DATE	POS	WKS	ARTIST—RECORD TITLE	LABEL & NO.
2/1/60	34	10	1. What a diff'rence a day makes! *What A Diff'rence A Day Makes* (8)	Mercury 20479
1/23/61	10	6	**2. Unforgettable**	Mercury 20572
7/28/62	33	4	3. Dinah '62	Roulette 25170

WASHINGTON, Grover Jr.

Born on 12/12/43 in Buffalo. Jazz-R&B saxophonist. Own band, The Four Clefs, at age 16. Much session work in Philadelphia, where he now resides.

DATE	POS	WKS	ARTIST—RECORD TITLE	LABEL & NO.
4/5/75	10	17	**1. Mister Magic** [I]	Kudu 20
11/22/75	10	7	**2. Feels So Good** [I]	Kudu 24
2/12/77	31	6	3. A Secret Place [I]	Kudu 32
2/4/78	11	9	4. Live At The Bijou [I-L]	Kudu 3637 [2]
11/18/78	35	5	5. Reed Seed [I] backed by the jazz ensemble Locksmith	Motown 910
5/19/79	24	6	6. Paradise [I]	Elektra 182
3/29/80	24	6	7. Skylarkin' [I]	Motown 933
1/24/81	5	27	▲ **8. Winelight** [I] *Just The Two Of Us* (2-with Bill Withers)	Elektra 305
1/23/82	28	5	9. Come Morning [I]	Elektra 562

DATE	POS	WKS	ARTIST—RECORD TITLE	LABEL & NO.
			WATERS, Roger	
			Born George Roger Waters on 9/6/43 in Cambridgeshire, England. Former leader/bassist of Pink Floyd. Went solo in 1983.	
6/2/84	31	7	1. The Pros and Cons of Hitch Hiking	Columbia 39290
9/19/92	21	3	2. Amused To Death	Columbia 47127
			WATLEY, Jody	
			Born on 1/30/59 in Chicago. Female vocalist of Shalamar (1977-84) and former dancer on TV's "Soul Train." Her godfather was Jackie Wilson. Won 1987 Best New Artist Grammy Award.	
4/4/87	10	44	▲ **1. Jody Watley**	MCA 5898
			Looking For A New Love (2)/*Don't You Want Me* (6)/ *Some Kind Of Lover* (10)	
4/22/89	16	17	● 2. Larger Than Life	MCA 6276
			Real Love (2)/*Friends* (9)/*Everything* (4)	
			WATSON, Johnny "Guitar"	
			Born on 2/3/35 in Houston. R&B-funk vocalist/guitarist/pianist. First recorded (as Young John Watson) for Federal in 1952.	
5/21/77	20	13	● A Real Mother For Ya	DJM 7
			WAYLON & WILLIE — see JENNINGS, Waylon, and/or NELSON, Willie	
			WEATHER REPORT	
			Jazz-fusion quintet formed in 1969 by Austrian-born Josef Zawinul (keyboards) and Wayne Shorter (sax). Zawinul was a member of Cannonball Adderley's combo for nine years; formed The Zawinul Syndicate in 1988.	
6/28/75	31	4	1. Tale Spinnin' [I]	Columbia 33417
4/30/77	30	5	▲ 2. Heavy Weather [I]	Columbia 34418
			WEAVERS, The	
			Legendary folk quartet: Pete Seeger, Lee Hays (died 8/26/81 [age 68]), Fred Hellerman and female lead Ronnie Gilbert. Revived and popularized folk music in the early '50s. Political blacklisting cut their recording career short, but the group's 1955 Carnegie Hall concert helped trigger a new folk boom and such Seeger-Hays songs as "If I Had A Hammer" kept it alive.	
3/13/61	24	1	The Weavers at Carnegie Hall [E-L]	Vanguard 9010
			recorded on Christmas Eve 1955	
			WEBB, Jack	
			Born on 4/2/20 in Santa Monica, California; died on 12/23/82. Actor/TV producer. Creator/director/star (Joe Friday) of "Dragnet" TV series (1952-59; 1967-70) and the movie *Pete Kelly's Blues*. Married to singer/actress Julie London (1945-53).	
9/3/55	2(2)	15	**Pete Kelly's Blues** [T-I]	RCA 1126
			Webb narrates the introduction to songs played by a seven-man jazz combo led by clarinetist Matty Matlock (same band that scored the movie; also see Ray Heindorf); Webb played Pete Kelly in the movie; however, his trumpet playing was dubbed by Dick Cathcart	
			WEEZER	
			Los Angeles-based alternative pop quartet: Rivers Cuomo (vocals, guitar), Brian Bell (guitar), Matt Sharp (bass) and Patrick Wilson (drums).	
12/31/94	16	9+	▲ Weezer	DGC 24629
			produced by Ric Ocasek	

DATE	POS	WKS	ARTIST—RECORD TITLE	LABEL & NO.
			WE FIVE	
			California pop quintet: Beverly Bivens (lead singer), Mike Stewart (brother of John Stewart), Pete Fullerton, Bob Jones and Jerry Burgan.	
12/11/65	32	6	You Were On My Mind	A&M 4111
			You Were On My Mind (3)	
			WEISBERG, Tim — see FOGELBERG, Dan	
			WEISSBERG, Eric	
			Bluegrass multi-instrumentalist. Worked with The Greenbriar Boys and The Tarriers folk groups. Prolific session man.	
2/17/73	1(3)	14	● **Dueling Banjos** [I]	Warner 2683
			ERIC WEISSBERG and STEVE MANDELL	
			except for the title song, all tunes performed by Weissberg and Marshall Brickman (previously released on album *New Dimensions in Banjo & Bluegrass*)	
			Dueling Banjos (2)	
			WELCH, Bob	
			Born on 7/31/46 in Los Angeles. Guitarist/vocalist with Fleetwood Mac (1971-74). Formed the British rock group Paris in 1976. His father, Robert L. Welch, was a major movie/TV producer.	
11/12/77	12	29	▲ 1. French Kiss	Capitol 11663
			Sentimental Lady (8)	
3/17/79	20	5	● 2. Three Hearts	Capitol 11907
			WELK, Lawrence	
			Born on 3/11/03 in Strasburg, North Dakota; died on 5/17/92 of pneumonia. Accordionist and polka/"sweet band" leader since the mid-1920s. Band's style labeled as "champagne music." Own national TV musical variety show began on 7/2/55 and ran on ABC until 9/4/71. New episodes in syndication from 1971 to 1982. Reruns are still enjoying immense popularity.	
1/28/56	5	11	**1. Lawrence Welk and His Sparkling Strings** [I]	Coral 57011
3/31/56	13	2	2. TV Favorites	Coral 57025
3/31/56	18	2	3. Shamrocks and Champagne	Coral 57036
5/12/56	6	17	**4. Bubbles In The Wine**	Coral 57038
			title song is Welk's theme song	
8/18/56	10	30	**5. Say It With Music** [I]	Coral 57041
			medleys of 36 dance favorites	
8/25/56	17	4	6. Champagne Pops Parade	Coral 57078
10/20/56	18	1	7. Moments To Remember [I]	Coral 57068
12/22/56	8	3	**8. Merry Christmas** [X]	Coral 57093
3/16/57	20	1	9. Pick-a-Polka! [I]	Coral 57067
5/20/57	17	5	10. Waltz with Lawrence Welk [I]	Coral 57119
			medleys of 24 favorite waltzes	
10/21/57	19	2	11. Lawrence Welk plays Dixieland [I]	Coral 57146
			featuring Pete Fountain on clarinet	
12/23/57	18	3	12. Jingle Bells [X]	Coral 57186
12/19/60	4	18	**13. Last Date** [I]	Dot 3350
1/30/61	1(11)	50	● **14. Calcutta!** [I]	Dot 3359
			Calcutta (1)	
8/7/61	2(1)	41	**15. Yellow Bird** [I]	Dot 3389
			above 2 feature Frank Scott on harpsichord	
1/13/62	4	43	**16. Moon River** [I]	Dot 3412
6/9/62	6	12	**17. Young World** [I]	Dot 3428

DATE	POS	WKS	ARTIST—RECORD TITLE	LABEL & NO.
9/29/62	9	10	**18. Baby Elephant Walk and Theme From The Brothers Grimm** [I]	Dot 3457
4/13/63	20	12	19. 1963's Early Hits [I]	Dot 25510
4/20/63	34	5	20. Waltz Time [I]	Dot 25499
9/7/63	33	6	21. Scarlett O'Hara [I]	Dot 25528
2/15/64	29	3	22. Wonderful! Wonderful! [I]	Dot 25552
5/16/64	37	3	23. Early Hits Of 1964 [I]	Dot 25572
12/31/66	12	18	● 24. Winchester Cathedral [I]	Dot 25774
			WELLS, Mary	
			Born on 5/13/43 in Detroit. Diagnosed with throat cancer, August 1990; died on 7/26/92. R&B vocalist. At age 17, presented "Bye Bye Baby," a tune she had written for Jackie Wilson, to Wilson's producer, Berry Gordy, Jr. Gordy signed her to his newly formed label, Motown. Wells was the first to have a Top 10 and #1 single for that label. Married for a time to Cecil Womack (brother of Bobby Womack).	
7/18/64	18	12	Greatest Hits [G] *The One Who Really Loves You* (8)/ *You Beat Me To The Punch* (9)/*My Guy* (1)	Motown 616
			WEST, BRUCE & LAING	
			Power-rock trio composed of former Mountain members Leslie West (guitar, vocals) and Corky Laing (drums), and Cream's Jack Bruce (bass).	
12/9/72	26	6	Why Dontcha	Windfall 31929
			WESTON, Paul	
			Born Paul Wetstein on 3/12/12 in Springfield, Massachusetts. Top arranger/conductor of mood music since 1934. Married to Jo Stafford. Won 1971 Trustees Grammy Award.	
10/29/55	15	2	1. Mood For 12 [I]	Columbia 693
9/1/56	12	5	2. Solo Mood [I]	Columbia 879
			above 2 feature same group of 12 big band soloists	
			WHAM! — see MICHAEL, George	
			WHISPERS, The	
			Los Angeles soul group formed in 1964. Consisted of Gordy Harmon, twin brothers Walter and Wallace "Scotty" Scott, Marcus Hutson and Nicholas Caldwell. First recorded for Dore in 1964. Harmon replaced in 1973 by Leaveil Degree, who was briefly a member of Friends of Distinction. The Scotts also recorded as Walter & Scotty since 1993. Group founded the Black Tie record label.	
2/9/80	6	17	▲ **1. The Whispers**	Solar 3521
2/14/81	23	11	● 2. Imagination	Solar 3578
4/3/82	35	4	● 3. Love Is Where You Find It	Solar 27
5/7/83	37	3	4. Love For Love	Solar 60216
7/25/87	22	12	▲ 5. Just Gets Better With Time *Rock Steady* (7)	Solar 72554
			WHITE, Barry	
			Born on 9/12/44 in Galveston, Texas; raised in Los Angeles. Soul singer/songwriter/keyboardist/producer/ arranger. With Upfronts vocal group, recorded for Lummtone in 1960. A&R man for Mustang/Bronco, 1966-67. Formed Love Unlimited in 1969, which included future wife Glodean James. Leader of 40-piece Love Unlimited Orchestra.	
6/2/73	16	10	● 1. I've Got So Much To Give *I'm Gonna Love You Just A Little More Baby* (3)	20th Century 407

DATE	POS	WKS	ARTIST—RECORD TITLE	LABEL & NO.
12/8/73	20	16	● 2. Stone Gon' *Never, Never Gonna Give Ya Up* (7)	20th Century 423
9/14/74	1(1)	13	● **3. Can't Get Enough** *Can't Get Enough Of Your Love, Babe* (1)/ *You're The First, The Last, My Everything* (2)	20th Century 444
4/26/75	17	8	● 4. Just Another Way To Say I Love You *What Am I Gonna Do With You* (8)	20th Century 466
11/29/75	23	5	● 5. Barry White's Greatest Hits　　　　　　[G]	20th Century 493
9/24/77	8	13	▲ **6. Barry White Sings For Someone You Love** *It's Ecstasy When You Lay Down Next To Me* (4)	20th Century 543
12/16/78	36	2	▲ 7. Barry White The Man	20th Century 571
10/22/94	20	16+	▲ 8. The Icon Is Love	A&M 0115
			WHITE, Karyn Born on 10/14/65. Prominent session singer from Los Angeles. Touring vocalist with O'Bryan in 1984. Recorded with jazz-fusion keyboardist Jeff Lorber in 1986. Married to superproducer Terry Lewis (member of The Time).	
1/28/89	19	17	▲ Karyn White *The Way You Love Me* (7)/*Superwoman* (8)/*Secret Rendezvous* (6)	Warner 25637
			WHITE LION New York-based rock band: Mike Tramp (Denmark native; vocals), James Lomenzo (bass), Vito Bratta (guitar) and Greg D'Angelo (drums; founding member of Anthrax). Lomenzo and D'Angelo left in 1991; replaced by Tommy Caradonna and Jimmy DeGrasso (ex-Y&T).	
3/5/88	11	56	▲² 1. Pride *Wait* (8)/*When The Children Cry* (3)	Atlantic 81768
7/15/89	19	13	● 2. Big Game	Atlantic 81969
			WHITEMAN, Paul Born on 3/28/1890 in Denver; died on 12/29/67. The most popular bandleader of the pre-swing era; had 32 #1 hits from 1920-34. Formed own band in 1919. Band featured jazz greats Henry Busse (trumpet), Ferde Grofe (piano, arranger) and Bix Beiderbecke (cornet). Vocalist Bing Crosby made his professional debut with Whiteman's band in 1926.	
1/19/57	20	1	Paul Whiteman/50th Anniversary reunion with many of the great alumni of the Whiteman Orchestra: Tommy & Jimmy Dorsey, Bing Crosby, Hoagy Carmichael, Jack Teagarden and others	Grand Award 901 [2]
			WHITESNAKE Ex-Deep Purple vocalist David Coverdale, who recorded solo as Whitesnake in 1977, formed British heavy-metal band in 1978. Coverdale fronted everchanging lineup. Early members included his Deep Purple bandmates, keyboardist Jon Lord (1978-84) and drummer Ian Paice (1979-81). Players in 1987 included John Sykes (guitar), Neil Murray (bass) and Aynsley Dunbar (former Jefferson Starship drummer). Sykes left in 1988 to form Blue Murder. Ex-Dio guitarist Vivian Campbell was a member from 1987-88; later with Riverdogs, Shadow King and Def Leppard. 1989 lineup included Steve Vai (David Lee Roth's former guitarist), Adrian Vandenberg (former guitarist of Vandenberg), Rudy Sarzo (bass) and Tommy Aldridge (drums). Lineup in 1994: Coverdale, Vandenberg, Sarzo, Warren De Martini (guitar), Paul Mirkovich (keyboards) and Denny Carmassi (former drummer of Heart). Coverdale married actress Tawny Kitaen on 2/17/89; divorced by 1992.	
8/25/84	40	2	▲² 1. Slide it in	Geffen 4018
4/25/87	2(10)	54	▲⁸ **2. Whitesnake** *Here I Go Again* (1)/*Is This Love* (2)	Geffen 24099
11/25/89	10	20	▲ 3. Slip Of The Tongue	Geffen 24249

DATE	POS	WKS	ARTIST—RECORD TITLE	LABEL & NO.
			WHITE ZOMBIE	
			Alternative-metal band formed in New York City by vocalist Rob Zombie and female bassist Sean Yseult. Added guitarist Jay Yuenger and revolving lineup of drummers. Band named after 1932 Bela Lugosi movie.	
10/2/93	**26**	9	▲ La Sexorcisto: Devil Music Volume One	Geffen 24460
			WHITTAKER, Roger	
			Born on 3/22/36 in Nairobi, Kenya. British Adult Contemporary singer.	
6/7/75	**31**	5	● "The Last Farewell" and other hits	RCA 0855
			WHO, The	
			Rock group formed in London in 1964. Consisted of Roger Daltrey (born 3/1/44, lead singer), Pete Townshend (born 5/19/45; guitar, vocals), John Entwistle (born 10/9/44; bass) and Keith Moon (born 8/23/47; drums). Originally known as The High Numbers in 1964. All but Moon had been in The Detours. Developed stage antics of destroying their instruments. *Tommy*, 1969 rock-opera album, became a movie in 1975. Solo work by members began in 1972. Moon died of a drug overdose on 9/7/78; replaced by Kenney Jones (formerly with Small Faces). *Quadrophenia*, 1973 rock opera album, became a movie in 1979. The Who's biographical movie *The Kids Are Alright* was released in 1979. Eleven fans trampled to death at a concert in Cincinnati on 12/3/79. Disbanded in 1982. Re-grouped at "Live Aid" in 1986. Daltrey, Townshend and Entwistle reunited with an ensemble of 15 for a U.S. tour in 1989. Jones formed The Law with Paul Rodgers in 1991. Inducted into the Rock and Roll Hall of Fame in 1990.	
11/30/68	**39**	2	1. Magic Bus-The Who On Tour [K]	Decca 75064
6/14/69	**4**	47	▲² **2. Tommy**	Decca 7205 [2]
			also see Rock Opera and Soundtrack versions	
6/6/70	**4**	24	▲² **3. Live At Leeds** [L]	Decca 79175
8/21/71	**4**	20	▲³ **4. Who's next**	Decca 79182
11/20/71	**11**	8	▲ **5. Meaty Beaty Big And Bouncy** [G]	Decca 79184
11/10/73	**2(1)**	18	▲ **6. Quadrophenia**	MCA 10004
			Townshend's second rock opera; movie version released in 1979	
11/2/74	**15**	8	● 7. Odds & Sods [K]	Track 2126
			previously unreleased recordings from 1964-72	
11/1/75	**8**	14	▲ **8. The Who By Numbers**	MCA 2161
9/9/78	**2(2)**	13	▲² **9. Who Are You**	MCA 3050
7/7/79	**8**	11	▲ **10. The Kids Are Alright** [S-L]	MCA 11005 [2]
			movie features interviews and performances from the group's past 15 years	
4/4/81	**4**	14	▲ **11. Face Dances**	Warner 3516
9/25/82	**8**	10	● **12. It's Hard**	Warner 23731
			WHODINI	
			New York rap group. Began as a duo of Jalil "Whodini" Hutchins and John Fletcher. Grandmaster Dee joined in 1986.	
1/26/85	**35**	5	▲ 1. Escape	Jive 8251
6/28/86	**35**	4	● 2. Back In Black	Jive 8407
10/31/87	**30**	6	● 3. Open Sesame	Jive 8494
			WILD CHERRY	
			White-funk band formed in Steubenville, Ohio, in the early '70s. Consisted of Robert Parissi (lead vocals, guitar), Bryan Bassett (guitar), Mark Avsec (keyboards), Allen Wentz (bass) and Ron Beitle (drums).	
8/7/76	**5**	15	▲ **Wild Cherry**	Sweet City 34195
			Play That Funky Music (1)	

DATE	POS	WKS	ARTIST—RECORD TITLE	LABEL & NO.
			WILDE, Kim	
			Born Kim Smith on 11/18/60 in Chiswick, England. Pop-rock singer. Daughter of singer Marty Wilde.	
6/13/87	40	2	Another Step	MCA 5903
			You Keep Me Hangin' On (1)	
			WILLIAMS, Andy	
			Born Howard Andrew Williams on 12/3/28 in Wall Lake, Iowa. Formed quartet with his brothers; eventually moved to Los Angeles. With Bing Crosby on hit "Swingin' On A Star," 1944. With comedienne Kay Thompson in the mid-1940s. Went solo in 1952. On Steve Allen's "The Tonight Show" from 1952-55. Own NBC-TV variety series from 1962-67; 1969-71. Appeared in the movie *I'd Rather Be Rich* in 1964. Formerly married to singer/actress Claudine Longet. One of America's greatest pop-MOR singers.	
1/25/60	38	1	1. Lonely Street	Cadence 3030
			Lonely Street (5)	
3/24/62	19	8	2. "Danny Boy" and other songs I love to sing	Columbia 8551
6/2/62	3	106	● **3. Moon River & Other Great Movie Themes**	Columbia 8609
11/10/62	16	22	4. Warm And Willing	Columbia 8679
4/20/63	1 (16)	61	● **5. Days of Wine and Roses**	Columbia 8815
			Can't Get Used To Losing You (2)	
2/1/64	9	16	● **6. The Wonderful World Of Andy Williams**	Columbia 8937
			with members of Williams's family	
5/23/64	5	27	● **7. The Academy Award Winning "Call Me Irresponsible"**	Columbia 8971
10/10/64	5	20	● **8. The Great Songs From "My Fair Lady" and other Broadway hits**	Columbia 9005
4/24/65	4	45	● **9. Dear Heart**	Columbia 9138
3/12/66	23	8	10. Andy Williams' Newest Hits [K]	Columbia 9183
6/11/66	6	18	● **11. The Shadow of Your Smile**	Columbia 9299
3/4/67	21	11	12. In The Arms Of Love	Columbia 9333
5/27/67	5	35	● **13. Born Free**	Columbia 9480
12/9/67	8	11	● **14. Love, Andy**	Columbia 9566
6/29/68	9	24	● **15. Honey**	Columbia 9662
5/31/69	9	10	● **16. Happy Heart**	Columbia 9844
11/22/69	27	6	● **17. Get Together With Andy Williams**	Columbia 9922
			with The Osmonds on 3 tracks	
2/27/71	3	16	▲ **18. Love Story**	Columbia 30497
			(Where Do I Begin) Love Story (9)	
5/20/72	29	8	● **19. Love Theme From "The Godfather"**	Columbia 31303
			WILLIAMS, Deniece	
			Born Deniece Chandler on 6/3/51 in Gary, Indiana. Soul vocalist/songwriter. Recorded for Toddlin' Town, early '60s. Member of Wonderlove, Stevie Wonder's backup group, from 1972-75. Also a popular Inspirational artist.	
3/5/77	33	6	● **1. This is Niecy**	Columbia 34242
7/29/78	19	8	● **2. That's What Friends Are For**	Columbia 35435
			JOHNNY MATHIS & DENIECE WILLIAMS	
5/15/82	20	7	3. Niecy	ARC 37952
			It's Gonna Take A Miracle (10)	
6/16/84	26	6	4. Let's Hear It For The Boy	Columbia 39366
			Let's Hear It For The Boy (1)	

Billy Vaughn's position as musical director for Dot Records offered him limitless recording possibilities. The much-loved orchestra leader produced 36 charting albums for the label between 1958–70. *Billy Vaughn Plays*, his third, peaked at No. 20 in 1959.

The Ventures were an exciting, guitar-based, instrumental band who left no possible theme unexplored. Found on 1961's *The Colorful Ventures* were such tracks as "Yellow Bird," "Bluer Than Blue" and "Silver City."

Bobby Vinton's popularity during the '60s drew a diverse lot of fans to his numerous Epic albums. *Satin Pillows and Careless*, one of his lesser efforts, reached only No. 110 in 1966 and dropped off the chart after five weeks.

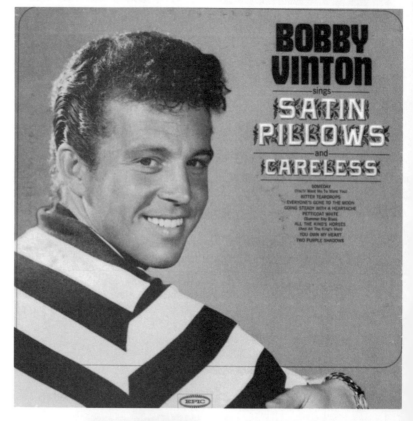

Dionne Warwicke's lengthy recording career never brought her a single No. 1 hit during the '60s. It wasn't until "Then Came You," her 1974 hit recorded with The Spinners and released on Atlantic, that she got her first taste of the top of the charts.

Lawrence Welk's 1956 album, *Say It With Music*, his third to reach the Top 10, featured dance medleys of "36 all time favorites." Twenty-four of the dedicated bandleader's numerous albums cracked the Top 40.

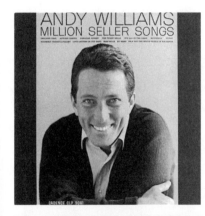

Andy Williams's *Million Seller Songs* preceded his all-time bestseller by only three months. *Days Of Wine And Roses* was released by Columbia in 1963, the year before the so-called "British invasion," and stayed in the No. 1 slot for 16 weeks.

Roger Williams, remembered by many baby boomers for his 1966 hit "Born Free," had been recording instrumental hits as far back as 1955. That year, his enormously successful "Autumn Leaves" was perched at No. 1 for four weeks. His 1962 *Greatest Hits* collection prominently featured his well-known version.

Nancy Wilson released a torrent of appealing product for Capitol during the '60s. *A Touch Of Today*, one of three charting albums she issued in 1966, climbed to No. 15.

Stevie Wonder's power as a singles artist is amply demonstrated by the relatively low charting of 1969's *For Once In My Life*. The album, which contained the Top 10 singles "Shoo-Be-Do-Be-Doo-Da-Day" and the title track, peaked at No. 50.

Neil Young's *Tonight's The Night*, containing the memorable title track dedicated to two of the singer's deceased friends, won critical raves upon its 1975 release. But the roughness of its sound alienated many fans of *Harvest*, his polished 1972 set.

DATE	POS	WKS	ARTIST—RECORD TITLE	LABEL & NO.
			WILLIAMS, Hank Jr.	
			Born Randall Hank Williams on 5/26/49 in Shreveport, Louisiana; raised in Nashville. Country singer/ songwriter/guitarist. Son of country music's first superstar, Hank Williams. Nicknamed "Bocephus" by his father. On the *Grand Ole Opry* since 1962. Injured in a climbing accident on 8/8/75 in Montana; returned to performing in 1977. Richard Thomas starred as Hank in his 1983 biographical TV movie "Living Proof: The Hank Williams Story." Hank, Jr., has charted over 40 Top 10 country singles.	
3/13/65	16	13	● 1. Your Cheatin' Heart [S]	MGM 4260
			movie is Hank Williams's life story (Hank is played by George Hamilton; songs sung by Hank, Jr.)	
9/12/87	28	3	▲ 2. Born To Boogie	Warner 25593
			WILLIAMS, Mason	
			Born on 8/24/38 in Abilene, Texas. Folk guitarist/songwriter/author/ photographer/TV comedy writer ("The Smothers Brothers Comedy Hour," 1967-69; "Saturday Night Live," 1980).	
8/17/68	14	8	The Mason Williams Phonograph Record	Warner 1729
			Classical Gas (2)	
			WILLIAMS, Robin	
			Born on 7/21/52 in Chicago. Actor/comedian. Mork of TV series "Mork & Mindy," 1978-82. Among his many movies: *The World According to Garp, Good Morning, Vietnam, Dead Poets Society, Hook* and *Mrs. Doubtfire*.	
7/28/79	10	12	● **Reality...What A Concept** [C]	Casablanca 7162
			WILLIAMS, Roger	
			Born Louis Weertz in 1925 in Omaha. Learned to play the piano by age three. Educated at Drake University, Idaho State University, and the Juilliard School of Music. Took lessons from Lenny Tristano and Teddy Wilson. Win on the TV show "Arthur Godfrey's Talent Scouts" led to recording contract.	
3/31/56	19	2	1. Roger Williams [I]	Kapp 1012
			album also released as *Autumn Leaves* / *Autumn Leaves* (1)	
8/25/56	19	3	2. Daydreams [I]	Kapp 1031
10/27/56	16	2	3. Roger Williams plays the wonderful Music of the Masters [I]	Kapp 1040
			classical melodies	
3/23/57	6	57	● **4. Songs Of The Fabulous Fifties** [I]	Kapp 5000 [2]
10/7/57	20	5	5. Almost Paradise [I]	Kapp 1063
11/4/57	19	4	6. Songs Of The Fabulous Forties [I]	Kapp 5003 [2]
3/31/58	4	61	● **7. Till** [I]	Kapp 1081
2/23/59	9	49	**8. Near You** [I]	Kapp 1112
			Near You (10)	
6/15/59	11	14	● 9. More Songs Of The Fabulous Fifties [I]	Kapp 1130
10/26/59	8	29	**10. With These Hands** [I]	Kapp 1147
12/28/59	12	2	11. Christmas Time [X-I]	Kapp 1164
4/4/60	25	10	12. Always [I]	Kapp 1172
12/19/60	5	12	**13. Temptation** [I]	Kapp 1217
10/23/61	35	2	14. Songs Of The Soaring '60s [I]	Kapp 1251
3/31/62	9	19	**15. Maria** [I]	Kapp 3266
11/17/62	27	4	16. Mr. Piano [I]	Kapp 3290
3/7/64	27	4	17. The Solid Gold Steinway [I]	Kapp 3354
7/30/66	24	11	18. I'll Remember You [I]	Kapp 3470

DATE	POS	WKS	ARTIST—RECORD TITLE	LABEL & NO.
12/17/66	7	23	● **19. Born Free** [I] *Born Free* (7)	Kapp 3501
			WILLIAMS, Vanessa	
			Born on 3/18/63 in Tarrytown, New York. In 1983, became the first black woman to win the Miss America pageant; relinquished crown after *Penthouse* magazine scandal. Married Ramon Hervey (manager of Babyface) in February 1987. Began hosting "Soul of VH-1" on video music TV channel in 1991. Starred in the Broadway production *Kiss of the Spider Woman*. Appeared in the movie *Harley Davidson & The Marlboro Man* and the TV mini-series "The Jacksons: An American Dream."	
4/1/89	38	4	● 1. The Right Stuff *Dreamin'* (8)	Wing 835694
3/7/92	17	18	▲² 2. The Comfort Zone *Save The Best For Last* (1)	Wing 843522
			WILLIS, Bruce	
			Born on 3/19/55 in Penns Grove, New Jersey. Played David Addison on TV's "Moonlighting." Starred in the *Die Hard* movies and others. Child's voice in the *Look Who's Talking* movies. Married actress Demi Moore on 11/21/87.	
2/21/87	14	11	● The Return Of Bruno *Respect Yourself* (5)	Motown 6222
			WILSON, Flip	
			Born Clerow Wilson on 12/8/33 in Jersey City, New Jersey. Black comedian. Host of own TV variety show, 1970-74. Also recorded as his female alter ego, Geraldine.	
2/17/68	34	5	1. Cowboys & Colored People [C]	Atlantic 8149
5/23/70	17	9	● 2. "The Devil made me buy this dress" [C]	Little David 1000
			WILSON, Hank — see RUSSELL, Leon	
			WILSON, Jackie	
			Born on 6/9/34 in Detroit; died on 1/21/84. Sang with local gospel groups; became an amateur boxer. Worked as solo singer until 1953; then joined Billy Ward's Dominoes as Clyde McPhatter's replacement. Solo since 1957. Godfather of Jody Watley. Cousin of Hubert Johnson of The Contours. Wilson collapsed from a stroke, on stage, at the Latin Casino in Cherry Hill, New Jersey, on 9/25/75; spent rest of his life in hospitals. Inducted into the Rock and Roll Hall of Fame in 1987.	
7/20/63	36	2	Baby Workout *Baby Workout* (5)	Brunswick 754110
			WILSON, Nancy	
			Born on 2/20/37 in Chillicothe, Ohio; raised in Columbus, Ohio. Jazz stylist with Rusty Bryant's Carolyn Club Band in Columbus. First recorded for Dot in 1956. Moved to New York City in 1959.	
7/7/62	30	5	1. Nancy Wilson/Cannonball Adderley **NANCY WILSON/CANNONBALL ADDERLEY**	Capitol 1657
4/20/63	18	21	2. Broadway-My Way	Capitol 1828
8/31/63	11	20	3. Hollywood-My Way	Capitol 1934
2/1/64	4	26	**4. Yesterday's Love Songs/Today's Blues**	Capitol 2012
6/13/64	10	24	**5. Today, Tomorrow, Forever**	Capitol 2082
9/19/64	4	18	**6. How Glad I Am**	Capitol 2155
2/27/65	24	18	7. The Nancy Wilson Show! [L] recorded at the Cocoanut Grove in Los Angeles	Capitol 2136
7/31/65	7	11	**8. Today-My Way**	Capitol 2321
10/16/65	17	8	9. Gentle Is My Love	Capitol 2351

DATE	POS	WKS	ARTIST—RECORD TITLE	LABEL & NO.
6/25/66	**15**	12	10. A Touch Of Today	Capitol 2495
10/29/66	**35**	3	11. Tender Loving Care	Capitol 2555
4/1/67	**35**	3	12. Nancy-Naturally	Capitol 2634
8/5/67	**40**	1	13. Just For Now	Capitol 2712
			WILSON PHILLIPS	
			Vocal/songwriting trio of sisters Carnie and Wendy Wilson, with Chynna Phillips. Carnie and Wendy's father is Brian Wilson (The Beach Boys). Phillips, the daughter of Michelle and John Phillips (The Mamas & The Papas), acted in the movie *Caddyshack II*.	
5/12/90	**2**(10)	69	▲⁵ **1. Wilson Phillips**	SBK 93745
			Hold On (1)/*Release Me* (1)/*Impulsive* (4)/*You're In Love* (1)	
6/20/92	**4**	12	▲ **2. Shadows And Light**	SBK 98924
			WINGER	
			Hard-rock quartet formed in New York City in 1986: Kip Winger (vocals, bass), Reb Beach, Rod Morgenstein (ex-Dixie Dregs) and Paul Taylor. Golden, Colorado, native Winger was a member of Alice Cooper's band.	
12/3/88	**21**	35	▲ 1. Winger	Atlantic 81867
8/18/90	**15**	11	▲ 2. In The Heart Of The Young	Atlantic 82103
			WINGS — see McCARTNEY, Paul	
			WINTER, Edgar, Group	
			Winter was born on 12/28/46 in Beaumont, Texas. Albino rock singer/ keyboardist/saxophonist. Younger brother of Johnny Winter. Edgar Winter Group included Dan Hartman (1972-76), Ronnie Montrose (1972-74) and Rick Derringer (1974-76).	
4/15/72	**23**	9	● 1. Roadwork [L]	Epic 31249 [2]
			EDGAR WINTER'S WHITE TRASH	
3/3/73	**3**	25	▲² **2. They Only Come Out At Night**	Epic 31584
			album introduces Ronnie Montrose and Dan Hartman in group *Frankenstein* (1)	
6/15/74	**13**	13	● 3. Shock Treatment	Epic 32461
			Rick Derringer replaces Montrose as lead guitarist (Derringer also appears on previous 2 albums)	
			WINTER, Johnny	
			Born on 2/23/44 in Leland, Mississippi. Blues-rock guitarist/vocalist. Both Johnny and brother Edgar Winter are albinos. A prominent '60s sessionman, Johnny toured with Muddy Waters and was a member of The Traits.	
5/17/69	**24**	8	1. Johnny Winter	Columbia 9826
5/17/69	**40**	1	2. The Progressive Blues Experiment	Imperial 12431
5/29/71	**40**	2	● 3. Live/Johnny Winter And [L]	Columbia 30475
5/5/73	**22**	11	4. Still Alive And Well	Columbia 32188
			WINTERS, Jonathan	
			Born on 11/11/25 in Dayton, Ohio. Comedian; master of improvisation. Own TV variety series, 1956-57; 1967-69; 1972-74. Also appeared on TV's "Mork & Mindy" and "Davis Rules."	
2/1/60	**18**	28	1. The Wonderful World Of Jonathan Winters [C]	Verve 15009
9/19/60	**25**	11	2. Down To Earth [C]	Verve 15011
7/3/61	**19**	6	3. Here's Jonathan [C]	Verve 15025

DATE	POS	WKS	ARTIST—RECORD TITLE	LABEL & NO.
			WINWOOD, Steve	
			Born on 5/12/48 in Birmingham, England. Rock singer/keyboardist/guitarist. Lead singer of Spencer Davis Group, Blind Faith and Traffic.	
7/30/77	**22**	10	1. Steve Winwood	Island 9494
2/14/81	**3**	26	▲ **2. Arc Of A Diver**	Island 9576
			While You See A Chance (7)	
9/4/82	**28**	6	3. Talking Back To The Night	Island 9777
7/26/86	**3**	60	▲³ **4. Back in the High Life**	Island 25448
			Higher Love (1)/*The Finer Things* (8)	
12/5/87	**26**	10	▲ 5. Chronicles [K]	Island 25660
			contains 10 cuts from his 4 Island albums	
			Valerie (9)	
7/9/88	**1**(1)	31	▲² **6. Roll With It**	Virgin 90946
			Roll With It (1)/*Don't You Know What The Night Can Do?* (6)	
12/1/90	**27**	7	● 7. Refugees of the Heart	Virgin 91405
			WITHERS, Bill	
			Born on 7/4/38 in Slab Fork, West Virginia. Soul vocalist/guitarist/composer. Moved to California in 1967; made demo records of his songs. Married to actress Denise Nicholas.	
9/25/71	**39**	1	1. Just As I Am	Sussex 7006
			Ain't No Sunshine (3)	
6/17/72	**4**	25	● **2. Still Bill**	Sussex 7014
			Lean On Me (1)/*Use Me* (2)	
2/4/78	**39**	2	● 3. Menagerie	Columbia 34903
			WOLF, Peter	
			Born Peter Blankfield on 3/7/46 in the Bronx. Lead singer of The J. Geils Band until 1983. Married actress Faye Dunaway on 8/7/74; divorced in 1979. Not to be confused with the producer of the same name.	
8/25/84	**24**	8	Lights Out	EMI America 17121
			WOMACK, Bobby	
			Born on 3/4/44 in Cleveland. Soul vocalist/guitarist/songwriter. Sang in family gospel group, The Womack Brothers. Group recorded for SAR as The Valentinos and The Lovers, 1962-64. Toured as guitarist with Sam Cooke. Backup guitarist on many sessions, including Wilson Pickett, The Box Tops, Joe Tex, Aretha Franklin and Janis Joplin. Married for a time to Sam Cooke's widow, Barbara. Bobby's brother, Cecil, and Sam Cooke's daughter, Linda, recorded as Womack & Womack. Nicknamed "The Preacher."	
8/25/73	**37**	1	1. Facts Of Life	United Art. 043
2/20/82	**29**	6	2. The Poet	Beverly G. 10000
			WONDER, Stevie	
			Born Steveland Morris on 5/13/50 in Saginaw, Michigan. Singer/songwriter/ multi-instrumentalist/ producer. Blind since birth. Signed to Motown in 1960; did backup work. First recorded in 1962; named "Little Stevie Wonder" by Berry Gordy, Jr. Married to Syreeta Wright from 1970-72. Near-fatal auto accident on 8/16/73. Winner of 17 Grammy Awards. In the movies *Bikini Beach* and *Muscle Beach Party*. Inducted into the Rock and Roll Hall of Fame in 1989.	
7/27/63	**1**(1)	13	**1. Little Stevie Wonder/The 12 Year Old Genius** **[L]**	Tamla 240
			LITTLE STEVIE WONDER	
			Fingertips (1)	
9/24/66	**33**	3	2. Up-Tight Everything's Alright	Tamla 268
			Uptight (Everything's Alright) (3)/*Blowin' In The Wind* (9)	
7/6/68	**37**	4	3. Greatest Hits [G]	Tamla 282

DATE	POS	WKS	ARTIST—RECORD TITLE	LABEL & NO.
11/1/69	**34**	4	4. My Cherie Amour *My Cherie Amour (4)/Yester-Me, Yester-You, Yesterday (7)*	Tamla 296
9/12/70	**25**	5	5. Signed Sealed & Delivered *Signed, Sealed, Delivered I'm Yours (3)/* *Heaven Help Us All (9)*	Tamla 304
6/10/72	**21**	11	6. Music Of My Mind	Tamla 314
12/30/72	**3**	30	**7. Talking Book** *Superstition (1)/You Are The Sunshine Of My Life (1)*	Tamla 319
8/25/73	**4**	58	**8. Innervisions** 1973 Album of the Year Grammy Award *Higher Ground (4)/Living For The City (8)*	Tamla 326
8/17/74	**1**(2)	11	**9. Fulfillingness' First Finale** 1974 Album of the Year Grammy Award *You Haven't Done Nothin (1)/Boogie On Reggae Woman (3)*	Tamla 332
10/16/76	**1**(14)	44	**10. Songs In The Key Of Life** 1976 Album of the Year Grammy Award; double album also includes a bonus 4-song, 7" EP *I Wish (1)/Sir Duke (1)*	Tamla 340 [2]
2/4/78	**34**	3	11. Looking Back [K] compilation of recordings from 1962-71	Motown 804 [3]
11/24/79	**4**	15	**12. Journey Through The Secret Life of Plants** *Send One Your Love (4)*	Tamla 371 [2]
11/15/80	**3**	25	▲ **13. Hotter Than July** *Master Blaster (Jammin') (5)*	Tamla 373
5/29/82	**4**	8	● **14. Stevie Wonder's Original Musiquarium I** [G] compilation of hits from 1972-82 *That Girl (4)*	Tamla 6002 [2]
9/29/84	**4**	21	▲ **15. The Woman in Red** [S] featuring Dionne Warwick on 3 songs *I Just Called To Say I Love You (1)*	Motown 6108
10/19/85	**5**	29	▲ **16. In Square Circle** *Part-Time Lover (1)/Go Home (10)*	Tamla 6134
12/12/87	**17**	13	▲ 17. Characters	Motown 6248
6/29/91	**24**	6	● 18. Music From The Movie Jungle Fever [S]	Motown 6291
			WOODBURY, Woody	
			Born in Fort Lauderdale, Florida, in 1927. Adult comedy storyteller.	
3/7/60	**10**	39	**1. Woody Woodbury Looks at love and life** [C]	Stereoddities 1
6/13/60	**16**	26	2. Woody Woodbury's Laughing Room [C]	Stereoddities 2
			WORLD PARTY	
			London-based group featuring keyboardist/vocalist/producer/engineer Karl Wallinger from North Wales (formerly of The Waterboys).	
3/28/87	**39**	3	Private Revolution	Chrysalis 41552
			WRECKX-N-EFFECT	
			Male rap group: Aqil Davidson, Markell Riley and Brandon Mitchell (died 1990 of gunshot fire). Riley is the brother of Guy member/prolific producer Teddy Riley.	
12/12/92	**9**	17	▲ **Hard Or Smooth** CD and cassette include bonus track *Rump Shaker (2)*	MCA 10566

DATE	POS	WKS	ARTIST—RECORD TITLE		LABEL & NO.
			WRIGHT, Betty		
			Born on 12/21/53 in Miami. Soul singer. In family gospel group, Echoes of Joy, from 1956. First recorded for Deep City in 1966. Hostess of TV talk shows in Miami.		
9/9/78	26	7	Betty Wright Live	[L]	Alston 4408
			WRIGHT, Gary		
			Born on 4/26/43 in Creskill, New Jersey. Pop-rock singer/songwriter/ keyboardist. Appeared in "Captain Video" TV series at age seven. In the Broadway play *Fanny*. Co-leader of rock group Spooky Tooth.		
2/14/76	7	35	▲ **1. The Dream Weaver**		Warner 2868
			Dream Weaver (2)/*Love Is Alive* (2)		
1/29/77	23	9	2. The Light of Smiles		Warner 2951
			WYNETTE, Tammy		
			Born Virginia Wynette Pugh on 5/5/42 in Itawamba County, Mississippi. With 20 #1 country hits, Wynette was dubbed "The First Lady of Country Music." Discovered by producer Billy Sherrill. Married to country star George Jones from 1969-75.		
11/8/69	37	2	▲ Tammy's Greatest Hits	[G]	Epic 26486
			# X		
			X CLAN		
			Brooklyn-based rap group: Professor X the Overseer, Grand Verbalizer Funkin-Lesson Brother J., Architect Tractitioner Paradise and Rhythm Provider Sugar Shaft. Professor X (Lumumba Carson) is the son of black activist Sonny Carson.		
6/6/92	31	2	Xodus-The New Testament		Polydor 513225
			XSCAPE		
			Female R&B quartet formed at the Tri-City Performing Arts School in Atlanta: sisters LaTocha and Tamika Scott, with Kandi Burruss and Tameka Cottle.		
10/30/93	17	14	▲ Hummin' Comin' At 'Cha		So So Def 57107
			Just Kickin' It (2)/*Understanding* (8)		
			# Y		
			YANKOVIC, "Weird Al"		
			Born on 10/24/59 in Lynwood, California. Novelty singer/accordionist. Specializes in song parodies. Starred in the 1989 movie *UHF*.		
3/31/84	17	11	● 1. "Weird Al" Yankovic In 3-D	[N]	Rock 'n' R. 39221
5/28/88	27	9	▲ 2. Even Worse	[N]	Rock 'n' R. 44149
5/2/92	17	9	● 3. Off The Deep End	[N]	Scotti Br. 75256
			YANNI		
			Born Yiannis Chryssolmalis in Kalamata, Greece. New Age keyboardist/ composer. National champion swimmer of Greece at age 14. Moved to Minneapolis in 1973 to earn psychology degree.		
12/15/90	29	7	▲ 1. Reflections Of Passion	[I-K]	Private M. 2067
			features selections from albums released from 1986-89		

DATE	POS	WKS	ARTIST—RECORD TITLE	LABEL & NO.
4/4/92	32	4	▲ 2. Dare to Dream [I] vocals on one track by Mona Lisa	Private M. 82096
5/22/93	24	8	▲ 3. In My Time [I]	Private M. 82106
3/26/94	5	34 +	▲² 4. **Live At The Acropolis** [L-I] with the Royal Philharmonic Concert Orchestra (of London); conducted by Shardad Rohani; recorded at the Herod Atticus Theatre in Athens, Greece, on 9/25/93	Private M. 82116
			YARBROUGH, Glenn Born on 1/12/30 in Milwaukee. Lead singer of The Limeliters (1959-63). Folk singer.	
7/10/65	35	3	Baby The Rain Must Fall	RCA 3422
			YARBROUGH & PEOPLES Dallas soul duo: Cavin Yarbrough and Alisa Peoples. Discovered by The Gap Band.	
2/14/81	16	11	● The Two Of Us	Mercury 3834
			YARDBIRDS, The Legendary rock group formed in Surrey, England, in 1963. Consisted of Keith Relf (died 5/14/76 by being electrocuted [age 33]; vocals, harmonica), Anthony "Top" Topham and Chris Dreja (guitars), Paul "Sam" Samwell-Smith (bass, keyboards) and Jim McCarty (drums). Formed as The Metropolitan Blues Quartet at Kingston Art School. Topham replaced by Eric Clapton in 1963. Clapton replaced by Jeff Beck in 1965. Samwell-Smith left in 1966; Dreja switched to bass; Jimmy Page (guitar) was added. Beck left in December 1966. Group disbanded in July 1968. Page formed The New Yardbirds in October 1968, which evolved into Led Zeppelin. Relf and McCarty formed Renaissance in 1969. Relf later in Armageddon, 1975; McCarty in Illusion, 1977.	
5/27/67	28	8	The Yardbirds' Greatest Hits [G]	Epic 26246
			YEARWOOD, Trisha Born on 9/19/64 in Monticello, Georgia. Country singer. Backing singer on Garth Brooks's first album. Married Robert Reynolds of The Mavericks on 5/21/94.	
8/17/91	31	4	▲² 1. Trisha Yearwood	MCA 10297
12/18/93	40	1	▲ 2. The Song Remembers When	MCA 10911
			YES Progressive-rock group formed in London in 1968. Consisted of Jon Anderson (vocals), Peter Banks (guitar), Tony Kaye (keyboards), Chris Squire (bass) and Bill Bruford (drums). Banks replaced by Steve Howe in 1971. Kaye (joined Badfinger in 1978) replaced by Rick Wakeman in 1971. Bruford left to join King Crimson; replaced by Alan White in late 1972. Wakeman replaced by Patrick Moraz in 1974; re-joined in 1976 when Moraz left. Wakeman and Anderson left in 1980; replaced by The Buggles' Trevor Horne (guitar) and Geoff Downes (keyboards). Group disbanded in 1980. Howe and Downes joined Asia. Re-formed in 1983 with Anderson, Kaye, Squire, White and South African guitarist Trevor Rabin. Anderson left group in 1988. Anderson, Bruford, Wakeman and Howe formed self-named group in early 1989. Yes reunited in 1991 with Anderson, Bruford, Wakeman, Howe, Kaye, Squire, White and Rabin. Bruford, Wakeman and Howe left group by 1994.	
1/22/72	40	1	● 1. The Yes Album	Atlantic 8243
2/5/72	4	21	● 2. **Fragile**	Atlantic 7211
10/21/72	3	15	● 3. **Close To The Edge**	Atlantic 7244
6/2/73	12	10	● 4. Yessongs [L]	Atlantic 100 [3]
2/9/74	6	11	● 5. **Tales From Topographic Oceans**	Atlantic 908 [2]
1/4/75	5	9	● 6. **Relayer**	Atlantic 18122

DATE	POS	WKS	ARTIST—RECORD TITLE	LABEL & NO.
3/29/75	17	5	7. Yesterdays [K] featuring cuts from the group's first 2 albums (uncharted) *Yes* and *Time and a Word*	Atlantic 18103
8/6/77	**8**	11	● **8. Going For The One**	Atlantic 19106
10/21/78	**10**	7	▲ **9. Tormato**	Atlantic 19202
9/13/80	18	7	10. Drama	Atlantic 16019
12/3/83	**5**	28	▲ **11. 90125** title refers to label number *Owner Of A Lonely Heart* (1)	Atco 90125
10/24/87	15	18	▲ 12. Big Generator	Atco 90522
7/15/89	30	7	● 13. Anderson, Bruford, Wakeman, Howe	Arista 90126
5/18/91	15	5	● 14. Union	Arista 8643
4/9/94	33	1	15. Talk	Victory 480033
			YOAKAM, Dwight Born on 10/23/56 in Pikesville, Kentucky. Country singer/songwriter. Member of The Buzzin' Cousins group, which appeared in the 1992 movie *Falling from Grace*. In spring 1993, had lead in the Peter Fonda-directed play *Southern Rapture* in Los Angeles.	
4/10/93	25	11	▲² This Time	Reprise 45241
			YOUNG, Jesse Colin Born Perry Miller on 11/11/44 in New York City. Folk-rock singer. Leader of The Youngbloods.	
7/20/74	37	3	1. Light Shine	Warner 2790
4/19/75	26	4	2. Songbird	Warner 2845
5/8/76	34	3	3. On The Road [L]	Warner 2913
			YOUNG, Neil Born on 11/12/45 in Toronto. Rock singer/songwriter/guitarist. Formed rock band The Mynah Birds, featuring lead singer Rick James, early '60s. Moved to Los Angeles in 1966; formed Buffalo Springfield. Went solo in 1969 with backing band Crazy Horse. Joined with Crosby, Stills & Nash, 1970-71. Appeared in the 1987 movie *Made in Heaven*. Reunited with Crosby, Stills & Nash in 1988 to record the *American Dream* album. Inducted into the Rock and Roll Hall of Fame in 1995.	
8/8/70	34	5	▲ 1. Everybody Knows This Is Nowhere *	Reprise 6349
9/19/70	**8**	21	▲² **2. After The Gold Rush**	Reprise 6383
3/4/72	**1 (2)**	25	▲⁴ **3. Harvest** *Heart Of Gold* (1)	Reprise 2032
11/3/73	22	6	● 4. Time Fades Away [L] guests: David Crosby and Graham Nash	Reprise 2151
8/10/74	16	9	● 5. On The Beach	Reprise 2180
7/26/75	25	5	6. Tonight's The Night	Reprise 2221
12/20/75	25	7	7. Zuma *	Reprise 2242
10/30/76	26	6	● 8. Long May You Run **STILLS-YOUNG BAND *M* (Stephen Stills)**	Reprise 2253
7/16/77	21	9	● 9. American Stars 'N Bars **NEIL YOUNG, CRAZY HORSE & THE BULLETS** guests: Linda Ronstadt and Emmylou Harris	Reprise 2261
10/28/78	**7**	11	● **10. Comes A Time**	Reprise 2266
7/28/79	**8**	17	▲ **11. Rust Never Sleeps ***	Reprise 2295
12/15/79	15	13	▲ 12. Live Rust * [L]	Reprise 2296 [2]
12/6/80	30	6	13. Hawks & Doves	Reprise 2297

DATE	POS	WKS	ARTIST—RECORD TITLE	LABEL & NO.
11/28/81	27	9	14. Re-ac-tor *	Reprise 2304
1/29/83	19	7	15. Trans	Geffen 2018
11/11/89	35	4	● 16. Freedom	Reprise 25899
10/6/90	31	3	17. Ragged Glory *	Reprise 26315
11/14/92	16	15	▲ 18. Harvest Moon	Reprise 45057
7/3/93	23	4	● 19. Unplugged [L]	Reprise 45310
			recorded on 2/7/93 on the MTV program "Unplugged"	
9/3/94	9	5	● **20. Sleeps With Angels** *	Reprise 45749
			*NEIL YOUNG & CRAZY HORSE	
			YOUNG, Paul	
			Born on 1/17/56 in Bedfordshire, England. Pop-rock vocalist/guitarist.	Columbia 39957
6/29/85	19	24	● The Secret Of Association	
			Everytime You Go Away (1)	
			YOUNG-HOLT UNLIMITED	
			Chicago instrumental soul group: Eldee Young (bass), Isaac "Red" Holt (drums; both of the Ramsey Lewis Trio) and Don Walker (piano). Walker left by 1968.	
2/1/69	9	14	**Soulful Strut** [I]	Brunswick 754144
			Soulful Strut (3)	
			YOUNG MC	
			Born Marvin Young on 5/10/67 in England; raised in Queens, New York. Rapper. Co-writer of Tone Loc's "Wild Thing" and "Funky Cold Medina." Graduated with economics degree from the University of Southern California.	
10/7/89	9	30	▲ **Stone Cold Rhymin'**	Delicious 91309
			Bust A Move (7)	

Z

DATE	POS	WKS	ARTIST—RECORD TITLE	LABEL & NO.
			ZAGER & EVANS	
			Folk-rock duo from Lincoln, Nebraska: Denny Zager and Rick Evans (both sing and play guitar).	RCA 4214
8/16/69	30	5	2525 (Exordium & Terminus)	
			In The Year 2525 (1)	
			ZAPP	
			Dayton, Ohio, funk band formed by the Troutman brothers: Roger ("Zapp"), Lester, Tony and Larry. "Bootsy" Collins produced and played on first session. Roger recorded solo as "Roger."	
10/4/80	19	7	● 1. Zapp	Warner 3463
			with "Bootsy" Collins (guitars)	
8/28/82	25	6	● 2. Zapp II	Warner 23583
9/24/83	39	2	3. Zapp III	Warner 23875
11/13/93	39	1	● 4. All The Greatest Hits [G]	Reprise 45143
			ZAPP & ROGER	

DATE	POS	WKS	ARTIST—RECORD TITLE	LABEL & NO.
			ZAPPA, Frank	
			Born Francis Vincent Zappa Jr. on 12/21/40 in Baltimore, Maryland, of Sicilian parentage; raised in California. Died on 12/4/93 of prostate cancer. Rock music's leading satirist. Singer/songwriter/ guitarist/activist. Formed The Mothers Of Invention in 1965. In the movies *200 Motels* and *Baby Snakes*. Father of Dweezil and Moon Unit Zappa (both performed in the 1991 Peace Choir, "Give Peace A Chance"). Inducted into the Rock and Roll Hall of Fame in 1995.	
4/13/68	30	4	1. We're Only In It For The Money	Verve 5045
			THE MOTHERS OF INVENTION album art work is a parody of The Beatles' *Sgt. Pepper's Lonely Hearts Club Band* album	
9/4/71	38	3	2. The Mothers/Fillmore East-June 1971 * [L]	Bizarre 2042
11/17/73	32	4	● 3. Over-nite Sensation *	DiscReet 2149
			*THE MOTHERS	
5/11/74	10	15	● **4. Apostrophe (')**	DiscReet 2175
11/9/74	27	3	5. Roxy & Elsewhere [L]	DiscReet 2202 [2]
			ZAPPA/MOTHERS	
8/2/75	26	5	6. One Size Fits All	DiscReet 2216
			FRANK ZAPPA AND THE MOTHERS OF INVENTION	
4/28/79	21	8	7. Sheik Yerbouti	Zappa 1501 [2]
9/29/79	27	5	8. Joe's Garage, Act I	Zappa 1603
7/17/82	23	6	9. Ship arriving too late to save a drowning witch	Barking P. 38066
			ZEBRA	
			New Orleans rock trio: Randy Jackson (lead singer), Felix Hanemann (bass) and Guy Gelso (drums).	
7/23/83	29	7	● Zebra	Atlantic 80054
			ZEVON, Warren	
			Born on 1/24/47 in Chicago. Parents were Russian immigrants. Rock singer/ songwriter/pianist. Recorded with female vocalist Tule Livingston as the duo Lyme & Cybelle in 1966. Worked as the keyboardist/ bandleader for The Everly Brothers shortly before their breakup. Wrote Linda Ronstadt's "Poor Poor Pitiful Me." Recorded with three R.E.M. members as The Hindu Love Gods in 1990.	
3/25/78	8	13	● **1. Excitable Boy**	Asylum 118
			produced by Jackson Browne	
3/15/80	20	8	2. Bad Luck Streak In Dancing School	Asylum 509
			ZHANÉ	
			Female duo formed at Philadelphia's Temple University: Renee Neufville and Jean Norris.	
3/12/94	37	2	● Pronounced Jah-Nay	Motown 6369
			Hey Mr. D.J. (6)	
			ZOMBIES, The	
			British rock quintet: Rod Argent (keyboards), Colin Blunstone (vocals), Paul Atkinson (guitar), Chris White (bass) and Hugh Grundy (drums). Group disbanded in late 1967. Argent formed the band Argent in 1969.	
5/1/65	39	1	The Zombies	Parrot 71001
			She's Not There (2)/*Tell Her No* (6)	

DATE	POS	WKS	ARTIST—RECORD TITLE	LABEL & NO.
			ZZ TOP	
			Boogie-rock trio formed in Houston in 1969. Consists of Billy Gibbons (vocals, guitar), Dusty Hill (vocals, bass) and Frank Beard (drums). All were born in 1949 in Texas. Gibbons had been lead guitarist in Moving Sidewalks, a Houston psychedelic-rock band. Hill and Beard had played in American Blues, based in Dallas. Group appeared in the movie *Back to the Future III*.	
9/29/73	8	24	● 1. Tres Hombres	London 631
			title is Spanish for three men	
5/31/75	10	21	● 2. Fandango! [L]	London 656
			side 1: "live"; side 2: studio	
1/29/77	17	8	● 3. Tejas	London 680
			title is Spanish for Texas	
12/22/79	24	14	▲ 4. Deguello	Warner 3361
			title is Spanish for beheading	
8/15/81	17	12	● 5. El Loco	Warner 3593
			title is Spanish for the crazy	
4/23/83	9	82	▲⁷ 6. Eliminator	Warner 23774
			Legs (8)	
			album named after a 1933 Ford coupe restored by Billy Gibbons	
11/16/85	4	36	▲⁴ 7. Afterburner	Warner 25342
			Sleeping Bag (8)	
11/3/90	6	21	▲ 8. Recycler	Warner 26265
5/2/92	9	13	▲² 9. Greatest Hits [G]	Warner 26846
2/5/94	14	6	▲ 10. Antenna	RCA 66317

SOUNDTRACKS

Each movie's stars are listed below the title. Also shown are the composer (cp), conductor (cd), lyricist (ly), music writer (mu), performer (pf) and songwriter [music & lyrics] (sw). The following symbols are also used in this section: [I] instrumental, [M] musical, [O] oldies, [R] reissue and [V] various artists.

DATE	POS	WKS	ARTIST—RECORD TITLE	LABEL & NO.
4/9/94	2(1)	20	▲² 1. Above The Rim [V]	Death Row/Int. 92359
			Duane Martin/Leon/2 Pac/Marlon Wayans	
			Regulate (2-Warren G. & Nate Dogg)	
			Advance To The Rear — see NEW CHRISTY MINSTRELS	
			Glenn Ford/Stella Stevens/Melvyn Douglas	
4/7/84	12	12	● 2. Against All Odds [I+V]	Atlantic 80152
			Rachel Ward/Jeff Bridges/James Woods/Alex Karras;	
			side 2: instrumentals; cp/pf: Larry Carlton and Michel Colombier	
			Against All Odds (Take A Look At Me Now) (1-Phil Collins)	
12/12/92	6	25	▲³ 3. Aladdin	Disney 60846
			animated movie, voices by: Robin Williams/Lea Salonga/Bruce Adler/Jonathan Freeman/Brad Kane; cp: Alan Menken; ly: Tim Rice/Howard Ashman (died 1991 [age 41])	
			A Whole New World (Aladdin's Theme) (1-Peabo Bryson and Regina Belle)	
12/5/60	7	15	4. Alamo, The [I+V]	Columbia 8358
			John Wayne/Richard Widmark/Laurence Harvey; cp/cd: Dimitri Tiomkin	
4/12/80	36	3	5. All That Jazz [M]	Casablanca 7198
			Roy Scheider/Jessica Lange/Ann Reinking/Ben Vereen; cd: Ralph Burns	

DATE	POS	WKS	ARTIST—RECORD TITLE	LABEL & NO.
3/15/80	7	15	● 6. **American Gigolo** [I+V] Richard Gere/Lauren Hutton/Hector Elizondo; side 2: instrumentals; cp/pf: Giorgio Moroder *Call Me* (1-Blondie)	Polydor 6259
10/6/73	10	41	▲³ 7. **American Graffiti** [V-O] Richard Dreyfuss/Ron Howard/Cindy Williams/Charles Martin Smith; director George Lucas's first major movie	MCA 8001 [2]
5/6/78	31	4	8. American Hot Wax [V-O] Tim McIntire/Fran Drescher/Laraine Newman/Jay Leno; based on the life of disc jockey Alan Freed; record 1: live; record 2: original '50s recordings	A&M 6500 [2]
7/10/82	35	7	▲ 9. Annie [M] Aileen Quinn (Annie)/Carol Burnett/Albert Finney/Tim Curry; mu: Charles Strouse; ly: Martin Charnin; cd: Ralph Burns	Columbia 38000
1/9/61	18	5	10. Apartment, The [I] Jack Lemmon/Shirley MacLaine/Fred MacMurray/Ray Walston; cp: Adolph Deutsch; cd: Mitchell Powell	United Art. 3105
			April Love — see BOONE, Pat Pat Boone/Shirley Jones	
4/13/57	1(10)	88	11. **Around The World In 80 Days** [I] David Niven/Cantinflas/Robert Newton/Shirley MacLaine; cp/cd: Victor Young; also see New World Theatre Orchestra version below	Decca 79046
10/21/57	8	4	12. **Around The World In 80 Days** [I] pf: New World Theatre Orchestra; not the original soundtrack (see version above)	Stereo-Fid. 2800
10/10/81	32	7	13. Arthur (The Album) [I+V] Dudley Moore/Liza Minnelli/John Gielgud; side 2: instrumentals; cp: Burt Bacharach *Arthur's Theme* (1-Christopher Cross)	Warner 3582
8/10/85	12	14	● 14. Back To The Future [V] Michael J. Fox/Christopher Lloyd/Lea Thompson/Crispin Glover *The Power Of Love* (1-Huey Lewis & The News)	MCA 6144
			Batman — see ELFMAN, Danny, and PRINCE Michael Keaton/Jack Nicholson/Kim Basinger/Robert Wuhl	
			Beach Party — see ANNETTE Annette Funicello/Frankie Avalon/Robert Cummings	
			Beaches — see MIDLER, Bette Bette Midler/Barbara Hershey/John Heard	
6/23/84	14	9	● 15. Beat Street, Volume 1 [V] Rae Dawn Chong/Guy Davis/John Chardiet	Atlantic 80154
12/14/91	19	24	▲² 16. Beauty and the Beast animated movie, voices by: Robby Benson/Jesse Corti/ Angela Lansbury/Paige O'Hara; cp: Alan Menken; ly: Howard Ashman (died 1991 [age 41]) *Beauty And The Beast* (9-Celine Dion & Peabo Bryson)	Disney 60618
4/25/60	6	48	17. **Ben-Hur** [I] Charlton Heston/Hugh Griffith; cp: Miklos Rozsa; cd: Carlo Savina; includes a full-color book about the movie	MGM 1
			Benny Goodman Story, The — see GOODMAN, Benny Steve Allen/Donna Reed/Herbert Anderson	
1/26/85	1(2)	36	▲² 18. **Beverly Hills Cop** [V] Eddie Murphy/Judge Reinhold/Lisa Eilbacher/John Ashton *Neutron Dance* (6-Pointer Sisters)/*The Heat Is On* (2-Glenn Frey)/*Axel F* (3-Harold Faltermeyer)	MCA 5547

DATE	POS	WKS	ARTIST—RECORD TITLE	LABEL & NO.
6/20/87	8	17	▲ **19. Beverly Hills Cop II** [V] Eddie Murphy/Judge Reinhold/Brigitte Nielsen/Ronny Cox *Shakedown* (1-Bob Seger)	MCA 6207
11/12/83	17	19	▲² 20. Big Chill, The [V-O] William Hurt/Glenn Close/Jobeth Williams/Jeff Goldblum/Kevin Kline	Motown 6062
8/10/91	28	5	21. Bill & Ted's Bogus Journey [V] Keanu Reeves/Alex Winter/William Sadler/Joss Ackland/George Carlin	Interscope 91725
2/2/63	33	6	22. Billy Rose's Jumbo [M] Doris Day/Stephen Boyd/Jimmy Durante/Martha Raye; mu: Richard Rodgers; ly: Lorenz Hart; cd: George Stoll	Columbia 2260
			Black Caesar — see BROWN, James Fred Williamson/Art Lund/Julius W. Harris/Gloria Hendry	
			Blue Hawaii — see PRESLEY, Elvis Elvis Presley (Chad Gates)/Joan Blackman/Angela Lansbury	
			Blues Brothers, The — see BLUES BROTHERS John Belushi/Dan Aykroyd/Carrie Fisher/Cab Calloway	
			Bodyguard, The — see HOUSTON, Whitney Whitney Houston/Kevin Costner/Gary Kemp/Bill Cobbs/Ralph Waite	
4/13/68	12	13	23. Bonnie And Clyde [I] Warren Beatty/Faye Dunaway/Gene Hackman/Estelle Parsons; cp: Charles Strouse; includes dialogue excerpts	Warner 1742
7/18/92	4	33	▲² **24. Boomerang** [V] Eddie Murphy/Halle Berry/Robin Givens/David Alan Grier *End Of The Road* (1-Boyz II Men)/*I'd Die Without You* (3-PM Dawn)	LaFace 26006
2/24/90	32	4	25. Born On The Fourth Of July [I+V] Tom Cruise/Kyra Sedgwick/Raymond J. Barry/Jerry Levine; side A: various artists; side B: instrumental; cp/cd: John Williams	MCA 6340
7/27/91	12	10	• 26. Boyz N The Hood [V] Ice Cube/Cuba Gooding, Jr./Morris Chestnut/Larry Fishburne	Qwest 26643
			Breakfast At Tiffany's — see MANCINI, Henry Audrey Hepburn/George Peppard/Patricia Neal	
3/30/85	17	13	• 27. Breakfast Club, The [V] Molly Ringwald/Anthony Michael Hall/Emilio Estevez/Judd Nelson *Don't You (Forget About Me)* (1-Simple Minds)	A&M 5045
6/16/84	8	14	▲ **28. Breakin'** [V] Lucinda Dickey/Adolfo Quinones/Michael Chambers *Breakin' ... There's No Stopping Us* (9-Ollie & Jerry)	Polydor 821919
1/10/70	16	26	• 29. Butch Cassidy And The Sundance Kid [I+V] Paul Newman/Robert Redford/Katharine Ross/Strother Martin; cp/cd: Burt Bacharach *Raindrops Keep Fallin' On My Head* (1-B.J. Thomas)	A&M 4227
5/11/63	2 (2)	41	**30. Bye Bye Birdie** [M] Ann-Margret/Jesse Pearson/Janet Leigh/Dick Van Dyke; mu: Charles Strouse; ly: Lee Adams; cd: Johnny Green; also see Original Cast ('60)	RCA 1081
5/12/73	25	9	• 31. Cabaret [M] Liza Minnelli/Michael York/Joel Grey; mu: John Kander; ly: Fred Ebb; also see Original Cast ('67)	ABC 752

DATE	POS	WKS	ARTIST—RECORD TITLE	LABEL & NO.
12/23/67	**11**	23	▲ 32. Camelot [M] Richard Harris/Vanessa Redgrave; mu: Frederick Loewe; ly: Alan Jay Lerner; cd: Alfred Newman; also see Original Cast ('61)/Living Strings/Percy Faith	Warner 1712
5/2/60	**3**	36	**33. Can-Can** [M] Frank Sinatra/Shirley MacLaine/Maurice Chevalier/Louis Jourdan; sw: Cole Porter; cd: Nelson Riddle	Capitol 1301
			Car Wash — see ROSE ROYCE Richard Pryor/Franklin Ajaye/Ivan Dixon/George Carlin	
2/25/56	**2**(1)	46	▲ **34. Carousel** [M] Gordon MacRae/Shirley Jones; mu: Richard Rodgers; ly: Oscar Hammerstein II; cd: Alfred Newman; also see Original Cast ('62-special version)	Capitol 694
6/10/67	**22**	9	35. Casino Royale [I] Peter Sellers/David Niven/Ursula Andress/Woody Allen; cp/cd: Burt Bacharach	Colgems 5005
			Charade — see MANCINI, Henry Cary Grant/Audrey Hepburn/Walter Matthau/James Coburn	
			Chariots Of Fire — see VANGELIS Ian Charleson/Ben Cross/Nigel Havers/Nick Farrell	
			Children Of Sanchez — see MANGIONE, Chuck Anthony Quinn/Dolores Del Rio/Katy Jurado	
			Clambake — see PRESLEY, Elvis Elvis Presley (Scott Heywood)/Shelley Fabares/Will Hutchins	
			Claudine — see KNIGHT, Gladys, & The Pips James Earl Jones/Diahann Carroll/Lawrence Hilton-Jacobs	
6/29/63	**2**(3)	14	**36. Cleopatra** [I] Elizabeth Taylor/Richard Burton/Rex Harrison; cp/cd: Alex North	20th Century 5008
4/8/72	**34**	5	37. Clockwork Orange, A [I] Malcolm McDowell/Patrick Magee; cp/cd: Walter Carlos	Warner 2573
1/21/78	**17**	8	● 38. Close Encounters Of The Third Kind [I] Richard Dreyfuss/Teri Garr; cp/cd: John Williams; includes bonus single of the theme song by John Williams	Arista 9500
5/17/80	**40**	1	● 39. Coal Miner's Daughter Sissy Spacek/Tommy Lee Jones/Beverly D'Angelo/Levon Helm; based on Loretta Lynn's life (Spacek plays Lynn); vocals performed by Spacek, D'Angelo and Helm	MCA 5107
9/3/88	**2**(1)	28	▲⁴ **40. Cocktail** [V] Tom Cruise/Bryan Brown/Elisabeth Shue *Don't Worry Be Happy* (1-Bobby McFerrin)/*Kokomo* (1-Beach Boys)	Elektra 60806
6/4/88	**31**	5	● 41. Colors [V] Sean Penn/Robert Duvall/Maria Conchita Alonso	Warner 25713
9/21/91	**8**	12	▲ **42. Commitments, The** Andrew Strong/Angeline Ball/Robert Arkins/Maria Doyle/ Bronagh Gallagher	MCA 10286
5/21/94	**1**(1)	13	▲ **43. Crow, The** [V] Brandon Lee/Ernie Hudson/Rochelle Davis/Michael Wincott	Atlantic/Int. 82519
12/1/58	**21**	1	44. Damn Yankees [M] Tab Hunter/Gwen Verdon/Ray Walston/Jean Stapleton; sw: Richard Adler and Jerry Ross; also see Original Cast ('55)	RCA 1047
7/28/90	**27**	7	● 45. Days Of Thunder [V] Tom Cruise/Robert Duvall/Randy Quaid/Nicole Kidman	DGC 24294

DATE	POS	WKS	ARTIST—RECORD TITLE	LABEL & NO.
1/22/55	**4**	16	**46. Deep In My Heart** **[M]** Jose Ferrer/Merle Oberon/Walter Pidgeon; cd: Adolph Deutsch; based on the life and melodies of composer Sigmund Romberg	MGM 3153
			Dick Tracy — see MADONNA ("I'm Breathless") Warren Beatty/Al Pacino/Madonna	
9/26/87	**1**(18)	68	▲¹¹ **47. Dirty Dancing** **[V]** Patrick Swayze/Jennifer Grey/Cynthia Rhodes/Jerry Orbach *(I've Had) The Time Of My Life* (1-Bill Medley & Jennifer Warnes)/*Hungry Eyes* (4-Eric Carmen)/*She's Like The Wind* (3-Patrick Swayze with Wendy Fraser)	RCA 6408
3/26/88	**3**	27	▲⁴ **48. Dirty Dancing, More** **[V-O]** 2nd volume released from the movie *Dirty Dancing*	RCA 6965
			Divine Madness — see MIDLER, Bette	
5/28/66	**1**(1)	115	● **49. Doctor Zhivago** **[I]** Omar Sharif/Julie Christie/Rod Steiger/Alec Guinness; cp/cd: Maurice Jarre	MGM 6
			Don't Knock The Twist — see CHECKER, Chubby Chubby Checker/Linda Scott	
			Doors, The — see DOORS, The Val Kilmer/Meg Ryan/Kevin Dillon/Kyle MacLachlan	
8/7/82	**37**	5	● **50. E.T. — The Extra-Terrestrial** **[I]** Henry Thomas/Peter Coyote/Dee Wallace/Drew Barrymore; cp/cd: John Williams	MCA 6109
10/18/69	**6**	41	● **51. Easy Rider** **[V]** Peter Fonda/Dennis Hopper/Jack Nicholson	Dunhill 50063
			Eddie And The Cruisers — see CAFFERTY, John Michael Pare/Tom Berenger/Ellen Barkin	
5/26/56	**1**(1)	99	**52. Eddy Duchin Story, The** **[S-I]** Tyrone Power/Kim Novak; pf: Carmen Cavallaro; biographical movie about the popular pianist/orchestra leader	Decca 8289
3/19/94	**33**	3	● **53. 8 Seconds** **[V]** Luke Perry/Stephen Baldwin/Cynthia Geary/Carrie Snodgress	MCA 10927
9/8/62	**35**	3	**54. El Cid** **[I]** Charlton Heston/Sophia Loren; cp/cd: Miklos Rozsa	MGM 3977
			Elvis-That's The Way It Is — see PRESLEY, Elvis	
5/17/80	**4**	17	● **55. Empire Strikes Back, The** **[I]** Mark Hamill/Harrison Ford/Carrie Fisher/Billy Dee Williams; cp/cd: John Williams; pf: London Symphony Orchestra	RSO 4201 [2]
8/15/81	**9**	14	● **56. Endless Love** **[I+V]** Brooke Shields/Martin Hewitt/Shirley Knight/Don Murray; cp: Jonathan Tunick/Lionel Richie *Endless Love* (1-Diana Ross & Lionel Richie)	Mercury 2001
1/16/61	**1**(14)	55	● **57. Exodus** **[I]** Paul Newman/Eva Marie Saint; cp/cd: Ernest Gold; pf: Sinfonia Of London Orchestra; also see The Hollywood Studio Orchestra	RCA 1058
			Experiment In Terror — see MANCINI, Henry Glenn Ford/Lee Remick/Stefanie Powers	
5/13/78	**5**	12	▲ **58. FM** **[V]** Michael Brandon/Eileen Brennan/Alex Karras/Martin Mull	MCA 12000 [2]
7/26/80	**7**	16	▲ **59. Fame** **[M]** Irene Cara/Eddie Barth/Maureen Teefy/Lee Curreri; inspired by the students of New York's High School of the Performing Arts *Fame* (4-Irene Cara)	RSO 3080

DATE	POS	WKS	ARTIST—RECORD TITLE	LABEL & NO.
			Ferry Cross The Mersey — see GERRY AND THE PACEMAKERS	
			Gerry and The Pacemakers/Cilla Black/Jimmy Saville	
1/1/72	**30**	4	● 60. Fiddler On The Roof [M]	United Art. 10900 [2]
			Topol/Norma Crane; mu: Jerry Bock; ly: Sheldon Harnick; cd: John Williams; also see Original Cast ('64)	
10/12/59	**22**	9	61. Five Pennies, The [M]	Dot 29500
			Danny Kaye/Louis Armstrong/Barbara Bel Geddes; based on the life of bandleader Loring "Red" Nichols	
			Flash Gordon — see QUEEN	
			Sam Jones/Max von Sydow/Melody Anderson/Topol	
5/7/83	**1**(2)	54	▲⁵ **62. Flashdance** [V]	Casablanca 811492
			Jennifer Beals/Michael Nouri/Marine Johan/Lilia Skala *Flashdance ... What A Feeling* (1-Irene Cara)/ *Maniac* (1-Michael Sembello)	
2/3/62	**15**	24	63. Flower Drum Song [M]	Decca 79098
			Nancy Kwan/James Shigeta/Miyoshi Umeki; mu: Richard Rodgers; ly: Oscar Hammerstein II; cd: Alfred Newman; also see Original Cast ('59)	
3/10/84	**1**(10)	27	▲⁸ **64. Footloose** [V]	Columbia 39242
			Kevin Bacon/Lori Singer/John Lithgow *Footloose* (1-Kenny Loggins)/ *Let's Hear It For The Boy* (1-Deniece Williams)/ *Almost Paradise* (7-Mike Reno & Ann Wilson)	
			For The Boys — see MIDLER, Bette	
			Bette Midler/James Caan/George Segal	
			For The First Time — see LANZA, Mario	
			Mario Lanza/Zsa Zsa Gabor	
7/23/94	**2**(5)	24	▲³ **65. Forrest Gump** [V]	Epic Sound. 66329 [2]
			Tom Hanks/Robin Wright/Gary Sinise/Mykelti Williamson/Sally Field	
			Frankie And Johnny — see PRESLEY, Elvis	
			Elvis Presley (Johnny)/Donna Douglas (Frankie)/Nancy Kovack	
			Friends — see JOHN, Elton	
			Sean Bury/Anicee Alvina	
7/25/64	**27**	6	66. From Russia with Love [I]	United Art. 5114
			Sean Connery/Daniela Bianchi/Lotte Lenya/Robert Shaw; cp/cd: John Barry	
			Fun in Acapulco — see PRESLEY, Elvis	
			Elvis Presley (Mike Windgren)/Ursula Andress/Elsa Cardenas	
			Funny Girl — see STREISAND, Barbra	
			Barbra Streisand/Omar Sharif	
			Funny Lady — see STREISAND, Barbra	
			Barbra Streisand/James Caan/Omar Sharif	
			G.I. Blues — see PRESLEY, Elvis	
			Elvis Presley (Tulsa McCauley)/Juliet Prowse/James Douglas	
9/8/90	**8**	13	▲ **67. Ghost** [I]	Varese S. 5276
			Patrick Swayze/Demi Moore/Whoopi Goldberg/Tony Goldwyn; cp/cd: Maurice Jarre	
7/14/84	**6**	17	▲ **68. Ghostbusters** [V]	Arista 8246
			Bill Murray/Dan Aykroyd/Sigourney Weaver/Harold Ramis *Ghostbusters* (1-Ray Parker, Jr.)	
7/8/89	**14**	10	● 69. Ghostbusters II [V]	MCA 6306
			Bill Murray/Dan Aykroyd/Sigourney Weaver/Harold Ramis *On Our Own* (2-Bobby Brown)	

DATE	POS	WKS	ARTIST—RECORD TITLE	LABEL & NO.
12/29/56	**16**	7	70. Giant [I] Elizabeth Taylor/Rock Hudson/James Dean/Jane Withers; cp/cd: Dimitri Tiomkin	Capitol 773
6/23/58	**1**(10)	78	● **71. Gigi** [M] Leslie Caron/Maurice Chevalier/Louis Jordan; ly: Alan Jay Lerner; mu: Frederick Loewe; cd: Andre Previn	MGM 3641
			Girl Happy — see PRESLEY, Elvis Elvis Presley (Rusty Wells)/Shelley Fabares/Gary Crosby	
			Girls! Girls! Girls! — see PRESLEY, Elvis Elvis Presley (Ross Carpenter)/Stella Stevens/Laurel Goodwin	
			Give my regards to Broad Street — see McCARTNEY, Paul Paul McCartney/Bryan Brown/Ringo Starr	
4/29/72	**21**	14	72. Godfather, The [I] Marlon Brando/Al Pacino/James Caan/Robert Duvall; cp: Nino Rota; cd: Carlo Savina	Paramount 1003
2/6/65	**1**(3)	36	**73. Goldfinger** [I] Sean Connery/Gert Frobe/Honor Blackman/Harold Sakata; cp/cd: John Barry *Goldfinger* (8-Shirley Bassey)	United Art. 5117
12/23/67	**24**	9	74. Gone With The Wind [I] Clark Gable/Vivien Leigh/Leslie Howard/Olivia de Havilland; taken directly from the movie soundtrack (premiered in 1939); cp/cd: Max Steiner	MGM 10
2/20/88	**10**	14	▲ **75. Good Morning, Vietnam** [V-O] Robin Williams/Forest Whitaker/Tung Thanh Tran/Bruno Kirby	A&M 3913
3/16/68	**4**	21	● **76. Good, The Bad And The Ugly, The** [I] Clint Eastwood/Lee Van Cleef; cp/cd: Ennio Morricone; also see Hugo Montenegro	United Art. 5172
			Graduate, The — see SIMON & GARFUNKEL Dustin Hoffman/Anne Bancroft/Katharine Ross	
			Graffiti Bridge — see PRINCE Prince/Morris Day/Ingrid Chavez/Jerome Benton	
5/27/78	**1**(12)	39	▲⁸ **77. Grease** [M] John Travolta/Olivia Newton-John/Stockard Channing/Jeff Conaway *You're The One That I Want* (1-John Travolta & Olivia Newton- John)/*Summer Nights* (5-John Travolta & Olivia Newton-John)/ *Hopelessly Devoted To You* (3-Olivia Newton-John)/ *Grease* (1-Frankie Valli)	RSO 4002 [2]
1/26/63	**10**	13	**78. Gypsy** [M] Rosalind Russell/Natalie Wood/Karl Malden; mu: Jule Styne; ly: Stephen Sondheim; also see Original Cast ('59)	Warner 1480
			Hard Day's Night, A — see BEATLES The Beatles/Wilfrid Brambell	
			Hard To Hold — see SPRINGFIELD, Rick Rick Springfield/Janet Eilber/Patti Hansen/Bill Mumy	
			Harum Scarum — see PRESLEY, Elvis Elvis Presley (Johnny Tyronne)/Mary Ann Mobley/Fran Jeffries	
			Hatari! — see MANCINI, Henry John Wayne/Red Buttons/Hardy Kruger	
			Having A Wild Weekend — see CLARK, Dave, Five The Dave Clark Five/Barbara Ferris	

DATE	POS	WKS	ARTIST—RECORD TITLE	LABEL & NO.
8/29/81	12	13	● 79. Heavy Metal [V] animated movie, voices by: John Candy/Joe Flaherty/Harold Ramis	Asylum 90004 [2]
2/3/58	25	1	80. Helen Morgan Story, The Ann Blyth/Paul Newman; vocals performed by Gogi Grant; cd: Ray Heindorf	RCA 1030
			Help! — see BEATLES The Beatles/Leo McKern/Eleanor Bron	
			Hey Boy! Hey Girl! — see PRIMA, Louis, & SMITH, Keely Louis Prima/Keely Smith/James Gregory	
			Hey, Let's Twist! — see DEE, Joey Joey Dee & The Starliters/Teddy Randazzo/Jo Ann Campbell	
8/25/56	5	28	81. High Society [M] Bing Crosby/Grace Kelly/Frank Sinatra; adapted from the play *The Philadelphia Story*; sw: Cole Porter *True Love* (3-Bing Crosby & Grace Kelly)	Capitol 750
			Hold On! — see HERMAN'S HERMITS Peter Noone/Shelley Fabares/Sue Ane Langdon	
9/12/92	18	6	● 82. Honeymoon In Vegas [V] James Caan/Nicolas Cage/Sarah Jessica Parker/Pat Morita	Epic Sound. 52845
			Honeysuckle Rose — see NELSON, Willie Willie Nelson/Dyan Cannon/Amy Irving/Slim Pickens	
4/20/63	4	34	● 83. How The West Was Won Gregory Peck/Henry Fonda/James Stewart/Debbie Reynolds; cd: Alfred Newman	MGM 5
			I Want To Live! — see MULLIGAN, Gerry Susan Hayward/Simon Oakland/Theodore Bikel	
			Imagine: John Lennon — see LENNON, John	
			It Happened At The World's Fair — see PRESLEY, Elvis Elvis Presley (Mike Edwards)/Joan O'Brien/Gary Lockwood	
10/15/94	17	10	▲ 84. Jason's Lyric [V] Forest Whitaker/Allen Payne/Jada Pinkett/BoKeem Woodbine	Mercury 522915
8/30/75	30	4	85. Jaws [I] Roy Scheider/Richard Dreyfuss/Robert Shaw; cp/cd: John Williams	MCA 2087
			Jazz Singer, The — see DIAMOND, Neil Neil Diamond/Laurence Olivier/Lucie Arnaz	
8/11/73	21	8	● 86. Jesus Christ Superstar [M] Ted Neeley/Yvonne Elliman/Carl Anderson/Barry Dennen; mu: Andrew Lloyd Webber; ly: Tim Rice; also see Rock Opera ('70)/Original Cast ('72)	MCA 11000 [2]
			Jonathan Livingston Seagull — see DIAMOND, Neil, and HARRIS, Richard James Franciscus/Juliet Mills	
10/2/93	17	8	● 87. Judgment Night [V] Emilio Estevez/Cuba Gooding Jr./Denis Leary/Stephen Dorff; CD includes bonus track	Immortal 57144
2/1/92	17	9	● 88. Juice [V] Omar Epps/Jermaine Hopkins/Khalil Kain/Tupac Shakur	MCA 10462

DATE	POS	WKS	ARTIST—RECORD TITLE	LABEL & NO.
3/9/68	**19**	11	89. Jungle Book, The animated movie, voices by: Phil Harris/Sebastian Cabot/ Louis Prima; based on Rudyard Kipling's *Mowgli* stories; sw: Richard M. Sherman and Robert B. Sherman	Disneyland 3948
			Jungle Fever — see WONDER, Stevie Wesley Snipes/Annabella Sciorra/Spike Lee/Ossie Davis	
7/3/93	**36**	3	● 90. Jurassic Park [I] Sam Neill/Laura Dern/Jeff Goldblum/Richard Attenborough; cp/cd: John Williams	MCA 10859
8/2/86	**30**	9	91. Karate Kid Part II, The [V] Ralph Macchio/Noriyuki "Pat" Morita/Martin Kove *Glory Of Love* (1-Peter Cetera)	United Art. 40414
			Kids Are Alright, The — see WHO, The	
7/21/56	**1**(1)	178	● 92. King And I, The [M] Yul Brynner/Deborah Kerr; mu: Richard Rodgers; ly: Oscar Hammerstein II; cd: Alfred Newman	Capitol 740
			King Creole — see PRESLEY, Elvis Elvis Presley (Danny Fisher)/Carolyn Jones/Walter Matthau	
11/6/61	**10**	24	93. King Of Kings [I] Jeffrey Hunter/Sibohan McKenna/Rip Torn; cp/cd: Miklos Rozsa; includes a full-color book about the movie	MGM 2
			Kissin' Cousins — see PRESLEY, Elvis Elvis Presley (Josh Morgan/Jodie Tatum)/Arthur O'Connell	
			La Bamba — see LOS LOBOS Lou Diamond Phillips/Esai Morales/Rosana DeSoto/Elizabeth Pena	
			Lady Sings The Blues — see ROSS, Diana Diana Ross/Billy Dee Williams/Richard Pryor	
6/26/93	**7**	14	▲ 94. Last Action Hero [V] Arnold Schwarzenegger/Austin O'Brien/F. Murray Abraham/Art Carney	Columbia 57127
			Last Waltz, The — see BAND, The	
3/23/63	**2**(2)	40	95. Lawrence Of Arabia [I] Peter O'Toole/Alec Guinness/Anthony Quinn; cp/cd: Maurice Jarre; pf: London Philharmonic Orchestra	Colpix 514
1/9/88	**31**	5	● 96. Less Than Zero [V] Robert Downey, Jr./Andrew McCarthy/Jami Gertz *Hazy Shade Of Winter* (2-Bangles)	Columbia 44042
			Let It Be — see BEATLES, The	
			Let's Do It Again — see STAPLE SINGERS, The Sidney Poitier/Bill Cosby/Jimmie Walker/John Amos	
6/18/94	**1**(9)	37 +	▲⁷ 97. Lion King, The [V] animated movie, voices by: Jonathan Taylor Thomas/Jeremy Irons/Matthew Broderick/James Earl Jones; mu: Elton John; ly: Tim Rice *Can You Feel The Love Tonight* (4-Elton John)	Walt Disney 60858
2/3/90	**32**	6	▲² 98. Little Mermaid, The animated movie, voices by: Jodi Benson/Pat Carroll/Samuel E. Wright; mu: Alan Menken; ly: Howard Ashman (died 1991 [age 41]); orchestration: Thomas Pasatieri; not available on vinyl	Disney 018
8/11/73	**17**	7	99. Live And Let Die [I] Roger Moore/Jane Seymour/Yaphet Kotto; cp/cd: George Martin *Live And Let Die* (2-Wings)	United Art. 100

DATE	POS	WKS	ARTIST—RECORD TITLE	LABEL & NO.
2/3/79	**39**	2	100. Lord Of The Rings, The [I] animated movie, voices by: Christopher Guard/William Squire/ John Hurt; based on the novels of J.R.R. Tolkien; cp/cd: Leonard Rosenman	Fantasy 1 [2]
8/29/87	**15**	9	● 101. Lost Boys, The [V] Kiefer Sutherland/Dianne Wiest/Jami Gertz/Jason Patric	Atlantic 81767
			Love Me Or Leave Me — see DAY, Doris Doris Day/James Cagney/Cameron Mitchell	
			Love Me Tender — see PRESLEY, Elvis Elvis Presley (Clint)/Richard Egan/Debra Paget	
1/23/71	**2**(6)	22	● 102. **Love Story** [I] Ali MacGraw/Ryan O'Neal/Ray Milland/John Marley; cp/cd: Francis Lai	Paramount 6002
			Loving You — see PRESLEY, Elvis Elvis Presley (Deke Rivers)/Lizabeth Scott/Dolores Hart	
			Mad Dogs & Englishmen — see COCKER, Joe	
9/21/85	**39**	2	103. Mad Max Beyond Thunderdome Mel Gibson/Tina Turner; cp/cd: Maurice Jarre *We Don't Need Another Hero (Thunderdome)* (2-Tina Turner)	Capitol 12429
			Magical Mystery Tour — see BEATLES, The	
12/13/75	**19**	10	104. Mahogany [I] Diana Ross/Billy Dee Williams/Anthony Perkins; cp/cd: Lee Holdridge *Theme From Mahogany (Do You Know Where You're Going To)* (1-Diana Ross)	Motown 858
			Main Event, The — see STREISAND, Barbra Barbra Streisand/Ryan O'Neal/Paul Sand/Whitman Mayo	
1/28/67	**10**	44	● 105. **Man And A Woman, A** [F] Jean-Louis Trintignant/Anouk Aimee; cp: Francis Lai	United Art. 5147
3/24/56	**2**(4)	17	106. **Man With The Golden Arm, The** [I] Frank Sinatra/Eleanor Parker/Kim Novak; cp/cd: Elmer Bernstein	Decca 78257
12/5/64	**1**(14)	78	● 107. **Mary Poppins** [M] Julie Andrews/Dick Van Dyke/David Tomlinson/Glynis Johns; sw: Richard M. Sherman and Robert B. Sherman; cd: Irwin Kostal	Buena Vista 4026
6/11/94	**35**	4	● 108. Maverick [V] Mel Gibson/Jodie Foster/James Garner/Graham Greene	Atlantic 82595
			Maximum Overdrive — see AC/DC Emilio Estevez/Pat Hingle/Laura Harrington/Yeardley Smith	
			McVicar — see DALTREY, Roger Roger Daltrey/Adam Faith/Cheryl Campbell	
6/12/93	**11**	14	▲ 109. Menace II Society [V] Tyrin Turner/Jada Pinkett/Bill Duke/Charles S. Dutton	Jive 41509
9/20/69	**19**	19	● 110. Midnight Cowboy [I+V] Dustin Hoffman/Jon Voight/Sylvia Miles; mu: John Barry *Everybody's Talkin'* (6-Nilsson)	United Art. 5198
7/18/92	**6**	11	▲ 111. **Mo' Money** [V] Damon Wayans/Marlon Wayans/Stacey Dash/Joe Santos/John Diehl *The Best Things In Life Are Free* (10-Luther Vandross & Janet Jackson)	Perspective 1004
7/27/63	**15**	13	112. Mondo Cane [I] documentary depicting various cultures around the world; cp/cd: Riz Ortolani and Nino Oliviero	United Art. 5105

DATE	POS	WKS	ARTIST—RECORD TITLE	LABEL & NO.
			Monterey Pop — see REDDING, Otis, and/or HENDRIX, Jimi	
			Muppet Movie, The — see CHILDREN'S ALBUMS	
			Jim Henson/Frank Oz	
11/5/94	**1**(2)	16	▲ **113. Murder Was The Case** **[V]**	Death Row 92484
			Snoop Doggy Dogg/Charlie Murphy/C Style/Freeze Luv; Dr. Dre directed this short-form movie that was based on lyrics of same title by Snoop Doggy Dogg	
8/11/62	**2**(6)	35	● **114. Music Man, The** **[M]**	Warner 1459
			Robert Preston/Shirley Jones/Buddy Hackett; cp: Meredith Willson; cd: Ray Heindorf; also see Original Cast ('58)	
1/5/63	**14**	11	115. Mutiny On The Bounty **[I]**	MGM 4
			Marlon Brando/Trevor Howard/Richard Harris; cp: Bronislau Kaper; cd: Robert Armbruster; includes a full-color souvenir book	
10/31/64	**4**	77	● **116. My Fair Lady** **[M]**	Columbia 2600
			Audrey Hepburn/Rex Harrison/Stanley Holloway; mu: Frederick Loewe; ly: Alan Jay Lerner; cd: Andre Previn; also see Percy Faith/Sammy Kaye/Andy Williams/ Original Cast ('56)	
9/17/94	**19**	6	● 117. Natural Born Killers **[V]**	Nothing/Int. 92460
			Woody Harrelson/Juliette Lewis/Robert Downey Jr./Tommy Lee Jones; produced by Trent Reznor (Nine Inch Nails)	
1/30/61	**2**(5)	53	**118. Never On Sunday** **[I]**	United Art. 5070
			Melina Mercouri/Jules Dassin; cp/cd: Manos Hadjidakis	
4/6/91	**2**(1)	19	▲ **119. New Jack City** **[V]**	Giant 24409
			Wesley Snipes/Ice-T/Chris Rock/Mario Van Peebles/Judd Nelson; CD includes bonus cut *I Wanna Sex You Up* (2-Color Me Badd)	
			Nighthawks — see EMERSON, Keith	
			Sylvester Stallone/Rutger Hauer/Billy Dee Williams	
12/4/82	**38**	3	120. Officer And A Gentleman, An **[V]**	Island 90017
			Richard Gere/Debra Winger/David Keith/Louis Gossett, Jr. *Up Where We Belong* (1-Joe Cocker & Jennifer Warnes)	
9/17/55	**1**(4)	229	▲² **121. Oklahoma!** **[M]**	Capitol 595
			Gordon MacRae/Shirley Jones; mu: Richard Rodgers; ly: Oscar Hammerstein II; cd: Jay Blackton	
5/10/69	**20**	8	● **122. Oliver!** **[M]**	Colgems 5501
			Mark Lester (Oliver)/Ron Moody/Jack Wild/Oliver Reed sw: Lionel Bart; cd: John Green; also see Original Cast ('62)	
			One-Trick Pony — see SIMON, Paul	
			Paul Simon/Blair Brown/Rip Torn	
4/26/86	**38**	2	● **123. Out Of Africa** **[I]**	MCA 6158
			Meryl Streep/Robert Redford/Klaus Maria Brandauer; cp/cd: John Barry	
12/6/69	**28**	4	● **124. Paint Your Wagon** **[M]**	Paramount 1001
			Lee Marvin/Clint Eastwood/Jean Seberg; mu: Frederick Loewe; ly: Alan Jay Lerner; cd: Nelson Riddle	
9/23/57	**9**	14	**125. Pajama Game, The** **[M]**	Columbia 5210
			Doris Day/John Raitt; sw: Richard Adler and Jerry Ross; cd: Ray Heindorf	
			Pal Joey — see SINATRA, Frank	
			Frank Sinatra/Rita Hayworth/Kim Novak	
			Paradise, Hawaiian Style — see PRESLEY, Elvis	
			Elvis Presley (Rick Richards)/Suzanne Leigh/James Shigeta	

DATE	POS	WKS	ARTIST—RECORD TITLE		LABEL & NO.
			Pat Garrett & Billy The Kid — see DYLAN, Bob		
			James Coburn/Kris Kristofferson/Jason Robards		
1/29/94	**12**	16	▲ 126. Philadelphia	[V]	Epic Sound. 57624
			Tom Hanks/Denzel Washington/Jason Robards/Mary Steenburgen		
			Streets Of Philadelphia (9-Bruce Springsteen)		
5/5/56	**6**	18	**127. Picnic**	**[I]**	Decca 78320
			William Holden/Kim Novak/Rosalind Russell; cp: George Duning; cd: Morris Stoloff		
			Moonglow and Theme From Picnic (1-Morris Stoloff)		
			Pink Panther, The — see MANCINI, Henry		
			Peter Sellers/David Niven/Robert Wagner/Capucine		
7/31/93	**23**	5	● 128. Poetic Justice	[V]	Epic Sound. 57131
			Janet Jackson/Tupac Shakur/Tyra Ferrell/Regina King/Joe Torry; CD includes 2 bonus tracks		
8/3/59	**8**	47	● **129. Porgy and Bess**	**[M]**	Columbia 2016
			Sidney Poitier/Dorothy Dandridge; mu: George Gershwin; ly: DuBose Heyward and Ira Gershwin; cd: Andre Previn; also see Harry Belafonte/Percy Faith/Lena Horne		
3/22/86	**5**	17	● **130. Pretty In Pink**	**[V]**	A&M 3901
			Molly Ringwald/Jon Cryer/Andrew McCarthy/Harry Dean Stanton		
			If You Leave (4-Orchestral Manoeuvres In The Dark)		
4/21/90	**4**	43	▲³ **131. Pretty Woman**	**[V]**	EMI 93492
			Richard Gere/Julia Roberts/Ralph Bellamy/Jason Alexander		
			It Must Have Been Love (1-Roxette)/ *King Of Wishful Thinking* (8-Go West)		
11/5/94	**21**	15+	▲ 132. Pulp Fiction	[V]	MCA 11103
			John Travolta/Samuel L. Jackson/Uma Thurman/Bruce Willis		
			Purple Rain — see PRINCE		
			Prince/Apollonia Kotero/Morris Day		
			Pure Country — see STRAIT, George		
			George Strait/Lesley Ann Warren/Isabel Glasser		
4/15/89	**31**	5	133. Rain Man	[V]	Capitol 91866
			Dustin Hoffman/Tom Cruise/Valeria Golino		
			Rainbow Bridge — see HENDRIX, Jimi		
			Rattle And Hum — see U2		
3/12/94	**13**	31	134. Reality Bites	[V]	RCA 66364
			Winona Ryder/Ethan Hawke/Ben Stiller/Janeane Garofalo		
			Baby, I Love Your Way (6-Big Mountain)/ *Stay (I Missed You)* (1-Lisa Loeb & Nine Stories)		
6/18/83	**20**	6	135. Return Of The Jedi	[I]	RSO 811767
			Mark Hamill/Harrison Ford/Carrie Fisher/Billy Dee Williams; cp/cd: John Williams; pf: London Symphony Orchestra		
			Richard Pryor Live On The Sunset Strip — see PRYOR, Richard		
7/20/91	**5**	13	▲ **136. Robin Hood: Prince Of Thieves**	**[I]**	Morgan Cr. 20004
			Kevin Costner/Morgan Freeman/Christian Slater/Alan Rickman; cp/cd: Michael Kamen		
			(Everything I Do) I Do It For You (1-Bryan Adams)		
3/9/57	**16**	9	137. Rock, Pretty Baby		Decca 8429
			Sal Mineo/John Saxon/Luana Patten; cp: Henry Mancini; pf: Jimmy Daley & The Ding-A-Lings		

DATE	POS	WKS	ARTIST—RECORD TITLE	LABEL & NO.
4/23/77	**4**	14	▲ **138. Rocky** **[I]** Sylvester Stallone/Talia Shire/Carl Weathers/Burgess Meredith; cp/cd: Bill Conti *Gonna Fly Now* (1-Bill Conti)	United Art. 693
7/24/82	**15**	10	● 139. Rocky III **[I+V]** Sylvester Stallone/Talia Shire/Mr. T/Burt Young; cp/cd: Bill Conti *Eye Of The Tiger* (1-Survivor)	Liberty 51130
12/28/85	**10**	16	▲ **140. Rocky IV** **[V]** Sylvester Stallone/Talia Shire/Dolph Lundgren/Burt Young *Burning Heart* (2-Survivor)/*Living In America* (4-James Brown)	Scotti Br. 40203
6/30/62	**5**	20	**141. Rome Adventure** **[I]** Troy Donahue/Suzanne Pleshette/Angie Dickinson; cp: Max Steiner; side 2: *Neapolitan Favorites* by The Cafe Milano Orchestra *Al Di La* (6-Emilio Pericoli)	Warner 1458
5/3/69	**2**(2)	31	▲ **142. Romeo & Juliet** Leonard Whiting/Olivia Hussey; cp/cd: Nino Rota; includes dialogue highlights	Capitol 2993
			Rose, The — see MIDLER, Bette Bette Midler/Alan Bates/Frederic Forrest	
			Roustabout — see PRESLEY, Elvis Elvis Presley (Charlie Rogers)/Barbara Stanwyck/Joan Freeman	
			Rush — see CLAPTON, Eric Jason Patric/Jennifer Jason Leigh/Sam Elliott/Max Perlich	
7/19/86	**20**	9	● 143. Ruthless People **[V]** Danny DeVito/Bette Midler/Judge Reinhold/Helen Slater *Modern Woman* (10-Billy Joel)	Epic 40398
			Saint — see St.	
			Saturday Night Fever — see BEE GEES John Travolta/Karen Gorney/Donna Pescow	
			Serenade — see LANZA, Mario Mario Lanza/Joan Fontaine/Vincent Price/Vincent Edwards	
			Seven Hills Of Rome — see LANZA, Mario Mario Lanza/Renato Roscel/Marisa Allasio	
8/12/78	**5**	12	▲ **144. Sgt. Pepper's Lonely Hearts Club Band** **[M]** Peter Frampton/Bee Gees/George Burns/Steve Martin; sw: John Lennon and Paul McCartney; movie inspired by The Beatles *Sgt. Pepper's ...* album *Got To Get You Into My Life* (9-Earth, Wind & Fire)	RSO 4100 [2]
			Shaft — see HAYES, Isaac Richard Roundtree/Moses Gunn/Gwenn Mitchell	
			Sing Boy Sing — see SANDS, Tommy Tommy Sands/Lili Gentle/Edmond O'Brien	
			Singing Nun, The — see REYNOLDS, Debbie Debbie Reynolds/Ricardo Montalban/Greer Garson	
8/22/92	**6**	13	▲ **145. Singles** **[V]** Matt Dillon/Bridget Fonda/Campbell Scott/Kyra Sedgwick	Epic 52476
7/18/92	**40**	2	● 146. Sister Act **[I+V]** Whoopi Goldberg/Maggie Smith/Harvey Keitel; cp/cd: Marc Shaiman	Hollywood 61334
7/17/93	**1**(1)	34	▲³ **147. Sleepless In Seattle** **[V]** Tom Hanks/Meg Ryan/Rosie O'Donnell	Epic Sound. 53764
6/19/93	**23**	8	● 148. Sliver **[V]** Sharon Stone/William Baldwin/Tom Berenger/Martin Landau	Virgin 88064

DATE	POS	WKS	ARTIST—RECORD TITLE	LABEL & NO.
			Song Remains The Same, The — see LED ZEPPELIN	
4/10/65	**1**(2)	161	● **149. Sound Of Music, The** [M]	RCA 2005
			Julie Andrews/Christopher Plummer; story of Maria Von Trapp's family; mu: Richard Rodgers; ly: Oscar Hammerstein II; cd: Irwin Kostal; also see Original Cast ('59)	
3/31/58	**1**(31)	161	● **150. South Pacific** [M]	RCA 1032
			Rossano Brazzi/Mitzi Gaynor/John Kerr; mu: Richard Rodgers; ly: Oscar Hammerstein II; cd: Alfred Newman	
			Sparkle — see FRANKLIN, Aretha	
			Irene Cara/Philip Thomas/Lonette McKee	
			Spinout — see PRESLEY, Elvis	
			Elvis Presley (Mike McCoy)/Shelley Fabares/Diane McBain	
11/5/77	40	2	151. Spy Who Loved Me, The [I]	United Art. 774
			Roger Moore/Barbara Bach/Richard Kiel; cp/cd: Marvin Hamlisch	
			Nobody Does It Better (2-Carly Simon)	
8/10/85	21	11	● 152. St. Elmo's Fire [V]	Atlantic 81261
			Emilio Estevez/Rob Lowe/Andrew McCarthy/Demi Moore/Judd Nelson	
			St. Elmo's Fire (Man In Motion) (1-John Parr)	
			St. Louis Blues — see COLE, Nat "King"	
			Nat "King" Cole/Eartha Kitt/Pearl Bailey/Cab Calloway	
11/22/86	31	11	● 153. Stand By Me [V-O]	Atlantic 81677
			Wil Wheaton/River Phoenix/Corey Feldman/Jerry O'Connell	
			Stand By Me (9-Ben E. King)	
			Star Is Born, A — see STREISAND, Barbra	
			Barbra Streisand/Kris Kristofferson	
7/2/77	▲ **2**(3)	22	▲ **154. Star Wars** [I]	20th Century 541 [2]
			Mark Hamill/Harrison Ford/Carrie Fisher/Alec Guinness; cp/cd: John Williams; pf: London Symphony Orchestra;	
			Star Wars (Main Title) (10); also see Meco	
1/21/78	36	2	● 155. Star Wars, The Story Of	20th Century 550
			storyline excerpts from the movie; narrator: Roscoe Lee Browne	
5/19/62	12	15	156. State Fair [M]	Dot 29011
			Pat Boone/Ann-Margret/Bobby Darin; mu: Richard Rodgers; ly: Oscar Hammerstein II; cd: Alfred Newman	
			Staying Alive — see BEE GEES	
			John Travolta/Cynthia Rhodes	
7/14/84	32	6	157. Streets Of Fire [V]	MCA 5492
			Michael Pare/Diane Lane/Rick Moranis/Amy Madigan	
			I Can Dream About You (6-Dan Hartman)	
			Superfly — see MAYFIELD, Curtis	
			Ron O'Neal/Carl Lee/Julius Harris	
			Sweet Dreams — see CLINE, Patsy	
			Jessica Lange/Ed Harris/Ann Wedgeworth	
11/24/84	34	4	● 158. Teachers [V]	Capitol 12371
			Nick Nolte/JoBeth Williams/Judd Hirsch/Ralph Macchio	
5/5/90	13	11	▲ 159. Teenage Mutant Ninja Turtles [V]	SBK 91066
			Judith Hoag/Elias Koteas	
5/4/91	30	5	● 160. Teenage Mutant Ninja Turtles II — The Secret Of The Ooze [V]	SBK 96204
			Paige Turco/David Warner; above 2 movies are based on the live action/animatronics characters created by Kevin Eastman and Peter Laird	

DATE	POS	WKS	ARTIST—RECORD TITLE	LABEL & NO.
5/20/78	10	15	▲ 161. Thank God It's Friday [V] Jeff Goldblum/Valerie Landsburg/Debra Winger; includes bonus 12" single *Last Dance* (3-Donna Summer)	Casablanca 7099 [2]
			That's The Way Of The World — see EARTH, WIND & FIRE Harvey Keitel/Ed Nelson/Cynthia Bostwick/Bert Parks	
1/22/55	6	8	162. There's No Business Like Show Business [M] Ethel Merman/Donald O'Connor/Dan Dailey; sw: Irving Berlin	Decca 8091
5/13/67	16	12	● 163. Thoroughly Modern Millie [M] Julie Andrews/Mary Tyler Moore/Carol Channing; cd: Andre Previn	Decca 71500
1/22/66	10	13	164. Thunderball [I] Sean Connery/Claudine Auger/Adolfo Celi; cp/cd: John Barry	United Art. 5132
11/15/80	37	4	165. Times Square [V] Tim Curry/Trini Alvarado/Robin Johnson	RSO 4203 [2]
11/11/67	16	11	166. To Sir, With Love [I+V] Sidney Poitier/Judy Geeson/Christian Roberts/Lulu; cp/cd: Ron Grainer *To Sir With Love* (1-Lulu)	Fontana 67569
5/30/64	38	3	167. Tom Jones [I] Albert Finney/Susannah York/Hugh Griffith; cp/cd: John Addison	United Art. 5113
4/12/75	2(1)	19	● 168. Tommy [M] Roger Daltrey/Ann-Margret/Oliver Reed/Elton John; rock opera; all but 4 songs written by Pete Townshend; also see The Who and Rock Opera ('72)	Polydor 9502 [2]
6/14/86	1(5)	33	▲⁷ 169. Top Gun [V] Tom Cruise/Kelly McGillis/Val Kilmer/Anthony Edwards *Danger Zone* (2-Kenny Loggins)/*Take My Breath Away* (1- Berlin)	Columbia 40323
			Trouble Man — see GAYE, Marvin Robert Hooks/Paul Winfield/Ralph Waite/Paula Kelly	
12/24/83	26	8	▲ 170. Two Of A Kind [V] John Travolta/Olivia Newton-John/Charles Durning/Scatman Crothers *Twist Of Fate* (5-Olivia Newton-John)	MCA 6127
10/5/68	24	11	● 171. 2001: A Space Odyssey [I] Gary Lockwood/Keir Dullea; features classical music by various orchestras	MGM 13
			Under The Cherry Moon — see PRINCE Prince/Jerome Benton/Kristin Scott Thomas/Steven Berkoff	
8/15/64	11	16	172. Unsinkable Molly Brown, The [M] Debbie Reynolds/Harve Presnell; sw: Meredith Willson; cd: Robert Armbruster; also see Original Cast ('60)	MGM 4232
6/7/80	3	23	▲ 173. Urban Cowboy [V] John Travolta/Debra Winger/Scott Glenn/Madolyn Smith *Lookin' For Love* (5-Johnny Lee)	Asylum 90002 [2]
2/24/68	11	9	174. Valley Of The Dolls Barbara Parkins/Patty Duke/Sharon Tate/Susan Hayward; sw: Dory & Andre Previn; cd: Johnny Williams	20th Century 4196
7/13/85	38	4	175. View To A Kill, A [I] Roger Moore/Tanya Roberts/Christopher Walken/Grace Jones; cp/cd: John Barry *A View To A Kill* (1-Duran Duran)	Capitol 12413

DATE	POS	WKS	ARTIST—RECORD TITLE	LABEL & NO.
3/23/85	**11**	12	▲ 176. Vision Quest **[V]** Matthew Modine/Linda Fiorentino/Michael Schoeffling *Only The Young* (9-Journey)/*Crazy For You* (1-Madonna)	Geffen 24063
9/8/62	**33**	2	177. Walk On The Wild Side **[I]** Laurence Harvey/Jane Fonda/Capucine; cp/cd: Elmer Bernstein	Ava 4
			Wattstax — see CONCERTS/FESTIVALS	
3/2/74	**20**	5	● 178. Way We Were, The **[I]** Barbra Streisand/Robert Redford/Bradford Dillman; cp: Marvin Hamlisch	Columbia 32830
3/7/92	**1**(2)	16	▲ **179. Wayne's World** **[V]** Mike Myers/Dana Carvey/Rob Lowe/Tia Carrere *Bohemian Rhapsody* (2-Queen)	Reprise 26805
11/20/61	**1**(54)	144	▲³ **180. West Side Story** **[M]** Natalie Wood/Richard Beymer/Rita Moreno/George Chakiris; mu: Leonard Bernstein; ly: Stephen Sondheim; cd: Johnny Green; also see Ferrante & Teicher/Stan Kenton/Original Cast ('58)	Columbia 2070
			What's Love Got To Do With It — see TURNER, Tina Angela Bassett/Laurence Fishburne	
8/21/65	**14**	10	181. What's New Pussycat? **[I+V]** Peter Sellers/Peter O'Toole; mu: Burt Bacharach; ly: Hal David *What's New Pussycat?* (3-Tom Jones)	United Art. 5117
12/7/85	**17**	12	● 182. White Nights **[V]** Mikhail Baryshnikov/Gregory Hines/Geraldine Page/Helen Mirren *Separate Lives* (1-Phil Collins & Marilyn Martin)	Atlantic 81273
			Who's That Girl — see MADONNA Madonna/Griffin Dunne/Haviland Morris/John McMartin/Sir John Mills	
5/8/93	**32**	2	183. Who's The Man? **[V]** Doctor Dre/Ed Lover	Uptown 10794
			Wild Angels, The — see ALLAN, Davie Peter Fonda/Nancy Sinatra/Bruce Dern/Dianne Ladd; cp/cd: Mike Curb	
9/21/68	**12**	12	184. Wild In The Streets Christopher Jones/Diana Varsi/Shelley Winters/Richard Pryor; sw: Barry Mann/Cynthia Weil; cd: Mike Curb	Tower 5099
11/25/78	**40**	1	● 185. Wiz, The **[M]** Diana Ross/Michael Jackson; sw: Charlie Smalls; cd: Quincy Jones; a soul musical version of *The Wizard of Oz*	MCA 14000 [2]
			Woman in Red, The — see WONDER, Stevie Gene Wilder/Charles Grodin/Judith Ivey/Gilda Radner	
			Woodstock — see CONCERTS/FESTIVALS	
			Xanadu — see NEWTON-JOHN, Olivia, and/or ELECTRIC LIGHT ORCHESTRA Olivia Newton-John/Michael Beck/Gene Kelly	
			Yellow Submarine — see BEATLES, The	
			Yentl — see STREISAND, Barbra Barbra Streisand/Mandy Patinkin/Amy Irving	
11/5/77	**17**	5	● 186. You Light Up My Life Didi Conn/Joe Silver/Melanie Mayron; cp/cd: Joseph Brooks	Arista 4159
8/19/67	**27**	6	187. You Only Live Twice **[I]** Sean Connery/Donald Pleasence; cp/cd: John Barry	United Art. 5155

Aladdin's 1992 soundtrack won kudos, and many awards, for its songs by Alan Menken, Howard Ashman and Tim Rice. Featuring Peabo Bryson & Regina Belle's No. 3 hit, "A Whole New World," the album climbed all the way to No. 6.

Around The World In 80 Days tied with Elvis Presley's *Loving You* as the highest-charting album of 1957. Each disc held the No. 1 position for a total of 10 weeks.

Beauty and the Beast's soundtrack, issued by Disney Records in 1991, was a multi-platinum seller that included a special version of the title song performed by Celine Dion & Peabo Bryson. Released as a single, the song climbed to No. 9.

Dirty Dancing's phenomenal 18-week stay at No. 1 during 1987–88 was one of the biggest stories in the industry. The record's astounding popularity inspired both a sequel, 1988's *More Dirty Dancing*, and an actual tour.

Exodus's much-heard soundtrack claimed the No. 1 position for 14 weeks in 1961. Hit versions of the theme were released the same year by Ferrante & Teicher, Mantovani and jazz saxophonist Eddie Harris.

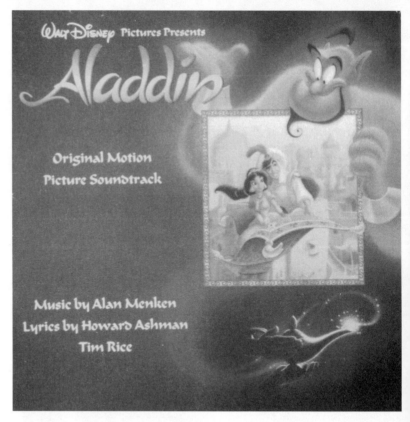

Footloose was a 1984 chart sensation that lingered for a total of 153 weeks and included hit singles by Kenny Loggins, Deniece Wiliams, Mike Reno & Ann Wilson, Shalamar and Bonnie Tyler.

Gigi's 1958 soundtrack offered original songs by Alan Jay Lerner and Frederick Loewe and spent 10 weeks at No. 1. The album's cover was later featured on British versions of Pink Floyd's *Ummagumma*, though airbrushed out in the U.S.

Grease provided four Top 10 hits that helped shape the sound of late '70s radio: Frankie Valli's No. 1 version of the title track, star Olivia Newton-John's "Hopelessly Devoted To You" and her dual duets with John Travolta: "Summer Nights" and the No. 1 "You're The One That I Want."

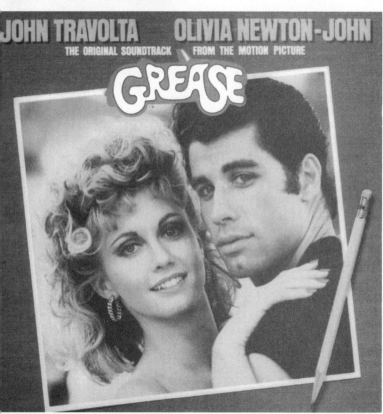

Mary Poppins produced an upbeat soundtrack in 1964 that stayed No. 1 for 14 weeks. Boasting the much-remembered tune "Super-cali-fragil-istic-expi-ali-docious," sung by stars Julie Andrews and Dick Van Dyke, the album also contained "Chim Chim Cher-ee," since covered by a host of jazz instru-mentalists.

Sleepless in Seattle's soundtrack was a multi-platinum sensation upon its 1993 release, climbing to No. 1 and offering a varied mixture of material by such diverse artists as Tammy Wynette, Louis Armstrong, Harry Connick, Jr., and Jimmy Durante.

DATE	POS	WKS	ARTIST—RECORD TITLE	LABEL & NO.
			Young At Heart — see DAY, Doris Doris Day/Frank Sinatra/Gig Young Young Guns II — see BON JOVI, Jon Emilio Estevez/Kiefer Sutherland/Lou D. Phillips/Christian Slater Your Cheatin' Heart — see WILLIAMS, Hank Jr. George Hamilton/Susan Oliver/Red Buttons/Arthur O'Connell	
7/17/65	**26**	23	188. Zorba The Greek [I] Anthony Quinn/Irene Papas; cp/cd: Mikis Theodorakis	20th Century 4167
			SOUNDTRACK COMPILATIONS	
1/23/61	**2**(3)	63	**1. Great Motion Picture Themes** [I] *Exodus* (Ferrante & Teicher)/*Never On Sunday* (Don Costa)	United Art. 3122
6/23/62	**31**	3	2. Original Motion Picture Hit Themes *Town Without Pity* (Gene Pitney)/*Tonight* (Ferrante & Teicher)	United Art. 3197
			ORIGINAL CASTS The original cast stars are listed below the title. Also shown are the lyricist (ly), music writer (mu) and songwriter (sw).	
4/21/62	**21**	6	1. All American Ray Bolger/Eileen Herlie/Ron Husmann; mu: Charles Strouse; ly: Lee Adams	Columbia 2160
12/30/57	**12**	5	2. Annie Get Your Gun Mary Martin/John Raitt; sw: Irving Berlin; San Francisco/ Los Angeles production selected by NBC for a TV spectacular; introduced on Broadway in 1946, starring Ethel Merman	Capitol 913
2/9/57	**20**	1	3. Bells Are Ringing Judy Holliday/Sydney Chaplin; mu: Jule Styne; ly: Betty Comden and Adolph Green	Columbia 5170
7/18/60	**12**	21	4. Bye Bye Birdie Chita Rivera/Dick Van Dyke/Kay Medford/Dick Gautier (Conrad Birdie); mu: Charles Strouse; ly: Lee Adams; also see Soundtrack ('63)	Columbia 5510
3/25/67	**37**	3	5. Cabaret Jill Haworth/Jack Gilford/Bert Convy/Lotte Lenya; mu: John Kander; ly: Fred Ebb; also see Soundtrack ('72)	Columbia 3040
1/23/61	**1**(6)	151	● **6. Camelot** Richard Burton/Julie Andrews/Robert Goulet; mu: Frederick Loewe; ly: Alan Jay Lerner; also see Percy Faith and Soundtrack ('67)	Columbia 2031
6/12/61	**1**(1)	30	**7. Carnival** Anna Maria Alberghetti/James Mitchell; sw: Bob Merrill	MGM 3946
11/17/62	**12**	12	8. Carousel version of the Rodgers & Hammerstein musical; produced by Enoch Light; featuring vocalists Alfred Drake and Roberta Peters; also see Soundtrack ('56)	Command 843
4/29/57	**15**	1	9. Cinderella Julie Andrews; mu: Richard Rodgers; ly: Oscar Hammerstein II; a special CBS-TV production (3/31/57)	Columbia 5190
6/11/55	**6**	12	**10. Damn Yankees** Gwen Verdon/Stephen Douglass/Ray Walston; sw: Richard Adler and Jerry Ross; also see Soundtrack ('58)	RCA 1021
3/6/61	**12**	11	11. Do Re Mi Phil Silvers/Nancy Walker; mu: Jule Styne; ly: Betty Comden and Adolph Green	RCA 2002

DATE	POS	WKS	ARTIST—RECORD TITLE	LABEL & NO.
6/12/82	**11**	15	● 12. Dreamgirls Jennifer Holliday/Loretta Devine/Cleavant Derricks; mu: Henry Krieger; ly: Tom Eyen	Geffen 2007
			Evening With Mike Nichols And Elaine May, An — see NICHOLS, Mike, & Elaine May	
1/22/55	**7**	2	**13. Fanny** Ezio Pinza/Walter Slezak/Florence Henderson; sw: Harold Rome (died 10/26/93 [age 85] from a stroke)	RCA 1015
12/26/64	**7**	60	▲² **14. Fiddler On The Roof** Zero Mostel/Maria Karnilova/Beatrice Arthur; mu: Jerry Bock; ly: Sheldon Harnick; also see Soundtrack ('71)	RCA 1093
1/11/60	**7**	32	**15. Fiorello!** Tom Bosley/Patricia Wilson/Ellen Hanley/Howard Da Silva; mu: Jerry Bock; ly: Sheldon Harnick	Capitol 1321
1/12/59	**1(3)**	67	● **16. Flower Drum Song** Miyoshi Umeki/Larry Blyden/Pat Suzuki; mu: Richard Rodgers; ly: Oscar Hammerstein II; also see Soundtrack ('61)	Columbia 2009
			Funny Girl — see STREISAND, Barbra Barbra Streisand/Sydney Chaplin/Kay Medford	
2/15/64	**33**	3	17. Girl Who Came To Supper, The Jose Ferrer/Florence Henderson; sw: Noel Coward	Columbia 2420
7/8/72	**34**	12	● 18. Godspell Stephen Nathan/Robin Lamont; sw: Stephen Schwartz; based upon the gospel according to St. Matthew	Bell 1102
2/13/65	**36**	3	19. Golden Boy Sammy Davis, Jr./Billy Daniels; mu: Charles Strouse; ly: Lee Adams	Capitol 2124
7/20/59	**13**	41	20. Gypsy Ethel Merman/Jack Klugman/Sandra Church; mu: Jule Styne; ly: Stephen Sondheim; based on memoirs of Gypsy Rose Lee; also see Soundtrack ('62)	Columbia 2017
11/23/68	**1(13)**	59	● **21. Hair** Gerome Ragni/James Rado/Lynn Kellogg; mu: Galt MacDermot; ly: Gerome Ragni and James Rado	RCA 1150
2/29/64	**1(1)**	58	● **22. Hello, Dolly!** Carol Channing/David Burns/Eileen Brennan; sw: Jerry Herman	RCA 1087
1/18/64	**38**	1	23. Here's Love Janis Paige/Craig Stevens; sw: Meredith Willson; based on *Miracle On 34th Street*	Columbia 2400
12/18/61	**19**	19	24. How To Succeed In Business Without Really Trying Robert Morse/Rudy Vallee; sw: Frank Loesser	RCA 1066
12/5/60	**9**	9	**25. Irma La Douce** Elizabeth Seal/Keith Michell/Clive Revill mu: Marguerite Monnot; original ly: Alexandre Breffort	Columbia 2029
1/8/72	**31**	4	26. Jesus Christ Superstar Ben Vereen/Jeff Fenbolt/Yvonne Elliman/Bob Bingham; mu: Andrew Lloyd Webber; ly: Tim Rice; also see Rock Opera ('70)/Soundtrack ('73)	Decca 1503
12/29/56	**19**	3	27. Li'l Abner Edith Adams/Peter Palmer/Howard St. John/Stubby Kaye; mu: Gene de Paul; ly: Johnny Mercer	Columbia 5150
8/20/66	**23**	14	● 28. Mame Angela Lansbury/Beatrice Arthur; sw: Jerry Herman; based on the movie *Auntie Mame*	Columbia 3000

DATE	POS	WKS	ARTIST—RECORD TITLE	LABEL & NO.
2/18/67	**31**	13	● 29. Man of La Mancha Richard Kiley/Irving Jacobson/Joan Diener; mu: Mitch Leigh; ly: Joe Darion; an adaptation of *Don Quixote*	Kapp 4505
11/20/61	**10**	27	**30. Milk And Honey** Robert Weede/Mimi Benzell/Molly Picon; sw: Jerry Herman	RCA 1065
8/4/56	**11**	4	31. Most Happy Fella, The Robert Weede/Jo Sullivan; sw: Frank Loesser	Columbia 2330
12/1/62	**14**	13	32. Mr. President Robert Ryan/Nanette Fabray; sw: Irving Berlin	Columbia 2270
2/24/58	**1**(12)	123	▲ **33. Music Man, The** Robert Preston/Barbara Cook; sw: Meredith Willson; also see Soundtrack ('62)	Capitol 990
4/28/56	**1**(15)	292	▲³ **34. My Fair Lady** Rex Harrison/Julie Andrews; mu: Frederick Loewe; ly: Alan Jay Lerner; adapted from Bernard Shaw's *Pygmalion*; also see Soundtrack ('64)	Columbia 5090
8/5/57	**17**	3	35. New Girl in Town Gwen Verdon/Thelma Ritter/George Wallace; sw: Bob Merrill	RCA 1027
4/28/62	**5**	27	**36. No Strings** Richard Kiley/Diahann Carroll; sw: Richard Rodgers	Capitol 1695
11/3/62	**4**	53	● **37. Oliver!** Clive Revill/Georgia Brown/Bruce Prochnik (Oliver); sw: Lionel Bart; also see Soundtrack ('68)	RCA 2004
2/15/64	**37**	2	38. 110 In The Shade Robert Horton/Inga Swenson/Stephen Douglass; mu: Harvey Schmidt; ly: Tom Jones	RCA 1085
4/2/55	**4**	8	**39. Peter Pan** Mary Martin/Cyril Ritchard; mu: Mark Charlap and Jule Styne; ly: Carolyn Leigh/Betty Comden/Adolph Green	RCA 1019
3/5/88	**33**	4	▲³ **40. Phantom Of The Opera, The** Michael Crawford/Sarah Brightman/Steve Barton; original London cast; mu: Andrew Lloyd Webber; ly: Charles Hart	Polydor 831273 [2]
1/6/62	**36**	2	41. Sail Away Elaine Stritch/James Hurst; sw: Noel Coward	Capitol 1643
6/22/63	**15**	8	42. She Loves Me Barbara Cook/Daniel Massey/Barbara Baxley/Jack Cassidy; mu: Jerry Bock; ly: Sheldon Harnick	MGM 4118 [2]
4/16/55	**9**	6	**43. Silk Stockings** Hildegarde Neff/Don Ameche/Gretchen Wyler; sw: Cole Porter	RCA 1016
12/21/59	**1**(16)	168	● **44. Sound Of Music, The** Mary Martin/Theodore Bikel; mu: Richard Rodgers; ly: Oscar Hammerstein II; also see Soundtrack ('65)	Columbia 2020
11/24/62	**3**	22	**45. Stop The World-I Want To Get Off** Anthony Newley/Anna Quayle; sw: Leslie Bricusse and Anthony Newley	London 88001
1/9/61	**15**	8	46. Tenderloin Maurice Evans/Ron Husmann/Wayne Miller/Eileen Rodgers; mu: Jerry Bock; ly: Sheldon Harnick	Capitol 1492
12/26/60	**6**	35	**47. Unsinkable Molly Brown, The** Tammy Grimes/Harve Presnell; sw: Meredith Willson; also see Soundtrack ('64)	Capitol 1509
3/17/58	**5**	119	● **48. West Side Story** Carol Lawrence/Larry Kert/Chita Rivera/Art Smith; mu: Leonard Bernstein; ly: Stephen Sondheim; also see Ferrante & Teicher/Stan Kenton/Soundtrack ('61)	Columbia 5230

DATE	POS	WKS	ARTIST—RECORD TITLE	LABEL & NO.
5/9/64	**28**	3	49. What Makes Sammy Run? Steve Lawrence/Sally Ann Howes/Robert Alda; sw: Ervin Drake	Columbia 2440
1/23/61	**6**	32	**50. Wildcat** Lucille Ball/Keith Andes; mu: Cy Coleman; ly: Carolyn Leigh	RCA 1060

TELEVISION SHOWS/MINI SERIES

The stars of the show are listed directly below the title.

DATE	POS	WKS	ARTIST—RECORD TITLE	LABEL & NO.
11/27/71	**8**	12	● **1. All In The Family** [C] Carroll O'Connor/Jean Stapleton/Rob Reiner/Sally Struthers; comedy excerpts from the show	Atlantic 7210
			Barney — see CHILDREN'S ALBUMS	
12/11/93	**5**	10	▲ **2. Beavis & Butt-head Experience, The** [V] Beavis & Butt-head are the animated stars of the same-named MTV music video/cartoon series; their creator, Mike Judge, does both voices; album features duo's comments between tracks with their vocals on two of the tracks	Geffen 24613
8/23/69	**18**	8	3. Dark Shadows [I] Jonathan Frid/David Selby; cp/cd: Robert Cobert	Philips 314
11/28/92	**40**	2	● 4. Heights, The Alex Desert/Ken Garito/Cheryl Pollack/Charlotte Ross; songs by the cast *How Do You Talk To An Angel* (1)	Capitol 80328
			Here's Johnny — see Tonight Show	
10/12/85	**1**(11)	22	▲⁴ **5. Miami Vice** [V] Don Johnson/Philip Michael Thomas *Miami Vice* (1-Jan Hammer)/*You Belong To The City* (2-Glenn Frey)	MCA 6150
			Mr. Lucky — see MANCINI, Henry John Vivyan/Ross Martin/Pippa Scott	
5/9/60	**30**	2	6. One Step Beyond, Music From [I] from the "Alcoa Presents" TV series hosted by John Newland; cd: Harry Lubin; pf: Berlin Symphony Orchestra	Decca 8970
			Peter Gunn — see MANCINI, Henry Craig Stevens/Herschel Bernardi/Lola Albright	
			Roaring 20's, The — see PROVINE, Dorothy Dorothy Provine/Donald May/Rex Reason	
			Roots — see JONES, Quincy LeVar Burton/John Amos/Leslie Uggams/Ben Vereen	
2/5/77	**38**	3	7. Saturday Night Live [C] John Belushi/Dan Aykroyd/Chevy Chase/Jane Curtin/Gilda Radner	Arista 4107
4/20/59	**3**	27	**8. 77 Sunset Strip** [I] Efrem Zimbalist, Jr./Roger Smith/Ed "Kookie" Byrnes; musical director: Warren Barker	Warner 1289
1/12/74	**34**	7	9. Sunshine Cliff DeYoung/Christina Raines; cp: John Denver; vocals by Cliff DeYoung; from the CBS-TV movie	MCA 387
1/18/75	**30**	3	● 10. Tonight Show, Here's Johnny — Magic Moments From The [C] actual musical and comedy excerpts from the TV show hosted by Johnny Carson from 10/1/62-5/22/92	Casablanca 1296 [2]
10/6/90	**22**	10	● 11. Twin Peaks [I] Kyle McLachlan/Michael Ontkean/Joan Chen/Sherilyn Fenn; instrumental except for 3 vocal tracks by Julee Cruise; lyrics and co-production by show's director David Lynch; cp/cd: Angelo Badalamenti	Warner 26316

DATE	POS	WKS	ARTIST—RECORD TITLE	LABEL & NO.
11/10/58	**2** (4)	50	**12. Victory At Sea, Vol. 2** [I]	RCA 2226
9/25/61	**7**	19	**13. Victory At Sea, Vol. 3** [I]	RCA 2523
			above 2 are orchestral suites from the NBC-TV series that featured actual footage of World War II naval battles; cp: Richard Rodgers; cd: Robert Russell Bennett	
			TELEVISION SPECIALS:	
			Aloha From Hawaii via Satellite — see PRESLEY, Elvis	
			Cinderella — see ORIGINAL CASTS	
			Elvis — see PRESLEY, Elvis	
			Elvis In Concert — see PRESLEY, Elvis	
			Goin' Back To Indiana — see JACKSON 5	
			Liza With A "Z" — see MINNELLI, Liza	
			Movin' With Nancy — see SINATRA, Nancy	
			On Broadway — see SUPREMES, The and/or TEMPTATIONS, The	
			Point!, The — see NILSSON	
			Really Rosie — see KING, Carole	
			TCB — see SUPREMES, The and/or TEMPTATIONS, The	
			Temptations Show, The — see TEMPTATIONS, The	
			COMPILATIONS BY RECORD LABEL	
			A sampling of artists and songs are listed below many titles.	
			ATLANTIC	
11/24/56	**20**	2	1. Rock & Roll Forever	Atlantic 1239
			14 selections by Atlantic's top R&B artists	
9/2/67	**12**	14	2. Super Hits, The	Atlantic 501
			Respect Aretha Franklin/*Good Lovin'* Young Rascals	
			CAPITOL	
6/1/59	**5**	3	**3. What's New? on Capitol Stereo, vol. 1**	Capitol SN-1
			preview of 12 new Capitol stereo albums	
			COLUMBIA	
6/12/61	**1** (9)	39	**4. Stars For A Summer Night**	Columbia 1 [2]
			25 performances by 22 pop and classical artists	
			END	
2/27/61	**19**	2	5. 12 + 3 = 15 Hits	End 310
			Flamingos/Chantels/Little Anthony & The Imperials/Dubs	
			ORIGINAL SOUND	
9/28/59	**12**	61	6. Oldies But Goodies	Original Snd. 5001
			Earth Angel Penguins/*In The Still Of The Night* 5 Satins	
9/11/61	**12**	20	7. Oldies But Goodies, Vol. 3	Original Snd. 5004
			Come Go With Me Dell-Vikings/*Sea Cruise* Frankie Ford	
8/4/62	**15**	11	8. Oldies But Goodies, Vol. 4	Original Snd. 5005
			Silhouettes Rays/*Blue Suede Shoes* Carl Perkins	
7/6/63	**16**	14	9. Oldies But Goodies, Vol. 5	Original Snd. 5007
			Alley-Oop Hollywood Argyles/*Little Star* Elegants	

DATE	POS	WKS	ARTIST—RECORD TITLE	LABEL & NO.
2/15/64	**31**	3	10. Oldies But Goodies, Vol. 6 *Raindrops* Dee Clark/*Quarter To Three* Gary U.S. Bonds	Original Snd. 5011
			RCA	
10/15/55	**9**	9	**11. Pop Shopper** 12 selections from RCA Victor's album releases	RCA 13
11/30/59	**2**(7)	39	● **12. 60 Years Of Music America Loves Best** performances by RCA Victor artists, from Enrico Caruso to Harry Belafonte	RCA 6074 [2]
10/31/60	**6**	12	**13. 60 Years Of Music America Loves Best, Volume II** 30 performances by RCA artists, from John Sousa to Eddie Fisher	RCA 6088 [2]
9/25/61	**5**	12	**14. 60 Years Of Music America Loves Best, Volume III (Popular)** *Frenesi* Artie Shaw/*Night And Day* Frank Sinatra	RCA 1509
			COMPILATIONS BY RADIO/TV PERSONALITIES	
			CLARK, Dick Born on 11/30/29 in Mt. Vernon, New York. Host of TV's "American Bandstand" from 1956-1989.	
8/11/73	**27**	7	● 1. Dick Clark/20 Years Of Rock N' Roll original hits from 1953-72	Buddah 5133 [2]
			MURRAY THE K Real name: Murray Kaufman. Legendary New York-area D.J. Died on 2/21/82 (age 60).	
1/27/62	**26**	7	2. Murray the K's Blasts From The Past *Sweet Little 16* Chuck Berry/*Bo Diddley* Bo Diddley	Chess 1461
			CONCERTS/FESTIVALS	
9/11/93	**40**	1	● 1. Bob Dylan — The 30th Anniversary Concert Celebration Dylan compositions performed by Johnny Cash, Eric Clapton, Bob Dylan, George Harrison, John Mellencamp, Willie Nelson, Tom Petty, Stevie Wonder, Neil Young and 19 other artists on 10/16/92 at Madison Square Garden in New York City	Columbia 53230 [2]
			Concert For Bangla Desh, The — see HARRISON, George	
8/26/72	**40**	2	2. Fillmore: The Last Days Bill Graham's Fillmore-San Francisco rock shows ran from 11/6/65-7/4/71; album includes a booklet and 7" interview record; Graham was killed in a helicopter crash on 10/25/91 (age 60)	Fillmore 31390 [3]
			Last Waltz, The — see BAND, The	
			Monterey International Pop Festival — see REDDING, Otis, and/or HENDRIX, Jimi	
3/24/73	**28**	6	● 3. Wattstax: The Living Word [S] "live" concert held in August 1972 in Los Angeles	Stax 3010 [2]
6/6/70	**1**(4)	36	▲² **4. Woodstock** [S] movie of historic rock festival near Woodstock, New York, on August 15-17, 1969	Cotillion 500 [3]
4/10/71	**7**	9	● **5. Woodstock Two** [S] more songs from the festival	Cotillion 400 [2]

DATE	POS	WKS	ARTIST—RECORD TITLE	LABEL & NO.
			BENEFIT RECORDINGS	
5/2/81	**36**	3	1. Concerts For The People Of Kampuchea [L]	Atlantic 7005 [2]
			benefit concert held December 26-29, 1979, in London; The Who/Paul McCartney/The Pretenders/The Clash/Elvis Costello	
5/18/91	**24**	1	2. Deadicated	Arista 8669
			original Grateful Dead compositions performed by Los Lobos/ Bruce Hornsby/Elvis Costello/Dwight Yoakam/Jane's Addiction and others; portion of proceeds benefits rain-forest preservation	
6/15/91	**31**	4	● 3. For Our Children	Disney 60616
			benefit for the Pediatric AIDS Foundation; Bob Dylan/Sting/Paul McCartney/Paula Abdul and 18 other stars perform children's songs	
6/22/91	**38**	1	● 4. Club MTV Party To Go — Volume One	Tommy Boy 1037
			l2 hits by M.C. Hammer/Vanilla Ice/Paula Abdul and others; portion of proceeds donated to the AMC Cancer Research Center	
7/4/92	**19**	11	▲ 5. MTV: Party To Go Volume 2	Tommy Boy 1053
			dance-hit remixes by Boyz II Men/Color Me Badd/The KLF & others; portion of proceeds donated to the AMC Cancer Research Center	
7/24/93	**29**	5	● 6. MTV: Party To Go Volume 3	Tommy Boy 1074
			dance-hit remixes by Sir Mix-A-Lot/Madonna/Jodeci and 7 others; portion of proceeds donated to the AMC Cancer Research Center	
7/24/93	**35**	2	● 7. MTV: Party To Go Volume 4	Tommy Boy 1075
			dance-hit remixes by TLC/En Vogue/Kris Kross and 7 others; portion of proceeds donated to AMC Cancer Research Center	
7/9/94	**36**	1	● 8. MTV: Party To Go Volume 5	Tommy Boy 1097
			dance-hit remixes by Dr. Dre/K7/SWV/Tag Team/Tony Toni Tone and 7 others; portion of proceeds donated to AMC Cancer Research Center	
1/5/80	**19**	9	● 9. No Nukes/The MUSE Concerts For A Non-Nuclear Future [L]	Asylum 801 [3]
			benefit concerts recorded at New York's Madison Square Garden September 19-23, 1979; Jackson Browne/Bruce Springsteen/Tom Petty and others	
1/5/91	**38**	3	10. Red Hot + Blue	Chrysalis 21799
			tribute to Cole Porter with proceeds benefitting AIDS research; Sinead O'Connor/Debbie Harry/Iggy Pop/U2/Jody Watley and 17 others	
4/17/82	**29**	5	11. Secret Policeman's Other Ball/The Music, The [L]	Island 9698
			benefit concert recorded in London for Amnesty International; Sting/Jeff Beck & Eric Clapton/Phil Collins/Donovan	
			Very Special Christmas, A — see CHRISTMAS (Top Pop Albums Chart-Various)	
			Very Special Christmas 2, A — see CHRISTMAS (Top Pop Albums Chart-Various)	
			TRIBUTE RECORDINGS	
10/30/93	**3**	23	▲³ **1. Common Thread: The Songs Of The Eagles**	Giant 24531
			portion of the proceeds benefits the Walden Woods Project for the preservation of forestland near Henry David Thoreau's Walden Pond; Eagles hits performed by Clint Black/Brooks & Dunn/Vince Gill/Alan Jackson/Travis Tritt/Tanya Tucker and 7 other country stars	
			DYLAN, Bob — see CONCERTS/FESTIVALS	

DATE	POS	WKS	ARTIST—RECORD TITLE	LABEL & NO.
7/9/94	**19**	2	● 2. Kiss My Ass: Classic Kiss Regrooved Kiss' hits performed by Anthrax, Garth Brooks, Gin Blossoms, Lenny Kravitz and others; also available as "Kiss My A**: Classic Kiss Regrooved" on Mercury 522393	Mercury 522123
11/27/93	**28**	2	● 3. Stone Free: A Tribute To Jimi Hendrix 14 Hendrix songs performed by artists including The Cure/Eric Clapton/Spin Doctors/P.M. Dawn/Living Colour/Belly	Reprise 45438
			CONCEPT ALBUMS	
2/14/76	**10**	14	▲² **1. Outlaws, The** **WAYLON JENNINGS/WILLIE NELSON/JESSI COLTER/TOMPALL GLASER**	RCA 1321
3/19/94	**18**	13	▲ 2. Rhythm Country And Blues classic hits performed by pairings of country and R&B stars such as Vince Gill and Gladys Knight, Al Green and Lyle Lovett, Natalie Cole and Reba McEntire, and others	MCA 10965
11/9/91	**18**	19	▲ 3. Two Rooms — Celebrating The Songs Of Elton John & Bernie Taupin John/Taupin compositions performed by a host of superstars	Polydor 845750
			ROCK OPERAS	
			Godspell — see ORIGINAL CASTS	
			Hair — see ORIGINAL CASTS	
11/21/70	**1(3)**	65	● **1. Jesus Christ Superstar** a rock opera; mu: Andrew Lloyd Webber; ly: Tim Rice; pf: Ian Gillan/Murray Head/Yvonne Elliman; also see Soundtrack and Original Cast versions	Decca 7206 [2]
12/23/72	**5**	13	● **2. Tommy** rock opera written by Pete Townshend (The Who); pf: Pete Townshend/Roger Daltrey/Rod Stewart/Ringo Starr; also see The Who and Soundtrack versions	Ode 99001 [2]
			DANCE/DISCO COMPILATIONS	
8/18/79	**21**	6	● Night At Studio 54, A specially sequenced disco favorites at the New York club	Casablanca 7161 [2]
			JAZZ COMPILATIONS	
7/9/55	**5**	10	**I Like Jazz!** [K] a sampling of the development of jazz (ragtime, swing, etc.)	Columbia 1
			CHILDREN'S ALBUMS	
			BARNEY	
9/18/93	**9**	16	▲² **1. Barney's Favorites — Volume 1** [TV] pf: Bob West/Julie Johnson; songs from the popular PBS series For Our Children — see BENEFIT RECORDINGS	SBK 27114
			DISNEY	
7/23/94	**40**	1	▲ 2. Lion King Sing-Along, The features original cast recordings from *The Lion King* movie and a 20-page, illustrated lyric book; available only on cassette	Walt Disney 60857
5/24/80	**35**	4	▲ 3. Mickey Mouse Disco disco songs performed by session musicians	Disneyland 2504
			SESAME STREET/MUPPETS	
8/29/70	**23**	9	● 4. Sesame Street Book & Record, The [TV] pf: Bob McGrath/Loretta Long/Jim Henson/Frank Oz/Carroll Spinney; songs from the popular PBS series	Columbia 1069

DATE	POS	WKS	ARTIST—RECORD TITLE	LABEL & NO.
10/27/79	32	5	● 5. Muppet Movie, The [S] pf: Jim Henson/Frank Oz/Jerry Nelson	Atlantic 16001
12/22/79	26	4	▲ 6. Christmas Together, A [X] **JOHN DENVER & THE MUPPETS** Christmas charts: 10/'83	RCA 3451
1/9/61	19	3	## MISCELLANEOUS 7. Alice In Wonderland: The Mad Tea Party/The Lobster Quadrille [T] **CYRIL RITCHARD** Ritchard (died 12/18/77 [age 79]) reads and sings selections from the classic story	Riverside 1406
			## CLASSICAL COMPILATIONS Various artist compilations.	
9/25/61	6	9	**1. 60 Years Of Music America Loves Best, Volume III (Red Seal)** Caruso/Fiedler/Toscanini and 9 other classical greats	RCA 2574
5/25/63	39	3	2. Sound of Genius, The 19 favorites by 18 of Columbia's greatest classical artists	Columbia SGS 1 [2]
6/16/62	24	9	3. Summer Festival 19 favorites by 20 of RCA's greatest classical artists	RCA 6097 [2]
			## COMEDY ALBUMS Comedy-concept productions.	
1/26/63	27	4	1. Other Family, The Larry Foster/Marty Brill/Toby Deane	Laurie 5000
11/12/66	40	2	2. Our Wedding Album or The Great Society Affair Kenny Solms/Gail Parent/Fannie Flagg/Robert Klein/Jo Ann Worley; spoof of President Johnson's family	Jamie 3028
1/26/63	35	4	3. President Strikes Back!, The Marc London/Sylvia Miles; an answer album to Vaughn Meader's *The First Family*	Kapp 1322
12/4/65	3	14	● **4. Welcome to the LBJ Ranch!** featuring the actual recorded voices of political leaders	Capitol 2423
5/7/66	22	5	5. When You're In Love The Whole World Is Jewish Betty Walker/Lou Jacobi/Frank Gallop/Valerie Harper/Bob McFadden	Kapp 4506
10/23/65	9	14	**6. You Don't Have To Be Jewish** Betty Walker/Lou Jacobi/Frank Gallop	Kapp 4503
			## AEROBIC INSTRUCTORS	
			### FONDA, Jane	
7/17/82	15	27	▲² Jane Fonda's Workout Record Jacksons/REO Speedwagon/Brothers Johnson/Boz Scaggs	Columbia 38054 [2]
			## SPECIALTY ALBUMS The following albums, because of their unusual content, are listed in this section and are categorized with special headings.	
			### CARS	
2/29/64	27	2	1. Big Sounds Of The Drags!, The actual sounds of drag racing at a quarter-mile track	Capitol 2001
7/27/63	7	31	**2. Shut Down** *Shut Down* Beach Boys/*Black Denim Trousers* Cheers, and 10 other car songs	Capitol 1918

DATE	POS	WKS	ARTIST—RECORD TITLE	LABEL & NO.
5/26/56	9	9	**MINSTREL SHOW** **3. Gentlemen, Be Seated!** recreation of a complete minstrel show; cd: Allen Roth; pf: Gordon Goodman/Osie Johnson/John Neher/Quartones	Epic 3238
10/15/88	31	3	**OLYMPICS** ● 4. 1988 Summer Olympics Album / One Moment In Time features tracks by 11 artists especially written and recorded for the NBC-TV broadcast of the 1988 Summer Olympic Games *One Moment In Time* (5-Whitney Houston)	Arista 8551
8/15/92	32	2	5. Barcelona Gold songs broadcast on TV during the 1992 Summer Olympics in Barcelona; Madonna/En Vogue/Damn Yankees/INXS/Rod Stewart *This Used To Be My Playground* (1-Madonna)	Warner 26974
3/29/69	31	7	**RADIO** 6. Themes Like Old Times features 180 of the most famous original radio themes	Viva 36018 [2]
			CHRISTMAS (Top Pop Albums Chart-Various Artists) The following various artist/specialty Christmas albums made *Billboard*'s regular Top Pop Albums charts:	
12/30/57	19	3	1. Merry Christmas　　　　　　　　[EP] 7" EP (originally released as a 10" album in 1952)	Coral 82003
12/5/87	20	7	▲² 2. Very Special Christmas, A Christmas songs contributed by 15 rock superstars; proceeds donated to the Special Olympics; Christmas charts: 1/'87, 1/'88, 4/'89, 5/'90, 3/'91, 5/'92, 9/'93, 9/'94	A&M 3911
11/28/92	7	7	▲ **3. Very Special Christmas 2, A** proceeds donated to the Special Olympics; Tom Petty/Randy Travis/Aretha Franklin/Extreme/Wilson Phillips and 18 others; Christmas charts: 2/'92, 6/'93, 8/'94	A&M 31454
			CHRISTMAS (Billboard's Special Christmas Charts) For the years 1963 through 1973, *Billboard* didn't chart Christmas albums on its Top Pop Albums charts. Instead, it issued special Christmas charts for 3-4 weeks during each Christmas season. These special charts were discontinued from 1974 through 1982 when *Billboard* again charted Christmas albums on its regular album charts. Since 1983, *Billboard* again issued special Christmas charts; however, it also listed the best-selling Christmas albums on its Top Pop Albums charts. The following list includes only those albums that made the Top 10 of *Billboard*'s special Christmas Albums chart, and never made *Billboard*'s Top Pop Albums charts. For Christmas albums that made both *Billboard*'s Top Pop Albums chart and the special Christmas charts, the peak position/year charted data achieved on the special Christmas charts is noted below the album title in the main artist section. Even though only the Top 10 albums are listed here, the special Christmas charts were researched in full and include all peak position/year charted data for these albums (if they charted for more than one season). The debut date is the earliest date the album appeared on the charts, even if it did not appear in the Top 10. The weeks charted total includes all weeks charted, not just weeks in the Top 10.	
12/19/87	10	3	**AIR SUPPLY** **1. Christmas Album, The** 17/'87, 10/'88	Arista 8528

DATE	POS	WKS	ARTIST—RECORD TITLE	LABEL & NO.
12/7/68	1(2)	10	**ALPERT, Herb & The Tijuana Brass** ● **2. Herb Alpert & The Tijuana Brass Christmas Album** [I] 1/'68, 6/'69, 17/'70	A&M 4166
12/2/67	9	6	**ANDREWS, Julie** **3. Christmas Treasure, A** with the orchestra, harpsichord and arrangements of Andre Previn; 9/'67, 52/'68	RCA 3829
12/3/66	6	12	**BAEZ, Joan** **4. Noel** 6/'66, 10/'67, 11/'71, 14/'72, 12/'73	Vanguard 79230
12/5/64	6	13	**BEACH BOYS, The** ● **5. Beach Boys' Christmas Album, The** 6/'64, 7/'65, 26/'66, 72/'67, 14/'68 *Little Saint Nick/The Man With All The Toys*	Capitol 2164
12/14/68	10	3	**BENNETT, Tony** **6. Snowfall/The Tony Bennett Christmas Album**	Columbia 9739
12/19/70	9	2	**BOSTON POPS ORCHESTRA/ARTHUR FIEDLER** **7. Christmas Festival, A** [I]	Polydor 5004
12/25/71	6	1	**BRADY BUNCH** **8. Merry Christmas from the Brady Bunch**	Paramount 5026
12/13/69	10	3	**BROWN, James** **9. Soulful Christmas, A**	King 1040
12/7/68	1(2)	10	**CAMPBELL, Glen** ● **10. That Christmas Feeling** 1/'68, 4/'69, 23/'70, 14/'71	Capitol 2978
12/13/69	7	5	**CASH, Johnny** **11. Christmas Spirit, The** 7/'69, 14/'70	Columbia 8917
12/7/63	9	13	**CHIPMUNKS, The** **12. Christmas with the Chipmunks, Vol. 2** [N] 9/'63, 18/'64, 18/'67, 31/'68	Liberty 7334
11/30/63	1(2)	85	**COLE, Nat King** ● **13. Christmas Song, The** 6/'63, 12/'64, 8/'65, 8/'66, 3/'67, 5/'68, 1/'69, 4/'70, 3/'71, 1/'72, 5/'73, 5/'83, 5/'85, 6/'87, 6/'88, 8/'89, 6/'90, 4/'91, 8/'92, 12/'93, 12/'94	Capitol 1967
12/5/70	5	5	**COMO, Perry** ● **14. Perry Como Christmas Album, The** 5/'70, 18/'73	RCA 4016
12/25/65	10	8	**CONNIFF, Ray** **15. Here We Come A-Caroling** 17/'65, 15/'66, 10/'70	Columbia GP 3

DATE	POS	WKS	ARTIST—RECORD TITLE	LABEL & NO.
			CROSBY, Bing	
12/12/64	**9**	3	**16. 12 Songs of Christmas** **BING CROSBY/FRANK SINATRA/FRED WARING**	Reprise 2022
12/5/92	**8**	19	**17. It's Christmas Time** **BING CROSBY/FRANK SINATRA/NAT KING COLE** 8/'92, 17/'93, 12/'94	Laserlight 15152
			DOMINGO, Placido	
12/15/84	**9**	1	**18. Christmas with Placido Domingo** with the Vienna Symphony Orchestra	CBS 37245
			ELMO & PATSY	
12/19/87	**8**	13	**19. Grandma Got Run Over By A Reindeer** 8/'87, 12/'88, 24/'89, 28/'91	Epic 39931
			FELICIANO, Jose	
12/1/73	**3**	4	**20. Jose Feliciano**	RCA 4421
			GARY, John	
12/5/64	**3**	17	**21. John Gary Christmas Album, The** 3/'64, 11/'65, 18/'66, 32/'67, 20/'68	RCA 2940
			GORME, Eydie, and The Trio Los Panchos	
12/3/66	**9**	4	**22. Navidad means Christmas** [F]	Columbia 9357
			GOULET, Robert	
11/30/63	**4**	16	**23. This Christmas I Spend With You** 4/'63, 5/'64, 17/'65, 90/'67, 30/'68	Columbia 8876
			GRANT, Amy	
12/21/85	**5**	22	**24. Christmas Album, A** 9/'85, 12/'87, 13/'88, 25/'89, 5/'91, 16/'92	A&M 5057
			GUARALDI, Vince, Trio	
12/19/87	**9**	32	**25. Charlie Brown Christmas, A** 13/'87, 9/'88, 9/'89, 9/'90, 18/'91, 16/'92, 23/'93, 22/'94	Fantasy 8431
			HAGGARD, Merle	
12/8/73	**4**	3	**26. Merle Haggard's Christmas Present** **(Something Old, Something New)**	Capitol 11230
			JACKSON, Mahalia	
12/13/69	**2**(1)	3	**27. Christmas with Mahalia**	Columbia 9727
			JACKSON 5	
12/5/70	**1**(6)	16	**28. Christmas Album** 1/'70, 2/'71, 1/'72, 1/'73	Motown 713
			JUDDS, The	
12/19/87	**9**	20	**29. Christmas Time with The Judds** 9/'87, 9/'88, 29/'89, 26/'90, 12/'91, 24/'92, 29/'93	RCA 6422
			KAEMPFERT, Bert, and his orchestra	
11/30/63	**6**	16	**30. Christmas Wonderland** [I] 6/'63, 34/'64, 38/'65, 21/'66, 62/'67, 38/'68	Decca 74441
			KING FAMILY, The	
12/18/65	**8**	2	**31. Christmas With The King Family**	Warner 1627

DATE	POS	WKS	ARTIST—RECORD TITLE	LABEL & NO.
12/5/64	7	18	**LEE, Brenda** 32. Merry Christmas from Brenda Lee 15/'64, 17/'65, 20/'66, 58/'67, 33/'68, 7/'72	Decca 74583
12/19/64	8	15	**LEWIS, Ramsey, Trio** 33. More Sounds of Christmas **[I]** 8/'64, 16/'65, 14/'66, 49/'67, 41/'68	Argo 745
12/15/84	8	2	**MANDRELL, Barbara** 34. Christmas At Our House	MCA 5519
12/14/63	7	15	**MANTOVANI And His Orchestra** 35. Christmas Greetings From Mantovani **[I]** 7/'63, 23/'65, 42/'66, 20/'67, 10/'68	London 338
12/3/66	1(1)	19	**MARTIN, Dean** ● 36. Dean Martin Christmas Album, The 1/'66, 2/'67, 4/'68, 10/'69, 14/'70	Reprise 6222
12/5/64	8	11	**MARTINO, Al** 37. Merry Christmas, A 8/'64, 19/'65, 59/'66, 23/'67	Capitol 2165
11/30/63	2(2)	20	**MATHIS, Johnny** 38. Sounds Of Christmas 2/'63, 7/'64, 13/'65, 45/'66, 18/'67, 11/'68	Mercury 60837
12/6/69	1(1)	20	● 39. Give Me Your Love For Christmas 1/'69, 3/'70, 5/'71, 3/'72, 19/'73, 19/'87, 18/'88	Columbia 9923
12/21/63	8	12	**MORMON TABERNACLE CHOIR, The** ● 40. Joy Of Christmas, The with Leonard Bernstein conducting the New York Philharmonic; 12/'63, 32/'64, 8/'65, 62/'66, 106/'67, 28/'68, 20/'70	Columbia 6499
12/18/65	5	8	41. Handel: Messiah with Eugene Ormandy conducting the Philadelphia Orchestra; Eileen Farrell (soprano)/William Warfield (baritone); 21/'65, 8/'70, 12/'71, 5/'72	Columbia 607 [2]
12/2/67	1(1)	25	**NABORS, Jim** ● 42. Jim Nabors' Christmas Album 7/'67, 7/'68, 1/'69, 3/'70, 6/'71, 5/'72, 20/'73	Columbia 9531
12/21/63	5	8	**NEW CHRISTY MINSTRELS, The** 43. Merry Christmas! 5/'63, 17/'64, 53/'65, 65/'66, 116/'67	Columbia 2096
12/21/85	9	2	**NEW EDITION** 44. Christmas All Over The World	MCA 39040
12/3/66	10	10	**NEWTON, Wayne** 45. Songs For A Merry Christmas 10/'66, 29/'67, 40/'68	Capitol 2588
12/4/71	1(4)	7	**PARTRIDGE FAMILY** ● 46. Partridge Family Christmas Card, A 1/'71, 9/'72	Bell 6066

DATE	POS	WKS	ARTIST—RECORD TITLE	LABEL & NO.
12/17/83	6	20	**PAVAROTTI, Luciano** ● 47. **O Holy Night** with Kurt Adler conducting the National Philharmonic; recorded in 1976; 7/'83, 6/'84, 21/'88, 19/'89, 20/'90, 14/'91, 22/'92	London 26473
12/5/70	2(9)	58	**PRESLEY, Elvis** 48. **Elvis' Christmas Album** originally issued in 1957 on LOC-1035 (red cover) as a gatefold with a 10-page booklet of color photos (made Pop charts); reissued in 1958 on LPM-1951 (blue cover, without gatefold and photos; also made Pop charts); reissued in 1970 on Camden CAL-2428 (omitting 4 songs and adding 2 more); reissued in 1975 on Pickwick/Camden CAS-2428 (didn't chart); original gatefold package reissued in 1985 on RCA 1-5486 (made Pop charts); 5/'63, 3/'64, 2/'65, 2/'66, 3/'67, 3/'68, 2/'69, 2/'70, 9/'72, 6/'85, 11/'87, 10/'88, 22/'89, 22/'90, 29/'92, 27/'94	RCA 1951
12/4/71	1(3)	12	▲ 49. **Elvis sings The Wonderful World of Christmas** an all new Christmas LP (recorded May 1971); 2/'71, 1/'72, 1/'73	RCA 4579
12/12/70	5	9	**PRIDE, Charley** 50. **Christmas in My Home Town** 8/'70, 5/'71, 8/'72, 15/'73	RCA 4406
12/2/67	2(1)	11	**RAWLS, Lou** 51. **Merry Christmas Ho! Ho! Ho!** 2/'67, 22/'68, 18/'69, 26/'70	Capitol 2790
12/2/67	10	5	**REVERE, Paul, & The Raiders** 52. **Christmas Present ... And Past, A**	Columbia 9555
12/7/68	8	6	**SHAW, Robert, Chorale and Orchestra** 53. **Handel: Messiah** *Messiah* was composed by George Frideric Handel from 8/22-9/14, 1741; 8/'68, 17/'69	RCA 6175 [3]
12/5/70	2(1)	5	**SHERMAN, Bobby** 54. **Bobby Sherman Christmas Album** 2/'70, 11/'71	Metromedia 1038
12/11/65	5	11	**SIMEONE, Harry, Chorale** 55. **O Bambino/The Little Drummer Boy** includes Simeone's new recording of "The Little Drummer Boy"; 16/'65, 5/'66, 9/'72, 7/'73	Kapp 3450
			SINATRA, Frank — see CROSBY, Bing	
12/6/69	3	4	**SINATRA FAMILY** 56. **Sinatra Family Wish You A Merry Christmas, The** Frank and daughters Nancy & Tina, and son Frank, Jr.	Reprise 1026
12/5/64	8	4	**SMITH, Jimmy** 57. **Christmas '64** [I]	Verve 8604
12/11/65	6	12	**SUPREMES, The** 58. **Merry Christmas** 6/'65, 13/'66, 19/'67, 26/'70	Motown 638

DATE	POS	WKS	ARTIST—RECORD TITLE	LABEL & NO.
			TEMPTATIONS, The	
12/5/70	4	7	59. Temptations' Christmas Card, The	Gordy 951
			7/'70, 7/'71, 4/'72	
12/17/83	6	30	60. Give Love At Christmas	Gordy 998
			6/'83, 14/'87, 12/'88, 17/'89, 13/'90, 20/'92, 22/'93, 25/'94	
			VENTURES, The	
12/11/65	9	9	61. Ventures' Christmas Album, The [I]	Dolton 8038
			9/'65, 32/'66, 32/'67, 15/'69	
			WARING, Fred — see CROSBY, Bing	
			WILLIAMS, Andy	
11/30/63	1(9)	34	● 62. Andy Williams Christmas Album, The	Columbia 8887
			1/'63, 1/'64, 1/'65, 60/'66, 6/'67, 17/'68, 30/'69, 4/'70, 4/'71, 8/'72, 6/'73	
12/18/65	1(3)	20	● 63. Merry Christmas	Columbia 9220
			5/'65, 1/'66, 20/'67, 4/'68, 1/'69, 19/'70	
			CHRISTMAS (Billboard's Christmas Charts- Various)	
12/9/72	7	12	1. Christmas Album, The	Columbia 30763 [2]
			Barbra Streisand/Mahalia Jackson/Johnny Mathis/Frank Sinatra/Tony Bennett/Johnny Cash and 14 others; 7/'72, 10/'73, 19/'91, 28/'92	
12/1/73	7	4	2. Christmas Greetings from Nashville	RCA 0262
			features Eddy Arnold/Chet Atkins/Jim Reeves and 7 others	
12/7/91	8	9	3. 50 All-Time Christmas Favorites	Madacy 10 [2]
			all songs performed by studio vocalists and musicians; 8/'91, 16/'92	
12/8/73	1(1)	4	4. Motown Christmas, A	Motown 795 [2]
			The Temptations/Stevie Wonder/The Jackson Five/The Miracles/The Supremes; 1/'73, 26/'87	
12/5/70	7	4	5. Peace On Earth	Capitol 585 [2]
			Beach Boys/Glen Campbell/Nat King Cole/Lettermen and 13 others	
12/23/72	6	5	6. Phil Spector's Christmas Album	Apple 3400
			reissue of *A Christmas Gift For You* (Philles/1963); The Crystals/The Ronettes/Darlene Love/Bob B. Soxx & The Blue Jeans; 6/'72, 8/'73, 25/'87	
12/21/68	8	8	7. Soul Christmas	Atco 269
			Otis Redding/Clarence Carter/Joe Tex and 5 others; 13/'68, 8/'69, 8/'70	

THE
RECORD
HOLDERS

THE TOP 100 ARTISTS OF THE ROCK ERA

Prv. Rank	New Rank	Artist		Points	Prv. Rank	New Rank	Artist		Points
(1)	1.	THE BEATLES	■	3304	(22)	26.	ENOCH LIGHT	●	938
(2)	2.	ELVIS PRESLEY	●	2699	(23)	27.	THE MONKEES		926
(3)	3.	FRANK SINATRA		2438	(25)	28.	STEVIE WONDER		913
(4)	4.	THE ROLLING STONES	■	2205	(27)	29.	THE TEMPTATIONS	■■■■	893
(5)	5.	BARBRA STREISAND		1966	(28)	30.	LAWRENCE WELK	●	892
(6)	6.	THE KINGSTON TRIO	■	1757	(26)	31.	RAY CONNIFF		891
(7)	7.	ELTON JOHN		1577	(33)	★32.	EAGLES		884
(8)	8.	JOHNNY MATHIS		1422	(36)	★33.	ROD STEWART		859
(9)	9.	HERB ALPERT/THE TIJUANA BRASS		1345	(29)	34.	RAY CHARLES		852
(10)	10.	HARRY BELAFONTE		1320	(49)	★35.	ERIC CLAPTON		844
(11)	11.	MITCH MILLER		1316	(30)	36.	THE BEACH BOYS	■	832
(18)	★12.	MICHAEL JACKSON		1151	(31)	37.	SIMON & GARFUNKEL		826
(12)	13.	CHICAGO	■	1136	(37)	38.	BRUCE SPRINGSTEEN		803
—	★14.	GARTH BROOKS		1113	(47)	★39.	MADONNA		796
(15)	15.	PAUL McCARTNEY/WINGS	■	1102	(34)	40.	PETER, PAUL & MARY		786
(13)	16.	BOB DYLAN		1086	(42)	★41.	PINK FLOYD		776
(14)	17.	ANDY WILLIAMS		1063	(35)	42.	THE SUPREMES	■	774
(24)	★18.	PRINCE		1052	(38)	43.	JEFFERSON AIRPLANE/STARSHIP	■	724
(55)	★19.	WHITNEY HOUSTON		1046	(40)	44.	NEIL DIAMOND		715
(17)	20.	HENRY MANCINI	●	1021	(41)	45.	CAROLE KING		671
(21)	21.	LED ZEPPELIN	■	1014	(43)	46.	BILLY VAUGHN	●	660
(16)	22.	MANTOVANI	●	1009	(66)	★47.	U2		650
(19)	23.	BEE GEES		1008	(61)	★48.	VAN HALEN		650
(20)	24.	FLEETWOOD MAC		1001	(44)	49.	ARETHA FRANKLIN		650
(32)	★25.	BILLY JOEL		939	(45)	50.	LINDA RONSTADT		634

POINT SYSTEM

An artist's rank is determined by a point system wherein each Top 40 album is assigned a value based on its chart performance. Each album's point total is tabulated using the following formula:

1. Each artist's Top 40 albums are awarded points based on their highest charted position:

#1	=	50 points for its first week at #1, plus 15 points for each additional week at #1
#2	=	40 points
#3	=	30
#4-5	=	25
#6-10	=	20
#11-20	=	15
#21-30	=	10
#31-40	=	5

2. Total weeks charted in Top 40 are added in.

Ties are broken based on which artist had the most No. 1 hits, and then most Top 10 hits.

When two artists combine for a hit album, such as Diana Ross and Marvin Gaye, the full point value is given to each artist. Artists such as Simon & Garfunkel, Hall & Oates and Loggins & Messina are considered regular recording teams, and their points are not split or shared by either of the artists individually.

Headings And Special Symbols:

Prv. Rank: Artist ranking in previous edition of **Top 40 Hits**

New Rank: Artist ranking in new edition of **Top 40 Hits**

- ● = **Deceased Solo Artist**
- ■ = **Deceased Group Member** The total number of square symbols indicates the total number of deceased members.
- ★ = Indicates that artist ranks higher in new edition than previous edition.
  Previous rank is shown in parentheses to the left of the new rank.
- — = Indicates that artist did not rank in the Top 100 Artists of the previous edition.

THE TOP 100 ARTISTS OF THE ROCK ERA

Prv. Rank	New Rank	Artist		Points
(46)	51.	SANTANA		632
(53)	52.	JOHN DENVER		619
(48)	53.	NAT "KING" COLE	●	617
—	★54.	MARIAH CAREY		616
(50)	55.	ROGER WILLIAMS		613
(51)	56.	THE MOODY BLUES		604
(52)	57.	JETHRO TULL	■	584
(54)	58.	EARTH, WIND & FIRE		583
—	★59.	HAMMER/MC HAMMER		549
(56)	60.	THE POLICE		538
(74)	★61.	QUEEN	■	534
(58)	62.	GEORGE HARRISON		530
(72)	★63.	JOHN COUGAR MELLENCAMP		530
(59)	64.	FOREIGNER		529
(60)	65.	CREEDENCE CLEARWATER REVIVAL	■	520
—	★66.	GEORGE MICHAEL/WHAM!		518
—	★67.	AEROSMITH		512
(62)	68.	DONNA SUMMER		511
(99)	★69.	BON JOVI		506
(63)	70.	JOHN LENNON	☻	504
(67)	71.	THE DOORS	■	504
(57)	72.	DIANA ROSS		498
(64)	73.	GLEN CAMPBELL		498
—	★74.	DEF LEPPARD	■	494
—	★75.	JANET JACKSON		491
(79)	★76.	BOB SEGER & THE SILVER BULLET BAND		487
(89)	★77.	NEIL YOUNG		487
(91)	★78.	PHIL COLLINS		484
(65)	79.	THE DOOBIE BROTHERS	■	484
—	★80.	GUNS N' ROSES		473
(76)	81.	JAMES TAYLOR		473
(70)	82.	JIMI HENDRIX	●	471
(69)	83.	HEART		464
(68)	84.	THE WHO	■	464
(71)	85.	CAT STEVENS		458
—	★86.	TOM PETTY & THE HEARTBREAKERS		455
(73)	87.	DARYL HALL & JOHN OATES		449
(75)	88.	JOAN BAEZ		444
(78)	89.	BARRY MANILOW		440
(77)	90.	BOB NEWHART		437
(92)	★91.	KISS	■	435
(80)	92.	REO SPEEDWAGON		429
(81)	93.	GRAND FUNK RAILROAD		428
(85)	94.	DAVID BOWIE		428
(82)	95.	KENNY ROGERS		427
(83)	96.	THE JACKSON 5/THE JACKSONS		426
(84)	97.	THREE DOG NIGHT		425
(86)	98.	CROSBY, STILLS & NASH (& YOUNG)		422
—	★99.	AC/DC	■	421
(87)	100.	TENNESSEE ERNIE FORD	●	419

THE TOP 25 ARTISTS BY DECADE

ARTIST	POINTS	ARTIST	POINTS
THE FIFTIES (1955-59)		**THE SIXTIES**	
1. HARRY BELAFONTE	1103	1. THE BEATLES	2817
2. FRANK SINATRA	1015	2. ELVIS PRESLEY	1469
3. ELVIS PRESLEY	927	3. FRANK SINATRA	1281
4. JOHNNY MATHIS	851	4. HERB ALPERT/THE TIJUANA BRASS	1260
5. THE KINGSTON TRIO	749	5. THE KINGSTON TRIO	1008
6. MITCH MILLER	747	6. ANDY WILLIAMS	999
7. MANTOVANI	572	7. ENOCH LIGHT	931
8. ROGER WILLIAMS	418	8. THE MONKEES	904
9. TENNESSEE ERNIE FORD	384	9. RAY CHARLES	852
10. DORIS DAY	356	10. BARBRA STREISAND	842
11. JACKIE GLEASON	341	11. PETER, PAUL & MARY	760
12. NAT "KING" COLE	338	12. THE ROLLING STONES	758
13. PAT BOONE	327	13. THE SUPREMES	747
14. LAWRENCE WELK	286	14. HENRY MANCINI	727
15. HENRY MANCINI	280	15. THE BEACH BOYS	643
16. VAN CLIBURN	273	16. RAY CONNIFF	629
17. RAY CONNIFF	262	17. LAWRENCE WELK	606
18. PERRY COMO	216	18. THE TEMPTATIONS	581
19. BILLY VAUGHN	211	19. MITCH MILLER	569
20. MARTIN DENNY	207	20. SIMON & GARFUNKEL	539
21. RICKY NELSON	195	21. JOHNNY MATHIS	510
22. SAMMY DAVIS, JR.	186	22. BILLY VAUGHN	449
23. THE FOUR FRESHMEN	151	23. BOB NEWHART	437
24. BING CROSBY	146	24. MANTOVANI	437
25. SHELLEY BERMAN	145	25. GLEN CAMPBELL	398

THE TOP 25 ARTISTS BY DECADE

ARTIST	POINTS	ARTIST	POINTS
## THE SEVENTIES		## THE EIGHTIES	
1. ELTON JOHN	1329	1. PRINCE	881
2. CHICAGO	944	2. MICHAEL JACKSON	860
3. PAUL McCARTNEY/WINGS	833	3. BRUCE SPRINGSTEEN	632
4. BEE GEES	831	4. WHITNEY HOUSTON	574
5. THE ROLLING STONES	820	5. MADONNA	566
6. EAGLES	769	6. THE ROLLING STONES	550
7. FLEETWOOD MAC	732	7. BILLY JOEL	501
8. LED ZEPPELIN	720	8. THE POLICE	499
9. CAROLE KING	671	9. U2	473
10. BOB DYLAN	642	10. JOHN COUGAR MELLENCAMP	454
11. BARBRA STREISAND	628	11. GEORGE MICHAEL/WHAM!	451
12. JOHN DENVER	596	12. VAN HALEN	450
13. STEVIE WONDER	592	13. PHIL COLLINS	427
14. PINK FLOYD	536	14. REO SPEEDWAGON	404
15. ROD STEWART	524	15. BARBRA STREISAND	399
16. JETHRO TULL	511	16. BON JOVI	372
17. SANTANA	504	17. MEN AT WORK	361
18. NEIL DIAMOND	486	18. JOURNEY	348
19. GEORGE HARRISON	466	19. FOREIGNER	347
20. CAT STEVENS	458	20. PAT BENATAR	340
21. EARTH, WIND & FIRE	457	21. LIONEL RICHIE	330
22. ERIC CLAPTON	426	22. DEF LEPPARD	327
23. DONNA SUMMER	421	23. BOB SEGER & THE SILVER BULLET BAND	325
24. JEFFERSON STARSHIP	416	24. DARYL HALL & JOHN OATES	322
25. GRAND FUNK RAILROAD	410	25. JANET JACKSON	314
## THE NINETIES			
1. GARTH BROOKS	1113		
2. MARIAH CAREY	616	Ties are broken based on which artist had the most No. 1	
3. HAMMER	516	hits, then most Top 10 hits, and finally, most Top 40 hits.	
4. WHITNEY HOUSTON	472		
5. BILLY RAY CYRUS	392		
6. PEARL JAM	338		
7. VANILLA ICE	328		
8. NIRVANA	265		
9. R.E.M. 262			
10. MICHAEL BOLTON	256		
11. BOYZ II MEN	239		
12. ERIC CLAPTON	230		
13. MADONNA	230		
14. ICE CUBE	215		
15. GUNS N' ROSES	212		
16. REBA McENTIRE	199		
17. KENNY G	196		
18. STONE TEMPLE PILOTS	196		
19. METALLICA	191		
20. NATALIE COLE	180		
21. U2	177		
22. JANET JACKSON	177		
23. SINEAD O'CONNOR	170		
24. DEF LEPPARD	167		
25. BONNIE RAITT	161		

TOP ARTIST ACHIEVEMENTS*

ARTIST	TOTAL	ARTIST	TOTAL
THE MOST WEEKS AT NO. 1		**THE MOST NO. 1 ALBUMS**	
1. THE BEATLES	119	1. THE BEATLES	15
2. ELVIS PRESLEY	64	2. ELVIS PRESLEY	9
3. MICHAEL JACKSON	47	3. THE ROLLING STONES	9
4. THE KINGSTON TRIO	46	4. BARBRA STREISAND	7
5. WHITNEY HOUSTON	45	5. ELTON JOHN	7
6. ELTON JOHN	39	6. PAUL McCARTNEY/WINGS	7
7. THE ROLLING STONES	38	7. LED ZEPPELIN	6
8. HARRY BELAFONTE	37	8. THE KINGSTON TRIO	5
9. GARTH BROOKS	37 +	9. HERB ALPERT/THE TIJUANA BRASS	5
10. FLEETWOOD MAC	37	10. CHICAGO	5
11. THE MONKEES	37	11. EAGLES	5
12. PRINCE	33	12. FRANK SINATRA	4
13. BEE GEES	31	13. GARTH BROOKS	4
14. EAGLES	29	14. BILLY JOEL	4
15. LED ZEPPELIN	28	15. THE MONKEES	4
16. HERB ALPERT/THE TIJUANA BRASS	26	16. BRUCE SPRINGSTEEN	4
17. SIMON & GARFUNKEL	26	17. PINK FLOYD	4
18. BARBRA STREISAND	23	18. U2	4
19. CHICAGO	22	19. MITCH MILLER	3
20. PAUL McCARTNEY/WINGS	22	20. MICHAEL JACKSON	3
21. HENRY MANCINI	22	21. BOB DYLAN	3
22. PINK FLOYD	22	22. PRINCE	3
23. M.C. HAMMER/HAMMER	21	23. WHITNEY HOUSTON	3
24. FRANK SINATRA	20	24. BEE GEES	3
25. ENOCH LIGHT	20	25. FLEETWOOD MAC	3
26. BRUCE SPRINGSTEEN	19	26. STEVIE WONDER	3
27. CAROLE KING	19	27. ERIC CLAPTON	3
28. MARIAH CAREY	19	28. SIMON & GARFUNKEL	3
29. BILLY JOEL	18	29. MADONNA	3
30. U2	18	30. THE SUPREMES	3
31. STEVIE WONDER	17	31. CAROLE KING	3
32. THE POLICE	17	32. VAN HALEN	3
33. BILLY RAY CYRUS	17	33. LINDA RONSTADT	3
34. DORIS DAY	17	34. JOHN DENVER	3
		35. DONNA SUMMER	3
		36. JOHN LENNON	3
		37. JANET JACKSON	3
		38. CROSBY, STILLS & NASH (& YOUNG)	3
		39. ALLAN SHERMAN	3
		40. NIRVANA	3

TOP ARTIST ACHIEVEMENTS

ARTIST	POINTS	ARTIST	POINTS
THE MOST TOP 10 ALBUMS		**THE MOST TOP 40 ALBUMS**	
1. FRANK SINATRA	33	1. FRANK SINATRA	51
2. THE ROLLING STONES	32	2. ELVIS PRESLEY	49
3. ELVIS PRESLEY	25	3. BARBRA STREISAND	38
4. THE BEATLES	24	4. THE ROLLING STONES	35
5. BARBRA STREISAND	24	5. JOHNNY MATHIS	31
6. JOHNNY MATHIS	18	6. BOB DYLAN	30
7. MITCH MILLER	17	7. MANTOVANI	30
8. THE KINGSTON TRIO	14	8. THE BEATLES	28
9. ELTON JOHN	14	9. ELTON JOHN	28
10. BOB DYLAN	14	10. THE TEMPTATIONS	28
11. MANTOVANI	13	11. RAY CONNIFF	28
12. THE BEACH BOYS	13	12. LAWRENCE WELK	24
13. NEIL DIAMOND	13	13. MITCH MILLER	23
14. CHICAGO	12	14. NEIL DIAMOND	23
15. PAUL McCARTNEY/WINGS	12	15. ERIC CLAPTON	22
16. ANDY WILLIAMS	12	16. JEFFERSON AIRPLANE/STARSHIP	21
17. RAY CONNIFF	12	17. ARETHA FRANKLIN	21
18. HERB ALPERT/THE TIJUANA BRASS	10	18. PAUL McCARTNEY/WINGS	20
19. LED ZEPPELIN	10	19. THE BEACH BOYS	20
20. BILLY JOEL	10	20. NEIL YOUNG	20
21. STEVIE WONDER	10	21. THE KINGSTON TRIO	19
22. THE TEMPTATIONS	10	22. ANDY WILLIAMS	19
23. LAWRENCE WELK	10	23. ROD STEWART	19
24. LINDA RONSTADT	10	24. THE SUPREMES	19
25. HARRY BELAFONTE	9	25. ROGER WILLIAMS	19
26. PRINCE	9	26. CHICAGO	18
27. HENRY MANCINI	9	27. STEVIE WONDER	18
28. BRUCE SPRINGSTEEN	9	28. BILLY VAUGHN	18
29. MADONNA	9	29. KISS	18
30. VAN HALEN	9	30. NAT "KING" COLE	17
31. THE WHO	9	31. JETHRO TULL	17
		32. DAVID BOWIE	17
		33. THE VENTURES	17

*Ties are broken based on the artists' rank in the "Top 100 Artists of the Rock Era" section.

+Subject to change since album was still at the No. 1 position as of the 2/25/95 cutoff date.

THE TOP 100 ALBUMS OF THE ROCK ERA

Following is a listing, in rank order, of the top No. 1 albums from January, 1955, through December, 1994. The ranking is based on this order: total weeks at No. 1, total weeks in the Top 10, total weeks in the Top 40, and finally, total weeks charted.

Columnar headings show the following data:

PK YR:	Year album reached its peak position
WEEKS CH:	Total weeks charted
WEEKS 40:	Total weeks in the Top 40
WEEKS 10:	Total weeks in the Top 10
WEEKS #1:	Total weeks album held the No. 1 position
+:	subject to change since album was still charted as of the 2/25/95 cutoff date

PK YR	CH	WEEKS 40	10	#1	TITLE/ARTIST
62	198	144	106	54	1. WEST SIDE STORY…Soundtrack
83	122	91	78	37	2. THRILLER…Michael Jackson
58	262	161	90	31	3. SOUTH PACIFIC…Soundtrack
56	99	72	58	31	4. CALYPSO…Harry Belafonte
77	134	60	52	31	5. RUMOURS…Fleetwood Mac
78	120	54	35	24	6. SATURDAY NIGHT FEVER…Bee Gees/Soundtrack
84	72	42	32	24	7. PURPLE RAIN…Prince And The Revolution/Soundtrack
90	108	70	52	21	8. PLEASE HAMMER DON'T HURT 'EM…M.C. Hammer
92	117 +	76	39	20	9. THE BODYGUARD…Whitney Houston/Soundtrack
61	79	53	39	20	10. BLUE HAWAII…Elvis Presley/Soundtrack
91	132	70	50	18	11. ROPIN' THE WIND…Garth Brooks
87	96	68	48	18	12. DIRTY DANCING…Soundtrack
67	70	45	25	18	13. MORE OF THE MONKEES…The Monkees
92	97	59	43	17	14. SOME GAVE ALL…Billy Ray Cyrus
83	75	50	40	17	15. SYNCHRONICITY…The Police
55	28	28	25	17	16. LOVE ME OR LEAVE ME…Doris Day/Soundtrack
60	276	168	105	16	17. THE SOUND OF MUSIC…Original Cast
90	67	39	26	16	18. TO THE EXTREME…Vanilla Ice
63	107	61	23	16	19. DAYS OF WINE AND ROSES…Andy Williams
56	480	292	173	15	20. MY FAIR LADY…Original Cast
71	302	68	46	15	21. TAPESTRY…Carole King
67	175	63	33	15	22. SGT. PEPPER'S LONELY HEARTS CLUB BAND…The Beatles
82	90	48	31	15	23. BUSINESS AS USUAL…Men At Work
59	118	43	31	15	24. THE KINGSTON TRIO AT LARGE…The Kingston Trio
81	101	50	30	15	25. HI INFIDELITY…REO Speedwagon
80	123	35	27	15	26. THE WALL…Pink Floyd
65	114	78	48	14	27. MARY POPPINS…Soundtrack
86	162	78	46	14	28. WHITNEY HOUSTON…Whitney Houston
60	108	67	44	14	29. THE BUTTON-DOWN MIND OF BOB NEWHART…Bob Newhart
61	89	55	38	14	30. EXODUS…Soundtrack
76	80	44	35	14	31. SONGS IN THE KEY OF LIFE…Stevie Wonder
62	101	59	33	14	32. MODERN SOUNDS IN COUNTRY AND WESTERN MUSIC…Ray Charles
64	51	40	28	14	33. A HARD DAY'S NIGHT…The Beatles/Soundtrack
60	124	105	43	13	34. PERSUASIVE PERCUSSION…Enoch Light/Terry Snyder And The All-Stars
61	95	73	37	13	35. JUDY AT CARNEGIE HALL…Judy Garland
66	78	49	32	13	36. THE MONKEES…The Monkees

THE TOP 100 ALBUMS OF THE ROCK ERA

PK YR	CH	WEEKS 40	10	#1	TITLE/ARTIST
69	151	59	28	13	37. HAIR…Original Cast
58	245	123	66	12	38. THE MUSIC MAN…Original Cast
88	87	69	51	12	39. FAITH…George Michael
62	96	69	46	12	40. BREAKFAST AT TIFFANY'S…Henry Mancini/Soundtrack
60	73	42	29	12	41. SOLD OUT…The Kingston Trio
78	77	39	29	12	42. GREASE…Soundtrack
62	49	26	17	12	43. THE FIRST FAMILY…Vaughn Meader
91	113	66	49	11	44. MARIAH CAREY…Mariah Carey
61	64	50	33	11	45. CALCUTTA!…Lawrence Welk
87	85	51	31	11	46. WHITNEY…Whitney Houston
69	129	32	27	11	47. ABBEY ROAD…The Beatles
64	71	27	21	11	48. MEET THE BEATLES!…The Beatles
85	34	22	18	11	49. MIAMI VICE…TV Soundtrack
89	175	78	64	10	50. FOREVER YOUR GIRL…Paula Abdul
57	88	88	54	10	51. AROUND THE WORLD IN 80 DAYS…Soundtrack
58	172	78	54	10	52. GIGI…Soundtrack
76	97	55	52	10	53. FRAMPTON COMES ALIVE!…Peter Frampton
56	48	48	43	10	54. ELVIS PRESLEY…Elvis Presley
59	119	47	43	10	55. THE MUSIC FROM PETER GUNN…Henry Mancini/TV Soundtrack
81	81	52	34	10	56. 4…Foreigner
60	111	46	29	10	57. G.I. BLUES…Elvis Presley/Soundtrack
84	61	27	20	10	58. FOOTLOOSE…Soundtrack
60	60	27	20	10	59. STRING ALONG…The Kingston Trio
57	29	29	19	10	60. LOVING YOU…Elvis Presley/Soundtrack
63	39	22	18	10	61. THE SINGING NUN…The Singing Nun
70	85	24	17	10	62. BRIDGE OVER TROUBLED WATER…Simon and Garfunkel
74	104	20	11	10	63. ELTON JOHN - GREATEST HITS…Elton John
85	97	55	37	9	64. BROTHERS IN ARMS…Dire Straits
87	103	58	35	9	65. THE JOSHUA TREE…U2
66	129	59	32	9	66. WHAT NOW MY LOVE…Herb Alpert & The Tijuana Brass
82	64	35	27	9	67. ASIA…Asia
68	69	47	26	9	68. THE GRADUATE…Simon & Garfunkel/Soundtrack
82	120	40	22	9	69. AMERICAN FOOL…John Cougar
94	37+	37+	22	9	70. THE LION KING…Soundtrack
81	58	30	22	9	71. TATTOO YOU…The Rolling Stones
61	40	39	21	9	72. STARS FOR A SUMMER NIGHT…Various Artists
79	57	36	21	9	73. THE LONG RUN…Eagles
60	86	35	19	9	74. NICE 'N' EASY…Frank Sinatra
70	69	26	19	9	75. COSMO'S FACTORY…Creedence Clearwater Revival
65	71	38	16	9	76. BEATLES '65…The Beatles
65	44	33	15	9	77. HELP!…The Beatles/Soundtrack
68	155	25	15	9	78. THE BEATLES [WHITE ALBUM]…The Beatles
71	42	23	15	9	79. PEARL…Janis Joplin
72	51	20	13	9	80. CHICAGO V…Chicago

THE TOP 100 ALBUMS OF THE ROCK ERA

PK YR	CH	WEEKS 40	10	#1	TITLE/ARTIST
65	185	141	61	8	81. WHIPPED CREAM & OTHER DELIGHTS...Herb Alpert's Tijuana Brass
58	204	128	53	8	82. SING ALONG WITH MITCH...Mitch Miller & The Gang
86	94	60	46	8	83. SLIPPERY WHEN WET...Bon Jovi
89	78	61	41	8	84. GIRL YOU KNOW IT'S TRUE...Milli Vanilli
73	103	43	36	8	85. GOODBYE YELLOW BRICK ROAD...Elton John
93	76+	50	33	8	86. MUSIC BOX...Mariah Carey
57	94	55	31	8	87. LOVE IS THE THING...Nat "King" Cole
77	107	32	28	8	88. HOTEL CALIFORNIA...Eagles
59	126	40	26	8	89. HERE WE GO AGAIN!...The Kingston Trio
80	74	27	24	8	90. DOUBLE FANTASY...John Lennon/Yoko Ono
78	76	34	22	8	91. 52ND STREET...Billy Joel
68	66	29	19	8	92. CHEAP THRILLS...Big Brother And The Holding Company
68	91	30	14	8	93. MAGICAL MYSTERY TOUR...The Beatles
63	32	24	12	8	94. MY SON, THE NUT...Allan Sherman
62	185	112	85	7	95. PETER, PAUL AND MARY...Peter, Paul and Mary
84	139	96	84	7	96. BORN IN THE U.S.A. ...Bruce Springsteen
69	109	66	50	7	97. BLOOD, SWEAT & TEARS...Blood, Sweat & Tears
61	57	57	42	7	98. STEREO 35/MM...Enoch Light And The Light Brigade
58	125	76	39	7	99. TCHAIKOVSKY: PIANO CONCERTO NO. 1...Van Cliburn
85	123	70	31	7	100. NO JACKET REQUIRED...Phil Collins

THE TOP ALBUMS BY DECADE

PK YR	CH	WEEKS 40	10	#1	TITLE/ARTIST
					FIFTIES (1955-59)
58	262	161	90	31	1. SOUTH PACIFIC…Soundtrack
56	99	72	58	31	2. CALYPSO…Harry Belafonte
55	28	28	25	17	3. LOVE ME OR LEAVE ME…Doris Day/Soundtrack
56	480	292	173	15	4. MY FAIR LADY…Original Cast
59	118	43	31	15	5. THE KINGSTON TRIO AT LARGE…The Kingston Trio
58	245	123	66	12	6. THE MUSIC MAN…Original Cast
57	88	88	54	10	7. AROUND THE WORLD IN 80 DAYS…Soundtrack
58	172	78	54	10	8. GIGI…Soundtrack
56	48	48	43	10	9. ELVIS PRESLEY…Elvis Presley
59	119	47	43	10	10. THE MUSIC FROM PETER GUNN…Henry Mancini/TV Soundtrack
57	29	29	19	10	11. LOVING YOU…Elvis Presley/Soundtrack
58	204	128	53	8	12. SING ALONG WITH MITCH…Mitch Miller & The Gang
57	94	55	31	8	13. LOVE IS THE THING…Nat "King" Cole
59	126	40	26	8	14. HERE WE GO AGAIN!…The Kingston Trio
58	125	76	39	7	15. TCHAIKOVSKY: PIANO CONCERTO NO. 1…Van Cliburn
56	62	62	54	6	16. BELAFONTE…Harry Belafonte
55	27	27	24	6	17. STARRING SAMMY DAVIS, JR. …Sammy Davis, Jr.
59	295	40	38	5	18. HEAVENLY…Johnny Mathis
56	32	32	24	5	19. ELVIS…Elvis Presley
58	120	55	19	5	20. FRANK SINATRA SINGS FOR ONLY THE LONELY…Frank Sinatra
59	63	46	19	5	21. EXOTICA…Martin Denny
58	71	50	18	5	22. COME FLY WITH ME…Frank Sinatra
56	305	229	116	4	23. OKLAHOMA!…Soundtrack
57	7	7	6	4	24. ELVIS' CHRISTMAS ALBUM…Elvis Presley
58	490	178	57	3	25. JOHNNY'S GREATEST HITS…Johnny Mathis
59	151	67	17	3	26. FLOWER DRUM SONG…Original Cast
55	23	23	22	2	27. LONESOME ECHO…Jackie Gleason
58	33	33	18	2	28. RICKY…Ricky Nelson
55	20	20	18	2	29. CRAZY OTTO…Crazy Otto
58	5	5	3	2	30. CHRISTMAS SING-ALONG WITH MITCH…Mitch Miller & The Gang
56	277	178	78	1	31. THE KING AND I…Soundtrack
56	99	99	49	1	32. THE EDDY DUCHIN STORY…Soundtrack
59	231	113	43	1	33. FILM ENCORES…Mantovani and his orchestra
58	195	114	22	1	34. THE KINGSTON TRIO…The Kingston Trio
57	7	7	6	1	35. MERRY CHRISTMAS…Bing Crosby
					SIXTIES
62	198	144	106	54	1. WEST SIDE STORY…Soundtrack
61	79	53	39	20	2. BLUE HAWAII…Elvis Presley/Soundtrack
67	70	45	25	18	3. MORE OF THE MONKEES…The Monkees
60	276	168	105	16	4. THE SOUND OF MUSIC…Original Cast
63	107	61	23	16	5. DAYS OF WINE AND ROSES…Andy Williams
67	175	63	33	15	6. SGT. PEPPER'S LONELY HEARTS CLUB BAND…The Beatles
65	114	78	48	14	7. MARY POPPINS…Soundtrack
60	108	67	44	14	8. THE BUTTON-DOWN MIND OF BOB NEWHART…Bob Newhart
61	89	55	38	14	9. EXODUS…Soundtrack
62	101	59	33	14	10. MODERN SOUNDS IN COUNTRY AND WESTERN MUSIC…Ray Charles
64	51	40	28	14	11. A HARD DAY'S NIGHT…The Beatles/Soundtrack
60	124	105	43	13	12. PERSUASIVE PERCUSSION…Enoch Light/Terry Snyder and The All-Stars
61	95	73	37	13	13. JUDY AT CARNEGIE HALL…Judy Garland
66	78	49	32	13	14. THE MONKEES…The Monkees

THE TOP ALBUMS BY DECADE

PK YR	CH	WEEKS 40	10	#1	TITLE/ARTIST
69	151	59	28	13	15. HAIR…Original Cast
62	96	69	46	12	16. BREAKFAST AT TIFFANY'S…Henry Mancini/Soundtrack
60	73	42	29	12	17. SOLD OUT…The Kingston Trio
62	49	26	17	12	18. THE FIRST FAMILY…Vaughn Meader
61	64	50	33	11	19. CALCUTTA!…Lawrence Welk
69	129	32	27	11	20. ABBEY ROAD…The Beatles
64	71	27	21	11	21. MEET THE BEATLES!…The Beatles
60	111	46	29	10	22. G.I. BLUES…Elvis Presley/Soundtrack
60	60	27	20	10	23. STRING ALONG…The Kingston Trio
63	39	22	18	10	24. THE SINGING NUN…The Singing Nun
66	129	59	32	9	25. WHAT NOW MY LOVE…Herb Alpert & The Tijuana Brass
68	69	47	26	9	26. THE GRADUATE…Simon & Garfunkel/Soundtrack
61	40	39	21	9	27. STARS FOR A SUMMER NIGHT…Various Artists
60	86	35	19	9	28. NICE 'N' EASY…Frank Sinatra
65	71	38	16	9	29. BEATLES '65…The Beatles
65	44	33	15	9	30. HELP!…The Beatles/Soundtrack
68	155	25	15	9	31. THE BEATLES [WHITE ALBUM]…The Beatles
65	185	141	61	8	32. WHIPPED CREAM & OTHER DELIGHTS…Herb Alpert's Tijuana Brass
68	66	29	19	8	33. CHEAP THRILLS…Big Brother And The Holding Company
68	91	30	14	8	34. MAGICAL MYSTERY TOUR…The Beatles
63	32	24	12	8	35. MY SON, THE NUT…Allan Sherman
62	185	112	85	7	36. PETER, PAUL AND MARY…Peter, Paul and Mary
69	109	66	50	7	37. BLOOD, SWEAT & TEARS…Blood, Sweat & Tears
61	57	57	42	7	38. STEREO 35/MM…Enoch Light And The Light Brigade
69	98	29	24	7	39. LED ZEPPELIN II…Led Zeppelin
68	66	40	20	7	40. BOOKENDS…Simon & Garfunkel

SEVENTIES

PK YR	CH	WEEKS 40	10	#1	TITLE/ARTIST
77	134	60	52	31	1. RUMOURS…Fleetwood Mac
78	120	54	35	24	2. SATURDAY NIGHT FEVER…Bee Gees/Soundtrack
71	302	68	46	15	3. TAPESTRY…Carole King
76	80	44	35	14	4. SONGS IN THE KEY OF LIFE…Stevie Wonder
78	77	39	29	12	5. GREASE…Soundtrack
76	97	55	52	10	6. FRAMPTON COMES ALIVE!…Peter Frampton
70	85	24	17	10	7. BRIDGE OVER TROUBLED WATER…Simon and Garfunkel
74	104	20	11	10	8. ELTON JOHN - GREATEST HITS…Elton John
79	57	36	21	9	9. THE LONG RUN…Eagles
70	69	26	19	9	10. COSMO'S FACTORY…Creedence Clearwater Revival
71	42	23	15	9	11. PEARL…Janis Joplin
72	51	20	13	9	12. CHICAGO V…Chicago
73	103	43	36	8	13. GOODBYE YELLOW BRICK ROAD…Elton John
77	107	32	28	8	14. HOTEL CALIFORNIA…Eagles
78	76	34	22	8	15. 52ND STREET…Billy Joel
76	51	27	21	7	16. WINGS AT THE SPEED OF SOUND…Wings
79	41	28	18	7	17. IN THROUGH THE OUT DOOR…Led Zeppelin
72	48	26	17	7	18. AMERICAN PIE…Don McLean
75	43	24	17	7	19. CAPTAIN FANTASTIC AND THE BROWN DIRT COWBOY…Elton John
71	38	22	14	7	20. ALL THINGS MUST PASS…George Harrison
70	88	40	30	6	21. ABRAXAS…Santana
79	88	48	26	6	22. BREAKFAST IN AMERICA…Supertramp
77	51	28	18	6	23. A STAR IS BORN…Barbra Streisand/Soundtrack
79	55	26	18	6	24. SPIRITS HAVING FLOWN…Bee Gees
79	49	26	16	6	25. BAD GIRLS…Donna Summer

THE TOP ALBUMS BY DECADE

PK YR	CH	WEEKS 40	10	#1	TITLE/ARTIST
75	41	15	12	6	26. PHYSICAL GRAFFITI...Led Zeppelin
74	93	42	19	5	27. YOU DON'T MESS AROUND WITH JIM...Jim Croce
75	56	43	18	5	28. ONE OF THESE NIGHTS...Eagles
72	61	25	18	5	29. HONKY CHATEAU...Elton John
79	87	30	16	5	30. MINUTE BY MINUTE...The Doobie Brothers
77	47	23	16	5	31. SIMPLE DREAMS...Linda Ronstadt
73	56	24	15	5	32. BROTHERS AND SISTERS...The Allman Brothers Band
74	41	23	15	5	33. THE STING...Marvin Hamlisch/Soundtrack
79	40	22	15	5	34. GET THE KNACK...The Knack
72	54	26	14	5	35. FIRST TAKE...Roberta Flack
73	71	23	14	5	36. NO SECRETS...Carly Simon
75	72	22	13	5	37. CHICAGO IX - CHICAGO'S GREATEST HITS...Chicago
72	40	22	13	5	38. AMERICA...America
76	35	17	13	5	39. DESIRE...Bob Dylan
76	133	57	12	5	40. EAGLES/THEIR GREATEST HITS 1971-1975...Eagles

EIGHTIES

PK YR	CH	WEEKS 40	10	#1	TITLE/ARTIST
83	122	91	78	37	1. THRILLER...Michael Jackson
84	72	42	32	24	2. PURPLE RAIN...Prince And The Revolution/Soundtrack
87	96	68	48	18	3. DIRTY DANCING...Soundtrack
83	75	50	40	17	4. SYNCHRONICITY...The Police
82	90	48	31	15	5. BUSINESS AS USUAL...Men At Work
81	101	50	30	15	6. HI INFIDELITY...REO Speedwagon
80	123	35	27	15	7. THE WALL...Pink Floyd
86	162	78	46	14	8. WHITNEY HOUSTON...Whitney Houston
88	87	69	51	12	9. FAITH...George Michael
87	85	51	31	11	10. WHITNEY...Whitney Houston
85	34	22	18	11	11. MIAMI VICE...TV Soundtrack
89	175	78	64	10	12. FOREVER YOUR GIRL...Paula Abdul
81	81	52	34	10	13. 4...Foreigner
84	61	27	20	10	14. FOOTLOOSE...Soundtrack
85	97	55	37	9	15. BROTHERS IN ARMS...Dire Straits
87	103	58	35	9	16. THE JOSHUA TREE...U2
82	64	35	27	9	17. ASIA...Asia
82	120	40	22	9	18. AMERICAN FOOL...John Cougar
81	58	30	22	9	19. TATTOO YOU...The Rolling Stones
86	94	60	46	8	20. SLIPPERY WHEN WET...Bon Jovi
89	78	61	41	8	21. GIRL YOU KNOW IT'S TRUE...Milli Vanilli
80	74	27	24	8	22. DOUBLE FANTASY...John Lennon/Yoko Ono
84	139	96	84	7	23. BORN IN THE U.S.A. ...Bruce Springsteen
85	123	70	31	7	24. NO JACKET REQUIRED...Phil Collins
89	63	40	27	7	25. THE RAW & THE COOKED...Fine Young Cannibals
87	68	37	19	7	26. LICENSED TO ILL...Beastie Boys
80	51	20	14	7	27. EMOTIONAL RESCUE...The Rolling Stones
86	26	15	11	7	28. BRUCE SPRINGSTEEN & THE E STREET BAND LIVE/1975-85... Bruce Springsteen & The E Street Band
88	133	96	78	6	29. HYSTERIA...Def Leppard
89	97	69	45	6	30. DON'T BE CRUEL...Bobby Brown
87	87	54	39	6	31. BAD...Michael Jackson
80	73	35	25	6	32. GLASS HOUSES...Billy Joel
80	110	43	22	6	33. AGAINST THE WIND...Bob Seger & The Silver Bullet Band
89	77	31	16	6	34. LIKE A PRAYER...Madonna
82	72	38	15	6	35. BEAUTY AND THE BEAT...Go-Go's

THE TOP ALBUMS BY DECADE

PK YR	CH	WEEKS 40	10	#1	TITLE/ARTIST
88	38	23	14	6	36. RATTLE AND HUM…U2/Soundtrack
89	34	17	10	6	37. BATMAN…Prince/Soundtrack
88	147	78	52	5	38. APPETITE FOR DESTRUCTION…Guns N' Roses
85	83	55	32	5	39. SONGS FROM THE BIG CHAIR…Tears For Fears
86	82	52	25	5	40. TRUE BLUE…Madonna

NINETIES

PK YR	CH	WEEKS 40	10	#1	TITLE/ARTIST
90	108	70	52	21	1. PLEASE HAMMER DON'T HURT 'EM…M.C. Hammer
92	117+	76	39	20	2. THE BODYGUARD…Whitney Houston/Soundtrack
91	132	70	50	18	3. ROPIN' THE WIND…Garth Brooks
92	97	59	43	17	4. SOME GAVE ALL…Billy Ray Cyrus
90	67	39	26	16	5. TO THE EXTREME…Vanilla Ice
91	113	66	49	11	6. MARIAH CAREY…Mariah Carey
94	37+	37+	22	9	7. THE LION KING…Soundtrack
93	76+	50	33	8	8. MUSIC BOX…Mariah Carey
92	64	35	17	7	9. THE CHASE…Garth Brooks
93	91+	52	36	6	10. JANET.…Janet Jackson
90	52	27	16	6	11. I DO NOT WANT WHAT I HAVEN'T GOT…Sinead O'Connor
92	65	31	15	5	12. ADRENALIZE…Def Leppard
91	110	49	14	5	13. UNFORGETTABLE WITH LOVE…Natalie Cole
93	67	28	14	5	14. VS. …Pearl Jam
93	76+	25	8	5	15. IN PIECES…Garth Brooks
91	183+	85	30	4	16. METALLICA…Metallica
94	24+	24+	24+	4	17. II…Boyz II Men
91	117	47	18	4	18. DANGEROUS…Michael Jackson
94	45+	20	9	4	19. THE DIVISION BELL…Pink Floyd
93	129+	52	38	3	20. UNPLUGGED…Eric Clapton
90	90	50	20	3	21. …BUT SERIOUSLY…Phil Collins
93	56	35	18	3	22. RIVER OF DREAMS…Billy Joel
93	64+	31	17	3	23. DOGGY STYLE…Snoop Doggy Dogg
94	36+	36+	16	3	24. PURPLE…Stone Temple Pilots
91	74	26	12	3	25. FOR UNLAWFUL CARNAL KNOWLEDGE…Van Halen
90	185	40	11	3	26. NICK OF TIME…Bonnie Raitt
94	14	10	6	3	27. MIRACLES - THE HOLIDAY ALBUM…Kenny G
94	64+	63+	30	2	28. THE SIGN…Ace Of Base
92	171+	50	28	2	29. NEVERMIND…Nirvana
92	65	45	25	2	30. TOTALLY KROSSED OUT…Kris Kross
91	109	48	22	2	31. OUT OF TIME…R.E.M.
94	47+	47+	17	2	32. NOT A MOMENT TOO SOON…Tim McGraw
91	70	41	16	2	33. SPELLBOUND…Paula Abdul
91	106	30	16	2	34. USE YOUR ILLUSION II…Guns N' Roses
94	14+	14+	14+	2	35. HELL FREEZES OVER…Eagles
94	83+	59	11	2	36. TONI BRAXTON…Toni Braxton
93	56	18	10	2	37. BLACK SUNDAY…Cypress Hill
92	47	16	9	2	38. WAYNE'S WORLD…Soundtrack
93	40	15	7	2	39. ZOOROPA…U2
94	20+	20+	6	2	40. MONSTER…R.E.M.

+subject to change since album was still charted as of the 2/25/95 cutoff date

NO. 1 ALBUMS LISTED CHRONOLOGICALLY

This section lists in chronological order, by peak date, all of the 409 albums that hit the No. 1 position on *Billboard's Top Pop Albums* chart from 1955-1994.

For the years 1958 through 1963, when separate stereo and mono charts were published each week, there are special columns on the right side of the page to show the weeks each album held the No. 1 spot on each of these pop charts. If an album peaked at No. 1 on both the mono and stereo charts in the same week, it is counted as only one week at No. 1. Therefore, the grand total of an album's weeks at No. 1 on all charts may equal more than the total shown on the left side of the page.

The date shown is the earliest date that an album hit No. 1 on any of the three pop charts. Some dates are duplicated because different albums peaked at No. 1 on the same date on different charts.

DATE: Date album first hit the No. 1 position
WKS: Total weeks album held the No. 1 position
    †: Album appeared nonconsecutively at the No. 1 position
    ★: Album debuted at No. 1

CHARTS COLUMN:
  1 CH: One chart published
    ST: Stereo chart
  MO: Mono chart

The No. 1 album of each year is shown in **bold type** and is based on total weeks at the No. 1 spot. Ties are broken by total weeks charted. The album qualifies for the award only in the year that it first peaked at No. 1.

DATE	WKS	ALBUM TITLE	ARTIST
		1955	
5/28	2	1. Crazy Otto	Crazy Otto
6/11	6	2. Starring Sammy Davis, Jr.	Sammy Davis, Jr.
7/23	2	3. Lonesome Echo	Jackie Gleason
8/6	17	4. **Love Me Or Leave Me**	Doris Day/Soundtrack
		Two albums from 1954 continued into 1955 at the No. 1 spot: *The Student Prince*, Mario Lanza (eighteen weeks), and *Music, Martinis And Memories*, Jackie Gleason (two weeks). For all of 1955 and up to 3/24/56, the album chart was published mainly on a biweekly basis. The chart was considered "frozen" for a nonpublished week; therefore, each position on the published chart was counted twice. In addition to these biweekly "frozen" charts, there were five other weeks of unpublished charts that did not count toward weeks at the No. 1 spot.	
		1956	
1/28	4	1. Oklahoma!	Soundtrack
3/24	6	2. Belafonte	Harry Belafonte
5/5	10	3. Elvis Presley	Elvis Presley
7/14	15†	4. My Fair Lady	Original Cast
		Peaked at No. 1 in four consecutive years: 1956 (eight wks.), 1957 (one wk.), 1958 (three wks.), & 1959 (three wks.-Stereo chart)	
9/8	31†	5. **Calypso**	Harry Belafonte
10/6	1	6. The King And I	Soundtrack
10/13	1	7. The Eddy Duchin Story	Soundtrack
12/8	5	8. Elvis	Elvis Presley
		Beginning with 3/24/56, *Billboard* published the album chart on a weekly basis. From the first of the year to that date, there were two published charts, two frozen charts, and seven weeks of unpublished charts.	

DATE	WKS	ALBUM TITLE	ARTIST
		1957	
5/27	8	1. Love Is The Thing	Nat "King" Cole
7/22	10†	2. **Around The World In 80 Days**	Soundtrack
7/29	10	3. Loving You	Elvis Presley/Soundtrack
12/16	4†	4. Elvis' Christmas Album	Elvis Presley
12/30	1	5. Merry Christmas	Bing Crosby

DATE	WKS	ALBUM TITLE	ARTIST	CHARTS		
		1958		1CH	ST	MO
1/20	2	1. Ricky	Ricky Nelson	2	—	—
2/10	5	2. Come fly with me	Frank Sinatra	5	—	—
3/17	12†	3. The Music Man	Original Cast	12	—	—
5/19	31†	4. **South Pacific**	Soundtrack	3	28	—
		Three wks. No. 1 in 1958; twenty-eight wks. No. 1 on Stereo charts beginning 5/25/59				
6/9	3†	5. Johnny's Greatest Hits	Johnny Mathis	3	—	—
7/21	10†	6. Gigi	Soundtrack	6	—	4
		Three wks. No. 1 in 1958; three wks. No. 1 in 1959; and four wks. No. 1 on Mono charts beginning 5/29/59				
8/11	7†	7. Tchaikovsky: Piano Concerto No. 1	Van Cliburn	7	—	—
10/6	8†	8. Sing Along With Mitch	Mitch Miller & The Gang	8	—	—
10/13	5	9. Frank Sinatra sings for Only The Lonely	Frank Sinatra	5	—	—
11/24	1	10. The Kingston Trio	The Kingston Trio	1	—	—
12/29	2	11. Christmas Sing-Along With Mitch	Mitch Miller & The Gang	2	—	—
		1959				
2/2	3	1. Flower Drum Song	Original Cast	3	—	—
2/23	10	2. The Music From Peter Gunn	Henry Mancini	10	—	—
		5/25/59: Separate Stereo and Mono charts begin				
6/22	5	3. Exotica	Martin Denny	—	—	5
7/13	1	4. Film Encores	Mantovani and his orchestra	—	1	—
7/27	15	5. **The Kingston Trio At Large**	The Kingston Trio	—	—	15
11/9	5	6. Heavenly	Johnny Mathis	—	—	5
12/14	8	7. Here We Go Again!	The Kingston Trio	—	2	8
		1960				
1/11	1	1. The Lord's Prayer	Mormon Tabernacle Choir	—	1	—
1/25	16	2. **The Sound Of Music**	Original Cast	—	15	12
4/25	13†	3. Persuasive Percussion	Enoch Light/Terry Snyder and The All-Stars	—	13	—
5/2	2†	4. Theme from A Summer Place	Billy Vaughn and his orchestra	—	—	2
5/9	12†	5. Sold Out	The Kingston Trio	—	3	10
7/25	14†	6. The Button-Down Mind Of Bob Newhart	Bob Newhart	—	—	14
8/29	10†	7. String Along	The Kingston Trio	—	10	5
10/24	9†	8. Nice 'n' Easy	Frank Sinatra	—	9	1
12/5	10	9. G.I. Blues	Elvis Presley/Soundtrack	—	2	8

DATE	WKS	ALBUM TITLE	ARTIST	CHARTS		
		1961		**1CH**	**ST**	**MO**
1/9	1	1. The Button-Down Mind Strikes Back!	Bob Newhart	—	—	1
1/16	5†	2. Wonderland By Night	Bert Kaempfert and his orchestra	—	—	5
1/23	14†	3. Exodus	Soundtrack	—	14	3
3/13	11†	4. Calcutta!	Lawrence Welk	—	11	8
6/5	6	5. Camelot	Original Cast	—	—	6
7/17	9	6. Stars For A Summer Night	Various Artists	—	9	4
7/17	1	7. Carnival	Original Cast	—	—	1
8/21	3	8. Something for Everybody	Elvis Presley	—	—	3
9/11	13	9. Judy At Carnegie Hall	Judy Garland	—	9	13
11/20	7	10. Stereo 35/MM	Enoch Light & The Light Brigade	—	7	—
12/11	20	11. **Blue Hawaii**	Elvis Presley/Soundtrack	—	4	20
		1962				
1/13	1	1. Holiday Sing Along With Mitch	Mitch Miller And The Gang	—	1	—
2/10	12†	2. Breakfast At Tiffany's	Henry Mancini/Soundtrack	—	12	—
5/5	54†	3. **West Side Story** Most weeks at No. 1 for the 1955-94 era	Soundtrack	—	53	12
6/23	14	4. Modern Sounds In Country And Western Music	Ray Charles	—	1	14
10/20	7†	5. Peter, Paul and Mary Returned to the No. 1 spot for one week on 10/26/63	Peter, Paul and Mary	1	—	6
12/1	2	6. My Son, The Folk Singer	Allan Sherman	—	—	2
12/15	12	7. The First Family	Vaughn Meader	—	—	12
		1963				
3/9	1	1. Jazz Samba	Stan Getz/Charlie Byrd	—	—	1
3/9	1	2. My Son, The Celebrity	Allan Sherman	—	1	—
3/16	5	3. Songs I Sing On The Jackie Gleason Show	Frank Fontaine	—	—	5
5/4	16	4. **Days of Wine and Roses**	Andy Williams	1	11	15
		8/17/63: Stereo & Mono charts combined into one single chart				
8/24	1	5. Little Stevie Wonder/The 12 Year Old Genius	Stevie Wonder	1	—	—
8/31	8	6. My Son, The Nut	Allan Sherman	8	—	—
11/2	5	7. In The Wind	Peter, Paul and Mary	5	—	—
12/7	10	8. The Singing Nun	The Singing Nun	10	—	—

DATE	WKS	ALBUM TITLE	ARTIST
		1964	
2/15	11	1. Meet The Beatles!	The Beatles
5/2	5	2. The Beatles' Second Album	The Beatles
6/6	1	3. Hello, Dolly!	Original Cast
6/13	6	4. Hello, Dolly!	Louis Armstrong
7/25	14	5. **A Hard Day's Night**	The Beatles/Soundtrack
10/31	5	6. People	Barbra Streisand
12/5	4	7. Beach Boys Concert	The Beach Boys

DATE	WKS	ALBUM TITLE	ARTIST
		1965	
1/2	1	1. Roustabout	Elvis Presley/Soundtrack
1/9	9	2. Beatles '65	The Beatles
3/13	14†	3. **Mary Poppins**	Soundtrack
3/20	3	4. Goldfinger	Soundtrack
7/10	6	5. Beatles VI	The Beatles
8/21	3	6. Out Of Our Heads	The Rolling Stones
9/11	9	7. Help!	The Beatles/Soundtrack
11/13	2	8. The Sound Of Music	Soundtrack
11/27	8†	9. Whipped Cream & Other Delights	Herb Alpert's Tijuana Brass
		1966	
1/8	6	1. Rubber Soul	The Beatles
3/5	6†	2. Going Places	Herb Alpert And The Tijuana Brass
3/12	5	3. Ballads of the Green Berets	SSgt Barry Sadler
5/21	1	4. If You Can Believe Your Eyes And Ears	The Mamas And The Papas
5/28	9†	5. What Now My Love	Herb Alpert & The Tijuana Brass
7/23	1	6. Strangers In The Night	Frank Sinatra
7/30	5	7. "Yesterday"…And Today	The Beatles
9/10	6	8. Revolver	The Beatles
10/22	2	9. The Supremes A' Go-Go	The Supremes
11/5	1	10. Doctor Zhivago	Soundtrack
11/12	13	11. **The Monkees**	The Monkees
		1967	
2/11	18	1. **More Of The Monkees**	The Monkees
6/17	1	2. Sounds Like	Herb Alpert & The Tijuana Brass
6/24	1	3. Headquarters	The Monkees
7/1	15	4. Sgt. Pepper's Lonely Hearts Club Band	The Beatles
10/14	2	5. Ode To Billie Joe	Bobbie Gentry
10/28	5	6. Diana Ross and the Supremes Greatest Hits	The Supremes
12/2	5	7. Pisces, Aquarius, Capricorn & Jones Ltd.	The Monkees
		1968	
1/6	8	1. Magical Mystery Tour	The Beatles
3/2	5	2. Blooming Hits	Paul Mauriat and his orchestra
4/6	9†	3. The Graduate	Simon & Garfunkel/Soundtrack
5/25	7†	4. Bookends	Simon & Garfunkel
7/27	2	5. The Beat Of The Brass	Herb Alpert & The Tijuana Brass
8/10	4	6. Wheels Of Fire	Cream
9/7	4†	7. Waiting For The Sun	The Doors
9/28	1	8. Time Peace/The Rascals' Greatest Hits	The Rascals
10/12	8†	9. Cheap Thrills	Big Brother And The Holding Company
11/16	2	10. Electric Ladyland	Jimi Hendrix Experience
12/21	5†	11. Wichita Lineman	Glen Campbell
12/28	9†	12. **The Beatles [White Album]**	The Beatles

DATE	WKS	ALBUM TITLE	ARTIST
and spanning		**1969**	
2/8	1	1. TCB	The Supremes with The Temptations
3/29	7†	2. Blood, Sweat & Tears	Blood, Sweat & Tears
4/26	13	3. **Hair**	Original Cast
8/23	4	4. Johnny Cash At San Quentin	Johnny Cash
9/20	2	5. Blind Faith	Blind Faith
10/4	4	6. Green River	Creedence Clearwater Revival
11/1	11†	7. Abbey Road	The Beatles
12/27	7†	8. Led Zeppelin II	Led Zeppelin
		1970	
3/7	10	1. **Bridge Over Troubled Water**	Simon and Garfunkel
5/16	1	2. Deja Vu	Crosby, Stills, Nash & Young
5/23	3	3. McCartney	Paul McCartney
6/13	4	4. Let It Be	The Beatles/Soundtrack
7/11	4	5. Woodstock	Various Artists/Soundtrack
8/8	2	6. Blood, Sweat & Tears 3	Blood, Sweat & Tears
8/22	9	7. Cosmo's Factory	Creedence Clearwater Revival
10/24	6†	8. Abraxas	Santana
10/31	4	9. Led Zeppelin III	Led Zeppelin
		1971	
1/2	7	1. All Things Must Pass	George Harrison
2/20	3†	2. Jesus Christ Superstar	Various Artists
2/27	9	3. Pearl	Janis Joplin
5/15	1	4. 4 Way Street	Crosby, Stills, Nash & Young
5/22	4	5. Sticky Fingers	The Rolling Stones
6/19	15	6. **Tapestry**	Carole King
10/2	4	7. Every Picture Tells A Story	Rod Stewart
10/30	1	8. Imagine	John Lennon
11/6	1	9. Shaft	Isaac Hayes/Soundtrack
11/13	5	10. Santana III	Santana
12/18	2	11. There's A Riot Goin' On	Sly & The Family Stone
		1972	
1/1	3	1. Music	Carole King
1/22	7	2. American Pie	Don McLean
3/11	2	3. Harvest	Neil Young
3/25	5	4. America	America
4/29	5	5. First Take	Roberta Flack
6/3	2	6. Thick As A Brick	Jethro Tull
6/17	4	7. Exile On Main St.	The Rolling Stones
7/15	5	8. Honky Chateau	Elton John
8/19	9	9. **Chicago V**	Chicago
10/21	4	10. Superfly	Curtis Mayfield/Soundtrack
11/18	3	11. Catch Bull At Four	Cat Stevens
12/9	5	12. Seventh Sojourn	The Moody Blues

DATE	WKS	ALBUM TITLE	ARTIST
		1973	
1/13	5	1. No Secrets	Carly Simon
2/17	2	2. The World Is A Ghetto	War
3/3	2	3. Don't Shoot Me I'm Only The Piano Player	Elton John
3/17	3	4. Dueling Banjos	Eric Weissberg
4/7	2	5. Lady Sings The Blues	Diana Ross/Soundtrack
4/21	1	6. Billion Dollar Babies	Alice Cooper
4/28	1	7. The Dark Side Of The Moon	Pink Floyd
5/5	1	8. Aloha from Hawaii via Satellite	Elvis Presley
5/12	2	9. Houses Of The Holy	Led Zeppelin
5/26	1	10. The Beatles/1967-1970	The Beatles
6/2	3	11. Red Rose Speedway	Paul McCartney & Wings
6/23	5	12. Living In The Material World	George Harrison
7/28	5†	13. Chicago VI	Chicago
8/18	1	14. A Passion Play	Jethro Tull
9/8	5	15. Brothers And Sisters	The Allman Brothers Band
10/13	4	16. Goats Head Soup	The Rolling Stones
11/10	8	17. **Goodbye Yellow Brick Road**	Elton John
		1974	
1/5	1	1. The Singles 1969-1973	Carpenters
1/12	5	2. You Don't Mess Around With Jim	Jim Croce
2/16	4	3. Planet Waves	Bob Dylan
3/16	2	4. The Way We Were	Barbra Streisand
3/30	3†	5. John Denver's Greatest Hits	John Denver
4/13	4†	6. Band On The Run	Paul McCartney & Wings
4/27	1	7. Chicago VII	Chicago
5/4	5	8. The Sting	Marvin Hamlisch/Soundtrack
6/22	2	9. Sundown	Gordon Lightfoot
7/13	4	10. Caribou	Elton John
8/10	1	11. Back Home Again	John Denver
8/17	4	12. 461 Ocean Boulevard	Eric Clapton
9/14	2	13. Fulfillingness' First Finale	Stevie Wonder
9/28	1	14. Bad Company	Bad Company
10/5	1	15. Endless Summer	The Beach Boys
10/12	1	16. If You Love Me, Let Me Know	Olivia Newton-John
10/19	1	17. Not Fragile	Bachman-Turner Overdrive
10/26	1	18. Can't Get Enough	Barry White
11/2	1	19. So Far	Crosby, Stills, Nash and Young
11/9	1	20. Wrap Around Joy	Carole King
11/16	1	21. Walls And Bridges	John Lennon
11/23	1	22. It's Only Rock 'N Roll	The Rolling Stones
11/30	10	23. **Elton John — Greatest Hits**	Elton John
		1975	
2/8	1	1. FireOhio Players	
2/15	1	2. Heart Like A Wheel	Linda Ronstadt
2/22	1	3. AWB	AWB (Average White Band)
3/1	2	4. Blood On The Tracks	Bob Dylan
3/15	1	5. Have You Never Been Mellow	Olivia Newton-John
3/22	6	6. Physical Graffiti	Led Zeppelin

DATE	WKS	ALBUM TITLE	ARTIST
	**1975 CONTINUED**		
5/3	2	7. Chicago VIII	Chicago
5/17	3	8. That's The Way Of The World	Earth, Wind & Fire/Soundtrack
6/7★	7†	9. **Captain Fantastic And The Brown Dirt Cowboy**	Elton John
7/19	1	10. Venus And Mars	Wings
7/26	5	11. One Of These Nights	Eagles
9/6	4†	12. Red Octopus	Jefferson Starship
9/13	1	13. The Heat Is On	The Isley Brothers
9/20	1	14. Between The Lines	Janis Ian
10/4	2	15. Wish You Were Here	Pink Floyd
10/18	2	16. Windsong	John Denver
11/8★	3	17. Rock Of The Westies	Elton John
12/6	1	18. Still Crazy After All These Years	Paul Simon
12/13	5	19. Chicago IX - Chicago's Greatest Hits	Chicago
	**1976**		
1/17	3	1. Gratitude	Earth, Wind & Fire
2/7	5	2. Desire	Bob Dylan
3/13	5†	3. Eagles/Their Greatest Hits 1971-1975	Eagles
4/10	10†	4. Frampton Comes Alive!	Peter Frampton
4/24	7†	5. Wings At The Speed Of Sound	Wings
5/1	2	6. Presence	Led Zeppelin
5/15	4†	7. Black And Blue	The Rolling Stones
7/31	2	8. Breezin'	George Benson
9/4	1	9. Fleetwood Mac	Fleetwood Mac
10/16★	14†	10. **Songs In The Key Of Life**	Stevie Wonder
	**1977**		
1/15	8†	1. Hotel California	Eagles
1/22	1	2. Wings Over America	Wings
2/12	6	3. A Star Is Born	Barbra Streisand/Soundtrack
4/2	31†	4. **Rumours**	Fleetwood Mac
7/16	1	5. Barry Manilow/Live	Barry Manilow
12/3	5	6. Simple Dreams	Linda Ronstadt
	**1978**		
1/21	24	1. **Saturday Night Fever**	Bee Gees/Soundtrack
7/8	1	2. City to City	Gerry Rafferty
7/15	2	3. Some Girls	The Rolling Stones
7/29	12†	4. Grease	Soundtrack
9/16	2†	5. Don't Look Back	Boston
11/4	1	6. Living In The USA	Linda Ronstadt
11/11	1	7. Live And More	Donna Summer
11/18	8†	8. 52nd Street	Billy Joel
	**1979**		
1/6	3	1. Barbra Streisand's Greatest Hits, Volume 2	Barbra Streisand
2/3	1	2. Briefcase Full Of Blues	Blues Brothers
2/10	3	3. Blondes Have More Fun	Rod Stewart
3/3	6†	4. Spirits Having Flown	Bee Gees
4/7	5†	5. Minute By Minute	The Doobie Brothers

DATE	WKS	ALBUM TITLE	ARTIST
		1979 CONTINUED	
5/19	6†	6. Breakfast In America	Supertramp
6/16	6†	7. Bad Girls	Donna Summer
8/11	5	8. Get The Knack	The Knack
9/15	7	9. In Through The Out Door	Led Zeppelin
11/3	9	10. **The Long Run**	Eagles
		1980	
1/5	1	1. On The Radio-Greatest Hits-Volumes I & II	Donna Summer
1/12	1	2. Bee Gees Greatest	Bee Gees
1/19	15	3. **The Wall**	Pink Floyd
5/3	6	4. Against The Wind	Bob Seger & The Silver Bullet Band
6/14	6	5. Glass Houses	Billy Joel
7/26	7	6. Emotional Rescue	The Rolling Stones
9/13	1	7. Hold Out	Jackson Browne
9/20	5	8. The Game	Queen
10/25	3†	9. Guilty	Barbra Streisand
11/8	4	10. The River	Bruce Springsteen
12/13	2	11. Kenny Rogers' Greatest Hits	Kenny Rogers
12/27	8	12. Double Fantasy	John Lennon/Yoko Ono
		1981	
2/21	15†	1. **Hi Infidelity**	REO Speedwagon
4/4	3†	2. Paradise Theater	Styx
6/27	4	3. Mistaken Identity	Kim Carnes
7/25	3	4. Long Distance Voyager	The Moody Blues
8/15	1	5. Precious Time	Pat Benatar
8/22	10†	6. 4 Foreigner	
9/5	1	7. Bella Donna	Stevie Nicks
9/12	1	8. Escape	Journey
9/19	9	9. Tattoo You	The Rolling Stones
12/26	3	10. For Those About To Rock We Salute You	AC/DC
		1982	
2/6	4	1. Freeze-Frame	The J. Geils Band
3/6	6	2. Beauty And The Beat	Go-Go's
4/17	4	3. Chariots Of Fire	Vangelis/Soundtrack
5/15	9†	4. Asia	Asia
5/29	3	5. Tug Of War	Paul McCartney
8/7	5	6. Mirage	Fleetwood Mac
9/11	9	7. American Fool	John Cougar
11/13	15	8. **Business As Usual**	Men At Work
		1983	
2/26	37†	1. **Thriller**	Michael Jackson
6/25	2	2. Flashdance	Soundtrack
7/23	17†	3. Synchronicity	The Police
11/26	1	4. Metal Health	Quiet Riot
12/3	3	5. Can't Slow Down	Lionel Richie

DATE	WKS	ALBUM TITLE	ARTIST
1984			
4/21	10	1. Footloose	Soundtrack
6/30	1	2. Sports	Huey Lewis And The News
7/7	7†	3. Born In The U.S.A.	Bruce Springsteen
8/4	24	4. **Purple Rain**	Prince And The Revolution/Soundtrack
1985			
2/9	3	1. Like A Virgin	Madonna
3/2	3	2. Make It Big	Wham!
3/23	1	3. Centerfield	John Fogerty
3/30	7†	4. No Jacket Required	Phil Collins
4/27	3	5. We Are The World	USA for Africa
6/1	3	6. Around the World in a Day	Prince & The Revolution
6/22	2	7. Beverly Hills Cop	Soundtrack
7/13	5†	8. Songs From The Big Chair	Tears For Fears
8/10	2	9. Reckless	Bryan Adams
8/31	9	10. Brothers In Arms	Dire Straits
11/2	11†	11. **Miami Vice**	TV Soundtrack
12/21	1	12. Heart	Heart
1986			
1/25	3	1. The Broadway Album	Barbra Streisand
2/15	2	2. Promise	Sade
3/1	1	3. Welcome To The Real World	Mr. Mister
3/8	14†	4. **Whitney Houston**	Whitney Houston
4/26	3	5. 5150	Van Halen
7/5	2	6. Control	Janet Jackson
7/19	1	7. Winner In You	Patti LaBelle
7/26	5†	8. Top Gun	Soundtrack
8/16	5	9. True Blue	Madonna
9/27	2	10. Dancing On The Ceiling	Lionel Richie
10/18	1	11. Fore!	Huey Lewis & The News
10/25	8†	12. Slippery When Wet	Bon Jovi
11/1	4	13. Third Stage	Boston
11/29★	7	14. Bruce Springsteen & The E Street Band Live/ 1975-85	Bruce Springsteen & The E Street Band
1987			
3/7	7	1. Licensed To Ill	Beastie Boys
4/25	9	2. The Joshua Tree	U2
6/27★	11	3. Whitney	Whitney Houston
9/12	2	4. La Bamba	Los Lobos/Soundtrack
9/26★	6	5. Bad	Michael Jackson
11/7	1	6. Tunnel of Love	Bruce Springsteen
11/14	18†	7. **Dirty Dancing**	Soundtrack
1988			
1/16	12†	1. **Faith**	George Michael
1/23	2	2. Tiffany	Tiffany
6/25	4	3. OU812	Van Halen

DATE	WKS	ALBUM TITLE	ARTIST
		1988 CONTINUED	
7/23	6†	4. Hysteria	Def Leppard
8/6	5†	5. Appetite For Destruction	Guns N' Roses
8/20	1	6. Roll With It	Steve Winwood
8/27	1	7. Tracy Chapman	Tracy Chapman
10/15	4	8. New Jersey	Bon Jovi
11/12	6	9. Rattle And Hum	U2/Soundtrack
12/24	4	10. Giving You The Best That I Got	Anita Baker
		1989	
1/21	6†	1. Don't Be Cruel	Bobby Brown
3/11	5	2. Electric Youth	Debbie Gibson
4/15	1	3. Loc-ed After Dark	Tone Loc
4/22	6	4. Like A Prayer	Madonna
6/3	7	5. The Raw & The Cooked	Fine Young Cannibals
7/22	6	6. Batman	Prince/Soundtrack
9/2	1	7. Repeat Offender	Richard Marx
9/9	2	8. Hangin' Tough	New Kids On The Block
9/23	8†	9. Girl You Know It's True	Milli Vanilli
10/7	10†	10. **Forever Your Girl**	Paula Abdul
10/14	2	11. Dr. Feelgood	Motley Crue
10/28	4	12. Janet Jackson's Rhythm Nation 1814	Janet Jackson
12/16	1	13. Storm Front	Billy Joel
		1990	
1/6	3	1. …But Seriously	Phil Collins
4/7	3	2. Nick Of Time	Bonnie Raitt
4/28	6	3. I Do Not Want What I Haven't Got	Sinead O'Connor
6/9	21	4. **Please Hammer Don't Hurt 'Em**	M.C. Hammer
6/30	1	5. Step By Step	New Kids On The Block
11/10	16	6. To The Extreme	Vanilla Ice
		1991	
3/2	11	1. Mariah Carey	Mariah Carey
5/18	2†	2. Out Of Time	R.E.M.
		5/25/91: Billboard begins compiling the pop albums chart based on actual units sold. The data is provided by SoundScan Inc. and is collected by point-of-sale scanning machines that read the UPC bar code	
5/25	1	3. Time, Love & Tenderness	Michael Bolton
6/8	2	4. Spellbound	Paula Abdul
6/22	1	5. EFIL4ZAGGIN	N.W.A.
6/29★	1	6. Slave To The Grind	Skid Row
7/6★	3	7. For Unlawful Carnal Knowledge	Van Halen
7/27	5	8. Unforgettable With Love	Natalie Cole
8/31★	4	9. Metallica	Metallica
9/28★	18†	10. **Ropin' The Wind**	Garth Brooks
10/5★	2	11. Use Your Illusion II	Guns N' Roses
12/7★	1	12. Achtung Baby	U2
12/14★	4	13. Dangerous	Michael Jackson

DATE	WKS	ALBUM TITLE	ARTIST
1992			
1/11	2†	1. Nevermind	Nirvana
4/4	2	2. Wayne's World	Soundtrack
4/18★	5	3. Adrenalize	Def Leppard
5/23	2†	4. Totally Krossed Out	Kris Kross
5/30★	1	5. The Southern Harmony And Musical Companion	The Black Crowes
6/13	17	6. Some Gave All	Billy Ray Cyrus
10/10★	7†	7. The Chase	Garth Brooks
11/21	1	8. Timeless (The Classics)	Michael Bolton
12/5★	1	9. The Predator	Ice Cube
12/12	20	10. **The Bodyguard**	Whitney Houston/Soundtrack
1993			
3/13	3	1. Unplugged	Eric Clapton
4/10★	1	2. Songs Of Faith And Devotion	Depeche Mode
5/8★	1	3. Get A Grip	Aerosmith
6/5★	6	4. janet.	Janet Jackson
7/17★	1	5. Back To Broadway	Barbra Streisand
7/24★	2	6. Zooropa	U2
8/7★	2	7. Black Sunday	Cypress Hill
8/21	1	8. Sleepless In Seattle	Soundtrack
8/28★	3	9. River Of Dreams	Billy Joel
9/18★	5†	10. In Pieces	Garth Brooks
10/9★	1	11. In Utero	Nirvana
10/30	1	12. Bat Out Of Hell II: Back Into Hell	Meat Loaf
11/6★	5	13. Vs.	Pearl Jam
12/11★	3†	14. Doggy Style	Snoop Doggy Dogg
12/25	8†	15. **Music Box**	Mariah Carey
1994			
2/12★	1	1. Jar Of Flies	Alice In Chains
2/19	1	2. Kickin' It Up	John Michael Montgomery
2/26	2†	3. Toni Braxton	Toni Braxton
3/26★	1	4. Superunknown	Soundgarden
4/2	2†	5. The Sign	Ace Of Base
4/9★	1	6. Far Beyond Driven	Pantera
4/16	1	7. Longing In Their Hearts	Bonnie Raitt
4/23★	4	8. The Division Bell	Pink Floyd
5/21	2	9. Not A Moment Too Soon	Tim McGraw
6/4	1	10. The Crow	Soundtrack
6/18★	1	11. Ill Communication	Beastie Boys
6/25★	3	12. Purple	Stone Temple Pilots
7/16	9	13. **The Lion King**	Soundtrack
9/17★	4†	14. II	Boyz II Men
10/1★	1	15. From The Cradle	Eric Clapton
10/15★	2	16. Monster	R.E.M.
11/5★	2	17. Murder Was The Case	Soundtrack
11/19★	1	18. MTV Unplugged In New York	Nirvana
11/26★	2	19. Hell Freezes Over	Eagles
12/10	3†	20. Miracles — The Holiday Album	Kenny G
12/24	1	21. Vitalogy	Pearl Jam

ALBUMS OF LONGEVITY

Albums Charted 60 Weeks Or More In The Top 40

PK YR	WKS T40	PK POS	PK WKS	WKS T10	RANK	TITLE...Artist
56	292	1	15	173	1.	MY FAIR LADY...Original Cast
56	229	1	4	116	2.	OKLAHOMA!...Soundtrack
58	178	1	3	57	3.	JOHNNY'S GREATEST HITS...Johnny Mathis
56	178	1	1	78	4.	THE KING AND I...Soundtrack
60	168	1	16	105	5.	THE SOUND OF MUSIC...Original Cast
58	161	1	31	90	6.	SOUTH PACIFIC...Soundtrack
65	161	1	2	109	7.	THE SOUND OF MUSIC...Soundtrack
61	151	1	6	87	8.	CAMELOT...Original Cast
62	144	1	54	106	9.	WEST SIDE STORY...Soundtrack
65	141	1	8	61	10.	WHIPPED CREAM & OTHER DELIGHTS...Herb Alpert's Tijuana Brass
57	138	2	3	53	11.	HYMNS...Tennessee Ernie Ford
58	128	1	8	53	12.	SING ALONG WITH MITCH...Mitch Miller & The Gang
92	126	3	2	36	13.	NO FENCES...Garth Brooks
58	123	1	12	66	14.	THE MUSIC MAN...Original Cast
62	119	5	5	32	15.	WEST SIDE STORY...Original Cast
59	117	4	1	14	16.	MORE SING ALONG WITH MITCH...Mitch Miller & The Gang
66	115	1	1	71	17.	DOCTOR ZHIVAGO...Soundtrack
58	114	1	1	22	18.	THE KINGSTON TRIO...The Kingston Trio
59	113	1	1	43	19.	FILM ENCORES...Mantovani and his orchestra
62	112	1	7	85	20.	PETER, PAUL AND MARY...Peter, Paul and Mary
66	107	1	6	48	21.	GOING PLACES...Herb Alpert And The Tijuana Brass
63	106	3	1	22	22.	MOON RIVER & OTHER GREAT MOVIE THEMES...Andy Williams
60	105	1	13	43	23.	PERSUASIVE PERCUSSION...Enoch Light/Terry Snyder and The All-Stars
92	100	2	4	35	24.	TEN...Pearl Jam
56	99	1	1	49	25.	THE EDDY DUCHIN STORY...Soundtrack
61	98	8	1	10	26.	KNOCKERS UP!...Rusty Warren
84	96	1	1	84	27.	BORN IN THE U.S.A. ...Bruce Springsteen
88	96	1	7	78	28.	HYSTERIA...Def Leppard
83	91	1	6	78	29.	THRILLER...Michael Jackson
57	88	1	37	54	30.	AROUND THE WORLD IN 80 DAYS...Soundtrack
69	87	4	10	49	31.	IN-A-GADDA-DA-VIDA...Iron Butterfly
61	86	2	1	26	32.	TIME OUT FEATURING "TAKE FIVE"...Dave Brubeck Quartet
60	86	3	1	22	33.	BELAFONTE AT CARNEGIE HALL...Harry Belafonte
91	85	1	1	30	34.	METALLICA...Metallica
62	83	5	4	31	35.	I LEFT MY HEART IN SAN FRANCISCO...Tony Bennett
83	82	9	1	1	36.	ELIMINATOR...ZZ Top
80	81	6	3	15	37.	CHRISTOPHER CROSS...Christopher Cross
65	78	1	14	48	38.	MARY POPPINS...Soundtrack
86	78	1	14	46	39.	WHITNEY HOUSTON...Whitney Houston
89	78	1	10	64	40.	FOREVER YOUR GIRL...Paula Abdul
58	78	1	10	54	41.	GIGI...Soundtrack
88	78	1	5	52	42.	APPETITE FOR DESTRUCTION...Guns N' Roses
83	78	1	3	59	43.	CAN'T SLOW DOWN...Lionel Richie
63	78	8	1	6	44.	THE BARBRA STREISAND ALBUM...Barbra Streisand
89	77	1	4	35	45.	JANET JACKSON'S RHYTHM NATION 1814...Janet Jackson
86	77	1	2	37	46.	CONTROL...Janet Jackson
91	77	1	1	38	47.	TIME, LOVE & TENDERNESS...Michael Bolton
65	77	4	2	30	48.	MY FAIR LADY...Soundtrack
68	77	5	1	32	49.	ARE YOU EXPERIENCED?...Jimi Hendrix Experience
92	76	1	20	39	50.	THE BODYGUARD...Whitney Houston/Soundtrack
58	76	1	7	39	51.	TCHAIKOVSKY: PIANO CONCERTO NO. 1...Van Cliburn
59	74	4	2	14	52.	OPEN FIRE, TWO GUITARS...Johnny Mathis
61	73	1	13	37	53.	JUDY AT CARNEGIE HALL...Judy Garland
56	72	1	31	58	54.	CALYPSO...Harry Belafonte
87	72	11	2	0	55.	RAPTURE...Anita Baker
89	71	1	2	45	56.	HANGIN' TOUGH...New Kids On The Block

ALBUMS OF LONGEVITY

Albums Charted 60 Weeks Or More In The Top 40

PK YR	WKS T40	PK POS	PK WKS	WKS T10	RANK	TITLE...Artist
84	71	1	1	42	57.	SPORTS...Huey Lewis And The News
63	71	2	9	50	58.	(MOVING)...Peter, Paul and Mary
84	71	3	11	39	59.	PRIVATE DANCER...Tina Turner
59	71	4	2	11	60.	STILL MORE! SING ALONG WITH MITCH...Mitch Miller & The Gang
90	70	1	21	52	61.	PLEASE HAMMER DON'T HURT 'EM...M.C. Hammer
91	70	1	18	50	62.	ROPIN' THE WIND...Garth Brooks
85	70	1	7	31	63.	NO JACKET REQUIRED...Phil Collins
78	70	2	6	19	64.	THE STRANGER...Billy Joel
91	70	3	1	28	65.	COOLEYHIGHHARMONY...Boyz II Men
62	70	10	4	4	66.	JOAN BAEZ IN CONCERT...Joan Baez
62	70	13	1	0	67.	JOAN BAEZ, VOL. 2...Joan Baez
88	69	1	12	51	68.	FAITH...George Michael
62	69	1	12	46	69.	BREAKFAST AT TIFFANY'S...Henry Mancini/Soundtrack
89	69	1	6	45	70.	DON'T BE CRUEL...Bobby Brown
93	69	1	1	12	71.	GET A GRIP...Aerosmith
90	69	2	10	52	72.	WILSON PHILLIPS...Wilson Phillips
60	69	2	5	27	73.	PROVOCATIVE PERCUSSION...Enoch Light & The Light Brigade
87	68	1	18	48	74.	DIRTY DANCING...Soundtrack
71	68	1	15	46	75.	TAPESTRY...Carole King
76	68	1	1	37	76.	FLEETWOOD MAC...Fleetwood Mac
60	67	1	14	44	77.	THE BUTTON-DOWN MIND OF BOB NEWHART...Bob Newhart
59	67	1	3	17	78.	FLOWER DRUM SONG...Original Cast
91	66	1	11	49	79.	MARIAH CAREY...Mariah Carey
69	66	1	7	50	80.	BLOOD, SWEAT & TEARS...Blood, Sweat & Tears
85	66	1	2	40	81.	RECKLESS...Bryan Adams
93	66	2	11	35	82.	BREATHLESS...Kenny G
64	66	3	8	24	83.	HONEY IN THE HORN...Al Hirt
60	66	6	3	21	84.	ENCORE OF GOLDEN HITS...The Platters
60	66	7	1	1	85.	PARTY SING ALONG WITH MITCH...Mitch Miller and The Gang
71	65	1	3	41	86.	JESUS CHRIST SUPERSTAR...Various Artists
88	65	3	4	22	87.	KICK...INXS
67	65	5	2	14	88.	THE TEMPTATIONS GREATEST HITS...The Temptations
84	65	8	2	6	89.	BREAK OUT...Pointer Sisters
67	63	1	15	33	90.	SGT. PEPPER'S LONELY HEARTS CLUB BAND...The Beatles
94	63+	1	2	30	91.	THE SIGN...Ace Of Base
73	63	1	1	27	92.	THE DARK SIDE OF THE MOON...Pink Floyd
61	63	2	3	35	93.	GREAT MOTION PICTURE THEMES...Soundtrack Compilations
88	63	8	2	4	94.	RICHARD MARX...Richard Marx
56	62	1	6	54	95.	BELAFONTE...Harry Belafonte
83	62	4	5	30	96.	AN INNOCENT MAN...Billy Joel
84	62	4	4	21	97.	SHE'S SO UNUSUAL...Cyndi Lauper
63	61	1	16	23	98.	DAYS OF WINE AND ROSES...Andy Williams
89	61	1	8	41	99.	GIRL YOU KNOW IT'S TRUE...Milli Vanilli
86	61	3	2	26	100.	INVISIBLE TOUCH...Genesis
58	61	4	1	3	101.	TILL...Roger Williams
91	61	10	1	1	102.	HEART IN MOTION...Amy Grant
59	61	12	2	0	103.	OLDIES BUT GOODIES...Various Artists
77	60	1	31	52	104.	RUMOURS...Fleetwood Mac
86	60	1	8	46	105.	SLIPPERY WHEN WET...Bon Jovi
91	60	2	7	29	106.	GONNA MAKE YOU SWEAT...C & C Music Factory
86	60	3	2	14	107.	BACK IN THE HIGH LIFE...Steve Winwood
66	60	4	2	17	108.	PARSLEY, SAGE, ROSEMARY AND THYME...Simon & Garfunkel
65	60	7	2	3	109.	FIDDLER ON THE ROOF...Original Cast

Ties are broken in this order: peak position, weeks at peak position, and finally, weeks in Top 10.

+subject to change since album was still in the Top 40 as of the 2/25/95 cutoff date

THE BILLBOARD CHARTS FROM TOP TO BOTTOM!

Only Joel Whitburn's Record Research Books List Every Record To Ever Appear On Every Major Billboard Chart.

When the talk turns to music, more people turn to Joel Whitburn's Record Research Collection than to any other reference source.

That's because these are the **only** books that get right to the bottom of *Billboard*'s major charts, with **complete, fully accurate chart data on every record ever charted.** So they are quoted with confidence by DJ's, music-show hosts, program directors, collectors and other music enthusiasts worldwide.

Each book lists every record's significant chart data, such as peak position, debut date, peak date, weeks charted, label, record number and much more, all conveniently arranged for fast, easy reference. Most books also feature artist biographies, record notes, RIAA Platinum/Gold Record certifications, top artist and record achievements, all-time artist and record rankings, a chronological listing of all #1 hits, and additional in-depth chart information.

Joel Whitburn's Record Research Collection. #1 on **everyone's** hit list.

TOP POP SINGLES 1955-1993
Over 20,000 Pop singles — every "Hot 100" hit — arranged by artist. Features thousands of artist biographies and countless titles notes. 912 pages. $74.95 Hardcover/$64.95 Softcover.

POP SINGLES ANNUAL 1955-1994
A year-by-year ranking, based on chart performance, of over 20,000 Pop hits. Over 850 pages. $69.95 Hardcover/ $59.95 Softcover.

POP HITS 1940-1954
Compiled strictly from *Billboard* and divided into two easy-to-use sections — one lists all the hits artist by artist and the other year by year. Filled with artist bios, title notes and many special sections. 414 pages. Hardcover. $54.95.

POP MEMORIES 1890-1954
Unprecedented in depth and dimension. An artist-by-artist, title-by-title chronicle of the 65 formative years of recorded popular music. Fascinating facts and statistics on over 1,600 artists and 12,000 recordings, compiled directly from America's popular music charts, surveys and record listings. 660 pages. Hardcover. $59.95.

TOP POP ALBUMS 1955-1992
An artist-by-artist history of the over 17,000 LPs that ever appeared on *Billboard*'s Pop albums charts, with a complete A-Z listing below each artist of <u>every</u> track from <u>every</u> charted album by that artist. 976 pages. Hardcover. $79.95.

TOP POP ALBUM TRACKS 1955-1992
An all-inclusive, alphabetical index of every song track from every charted music album, with the artist's name and the album's chart debut year. 544 pages. Hardcover. $44.95.

BILLBOARD HOT 100/POP SINGLES CHARTS:

THE EIGHTIES 1980-1989
THE SEVENTIES 1970-1979
THE SIXTIES 1960-1969

Three complete collections of the actual weekly "Hot 100" charts from each decade, reproduced in black-and-white at 70% of original size. Over 550 pages each. Deluxe Hardcover. $79.95 each.

POP CHARTS 1955-1959

Reproductions of every weekly Pop singles chart *Billboard* published from 1955 through 1959 ("Best Sellers," "Jockeys," "Juke Box," "Top 100" and "Hot 100"). 496 pages. Deluxe Hardcover. $79.95.

BILLBOARD POP ALBUM CHARTS 1965-1969
The greatest of all album eras...straight off the pages of *Billboard*! Every weekly *Billboard* Pop albums chart, shown in its entirety, from 1965 through 1969. All charts reproduced in black-and-white at 70% of original size. 496 pages. Deluxe Hardcover. $79.95.

TOP COUNTRY SINGLES 1944-1993
The complete history of the most genuine of American musical genres, with an artist-by-artist listing of every "Country" single ever charted. 624 pages. Hardcover. $59.95.

TOP R&B SINGLES 1942-1988
Every "Soul," "Black," "Urban Contemporary" and "Rhythm & Blues" charted single, listed by artist. 624 pages. $59.95 Hardcover/$49.95 Softcover.

TOP ADULT CONTEMPORARY 1961-1993
America's leading listener format is covered hit by hit in this fact-packed volume. Lists, artist by artist, the complete history of *Billboard*'s "Easy Listening" and "Adult Contemporary" charts. 368 pages. Hardcover. $39.95.

BUBBLING UNDER THE HOT 100 1959-1985
Here are 27 years of *Billboard*'s unique and intriguing "Bubbling Under" chart, listed by artist. Also features "Bubbling Under" titles that later hit the "Hot 100." 384 pages. Hardcover. $34.95.

BILLBOARD SINGLES REVIEWS 1958
Reproductions of every weekly 1958 record review *Billboard* published for 1958. Reviews of nearly 10,000 record sides by 3,465 artists. 280 pages. Softcover. $29.95.

TOP POP SINGLES CD GUIDE 1955-1979
This comprehensive guide tells you exactly where to find CD versions of past hits by your favorite Pop artists, with a complete listing of all 1955-1979 charted Pop records that are available on CD. 288 pages. Softcover. $24.95.

BILLBOARD TOP 1000 x 5
Here for the first time ever are five complete separate rankings — from #1 right down through #1000 — of the all-time top charted hits of Pop Music 1955-1993, Pop Music 1940-1955, Adult Contemporary Music 1961-1993, R&B Music 1942-1993, and Country Music 1944-1993. 272 pages. Softcover. $24.95.

DAILY #1 HITS 1940-1992
A desktop calendar of a half-century of #1 pop records. Lists one day of the year per page of every record that held the #1 position on the Pop singles charts on that day for each of the past 53+ years. 392 pages. Spiral-bound softcover. $24.95.

BILLBOARD #1s 1950-1991
A week-by-week listing of every #1 single and album from *Billboard*'s Pop, R&B, Country and Adult Contemporary charts. 336 pages. Softcover. $24.95.

MUSIC YEARBOOKS 1994/1993
Comprehensive, yearly updates on *Billboard*'s major singles and albums charts. Various page lengths. Softcover. $29.95 each.

VIDEO YEARBOOKS 1994/1993
Complete yearly recaps of 1994 and 1993 charted videocassettes. Various page lengths. Softcover. $19.95 each.

MUSIC & VIDEO YEARBOOKS
1992/1991/1990/1989
Comprehensive, yearly updates on *Billboard*'s major singles, albums and videocassettes charts. Various page lengths. Softcover. $29.95 each.

For complete book descriptions and ordering information, call, write or fax today.

RECORD RESEARCH INC.
P.O. Box 200
Menomonee Falls, WI 53052-0200 U.S.A.
Phone: 414-251-5408 / Fax: 414-251-9452